FOR THE ENRICHMENT OF ALL
WOMEN IN SPORT

DEDICATION

To my mother, Edythe A. Wells, and in memory of my father, Harold E. Wells.
To a mentor, Eunice E. Way.
They showed me the way.
And to my special friends, D.D., K.C., M.C.P., N.F., and A.N.-H.
They gave me love and support.

WOMEN, SPORT, & PERFORMANCE

A PHYSIOLOGICAL PERSPECTIVE

Second Edition

Christine L. Wells, PhD
Arizona State University

Human Kinetics Books

Library of Congress Cataloging-in-Publication Data

Wells, Christine L., 1938-
  Women, sport, & performance / by Christine L. Wells--2nd ed.
    p. cm.
  Includes bibliographical references and index.
    ISBN: 0-87322-303-9 (cloth)   ISBN: 0-88011-724-9 (paper)
    1. Sports--Physiological aspects.   2. Women--Physiology.
  3. Exercise for women.   I. Title.   II. Title: Women, sport, and
  performance.
  RC1235.W447   1991   90-39652
  612'.044'082--dc20   CIP

ISBN: 0-87322-303-9 (cloth)   ISBN: 0-88011-724-9 (paper)

Copyright © 1991, 1985 by Christine L. Wells

Interior photo credits: page xii (top): Karlis, *The Daily Illini*, Champaign, IL. Page xii (bottom): Craig Cotton, *The Daily Illini*. Page 3 (left): Marcy Bright, *The Daily Illini*. Page 3 (right): Andy Kokodynski, *The Daily Illini*. Page 19 (left): *The Daily Illini*. Page 19 (right): Claudio Gratton, *The Daily Illini*. Page 35 (left): Gary Eifert, *The Daily Illini*. Page 35 (right): Nora Hipolito, *The Daily Illini*. Pages 50, 85, 159, and 307: CLEO, St. Paul, MN. Page 53: David Roback, courtesy of Smith College, Office of Sports Information, Northampton, MA. Page 75: Lee Ferguson Photography, Phoenix, AZ, courtesy of the Department of Dance, Arizona State University. Page 97: © 1986 Ken Akers (from the photo files of Arizona State University). Pages 107 and 192: courtesy of Pennsylvania State University. Pages 126, 181, and 195: courtesy of The U.S. National Senior Sports Classic—The Senior Olympics. Page 129: Valerie Rose Hall. Page 219: Kevin Mulhall, *The Daily Illini*. Page 236: Lisa Davis, *The Daily Illini*. Page 239: Kristin Oostendorf, *The Daily Illini*. Page 261: Stephen Warmowski, *The Daily Illini*. Page 277: Phil Messersmith, *The Daily Illini*.

Developmental Editor: Marie Roy; **Assistant Editor:** Kari Nelson; **Copyeditor:** Bruce Owens; **Proofreader:** Laurie McGee; **Photo Editor:** Valerie Hall; **Production Director:** Ernie Noa; **Typesetters:** Brad Colson, Sandra Meier, Yvonne Winsor, Angie Snyder, Kathy Fuoss; **Text Designer:** Keith Blomberg; **Text Layout:** Denise Lowry, Tara Welsch; **Cover Designer:** Jack Davis; **Printer:** Versa Press

Printed in the United States of America   10 9 8 7 6 5 4 3 2 1

Human Kinetics
Web site: http://www.humankinetics.com/

United States: Human Kinetics, P.O. Box 5076
Champaign, IL 61825-5076
1-800-747-4457
e-mail: humank@hkusa.com

Canada: Human Kinetics, Box 24040
Windsor, ON N8Y 4Y9
1-800-465-7301 (in Canada only)
e-mail: humank@hkcanada.com

Europe: Human Kinetics, P.O. Box IW14
Leeds LS16 6TR, United Kingdom
(44) 1132 781708
e-mail: humank@hkeurope.com

Australia: Human Kinetics
57A Price Avenue, Lower Mitcham
South Australia 5062
(08) 277 1555
e-mail: humank@hkaustralia.com

New Zealand: Human Kinetics, P.O. Box 105-231
Auckland 1
(09) 523 3462
e-mail: humank@hknewz.com

Contents

Preface

When I began nearly a decade ago doing the literature research necessary for writing the first edition of *Women, Sport, and Performance*, I didn't know just how much information I would find on topics like exercise and pregnancy, menopause, and osteoporosis. Sometimes what I found was based on myth or misconception rather than scientific fact; omitting such information often meant limiting or dating what I could actually publish. But I am happy to say that research pertaining both directly and indirectly to the woman in sport has become very productive since my initial literature review. New information is continually available on sport and exercise that relates to the specific concerns of women. Most recently attention has been directed to a possible correlation between athletic amenorrhea and bone health.

It is encouraging to see not only so much research focused on the exercising woman but also that the quality of this research is generally quite good. In light of the wealth of new studies, I have extensively revised *Women, Sport, and Performance* for its second edition. Most of the dated material has been removed, and considerable new material added. The issues of perhaps greatest significance include athletic amenorrhea, bone health, eating disorders, pregnancy, and menopause. I have revised the sections on those topics, putting more emphasis on the female's full life span and discussing childhood, menarche, and adolescent and masters athletes.

The intended audience continues to be exercise scientists, sports medicine experts, physical education teachers, coaches, athletes, and any others interested in the female's physiological responses to exercise. A general understanding of human anatomy and physiology is assumed, but for those with only a basic background I have tried to explain scientific terms and mechanisms as clearly as possible. The glossary of terms and the list of abbreviations may prove helpful to readers who are unfamiliar with the jargon of exercise physiology.

This book attempts to present a balance of introductory information (chapter 4: "The Menstrual Cycle: A Unique Function"), the latest concepts in research (chapter 8: "Athletic Amenorrhea"), and practical material (chapter 7: "Menstruation and Sport: Practical Implications").

The book focuses on the physiological adaptations of the human female to exercise and is divided into five parts. The first deals with the differences and similarities between the sexes. Three chapters are devoted to this topic: Morphological, physiological, and performance differences are discussed, with the emphasis being the growth and development of both young girls and mature women. In fact, throughout the book I have attempted to include information that is relevant to the female of all ages and of all experience and skill levels, not solely the woman athlete.

Part II covers exercise and menstrual function. Five chapters expand on material to which most books give only a few cursory pages. Chapter 4 is a basic explanation of the anatomy and physiology of the female reproductive system. Teachers may find this chapter extremely helpful in preparing a course or a series of classes on this topic.

It may also prove useful to dispel various myths encountered about physical activity and the female's reproductive functions. Chapters 5 and 6 are reversals of each other. Whereas chapter 5 describes the effects of menstrual function on performance, chapter 6 describes the effects of exercise on menstrual function. Chapter 8 explores the literature on athletic amenorrhea extensively and presents the pros and cons of most theories of athletic amenorrhea.

Part III presents the effects of exercise on the nonmenstruating woman, that is, the pregnant or lactating woman, the woman experiencing menopause, and the older, postmenopausal woman. This material has perhaps never been presented in such a comprehensive manner. Because there have been no reports that exercise during pregnancy is deleterious, investigators and human-subject review committees are becoming less restrictive about research efforts that focus directly on the effects of exercise on the pregnant woman and her developing fetus. Almost everything known about exercise and pregnancy had been surmised from laboratory models of pregnant ewes or rats. Unfortunately, neither is a particularly useful model for the study of human pregnancy. Now, more research is being focused directly on the pregnant woman. Increasing attention is also being given to the effects of menopause on health issues and to the physiological capacities of older women. I find it wonderful to see so many women entering masters-level competition. It will be exciting to watch women's performance records change as today's young, highly trained athletes become masters competitors.

Nutritional information, whether general in nature or specific to exercise, is always a topic of great interest to women, and I address it in Part IV. Chapter 12 covers nutritional guidelines for promoting health and preventing disease as well as topics of particular interest to the athlete, like iron deficiency. Chapter 13 discusses obesity, the major eating disorder among women who are characteristically inactive, as well as anorexia nervosa and bulimia, psychogenic eating behaviors seen in some highly active women.

Part V is devoted to the athletic woman. Muscular, metabolic, and cardiovascular adaptations to training during preadolescence, adolescence, adulthood, middle age, and post-menopausal years are discussed, as is the limited information available on detraining. Chapter 15, which covers athletic injuries, begins by discussing the relative injury rates of men and women in various sports and then emphasizes injuries that are specific to women. Chapter 16 comprehensively reviews the characteristics of highly trained, successful female athletes of all ages. Such topics as body composition and build, cardiorespiratory endurance, strength, and anaerobic power are covered. Chapter 17, a new chapter for this edition, discusses health issues related to inactivity and to very high levels of physical training. The purpose of this final chapter is to point the way for future research.

I remain confident that as women of all ages become increasingly active and successful in their sport endeavors—whether as serious competitors, social-recreational participants, or physical fitness and health enthusiasts—they will continue to probe for information about themselves, their well-being, and their performance. The female athlete is a beautiful being, and she deserves to achieve the full measure of her potential. It is my hope that this book will assist her to do just that.

Christine L. Wells, PhD

Acknowledgments

A number of people contributed significantly to this second edition of *Women, Sport, and Performance*. In particular, I thank Anne B. Loucks, Emily M. Haymes, Barbara L. Drinkwater, Patty S. Freedson, Mona Shangold, and N. Peggy Burke for reading the first edition and providing suggestions and comments for improving the manuscript.

Marie Roy served as developmental editor for this edition and was a constant source of encouragement. Her deadlines kept me working when I occasionally wanted to quit.

N. Peggy Burke read every word of the revised text and made numerous corrections and suggestions for improvement. She also kept me humble when my opinions ran rampant. I am much in her debt.

And last, but certainly not least, I drew considerable inspiration for completing this edition from the hundreds of women I have met at professional meetings, from my graduate students at Arizona State University, and from the women I have met at various running and triathlon competitions. Without their inspiration, I could not have completed this book, which, in turn, I hope will inspire them.

PART I

Differences Between Women and Men

Unlike other books dealing with the physiological aspects of physical performance, this book focuses rather exclusively on women. The fact that this book is necessary speaks to the notion that accurate information regarding women is either severely limited or not sufficiently indexed to be readily available to people who are especially interested in such matters. Although considerable material is available on physical performance by young men, relatively little performance data are available on girls or women. Is such a compilation of information necessary? Are girls and women just a smaller version of boys and men? Are there structural and functional differences between the sexes that make each sex truly unique in terms of performance?

Part I of this book is concerned with such questions. Chapter 1 begins by attempting to place the term *differences* in proper perspective. It points out that significant "variations" in morphological (structural) characteristics occur *within* each sex that are often greater than or as great as "differences" *between* the sexes. Following this generalized discussion is a description of growth patterns and skeletal differences between the sexes in relation to factors influencing human performance. The development of the secondary sexual characteristics is presented, as is a description of differences in body composition throughout the life span.

Chapter 2 proceeds with a discussion of the physiological, or functional, differences between the sexes that are important to physical performance. Cardiorespiratory, metabolic, and skeletal muscle differences and similarities are presented in relation to such variables as oxygen uptake, cardiac output, and anaerobic threshold. Data from both athletic and nonathletic populations are included. Finally, the myth that women are especially equipped for endurance performance because of their extra supply of body fat is refuted.

Chapter 3 deals exclusively with factors that influence performance. Muscular strength and strength training are discussed with special reference to differences between the sexes in muscular hypertrophy. Motor performance, as measured by the AAHPERD fitness test items, is compared between boys and girls ages 10 to 17. Outstanding athletic performances are also discussed, and men's and women's world records in track and swimming events from 1963 to 1989 are compared.

Chapter 1

Morphological Differences and Similarities

Largely as a consequence of the women's movement and the resulting efforts to achieve greater equality in all aspects of life, many questions have been raised regarding the ability of girls and women to perform the same tasks as boys and men. This issue has considerable significance in regard to military duty, police and fire-fighting work, heavy industry and construction, physical education in schools and colleges, and athletic competition at all ages. Today, public law (Title IX of the Educational Amendments of 1972) mandates that girls and women shall have opportunities equal to those of boys and men in physical education and athletics in public schools and colleges. (It is unfortunate that the Supreme Court's Grove City decision inhibited the enforcement of that law for several years. Recent passage of the Civil Rights Restoration Act has largely restored Title IX.) Nevertheless, questions raised about physical and physiological differences have serious moral and economic overtones and do not simply indicate a passing academic interest. It is not so much the actual differences that are of major importance, however, as it is the *meaning* of these differences in terms of equal opportunity and enhanced quality of life.

In fact, differences in body conformation (morphology) between mature males and females are far less marked in *Homo sapiens* than in many other animals. In many species, the differences between the sexes are often so great that males and females do not even appear to belong to the same species. Even among the animals most similar to us (primates such as the orangutan, gorilla, and baboon), sexual differences in such features as head size, hair growth, dentition, general stature, and physique are very much exaggerated. Individually, however, humans are probably the most highly variable of all species.

Normal Distribution

Although many structural and functional variations exist between the sexes, these variations should be considered from the point of view of the *normal*

distribution. Most physical factors or variables are distributed along a *normal curve* (see Figure 1.1), in which the mean, or average, value for each population is approximately in the center of the range of values for that variable. The width of such a curve represents the amount of variability within the population. A very informative measure of variability is called the *standard deviation (SD)*, which represents the distance that each score lies away from the *mean (M)*. An example is the height of girls at a particular age. The normal curve indicates that height is distributed rather evenly around an average value. For that age, many girls are either taller or shorter than the average height. When two *different* groups are compared, we are essentially comparing *two* normal distributions. If the two groups are distinctly different, the distribution of values for the variable being examined will overlap very little (as in Figure 1.2) or not at all. Figure 1.2 shows that Population A is distinctly different from Population B in regard to the variable the two curves represent. In other words, Population B displays higher values for variable *x* than does Population A.

Figure 1.3 illustrates the curves that are formed when most differences between the sexes are plotted for adult humans. The figure indicates two

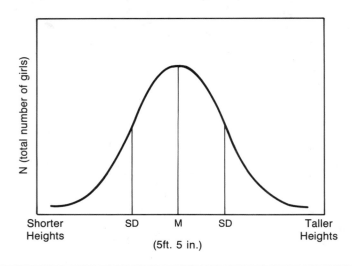

Figure 1.1   The normal curve.

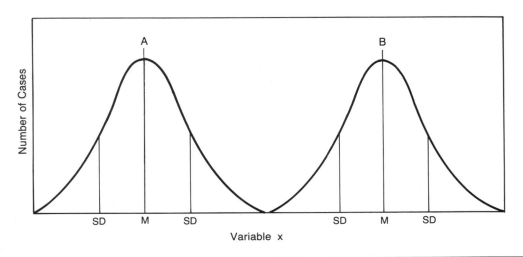

Figure 1.2 Two distinctly different populations.

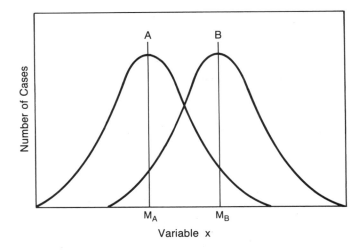

Figure 1.3 Two populations with many individuals of each population having identical values for the variable in question.

superimposed normal distributions. Note the large overlap between the two groups. For many variables, the difference between men and women is *statistically significant* but relatively small. Figure 1.3 indicates that a large number of individuals in Population A possess the same value for a certain variable (x) as a large number of individuals in Population B. More specifically, distributions such as those displayed in Figure 1.3 indicate that although there are many differences among humans, there are far more similarities than differences. For example, although the average woman is shorter and smaller than the average man, many women are taller and larger than many men. Although the average man has wider shoulders and narrower hips than the average woman, some men have narrower shoulders and wider hips than some women.

Frequency distributions such as these also show that differences in size, shape, and stature between two individuals of the same sex are often greater than differences between two individuals of the opposite sex. It is also evident that many people do not possess the characteristics of the so-called average man or woman.

Why Do Sex Differences Exist?

Wyrick (1971) has pointed out at least two basic potential causes for sex differences: environmental-experiential and biological. This chapter is primarily about biological differences. Ideally, once the exact nature and the extent of biological sex differences are understood, we can better understand the ways in which environmental influences and experiences shape the way we live and the limitations we impose on ourselves. In this way, we can better understand how to minimize or maximize these influences. It is important to know whether the environment is "creating differences between the sexes that do not biologically exist, or whether it is obscuring the function of existing biological sex differences by exerting social pressures toward egalitarianism" (Wyrick, 1971, p. 21).

Of the approximately 10 trillion cells that make up the human body, only those that make up the reproductive system result in physical differences between men and women. Only the hormones of the reproductive system are dedicated exclusively to the survival of the species and account for variation between the sexes (Sloane, 1980). The functioning of the remaining cells is dedicated to the survival of the individual. No one, for example, can distinguish a woman's liver, kidney, heart, or brain from that of a man's when the organ is lying on a laboratory table. Many might guess that the larger organ was a man's, but the size of the organ is more related to the size of the total body from which it came than from the sex of the body.

Even with this background and common understanding, I have found that sex differences and similarities are difficult to discuss. That is, the words *generally, usually, on the average*, and so on seemed to keep emerging. After much pulling of hair and gnashing of teeth, I finally decided I had to charge full steam ahead or never write this book at all. So, please bear with all the hedging of terms in this chapter (and the next) and accept the spirit with which this book is written—that, although there are many sex differences that are both physical and physiological, there are also many, many sex similarities.

The rest of this chapter presents information on variations between the sexes that are basically structural (i.e., anatomical), and I have chosen to use the word *morphological* to describe them. Chapter 2 deals with variations that are more functional, or physiological, than morphological. The distinction, of course, is strictly arbitrary.

Growth Differences

Of the numerous sex differences in body size and shape, the most striking of these arise at adolescence: the man's greater height and wider shoulders and the woman's proportionately wider hips and larger layer of subcutaneous fat. However, some morphological sex differences (dimorphisms) develop before puberty. Three ways in which these originate follow:

1. By differential growth rates operating at specific developmental phases (i.e., infancy or adolescence)
2. By differential growth rates operating throughout growth (i.e., from birth or before)
3. By the direct result of differential hormone secretion and specificity of target-organ responses (i.e., sexual maturation and the development of secondary sex characteristics)

An example of the first mechanism is the four-phase growth pattern of height and weight: a rapid gain in infancy and early childhood; a slower, relatively constant gain in middle childhood; a rapid gain during adolescence; and a slow increase and eventual cessation of growth at adulthood (Malina, 1988, p. 121). Most dimensions of the body (sitting height, leg length, shoulder and hip widths, limb circumferences, and muscle mass) follow such a pattern. What may vary from variable to variable (as well as from individual to individual) is the initiation, duration, and rate of each growth curve. The maximum increase in weight, for example, occurs after the maximum growth in height, whereas maximum growth in leg length occurs early in the growth spurt and before that for sitting height or trunk length.

At birth, the boy has slightly greater length than the girl, but the girl is more advanced in skeletal ossification (development) and other signs of maturity than the boy. At any given chronological age, "girls are further along their road to maturity than boys" (Tanner, 1962, pp. 40-41)—they are of greater physiological age. Growth curves are more or less parallel until approximately 9 to 12 years of age, at which time the body mass of girls is similar to or even slightly greater than that of boys. Height is similar, but usually differences of about 1 to 2 kg in the strength of various muscle groups favor boys. The gain in height is usually consistent in boys from 6 to 13 years of age and in girls until the adolescent growth spurt (around age 11). At that time, girls surge ahead of boys in height and weight. Within a couple of years (around age 13), boys begin the adolescent growth spurt. Peak height velocity in girls ranges between 10.2 and 13.6 years and in boys between 12.3 and 16.9 years (Brook, 1985, pp. 17, 20). Linear growth in the girl usually decelerates with menarche (beginning of menstruation) between 12 and 14 years, whereas breadth increases. After menarche, the girl will gain 2 more inches of height. Until recently, the trend was for pubertal development to appear about 4 months earlier in each successive generation. Earlier sexual maturation in the female also signifies earlier onset of the

secondary sex characteristics, which are regulated by the hormones of the reproductive system. The extra years of physical growth under the influence of human growth hormone (HGH, or somatotropin) before sexual maturity accounts for the larger size of the adult male. When growth ends, young men are usually 10% taller than young women.

The pattern of body weight development is similar to that for height. The earlier acceleration in pubertal growth gives the girl a 4- to 5-lb advantage in weight by midadolescence. The boy, however, usually catches up by age 15 and soon surpasses the girl. At full sexual maturity, the male outweighs the female by approximately 25 lb. Differences in bone structure and muscle mass mostly account for this additional weight.

Skeletal Comparisons

Ossification is the process during which bone salts are deposited in the matrix (inner portion) of the long bones, resulting in a hardening of the bone and a closure (union) of the primary and secondary growth centers. X rays of the hand are used to assess the degree of ossification, a measure of skeletal maturity. Nutrition, health, and hormonal secretions of the endocrine glands are some of the factors that alter the rate of ossification. At adolescence, girls are usually 2 years ahead of boys in bone ossification because estrogen hastens the closing of the growth plates (epiphyses) in the long bones. Therefore, the female has a shorter growth period. Generally, growth in the length of the long bones is completed 1 to 3 years earlier in the female than in the male. In the female, ossification is completed by approximately age 18 but not until about age 21 or 22 in the male.

Late-maturing girls have a longer period of skeletal growth than early-maturing girls, and consequently, greater height and longer legs and arms. In terms of the general appearance of the skeleton, the male is more rugged—bones are more massive and dense, long bones are longer, and joints are larger and have a more extensive articular surface. One exception is that the knee joint of the female is generally wider, possibly providing more stability relative to her body size. In general, the adult male is more or less wedge shaped with wide shoulders and narrow hips, whereas the female generally has a wide pelvis in relation to the width of her shoulders.

Shoulder width in girls exceeds that of boys until approximately age 15. Chest circumference after about 3 years of age is greater in the boy up to around age 12 or 13. Because of the female's earlier adolescent growth spurt, she will momentarily surpass the boy in chest circumference until he catches up and surpasses her measurements during his growth spurt. By age 16, boys exhibit broader chests than girls.

Young children often appear to have very prominent abdomens. Trunk features take on a more proportioned appearance as height increases in late childhood. With sexual maturity, the male has the larger thorax, and the female the larger abdomen. The larger abdominal cavity of the female is probably to support the additional organs of reproduction.

Mean leg length does not differ between the sexes in preadolescence. During the adolescent growth spurt, however, the major gain in height is due to the lengthening of the legs and not of the trunk. Leg length is approximately 52% of the height of the adult male and 51.2 % of the height of the adult female. This very small relative difference exists mostly in the lower segment of the limb; the lower leg of the female is relatively shorter than the lower leg of the male. Also, the male's foot is usually of greater length and breadth.

Boys have longer arms than girls, largely because of the longer forearms of the boy. The upper arm in the female is shorter than her forearm. In adults of the same height, the upper arm is longer in the male. In general, body measurements (stature, sitting height, head circumference, etc.) of the adult female average 92% of the body measurements of the adult male (Sloane, 1980).

Center of Gravity

One often reads overgeneralized statements (in kinesiology textbooks, sport technique books, and the lay press) implying that inferior sport performance in women is the result of structural differences between the sexes. One example has been the notion that a woman's center of gravity is significantly lower than a man's and consequently that she is handicapped in jumping and running activities. Atwater (1988) reviewed the literature on comparisons of center of gravity to see if those notions were correct. The *center of gravity* (or center of mass) represents a balance point of the body that is located at the intersection of the three primary planes: sagittal, frontal, and transverse. Basically, she found several studies that showed a difference of about 1 % in the average height of the center of gravity for males and females. The actual difference in height of the center of gravity was determined more by the individual's height and body type than by sex. For a man and woman of identical standing height and athletic body type, the difference in center of gravity would probably be less than 1 in. Intuitively, we know that tall people excel in skills that require a high center of gravity and that shorter people excel in skills that require a low center of gravity. Suggestions that women should adopt special techniques for jumping or throwing skills because of differences in the location of their centers of gravity do not seem warranted.

Pelvic Differences

Sex differences in the pelvis have been studied extensively. Generally, the male pelvis is larger than the female's except for the dimensions of the *true pelvis*, which must accommodate the full-term fetal head during delivery. Pelvic measurements, however, show as much variation as other skeletal measurements in humans: No two pelvises are alike, for there is often as much variation in the size and shape of the pelvis among women as there is between the sexes.

Classification

Several classification systems have been devised to describe the normal range of variation in the male and female pelvises. One system is based on X-ray determinations of the dimensions of the pelvic inlet (see Figure 1.4). In the *gynecoid*, or true female pelvis, the inlet is round and roomy, and the pubic arch is almost a 90% angle. This pelvic type accommodates an easy delivery and is usually pictured in anatomy books for comparison with typical male pelvises. Approximately 50% of all women have this type of pelvis. The *android* pelvis has a heart-shaped inlet and narrow sidewalls, making it difficult to deliver a baby. It is common in men, and approximately one third

of white women and 10% to 15% of black women have this type of pelvis. The *anthropoid* pelvis, also common in men, occurs in 20% to 30% of white women and nearly 50% of black women. In the anthropoid, the inlet is oval and the sacrum long. A relatively rare type of pelvis with a shallow, wide cavity is the *platypelloid* pelvis. However, as long as the fetal head can pass through the pelvic inlet, this type of pelvis will not cause difficulty at delivery. In some cases, the pelvic structure may be a mixed classification, the anterior part being similar to one type and the posterior part more like another. A very narrow pelvis may result from poor nutrition, injury, or some disease process. Such a pelvis is said to be *contracted* and could cause *dystocia*, or long and difficult labor. A cesarean section, by which the fetus is removed by surgical incision of the abdomen and uterus, may be necessary.

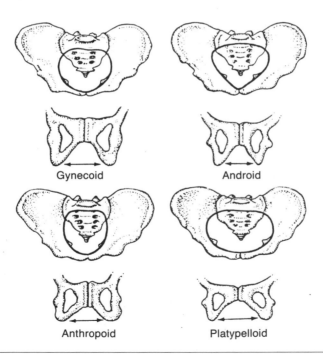

Figure 1.4 The Caldwell–Moloy classification of pelvises. *Note.* From *Biology of Women* (p. 21) by E. Sloane, 1980, New York: John Wiley & Sons, Inc. Copyright 1980 by John Wiley & Sons, Inc. Reprinted by permission.

Pelvic Tilt

The angle of pelvic inclination, called *pelvic tilt*, is subject to considerable individual variation (see Figure 1.5). In women, it is frequently exaggerated because of differences in the dimension of the true pelvis. As a result of increased pelvic tilt, the spinal curvature in the lumbar (lowest) area of the spine is increased in a forward direction to compensate and to maintain the center of gravity. This causes the buttocks of the female to be more prominent than that of the male. The tendency for fat pads to form over the hips also serves to accentuate the width of the female pelvis.

Backache and the Pelvis

People with a larger angle of pelvic inclination will also have a greater curvature of the lumbar spine. Anything that places strain on the lumbar area (e.g., the protruding abdomen of pregnancy or obesity) will likely result in lower back pain. An estimated 50% to 60% of the population has had at least one episode of back trouble at one time or another. Women, however, more frequently suffer from chronic backache than men.

The delivery of a baby puts unusual strain on the muscles and ligaments surrounding the sacroiliac joints. This occurs even though these ligaments and joints have been ''unlocked'' and allowed to stretch under the influence of hormonal action to provide more mobility at childbirth. These changes regress following the birth of the baby, but it may take a long time for these muscles, ligaments, and joints to return to their normal prepregnancy condition. Many women experience chronic lower back pain in the interim.

Most backache in women that is not associated with childbirth or pregnancy is muscular pain resulting from poor posture, faulty body mechanics, or both. Occasionally, the ligaments supporting the spinal column are traumatically stretched from lifting heavy objects incorrectly (e.g., bending forward with the knees straight). This sudden strain can produce muscle spasm and backache. Osteoarthritis or degenerative joint disease, which often occurs after the fourth decade of life, may also lead to chronic lower back pain.

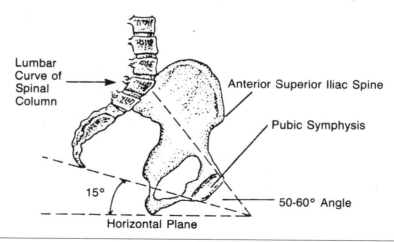

Lumbar Curve of Spinal Column

Anterior Superior Iliac Spine

Pubic Symphysis

15°

50-60° Angle

Horizontal Plane

Figure 1.5 Angle of pelvic inclination. When standing erect, the whole pelvis is tilted forward, and the pelvic canal is directed backward relative to the abdominal cavity and the torso. The greater the tilt of the pelvis, the greater the forward curve in the lower back. *Note.* From *Biology of Women* (p. 23) by E. Sloane, 1980, New York: John Wiley & Sons, Inc. Copyright 1980 by John Wiley & Sons, Inc. Reprinted by permission.

Supposed Consequences of a Wide Pelvis

Women are more frequently seen with knock-knees than are men because of the way in which the head of the femur fits into the cup-shaped socket (acetabulum) of the pelvis. In the male, the angle formed between the neck of the femur and the shaft of the femur is approximately 125° (see Figure 1.6). This allows the femur to swing clear of the pelvis when the leg is moved. Because the pelvis in women is generally wider and the femur shorter, the angle between the neck of the femur and the shaft bone is less than 125°. The smaller this angle, the more the shaft of the long bone will slope inward and the closer the knees will be.

The greater angle of the femur from the vertical increases the *Q angle* (see Figure 1.7), which is the intersection of two lines in the midpatellar region, one drawn down the femur in the direction of the quadriceps pull and the other drawn up the tibia from the tibial tuberosity. A Q angle greater than 15° is thought to predispose a person to patellar problems such as lateral instability or chondromalacia (generalized knee pain and grating sounds). When a person with an increased Q angle contracts the quadriceps, the patella is forced to track laterally in the patellofemoral groove (Hunter, 1988). Consequently, women with average or wider pelvic widths may be predisposed to knee problems in sports that require jumping, running, or sudden shifts of direction. There may also be a tendency toward greater lateral shifting of the pelvis during running.

Another supposed consequence of a wide pelvic structure is that the forearms must angle outward more sharply to clear the hips. Popular opinion has perpetuated the notion that a larger "carrying angle" of the arms in women limits their ability in throwing skills. Beals (1976) measured this angle from X rays of males and females in four age-groups: 0 to 4 years, 5 to 11 years, 12 to 15 years, and adults. He found no significant differences in carrying angle between the sexes at any age-group. Therefore, differences in throwing

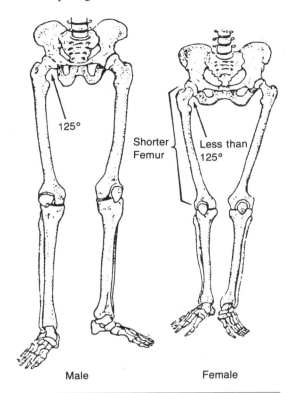

Figure 1.6 The femoral angle is less than 125° in some women, giving women a greater tendency to knock-knees. *Note.* From *Biology of Women* (p. 24) by E. Sloane, 1980, New York: John Wiley & Sons, Inc. Copyright 1980 by John Wiley & Sons, Inc. Reprinted by permission.

performance cannot be attributed to differences in the carrying angle of the arm.

Puberty and the Development of Secondary Sex Characteristics

The transition from childhood to adulthood is most obviously marked by the acquisition of reproductive capacity. Puberty occurs as the result of the secretion of pituitary hormones (gonadotropins) that act to stimulate the development of the primary sex

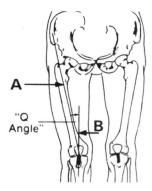

Figure 1.7 The Q angle is formed by a line (A) extending from the anterior superior iliac spine to the midpoint of the patella and a line (B) from that same midpoint on the patella to the site of the attachment of the patellar tendon on the tibial tuberosity. *Note.* From ''Biomechanics and the Female Athlete'' by A.E. Atwater. In *Sport Science Perspectives for Women* (p. 7) by J. Puhl, C.H. Brown, and R.O. Voy (Eds.), 1988, Champaign, IL: Human Kinetics Books. Copyright 1988 by Human Kinetics Publishers, Inc. Reprinted by permission.

organs: the testes and the ovary. Eventually, the testes produce and secrete mainly androgens in the male, and the ovaries produce and secrete mainly estrogens and progesterone in the female. As reproductive ability is attained, the testes are able to produce spermatozoa. The male is able to have erections and ejaculations and is able to father a child. In contrast, females have menstrual cycles, whereby one egg per month is developed; as a result, she can become pregnant, give birth, and lactate. Many other significant sex differences besides reproductive capacities develop with puberty. These differences, which produce the characteristic sexual dimorphism seen in adulthood, result from the actions of the sex hormones (androgens and estrogens) not only in the sex organs themselves but also on many other target tissues common to both sexes. Developmental changes in the skeleton, breasts, hair follicles, and fat and lean tissues are quantitative rather than qualitative, however, and the secondary sex characteristics are merely a matter of degree.

With sexual maturation comes a tremendous increase in the rates of growth of various body parts. This acceleration results in changes in the skeleton and in the relative amounts of bone, muscle, and fat. In girls, the first outward sign of the onset of puberty is the development of the breasts (budding). This can occur any time from ages 8-1/2 to 13-1/2 years. The growth of pubic hair is usually the next sign and is followed about a year later by the appearance of underarm hair. About a year after breast budding, a girl reaches the peak of her adolescent growth spurt, and *menarche* (first menstrual period) occurs a year or so later. The average age for menarche in the United States is 12.8 years. This is no longer significantly different from the age at which her mother first menstruated. Previously, the age of menarche had steadily declined since data were first tabulated in the mid-19th century. Stabilization of the age of menarche is thought to be due to the better nutrition and general health enjoyed by large numbers of people in the world today.

In boys, the first sign of the onset of sexual maturation (testicular enlargement) appears later than it does in girls. The growth of pubic hair follows. The penis begins to grow rapidly approximately a year later. Underarm and facial hair usually develop 2 years after the development of pubic hair, but there is considerable individual variation.

With puberty, the increasing amounts of estrogen hasten the closing of the growth plates (epiphyses) in the bones of females. Consequently, girls complete their growth in height 2 years earlier than boys. At age 18, when the long bones stop growing in females, the average American young woman is 5 ft, 4-1/2 in. tall and weighs 123 lb. Her male counterpart is 5 ft, 9 in. tall and weighs 150 lb (Sloane, 1980). The male, however, will continue to grow until his early 20s, when his long bones, under the influence of testosterone, will cease growing. Males, then, end up approximately 10% taller because they have had about 2 years longer to grow.

Furthermore, males develop a larger larynx and a deeper voice, greater facial bone growth leading to more prominent features, a ruddier and coarser complexion, and more hair on the face and progressively less on the scalp. The shoulders and thoracic cage grow more rapidly in boys than in girls during this period; consequently, men have wider shoulders relative to hip width than women. As the boy matures, he loses fat and gains muscle mass and bone density. Females gain less muscle and bone but continue to gain fat (some excessively). In the female, fat is distributed differentially on the hips, buttocks, and breasts.

Physique

Physique refers to the general conformation of an individual's body. The most commonly used method of physique assessment is based on the premise that the body has three major components, or dimensions: fatness, or *endomorphy*; muscularity, or *mesomorphy*; and linearity, or *ectomorphy*. Because everyone has each of these components to some degree, a rating procedure can be used to describe morphology, or physique. A *somatotype* is a characterization of physique in terms of the three components previously outlined.

In early childhood, girls tend to have higher ratings for endomorphy and boys higher ratings for mesomorphy (Malina, 1980). The distribution of somatotype ratings indicates that there are more endomorphic girls than boys and more mesomorphic boys than girls. This represents a sex difference that is probably of genetic origin.

In boys, adolescence is characterized by a major development in the mesomorphic component, a reduction in the endomorphic component, and an increase in the ectomorphic component. In girls, however, adolescence corresponds to a primary development in endomorphy, a small increase in mesomorphy, and a reduction of ectomorphy. Therefore, in adulthood, men are generally more mesomorphic than women who are more endomorphic than men.

Both male and female athletes are less endomorphic and more mesomorphic than their respective nonathletic age-groups. The overall somatotype

ratings for the 1976 women (Montreal) Olympians were 2.8 for endomorphy, 3.8 for mesomorphy, and 3.1 for ectomorphy. University students' ratings were 4.0, 3.5, and 2.9, respectively. The ratings for the 1976 men Olympians were 2.1, 5.2, and 2.6 and for the university students 2.8, 4.9, and 2.8, respectively (Carter, 1981).

Body Composition

This section discusses sex differences in body composition and provides the basic framework for a later discussion on performance differences with sex, age, and state of training. Therefore, a brief description of *indirect methods* of estimating body composition is necessary.

Definitions

Body composition refers to the internal makeup of the body. Most indirect procedures to estimate body composition rely on a two-component model that divides the body into fat and lean masses. The following definitions were provided by Sady and Freedson (1984):

Lean body mass (LBM)—The mass of a body less all but essential fat

Fat-free mass (FFM)—The mass of a body less the ether-extractable fat (this still contains a small percentage of essential fat)

Adipose tissue—The tissues that contain fat (triglyceride), adipocytes (fat cells that contain some water), and supportive connective tissue

Essential fat—The fat (lipids such as lecithin and phospholipids) required for normal physiological functioning that is contained in bone marrow, heart, lung, liver, spleen, kidney, intestinal, muscle, and central nervous system tissues

Storage fat—The major fat depot that accumulates in adipose tissue (serves as a nutritional reserve and as protection for internal organs) and that includes subcutaneous fat deposits

Sex-specific fat—The fat that is specific to females

(sometimes included in the essential fat classification) and thought to be associated with hormone synthesis for reproduction

Body cell mass—The actively metabolizing cell mass (excluding extracellular tissues) that is considered a constant fraction of FFM

Methods

The underwater-weighing method (hydrostatic weighing) of estimating body composition is considered by most researchers to be the criterion method (i.e., the method from which the other methods are derived) and is based on the difference between body weight on land and body weight in water. The major problem with this method (as well as the other methods) is the underlying assumption that so-called biological constants are consistent with age, sex, race, state of hydration, health status, and level of training. Although fat density seems biologically stable (0.9007 g • cc^{-1}), the lean component is known to fluctuate with the previously mentioned factors. Therefore, the usual value for the density of lean tissue of 1.100 g • cc^{-1} is not really a constant but rather an average for the "typical" person (Sady & Freedson, 1984). This means that underwater-weighing estimates of body composition are likely to be subject to error for children, postmenopausal women, extra-lean or extra-fat persons, and various racial groups (e.g., blacks have a higher bone density than whites). Nevertheless, this method provides the best *estimate* we have, so values obtained by underwater weighing are emphasized throughout this book.

Another method of assessing body composition for which there are considerable data in the literature is the skinfold method. This technique is typically based on two to seven skinfold measurements (obtained with a skinfold caliper) that are incorporated into a multiple regression equation that indirectly estimates body density (Db) and from which (as with underwater weighing) percent body fat is obtained:

$$\% \text{ fat} = \left(\frac{4.950}{\text{Db}} - 4.500\right) \times 100 \text{ (Siri method)}$$

or

$$\% \text{ fat} = \left(\frac{4.570}{\text{Db}} - 4.142\right) \times 100 \text{ (Brozek method)}$$

Since this technique is based on underwater weighing, it is no better (in fact it is less accurate) than underwater weighing because subcutaneous fat is not distributed in the same pattern in all individuals. Skinfolds accurately determine where subcutaneous storage fat is distributed but do not give a very good estimate of an individual's total percent body fat. Other currently popular methods, such as bioelectrical impedance and infrared fat analysis, possess essentially similar inherent weaknesses at this point in their development.

Sex Differences

Now that some basic information has been discussed, it is appropriate to examine sex differences by age classification. Figure 1.8 indicates that males have higher body density values than females at all ages and consequently lower percentages of body fat. Small differences in body fat and LBM emerge very early in life, perhaps as early as 3 or 4 years of age (more information on body fat in children is covered in chapter 3). Lean body mass increases from about 25 kg at 10 years to about 42 kg at 16 years in girls, whereas muscle mass increases from about 12 kg at 9 years to 23 kg at 15 years (Malina, 1988). These variables increase only slightly in late adolescence, that is, to about 43 kg and 24 kg at ages 17 and 18, respectively. Thus the gain in LBM and muscle mass in adolescence is not as large in girls as in boys. By late adolescence, girls have attained about two thirds of the estimated values of boys (Malina, 1988). During puberty, both sexes acquire more fat, but the total (and relative) amount is much greater in girls than boys and the distribution of body fat rather different (Brook, 1985, pp. 12-13). In childhood, subcutaneous fat overlying the limbs is considerably greater than over the trunk. During puberty, boys lose limb fat but gain trunk fat. In girls the loss of limb fat is less marked, and fat accumulates around the shoulders, hips, and but-

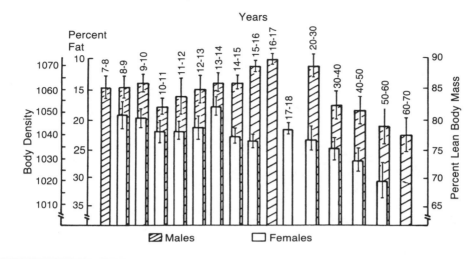

Figure 1.8 Changes in relative body fat with age for males and females. *Note.* From "Body Composition and Exercise During Growth and Development" by J. Pařízková. In *Physical Activity: Human Growth and Development* (p. 98) by G.L. Rarick (Ed.), 1973, New York: Academic Press, Inc. Copyright 1973 by Academic Press, Inc. Reprinted by permission.

tocks. In addition, the higher levels of androgenic hormones in the male following the adolescent growth spurt are thought to be responsible for the considerable increase in lean body tissue (mostly muscle mass) that occurs at that time. Fat tissue often decreases as well. The higher levels of estrogenic hormones in the adolescent and adult female are at least partially responsible for the higher percentage of fat tissue in the female body. The mature woman has a higher amount of *essential* body fat because of the fat tissue in the breast and other sex-specific tissues and organs. The absolute level of *storage* fat may equal that of men, but because the total body weight of the woman is less than that of the man, her *relative* storage fat is greater (Table 1.1).

Adult women have about 8% to 10% more body fat than men. Sparling (1980) reported values from about 13% to 16% and from 22% to 26% for young men and women, respectively. According to the data in Table 1.1, sex differences in storage fat are small, accounting for only a 3% difference in the percentage of total body weight. Absolute differences in body fat are negligible. The fat component that accounts for the largest propor-

tion of the difference in total fat is in sex-specific fat and is estimated to be about 5% of a woman's total weight (Katch, Campaigne, Freedson, & Sady, 1980).

Relative body fat varies with physical activity level as well as with sex and age. Highly active individuals of both sexes tend to be leaner than those who are less active. Highly active females are often much leaner than sedentary males. With the exception of some tennis players and field-event participants (see Table 1.2), female athletes are leaner than their college-age counterparts (22% to 25% body fat) and often leaner than average college-age men (15% to 18%). The difference in percent body fat is usually less between male and female athletes of the same sport than between males and females in the general population (see Table 1.2). In elite endurance athletes, the sex difference in percent body fat is often no more than 2% to 6%, a small difference that may reflect true biological differences, factors of specific genetic endowment, or both. The larger differences seen with more "typical" people (8% to 10%) may be related to differences in physical activity levels and sociocultural influences.

Table 1.1   Body Composition of Typical Adult Men and Women

Characteristics	Reference man[a]	Reference woman[a]	Reference woman[b]
Height	68.5	64.5	64.5
Weight	70.0	56.8	56.8
Muscle	31.4 (44.8%)	20.5 (36.0%)	21.0 (37.0%)
Bone	10.5 (14.9%)	6.8 (12.0%)	8.0 (14.0%)
Storage fat	8.4 (12.0%)	8.5 (15.0%)	8.5 (15.0%)
Essential fat	2.1 (3.0%)	6.8 (12.0%)	2.3 (4.0%)
Sex-specific fat	—	—	2.8 (5.0%)
Total fat	10.5 (15.0%)	15.3 (27.0%)	13.6 (24.0%)
Remainder	17.7 (25.3%)	14.2 (25.0%)	14.2 (25.0%)

Note. Height is given in inches, remaining characteristics are given in kilograms.

[a]Adapted from Lamb (1984). Data from Behnke (1969).

[b]Data from Katch, Campaigne, Freedson, and Sady (1980).

Table 1.2   Relative Body Fat Values for Athletes in Various Sports

Sports	Relative fat (%) Males	Females
Sprint running	3-6	9-11
Distance running	4-11	6-15
Gymnastics	5-10	8-12
Swimming		
Sprinting	6-10	8-12
Distance	8-12	10-14
Basketball	8-12	12-16
Baseball and softball	12-16	14-18
Bicycling	8	15
Orienteering	16	19
Rowing	11-14	9
Tennis	12-16	15-20
Track-and-field events		
Hurdles	5-6	16
Jumping	7	17
Discus	16-18	24
Shot put	16-20	28
Skiing		
Alpine	10-15	21
Cross-country	8-10	15-22

Note. Adapted from Wilmore (1977, p. 137).

Carter (1981) analyzed the skinfold fat patterns of 1976 (Montreal) Olympians. The women displayed a more consistent profile among the sports than the men. In order of fatness, the skinfold sites ranked as follows: front thigh (fattest), triceps/medial calf/umbilical, subscapular, and anterior suprailiac (thinnest). For the men, the order was generally as follows: thigh (fattest), umbilical/subscapular, triceps, medial calf, and anterior suprailiac (thinnest).

As middle age approaches, percent body fat gradually increases in both sexes. For men, one study reported an increase in body fat from approximately 18% at ages 18 to 25 to 36% at ages 65 to 85 (Novak, 1972). Fat-free mass subsequently declined from 82% body weight to 63%. For women, percent body fat increased from 33% at ages 18 to 25 to 44% at ages 65 to 85. Fat-free mass decreased from 67% to 55%. Similar decreases in body cell mass were noted.

Ratios of subcutaneous (S) fat to visceral (V) fat (determined by computed axial tomography) were determined in men and women from ages 20 to over 60 (Enzi et al., 1986). The S:V ratios were significantly higher (two to three times) in women than in men at all ages at both the thoracic and the abdominal areas. With age, S:V ratios increased in both sexes at the thoracic level in middle age (40-59) and then decreased after 60 years of age. The ratio decreased slightly with age at the abdominal level.

These results indicate that in young subjects, fat tissue is located mainly in the subcutaneous depots, particularly in women. After age 60, however, fat distribution becomes more internal, which may be related to relatively more androgenic hormonal activity than estrogenic activity (see chapter 10). The S:V ratio in postmenopausal women was significantly lower than in premenopausal women. With obesity, women tend to store fat preferentially in the subcutaneous abdominal area, whereas men tend to store fat in the visceral depots.

Summary

When full maturity is reached, the average woman is 5 in. shorter, 30 to 40 lb lighter in total weight, and considerably fatter (25% rather than 15% relative body fat) than the average man (see Table 1.3). The man will have broader shoulders, narrower hips, and a larger chest girth relative to his total body size. Sex differences in adult height are due primarily to the fact that boys grow over a longer period of time than girls. Sex differences in body structures are relatively minor before adolescence.

Sex differences in the adolescent growth spurt produce the characteristic sexual dimorphism seen in adulthood. Broadening of the shoulders relative to the hips is a characteristic of male adolescence, whereas broadening of the hips relative to the shoulders and waist is characteristic of female adolescence.

On the average, the male will have the greater proportion of his subcutaneous fat in the abdominal and upper regions of his body, whereas the female will carry substantially more of her fat in the hips and lower regions of her body. The woman's hips will be essentially equal to the man's in width even though the width of other regions of the body are approximately 10% larger in the man. The average woman will tend toward more endomorphy (fatness), whereas the average man will tend toward more mesomorphy (muscularity) and ectomorphy (linearity). The average young woman will have

Table 1.3   Summary of Some Morphological Differences Between the Sexes in Relation to Exercise Performance

Characteristics	Results
Skeletal system	
Women usually are smaller and shorter	Lighter body frame
Women have a wider pelvis, the thighs slant inward toward the knees, and the lower leg bones are less bowed than in men	Different running mechanics; some believe more prone to injury because of knee instability
Women have shorter limbs (relative to body length)	Shorter lever arms for movement (important for use of implements)
Women have narrower shoulders with more slope	Different mechanics of upper limb musculature
Body composition	
Women have a larger percent body fat and concentration of subcutaneous adipose tissue	Contours more rounded and less angular
Women have less LBM (less bone and muscle)	Physique less mesomorphic and more endomorphic Less metabolically active tissue More buoyant
Women have a smaller muscle mass	Lower absolute strength

approximately 22% to 26% relative body fat, whereas the young man will average between 12% and 16% relative body fat. The woman will have both a lower absolute lean body weight and a higher absolute fat weight.

To what extent these differences are truly biological or genetic has not been determined. Possibly, environmental or cultural factors are of major importance. Some evidence indicates that each of these factors makes a significant contribution to the differences observed. For example, women who engage in high-intensity endurance training have been shown to approach the relative body fat values observed in male athletes. On the other hand, average relative fat values for the fully mature woman are considerably above the values that many consider ideal. The sedentary lifestyle acquired by the average woman following puberty undoubtedly accounts for much of this excess adiposity.

Chapter 2

Physiological Differences and Similarities

Although morphological differences between the sexes are of considerable interest, it is likely that physiological differences are more important in terms of physical performance. As you will see, however, physiological differences are often due to differences in such factors as body size and composition. Thus, morphological and physiological differences are very much interrelated and may produce variations in performance between the sexes. Differences and similarities in performance are discussed in chapter 3.

Basal Metabolism

Metabolic rate, or *metabolism*, represents the conversion of food to energy for use by the body. *Basal metabolic rate* (BMR) is the rate of energy conversion measured under precise basal conditions (total quiet and supine rest) and represents the lowest metabolic rate that an individual attains during a 24-h period. Basal metabolic rate is usually expressed in terms of the caloric expenditure of the body relative to body surface area and represents the minimum amount of heat (calories) that must be produced to stay alive. Metabolic rate, of course, will increase in direct proportion to one's level of activity.

Basal metabolic rate decreases approximately 1% to 3% per decade from the age of 3 through 80. Until adulthood, this decrease is thought to represent improved metabolic efficiency. After about age 30, this decrease is due to a reduction in lean body mass (LBM). From just before puberty and throughout the rest of life, BMR is lower in the female than in the male, to a great extent because of the greater LBM of the male and the greater proportion of relatively inactive (metabolically) adipose tissue of the female. The BMR of young women usually averages about 37 kilocalories per square meter of body surface area per hour ($kcal \cdot m^{-2} \cdot h^{-1}$). Over a 24-h period, basal rates range from 1,200 to 1,400 kcal. In young men of comparable body structure, BMR averages 40 $kcal \cdot m^{-2} \cdot h^{-1}$, which corresponds to approximately 1,700 kcal for a 24-h period. Whereas a moderately active young woman requires about 2,400 kcal per day to maintain her body weight, the active young man requires about 3,000 to 3,200 kcal per day. Again, however, there are wide individual differences and much overlapping of values between boys and girls and between men and women. When BMR is calculated in terms of lean muscle mass rather than body surface area, the difference disappears (DeVries, 1980). One's BMR has little bearing on the effectiveness or efficiency of muscular activity.

Oxygen Uptake

Oxygen uptake ($\dot{V}O_2$) is the term used to represent the quantity of oxygen consumed by the body at any moment in time. It is usually measured over a period of 1 to 5 min by collecting one's expired air and is expressed in terms of liters of oxygen utilized by the body's cells per minute ($L \cdot min^{-1}$). The rate at which metabolic processes proceed dictates one's need for oxygen.

Maximal oxygen uptake ($\dot{V}O_2max$) is widely accepted as the best single measure of cardiovascular fitness and maximal *aerobic power*. Although ignoring several important factors contributing to overall fitness (such as strength and flexibility), the assumption that high $\dot{V}O_2max$ indicates superior physical fitness can be justified on several counts. For one, there is a strong positive relationship between $\dot{V}O_2max$ and total work output (Åstrand & Rodahl, 1977). For another, $\dot{V}O_2max$ provides a very good estimate of the potential of the cardiovascular system and one's endurance capacity (Shephard, 1977).

Few studies have shown significant sex differences in $\dot{V}O_2max$ until approximately age 11 or 12. With puberty, the girl's rate of improvement in $\dot{V}O_2max$ usually declines, coinciding with her lesser development of LBM and greater deposition of adipose tissue. Peak $\dot{V}O_2max$ values in both sexes are most frequently observed between the ages of 16 and 20 and are followed by a gradual decline (see Figure 2.1). However, peak values for $\dot{V}O_2max$ occurred at age 11 in Canadian girls (46 $ml \cdot kg^{-1} \cdot min^{-1}$) and at age 14 in Canadian boys (54 $ml \cdot kg^{-1} \cdot min^{-1}$). Sex differences were statistically significant after age 12 (MacDougall, Roche, Bar-Or, & Moroz, 1983).

Many factors affect cardiovascular or cardiorespiratory endurance as reflected by maximal aerobic power ($\dot{V}O_2max$). The following model is modified from that suggested by Pate and Kriska (1984):

1. Body weight and composition
   a. Active muscle mass
   b. Fat weight
2. Maximal systemic oxygen transport
   a. Maximal cardiac output ($\dot{Q}max$)
      (i) Maximal heart rate (HRmax)
      (ii) Maximal stroke volume (SVmax)
   b. Oxygen-carrying capacity (hemoglobin concentration)
3. Skeletal muscle oxidative capacity

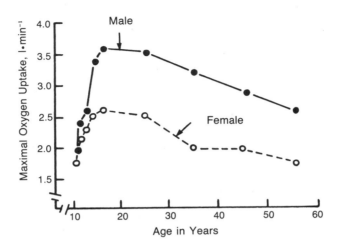

Figure 2.1 Maximal oxygen uptake as a function of age in males and females. Reprinted with permission of Macmillan Publishing Company from *Fitness, Health, and Work Capacity* by L.A. Larson (Ed.). Copyright © 1974 by Macmillan Publishing Co., Inc. (Figure is from p. 408 of L. Hermansen's chapter.)

Effects of Body Weight and Composition

It is well established that $\dot{V}O_2$max is largely dependent on one's body weight and active skeletal muscle mass. Because women are generally smaller and lighter in body size, weight, and LBM than men, it would be expected that $\dot{V}O_2$max expressed in absolute terms (i.e., L · min^{-1}) would be lower in women. Sparling (1980) completed an in-depth analysis of 15 comparisons of $\dot{V}O_2$max and body composition in men and women. His report is the best analysis to date of sex differences in maximal aerobic power. Sparling reported that approximately 66% of the variation in absolute $\dot{V}O_2$max was accounted for by simply knowing the sex of the subjects. On the average, the men's values for $\dot{V}O_2$max were 56% higher than the women's values.

Maximal oxygen uptake is often expressed in relative terms, that is, in milliliters of oxygen per kilogram of body weight per minute (ml · kg^{-1} · min^{-1}). Using this relative expression of $\dot{V}O_2$max reduces the apparent sex difference in maximal aerobic power to approximately 20% to 30%. When Sparling (1980) examined the sex difference

in $\dot{V}O_2$max expressed relative to body weight, the variance accounted for was 49%; that is, almost 50% of the variation was still unexplained by knowing the sex of the subjects. The men's values for $\dot{V}O_2$max averaged 28% higher than those of the women. Thus, part of the sex difference in $\dot{V}O_2$max is related to differences in body size and weight.

Aerobic power expressed per unit of body weight is of important practical significance because it is the best overall indicator of physical working capacity in weight-bearing exercise such as walking, running, bench stepping, and stair or hill climbing. Because women remain at a distinct disadvantage in certain occupational and athletic tasks, even when body weight is accounted for, it is important to understand the basis for this sex difference. One factor known to influence $\dot{V}O_2$max during weight-bearing work is relative body fatness. Body fat is essentially dead weight in that it contributes to the load carried (i.e., body weight) but not to the absolute $\dot{V}O_2$max (i.e., it does no work). Because the adult female has about 10% more relative body fat than the adult male, part of the difference between men and women in relative $\dot{V}O_2$max (ml • kg^{-1} • min^{-1}) is due to sex differences in fat.

If $\dot{V}O_2$max is expressed relative to fat-free weight (ml • kg FFW^{-1} • min^{-1}) instead of total body weight, the sex difference in $\dot{V}O_2$max is further reduced to approximately 15% on the average and in some cases to statistical nonsignificance. Sparling (1980) reported that the variance accounted for between men and women was reduced to 35% and that the men's values for $\dot{V}O_2$max (ml • kg FFW^{-1} • min^{-1}) were 12% to 15% higher than the women's values. This suggests that differences in body composition account for much but not all of the sex difference in $\dot{V}O_2$max.

By expressing $\dot{V}O_2$max relative to FFW, we are considering only that body tissue that contributes to the work done. Of course, comparing $\dot{V}O_2$max in terms of the fat-free body mass (or LBM) is merely an academic exercise in terms of actual performance because no way has yet been found to leave part of one's body behind at the starting line.

Cureton and Sparling (1980) added external weight to men in an attempt to duplicate the excess fat weight of women. Their study showed that sex differences were reduced by 30% when extra weight was added to the men. They concluded that the ''greater, essential, sex-specific fat of women is one determinant of the sex difference in metabolic responses to exercise and distance running performance'' (p. 293).

Washburn and Seals (1984) studied peak values of oxygen uptake ($\dot{V}O_2$) during arm cranking in men and women. When $\dot{V}O_2$ was expressed in liters per minute (L • min^{-1}) or milliliters per unit of body weight (ml • kg^{-1} • min^{-1}), the men had significantly higher values. However, when $\dot{V}O_2$ was expressed relative to the volume of the arms and shoulders, no significant difference was found, suggesting no sex-related differences in the ability of skeletal muscle to utilize oxygen during arm exercise. Washburn and Seals believe that the differences in $\dot{V}O_2$max between men and women are largely a function of the size of the contracting muscle mass.

Sparling (1980) reported that the sex difference in $\dot{V}O_2$max between trained men and women was less than that in the untrained subjects when expressed in liters per minute and milliliters per unit of body weight but not when expressed relative to FFW.

Maximal Systemic Oxygen Transport

Although the primary limiting factor of $\dot{V}O_2$max has been debated for years, most believe it is cardiac output, or the quantity of blood pumped by the heart per minute. Cardiac output ($\dot{Q}$) is the product of heart rate (HR) and stroke volume (SV).

Mostly as a result of her smaller body size, the woman has a smaller heart (heart volume) than does a man of the same age. Because of her smaller proportion of muscle tissue and larger fraction of adipose tissue, the ratio of heart weight to body weight is different between the sexes. From about the ages of 10 until 60, the average ratio for women is approximately 85% to 90% of the value for men. There is less difference in heart volume between trained men and women than between untrained subjects when heart volume is expressed in milliliters per unit of body weight (Fox & Mathews, 1981). The woman's smaller heart (in both absolute and relative terms) results in a smaller maximal SV during exercise than in men (Åstrand, Cuddy, Saltin, & Stenberg, 1964) and contributes to a sex difference in $\dot{Q}$max and thus $\dot{V}O_2$max. Furthermore, because SV is limited by heart volume, a woman's HR is usually higher than a man's at a given submaximal $\dot{Q}$. Often, the woman's HR is 5 to 8 beats per minute (bpm) faster than the man's at an equal exercise load. For both women and men, maximal HR decreases with advancing age.

In terms of maximal cardiac output ($\dot{Q}$max), there is a difference of approximately 30% between the sexes, men being able to deliver a larger $\dot{Q}$max. Much of this difference appears to be related to his larger heart volume and, consequently, larger SV because little or no difference is seen in maximal heart rate (HRmax) between the sexes (Drink-water, 1973).

Freedson, Katch, Sady, and Weltman (1979) measured $\dot{Q}$ differences in men and women matched for aerobic fitness as they performed low-intensity bicycle ergometer exercise. At a work load equivalent to 35% of maximum, the men had significantly lower values for $\dot{Q}$ and SV and higher values for arterial-venous oxygen difference $(a - \bar{v}O_2$, the variable that indicates the amount of oxygen extracted from the blood). When these variables were expressed relative to lean body weight, the differences between the sexes were not significant. The authors suggested that the observed differences in $\dot{Q}$ were due to differences in lean body weight. Another study, however, reported somewhat different results. In fact, Becklake, Frank, Dagenais, Ostiguy, and Guzman

(1965) reported that at submaximal work requiring equal levels of $\dot{V}O_2$, women in their 20s and 30s had lower a $\bar{v}O_2$ differences and higher $\dot{Q}$s than men of the same age. No differences in SV were seen in this study, but the women had higher HRs. Åstrand et al. (1964) found that the $\dot{Q}$ required to transport 1 L of oxygen during a submaximal work load requiring a $\dot{V}O_2$ of 1.5 L • min^{-1} was 9 L of blood for women (arterial O_2 content = 16.7 ml • 100 ml^{-1}) and 8 L for men (arterial O_2 content = 19.2 ml • 100 ml^{-1}). This is illustrated in Figure 2.2, which also shows that men can achieve higher $\dot{Q}$max values than women.

The principal variable influencing the oxygen-carrying capacity of the blood is the concentration of hemoglobin (Hb), the oxygen-carrying molecule contained in the red blood cells. Adult men have approximately 6% more red blood cells and 10%

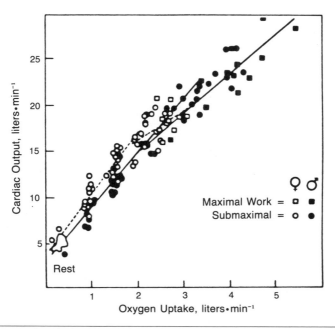

Figure 2.2 Cardiac output in relation to oxygen uptake at rest, during submaximal work, and during maximal exercise on a bicycle ergometer. Regression lines (broken lines for women) were calculated for experiments where the oxygen uptake was (1) below 70% and (2) about 70% of the individual's maximum. *Note.* From "Cardiac Output During Submaximal and Maximal Work" by P.-O. Åstrand, T.E. Cuddy, B. Saltin, and J. Stenberg, 1964, *Journal of Applied Physiology,* **19,** p. 271. Copyright 1964 by The American Physiological Society. Reprinted by permission.

to 15% more Hb per 100 ml of blood than women (Åstrand & Rodahl, 1977; DeVries, 1980). Consequently, women generally possess a lower oxygen-carrying capacity than men. This means that for any given level of $\dot{V}O_2$ (or metabolic activity), women must either deliver more blood to the tissues to supply the same quantity of oxygen or extract a greater quantity of oxygen from the blood provided.

Studying the relationship between oxygen-carrying capacity and $\dot{Q}$, Freedson (1981) reported a negative correlation between Hb concentration and $\dot{Q}$ at submaximal exercise intensities (54% and 69% $\dot{V}O_2$max). Her data showed that 69% of the variance in submaximal $\dot{Q}$ could be explained by differences in Hb concentrations.

Cureton et al. (1986) experimentally equalized the Hb concentrations [Hb] of male and female subjects. Before they reduced the men's [Hb], $\dot{V}O_2$max was 47% (L • min^{-1}) and 11.5% (ml • kg^{-1} • min^{-1}) higher in the men. Equalizing [Hb] reduced the mean $\dot{V}O_2$max of the men by 7.5% (L • min^{-1}) and 6.9% (ml • kg^{-1} • min^{-1}), which was less than predicted from proportional changes in the oxygen content of the arterial blood and a$-\bar{v}O_2$ difference during maximal exercise. The investigators concluded that the sex difference in [Hb] accounts for a significant but relatively small portion of the sex difference in $\dot{V}O_2$max.

Skeletal Muscle Oxidative Capacity

Oxygen is consumed primarily in the mitochondria of active skeletal muscle fibers during exercise. Succinic dehydrogenase (SDH) seems to be the muscle mitochondrial enzyme that best correlates with maximal aerobic power. Two studies from the same laboratory (Costill, Fink, Getchell, Ivy, & Witzmann, 1979; Costill et al., 1976) reported higher SDH activity in men runners than in equally well trained women runners. Although additional research is needed before a general conclusion can be reached, these studies suggest that men may manifest a greater muscle metabolic adaptation to endurance training than women (Pate & Kriska, 1984).

Additional Factors Possibly Affecting $\dot{V}O_2$max

Other factors for which there is a sex difference include blood pressure, oxygen pulse, respiratory volumes, and physical conditioning.

Systolic blood pressure (the contracting, emptying phase) usually increases with puberty. In girls, however, systolic blood pressure increases less than in boys and may even decrease until young adulthood. After menopause, systolic pressure may increase slightly over that of the adult male. Overall, fewer women suffer from essential hypertension (elevated blood pressure of unknown origin) than men.

Oxygen pulse represents the quantity of oxygen utilized by the body per heartbeat. It is a relative measure of the efficiency of the heart and the respiratory system. Many factors are involved, including blood volume, the Hb content of blood, $\dot{Q}$, body size, $\dot{V}O_2$, and HR. Until approximately age 15, there are essentially no sex differences in oxygen pulse at equal work rates. After this age, however, $\dot{V}O_2$max usually continues to improve in the male, and greater differences in HR are seen. Consequently, oxygen pulse values are often significantly higher in the adult male. Of course, physical fitness plays a large role in this variable, and many large individual differences are seen.

Respiratory volumes are not generally considered a limiting factor for $\dot{V}O_2$max at sea level or at low altitudes. However, a considerable sex difference exists for these variables. Because of her smaller body size, the postpubertal female has a smaller thorax than the postpubertal male. Thorax size corresponds fairly closely with *vital capacity* (VC), the maximal volume of air that can be moved through the lungs from a maximal inspiration to a maximal expiration. Thorax size is also related to *residual volume* (RV), the volume of air that remains in the lungs following maximal expiration. Because VC and RV are smaller in the female, *total lung capacity* (TLC) is also smaller. Figure 2.3 illustrates the subdivisions of TLC. The average respiratory volumes of adult men and women are shown in Table 2.1.

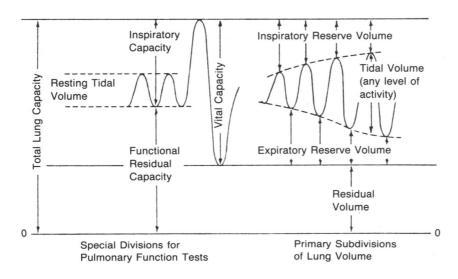

Figure 2.3   Subdivisions of the lung volume. *Note*. From "Standardization of Definitions and Symbols in Respiratory Physiology" by J.R. Pappenheimer et al., 1950, *Federation Proceedings, 9*, pp. 602-605. Copyright 1950 by Federation of American Societies for Experimental Biology. Reprinted by permission.

Generally, an adult female has about a 10% smaller *maximal breathing capacity* (MBC) than a male of comparable age. This is measured by breathing as deeply and rapidly as possible for 10 to 15 s and represents the maximal quantity of air that one can move. *Respiratory minute volume* ($\dot{V}_E$) is the volume of air breathed per minute at rest or while exercising. At the same submaximal $\dot{V}_E$, women usually display a smaller *tidal volume* and a faster *respiratory rate* than men ($\dot{V}_E$ = tidal volume × respiratory rate).

Earlier studies indicated that men tend to breathe more abdominally; that is, they use their diaphragms more than women. Perhaps this was a cultural difference; if so, this difference may not exist today (women no longer wear corsets that restrict abdominal movements). Physical training tends to produce more diaphragmatic breathing in both sexes. Apparently, diaphragmatic breathing is more economical than breathing predominantly with upper chest movements.

Physical conditioning and habitual physical activity is another factor that greatly influences $\dot{V}O_2$max. Considerable variation is seen in the

Table 2.1   Average Respiratory Volumes of Adult Men and Women

	Males (20-30 yr 1.7 M²BSA)	Females (20-30 yr 1.6 M²BSA)
Inspiratory capacity	3,600	2,400
Expiratory reserve volume	1,200	800
Vital capacity	4,800	3,200
Residual volume	1,200	1,000
Functional reserve capacity	2,400	1,800
Total lung capacity	6,000	4,200
RV/TLC × 100	20%	24%

Note. Values are approximate and expressed in milliliters. BSA = body surface area in meters. From *The Lung: Clinical Physiology and Pulmonary Function Tests* (2nd ed., p. 16) by J.H. Comroe, Jr., et al., 1962, Chicago: Year Book Medical Publishers. Copyright 1962 by Year Book Medical Publishers, Inc. Reprinted by permission.

aerobic capacity of children and adults that is thought to be related to one's lifestyle. Habitually active people have higher $\dot{V}O_2$max values (regardless of form of expression) than the sedentary. In fact, physical activity level usually overrides the

Table 2.2   Norms for $\dot{V}O_2$max (Maximal Aerobic Power in L • min^{-1} and ml • kg^{-1} • min^{-1}) for Adult Men and Women

Age	Low	Fair	Women Average	Good	High
20-29	1.69 (28)	1.70-1.99 (29-34)	2.00-2.49 (35-43)	2.50-2.79 (44-48)	2.80+ (49+)
30-39	1.59 (27)	1.60-1.89 (28-33)	1.90-2.39 (34-41)	2.40-2.69 (42-47)	2.70+ (48+)
40-49	1.49 (25)	1.50-1.79 (26-31)	1.80-2.29 (32-40)	2.30-2.59 (41-45)	2.60+ (46+)
50-65	1.29 (21)	1.30-1.59 (22-28)	1.60-2.09 (29-36)	2.10-2.39 (37-41)	2.40+ (42+)

Age	Low	Fair	Men Average	Good	High
20-29	2.79 (38)	2.80-3.09 (39-43)	3.10-3.69 (44-51)	3.70-3.99 (52-56)	4.00+ (57+)
30-39	2.49 (34)	2.50-2.79 (35-39)	2.80-3.39 (40-47)	3.40-3.69 (48-51)	3.70+ (52+)
40-49	2.19 (30)	2.20-2.49 (31-35)	2.50-3.09 (36-43)	3.10-3.39 (44-47)	3.40+ (48+)
50-59	1.89 (25)	1.90-2.19 (26-31)	2.20-2.79 (32-39)	2.80-3.09 (40-43)	3.10+ (44+)
60-69	1.59 (21)	1.60-1.89 (22-26)	1.90-2.49 (27-35)	2.50-2.79 (36-39)	2.80+ (40+)

Note. Figures in parentheses are milliliters of oxygen per kilogram body weight. From "Aerobic Work Capacity in Men and Women With Special Reference to Age" by I. Åstrand, 1960, *Acta Physiologica Scandinavica,* 49(Suppl. 169), pp. 2a-11a. Reprinted by permission of *Acta Physiologica Scandinavica.*

effect of sex. Most highly active females have better maximal aerobic capacities than males of the same age who are inactive.

$\dot{V}O_2$max Standards for the Nonathletic Population

In 1960, Irma Åstrand published standards for $\dot{V}O_2$max for men and women aged 20 to 65 (see Table 2.2). Although these norms have proven very useful, most exercise physiologists in the United States have found that the American population is less fit than the Scandinavian population, for which these norms were originally developed. Wilmore (1977) stated that the college-age American woman exhibits a $\dot{V}O_2$max between 30 and 44 ml • kg^{-1} • min^{-1}, whereas the mean value for men ranges between 45 and 53 ml • kg^{-1} • min^{-1}.

Sex Differences in $\dot{V}O_2$max in Athletic Populations

Table 2.3 presents the range of $\dot{V}O_2$max values reported in the literature for men and women classified as athletes. Comparison of this data with the standards of Åstrand (1960) in Table 2.2 illustrates the previous statement that highly active women have better maximal aerobic capacities than inactive men of the same age. This table also points out the range of $\dot{V}O_2$max values found in athletic groups within each sex. Note the range of $\dot{V}O_2$max values found among participants in different sports and the large overlap in values between male and female athletes. Female long-distance skiers and runners, for example, have a much higher maximal aerobic capacity than males who excel in tennis, baseball, football, and ice hockey.

Anaerobic Capacity and Blood Lactate

Very strenuous high-intensity exercise requires energy production (ATP per second) at a rate faster

Table 2.3 Comparative V̇O₂max Values for Athletes in Various Sports

Sports	V̇O₂max (ml · kg⁻¹ · min⁻¹)
Men	
Cross-country skiers	70-94
Long-distance runners:	
Collegiate runners	60-70
Average runners	55-62
Elite marathon runners	70-75
Elite middle-distance runners	76-84
Rowers	58-75
Bicyclists	55-70
Long-distance swimmers	48-68
Gymnasts	48-64
Speed skaters	50-75
Ice hockey players	50-60
Football players	45-64
Baseball players	45-55
Tennis players	42-56
Women	
Cross-country skiers	56-74
Average marathon runners	50-55
Olympic distance runners	55-62
National class distance runners	58-72
Pentathletes	43-52
Rowers	41-58
Distance swimmers	45-60
Speed skaters	40-52
Sprinters	38-52
Basketball players	35-45

Note. Adapted from Wilmore (1977, p. 41).

than can be produced aerobically (in the presence of oxygen). *Anaerobic* forms of metabolism are used extensively, but not exclusively, in high-intensity exercise that lasts for only a brief period of time (i.e., 30 s to 3 min) or for longer periods at somewhat lower levels of intensity to supplement aerobic metabolism. *Anaerobic glycolysis* (the anaerobic breakdown of glucose or glycogen)

results in the production of lactic acid. The concentration of blood lactic acid is a function of the production of lactate through anaerobic glycolysis and the removal of lactate through oxidation and other processes. The lactic acid measured in the blood is used as an indicator of the degree of *anaerobiosis* that has occurred. The term *lactate threshold* (LT) is used here to describe the level of exercise at which blood lactate rises above 4 mM. This point is most often expressed as a percentage of maximal aerobic power and is sometimes referred to in the literature as *anaerobic threshold* (AT). Because anaerobic energy production is far less efficient than aerobic metabolism, exercise beyond the LT is associated with fatigue, and sustained performance becomes limited. Performance in some distance or endurance events can be better predicted from LT than from V̇O₂max when comparing similarly trained individuals.

Relatively little is known about the anaerobic capacity, *anaerobic power*, or LT levels of girls and women. It is known that maximal postexercise lactate levels in children are lower than in adults and that boys usually reach higher levels than girls (Cunningham, 1980). Sex differences in blood lactate during rest or following maximal exercise, however, have not been reported in adults (Lamb, 1978). Women may have a lower lactate-formation capacity because of their smaller muscle mass (see following section), but at this point any observed differences in LT and peak lactate are due mainly to differences in the levels or the type of training of men and women athletes. Research is very limited on this topic.

Lactate threshold expressed in terms of percent of V̇O₂max does not differ between the sexes but is reached by most women and girls at a lower absolute work load. At equal submaximal work loads above that point, women have higher blood lactate levels than men. This indicates that the work required a larger anaerobic component and that the work load was more stressful for the woman. When work loads are expressed relative to aerobic power (i.e., percent of V̇O₂max), blood lactate concentrations are not different.

Metabolic Differences in Submaximal Exercise

The study of the oxygen cost of submaximal exercise has attracted considerable attention in recent years. The concepts of *efficiency* (the ratio between work output and energy input) and *economy* (the oxygen cost of a submaximal exercise load) are important to performance and have been observed to vary considerably among individuals, even those with very similar levels of maximal aerobic power. The notion that men and women may differ in exercise efficiency has been addressed during ergometer cycling and treadmill walking and running.

$\dot{V}O_2$ (L • min^{-1}) for ergometer cycling has been observed to be lower in women than men in most studies (Pate & Kriska, 1984). Most likely, these differences, which tended to be quite small, can be accounted for by differences in body weight. Two explanations have been offered:

1. The man's larger body weight is associated with a larger resting metabolic rate (which was not accounted for).
2. The man's heavier leg weight could be associated with a higher rate of internal work in moving the legs while cycling.

Although it appears that women are more efficient than men in stationary ergometer exercise, this may not apply to cycling in which the bicycle and the participant are moved translationally.

Circulatory Responses

Zwiren, Cureton, and Hutchinson (1983) studied circulatory responses (but not economy) to submaximal ergometer exercise in equally trained male and female runners and swimmers. Cardiac output, HR, SV, and $a-\bar{v}O_2$ difference were determined at 30%, 50%, 70%, and 90% of $\dot{V}O_2$max. Mean differences were smaller than previously reported, which may indicate that there was a significant difference in the earlier studies between the men and women in habitual physical activity and physical fitness. The investigators concluded that the previously reported magnitude of sex-related differences in circulatory responses to submaximal exercise may have been a consequence of the different levels of physical conditioning between the two groups. This is a matter to which all readers of the scientific literature should pay particular attention, as will be seen in the following discussion.

Efficiency and Economy

The literature is in disagreement regarding sex differences in efficiency of treadmill walking and running. Booyens and Keatinge (1957) reported that women, walking at 91 and 107 m • min^{-1}, expended 10% less energy than men. Durnin and Namyslowski (1958) found that men and women walked with equal metabolic cost on a treadmill at zero grade and at a 10% grade. Gehlsen and Dill (1977) compared the performance of men and women in grade walking in two groups having the same averages for age, height, and weight. Despite these uniformities, the women had a lower $\dot{V}O_2$ while standing at rest (by 13%) and when walking at 80 m • min^{-1} on a 7% grade (by 3.6%). The difference while grade walking was almost entirely accounted for by the women's lower resting $\dot{V}O_2$. After the resting $\dot{V}O_2$ values were subtracted from the grade walking values, the rate of net $\dot{V}O_2$ was not significantly different.

Bransford and Howley (1977) reported that both trained and untrained men were more economical than trained and untrained women during treadmill running, but there were significant differences in the relative experience of the *trained* groups. In contrast, Daniels, Krahenbuhl, Foster, Gilbert, and Daniels (1977) and Wells, Hecht, and Krahenbuhl (1981) found no significant differences in the metabolic costs of submaximal running (ml • kg^{-1} • min^{-1}) between highly trained men and women distance runners of relatively equal ability and fitness. These investigators attributed the sex differences in running performances at middle- and long-distance races to differences in $\dot{V}O_2$max.

Pate, Barnes, and Miller (1985) conducted a study that compared absolute performance-matched men and women distance runners (rather than comparable relative performance levels as in Daniels et al., 1977, and Wells et al., 1981). The sexes did not differ in percent body fat, relative $\dot{V}O_2$max, or running economy (ml $\cdot$ kg^{-1} $\cdot$ min^{-1}) at speeds of 161 to 228 m $\cdot$ min^{-1}.

Although the issue of the running economy of women compared to men is not fully resolved, such factors as a wider pelvis, shorter legs, more oblique femurs, a larger ratio of leg weight to body weight, greater fat deposition on the thigh, and a higher stride frequency at a given speed have been suggested to contribute to a less mechanically efficient running gait in nonelite female performers (Daniels et al., 1977; Pate & Kriska, 1984).

Because female competitors have lower $\dot{V}O_2$max, they are working at a higher percentage of their $\dot{V}O_2$max during a standard work load such as a given submaximal running speed. Since blood lactate accumulation is determined largely by the percent of $\dot{V}O_2$max used during exercise, this disparity may contribute to sex differences in long-distance running performance.

In summary, during a standardized submaximal work task, the absolute value of $\dot{V}O_2$ for the woman will be lower than that of the man because of smaller body size and LBM. When the aerobic demand is expressed relative to body weight, the cost is likely to be equal, but the percentage of $\dot{V}O_2$max will be higher for the woman (if the man's $\dot{V}O_2$max is higher). Very likely, the woman will compensate for the smaller amount of oxygen in her arterial blood (due to less Hb and smaller blood volume) by increasing her $\dot{Q}$ above the man's. Her HR will probably be higher than a man's because comparatively little of the increase in $\dot{Q}$ will be accounted for by an increase in SV. Finally, if the work load is above the anaerobic threshold, the woman's blood lactate will exceed the man's. Table 2.4 summarizes many of the differences and similarities in unmatched subjects discussed here.

Table 2.4   Differences and Similarities Between the Sexes in Response to Exercise

Variables	Rest	Standardized submaximal work	Relative (% $\dot{V}O_2$max) submaximal work	Maximal work
HR	Women higher	Women higher	Women same or higher	Women same
SV	Women lower	Women lower	Women lower	Women lower
$\dot{Q}$	Women lower	Women higher	Women lower	Women lower
$a - \bar{v}O_2$	Women same or lower	Women higher	Women lower	Women lower
$\dot{V}O_2$	Women lower	Women lower (% $\dot{V}O_2$max higher)	Same percent $\dot{V}O_2$max	Women lower
LA	Women same	Women higher	Same percent $\dot{V}O_2$max	Women same or lower

Note. Derived from data from Åstrand, Cuddy, Saltin, and Stenberg (1964) and Zwiren, Cureton, and Hutchinson (1983).

Fat Metabolism

A few years ago, Ernst van Aaken proposed that women were especially adapted for endurance performance because they had a special ability to metabolize fat. Because women—even highly trained long-distance runners—have more fat than men, van Aaken believed that this meant that women would surpass men in long-distance running performance. Widespread throughout Europe, his statements about this were proclaimed in the United States by pathologist Joan Ullyot (1976) in a book titled *Women's Running*.

Endurance training, especially that characterized by slow long-distance running, is well known to enhance lipid metabolism in exercising skeletal muscle. No sex differences in this factor, however, have been detected (Bransford & Howley, 1979; Costill et al., 1979). In one study, male and female runners of similar $\dot{V}O_2$max and training mileage ran for 1 h at a speed requiring 70% of their $\dot{V}O_2$max. Muscle biopsies were obtained from the gastrocnemius muscle. No differences were found in the percentages of the various kinds of muscle tissue (see next section). Although there was wide individual variability, the men and women derived similar fractions of their energy from lipids (fats) during the hour run. There were also no sex differences in serum free fatty acid (FFA) or glycerol concentrations during the runs. In vitro lipid oxidation was significantly less in the women's muscle samples. It was suggested that this was due to the women's lesser mitochondrial density. The investigators believe that the differences in enzyme activities and the in vitro measurement of lipid oxidation had no functional effect on the utilization of lipids during the submaximal run (Costill et al., 1979). In sum, although the notion that women can mobilize and utilize their body fats more advantageously than men is attractive and seemed reasonable, it has not been supported by research.

Muscle Tissue

Muscle fibers are usually classified according to their contractile properties. Slow-twitch muscle fibers are red in color because of their high concentration of myoglobin, a reddish molecule with a similar oxygen-carrying function as Hb. These fibers possess large quantities of enzymes specific to oxidative or aerobic metabolism and are said to be fatigue resistant. As such, they are utilized (recruited) for prolonged, submaximal work characterized as endurance exercise. Fast-twitch fibers are paler because of their low concentration of myoglobin but possess high concentrations of enzymes specific to anaerobic glycolysis. These fibers are capable of producing large quantities of lactic acid; consequently, they fatigue rapidly. Fast-twitch fibers are utilized for more intensive exercise (characterized as power exercise) than are slow-twitch fibers. Hence, slow-twitch fibers are said to be oxidative (or aerobic) and fast-twitch fibers glycolytic (or anaerobic). Fast-twitch fibers have been further classified into fast-twitch oxidative-glycolytic (FOG) fibers and fast-twitch glycolytic (FG) fibers because some fast-twitch fibers possess greater oxidative capacity than others.

Although it is well established that the male has a larger muscle mass than the female after puberty because of higher levels of androgenic hormones (mainly testosterone), studies have failed to find sex differences in the relative distribution of the various types of slow- and fast-twitch muscle fibers (Costill et al., 1976, 1979; Edstrom & Nystrom, 1969; Prince, Hikida, & Hagerman, 1977). Sedentary men and women have about 50% slow-twitch fibers in the vastus lateralis muscle, but this varies widely among individuals (Byrnes, 1988). When fiber area is compared, men have larger slow-twitch and fast-twitch fibers than women. Therefore, the larger muscle mass of the adult male is due not to differences in distribution of fast- or slow-twitch muscle fibers but to differences in the size (cross-sectional area) of the muscle fibers. The fast-twitch fibers of both trained and untrained men are usually larger than their slow-twitch fibers, but in untrained women the two types of fibers are about the same size (Brooke & Engel, 1969), presumably because untrained women are typically less involved in activities that require the type of forceful contractions that are needed to develop their fast-twitch fibers. Therefore, sex differences in fiber size may be partly due to differences in physical activity patterns. The larger muscle mass of the male provides an obvious advantage in terms of strength and power, a topic discussed in chapter 3.

With aging, relative fiber distribution remains constant, but differential changes occur in fiber area (Byrnes, 1988). Although slow-twitch fiber area remains constant in both sexes, fast-twitch fiber number and size decrease in men by age 80. Changes do not seem to be as pronounced in women, probably because their fast-twitch fibers are not as well developed.

Successful athletes in most sports have mixed muscle fiber distributions that are similar to the average population. However, there appears to be a relationship between muscle fiber composition and performance in some activities (for reviews of this topic, see Byrnes, 1988, and Puhl, 1986). In sports in which fiber distribution patterns seem specific (see Figure 2.4), female athletes seem to have muscle fiber ratio patterns similar to male athletes of the same sport.

Although it is well known that men experience considerable muscular *hypertrophy* (increase in size) as a result of strength training, women do not seem to do so. However, studies on female athletes have shown that they have larger slow- and fast-twitch fibers than untrained women (Prince et al., 1977) and that some female athletes have fast-twitch fibers that are larger than their slow-twitch fibers—a pattern similar to that found in men (Costill et al., 1976; Puhl, 1986). Burke, Cerny, Costill, and Fink (1977) found that highly trained women cyclists had significantly larger fibers than active women and untrained men. These findings suggest that women are capable of significant increases in muscle fiber hypertrophy given sufficient training.

Thermoregulation

As previously described, women have a different morphological configuration than men. Some of these features, plus other factors outlined in Table 2.5, have a direct effect on thermoregulation in the heat and cold. For a more extensive treatment of this topic, refer to Drinkwater (1986), Haymes (1984, 1988b), Haymes and Wells (1986), Nunneley (1978), Wagner and Horvath (1985a, 1985b), and Wells (1977).

Early studies that compared responses of men and women to heat stress concluded that the woman was less tolerant of exercise in the heat. However, it became evident that the female subjects were considerably less physically fit than the male subjects. Furthermore, these studies utilized standardized exercise loads, which meant that the women were exercising at a higher percentage of their $\dot{V}O_2$max. Core temperature is now known to be directly proportional to relative exercise intensity (percent $\dot{V}O_2$max). Numerous studies conducted since 1980 have shown that men and women exercising at the same relative intensity tolerate heat equally well.

One of the most important items listed in Table 2.5 is the woman's larger ratio of surface area to mass. Body surface area (BSA) is important for heat exchange (either heat gain or heat loss). Body mass is important for heat production. A larger BSA will result in more heat gain through radiation, conduction, and convection from the environment under hot conditions and will allow a rapid loss of heat under cold conditions. In dry heat, a large BSA offers a considerable advantage because the evaporation of sweat is enhanced, providing an excellent cooling effect. In humid heat, a large BSA offers no advantage in terms of sweat evaporation but should allow for more heat dissipation through the skin as long as the skin temperature exceeds the ambient temperature. In the cold, a large ratio of BSA to body mass offers a distinct disadvantage in terms of heat loss from the body core, but it appears that the woman's thicker layer of subcutaneous fat provides an important insulating effect that more than compensates for the loss. In addition, a smaller body (everything else being the same) will have a lower thermal mass, so the smaller person will lose or gain heat more rapidly,

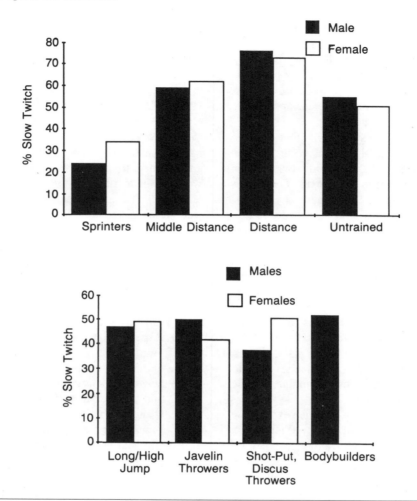

Figure 2.4 A summary from several sources of the muscle fiber composition of male and female track athletes. *Note*. From ''Female and Male Skeletal Muscle Fiber Composition and Performance'' by W.C. Byrnes. In *Sport Science Perspectives for Women* (pp. 29, 30) by J. Puhl, C.H. Brown, and R.O. Voy (Eds.), 1988, Champaign, IL: Human Kinetics Books. Copyright 1988 by Human Kinetics Publishers, Inc. Reprinted by permission. Data from Costill, Daniels, et al. (1976); Costill, Fink, and Pollock (1976); Edgerton, Smith, and Simpson (1975); Gregor et al. (1979); Saltin et al. (1977); and Schantz et al. (1983).

depending on the thermal gradient between the body and the environment.

In the final analysis, it appears that cardiovascular fitness is probably the most important variable in terms of heat tolerance because the effector mechanisms (vasodilation and sweating) depend greatly on the maintenance of Q̇ and total peripheral resistance. Individuals with low levels of cardiovascular fitness are rather intolerant of heat stress, as are people with coronary disease or obesity. When men and women are matched for fitness, level of acclimatization, or both, there does not appear to be a significant difference in heat tolerance. However, the mechanisms used by men

Table 2.5 Factors That Affect Thermoregulation in Women Compared to Men

Characteristics	Results
Smaller body mass; less lean body tissue; lower absolute $\dot{V}O_2$max	Lower heat production
Larger SA:Mass	In hot environment: Higher rate of heat gain via R, C, K In cold environment: Higher rate of heat loss via R, C, K, E Higher ratio of evaporative surface to metabolically active tissue Low thermal mass: Will gain or lose heat rapidly
Thicker layer of subcutaneous fat (but less proportionately on trunk than on legs)	Extra insulation (but less relative protection of body core); improved tolerance of cold air or water In cold, lower T_{sk}
Threshold for shivering set at higher T_c and T_{sk}	Earlier onset of shivering
More vasoconstriction in extremities in cold	Protects core, but greater risk of frost bite
Higher skin temperature	Reduces core to skin temperature gradient, thus reducing heat exchange
Smaller girth of extremities	Proportionately larger surface area for heat loss
Requires higher T_c and T_{sk} to initiate sweating	Higher heat storage before sweating
Possible lower fitness level	Less cardiac reserve; possible compromise to exercise in the heat

Note. SA = surface area, T_{sk} = skin temperature, R = radiation, C = convection, K = conduction, E = evaporation, and T_c = core temperature.

and women to dissipate body heat may be somewhat different, probably because of the factors listed in Table 2.5. The most notable difference appears to be that women generally do not sweat as much as men unless they are physically trained or heat acclimatized. In summary, fitness level and acclimatization seem to be more important factors than sex when assessing response to heat stress.

In a cold environment, women generally are less able to produce heat through either exercise or shivering because of less lean body tissue. However, their additional subcutaneous fat provides more tissue insulation. In the cold, men tend to maintain a lower HR, higher SV, and higher mean arterial blood pressure than women, but there are

no distinct differences in cold tolerance when the subjects are matched for aerobic fitness or exercise at the same relative work load.

Summary

Table 2.6 summarizes some of the physiological differences between the sexes. The net result of these differences is that women have lower *absolute* maximal aerobic capacity and muscular strength than men. However, when these parameters are examined in *relative* terms such as body weight or LBM, much of the variation between the sexes is explained. This indicates that the morphological differences discussed in chapter 1 are

Table 2.6   Summary of Some Physiological Differences Between the Sexes

Characteristics	Results
Cardiovascular system	
Women have lower blood volume, fewer RBCs ($\approx 6\%$ fewer), and less HB ($\approx 15\%$ fewer)	Lower total oxygen-carrying capacity of blood
Women have smaller hearts	Higher HR, smaller SV, and lower oxygen pulse for given $\dot{Q}$ and $\dot{V}O_2$
Women have lower $\dot{Q}$max	Lower $\dot{V}O_2$max (20%-25% lower)
Respiratory system	
Women have a smaller thorax	Lower VC, TV, RV, and MBC
Women have less lung tissue	Lower $\dot{V}_E$max
Muscular system	
No differences in the distribution of slow- and fast-twitch fibers	
Women have smaller muscle mass (fewer fibers and smaller fibers)	40%-60% weaker in upper body strength, 25% weaker in lower body strength

largely responsible for the more functional differences discussed in this chapter.

Physiological differences are smaller among well-trained male and female athletes within the same sport than within the general population. This implies that much of the variation between the sexes may be attributable to behavioral factors as well as to strictly biological differences. It should be remembered that there are wide morphological, physiological, and behavioral variations within each sex.

Chapter 3

Performance Differences

The morphological (structural) and physiological (functional) differences and similarities between the sexes were presented and discussed in the two preceding chapters. Clearly, many functional differences are the results of basic differences in body size and composition. Because the cellular mechanisms that control the physiological and biochemical responses to exercise are identical for both sexes, slightly different quantitative responses can result in significant performance differences. This chapter examines various performance records of boys and girls and men and women and attempts to explain these differences in terms of the morphological and physiological differences previously presented.

Strength

Strength is directly related to the number and absolute size of the muscle fibers recruited. This explains most of the usual sex differences in strength seen after puberty. Therefore, men are usually stronger than women because they have more muscle mass. When muscular strength is expressed relative to LBM or to cross-sectional area of muscle, sex differences often disappear, a further indication that, qualitatively, there is no sex difference in the innate strength of muscle tissue. However, because strength increases faster in the male at puberty than does muscle size, differences in muscle size may not be the only explanation for sex differences in strength (Lamb, 1978).

Generally, the female after age 16 is about two thirds as strong as most males of her age. However, there are wide individual differences that may be due to differences in either physiological maturity or habitual activity patterns. At puberty, the boy experiences a rapid increase in strength, which is probably due to the influence of testosterone, the sex hormone known to stimulate muscle growth. Developmentally, the ratio of strength to body weight following puberty favors the male. This is due to the female's greater adiposity in relation to LBM rather than to differences in the structure or function of skeletal muscle itself. It is during this period of life, however, that one often sees changes in physical activity patterns between boys and girls. Boys usually remain physically active and often become intensely interested in sport and in the physical development of their bodies. Many girls, on the other hand, decrease their usual daily activity patterns, viewing it as childish or immature to play. Only those girls who become interested in competitive sport continue (and may even increase) their daily activity levels. Strength differences, in my opinion, are probably very much related to these possible differences in daily activity patterns.

Malina (1980) has shown that boys tend to have greater strength than girls at all ages. His data indicate that girls achieve strength values closest to those of boys at about ages 10 to 11. Following this, girls increase in strength at ages 11 through 17. A woman's strength will continue to increase until full maturity occurs at about age 30. A boy shows his greatest increase in strength at about 15 or 16 and continues gaining in strength until about 25.

Montoye and Lamphiear (1977) found large differences in grip strength and arm strength between the sexes in the community of Tecumseh, Michigan after the age of about 14 years (Figure 3.1). One of the most significant things about this study was the large number of individuals tested.

Table 3.1 expresses women's strength scores as a percentage of those of men found in the literature. The larger the value, the smaller the sex difference. As can be seen, the difference in strength between the sexes depends on the muscle group measured and to a lesser extent on the training status of the subjects. Generally, the strength differences between the sexes are larger in measures of upper body strength than lower. Wilmore (1974) speculated that upper body strength is relatively lower in women because women have not traditionally engaged in upper body strength activities as frequently as boys or men.

Sex differences in strength can also be evaluated by examining differences in strength in relation to body size (body weight) and body composition (strength per unit of lean body weight). In Figure 3.2, strength differences are expressed in terms of absolute strength, strength per unit of body weight, and strength per unit of lean body weight. A ratio less than 1 means that the men are stronger. This figure indicates that in relation to men, women are weakest in the chest, arms, and shoulders and strongest in the legs. This is also shown in Table 3.1. However, when strength is expressed in terms of total body weight or in terms of LBM (which closely approximates the total muscle mass), the difference between the sexes is reduced considerably. Heyward, Johannes-Ellis, and Romer (1986) studied sex differences in shoulder flexion and knee extension as a function of differences in lean

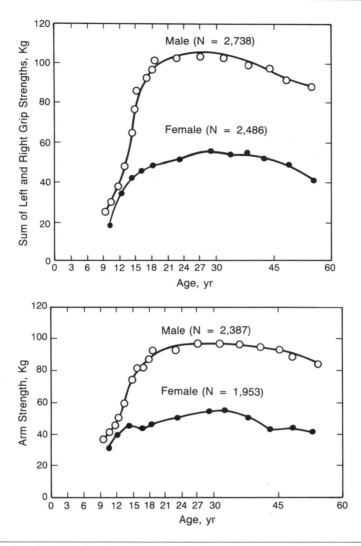

Figure 3.1 Changes in grip strength and arm strength with age. *Note*. Data from Mantoye and Lamphiear (1977, p. 109).

body mass and the distribution of muscle and subcutaneous fat in the body segments. They reported that strength in women and men did not differ significantly when differences in lean body mass, arm and thigh girths, and triceps and thigh skinfolds were statistically controlled. High strength scores were associated with high lean body weight and a large arm girth. In men, a substantial portion of both shoulder flexion and knee extension strength was explained by lean body mass alone. In women, strength variations were explained more adequately by including limb variables with lean body mass. They also reported that upper body strength was relatively more important than lower body strength in characterizing the sex differences.

Table 3.1   Ratio of Absolute Strength in Women and Men

References	Subjects	Ratio (%)
Handgrip		
Wilmore (1974)	Students	57
Laubach (1976)	Untrained	52
Bishop et al. (1987)	Swimmers	67
	Untrained	62
Bench press		
Wilmore (1974)	Students	37
Wilmore et al. (1978)	Students	50
Hosler & Morrow (1982)	Students	36
Bishop et al. (1987)	Swimmers	57
	Untrained	46
Leg press		
Wilmore (1974)	Students	73
Wilmore et al. (1978)	Students	47
Hosler & Morrow (1982)	Students	56
Bishop et al. (1987)	Swimmers	73
	Untrained	63
Flexion/extension		
Heyward et al. (1986)	Physically active	54[a]
Heyward et al. (1986)	Physically active	68[b]

Note. Ratio (%) = (female/male) × 100.

[a]Shoulder flexion.

[b]Knee extension.

Bishop, Cureton, and Collins (1987) studied sex differences in strength among swimmers and untrained subjects. Differences in absolute strength were generally smaller for the swimmers than for the nonathletes. Adjusting strength for FFW and for fat-free cross-sectional area of the limbs eliminated sex differences for all measures except curl and bench press scores. The combination of these variables accounted for an average of 97% of the sex-related variance in strength for both the swimmers and the nonathletes. These findings suggest that sex differences in muscular strength in equally trained men and women are almost entirely accounted for by differences in muscle size.

Anderson, Coté, Coyle, and Roby (1979) have obtained similar results. For isometric contractions and at slow speeds for isokinetic contractions, knee extensor strength expressed per unit of lean body mass was the same in men and women. However, at contraction speeds greater than 180° per second, the men were significantly stronger. This difference in power was also demonstrated in a jump-reach test. It is difficult to explain these results because differences in muscle fiber type and fiber recruitment patterns between the sexes have not been demonstrated.

Atwater (1988) stated that strength itself, plus the ability to apply it fast (speed and power), is critical for performing many sports. She cited throwing, running, and jumping as prime examples and gave specific illustrations of how strength, speed, and power interact with biomechanical factors, such as longer segment (bone) lengths, to partially explain sport performance differences between men and women.

Table 3.2 presents a comparison of the 1987 men's and women's U.S. Weightlifting Federation records for the common body weight classes. These represent elite performances for both sexes. The ratios of performance are only slightly higher than those in Table 3.1, and two outstanding clean-and-jerk performances (52- and 56-kg classes) can be noted. The average ratio of performance in the snatch was 61% and in the clean and jerk 65%. Mean values for weight lifted per kilogram of body weight were as follows:

- Snatch: 1.17 for women and 1.93 for men
- Clean and jerk: 1.56 for women and 2.41 for men

Very useful standard scores for women's weight-training classes have been provided by Kindig, Soares, Wisenbaker, and Mrvos (1984) in an article titled "Standard Scores for Women's Weight Training" (*The Physician and Sportsmedicine*, Vol. 12, No. 10, pp. 67-74) for the bench press, half squat, bent-arm pullover, military press, and dead lift. These standards are appropriate for young women of college age.

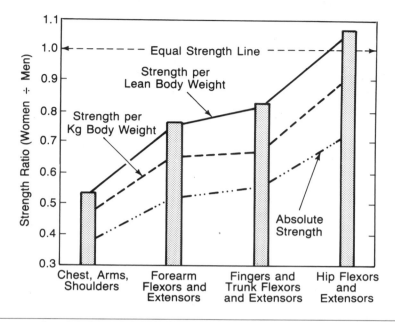

Figure 3.2 The strength ratio when strength in both sexes is expressed in terms of total body weight and lean body mass. *Note.* Data from Wilmore (1974, p. 135).

Strength Training

Although muscle size has been associated with muscular strength, hypertrophy (increase in muscle size or bulk) has been associated with gains in strength. It is well known that males experience both hypertrophy and increases in strength with intensive weight training. Women and girls, however, exhibit very little of the muscular hypertrophy exhibited by men and boys (after puberty) in response to weight training. Because muscular development is linked with plasma testosterone levels, males are capable of considerably greater gains in muscle bulk than are females. Nevertheless, females substantially increase in strength when placed on a progressive resistance weight-training program.

In one often-cited study (Wilmore, 1974), adult men and women participated in 10 weeks of intensive weight training. The men were stronger than the women. Both groups, however, made significant gains in strength in both absolute and relative terms. The changes in body composition were nearly identical for both groups: no change in total body weight, a substantial increase in lean body mass, and significant decreases in relative and total body fat. The degree of muscular hypertrophy was substantially greater in the men than in the women. In fact, the women gained only 1/4 in. on the upper body girth measurements (an insignificant amount). The relationships between absolute strength and girth size for men ranged from 0.63 to 0.77. For women, the correlations were much lower, ranging from 0.09 to 0.42. Wilmore concluded that muscular hypertrophy was not "a consistent or necessary consequence of strength training" (p. 138).

Another study (Brown & Wilmore, 1974) showed that although women responded to 6 months of maximum resistance training with large and significant strength gains, they showed only 0.4% and 2.0% increases in thigh and arm girths, respectively.

A major limitation of both these studies is the use of limb girth to study muscle hypertrophy.

Table 3.2   U.S. Weightlifting Federation Records as of November 1, 1987

Weight class	U.S. women's record[a]	U.S. men's record[a]	Ratio (in %, women/men)	kg lifted · kg BW^{-1}	
				Women	Men
52 kg					
S	60.0	90.5	66	1.15	1.74
C & J	85.0	115.0	74	1.63	2.21
Total	145.0	205.0	—	—	—
56 kg					
S	67.5	112.5	60	1.20	2.01
C & J	96.5	135.0	71	1.72	2.41
Total	160.0	242.5	—	—	—
60 kg					
S	73.0	115.0	63	1.22	1.92
C & J	95.0	152.5	62	1.58	2.54
Total	157.5	260.0	—	—	—
67.5 kg					
S	85.0	133.5	64	1.26	1.98
C & J	102.5	165.0	62	1.52	2.44
Total	185.0	297.5	—	—	—
75.0 kg					
S	80.0	152.5	52	1.06	2.03
C & J	104.0	182.5	57	1.39	2.43
Total	177.5	327.5	—	—	—
82.5 kg					
S	97.5	157.5	62	1.18	1.91
C & J	125.0	200.0	62	1.51	2.42
Total	220.0	355.0	—	—	—

Note. Ratio (%) = (female/male) × 100. S = snatch, C & J = clean and jerk, and BW = body weight. [a]Data expressed as kilograms.

Limb girth reflects the underlying subcutaneous fat as well as muscle mass. Women have more subcutaneous fat than men. It is quite possible that losses of subcutaneous fat were equal to or exceeded changes in muscle mass. Similar studies of the relationship between strength training and muscle mass in women should be undertaken with the sophisticated imaging techniques now available.

What about women bodybuilders? If women do not bulk up in response to weight lifting, how do these women develop such large muscles? There are at least five explanations for the rather remarkable muscular development seen in women bodybuilders. First, there is the element of genetic endowment. If one does not have the genetic potential for developing large muscles, no amount of physical training will result in the development of unusually large, prominent muscles. It is likely that successful bodybuilders have a larger than average proportion of fast-twitch muscle fibers because this type of skeletal muscle is most likely

Table 3.3   50th-Percentile Scores of U.S. Boys and Girls From the 1976 AAHPER Youth Fitness Test

	Ages							
	10	11	12	13	14	15	16	17
Flexed-knee sit-ups								
Boys	31	34	35	38	41	42	41	41
Girls	27	29	29	30	30	31	30	30
40-yd shuttle run (s)								
Boys	11.2	10.9	10.7	10.4	10.1	9.9	9.9	9.8
Girls	11.8	11.5	11.4	11.2	11.0	11.0	11.2	11.1
Standing long jump								
Boys	4' 11''	5' 2''	5' 5''	5' 9''	6' 2''	6' 8''	7' 0''	7' 2''
Girls	4' 8''	4' 11''	5' 0''	5' 3''	5' 4''	5' 5''	5' 3''	5' 5''
50-yd dash (s)								
Boys	8.2	8.0	7.8	7.5	7.2	6.9	6.7	6.6
Girls	8.6	8.3	8.1	8.0	7.8	7.8	7.9	7.9
600-yd run-walk (min:s)								
Boys	2:33	2:27	2:19	2:10	2:03	1:56	1:52	1:52
Girls	2:56	2:53	2:47	2:41	2:40	2:37	2:43	2:41

Note. Data from American Alliance for Health, Physical Education, Recreation and Dance (1976).

due to hypertrophy in response to progressive resistance training. Second, it is probable that both male and female bodybuilders utilize anabolic steroids to enhance muscular development. Of course, no one talks about this because it is both an illegal and unethical sporting practice. Still, it is common knowledge that male weight lifters and bodybuilders use steroids, and it is unlikely that serious female competitors totally ignore them. Third, the muscles of most women bodybuilders are not really as large as they look. In competitive bodybuilding, it is not so much the size of the muscle that gains points for the competitor as it is the shape and definition of the muscle. Bodybuilders use extremely careful training procedures to fully develop a muscle or muscle group so that it will "ripple" just right; therefore, it is not so much a matter of muscle size as muscle control. Furthermore, many bodybuilders use rather extreme dietary practices during training to reduce subcutaneous fat layers to further enhance the

element of muscle definition. In addition, bodybuilders will voluntarily dehydrate themselves before a competition so that the skin will be especially taut. Finally, these bodybuilders use "pumping up" techniques to engorge the muscle with blood, thus enlarging a muscle and making it pop out.

Physical Performance

Data on motor performance in children are extensive but are not thoroughly reviewed here. A few of what I consider the more important studies are described in the following section.

AAHPERD Fitness Test

A sample of American schoolchildren were given the AAHPER (now AAHPERD) fitness tests in 1957, 1965, and 1976. Considerable gains were made on the test items between 1957 and 1965; additional improvements in 1976 were minor. Table 3.3 shows the scores at the 50th percentile for ages 10 through 17.

The boys' median scores are better than the girls' at all ages. The differences between the sexes are small at ages 10 to 12 but after age 13 are more pronounced.

In 1980, AAHPERD published another physical fitness test manual. It was based not on motor performance but on health-related factors. The 50th-percentile scores for each age and sex are listed in Table 3.4 for some of the items. The boys' performance exceeded the girls' at all ages in the 1-mi run-walk (a measure of cardiorespiratory endurance) and the bent-knee sit-up (a measure of abdominal strength and endurance) after age 6. The girls were more flexible as assessed by the sit-and-reach test and fatter as assessed by the sum-of-triceps and subscapular skinfold measurements.

In 1985 ("Summary of Findings," 1985), the Office of Disease Prevention and Health Promotion, an agency of the U.S. Public Health Service, published results of the National Children and Youth Fitness Study I (NCYFS I) for children in Grades 5 through 12. Two years later, the study was repeated (some items were altered) for children aged 6 through 9 (NCYFS II; "Summary of Findings," 1987). The results of NCYFS I and II are compared with the common test items of the 1980 AAHPERD test in Table 3.4. Once again, the boys outperformed the girls at all ages on all variables. The earlier test results indicated that boys' performance on fitness tests tended to peak shortly after puberty and then plateau for the remaining school years, whereas girls' performance peaked at the onset of puberty and then rapidly declined ("Summary of Findings," 1985). The NCYFS I results, however, showed that boys did more sit-ups and had less body fat into the later teen years. One-mile run-walk times appeared to reach a plateau at a later age in the NCYFS I tests than in the 1980 AAHPERD tests for both boys and girls (at age 16 compared to age 14 in boys and at ages 16 to 17 compared to age 13 in girls). This could be interpreted as reflecting the increasing

national interest in physical fitness except for the fact that the 1985 (and the 1987) results indicated that American schoolchildren were less cardiovascularly fit (slower running times) and fatter (higher skinfold scores) than in 1980. Furthermore, the NCYFS results showed that American children have become fatter since the 1960s ("Summary of Findings," 1985, p. 48). The NCYFS skinfold sums were 2 to 3 mm thicker than in a 1960 sample studied by the National Center for Health Statistics, and the average triceps skinfold in the NCYFS I sample was significantly larger in 13 of the 16 sex- and age-groups.

A chin-up test was utilized in NCYFS I and a modified pull-up in NCYFS II to assess upper body strength and endurance. Chin-up scores for girls were dismal. Relatively few girls could complete even one chin-up (average score at age 10 was .9 and at age 18 was .6). Boys steadily increased from 2.7 at age 10 to 9.7 at age 18. The modified pull-up test of NCYFS II provided a more successful measurement of performance for girls. At age 6, the sex difference was 1.3 pull-ups and at age 9 was 2.6 pull-ups in favor of the boys.

Motor Skills

A typical description of sex differences in motor performance tasks across childhood and adolescence shows small differences favoring boys during the preschool years, a rapid improvement in performance as boys maintain an increasing advantage during the elementary school years, and an acceleration in performance by boys in the adolescent years (Nelson, Thomas, Nelson, & Abraham, 1986; Thomas & French, 1985).

Many have suggested (see, e.g., Thomas & French, 1985) that sex differences in motor performance in very young children may be the effect of environmental factors such as socialization by parents and teachers and of the child's modeling of what is perceived to be sex-appropriate behavior. After puberty, biology plays an important role in the development of morphological and physiological variables that result in the adolescent boy's

Table 3.4 50th-Percentile Scores of U.S. Boys and Girls From the 1980 AAHPERD Health Related Physical Fitness Test, the 1985 National Children and Youth Fitness Study I, and the 1987 National Children and Youth Fitness Study II

Year		5	6	7	8	9	10	11	12	13	14	15	16	17	18
							Ages								
One-mile run (min:s)															
1980	Boys	13:46	12:29	11:25	11:00	9:56	9:19	9:06	8:20	7:27	7:10	7:14	7:11	7:25	—
	Girls	15:08	13:46	12:30	12:00	11:12	11:06	10:27	9:47	9:27	9:35	10:05	10:45	9:47	—
1985	Boys	—	—	—	—	—	10:20	9:50	9:24	8:41	8:40	8:00	7:44	8:20	8:10
	Girls	—	—	—	—	—	11:38	11:52	11:30	11:05	10:42	11:14	11:03	11:00	11:20
1987	Boys	—	5:31[a]	5:10[a]	11:04	10:37	—	—	—	—	—	—	—	—	—
	Girls	—	5:48[a]	5:33[a]	11:58	11:35	—	—	—	—	—	—	—	—	—
Sit-ups (number in 60 s)															
1980	Boys	18	20	26	30	32	34	37	39	41	42	44	45	46	—
	Girls	19	22	25	29	29	32	34	36	35	35	37	33	37	—
1985	Boys	—	—	—	—	—	34.4	35.3	37.9	39.6	41.0	42.0	43.5	43.5	42.7
	Girls	—	—	—	—	—	31.4	31.6	33.7	33.6	34.8	34.6	35.1	35.1	35.4
1987	Boys	—	18.4	22.4	25.2	27.9	—	—	—	—	—	—	—	—	—
	Girls	—	17.8	21.4	23.9	25.5	—	—	—	—	—	—	—	—	—
Sit-and-reach (in.)															
1980	Boys	9.8	10.6	9.8	9.8	9.8	9.8	9.8	10.2	10.2	11.0	11.8	11.8	13.4	—
	Girls	10.6	10.6	10.6	11.0	11.0	11.0	11.4	11.8	12.2	13.0	14.1	13.4	13.8	—
1985	Boys	—	—	—	—	—	13.1	13.1	12.7	12.9	13.3	14.1	14.8	15.1	15.1
	Girls	—	—	—	—	—	14.4	14.8	15.5	16.1	16.4	17.0	17.5	17.2	17.1
1987	Boys	—	13.2	13.2	13.0	12.6	—	—	—	—	—	—	—	—	—
	Girls	—	14.1	14.4	14.1	14.0	—	—	—	—	—	—	—	—	—
Sum of triceps and subscapular skinfolds (mm)															
1980	Boys	—	12	12	13	14	14	16	15	15	14	14	14	15	—
	Girls	—	14	15	16	17	18	19	19	20	24	25	25	27	—
1985	Boys	—	—	—	—	—	20.9	21.2	21.6	20.1	20.1	20.1	19.4	20.1	20.2
	Girls	—	—	—	—	—	22.6	24.8	25.3	26.8	27.9	30.0	28.7	30.2	28.9
1987	Boys	—	15.6	16.7	18.4	20.5	—	—	—	—	—	—	—	—	—
	Girls	—	19.2	20.3	22.8	24.9	—	—	—	—	—	—	—	—	—

Note. 1980 data from American Alliance for Health, Physical Education, Recreation and Dance (1980). 1985 data from "Summary of Findings" (1985). 1987 data from "Summary of Findings" (1987).

[a]Half-mile run-walk.

having a distinct biological advantage in the performance of many tasks. Thomas and French (1985) theorized that if sex differences are small in early childhood but begin to increase in the elementary school years, environment seems to be the likely cause. This would be shown if remedial programs eliminated much of the difference. According to Thomas and French, biological factors are implicated if large sex differences are noted very early in childhood and cannot be reduced by instruction or training.

The most thorough analysis of this question—environment versus biology—took the form of a meta-analysis that involved 64 studies and 31,444 subjects (Thomas & French, 1985). It was concluded that, in 15 of the 20 tasks that were studied, sex differences before puberty were environmentally induced. This was based on small effect sizes and on observations that treatment, expectations, and practice opportunities differed by sex. Effect sizes at puberty in 6 tasks (dash, grip strength, long jump, shuttle run, sit-ups, and vertical jump) showed rapid increases that were probably associated with the increase in the boys' size and strength. However, differences in effect sizes for throwing began with biological differences and increased with an environmental factor: more practice opportunities for boys.

Investigators from the same laboratory (Nelson et al., 1986) further investigated sex differences in throwing in a hundred 5-year-old girls and boys. The children were tested on throwing for distance, rated on two components of throwing form (trunk rotation and foot action), and evaluated on eight biological characteristics. Analysis of covariance (ANCOVA) was used to evaluate sex differences by adjusting biological and environmental variables that were identified as predictive of throwing performance. The boys threw farther and had a more mature form. Sex alone accounted for 41% of the variance observed. A gain of 10% in accounted variance was found to be due to three biological variables (joint diameters, shoulder-to-hip ratio, and sum of skinfolds), whereas a gain of only 4% was due to an environmental variable (playing with older children). When the biological and environmental variables were combined, there was a gain of 12% accounted variance. The investigators concluded that differences in throwing performance appear to reflect biological characteristics even as early as 5 years of age.

The unpublished observations of Grimditch and Sockolov (as reported by Wilmore, 1977, p. 184) suggest a different conclusion. These results indicate that there are no performance differences between the ages of 3 and 12 for the softball throw with the nondominant arm. The dominant-arm results showed the usual differences. Grimditch and Sockolov had postulated that throwing differences between the sexes were the result of insufficient practice and experience by the girls; in other words, throwing differences were environmental rather than biological. They concluded that the softball throw for distance was biased in favor of boys because of different social and cultural expectations and that, when experience and practice were eliminated by using the nondominant arm, this motor task gave results identical to the other tasks.

Performance Studies on Adults

A 1975 law states that "standards required for appointment, training, graduation, and commissioning of female individuals shall be the same as those required for male individuals, except for those minimum essential adjustments in such performance standards because of physiological differences between male and female individuals." Consequently, the U.S. military academies have been struggling with the question, What minimum essential adjustments in performance standards are necessary?

Extensive testing has revealed significant differences between men and women cadets at West Point in the following performance variables: (a) arm bench press for power, (b) arm bench press for strength, (c) dominant-hand grip strength, and (d) leg press for strength and power. Both absolute and relative measures of $\dot{V}O_2$max were also significantly higher in the men (Stauffer, 1976).

Motor fitness performance measures were compared for men and women cadets at the U.S. Air Force Academy (Thomas & Riding, 1978). Following 1 year of training, the women generally made greater improvements on the test items than the men. In comparison to men, the women performed as follows:

- Push-ups   43% of men

- Standing long jump   80% of men
- 600-yd run   85% of men
- 2-min of sit-ups   86% of men

The U.S. Forest Sevice has also been interested in the question of sex differences in motor performance. Comparisons between mean performances of male and female firefighters revealed that the women performed as follows:

- Chin-ups   15% of men
- Push-ups   48% of men
- Sit-ups   87% of men

Reports from the field indicated that some men and women lacked the strength to build fire lines with hand tools and to pack heavy loads for prolonged periods. The investigators (Sharkey, Wilson, Whiddon, & Miller, 1978) suggested that women are generally at a disadvantage in occupations requiring a high level of muscular fitness.

Little data exist on the comparative abilities of men and women to perform tests of anaerobic power or capacity. One such test is the Margaria-Kalamen power (stair climbing) test. This test takes just hundredths of a second and is indicative of one's ability to utilize stored adenosine tri-phosphate (ATP) and creatine phosphate (CP) in the leg muscles. Figure 3.3 indicates that when results are plotted in kilogram meters per second per unit of body weight, there is no difference between men and women (Fox & Mathews, 1981, pp. 354-355). This means that performance differences are due to the smaller body size of the female and not to a lesser ability to utilize these energy sources.

Athletic Performance

An analysis of the National AAU Indoor Swimming Championships from 1971 through 1975 convinced Jackson and Jackson (1977) that the sex gap in top-level swimming was narrowing. They selected the 100-yd freestyle as an event involving speed and anaerobic capabilities and the 1,650-yd freestyle as representative of endurance and aerobic performance. The top 16 performers of each sex for each year and each event constituted their sample. The male swimmers were superior; however, the mean times between the sexes decreased each year. The percentage differences in the 100-yd freestyle were 14.4% in 1971 and 12.6%

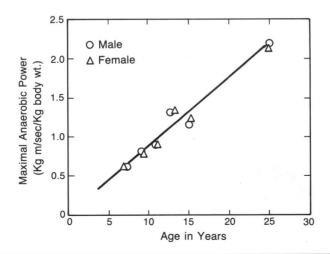

Figure 3.3 Anaerobic power in males and females. *Note.* Data from Davies, Barnes, and Godfrey (1974); Kalamen (1968); and Margaria, Aghemo, and Rovelli (1966).

in 1975; and the 1,650-yd freestyle differences were 8.6% in 1971 and 7.4% in 1975.

Performance differences in the Olympic Games were compared for men and women from 1960 to 1976 (Raine, 1978). Average improvement over those years was 2.6% for men and 4.7% for women. In comparison with men, the best event for women was the 100-m dash, with an average winning performance difference of 10.4%. The worst event for women was the long jump, with an average sex difference of 21.1%. Raine speculated that women would gradually close the performance gap to approximately 10% in track events.

A comparison of world records in track revealed that men were 8% to 15% faster than women in 1974; swimming records were somewhat closer,

Table 3.5   Comparison of World Records for Men and Women as of May 1989

Events	Women	Men	Ratio of performance (%)			
			1989	1984	1978[a]	1963[a]
Swimming (m)						
100 freestyle	54.73	48.42	88	90	89	90
200 freestyle	1:57.55	1:47.25	91	92	93	90
400 freestyle	4:03.85	3:46.95	93	93	94	89
1,500 freestyle	15:52.10	14:54.72	94	93	93	91
100 breaststroke	1:07.91	1:01.65	91	91	89	86
200 breaststroke	2:26.71	2:13.34	91	91	89	89
100 butterfly	57.93	52.84	91	94	91	86
200 butterfly	2:05.96	1:56.24	92	94	92	86
100 backstroke	1:00.59	54.51	90	91	90	88
200 backstroke	2:08.60	1:58.14	92	90	90	88
Running (m)						
100	10.49	9.83	94	92	91	89
200	21.34	19.72	92	91	—	—
400	47.60	43.29	91	91	89	85
800	1:53.28	1:41.73	90	90	90	86
1,500	3:52.47	3:29.46	90	91	90	—
3,000	8:22.62	7:32.10	90	89	89	—
10,000	30:13.74	27:13.81	90	87	—	—
Marathon	2:21:06	2:06:50	90	90	83	—
Field events (m)						
High jump	2.09	2.43	86	86	82	84
Long jump	7.52	8.90	84	83	79	80
Javelin	80.00	87.66	91[b]	75	—	—
Average ratio			90.5	89.6	89.0	87.1

Note. Ratio of performance = (men/women) × 100 for swimming and running. Ratio of performance = (women/men) × 100 for field events.

[a]Data from DeVries, 1980, p. 552.

[b]New javelin.

with women's performances ranging from 7% to 14% below men's records (Plowman, 1974).

Table 3.5 lists world records as of May 1989 for men and women in some swimming, track, and field events. The table shows that women have made substantial gains in athletic performance in recent years both in absolute terms and in relation to the performance of men. From 1963 to 1978, the average ratio of performance improved 1.9% (from 87.1% to 89.0%) over a period of 15 years. The average ratio of performance for 1984 was 89.6% for all events listed, 91.6% for the swimming events, and 89.8% for the running events, indicating a 0.6% improvement over a 6-year period. In 1989, the average performance ratio improved to 90.5%, representing a gain of 0.9% in 5 years. The average ratio of performance for the swimming events listed was 91.3% and for the running events 90.8%.

In relation to men, women perform least well in jumping or throwing events, which require a considerable degree of explosive power and strength. In running, women have been steadily improving in the longer road races such as the 10 km and marathon, and, now that the 3,000-m, and 10,000-m, and marathon races are Olympic events, there should be even more rapid improvement.

Further evidence of the steady improvement made by women in athletic performance and the narrowing gap between men's and women's performances is provided by an analysis of track and swimming records with special reference to the decade 1975 to 1986. The interested reader is referred to the full manuscript of Wells and Ballinger (1988), which was originally presented in late 1985. The following comments and illustrations are abstracted from that paper but are updated to late 1986.

From the world records of 1956, 1966, 1976, and 1986, running speed was calculated in meters per second for the 100-, 200-, 400-, 800-, and 1,500-m events. Percentage differences between men's and women's performances were determined using the following formula:

$$\frac{\text{men's speed} - \text{women's speed}}{\text{men's speed}} \times 100$$

The results in Table 3.6 reveal a steady decline in the percentage difference between men's and women's running speeds from 14.72% to 9.15% in those 30 years.

Table 3.6 Percentage Differences in Speed (m · s⁻¹) Between Men's and Women's World Records in Track Events by 10-Year Intervals

Events	1956	1966	1976	1986
100 m	11.40	9.91	9.62	7.74
200 m	11.20	11.90	10.76	10.86
400 m	15.67	13.48	11.00	7.89
800 m	15.43	13.87	9.98	9.35
1,500 m	19.89	16.21	10.07	9.92
Mean difference	14.72	13.07	10.29	9.15

Note. From "Women's Performances—The Last Decade" by C.L. Wells and D. Ballinger. In *Sport Science Perspectives for Women* (p. 222) by J. Puhl, C.H. Brown, and R.O. Voy (Eds.), 1988, Champaign, IL: Human Kinetics Books. Copyright 1988 by Human Kinetics Publishers. Adapted by permission.

Careful analysis of Table 3.6 suggested that the women's 200-m record might be the next record to be broken, and Florence Griffith-Joyner did just that in the 1988 Olympic Games. The current percentage difference in men's and women's running speeds for 200 m is 7.59%!

Table 3.7 shows the percentage of improvement in selected women's track-and-field records since 1956 in 10-year increments. The last column gives the total percentage improvement from the first world record. In the decade 1976 to 1985, the average rate of improvement slowed from 6.1% (1956 to 1965) to 3.8%. Total improvement from the first records continues to rise. The relatively small total percentage improvement in the 1,500-m event results from the fact that world records were not recognized for women until 1967.

Percentage differences in freestyle swimming speed (m · s⁻¹) for men's and women's world records from 1956 to 1986 are presented in Table

Table 3.7 Percentage Improvement in Women's Track-and-Field Records From 1956 to 1985

Events	1956-1965[a]	1966-1975	1976-1985	Totals from 1st year
100 m	1.8	2.7	.4	11.8 (1928)
200 m	2.2	3.1	1.8	14.5 (1927)
400 m	8.9	3.0	3.8	15.8 (1957)
800 m	3.1	4.2	3.5	17.2 (1928)
1,500 m	—	8.3	3.7	9.7 (1967)
High jump	8.3	2.6	5.3	22.9 (1928)
Javelin	12.5	9.6	8.2	96.1 (1928)
Mean	6.13	4.79	3.81	26.86

Note. From "Women's Performances—The Last Decade" by C.L. Wells and D. Ballinger. In *Sport Science Perspectives for Women* (p. 225) by J. Puhl, C.H. Brown, and R.O. Voy (Eds.), 1988, Champaign, IL: Human Kinetics Books. Copyright 1988 by Human Kinetics Publishers. Reprinted by permission.

[a]Data from Hodgkins and Skubic (1968, p. 39).

Table 3.8 Percentage Differences in Speed (m · s^{-1}) Between Men's and Women's Freestyle Swimming World Records by 10-Year Intervals

Events	1956[a]	1966[a]	1976	1986
100 m	11.05	10.05	10.02	10.73
200 m	11.19	11.34	9.77	8.60
400 m	7.01	9.37	8.40	7.46
800 m	9.54	8.56	7.73	6.43
1,500 m	13.95	8.41	8.32	7.22
Mean difference	10.55	9.55	8.85	8.09

Note. From "Women's Performances—The Last Decade" by C.L. Wells and D. Ballinger. In *Sport Science Perspectives for Women* (p. 226) by J. Puhl, C.H. Brown, and R.O. Voy (Eds.), 1988, Champaign, IL: Human Kinetics Books. Copyright 1988 by Human Kinetics Publishers. Adapted by permission.

[a]Data from Dyer (1977, p. 723).

3.8. The progressive decline in the mean difference in those 30 years reveals not only a steady improvement in women's records in relation to men's but also that the sex-performance difference is less in swimming than in running (see also Table 3.6).

The current rate of improvement in women's records exceeds the current improvement in men's records. Most likely, this will be true for many years to come. Performance is a reflection of the interrelationships between morphology, physiology, and environment (cultural attitudes and practices). The world records of women in many events may never equal the world records of men, but it is quite clear that social preconceptions (and not strictly biological limitations) have played a role in limiting women's achievements to date. As more of these preconceptions are dispelled, women's records will continue to improve, and men's and women's performances will become more similar. However, sport-specific differences are likely to remain. For example, sex differences in body composition may be an advantage to the woman in swimming and a disadvantage in running. The greater body fat in women provides buoyancy and reduces body drag in water as well as providing extra insulation against the cold. In running, however, having more body fat is a disadvantage because it does not contribute in any way to propelling the body forward. Instead, a larger amount of body fat is an extra burden to carry.

Sex Role Expectations

Sex role expectations have traditionally affected the habitual activity levels of males and females.

Because of social restraints, there are fewer opportunities for girls and women to exercise vigorously and regularly than there are for males. Until rather recently, it has not been socially acceptable for girls and women to really work up a sweat. High-level training for girls and women has been practically nonexistent. In fact, I suspect that few world-class female athletes are trained to the same extent as most world-class male athletes. Much of the published data on female athletes comes from the intercollegiate sector. Sparling (1980) stated that in the past these women were more comparable to moderately active college men than to men who were highly trained. Thus, a proper equating of male and female groups relative to habitual activity, conditioning, coaching exposure, or competitive experience is rare, perhaps even nonexistent. Such unintentional biasing of samples in the scientific literature has no doubt led to the publication of differences in physiological variables that are *not* solely attributable to biological differences between the sexes.

As more girls and women undertake serious conditioning and training and gain in international experience, many so-called physiological barriers will fall by the wayside. As rapidly as these barriers (mostly social preconceptions) disappear, women's performances will improve.

Absolute differences in strength between the sexes depends on the muscle group measured and the training status of the subjects. Larger differences between the sexes occur in upper rather than in lower body strength.

Physical fitness test scores continue to show that boys outperform girls in all measures except flexibility and that American schoolchildren are fatter and less cardiovascularly fit today than in the 1960s. Motor skill test scores indicate that sex differences exist at an early age. There is some evidence that skill differences are more related to environmental factors than to biological differences.

World-class performance differences are of interest because the individuals involved are highly trained and represent the best combination of environmental and biological factors available. Currently, performance ratios between the sexes are less than 10% and are continuing to decline. Women's world records in track and swimming are being lowered more rapidly than are men's. This implies that sex role expectations and environmental factors, such as opportunities for participation at an early age and the availability of expert coaching, play a major role in sex differences in sport performance.

Summary

Sex differences in muscular strength can be largely accounted for by differences in muscle mass.

PART II

Exercise and the Menstruating Woman

Many myths have been propagated regarding the supposed interrelationships of exercise and menstrual function. Although much has been written on the topic, there is still considerable confusion about any cause-and-effect relationships between the two. When speaking to physical educators, athletes, coaches, and physicians, I am often surprised by their lack of correct information and knowledge regarding menstrual function. It seems that this factor remains one of the major blocks to the participation of girls and women in competitive sports. Until recently, most of the International Olympic Committee members believed that sport training and competition were detrimental to proper reproductive functions in women. An opinion statement published by the American College of Sports Medicine (see the appendix) virtually eliminated the so-called medical objections to long-distance running by women; as a result, the 3,000-m and marathon races were added to the roster of the 1984 Olympic Games, as were the 5,000- and 10,000-m events in 1988. Obviously, considerable uncertainty exists about the effects of exercise on menstrual function and of menstrual function on exercise performance.

Part II, the major portion of this book, deals with exercise and menstrual function. Although there is still much to be learned about the interrelationships of these aspects of human life, it is clear that exercise in and of itself is not harmful to the reproductive function of young girls and women. It also becomes clear that menstruation has little effect on exercise performance.

Chapter 4 presents the anatomy and physiology of the female reproductive cycle in a fairly simple, didactic manner. This chapter is included to provide readers a common basis of understanding about menstrual function. Structural aspects of the reproductive system have been covered with care because some objections to sport participation by girls and women have revolved around the misconception that physical harm to reproductive organs was a likely occurrence. Particular attention was also given to describing the menstrual events in terms of the specific organs involved—the brain, the ovary, and the uterus—and to describing how these events and physiological changes are related to one another. The physiology of puberty and menarche has been added to this edition.

Chapter 5 describes the effects of the menstrual cycle on physical performance. This is a rather short chapter because there appears to be no conclusive evidence that menstrual function affects physical performance in most women.

Chapter 6 details the effects of exercise on menstrual function. The topics of puberty and menarche are presented because there is some evidence that physical performance and menarche are in some way interrelated. However, more research is needed. Is menarche delayed by strenuous athletic training, or are physically active young girls who mature at a later age than the average girl more suited for and, consequently, more active in athletic events? The incidence of amenorrhea in relation to physical training is discussed at length.

Chapter 7 deals with a variety of topics related to exercise and menstruation, such as the use of oral contraceptives to alter the menstrual cycle, the effects of oral contraceptives on performance, swimming during the menses, and various menstrual problems. Premenstrual syndrome and short luteal phase, two subjects of current interest, are also discussed.

Chapter 8 is devoted entirely to a discussion of the extremely complicated subject of athletic amenorrhea. It begins with an extensive review of the responses (both acute and chronic) of the reproductive hormones to exercise and is followed by a detailed discussion of some proposed mechanisms for these responses. Evidence that both supports and refutes various theories as to the etiology of athletic amenorrhea is explored. In this edition, material regarding the reversibility of athletic amenorrhea is provided, as is information regarding risks to bone health in the amenorrheic athlete.

Chapter 4

The Menstrual Cycle: A Unique Function

Negative attitudes and reactions to the menstrual cycle have proven difficult to alter. This is probably at least partially related to a general lack of knowledge about this complicated and confusing subject. The objective of this chapter is to present the basic anatomical and physiological knowledge about the menstrual cycle that is relevant to later discussion. It is hoped that this information will lead to a better understanding of how the female body works and, subsequently, do much to alleviate the fears and misconceptions that many have toward this important physiological function. Serious readers should refer to additional sources (such as medical textbooks of endocrinology and gynecology and scientific journals) for more detailed information. Only those topics that pertain to sport and reproductive physiology were selected for inclusion here.

This chapter is presented in two parts. The first deals with anatomical descriptions of the organs and tissues important to the female reproductive system, and the second outlines the function and regulation of that system. The chapters that immediately follow deal directly with the interactions between exercise and the menstrual cycle.

Anatomy of the Female Reproductive Cycle

A more accurate term for the menstrual cycle is the *female reproductive cycle*. This refers to the rhythmic changes that occur in the reproductive organs under the influence of hormones of the endocrine system.

The *endocrine system* (see Figure 4.1) constitutes the second major communication system of the human body (the first is the nervous system). It is made up of *endocrine glands*, which have no ducts or tubes and which secrete *hormones* (chemical control substances) directly into the extracellular space around the gland. These secretions diffuse into the blood through the capillaries or lymphatics. Each endocrine gland secretes a

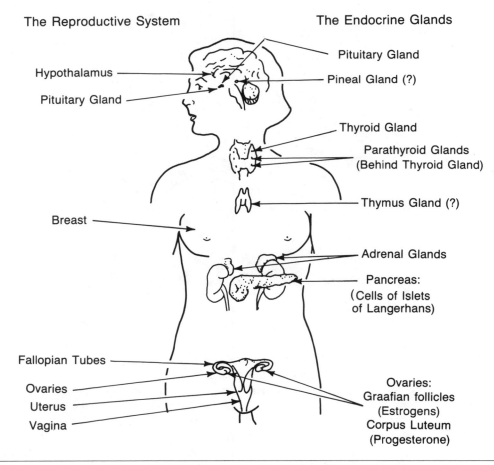

The Reproductive System

The Endocrine Glands

Hypothalamus

Pituitary Gland

Breast

Fallopian Tubes

Ovaries

Uterus

Vagina

Pituitary Gland

Pineal Gland (?)

Thyroid Gland

Parathyroid Glands (Behind Thyroid Gland)

Thymus Gland (?)

Adrenal Glands

Pancreas: (Cells of Islets of Langerhans)

Ovaries: Graafian follicles (Estrogens) Corpus Luteum (Progesterone)

Figure 4.1   The endocrine glands and reproductive system in a woman. *Note.* Adapted by permission. *Biology of Women* by E. Sloane. Delmar Publishers Inc., copyright 1985.

specific hormone or hormones designed to affect particular target organs or tissues.

The classic endocrine glands in the female are the pituitary, the thyroid, the parathyroid, the adrenal, the islets of Langerhans of the pancreas, and the ovaries. During pregnancy, the placenta is considered an endocrine gland. Many physiologists also consider the pineal and thymus glands to have endocrine functions. In Figure 4.1 the endocrine glands of the female are listed on the right. Listed on the left side of the figure are the endocrine glands and organs and tissues directly involved in the female reproductive cycle.

Figure 4.2 shows a lateral view of the female pelvic region. The anatomical relationships of the ovary, uterus, urinary bladder, vagina, pubic bone, and vulva are evident here. Figure 4.3 shows a frontal view. Notice the placement of the ovaries, uterus, and vagina within the pelvic cavity.

Support of the Pelvic Viscera

Standing erect and walking on two legs rather than four has been of primary importance to *Homo sapiens*. However, there is another side to the issue. The problem with erect posture is that gravity is constantly pulling everything downward. Anatomical modifications have occurred to compensate for this force; nevertheless, with advanced age, gravity sometimes wins the battle, and various organs begin to sag downward.

With upright posture, the abdominal and pelvic contents exert considerable pressure on the abdominal wall and the pelvic floor even when a person is motionless. With movement, the pressures increase as viscera are squeezed together and additional force is exerted against the pelvis. Contraction of the abdominal muscles during respiration, urination, or defecation increases these forces tremendously.

Three kinds of support exist for the abdomino-pelvic organs. The first is provided by the curvatures of the spine and the flare of the ilia of the pelvis (see Figures 4.2 and 4.3). The second form of support is provided by the folding of the peritoneal lining of the body cavity and the packing of connective tissue that attaches the viscera to the pelvis and holds everything in place. The final and most important support is provided underneath the pelvic organs. The muscles and connective tissues of the pelvic diaphragm stretch like

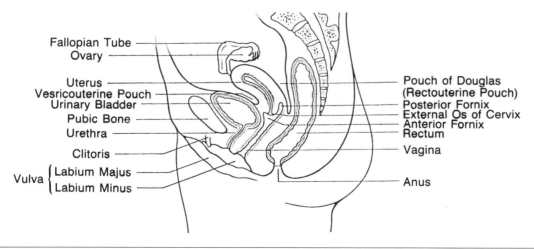

Figure 4.2 Lateral view of female reproductive organs of the pelvic cavity. *Note.* From *Biology of Women* (p. 31) by E. Sloane, 1980, New York: John Wiley & Sons, Inc. Copyright 1980 by John Wiley & Sons, Inc. Reprinted by permission.

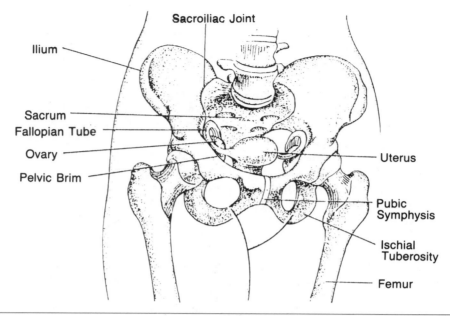

Figure 4.3 Frontal view of the reproductive organs within the pelvic cavity. *Note.* Adapted by permission. *Biology of Women* by E. Sloane. Delmar Publishers Inc., copyright 1985.

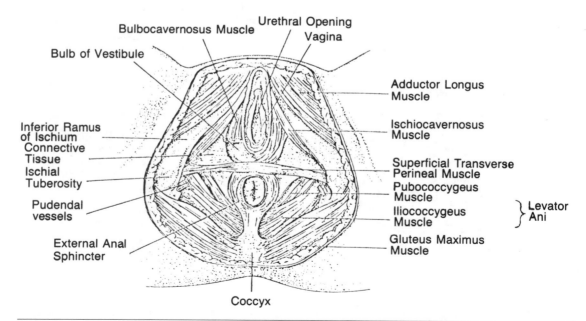

Figure 4.4 Muscles of the pelvic diaphragm. *Note.* From *Biology of Women* (p. 49) by E. Sloane, 1980, New York: John Wiley & Sons, Inc. Copyright 1980 by John Wiley & Sons, Inc. Reprinted by permission.

hammocks across the bony structures of the pelvic outlet (Figure 4.4). Openings exist in the pelvic diaphragm to provide exits for the urethra, the rectum, and the vagina. These openings are inherent weaknesses in the pelvic diaphragm; nevertheless, the pelvic floor is extremely strong. Occasionally, childbearing and childbirth (especially multiple pregnancies) strain the pelvic support systems sufficiently to allow the organs to protrude downward (prolapse). When this occurs, surgical correction is necessary. It should be evident from Figures 4.2-4.4 that the female reproductive organs are very well protected from injury due to jarring or sudden falls such as may occur with participation in sport.

Functions of Reproductive Structures

The relationship of the ovary, fallopian tube, uter-us, endometrium, and vagina are detailed in Figure 4.5.

Ovaries.   The ovaries produce discrete cell clusters called follicles, which in turn produce ova and hormones. They are small glands (approximately 3 cm long, 1.5 cm wide, and 1 cm thick) that are suspended in the pelvic cavity by ligaments and connective tissue. Their actual position is variable, especially after pregnancy, during which they are displaced from their original position.

The follicles arise from primordial germ cells, which are segregated from the rest of the body's cells as early as 10 days after fertilization. At about 20 weeks of fetal life, there are more than 7 million primary follicles. Most of these follicles undergo regression and degeneration. At birth, between 400,000 and 1,000,000 follicles are present, each containing an ovum known as a *primary oocyte*. The ovary is not a dormant organ during childhood

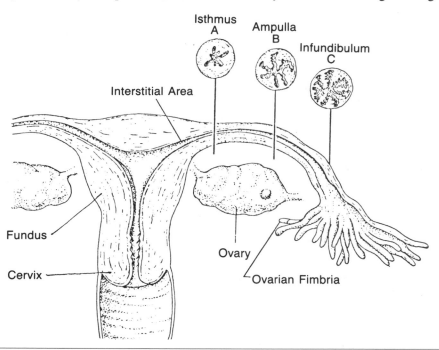

Figure 4.5   The relationship among the female reproductive organs of the pelvic cavity, frontal view. Occasionally ectopic (out-of-place) pregnancies occur in areas A, B, or C of the fallopian tubes. *Note.* From *Biology of Women* (p. 42) by E. Sloane, 1980, New York: John Wiley & Sons, Inc. Copyright 1980 by John Wiley & Sons, Inc. Reprinted by permission.

as was previously thought. Rather, follicular growth and atresia (regression) is an ongoing process. However, there is no indication of prepubertal hormonal secretion from this process in normal girls. By puberty, the number of follicles decrease to approximately 50,000. Only one of these is ovulated each month, a total of about 400 from puberty to menopause.

After puberty, each follicle that ovulates goes through a cycle of changes known as the *ovarian,* or *follicular, cycle* (see Figure 4.6). At the beginning of this cycle, a group of primary follicles undergo development, but only one completely matures. This becomes the dominant follicle, whereas the others regress. As the follicle develops, two distinct layers of cells are formed. The outermost layer, called the *theca cells,* synthesizes androgens (testosterone and androstenedione) and dominates during the follicular phase of the menstrual cycle. The *granulosa cells* are surrounded by theca cells and are able to aromatize (convert) the androgens produced by the theca cells to estrogens. Thus, the granulosa cells produce estro-

gens from the precursors provided by the theca cells.

Each follicle contains an ovum surrounded by granulosa cells. The ovum becomes larger as the follicle progresses through the ovarian cycle. Gradually, a mature *Graffian follicle* is formed with a large fluid-filled antrum (sac). Eventually, the ovum moves toward the outer surface of the ovary in preparation for ovulation. First, a bulge forms on the ovarian surface. Then the follicle ruptures, and the ovum, surrounded by its protective, nourishing cell layer (now called the *corona radiata*), floats into the peritoneal cavity with a rush of follicular fluid. Sometimes, ovulatory pain, called *mittleschemerz* (German for *middle pain*), occurs.

Exactly how the ovulated egg enters the fimbriated end of the fallopian tube is not known. However, if it is not fertilized within 24 h, the ovum will die. Meanwhile, the wall of the ruptured follicle collapses, and some of the cells produce a yellow pigment called *lutein*. The cells are now called *luteal cells* and the follicle the *corpus luteum*

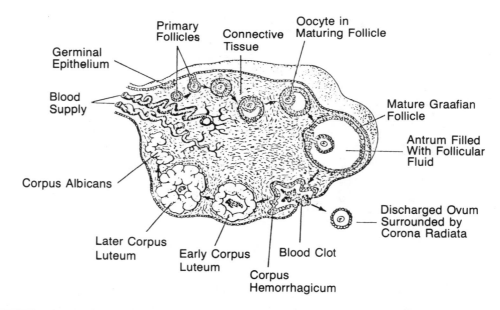

Figure 4.6 The ovarian cycle. *Note.* From *Biology of Women* (p. 46) by E. Sloane, 1980, New York: John Wiley & Sons, Inc. Copyright 1980 by John Wiley & Sons, Inc. Reprinted by permission.

(*yellow body*). The corpus luteum, which produces progesterone, achieves its peak of activity about 5 to 7 days following ovulation and its maximal development within 10 days. In pregnancy, the corpus luteum is maintained for 4 to 6 months, at which point the placenta takes over the production of progesterone and the corpus luteum regresses. If fertilization has not occurred, the corpus luteum begins to regress, eventually forming a white scar *(corpus albicans)* in the ovary within 7 to 10 months. When menopause occurs (see chapter 10), no further follicular development takes place.

Fallopian Tubes.   The oviducts, or fallopian tubes, contain many blood vessels, as well as smooth muscle arranged in longitudinal and circular patterns. The lining of the tube forms inner folds, the number of which vary in each section of the tube. The epithelium of the lining secretes a nutrient fluid that is necessary for the movement, fertilization, and sustenance of the ovum. Other cells in the lining have cilia (little hairlike processes) that beat toward the uterus to help the ovum progress into the uterine cavity. Movement of the ovum, however, is mainly due to the contraction of the circular and longitudinal muscles that create peristaltic waves along the tubes. This muscular activity, which peaks at ovulation, is influenced by hormones. Perhaps these contractions, together with the ciliary movement in the lining, act like a vacuum cleaner to pull the ovulated egg into the fallopian tube.

Fertilization of an ovum most often occurs in the isthmus of the fallopian tube. If conception occurs, the new embryo divides, begins developing, and passes into the uterine cavity. All this occurs within 4 days of ovulation. If the ovum is not fertilized, it disintegrates and is absorbed by the body. Occasionally, ectopic (out-of-placenta) pregnancies occur in the fallopian tubes (in areas A, B, or C in Figure 4.5).

Uterus.   The *uterus* is a hollow, muscular organ. Its upper, expanded part is called the *body*, or *fundus*; a lower, constricted part extends into the vagina and is called the *neck*, or *cervix*. The opening of the cervix into the vagina is called the *external os*. Although there is considerable variation in size, the nonpregnant uterus is about 3 in. long, 2 in. wide at the fundus, and 1 in. thick at its thickest part.

The uterus is very mobile and has more than one normal position. Because it lies between the bladder and rectum, its position depends on how distended these organs are, on posture, and on how many children have been born. The usual position is inclined forward.

The glands of the cervix secrete mucus. During the reproductive cycle, the physical properties of this mucus change as a result of the circulating hormones from the ovary. At the time of ovulation, the mucus is thin, clear, and secreted in large quantities. After ovulation, the mucus thickens, reaching a gelatinous state. These changes in cervical mucus are used as an index of hormonal activity and ovarian function.

The walls of the uterus are about 1/2 in. thick, solid, and made up of smooth muscle called the *myometrium*. The inside of the cavity is lined with epithelial tissue called the *endometrium*. It is this lining that undergoes cyclic changes during the reproductive cycle and that forms the site of implantation of the fertilized ovum if pregnancy occurs.

A unique characteristic of the uterus is its *endometrial cycle*. The large, superficial layer of the endometrium contains glands that respond to the steroid hormones that fluctuate throughout the reproductive cycle. It is this layer that is almost completely shed with menstruation. A thin basal layer of the endometrium does not undergo cyclic change. The endometrial cycle is described in the section on the physiology of the menstrual cycle.

Vagina.   The *vagina* is a distensible tube that passes upward from the vulva to the uterus. Its anterior and posterior walls form numerous transverse folds that enable it to withstand vigorous stresses during intercourse or childbirth. The *vaginal epithelium*, or inner lining, consists of many layers of cells containing blood vessels and nerves. It is a very strong and resistant protective lining. The deep basal cells are stimulated by estrogen. When little estrogen is present, as after menopause, the vaginal epithelium is thin and made up almost exclusively of basal cells. An index of estrogenic activity can be determined from a smear of cellular matter obtained from the vaginal epithelium. The shape, staining quality, and relative numbers of basal, intermediate, or superficial cells in the smear are telltale signs of steroid production. The smear can also be used in tests for cancer.

The normal vaginal discharge is a clear acid fluid containing sloughed-off cells of the superficial layer, some bacilli, and a small amount of cervical mucus from the cervical glands. This discharge, together with the outermost epithelial cells, protects the vagina from harmful bacteria. The bacilli that are normally present are absolutely

essential to normal vaginal health and must not be destroyed by chemical contraceptives, antibiotics, or excessive douching.

There is little sensation in the vagina because most of the nerve fibers supplying the organ originate from the autonomic nervous system. The *vulva*, however, is richly supplied with sensory nerve endings. If the lower part of the internal wall of the vagina is inflamed or infected (vaginitis), itching and burning is transferred to the vulva. If itching, burning, or an abnormal discharge is present, it is very likely that undesirable organisms have invaded the vagina.

Breast. The *breast*, or *mammary* gland, is also an organ of the female reproductive system (see Figure 4.7). Its glandular tissue consists of 15 to 25 lobes, each with an excretory duct to drain the

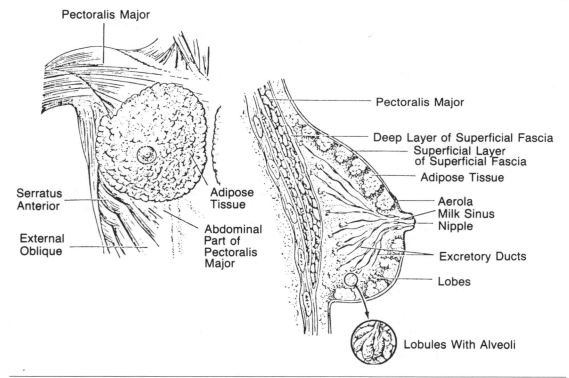

Figure 4.7 The human breast. *Note.* From *Biology of Women* (p. 165) by E. Sloane, 1980, New York: John Wiley & Sons, Inc. Copyright 1980 by John Wiley & Sons, Inc. Reprinted by permission.

lactiferous fluid to the nipple. This tissue responds to hormonal cycles and is capable of milk production following parturition (delivery of a child) in response to the pulsatile release of prolactin from the anterior pituitary gland. The lobes are supported by connective tissue. In the upper portion of the breast are the suspensory ligaments of Cooper (not true ligaments), which extend diagonally from the deep fascia overlying the chest muscles to the superficial fascia below the skin (not shown in Figure 4.7). There are differing opinions about *Cooper's ligaments*. Haycock (1988) stated that Cooper's ligaments do not support the breast but are merely connective tissue strands separating the glandular structures. Gehlsen and Stoner (1987, p. 13) stated that these "weak structures" provide the breast its primary support and maintain the breast with the nipple at the approximate level of the fifth intercostal space. Sloan (1980) stated that the stretching of Cooper's ligaments contributes to sagging, pendulous breasts (known as *ptosis*, or *Cooper's droop*).

The four stages of breast development are (a) immature (the adolescent breast); (b) glandular (the reproductive period, during which functioning tissue proliferates and is capable of lactation); (c) involutional (the shrinking of ducts and tubules due to the withdrawal of estrogen that occurs with menopause); and (d) atrophic (a sequel to the involutional breast that occurs at a more advanced state in the aging process).

Average glandular-stage breast size is 150 to 200 g and increases to 400 to 500 g during lactation. This increase in size and weight is largely the result of fluid production and accumulation.

The breast is mainly adipose tissue and contains differing amounts of fat, depending on age and nutritional status. This mammary fat constitutes a significant amount of the sex-specific fat mentioned in chapter 1. Campaigne (1977) found that the breast contributes about 4% to the total body fat and, at most, 12% to the theoretical quantity of sex-specific fat proposed by Behnke and Wilmore (1974). Regardless of breast size, women have about the same amount of glandular tissue.

Breast size and shape are determined by the relative amounts of fatty and connective tissue one has, which in turn is dependent on genetic and endocrine factors. Breast size has nothing to do with breast function. Women with small breasts are just as able to nurse a baby as are women with large breasts.

Menstrual Phases

The menstrual cycle is typically divided into three phases (see Figure 4.8). The first, the period of menstrual bleeding (*menses*), is called the *menstrual phase* and occurs from Days 1 to 4 (or 5). Menstrual bleeding, or *endometrial regression*, is usually referred to as the first phase of the cycle because of the simplicity of noting Day 1 (it actually marks the completion of the menstrual cycle). The second phase is called the *follicular, proliferative*, or *regenerative phase* and is characterized by the development of a mature follicle under the primary influence of the gonadotropins, *luteinizing hormone* (LH) and *follicle-stimulating hormone* (FSH), and by a thickening of the endometrial

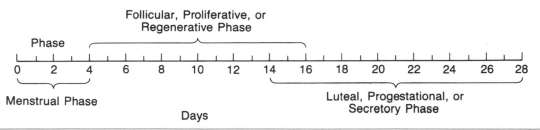

Figure 4.8 Phases of the menstrual cycle.

lining of the uterus under the influence of estrogen. The second half of the cycle is dominated by the hormone progesterone and is called the *luteal, progestational,* or *secretory phase.* This phase follows ovulation and continues until menstrual flow again occurs. It is characterized by the development of secretory glands in the endometrium and the predominance of the corpus luteum. The growth and development of the endometrial layer makes it possible for the uterus to support a fetus, which is the ultimate purpose of the menstrual cycle. Menstrual flow is the reversal of this growth-and-development process. The average length of the entire cycle is 28 days but may range from about 20 to 38 days. To avoid confusion, the mentrual phases are referred to here as the menstrual, follicular, and luteal phases.

Neuroendocrinology of the Menstrual Cycle

The menstrual cycle is under the hormonal control of the endocrine system as well as the neurogenic stimulus of the nervous system. The relatively new science of neuroendocrinology is the study of the interaction between the nervous and the endocrine systems. This interaction occurs primarily between the hypothalamus and the pituitary gland. Neurons in the hypothalamus produce *neurohormones,* or *releasing factors,* that are secreted into a capillary complex in the pituitary stalk and transported to the pituitary gland (see Figure 4.9). The release of these neurohormones is regulated by the feedback of endocrine hormones from target tissues (such as the gonads) as well as higher levels of the brain.

In the case of the menstrual cycle, hypothalamic neurons that project into the median eminence secrete *gonadotropin-releasing hormone* (GnRH) into the hypothalamic-pituitary portal vessels in the pituitary stalk (see Figure 4.9). From there, GnRH is transported by the blood to the anterior pituitary gland. Gonadotropin-releasing hormone is a peptide hormone that stimulates the release of the anterior pituitary hormones, LH and FSH.

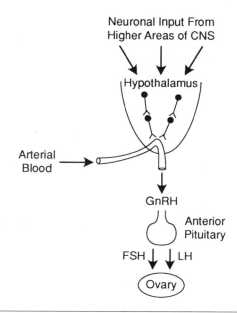

Figure 4.9   Schematic diagram of control of anterior pituitary secretions by the hypothalamus. *Note.* Adapted from *Clinical Neuroendocrinology* (2nd ed., p. 308) by J.B. Martin and S. Reichlin, 1987, Philadelphia: F.A. Davis. Copyright 1987 by F.A. Davis Co. Adapted by permission.

These hormones are called *gonadotropins* because their target organs are the gonads (in this case, the ovaries). They are also glycoprotein hormones (i.e., they have carbohydrate moieties) whose biological activity can be altered by different physiological conditions, including age and photoperiod. (The anterior pituitary produces other protein hormones, such as prolactin, from different cell clusters.) Both LH and FSH are released in a highly regulated pulsatile manner. Anterior pituitary function can also be controlled by a number of *neurotransmitters* that are released from neurons such as dopaminergic neurons in the arcuate nucleus of the hypothalamus. This is important because dopamine is an inhibitor of prolactin and possibly of LH.

The two major types of reproductive hormones in terms of chemical structure are protein, or peptide, hormones (as in the case of the gonadotropins), and steroid hormones, which are fat-soluble compounds secreted from the gonads and adrenal cortex (outermost part of the adrenal gland). Of major importance in female reproductive function are the steroid hormones estrogen and progesterone, which are secreted from the ovary.

Hormones control the activities of specific target cells or tissues. They circulate in the blood at very low concentrations, at least compared to concentrations of other biologically active substances. Therefore, two questions arise: (a) How do the target cells recognize the hormone that ultimately controls them? (b) How is the hormone itself regulated or controlled?

The first question of how a target cell recognizes its controlling hormone refers to the mechanism of hormone action. The answer is that *receptor sites* located on the membranes, in the cytoplasm, or in the nucleus of target cells are highly specific to and have a high affinity for the hormone acting on that tissue. The hormone binds to the receptor and transmits a chemical message to that area of the cell involved in the appropriate biological response. Exactly how the hormone-receptor complex activates the biological response differs, depending on the chemical structure of the hormone and the target cell, but the response often involves protein synthesis.

The second question of how the hormone itself is regulated is more complicated. In some instances, the nervous system directly stimulates an endocrine gland, causing it to release a hormone in response to a nervous impulse. For example, norepinephrine is released from the adrenal medulla in response to sudden emotional stress (e.g., fear, or the roar of the crowd during a competitive event). The neurogenic impulse causing the release of norepinephrine originates in the autonomic nervous system. However, in the case of a normal but highly regulated function such as the menstrual cycle, hormonal secretions are controlled by the blood levels of another hormone. If this hormone or substance serves to inhibit further hormonal secretion from the endocrine gland, it is called a *negative feedback mechanism*; if the hormone or substance signals an increase in the rate or quantity of the hormonal secretion, it is called a *positive feedback mechanism*.

Figure 4.10 illustrates short-loop and long-loop feedback. In the example on the left, prolactin, which has no major control over any peripheral endocrine gland, is regulated by prolactin-inhibiting factors and prolactin-releasing factors produced by the hypothalamus. Stimuli such as stress or suckling stimulate the release of prolactin-releasing factors from the hypothalamus, resulting in an increase of prolactin secretion from the anterior pituitary. High levels of prolactin, however, exert a negative feedback effect by promoting the release of prolactin-inhibiting factors from the hypothalamus that decrease prolactin secretion from the anterior pituitary. Long-loop negative feedback is shown in the example of estrogen (right side of Figure 4.10), which acts on a variety of target tissues. Here, an elevated estrogen concentration (the third hormone in the loop) exerts an inhibitory effect on GnRH as well as on LH and FSH, ultimately resulting in a lower concentration of estrogen.

Regulation of the Menstrual Cycle

The menstrual cycle is the result of highly regulated cyclic fluctuations of the protein hormones from the anterior pituitary that act on the ovary. These fluctuations are followed by corresponding fluctuations of steroid hormones from the ovary that act on the endometrium (see Figure 4.11).

The Role of the Hypothalamus and Anterior Pituitary Gland

The hypothalamus, located beneath the cerebral hemisphere, is part of an extremely important part of the brain known as the *limbic system*, which is concerned with emotional behavior (e.g., fear, anger, depression, elation, sexual desire, pleasure, and pain) and stress. The hypothalamus integrates the nervous and endocrine systems. Besides controlling the menstrual cycle, the hypothalamus

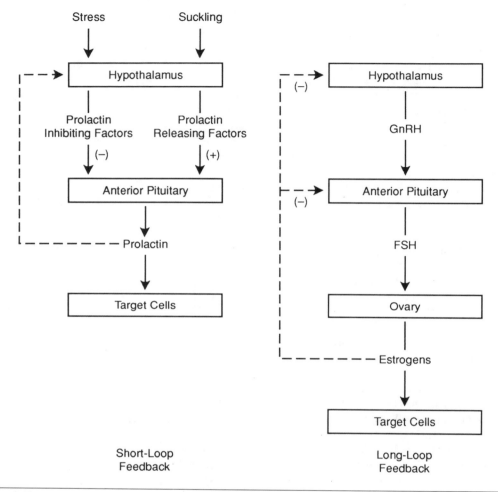

Figure 4.10 Examples of short-loop and long-loop feedback.

also controls such functions as hunger and satiety, thirst, body temperature regulation, and possibly body weight.

For a long time it was not known what stimulated the release of GnRH from the hypothalamus. It is now known that there are estrogen receptors (and perhaps progesterone receptors) in the hypothalamus and that there is a delicate reciprocal feedback relationship between ovarian estrogen and GnRH release as described previously (see Figures 4.9 and 4.10). The reason for mentioning the limbic system and the other functions of

the hypothalamus is to point out that the pulsatile release of GnRH may affect and be affected by many factors. The effect could be a delay or disruption of menstrual function. This is discussed further in chapter 8.

The Role of the Gonadotropins

Of the seven hormones known to be synthesized by the anterior pituitary gland, two are intricately involved in the menstrual cycle. These protein hormones—LH and FSH—are called gonadotropins because they regulate the gonads, the organs of

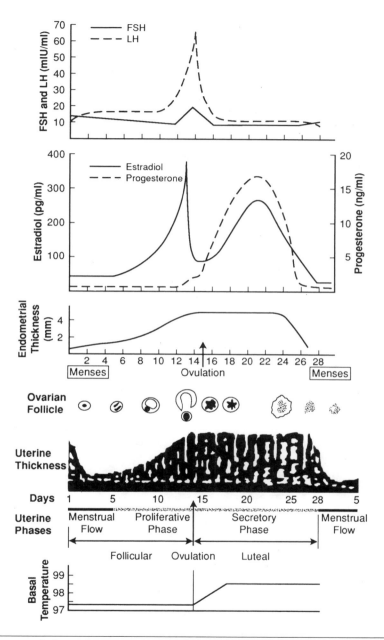

Figure 4.11 Summary of plasma hormone concentrations, endometrial and ovarian changes, and basal body temperature during the menstrual cycle. *Note.* Adapted from "Menstruation" by M.M. Shangold, in *Women and Exercise: Physiology and Sports Medicine* (p. 132) by M.M. Shangold and G. Mirkin (Eds.), 1988, Philadelphia: F.A. Davis, copyright 1988 by F.A. Davis Co.; adapted from *Human Physiology: The Mechanisms of Body Function* (4th ed., p. 572) by A.J. Vander, J.H. Sherman, and D.S. Luciano, 1985, New York: McGraw-Hill, copyright 1985 by McGraw-Hill, Inc. Adapted by permission of McGraw-Hill, Inc.

reproduction. Follicle-stimulating hormone stimulates the growth and development of the primary follicles in the ovary (and sperm production in the testes), whereas LH is responsible for estrogen production and secretion, ovulation, and corpus luteum formation (and stimulation of testosterone secretion from the testes). A third anterior pituitary hormone, prolactin, initiates and sustains milk production in the breasts after they have been prepared for lactation by the steroid hormones, estrogen and progesterone.

The growth and development of the ovarian follicle involves synergistic interaction between FSH, LH, androgens, estrogens, and the granulosa and theca cells of the ovary. Luteinizing hormone acts mainly on the theca cells, which synthesize androgens, which in turn are aromatized to estrogens by the granulosa cells (see Figure 4.12). Follicle-stimulating hormone acts mainly on the granulosa cells, which produce estrogens both directly and by aromatizing androgens (male sex hormones) provided by the theca cells. Thus, estrogen production and secretion requires theca and granulosa cells and both gonadotropins.

The Role of the Ovarian Steroids

The steroid hormones involved in female reproductive function are produced by the ovaries and during pregnancy by the placenta. The estrogens and progesterone are the female sex hormones and the androgens the male sex hormones. Actually, the ovaries produce all three sex hormones, but of course they produce a relatively small amount of androgens. The follicular structures of the ovary preferentially produce the *estrogens*, a general term used for substances that produce biological effects characteristic of estrogenic hormones. The three major forms of estrogen are *estradiol*, *estrone*, and *estriol*. The cells

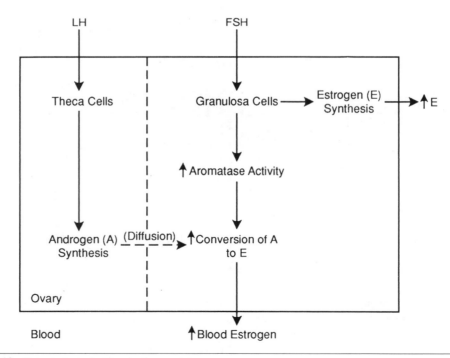

Figure 4.12   Estrogen production in the ovary.

of the corpus luteum produce *progesterone*, and the adrenal glands produce androgens.

The primary function of the estrogens in the menstrual cycle is to stimulate the growth of the uterine endometrium, resulting in an increase in both the number of cells (hyperplasia) and cell size (hypertrophy). Estrogens also exert major feedback effects on the secretion of GnRH and the gonadotropins. Low plasma concentrations of estrogen in the early follicular phase inhibit the hypothalamic neurons that secrete GnRH, thus inhibiting the release of gonadotropins from the anterior pituitary (this refers to the negative feedback loop shown in Figure 4.10). In the late follicular phase, however, the rise in estrogen concentrations (known as the *preovulatory estradiol surge)* causes the anterior pituitary cells to secrete more LH (and secondarily, FSH) in response to GnRH and may also stimulate the hypothalamic neurons that secrete GnRH. This positive feedback stimulation of LH (and FSH) secretion induces the LH surge, which causes ovulation.

The estrogens have many additional functions and affect many target tissues. In the cervical glands, the estrogens cause a clear, watery secretion that facilitates the passage of sperm. Uterine contractions are also affected. The lining of the fallopian tubes increases in thickness, and ciliary action is enhanced by the estrogens. In the breasts, duct tissue grows, and fat is deposited as a result of estrogenic action.

The estrogens also influence the exterior appearance of the body. Initially, the growth spurt at puberty is enhanced, but estrogens also cause the fusion of the epiphyseal growth plates at the ends of the long bones so that linear growth in height slows. The elevated estrogens of puberty also cause increased deposition of body fat, particularly in the breasts, buttocks, and thighs, resulting in the characteristic female figure.

Estrogens affect the woman's health by reducing the total blood cholesterol level and enhancing the high-density lipoprotein cholesterol fraction. These two factors are thought to be responsible for the lower incidence of coronary heart disease in premenopausal women than in men of the same age. Estrogen also affects women's bone structure and consequently bone health. This topic is discussed at length in later chapters.

The temperature-regulating and vasomotor functions of the hypothalamus are also influenced, resulting in the higher skin temperatures characteristic of the female and the lower basal body temperature of the first half of the menstrual cycle.

The effects of progesterone are not nearly so extensive. Its main function is to prepare the endometrial lining of the uterus for the implantation of a fertilized ovum, primarily by stimulating the secretions of endometrial glands. Progesterone also plays a role in the regulation of the menstrual cycle. High plasma concentrations of progesterone, in the presence of estrogen, inhibit the hypothalamic neurons that secrete GnRH, resulting in a negative feedback inhibition of FSH and LH secretion. Progesterone also inhibits uterine contractions so that an implanted ovum can be retained. Progesterone increases the glandular elements in the breasts, but actual production of milk is a function of prolactin. Cervical mucus becomes more viscous, thus preventing the passage of sperm through the cervical os as a result of elevated progesterone.

After ovulation, basal body temperature rises slightly. This rise is sometimes used as an indication that ovulation has occurred and has been attributed to progesterone. This hormone also causes an increase in the excretion of water and sodium from the kidney, so it is unlikely that progesterone is responsible for the water retention and bloating that some women experience during the last phase of the menstrual cycle.

Ovarian and Uterine Cycles

The ovarian cycle has already been discussed and illustrated (Figure 4.6). What remains is to correlate all the hormonal actions discussed previously with the ovarian cycle and the uterine endometrial cycle (which has not yet been described). Figure 4.11 should be very helpful if you refer to it during the following discussion.

Recall the purpose of the menstrual cycle. The ovarian cycle occurs to produce an ovum and can be divided into three phases: follicular, ovulatory, and luteal. The endometrial cycle occurs to provide a place to nourish and maintain a fertilized ovum and can be divided into three phases: menstrual, proliferative (or follicular), and secretory (or progestational or luteal); these do not correspond exactly to the phases of the ovarian cycle.

Follicular (Proliferative) Phase

At the beginning of the ovarian and endometrial cycles (Day 1 or before), the anterior pituitary responds to GnRH from the hypothalamus and begins to secrete increasing amounts of FSH and LH (in pulsatile fashion). A group of ovarian follicles responds to FSH and grows steadily. Full follicle development takes 17 to 25 days, which means that the process is initiated in the late luteal phase of the preceding menstrual cycle. Sometime within the first 5 days of the cycle, one follicle (or follicles in the case of multiple fraternal births) becomes dominant. Under the combined influence of FSH and LH, the follicle develops, synthesizes estrogen, and secretes it into the blood. During this time, the endometrium is in the menstrual phase (the bleeding period). Even so, estrogen from the developing follicle or follicles causes cell division in the endometrial lining to repair the denuded area. Regeneration of the previously sloughed-off superficial layer occurs rapidly, and within a few days of menses the entire uterine cavity is covered with new epithelial cells.

As a mature Graffian follicle develops and secretes more estrogen, the glandular cells of the endometrium rapidly proliferate (proliferative endometrial phase). The cellular layer, referred to as the *functionalis*, is extremely responsive to ovarian hormones. Initially, RNA and DNA synthesis is induced by estrogen, and epithelial and vascular cells grow rapidly. Blood vessels

then develop, elongating disproportionately faster than the increase in endometrial thickness. Consequently, they twist and coil and are thus referred to as *spiral arteries* and *spiral veins*.

At this time, the relatively low estrogen levels from the maturing follicle inhibit further production of LH and FSH through a negative feedback loop (see Figure 4.10). Eventually, estrogen levels rise sharply as the theca and granulosa cells become increasingly active (see Figure 4.12). The rapidly increasing estrogen concentrations now cause a positive feedback effect on the secretion of LH (and, secondarily, FSH). In some way, the high estrogen level acts directly on pituitary cells to enhance the sensitivity of the LH-releasing mechanism to GnRH. The high estrogen concentration may also act on the hypothalamus to increase the frequency of GnRH pulses. The resulting effect is the characteristic surge of LH (and FSH) just before ovulation, and, within hours, LH induces a variety of changes in the ovary and follicle, causing ovulation. Initially, follicle size increases markedly. This is followed by the onset of progesterone secretion by granulosa cells, a decrease in estrogen secretion (mid-cycle drop), and the appearance of enzymes that cause the rupture of the ovarian wall. Within 16 to 24 h of the LH peak, ovulation occurs (approximately Day 14 of a normal 28-day cycle).

Luteal (Secretory) Phase

Following its expulsion from the follicle, the ovum enters the fimbriated ends of a fallopian tube. The cells of the ruptured follicle undergo luteinization and become a corpus luteum, which produces both estrogen and progesterone and reaches a peak of activity about 8 days after ovulation.

During the 8 days of intense corpus luteum activity, the endometrium enters the progestational, or secretory, phase. The thickened endometrial lining continues to be highly responsive to progesterone, enzymes increase, and glandular tissues produce secretions (thus the term *secretory phase*). The glands of the superficial layer of the functionalis become dilated as they become filled with materials rich in glycogen, proteins, lipids, and enzymes. The highest level of metabolic activity occurs at about Day 21 or 22, by which time the endometrium has fully accomplished the task of providing a cushioned and nutritious site for the implantation of a fertilized ovum. If the ovum has been fertilized, implantation occurs at about this time.

The high progesterone levels secreted from the corpus luteum act on the hypothalamus to decrease the frequency of GnRH pulses, signaling a reduction in LH secretion from the anterior pituitary. During the luteal phase, FSH and LH are at their lowest levels, whereas estrogen and particularly progesterone are high. This appears to be a result of the negative feedback effects of the steroids on gonadotropic hormone secretions.

The mechanism for the demise of the corpus luteum is not fully understood, but it will regress if implantation of a fertilized ovum does not occur and there are no hormones from a developing embryo and placenta. What is known is that luteal function requires a continuous basal level of LH (FSH is not required) and that, as the corpus luteum ages, the level of LH receptors falls. A current hypothesis is that the corpus luteum produces a large quantity of prostaglandins that interfere with hormonal secretion and cell function. Possibly, the accumulation of estrogen in the corpus luteum inhibits gonadotropic action, and its function is terminated. With pregnancy, the corpus luteum is maintained for approximately 4 to 6 weeks, at which point the placenta takes over the production of progesterone and the corpus luteum regresses.

Menstrual Phase

If there is no pregnancy, and with the regression of the corpus luteum, estrogen and progesterone decrease rapidly, and their negative feedback effect is diminished. Both FSH and LH can again increase to initiate a new cycle. Before that happens, however, the most dramatic occurrence of all takes place: menstrual flow.

If the thick, superficial endometrial tissues are not supported by high levels of progesterone and estrogen, they undergo rapid decline and break down. As the superficial tissues regress, the spiral arteries become even more tortuously coiled, slowing the flow of blood. Some of the arteries momentarily constrict, stopping all blood flow to the endometrial tissues, which die as a result. When the arteries dilate again, blood escapes from the weakened and disintegrating top layers. As more of the endometrium disintegrates, pieces detach, and glandular secretions and blood slowly ooze into the uterine cavity. Menstrual hemorrhage and the sloughing off of the crumbling tissue results in a reorganization of the vascular bed and a stabilization of circulatory activity at the basal level of the endometrium. The bleeding is primarily arterial, but more tissue is lost than blood. The actual hemorrhaging occurs for a relatively short period of time, and approximately 50 ml of blood, glandular secretions, and tissue fragments flow from the uterine cavity and out the vagina (about 2-1/2 tablespoons of blood). Menstrual blood does not clot until it reaches the vagina because some of the clotting factors normally found in blood are destroyed by the enzymes of the uterus. The clots that appear with a heavy flow are a combination of red blood cell clumps, mucus, glycogen, and glycoproteins.

Breast tissues also respond to peaks of ovarian hormone secretion. Slight tenderness may occur at ovulation because of the retention of fluids in glandular tissue. This also tends to occur several days before menstruation. Relief is experienced with the onset of menstrual flow.

As you can see, the menstrual cycle is a complicated biological phenomenon. Emotional stress and exercise can affect this function. The effects of exercise on menstrual function and of menstrual function on exercise performance are discussed in the following chapters. However, now that the physiology of the menstrual cycle has been presented, the groundwork is laid for a discussion of puberty and menarche. Only with this background can the physiology of adolescence be properly understood.

There is considerably more agreement about the regulation of the menstrual cycle than about the control of puberty. The basic feedback mechanisms were explained previously, as were the effects of the steroid sex hormones, estrogen and progesterone. A clear understanding of the result of pubertal development should help you understand the process by which that result is attained. The remainder of this chapter is in part devoted to explaining how the adult menstrual cycle develops from the hormonal patterns of childhood.

Physiology of Puberty and Menarche

Early prepubertal children have low LH and FSH levels and show minimal evidence of pulsatile secretory activity. Initially, the prepubertal gonadal steroid hormone levels are able to keep the GnRH neurons pulsing at a slow rate, and FSH secretion is maintained at a higher level than LH secretion. The sensitivity of the negative feedback mechanism that is operative in early childhood is very high, and small amounts of circulating gonadal steroids are sufficient to maintain very low gonadotropin levels.

Hormonal Changes

With the onset of puberty, the hypothalamic neurons that release GnRH become progressively less sensitive to the suppressive effect of the gonadal steroids, and pulsatile LH secretion (and to a lesser extent FSH) markedly increases in response to increased intermittent secretory discharges of GnRH (the so-called *pulse generator*) during sleep. As the pulse generator accelerates, the young adolescent has more secretory episodes of LH (and FSH). The gonads respond by producing more gonadal steroids. Gradually, the increasing steroid levels effect significant changes in the prepubertal morphology, and secondary sex characteristics begin to develop. Eventually, pulsatile LH secretion begins to occur during waking, but the levels of LH remain dominant during sleep

until sexual maturation is complete.

Although the pubertal process begins with a diminished sensitivity to negative feedback at the level of the hypothalamus, maturation is not complete until the more complex positive feedback mechanism is operative and ovulation occurs. The major question here is, What stimulates the shift in feedback sensitivity? Many believe that it is adrenal maturation.

Adrenal androgen concentrations are low during early prepuberty. The increase in adrenal activity, called *adrenarche* (from the Greek word *arche* for *beginning*), begins at about age 6 with increases in the activity of dehydroepiandrosterone (DHEA), DHEA sulfate (DHEAS), and androstenedione. Both DHEA and androstenedione may act directly on the hypothalamus or indirectly by being converted to estrogen (aromatization). The factors responsible for heightened adrenal activity (which corresponds to the heightened hypothalamic activity) are unknown. However, because androstenedione can be peripherally converted in adipose tissue (fat) to estrone, it is probable that the increased levels of biologically active estrogen in the developing young girl are critical for further sexual maturation.

The pubertal process is an orderly one but shows a high degree of variability in its onset and completion. It begins with an acceleration of growth velocity (initiation of the growth spurt) after adrenarche. *Gonadarche* (from *gone*, Greek for *seed*) designates the period of hypothalamo-pituitary-ovarian activation. The progressive increase in the levels of adrenal androgens and ovarian estrogens is associated with the onset of *thelarche* (from *thele*, Greek for *nipple*), or breast development, and *pubarche*, which refers to the development of pubic and axillary hair. Breast and pubic hair development have been divided into five developmental stages (often known as the Tanner stages) that define the normal progression of adolescent sexual development. These stages are described in Table 4.1, which shows typical age ranges for normal female pubertal development. Figure 4.13 depicts a visualization of the Tanner developmental stages.

Table 4.1 Stages of Pubertal Development in the Female

Stages	Characteristics	Mean age (yr)
	Pubic hair development	
I	Prepubertal; no sexual hair	
II	Sparse growth of long, slightly pigmented hair over mons veneris or labia majora	11.7 (9.2-14.1)
III	Further darkening and coarsening of hair spread over the symphysis pubis	12.4 (10.2-14.6)
IV	Hair adult in character but not in distribution; not spread to medial surface of the thighs	13.0 (10.8-15.1)
V	Hair adult and extended to the medial thighs	14.4 (12.2-16.7)
	Breast development	
I	Prepubertal	
II	Breast budding; widening of areola with elevation of the breast and papilla as a small mound	11.1 (9.0-13.3)
III	Continued enlargement of both breast and areola but without separation of their contours	12.2 (10.0-14.3)
IV	Formation of the areola and papilla as a secondary mound projecting above the contour of the breast	13.1 (10.8-15.3)
V	Adult; projection of the papilla only; areola recessed to the contour of the breast (not all girls pass through Stage V; others may maintain Stage IV development)	15.3 (11.9-18.8)

Note. 95% confidence limits are in parentheses. From ''Pubertal Development in Endurance-Trained Female Athletes'' by A.D. Rogol. In *Competitive Sports for Children and Youth* (p. 174) by E.W. Brown and C.F. Branta (Eds.), 1988, Champaign, IL: Human Kinetics Books. Copyright 1988 by Human Kinetics Publishers, Inc. Reprinted by permission.

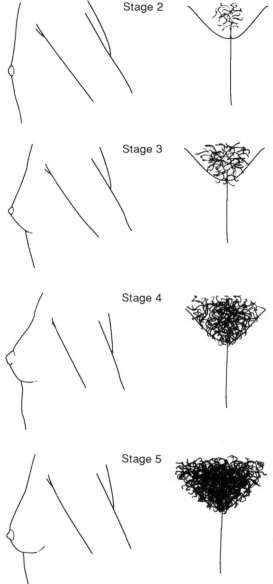

Figure 4.13 The Tanner stages for the development of pubic hair and breasts in young girls. *Note.* From ''Pubertal Changes in Adolescence'' by W.A. Daniel, Jr. In *Girls at Puberty* (pp. 59, 60) by J. Brooks-Gunn and A.C. Petersen (Eds.), 1983, New York: Plenum Press. Copyright 1983 by Plenum Press. Redrawn by permission.

Menarche, or the first menstrual flow, occurs at the mean age of 12.8 years in the United States (95% confidence limits for ages 9.0 to 13.3 years) (Rogol, 1988). Menarche occurs when the gonadotropic and ovarian hormones activate the ovarian-uterine axis. It has been estimated on the basis of basal body temperature and plasma progesterone measurements that about 55% to 90% of the cycles in the first two postmenarcheal years are anovulatory (Brisson, Dulac, Peronnet, & Ledoux, 1982). Figure 4.14 presents an integrated view of the different pubertal events.

The Critical Body Weight/Body Fat Theory

Frisch and Revelle (1970) noted that each pubertal event seemed to occur at an invariant mean body weight. The initiation of the adolescent growth spurt occurred at 30 kg, the time to peak height velocity at 39 kg, and menarche at 47 kg. Figure 4.15 integrates Frisch's body weight observations with Tanner's stages and chronological age and body weight.

Frisch and Revelle (1970, 1971) and Frisch, Revelle, and Cooke (1973) believe that a change in metabolic rate triggers the change in the sensitivity of the hypothalamus to steroids. Basal metabolic rate (BMR) is largely determined by the amount of heat produced by the vital organs. During the adolescent growth spurt, BMR per kilogram of body weight declines because the organs become a smaller proportion of the total body weight. The BMR is 35 kcal $\cdot$ kg^{-1} per day at the initiation of the growth spurt in girls (mean weight is 30 kg). At menarche, the BMR is 28 kcal $\cdot$ kg^{-1} per day (mean weight is 47 kg). Frisch believes this is due largely to an increase in body fat. From the initiation of the growth spurt to menarche, there is a 56% increase in total weight, a 42% increase in lean body weight, and a 125% increase in body fat. This results in a change in the ratio of fat to

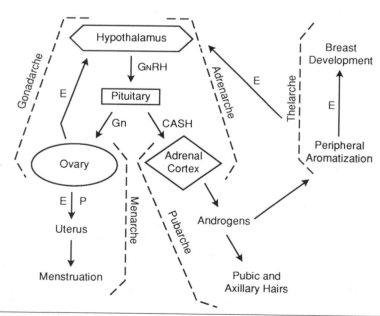

Figure 4.14 An integrated view of the different pubertal events. *Note.* From "The Onset of Menarche: A Late Event in Pubertal Progression to Be Affected by Physical Training" by G.R. Brisson, S. Dulac, F. Peronnet, and M. Ledoux, 1982, *Canadian Journal of Applied Sport Sciences*, **7**(2), p. 64. Copyright 1975 by Canadian Association of Sports Sciences. Reprinted by permission.

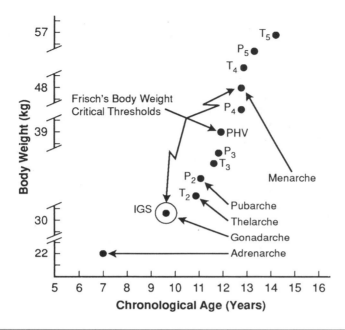

Figure 4.15 Integration of Frisch's critical weight hypothesis with Tanner's stages of pubertal development and chronological age. *Note.* From "The Onset of Menarche: A Late Event in Pubertal Progression to Be Affected by Physical Training" by G.R. Brisson, S. Dulac, F. Peronnet, and M. Ledoux, 1982, *Canadian Journal of Applied Sport Sciences,* **7**(2), p. 65. Copyright 1975 by Canadian Association of Sports Sciences. Reprinted by permission.

lean body weight from 1:5 at spurt initiation to 1:3 at menarche (Frisch et al., 1973).

Frisch et al. (1973) studied differences in body fat and lean body mass of early- and late-maturing girls. The late maturers (older age at menarche) had less body fat (22%) than the early maturers (25%), although the girls did not differ in lean body weight. This and other data led Frisch and McArthur (1974) to propose what has been termed the *critical fat theory*. They proposed that a "minimum level of stored, easily mobilized energy is necessary for ovulation and menstrual cycles in the human female" (p. 949). Specifically, they determined that the critical body fat percentage that was needed to initiate menses was 17% and that at age 18, when most women have ended their growth in height and are likely to be stable in weight, a 22% fat content is necessary to maintain normal menstrual function. Weight changes

associated with the cessation or restoration of menstrual function were in the range of 10% to 15% of body weight, mainly as a loss or gain of body fat.

A considerable amount of literature that is critical of Frisch's work has appeared in the scientific literature. Frisch and co-workers obtained their data by using an indirect methodology. Percent body fat was not measured with traditionally accepted methods but rather was estimated from Mellits and Cheek's (1970) estimation of total body water from height and weight. Frisch and co-workers did not even obtain the height and weight values they used at the exact age of menarche. The use of Mellits and Cheek's procedure to calculate relative body fat has been severely criticized by many investigators (e.g., Billewicz, Fellowes, & Hytten, 1976; Johnston, 1982; Johnston, Roche, Schell, & Wettenhall, 1975; Katch

& Katch, 1980; Loucks, Horvath, & Freedson, 1984; Scott, 1984; Scott & Johnston, 1982; Van't Hof & Roede, 1977). The methodology of Mellits and Cheek assumed that the biological constant for the water content of the fat-free body (FFB) is 72%, an assumption that most likely is not valid for children. Boileau et al. (1984) found that the percentage of water in the FFB progressively decreased from prepubescence to adulthood for both sexes at a rate approximating 0.38% per year. Actual values for white and black prepubescent girls were 76.0% and 75.4%, respectively, and for white and black postpubescent girls 73.3% and 74.1%, respectively. These differences are sufficient to overestimate body fatness by at least 3% to 4%. This is enough to lower the critical fat level if such a threshold exists.

Several studies have criticized Frisch's work for statistical reasons (e.g., Billewicz et al., 1976; Johnston et al., 1975; Trussell, 1978, 1980), a major problem being her interpretation of a descriptive measure of central tendency as a causative rather than merely an associated factor. Even if an "invariant" mean body weight or percent body fat does coincide with the occurrence of menarche, it does not necessarily follow that a critical threshold value exists. An outside variable indirectly related to the invariant variable may be the actual "causal" factor.

Several studies have been designed to experimentally verify Frisch's concept of a critical weight or level of body fat. These studies have shown that weight is not invariant at menarche (Johnston, Malina, & Galbraith, 1971; Johnston et al., 1975) and that early maturers tend to be heavier at a constant height than late maturers. Others who have dealt experimentally with age at menarche have concluded that menarche is not triggered by a set weight or body composition (Billewicz et al., 1976; Cameron, 1976; Crawford & Osler, 1975; Ellison, 1981a, 1981b).

Frisch's theory has been discussed here because it plays an important role in understanding menarche in young athletes. The possibility that strenuous training delays menarche is discussed in chapter 6.

Summary

This chapter presented basic information on the anatomy and physiology of the menstrual cycle. Emphasis was placed on the following points:

1. There is considerable anatomical protection for the pelvic organs of reproduction.
2. Hormonal regulation of the menstrual cycle involves a series of feedback mechanisms to properly coordinate events occurring in the hypothalamus, the pituitary gland, the ovaries, and the uterus.
3. The generation of GnRH pulses regulates the normal menstrual cycle and stimulates the attainment of menarche.
4. Sexual maturation, as characterized by breast and pubic hair development, is affected by the hypothalamic-pituitary-adrenal-ovarian axis.
5. The critical body weight/body fat theory is an inadequate explanation for the attainment of menarche.

Chapter 5

Effects of the Menstrual Cycle on Physical Performance

Many clinical and experimental investigations have dealt with menstrual function in women, and some have revealed interesting interrelationships between exercise and menstrual function. The objective of this chapter is to explore the question: How does the menstrual cycle affect exercise performance? The next chapter explores the reverse of this question: How does exercise affect the menstrual cycle? First, let's examine some of the physiological variations that may occur during a normal menstrual cycle and then see how performance may be influenced.

Physiological Variations Occurring With the Menstrual Cycle

Many biological variables show periodicity, that is, a tendency toward a characteristic, regularly repeating pattern. When there is synchronization with the 24-h cycle of light and darkness, the term *diurnal*, or *circadian* (about 1 day), is used. These rhythms can be disturbed by shifts of time zone (i.e., latitudinal travel) and sleep deprivation. There has been increasing interest in the extent to which disturbances in circadian rhythms can influence performance (for a limited treatment of this topic, see Haymes & Wells, 1986).

Certain body functions may show longer cycles, such as circalunar (about 28 days) or circa-annual (seasonal variations). A *biological rhythm* is considered endogenous if it persists under free-running conditions, that is, when the individual is not influenced by external signals (such as social contacts or changes in the natural environment). The human menstrual cycle is an excellent example of an endogenous biological rhythm.

Many physical, biochemical, or systemic changes have been reported to undergo variation consistent with phases of the menstrual cycle. However, not all investigators agree as to the direction of change or the degree of change.

Southam and Gonzaga (1965) extensively reviewed systematic changes reported during the menstrual cycle. They listed numerous changes but added the caveat that some of the changes they described required additional documentation with modern techniques. Some of the more persistent changes that could affect performance include the following:

- A premenstrual increase in body mass
- An increase in fasting blood glucose during menses
- An increase in habitual daily activity in the postmenstrual phase
- An increase in resting respiratory minute volume ($\dot{V}_E$) in the luteal phase

- A decrease in body temperature at the time of ovulation, followed by a sharp rise to a plateau higher than that reached during the follicular phase
- Premenstrual hyperemia of the breast with a corresponding increase in breast size
- Increased gastric motility during menstruation
- A decrease in red blood cell survival time in the luteal phase and a decrease in the number of platelets

The most consistent and important variation in physiological baseline that occurs in relation to the menstrual cycle is the alteration in basal body temperature mentioned in the previous chapter. After ovulation, basal temperature rises, remains slightly elevated throughout the luteal phase, and falls at menstrual flow. Variations in HR are less marked, but in some women HR is higher during the time that basal body temperature is elevated.

The increase in body mass (which has not been verified in all studies) probably has little if any effect on the performance of most tasks; however, when it does occur, the related sensations of heaviness may cause a deterioration of all-out effort.

Blood pressure is apparently too irregular or too responsive to other variables to consistently support a rhythmic cycle. Garlick and Bernauer (1968) reported considerable disagreement in the literature. Although some investigators have found blood pressure to be lowest at the onset of menses, others have reported that it is highest on the first 2 days of flow. Still others have reported that blood pressure is constant throughout the cycle.

Some investigators have reported changes in hematocrit, Hb, and red blood cell number with menstrual phase. The lowest values seem to correspond with menstrual flow. These changes, however, more likely reflect fluid volume shifts than changes in red cell production. Capillary and red cell fragility are known to change with hormonal fluctuation and are increased during menses.

The volume of the breasts significantly increases in the second half of normal (and contraceptive-controlled) menstrual cycles. The mean change in volume throughout the cycle was 100 ml under normal conditions and 66 ml when oral contraceptives were taken (Milligan, Drife, & Short, 1975). These changes in volume could be the result of hormonally controlled vascular and lymphatic changes or structural changes specifically related to progestational effects. Unfortunately, this study did not measure body weight changes, so it is not known whether increased breast volume is related to variations in total body weight. These changes in breast volume are probably related to the feelings of fullness and breast tenderness noted by many women during the late stages of the luteal phase.

Although it appears that systematic changes throughout the menstrual cycle are fairly extensive, it is also evident that there is considerable individual variation. Are these variations in physiological baseline significant enough to influence exercise performance during the menstrual cycle? The remainder of this chapter summarizes the literature dealing with this question. Findings are discussed in chronological order of publication, and studies of the nonathletic woman are discussed separately from those of highly trained athletes.

Menstrual Function and Performance in the Nonathlete

Investigations dealing with the influence of the menstrual cycle on performance are mostly equivocal. For example, although one study (Tuttle & Frey, 1930) reported that girls exhibited a more efficient HR response to step-test performance during the preflow and flow phases, another report from the same laboratory (Scott & Tuttle, 1932) found that the poorest ratings occurred during menstruation. In these studies, many individual differences were seen, and the overall conclusion was that differences were probably due to factors other than menstrual function.

No differences attributable to menstrual flow were found for static balance, grip strength, leg or back lift strength (Auster, 1944), and reaction time (Loucks & Thompson, 1968; Phillips, 1962) or for steadiness, movement time, blood pressure, and HR (Phillips, 1962). Phillips (1968) reported that menstrual phase did not affect HR or blood pressure either before or after exercise. Garlick and Bernauer (1968) reported lower resting values for HR, blood pressure, hematocrit, and hemoglobin on the 1st day of flow than on the 14th day of the cycle, but these cyclic changes were not evident after moderate exercise.

Slightly poorer performance in the vertical jump (explosive power) and the 100-yd shuttle run was reported in college women during the first 24 h of menses (Rockwell, 1962). Keenan (1958) reported that steadiness, weight shifting, and grip strength scores were lower on the first day of flow than during the middle of the cycle.

Dalton (1960) indicated that menstrual flow had a detrimental effect on school grades. Of particular significance was the indication that "times of stress" increased premenstrual symptoms, imposing a greater handicap on school performance. Johnson (1932) had previously demonstrated a drop in learning curves at the onset of menses and during menstrual flow in subjects learning to walk a tightwire. These results could indicate a drop in ability to concentrate or a loss of interest in what one is doing during the period of menstrual flow, perhaps because of negative attitudes that are often associated with menses (see introduction to chapter 7). It should be noted that the previous studies were completed during an era when menstruation was considered a disability.

In one carefully controlled study, variations in performance in the 12-min run-walk, $\dot{V}O_2$max, the 600-yd run-walk, and the 1.5-mi run-walk were not related to phases of the menstrual cycle (Doolittle & Engebretsen, 1972). The authors suggested that further investigation—including performance measures, a complete battery of physiological parameters, and frequent hormonal analysis throughout the cycle—is necessary to adequately determine the effect of the menstrual cycle on physical performance. No investigation of this scope has yet been attempted.

More recently, Stephenson, Kolka, and Wilkerson (1982a) reported the results of 6 subjects who completed a series of work loads to exhaustion on a bicycle ergometer on Days 2, 8, 14, 20, and 26 of their menstrual cycles. There were no differences relative to menstrual cycle day at any exercise intensity for $\dot{V}O_2$, carbon dioxide production, oxygen pulse, total respiratory volume, tidal volume, respiratory rate, or respiratory exchange ratio. Furthermore, there were no differences from one day to another for exercise time to exhaustion. The authors concluded that

> cyclic reproductive function of relatively fit human females does not affect the overall energy production over the entire range of metabolic intensities from rest through maximal exercise. In addition, the composite function of the . . . cardiovascular and respiratory systems . . . are also unaltered by reproduction changes occurring throughout the normal menstrual cycle. (p. 274)

In contrast to the stability of the metabolic measurements, however, changes were observed in the thermoregulatory variables. As expected, resting core temperature (T_{re}) increased during the luteal phase. This borderline elevation was also observed at all submaximal and maximal exercise loads during the luteal phase (Days 14 and 20). This dissociation of metabolic from thermoregulatory responses has not previously been documented (except in febrile males) and needs further study.

Table 5.1 presents a compilation of results from a number of studies documenting the effects of menstrual phase on exercise responses. Some of the studies listed are discussed in the next section because the subject pool represents trained women (athletes). Only the studies that utilized untrained women are discussed in this section.

Eston and Burke (1984) studied 21 physical education students with normal cycles during menses (the second or third day), the midfollicular phase (Days 6 to 9), the midluteal phase (6 to 9 days after ovulation determined by oral temperature changes), and the premenstrual phase (within 72 h preceding menses). The subjects performed 3-min work bouts on a bicycle ergometer at 70% to 90% $\dot{V}O_2$max. Body weight was higher in the premenstrual phase than the luteal and follicular phases. More important, however, no differences were observed in $\dot{V}O_2$, carbon dioxide production, ventilation, lactic acid concentration, HR, or rating of perceived exertion.

Hall-Jurkowski, Jones, Toews, and Sutton (1981) utilized a similar exercise task (cycling at 70% and 90% $\dot{V}O_2$max) for a much longer period (40 min). Although there were no differences among menstrual phases for ventilation, they reported an increase in endurance during the luteal phase compared to the follicular phase that they attributed to higher lactate values during the midfollicular phase. Note in Table 5.1 that the other investigators of lactate accumulation during exercise (Bonen et al., 1983; Gamberale et al., 1975; Lamont, 1986) reported no significant differences among menstrual phases.

Higgs and Robertson (1981) investigated the relationship of perceived exertion and menstrual phase at high levels of exercise intensity (90% and 100% $\dot{V}O_2$max). No differences were observed at 90% $\dot{V}O_2$max, but the pattern of responses was similar to the 100% $\dot{V}O_2$max load, in which perception of effort was higher during the premenstrual and menstrual phases and run time to exhaustion reduced. Gamberale et al. (1975) also reported that perceived exertion was elevated during menses, but their subjects were characterized by severe menstrual distress, and such perceptions are expected. Ratings of perceived exertion have been shown to be closely associated with HR.

The findings of Higgs and Robertson, however, indicated some dissociation of HR and perceived exertion. The correlation between these variables was lower during the premenstrual and menstrual phases than the other phases. As noted previously, neither Stephenson, Kolka, and Wilkerson (1982b) nor Eston and Burke (1984) found differences in perceived exertion with menstrual phase.

Table 5.1 Effects of Menstrual Phase on Exercise Responses

Variables	References	Types of exercise	Results	Cycle phase verification	Special notes
$\dot{V}O_2max$	Allsen et al. (1977)	TM run	No difference	C	—
	Schoene et al. (1981)	BE to exhaustion	No difference	T	Athletes & nonathletes
$\dot{V}O_2submax$	Eston & Burke (1984)	BE: 3 min; 70% & 90% $\dot{V}O_2max$	No difference	T	—
	Stephenson et al. (1982a)	BE: 4 loads	No difference	C	—
	Lamont (1986)	BE: 60 min, 70% $\dot{V}O_2max$	No difference	H	Active & untrained
$\dot{V}_E$	Schoene et al. (1981)	BE to exhaustion	Increase during luteal phase	T	Nonathletes & athletes
	Hall-Jurkowski et al. (1981)	BE: 40 min, 70% & 90% $\dot{V}O_2max$	No difference	T, H	—
	Stephenson et al. (1982a)	BE: 4 loads	No difference	C	—
	Eston & Burke (1984)	BE: 3 min, 70% & 90% $\dot{V}O_2max$	No difference	T	—
	Lamont (1986)	BE: 60 min, 70% $\dot{V}O_2max$	No difference	H	—
LA	Hall-Jurkowski et al. (1981)	BE: 40 min, 70% & 90% $\dot{V}O_2max$	Increase during midfollicular phase	T, H	—
	Gamberale et al. (1975)	BE: 12 min, 40% & 70% $\dot{V}O_2max$	No difference	—	—
	Bonen et al. (1983)	BE: 60 min, 40% & 80% $\dot{V}O_2max$	No difference	—	—
	Eston & Burke (1984)	BE: 3 min, 70% & 90% $\dot{V}O_2max$	No difference	T	—
	Lamont (1986)	BE: 60 min, 70% $\dot{V}O_2max$	No difference	H	—
RPE	Higgs & Robertson (1981)	R: 3 min, 100% $\dot{V}O_2max$	Increase during PM & M	—	—
		R: 3 min, 90% $\dot{V}O_2max$	No difference	C	—
	Gamberale et al. (1975)	R: 12 min, 40% & 70% $\dot{V}O_2max$	Increase during M	—	Subjects had severe menstrual distress

(Cont.)

Table 5.1   (Continued)

Variables	References	Types of exercise	Results	Cycle phase verification	Special notes
HR	Stephenson et al. (1982b)	BE: 4 loads	No difference	C	—
	Eston & Burke (1984)	BE: 3 min, 70% & 90% $\dot{V}O_2$max	No difference	T	—
	Eston & Burke (1984)	BE: 3 min, 70% & 90% $\dot{V}O_2$max	No difference	T	—
	Higgs & Robertson (1981)	BE: 90% & 100% $\dot{V}O_2$max	No difference	C	Two complete cycles assessed
Performance	Hall-Jurkowski et al. (1981)	BE: 40 min, 70% & 90% $\dot{V}O_2$max	Increase in endurance during luteal phase	T, H	—
	Higgs & Robertson (1981)	BE: > 100% $\dot{V}O_2$max	Decrease in R time during PM & M	C	—
	Brooks-Gunn et al. (1986)	100-yd freestyle 100-yd best event	Best times during M; Slowest times during PM	T —	Highly trained postmenarcheal adolescents ($n = 4$)
	Stephenson et al. (1982a)	BE: 4 loads	No difference in work time to exhaustion	C	—
	Schoene et al. (1981)	BE to exhaustion	Decrease in endurance during luteal phase No difference	T —	Nonathletes Athletes

Note. TM = treadmill, BE = bicycle ergometer, R = run, C = calendar day, T = oral temperature chart, H = hormonal analysis, $\dot{V}O_2$max = maximum oxygen uptake, $\dot{V}_E$ = minute ventilation volume, LA = lactic acid concentration, RPE = rating of perceived exertion, and HR = heart rate.

Menstrual Function and Performance in the Athlete

The previously reviewed studies utilized subjects of high school and college age who were free of menstrual disorders (with the exception of Gamberale et al., 1975) and who menstruated regularly. They also possessed no particular athletic ability. Studies of special interest in terms of physical performance are those that involve athletic groups such as intercollegiate teams, Olympic athletes, and nationally ranked competitors.

In college athletes, no differences were found in $\dot{V}O_2$max during four phases of the menstrual cycle (Allsen, Parsons, & Bryce, 1977). Consequently, the authors stated that there were no reasons for girls or women to alter their conditioning, training, or competitive activities at any time during the menstrual cycle.

Martin (1976) studied metabolic and cardiorespiratory responses to exercise in 9 nonathletes and 8 Ohio State University varsity athletes during three menstrual phases represented by Day 3 (menstrual phase), Day 13 (postmenstrual phase), and the 7th day following ovulation (premenstrual phase). No significant differences were found within the three menstrual phases at rest and during submaximal walking, maximal running, or recovery in the untrained group. Although there was a significantly higher hematocrit value in the trained group during the postmenstrual phase, this did not occur in the untrained group and was not accompanied by changes in Hb values. The trained group also demonstrated a higher $\dot{V}O_2$ (L • min^{-1} and ml • kg^{-1} • min^{-1}) during the postmenstrual phase during the walking part of the test. This difference did not persist during maximal running. Because the variations seen did not occur in both groups and disappeared with more strenuous exercise, Martin minimized the significance of the few changes seen. He stated, "It is reasonable to assume that there is little influence on maximal performance due to cyclic variation in any of the three phases of the menstrual cycle" (p. 70).

Progesterone has been implicated as an agent that causes hyperventilation during pregnancy and the luteal phase of the menstrual cycle. It is conceivable, therefore, that the endogenous surge of progesterone in the luteal phase could stimulate ventilatory drive during exercise. Because there is a high correlation between low ventilatory drive and outstanding athletic performance in runners and swimmers (Byrne-Quinn, Weil, Sodal, Filley, & Grover, 1971; Saunders, Leeder, & Rebuck, 1976), a progestational effect on ventilation could be deleterious to maximal performance. Schoene, Robertson, Pierson, and Peterson (1981) studied this problem in three groups of women. One group consisted of 6 outstanding athletes with normal menstrual cycles. A second group consisted of 6 sedentary controls with normal menstrual cycles,

and the third group of subjects were outstanding athletes who were amenorrheic.

In the normally menstruating subjects, resting and exercise ventilation values were elevated in the luteal phase (with corresponding high progesterone values). Hypoxic ventilatory responses (responses to breathing air that is low in oxygen) and hypercapnic ventilatory responses (responses to breathing air that is high in carbon dioxide) were increased in the luteal phase. The athletic subjects, however, showed a blunted response when compared with the sedentary control subjects. The responses of the amenorrheic subjects did not differ in the two test periods. The authors concluded that ventilatory responses were elevated in menstruating women during the luteal phase. Note that the other studies listed in Table 5.1 (untrained subjects) reported no differences in ventilation with menstrual phase.

Three variables were chosen to gauge exercise performance: $\dot{V}O_2$max, $\dot{V}CO_2$max, and maximum work time (T_{max}). The nonathletes had significantly ($p < .05$) lower $\dot{V}CO_2$max and T_{max} values during the luteal phase. Neither the menstruating nor the amenorrheic athletes, however, displayed phasic differences in these parameters. In addition, there were no differences between the phases in the onset of anaerobic threshold. The authors concluded that the study demonstrated that

women during the luteal phase . . . have augmented ventilatory responses to hypoxia and hypercapnia that effect an increase in ventilation during exercise. This increase in ventilation does not seem to affect adversely the exercise performance of trained athletes even though nonathletic controls were not able to reach as high a level of exercise during the luteal phase as they were during the follicular phase. (Schoene et al., 1981, p. 1305)

Even if minor differences with menstrual phase in physiological responses to exercise do occur, it does not necessarily follow that performance will be altered. Nevertheless, many athletes believe that menstruation negatively affects their performance.

Several surveys of the performance of outstanding athletes have been completed. In the 1930 (Prague) track-and-field championships for women, 29% of the competitors produced their "best performance" during menstrual flow, 63% had no change in performance, and 8% had a slight decline in performance during menses (Kral & Markalous, 1958).

Finnish sportswomen were surveyed at the Helsinki Olympic Games (Ingman, 1953). Five attained their record scores during menstrual flow, 20 reported that their performances were better than usual, 45 reported that their performances were unaffected by menstruation, and 39 reported that they performed worse during menses.

According to Jokl (1958), at least six gold medals in track and swimming events were won by women who were in their menstrual phases at the 1956 Olympic Games in Melbourne. Three women athletes—one in shot put, one in discus, and one in the 4 × 100-m track relay—were pregnant (2, 3, and 4 months, respectively).

In Hungarian athletes, Erdelyi (1962) found that 42% to 48% showed no change in performance during menstrual flow, that 30.7% showed poorer performance, and that 13% to 15% showed better performance than usual. Best performance was reported in the postmenstrual (follicular) phase, whereas worst performance occurred in the premenstrual (late luteal) phase and during the first 2 days of flow. Erdelyi found poor performances during menstruation in tennis players and rowers but that menses did not affect performance in ball games and sprinting. He explained these differences by stating that rowing and tennis performance required great effort over an extended period of time. Short-term effort, he believed, was less likely to be affected by menstruation. He acknowledged that performance during menses may well be influenced by psychological factors that are due to attitudes toward menstruation.

At the Tokyo Olympic Games, 54% of the women surveyed reported that they "sometimes" did not train during menses, and 12% reported that they "never" trained during menses (Zaharieva,

1965). Most of this latter category were swimmers. Thirty-one percent said they "sometimes" competed during menses. These are results of a 1964 survey, which probably could not be duplicated today. With competition as rigorous as it is now, a competitor cannot afford to take a few days off each month. This means that a woman choosing not to train or compete during her menses eliminates herself from an athletic career. Many of the Tokyo Olympians reported performing just as well during menses as in other phases of their cycles (37%), but 16.9% said they were "always bad" during their menstrual periods, and 28% reported that their performance "varies" during flow. Some 32% reported "feeling weak" during flow, and 10.8% expressed feelings of "nervousness." In terms of self-confidence, 63% were "normal," but 26% were "uncertain."

A classic study of Swedish girl swimmers (Åstrand et al., 1963) revealed that all girls competed if an event coincided with menstrual flow but that many temporarily discontinued their training during this time. Nearly half the girls performed worse during menstruation. Currently, I believe that very few female athletes interrupt their training schedules during menstrual flow.

Women on U.S. Olympic teams in 1964 and 1968 won gold medals and established world records during all menstrual phases, including menstruation (Thomas, 1974). This does not mean that all women can or will perform at maximal capacity at any time during their cycles. There are many individual differences, and athletic achievement is influenced by numerous physiological, psychological, and environmental factors that probably have more effect on performance than menstrual phase.

The only experimentally controlled study of athletic performance was reported by Brooks-Gunn, Gargiulo, and Warren (1986a). Performance times of 4 menstruating adolescent swimmers who competed at the national level were recorded twice per week for 12 weeks. Average performance times were calculated for the entire cycle, the midfollicular phase (a 10-day period after menstrual flow ceased), the premenstrual phase (a 4-day period before the onset of menstruation), and the menstrual phase (the duration of menses). The fastest times for the 100-yd freestyle (by .82 s) and the 100-yd best event (by .70 s) occurred during the menstrual phase. The slowest times occurred during the premenstrual phase (by .96 s and 1.32 s, respectively). Body temperatures were obtained to verify menstrual phase, and many of the cycles did not display an increase during the second half of the cycle. This suggests that many of the cycles were anovulatory.

The Moos Menstrual Distress Questionnaire revealed significantly higher arousal during the menstrual phase and lower arousal during the premenstrual phase. None of the subjects reported menstrual pain. Obviously, the results of this study need to be verified in older subjects who are known to be ovulating. The fact that these swimmers may not have been ovulating (plus the very small number of subjects) means that the results of this investigation should not be given too much weight.

Summarizing the earlier studies of athletic performance (or perception of performance) and cycle phase, Brooks-Gunn, Gargiulo, and Warren (1986b) stated that 40% to 60% of the athletes did not show cycle-related performance alterations and that 15% to 30% exhibited their worst performances in the menstrual phase, premenstrual phase, or both. The suggested mediators of cycle-related effects are the following:

• *Self-expectancies*. This is the notion that behavior is affected by one's expectations regarding that behavior. In this instance, if a woman expects to perform poorly as a result of negative feelings about menstruation (or the premenstrual period), she may indeed do so.

• *Cultural restrictions*. Menstrual flow is almost universally perceived as negative, even unclean. Many women believe that restrictions should be imposed on sports,

particularly swimming (and even bathing), during menstruation.

• *Menstrual symptoms*. Many women report negative symptoms during the menstrual and premenstrual phases. These reports may be systematically biased by a woman's awareness of the purpose of the questionnaire and by her perception of menstruation. The authors pointed out that retrospective reports seem to accentuate the association between phase and negative symptoms, whereas prospective reports often fail to show cyclic fluctuations. Obviously, women with dysmenorrhea, severe premenstrual tension, and water retention are less likely to put forth maximal effort than when they have no menstrual symptoms.

There is some evidence, however, that athletic women have a lesser incidence of dysmenorrhea and a generally better attitude toward menstruation than nonathletic women (this is discussed in a later chapter) and, therefore, that athletic women are not likely to have significant performance differences resulting from the mediators suggested previously. Many believe that regular aerobic exercise promotes menstrual health. Others believe that the menstrual cycles of highly trained athletes are likely to be affected in such a way that performance differences are unlikely (e.g., amenorrhea and anovulatory cycles). Still others believe that women who are likely to have performance decrements with menstruation do not become athletes in the first place.

Responses to Heat Stress During the Menstrual Cycle

It has been suggested that the elevation in basal body temperature during the luteal phase is the result of a higher hypothalamic "set point" temperature (Cunningham & Cabanac, 1971). If this is so, lower sweating rates and higher body temperatures would be expected in women who are exposed to high environmental temperatures during the latter half of the menstrual cycle. However, when young untrained and unacclimatized women walked in a hot-dry environment (48 °C/ 118 °F, 11 mm water vapor pressure) for 40 min (total exposure was 2 h) at a work load representing 50% $\dot{V}O_2$max, no menstrual phase differences were found for rectal temperature, mean skin and body temperatures, body heat content, sweating rate, evaporative heat loss, $\dot{V}O_2$, ventilation volume, and oxygen pulse (milliliters of oxygen per heart beat). Blood samples indicated no significant differences with menstrual phase in plasma proteins, lactic acid, or serum sodium or potassium (Wells, 1977; Wells & Horvath, 1973, 1974). These results were recently verified at a lower work load (30% $\dot{V}O_2$max) in three environments (28 °C, 35 °C, and 48 °C) (Horvath & Drinkwater, 1982). In an interesting study that compared pre- and postovulatory women (with normal menstrual cycles) with amenorrheic women, no differences were found in exercise responses to heat stress either before or after heat acclimation (Frye, Kamon, & Webb, 1982). These investigations firmly indicate that hormonal fluctuations either during the menstrual cycle or with amenorrhea do not influence responses to exercise in the heat.

With a few exceptions (e.g., in women with serious dysmenorrhea), physical performance is *not* altered by menstrual phase. However, some physiological and psychological biorhythms have sufficient influence on performance that they merit close study. There is possibly a phase of the cycle in which a particular athlete may be more or less efficient, but the differences are so small that in daily performance they are not noticeable. At elite levels of performance, these slight variations may be more significant. Some women athletes may be more keenly "tuned" to these small differences than others. In cases where this is true, training and competitive schedules should be adjusted accordingly. Certainly, a coach should individualize each athlete's training schedule rather than use the same schedule for an entire team. Many variables should be considered when planning such a schedule, and certainly the menstrual cycle is an important one. For some women (and maybe all), juxtaposing the menstrual cycle and the training schedule to plan when workouts are to be most strenuous, when "peaking" is to be achieved, and when rest is needed may be extremely important in maximizing performance.

Summary

There is no conclusive evidence to suggest that menstrual function affects physical performance.

Chapter 6

Effects of Exercise
on Menstrual Function

Chapter 5 reviewed how menstrual function affects exercise performance. This chapter deals with how exercise affects menstrual function, specifically, menarche and menstruation. The etiology of exercise-related menstrual "problems" and hormonal alterations with exercise are discussed in chapters 7 and 8. Only studies that deal with the incidence of amenorrhea and other menstrual dysfunctions in athletes are reviewed here.

Sport, Puberty, and Menarche

Puberty is the transition between childhood and adulthood. It is a period marked by many physiological and psychological changes associated with reproductive ability. Girls begin puberty about 2 years earlier than boys. This gives the pubescent girl of the same chronological age but of more advanced maturation a temporary advantage in athletic endeavors requiring skill and strength.

Menarche

Studies of twins and of mothers and daughters indicate a significant genetic component in the time of menarche. In addition, environmental sources of variation (e.g., nutritional status, socioeconomic background, family size, altitude, and certain disease states) are just as significant. Johnston (1974) and Malina (1978) have provided excellent reviews of these factors. The effects of exercise (heavy training) on pubertal development and age at menarche must be assessed with regard to these factors and the wide variations among individuals. This topic is one of considerable controversy and disagreement.

The mean age at menarche in the United States is 12.8 years (95% confidence limits 10.8 to 14.8) and is slightly later in many foreign countries. *Primary amenorrhea* is the term used for delayed menarche. Puberty is considered delayed in girls

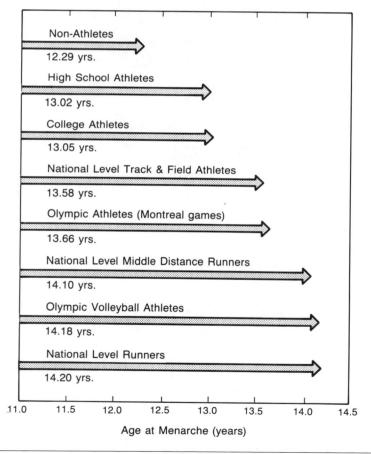

Figure 6.1   Age at menarche in non-athletes and athletes at different competitive levels. *Note.* Data from Feicht, Johnson, Martin, Sparkes, and Wagner (1978); Malina (1978); and Wakat and Sweeney (1979).

if they have not achieved the first stage of breast development (budding) by 13 years or if more than 5 years have elapsed between breast budding and menarche (Rogol, 1988).

Menarche has been reported to occur at a significantly later age in young female athletes than in her nonathletic counterparts (Malina, Spirduso, Tate, & Baylor, 1978; Märker, 1981). Malina et al. (1978) showed that high school and college track athletes had a later onset of menarche than sedentary control subjects and that nationally or internationally ranked athletes had later menarche than high school athletes (see Figure 6.1). Thus, there was an apparent association between a later age at menarche and a more advanced competitive level (and presumably more intensive training).

Märker (1981) provided mean ages, standard deviations, and ranges of menarcheal ages for elite European athletes (see Figure 6.2). The divers, figure skaters, and gymnasts experienced the latest menarche in this large sample of subjects. These studies seem to indicate that girls who engage in strenuous physical training experience a later age at menarche than the relatively inactive population and that the better performers (i.e., the more highly trained) have a later age at menarche than those who are not so extensively trained.

Age at menarche has not always been reported to be later in athletic groups. In their classic study on swimmers, Åstrand et al. (1963) reported that Swedish girl swimmers experienced menarche at an earlier age (12.9 years) than the average Swedish girl. Erdelyi (1962) reported that Hungarian national athletes experienced menarche at 13.6 years, the equivalent to the average for the Hungarian population. These studies, however, were completed when the scope and intensity of training for female athletes were not nearly as demanding as they are today. A study completed 20 years later (Stager, Robertshaw, & Miescher, 1984) concluded that competitive swimmers from the midwestern United States had a significantly later age at menarche than their nonathletic counterparts.

Warren (1980) and Frisch, Wyshak, and Vincent (1980) have intensively studied the onset and pubertal progression of young ballet dancers and found a later age at menarche and a high incidence of *secondary amenorrhea* (cessation of cycles). For 4 years, Warren (1980) monitored 15 ballerinas aged 13 to 15 who maintained a high level of activity

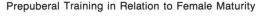
Prepuberal Training in Relation to Female Maturity

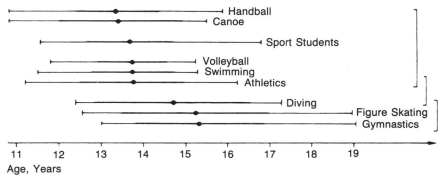

Figure 6.2 Mean values (•), standard deviations (heavy lines), and ranges of menarcheal ages of athletes from different sports. Markings at the right side indicate those groups for which the mean menarcheal ages are not significantly different. *Note.* From "Influence of Athletic Training on the Maturity Process of Girls" by K. Märker. In *Medicine and Sport* (Vol. 15, p. 119) by E. Jokl (Ed.), 1981, S. Karger AG, Basel. Copyright 1981 by S. Karger AG. Reprinted by permission.

from early adolescence. Menarche was markedly delayed, not occurring until age 15.4. This was significantly different from the normal (control) subjects (12.5 years) and the music students (12.6 years), who were chosen as subjects because of their intense career goals but relatively low levels of physical activity. Primary amenorrhea persisted in 2 dancers until age 18. Although all the dancers were premenarcheal, they had low to low-normal gonadotropin levels. The mean body weight and body fat values of the dancers were significantly less than those of controls. Onset of menses in 10 of the 15 dancers corresponded with a decrease in exercise or a forced rest of at least 2 months due to injury. During this time, weight gain was minimal, and body composition did not change. Reversal to the amenorrheic (no menses) state occurred in 11 of 13 subjects when they returned to usual exercise habits even though no change in body weight occurred.

It is interesting that a significant dichotomy in the usual order of pubertal development was noted in the dancers. Warren found that her subjects had delayed breast development and menarche, which is mediated by ovarian steroid hormones, but normal pubic hair development, which is mediated by adrenal androgenic hormones. The ballerinas also had increased long-bone growth. She interpreted these findings as showing a distinction between delayed puberty and adrenarche. Warren concluded that the severe energy demand (energy "drain") of ballet training rather than low body weight or body composition modulated hypothalamic activity and resulted in delayed menarche.

The maturation and body composition (assessed by skinfold technique) of Dutch gymnasts, swimmers, and normally active schoolgirls were studied to determine the relationship among these variables (Peltenburg, Erich, Bernink, Zonderland, & Huisveld, 1984). The onset of puberty (indicated in this study by breast budding, or the attainment of Tanner Stage 2) and age at menarche was 1 or 2 years later in the gymnasts than the swimmers or the schoolgirls. The gymnasts were also leaner and smaller in body build, which was interpreted

to be the result of self-selection and a delayed growth spurt. The swimmers and gymnasts in this study began training at about the same age, and the correlations between onset of training, pubertal development, and anthropometric variables were low.

However, some believe that age at menarche and the age at which training begins are important factors. Frisch et al. (1981) reported a delay in menarche of 0.4 years for each year of training before menarche in collegiate swimmers and runners. Figure 6.3 indicates the number of years of training before menarche in the European athletes mentioned previously (Märker, 1981). These data imply that the earlier a girl begins training, the later her menarche will be. However, an observational artifact may be operating here. In sports characterized by early entry (e.g., swimming, gymnastics, figure skating, and ballet), the later menarche occurs, the greater will be the number of years of training before menarche. Therefore, it would be expected that the relationship between years of training before menarche and age at menarche is linear (Stager et al., 1984).

It appears that physical activity level affects age at menarche. For example, both Dale, Gerlach, Martin, and Alexander (1979) and Malina, Harper, Avent, and Campbell (1973) have noted that girls who do not participate in interscholastic sports experience earlier menarche than their athletic classmates. Bedridden retarded children have been reported to reach menarche at an earlier age and have lower body fat than active retarded children (Osler & Crawford, 1973). Blind children also experience early menarche (Zacharias & Wurtman, 1964), presumably because of their lower activity levels.

In a brief survey of women running in the 1980 Boston Marathon and the Minneapolis-St. Paul Bonne Bell 10-km race, it was found that women who began running before menarche were more likely to experience delayed menarche than women who started training later in life. The average menarcheal age of the 31 respondents who began running before menarche was 15.1 years. The

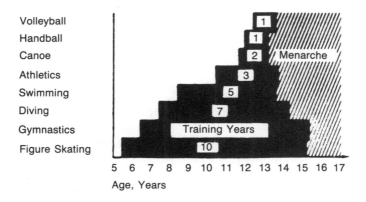

Figure 6.3 Number of years of training before menarche of female athletes. *Note*. From "Influence of Athletic Training on the Maturity Process of Girls" by K. Märker. In *Medicine and Sport* (Vol. 15, p. 121) by E. Jokl (Ed.), 1981, S. Karger AG, Basel. Copyright 1981 by S. Karger AG. Reprinted by permission.

average menarcheal age of the 281 respondents who began running after menarche was 12.9 years (Paul, 1983).

Hypotheses for Late Menarche

Two hypotheses have been offered to explain the apparent association between strenuous physical training and a later menarcheal age. The *critical body weight/body fat hypothesis* (proposed by Frisch, 1977a, 1977b; Frisch & Revelle, 1970, 1971; Frisch et al., 1973; and Frisch et al., 1980) has generated the most interest and attention in the literature. This hypothesis was explained in chapter 4, as was some of the criticism of it. Frisch believes that physical training causes a reduction in body fat, which, combined with dietary restrictions, causes excessive thinness that results in a decreased concentration and potency of circulating estrogens. This, she proposed, impairs hypothalamic function, causing a delay in menarche or a disruption in menstruation (Frisch, 1988).

An alternate, two-part hypothesis has been offered by Malina et al. (1978) and Malina (1983). (The interested reader is referred to the latter reference, which provides an excellent and extensive review of the international literature on menarche in athletes.) The first part of this hypothesis involves the *genetic disposition* for sport achievement. Malina suggested that the physical characteristics associated with delayed maturation in girls are more suitable for excellence in athletic performance. The late maturer, for example, has longer legs, narrower hips, less weight per unit of height, and less relative body fat than the early maturer. These factors would be advantageous to athletic performance with the possible exception of swimming, in which more body fat may be an advantage. If this is the case, then early-maturing girls would tend to be better swimmers. Note that there is disagreement about whether swimmers have a later age at menarche or essentially the same menarcheal age as untrained girls. In most sports, the late-maturing girls tend to perform at higher levels than their earlier maturing peers of the same age. Later menarche appears to be associated with factors that select for superior performance (Stager et al., 1984).

The second part of Malina's hypothesis relates to the socialization process: "The early maturing girl is perhaps socialized away from sports competition through a myriad of social- and status-related motives" (Malina et al., 1978, p. 221). This suggests that once a girl has developed the full sex characteristics of the adult woman, her interests shift from sport to more social goals. In short, for a variety of reasons, the early-maturing girl is likely to drop out of sport. The later maturing girl may not experience these social pressures and may (while continuing to be successful in sport because of her morphological assets) have increased motivation to compete and train.

Is a Late Age at Menarche Harmful?

No evidence to date has shown that young athletes with a later age at menarche fail to attain normal menstrual function and fertility. However, a relationship between later menarcheal age and the development of temporary menstrual dysfunctions is possible (see pp. 91 and 95).

Late pubertal development and the development of scoliosis and stress fractures later in life might also be related. Warren, Brooks-Gunn, Hamilton, Warren, and Hamilton (1986) studied 75 ballerinas (mean age 24.3 years) in whom the prevalence of scoliosis was 24%. The incidence of scoliosis rose with an increased age at menarche. The average age at menarche was 14.5 years for the entire sample. The dancers with scoliosis had a mean menarcheal age of 15.2 years. The incidence of fractures was 61% in this group of dancers, and it rose with increasing age at menarche. The dancers with stress fractures (69% of the fractures) achieved menarche at 15.6 years. The investigators suggested that a delay in menarche and prolonged intervals of amenorrhea reflect hypoestrogenism, which may predispose ballet dancers to scoliosis and stress fractures. The topic of hypoestrogenism and bone health is further discussed in chapters 8 and 10.

Summary of Evidence

Although many studies indicate that highly trained adolescent athletes have a later age at menarche than their age-matched counterparts, this does not necessarily mean that menarche is delayed by strenuous training. The phenomenon could well be an artifact. In most instances, the morphological characteristics associated with later maturity in females are those more suitable for athletic performance: slim hips, longer legs, low relative body fat, less weight per unit of height, and high lean body mass. Those variables associated with maturation of the reproductive system—gain in body fat, breast development, and widening of the hips—are also associated with a decline in performance. Perhaps a process of natural or self-selection is occurring and there is no exercise effect at all. Do early-maturing girls drop out of sport because of either a lack of success or social pressure? Would athletic girls have had a late menarche even if they were not athletic? Do late maturers make better athletes, or is there truly a delay in menarche that is due to athletic training? These questions require further investigation.

The remainder of this chapter focuses on the effects of exercise on menstrual function. The etiology of exercise-associated amenorrhea is discussed in chapter 8.

Early Studies of Menstrual Function in Athletes

Survey data from over 20 years ago have associated athletic training with menstrual irregularities. Of 729 Hungarian athletes studied by questionnaire, personal interview, and menstrual charting, 83.8% showed no "changes in menstrual function," whereas 5.02% noticed "favorable changes" and 11.13% "unfavorable changes" (Erdelyi, 1962, p. 174). Generally, *amenorrhea* (ā-men-o-'re-ah—absence or cessation of the menses) and *oligomenorrhea* (ol-i-go-men-o-'re-ah—scanty or infrequent menstruation) were more frequent among participants in sports (which were not identified) requiring "strenuous physical efforts." In this report, *dysmenorrhea* (dis-men-o-'re-ah—painful menstruation) was frequently "the consequence of participation in competition *during* the menstrual period" (p. 175; italics added) and was higher among swimmers than participants in other sports.

Erdelyi (1976) reported the results of some European studies that were impossible to locate. In one, 8.1% of the athletes surveyed reported unfavorable changes in their menstrual cycles due to sport participation (Stammer, 1943). Favorable effects occurred in 21.4% of the athletes, and 70.5% reported no change at all in menstrual function. Zhanel (cited in Erdelyi, 1976) found that fencers continued to compete during menstruation and that 87.2% reported no changes in menstruation. In this group, 12.8% reported moderate menstrual disturbances. Ingman (1953) reported that 16.8% of the Finnish sportswomen surveyed had unfavorable changes, 14% had favorable changes, and 69.2% had no changes in menstrual function. Few differences in menstrual symptoms were reported among physical education students participating in regular intense exercise, students exercising 2 to 4 h per week, and students who did not exercise at all (Rougier & Linquette, cited in Erdelyi, 1976).

Gendel (1976) reported that of 160 university freshmen, those who were most physically active had the fewest menstrual complaints. In studies such as this, however, and in studies comparing athletes with nonathletes, it is not known why the inactive women are inactive. It could be that women with menstrual complaints avoid physical activity. Therefore, it is not possible to conclude that inactivity causes menstrual dysfunction.

Erdelyi (1976) stated that some investigators have noted that girls who start intensive training *before* menarche have a higher incidence of menstrual disorders than do those who begin training *after* menarche. Others do not support that claim. Although Zaharieva (1972) contended that physical exertion does not affect the menstrual period or the phases of the cycle, Erdelyi (1976) stated that "any type of menstrual disorder—polymenorrhea, menorrhagia, scanty menstrual bleeding, oligomenorrhea, amenorrhea, completely irregular periods, dysmenorrhea, or a combination of these"—may be caused by "overly stressful sports activity" (p. 80). Of the athletes he studied, 9.3% had unfavorable menstrual changes, with the younger girls (15 to 17 years) having a higher incidence of menstrual problems than the adults (over 18 years). He stated the following:

Athletes in sports that required much physical effort and endurance have menstrual disorders more often. Generally speaking, amenorrhea, oligomenorrhea, scanty menstrual flow, or completely irregular periods are common in sports such as tennis, rowing, and skiing that require strenuous physical exertion over a sustained period of time. We found several female rowers who had irregular periods or complete amenorrhea during the rowing season, but these irregularities disappeared during the winter. Menorrhagia and dysmenorrhea are more often found as a possible consequence of participation in strenuous sports activities during menstruation. (p. 80)

No data or statistical comparisons accompanied this statement, however, and I am led to believe that these are merely Erdelyi's unsubstantiated opinions or impressions.

Many believe that sport participation has a favorable effect on dysmenorrhea. On the other hand, Erdelyi (1976) stated that certain sports, particularly swimming, may cause dysmenorrhea. His studies indicate that the incidence of dysmenorrhea among athletes is highest among swimmers.

Approximately one third of the Swedish girl swimmers studied by Åstrand et al. (1963) stated that strenuous swimming during menstruation caused pain in their lower abdomens. Perhaps of greater interest in this study was that pathogenic organisms were recovered from the vaginas of nearly one third of the swimmers. In regard to this last finding,

under unfavorable conditions, there is a risk of infection in the reproductive organs due to these bacteria . . . this applies particularly during menstruation, when conditions for bacterial growth are improved, owing to pH change, and to the fact that the cervical canal is open to the uterine cavity, in which the sloughing mucosa is a good soil for bacteria. (p. 36)

Furthermore, they stated that chilling water and intense physical exertion may lower the body's resistance to infection. They summarized their results regarding the menstrual cycle by saying, "It seems warranted on medical grounds to advise against swimming—both training and competition —during menstruation" (pp. 36-38). However, these women who had undergone 2.5 years of strenuous training were examined 10 years after discontinuing training and found to be normal in all respects, including gynecologic and obstetric observations (Eriksson et al., 1978). For more on swimming during menstruation, see chapter 7, pp. 98-99.

The early literature did not indicate that exercise influenced cyclic changes in uterine mucosa (Anderson, 1965; Hellebrandt & Meyer, 1939; Jokl, 1958). Occasional menstrual irregularity and an increase in flow were reported (Duentzer & Hellendall, 1930) to be the results of severe physical exertion. Because these reports came from young girls at an age at which menstrual irregularity is the rule rather than the exception, the authors thought it possible that these observations were the result of the emotional strain of competition rather than the physical activity itself.

At the Tokyo Olympic Games, sportswomen from 10 countries were surveyed (Zaharieva, 1965). These women were 16 to 33 years of age and were taking part in track-and-field events, swimming, gymnastics, and volleyball. Their active sporting careers ranged from 5 to 12 years of training and competition. The menstrual cycle was rhythmic in 92.4% of the sample with 4 of the youngest girls reporting irregular menstrual periods. One girl, a 19-year-old track-and-field participant, had no menses. The menstrual interval was normal in the majority (between 21 and 30 days) with 5 women reporting an interval exceeding 31 days. In 89% of these women, menses duration was 3 to 6 days. Menstrual flow was reported to be "moderate" by 63%, "profuse" by 15%, and "slight" by 15%. Some 38.5% reported that menstrual flow was not accompanied by pain, whereas 26% reported frequent menstrual distress.

Some 41.5% of these women reported changes in menstrual function after training and competition. (This part of the study was very vague.) Most of these "disturbances" were expressed as longer flow periods, greater loss of blood, and "colic" (dysmenorrhea? nausea?). However, 81.6% reported that their next menstrual period following a major competition event was "regular." Zaharieva concluded that training and competition did not essentially affect the menstrual cycle.

Several reports of decreased menstrual discomfort as a direct effect of exercise were found in the literature. It is often stated that mild physical exercise is a prophylactic for dysmenorrhea and that menstrual disorders are rather uncommon among active girls. In one example, a group of high school synchronized swimmers were compared with students with minimal swimming experience. The synchronized swimmers had less difficulty and less severity with dysmenorrhea than the nonswimmers (Anderson, 1965). For a more complete discussion of dysmenorrhea, see chapter 7, pp. 100-103.

Current Studies of Menstrual Function in Athletes

The fact that highly trained women athletes often have oligomenorrhea or amenorrhea has received considerable attention in recent years. It is difficult to estimate the significance of the problem. Whereas oligo-amenorrhea occurs in about 2% to 3% of the nonathletic, nonlactating, nonpregnant population, the prevalence of menstrual changes with athletic training has been variously estimated at figures ranging from 1% (Shangold & Levine, 1982) to 66% (Bonen & Keizer, 1984) (see Table 6.1). There are several reasons for such a wide range of findings:

- The stringency of the definition used for essential terms (e.g., *regular, irregular, oligomenorrhea, amenorrhea,* etc.) and because oligomenorrheic subjects are sometimes grouped with amenorrheic subjects.

Table 6.1 Prevalence of Athletic Amenorrhea

Population	N	Percent	Definition	Reference
Runners				
Cross-country	128	24.0	≤ 3 periods per year	Feicht et al. (1978)
Cross-country	38	44.7	No periods in previous 3 months	Wakat et al. (1982)
> 30 mi/wk	89	34.0	No definition provided	Dale, Gerlach, & Wilhite (1979)
5-30 mi/wk	22	23.0	No definition provided	Dale, Gerlach, & Wilhite (1979)
> 30 mi/wk	70	23.0	< 9 but > 4 per year (oligomenorrhea) < 3 periods per year (amenorrhea)	Gray & Dale (1983)
New York Marathon	270	1.0	< 1 period in previous 10 months	Shangold & Levine (1982)
Joggers	885	≈6.0	No definition provided	Speroff & Redwine (1980)
Marathon	237	25.7	≤ 3 periods per year	Sanborn et al. (1982)
Marathon (70 mi/wk)	67	19.0	≤ 2 periods per year	Glass et al. (1987)
Ballet dancers				
Students	69	18.8	At least 3 months with no periods	Frisch et al. (1980)
Professionals (29) and students (5)	34	44.0	At least 3 months with no periods	Calabrese et al. (1983)
Professionals	32	36.7	At least 3 months with no periods	Cohen et al. (1982)
Athletes				
College varsity	140	12.1	No periods in previous 3 months or < 4 periods per year	Carlberg et al. (1983)
Swimmers	197	12.3	≤ 3 periods per year	Sanborn et al. (1982)
Cyclists	33	12.1	≤ 3 periods per year	Sanborn et al. (1982)

Note. From "The Female Athlete and Menstrual Irregularity" by C.F. Sanborn and W.W. Wagner, Jr. In *Sport Science Perspectives for Women* (p. 113) by J. Puhl, C.H. Brown, and R.O. Voy (Eds.), 1988, Champaign, IL: Human Kinetics Books. Copyright 1988 by Human Kinetics Publishers, Inc. Adapted by permission.

- Variance in the methods used to gather and interpret information (e.g., questionnaire, interview, physical examination, and hormonal analysis)
- Differences in the ages of the subjects (e.g., postmenarcheal, young adult, and middle aged)
- Differences in the intensity of training in the subjects (e.g., differences in the training of recreational joggers and elite performers)
- Innate differences in the demands of the sport the subjects engage in (e.g., the energy demands and body-type requirements of ballet, gymnastics, and track differ significantly from the demands and body-type requirements of weight lifting, cycling, and swimming).

Table 6.1 presents a compilation of recent data on the prevalence of secondary amenorrhea in athletes. The column labeled "Definition" should receive as much attention from the reader as the column labeled "Percent." Definitions of amenorrhea generally range from the cessation of menstrual flow for more than 3 months to less than three menstrual periods per year. Table 6.1 indicates that the studies using more stringent definitions tended to report a lower prevalence of secondary amenorrhea.

It is suggested that the definitions of the following terms be adopted universally (Loucks & Horvath, 1985; Sanborn & Wagner, 1988):

- *regular, eumenorrheic*, or *cyclic*: menstrual bleeding that occurs regularly between 23 and 38 days
- *irregular* or *oligomenorrheic*: menstrual periods that occur once every 39 to 90 days
- *amenorrheic* or *acyclic*: menstrual periods that occur at intervals longer than 90 days

The methods used by each investigator also deserve special consideration. Much of the prevalence data has been obtained by retrospective questionnaire, which relies on a woman's recollection of her menstrual cycle. A woman may report more regular cycles than would be documented by careful record keeping. Individual follow-up interviews may improve the quality of the data originally obtained by questionnaire. Longitudinal studies requiring that the subject keep elaborate records may provide more valid information than retrospective questionnaires. Studies that utilize hormonal confirmation of menstrual status are relatively few but are generally considered the most reliable.

Subject selection is also important because it can cause variability in data. Self-selection may seriously skew results. Criteria for inclusion in a study and assignment to an experimental group should be explicitly stated (Loucks, 1986). Important factors such as gynecologic age (age since menarche), prior menstrual status, and coincident health problems should be ascertained.

There is a notably higher incidence of menstrual disruption in younger, highly motivated athletes (and dancers) than older athletes; in intensively training athletes than recreational athletes; and in athletes whose sports demand a particularly lean body type as opposed to those sports that do not. For example, the incidence of amenorrhea was higher among runners (25.7%) than among swimmers (12.3%) or cyclists (12.1%) (Sanborn, Martin, & Wagner, 1982) and very high in professional ballerinas (Cohen, May, Kim, & Ertel, 1980; Frisch et al., 1980).

Factors Related to Amenorrhea in Athletes

A number of variables have been associated by means of correlational analysis with the incidence of amenorrhea in athletes. Some have reported that menstrual irregularity was more common in younger than older athletes (Baker, Mathur, Kirk, & Williamson, 1981; Lutter, & Cushman, 1982; Speroff & Redwine, 1980). Some reported a high relationship between low body weight or low percent body fat and amenorrhea in athletes (Baker et al., 1981; Carlberg, Buckman, Peake, & Riedesel, 1983; Dale, Gerlach, & Wilhite, 1979; Lutter & Cushman, 1982; Schwartz et al., 1981). Others reported that only weight loss is an important factor (Dale, Gerlach, Martin, & Alexander, 1979; Speroff & Redwine, 1980).

Several studies have failed to find a relationship between weight or body composition and amenorrhea in athletes (Baker et al., 1981; Feicht, Johnson, Martin, Sparkes, & Wagner, 1978; Wakat, Sweeney, & Rogol, 1982). In amenorrheic ballerinas, menstrual function has been reported to return during vacations and periods of enforced rest even without a gain in body weight or fat (Abraham, Beaumont, Fraser, & Llewellyn-Jones, 1982; Warren, 1980).

Many have reported that training intensity (most often indicated by mileage completed) is a highly predictive variable (Dale, Gerlach, Martin, &

Alexander, 1979; Dale, Gerlach, & Wilhite, 1979; Feicht et al., 1978; Feicht, Martin, & Wagner, 1980; Lutter & Cushman, 1982). However, no association between training mileage and amenorrhea was reported by Baker et al. (1981), Speroff and Redwine (1980), or Wakat et al. (1982).

Other factors have also been implicated. Older age at menarche has been reported to be related in several studies (Baker et al., 1981; Feicht et al., 1978; Lutter & Cushman, 1982; Wakat et al., 1982) but not all (Dale, Gerlach, & Wilhite, 1979; Gray & Dale, 1983; Schwartz et al., 1981; Shangold & Levine, 1982). Intense training before menarche was a factor in some studies (Frisch et al., 1981; Waket et al., 1982). Prior gravidity (pregnancy) has been reported to be protective because it demonstrated hypothalamic maturity (Baker et al., 1981; Dale, Gerlach, & Wilhite, 1979). Two studies have reported that having had prior menstrual irregularities is a good predictor of amenorrhea in athletes (Schwartz et al., 1981; Shangold & Levine, 1982). Amenorrhea was reported to be significantly higher among athletes who participated in endurance training than among other female athletes (Carlberg et al., 1983; Dale, Gerlach, Martin, & Alexander, 1979). There may be a sport-specific correlation between incidence of amenorrhea and training distance (Sanborn et al., 1982).

Psychological stress has also been implicated. Amenorrheic middle-distance runners subjectively rated the months they trained as more intense (Feicht et al., 1978) and subjectively associated more stress with running (Schwartz et al., 1981) than did menstruating subjects. However, no significant differences were found in four psychological tests to assess depression, anxiety, compulsive behavior, hypochondria, and overall stress (Schwartz et al., 1981). Emotional stress was believed to have contributed to menstrual dysfunction among one group of athletes (Carlberg et al., 1983). Gray and Dale (1983) used the Schedule of Recent Experiences (SRE) questionnaire to quantify life stress in oligoamenorrheic and eumenorrheic (normally menstruating) runners. The SRE scores for life events for all run-ners was 323 but were not significantly correlated with the number of menstrual cycles.

Poor diet or nutritional status has long been known to affect menstrual function. Two studies have reported an extremely high prevalence of vegetarianism among amenorrheic runners (Brooks, Sanborn, Albrecht, & Wagner, 1984; Carlberg et al., 1983). Another study reported that amenorrheic runners consumed significantly less protein than eumenorrheic runners and nonrunning controls (Schwartz et al., 1981). Diets deficient in certain amino acids may affect neurotransmitter synthesis. This could be important in terms of the secretion of GnRH.

The effects of exercise on menstrual function is a complicated topic, and much remains unknown. Carefully designed cross-sectional and longitudinal studies need to be completed to unravel some of the remaining confusion regarding this topic.

Summary

The onset of puberty is influenced by genetic factors, nutrition, and general health. Menarche is the onset of menstrual flow and is associated with a maturing of the relationship among the hypothalamus, the pituitary gland, and the ovaries. Menarche has also been associated with change in the basal metabolic rate, a spurt in growth, and the deposition of increased amounts of body fat.

Many young athletes and dancers experience menarche at a later age than less active girls. This appears to be particularly prevalent in sports and dance that require high energy and low body weight. Although no physiological mechanism for this phenomenon has yet been found, one hypothesis is that the high energy demand of vigorous training prevents some girls from gaining sufficient body weight or fat to commence menstruation. Another hypothesis is that a later age at menarche is associated with body characteristics that favor athletic performance and that the observed later age at menarche in athletes is simply a matter of natural selection. Whether caused by physical training or merely an observational artifact, a later menarche appears to be associated with superior performance.

In some women, menstrual function appears to be adversely affected by strenuous training. At this time, the pathogenesis of these menstrual irregularities remains unknown, but many related factors (some probably important, others perhaps trivial) have been identified. The etiology of secondary amenorrhea in athletes is explored in chapter 8.

Chapter 7

Menstruation and Sport: Practical Implications

Early societies were not always kind to the menstruating woman. She was often treated as "unclean," and superstitions and taboos surrounding this completely normal physiological function persisted for centuries. Fortunately, we have passed the era when menstruation was viewed with fear and derision and sometimes even as a supernatural event. Even today, however, prevailing attitudes toward menstruation are less than positive. All one has to do is consider the euphemisms we use to describe menstruation to realize that. Rather than talking freely about menses, we get "sick," "the curse," our "period," the "monthlies," or a "visit from our friend" or we "fall off the roof." We even use the term *sanitary pad*, which implies uncleanliness. All these attest to the "sickness," the burden, or the uncomfortable nuisance of menstruation. So today's woman, even though she knows menstruation is not physically or psychologically incapacitating, has inherited modern versions of ancient myths, taboos, and superstitions. Consequently, it seems plausible that a menstruating girl may even today be excused from physical education classes or sports at school, excused from taking a shower, or not allowed to enter the pool.

Athletic Participation During Menstruation

The odds are about 1 out of 7 that a nonpregnant woman of menstrual age will be menstruating on any given day. Therefore, it is virtually impossible to schedule athletic events so that none of the contestants are menstruating. Menstrual synchrony has been reported in all-female living groups and by mothers, daughters, and sisters who live together (McClintock, 1971). It is interesting to speculate on the possibility of menstrual synchrony among team members who not only spend a great deal of time together but frequently have similar work-study-practice schedules.

The occasional attitude that vigorous exercise may be harmful during menstrual flow seems to have no basis. Physical activity is not a causative factor in dysmenorrhea or other menstrual discomforts (see the following discussion) and is certainly not harmful in terms of childbearing functions. Consequently, all former customs, superstitions, antiquated mores, or fears of harm should be put to rest. Whether a girl exercises during all phases of her menstrual cycle should be her own decision. She should certainly not be prevented from doing so or be compelled to do so.

Frequently, a poor attitude toward menstruation is passed on from mother to daughter. Quite often, girls ask to be excused from physical activity during menstrual flow (or their mothers ask for them). A good approach by the physical education teacher or coach is to ask the girl if she is really feeling ill. If she has serious dysmenorrhea, she should be referred to the school's medical personnel. If she does not (which is more likely the case), or if she is just vaguely uncomfortable, then she could be instructed to dress for activity and participate as much as she feels able. Chances are that she will be playing as vigorously as anyone else before the end of the class or practice period. A girl is more likely to develop a positive attitude toward exercise during her menses if she is not embarrassed in any way as a result of participation. Therefore, the teacher should allow plenty of opportunity for the girl to leave activity to attend to personal hygiene. Some girls may be in need of instruction regarding menstrual hygiene (refer to the section on menstrual hygiene).

Such premenstrual and menstrual symptoms as increased frequency of urination, increased peristalsis (causing temporary bowel irregularity), abdominal bloating, breast tenderness, backaches, headaches, and temporary weight gain from water retention may or may not interfere with performance. Some competitors may wish to alter their menstrual cycles to perform at a more advantageous time.

Swimming During Menstruation

A menstruating girl or woman should not be prevented from swimming. This statement immediately raises questions about the safety of others, the normal bacteriology of swimming pools, the type of menstrual protection used, and whether pool water can enter the vagina.

Pool water (in a body-sized tank) was analyzed after women swam at various times during their menstrual cycles using tampons or no menstrual protection (Robinton & Mood, 1966). The water showed marked variations in the number and types of bacteria shed by a swimmer, but these variations did not relate to differences in menstrual hygiene, menstrual flow, or personal hygiene.

A gram of tissue scraped from the skin contains as many as 530,000,000 bacteria (Marples, 1969). This is similar to the number found in a gram of fertile soil. Menstrual blood, on the other hand, is sterile and in no way unclean. Also, normal vaginal fluids do not contain pathogenic organisms. Menstrual and vaginal fluids are "cleaner" than nose, mouth, skin, or anal secretions, all of which represent a greater source of potentially harmful organisms than those from the vagina. Even if vaginal secretions were harmful, the ability of the vagina to exclude water (even almost immediately following childbirth) has been demonstrated (Siegel, 1960). Therefore, the possibility of contamination of a swimming pool by water entering and leaving the vagina is nil even without menstrual protection. Conversely, if water cannot enter the vagina, there can be no danger of vaginal contamination from dirty swimming water.

Just as a girl should not be forced to swim during her menstrual period, neither should she be forced to use a particular type of menstrual protection. So-called sanitary pads, of course, offer no "protection" during swimming and are totally impractical. Anderson's (1965) treatment of this topic is highly commendable. She pointed out that girls learn about internal menstrual protection (tampons) very early through mass media, other girls, or their mothers. Tampons are comfortable, and in today's rush to be "modern," most girls use them. Women who participate in aquatic sports consider tampons the method of choice. Perhaps parental permission should be required before tampons are supplied in the locker room, where sanitary pads should already be available. This consent is for the protection of the teacher, coach, and other school authorities rather than the student.

Menstrual Hygiene

The approximately 50 ml of blood, glandular secretions, and tissue lost during menstrual flow is sterile and odorless. Menstrual secretions develop odor and become a breeding ground for bacteria only when exposed to air. Therefore, the commonly used sanitary pad, or napkin, is actually the most unsanitary form of menstrual protection. As mentioned before, even the term *sanitary pad* associates menstruation with uncleanliness and impurity.

A more convenient, as well as sanitary, form of menstrual protection is the tampon. Although the newest of the commercial products, use of menstrual tampons is not new. Roman women, as well as women in Egypt and Africa, used rolls of soft wool, soft papyrus, and even grass internally.

According to Thomas (1974), physically active girls, particularly ballet dancers, used homemade menstrual tampons long before they were available commercially. These tampons provided examples for the industrial development of today's tampon.

There is little to fear about internal menstrual protection. The American Medical Association has long recognized the use of tampons and sanctioned their use by unmarried women. Religious authorities have investigated the subject of tampons and virginity with the resultant approval of tampons (Cavanaugh, 1963). Using a tampon with a cardboard or plastic applicator and sterile lubricating jelly makes it possible to painlessly stretch even a very small hymenal aperture. Visible evidence of virginity will still exist after tampon use. A normal vagina can accommodate one or even two "super-size" tampons inserted one at a time. Difficulty in insertion usually turns out to be more emotional than physical. Use of a sterile jelly will assist insertion. After a few months, the lubricating jelly should not be necessary.

Contraceptive Practices in Athletes

Contraceptive options for women include (a) oral contraceptive (OC) agents that aim at suppressing ovulation, (b) intrauterine devices (IUDs) that prevent implantation, (c) barrier methods (cervical cap, diaphragm, or condom, all used with spermicidal jelly or foam), (d) natural family planning methods of sexual participation, and (e) abstinence from sexual intercourse (Prior & Vigna, 1985). Jarrett and Spellacy (1983a) and Lutter (1983) have reported that the contraceptive practices of athletic women differ from those of sedentary women in their lower use of OCs and IUDs and higher use of barrier methods. Only 5% to 12% of athletic women use OCs (compared to about 40% in the general population of 1976). Few use IUDs because of menorrhagia (heavy bleeding) (see p. 104) and the high incidence of pelvic pain with exercise. Barrier methods, when used with full doses of spermicidal jelly, are almost as effective as OCs. They produce no side effects and can be used only when needed. The rhythm method of contraception offers special problems for athletes, many of whom are anovulatory, have luteal phase shortening (see p. 104), or have irregular menstrual periods. The spontaneous reversibility of anovulation, plus the common irregularity experienced by the athletic woman, makes this method quite risky (Prior & Vigna, 1985). Such methods as recording basal body temperature or cervical mucus changes to pinpoint ovulation may be unreliable because of lower hormonal levels in highly trained women. Abstinence from sexual activity may be used inadvertently by many athletes because the hormonal alterations that occur with intensive training may lower libido.

Effects of Oral Contraceptives on Performance

At least one reason for the reduced popularity of OCs among athletes is the strong belief by many that they hinder one's performance. Substantive evidence to support such a belief comes from four studies. Maximal oxygen uptake was significantly decreased in active women during OC use (Daggett, Davies, & Boobis, 1983; Notelovitz et al., 1987). Muscle biopsies revealed a significant reduction in mitochondrial citrate (an oxidative enzyme) with OC use but no change in postexercise muscle lactate or glycogen (Daggett et al., 1983). All values returned to normal with the cessation of OC use. Other studies have shown unfavorable changes in isometric strength and endurance time in OC users (Petrofsky, LeDonne, Rinehart, & Lind, 1976;

Wirth & Lohman, 1982). On the other hand, OC use in athletes results in predictable, asymptomatic menstrual cycles with no or reduced dysmenorrhea and premenstrual syndrome (see later sections) and reduced menstrual blood loss.

The use of OCs has been linked with a slightly increased risk of myocardial infarction, deep-vein thrombosis, and stroke in sedentary women. However, athletes may be at less risk than sedentary women because regular exercise is known to increase protective high-density lipoprotein cholesterol, reduce deleterious low-density lipoprotein cholesterol, lower total triglyceride levels, and activate the fibrinolytic system. In a study that was flawed by the lack of nonactive control groups, 5 runners who used OCs for 6 months were found to have lipid profiles similar to those of 6 eumenorrheic runners who did not use OCs (Gray, Harding, & Dale, 1983). Notelovitz et al. (1987) reported that although $\dot{V}O_2$ decreased in exercising women who used low doses of OCs, neither coagulation nor lipid-lipoprotein metabolism was altered. In addition, most trained women have lower arterial blood pressures, lower body fat, and higher lean body weight and do not smoke, all factors that put them at less risk.

Menstrual Problems

Dysmenorrhea

Dysmenorrhea, or painful menstruation, is one of the most common gynecologic complaints. It is estimated that more than 50% of menstruating women experience dysmenorrhea regularly, about 10% of whom have severe symptoms with incapacitation for 1 to 3 days each month (Dawood, 1987a). This means that about 600 million working hours may be lost annually (assuming that women make up 42% of the work force). Thus, dysmenorrhea is a truly significant malady.

Women aged 20 to 24 seem to be most severely disabled, but dysmenorrhea occurs in adolescence as well. In teenagers, the incidence of dysmenorrhea is estimated to be between 5% and 50%. In a study of over 5,000 adolescent girls (aged 10 to 20), 13% had dysmenorrhea on a regular basis; however, 46% had completely painless menstruation (Widholm, 1985). Within the first year of menarche, 7.2% had dysmenorrhea, and the incidence tripled to 26% by 5 years after menarche. When these data were analyzed according to chronological age, the frequency of dysmenorrhea increased from 36% at age 13 to 56% at age 20. Of course, this could be a statistical artifact in that the longer one menstruates, the higher the likelihood that a painful menses will occur. Overall absenteeism due to dysmenorrhea in adolescents was about 24%, and 3% were absent frequently.

Primary dysmenorrhea occurs when there is no macroscopically identifiable pelvic pathology (Dawood, 1987a). Onset usually occurs 6 to 12 months after menarche, when ovulatory cycles have been established. Discomfort is most severe on the first or second day of menses. Pain is spasmodic and strongest over the lower abdomen but may radiate to the back and inner thighs. Accompanying symptoms may include nausea and vomiting, diarrhea, and even syncope and collapse. Symptoms usually persist from a few hours to a day.

Current theory indicates that the pain of primary dysmenorrhea is due to myometrial ischemia (lack of blood) and subsequent hypoxia (lack of oxygen) secondary to abnormally increased uterine contractile activity. Women with this form of dysmenorrhea have significantly higher than normal levels of the prostaglandins PGE_2 and PGF_2 in their endometrial tissues and menstrual fluids (Dawood, 1987a). It is thought that high levels of these prostaglandins cause the uterus to undergo intense contractions that in turn obstruct blood flow. The resultant lack of oxygen at the tissue level causes pain. The prostaglandins may also sensitize nerve endings or pain receptors. The contractions, ischemia, and heightened sensitivity may all interact to create the moderate-to-severe pain of dysmenorrhea. The sometimes widespread symptoms of nausea, headache, backache, and diarrhea may be the effect of prostaglandins on other target organs, such as the stomach, intestinal muscles, and blood vessels. Figure 7.1 illustrates the proposed mechanism.

For many years, dysmenorrhea was treated as psychosomatic, as the response of a neurotic woman, or as something that was ''the woman's lot in life.'' Often the complaining woman was simply told that a pregnancy would solve her menstrual problems. Today, it is recognized that severe incapacitating menstrual pain is not normal and need not be tolerated. Severe symptomology demands a complete history and physical examination to determine whether uterine or ovarian pathology is responsible. If primary dysmenorrhea is the diagnosis, physicians now give prostaglandin inhibitors (such as aspirin, ibuprofen, and naproxen) to counter the action of the elevated prostaglandins produced by the uterus. These drugs apparently act to inhibit prostaglandin biosynthesis (see Figure 7.1). Prostaglandin inhibitors are very effective in treating dysmenorrhea, and most women get significant relief from symptoms.

Another successful but less desirable approach to the problem of dysmenorrhea is the use of OCs, the efficacy of which is presumably related to the inhibition of ovulation. Prostaglandin levels in anovulatory cycles are several times lower than in ovulatory cycles. The suppression of ovulation with OCs or other hormonal therapy results in almost uniform success in producing painless menstruation. Although effective, OCs for the relief of dysmenorrhea are not efficient as one must take 21 days worth of pills for 24 to 48 h of relief. Of course, if a woman wants to become pregnant, OCs are contraindicated. Furthermore, if one is concerned about the possibly harmful side effects of hormone therapy, the potential risks must be weighed against the benefits.

Several theories have been proposed to support the claim that exercise offers relief from primary dysmenorrhea. For example, it is known that exercise leads to higher levels of a class of plasma opioid peptides known as endorphins. These alleviate pain by binding to opiate receptors and thus may play a role in reducing menstrual pain. It has

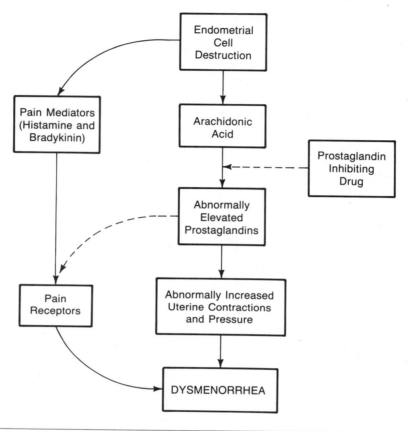

Figure 7.1   Proposed mechanism for the role of prostaglandins in the etiology of dysmenorrhea.

also been suggested that training may lead to a greater pain tolerance. If this is so, the athlete would be less aware of mild dysmenorrhea. Years ago it was thought that a shortening of the pelvic nerves or ligaments caused dysmenorrhea, so stretching exercises to lengthen these structures were prescribed. There is no clinical evidence to suggest that these stretching exercises either ''cured'' or prevented dysmenorrhea.

Linse and Lutter (1987) recently reviewed the literature on menstrual discomfort and exercise and found no substantial evidence that athletic women had less dysmenorrhea than inactive women or that exercise alleviated painful menstruation. They also administered a questionnaire to 420 women, most of whom were physically active. The incidence of

dysmenorrhea was independent of physical activity level. They concluded that most women experienced no change in menstrual symptoms with physical activity. Thus, most women should be advised that although there is no reason to avoid exercising while experiencing dysmenorrhea, they should not expect total pain relief.

In *secondary dysmenorrhea*, pelvic pathology is present. The causes of secondary dysmenorrhea may include (but are not limited to) endometriosis, pelvic inflammatory disease, use of an IUD, uterine polyps, ovarian cysts, and pelvic congestion syndrome. Secondary dysmenorrhea usually occurs years after menarche and may occur in women with anovulatory cycles.

Endometriosis, the most common cause of

secondary dysmenorrhea, is the occurrence of endometrial tissue outside the uterus. Sometimes, endometrial tissue is found on the ovaries, the fallopian tubes, the outer surface of the uterus, the ligaments supporting the uterus, the tissue surrounding the pelvic cavity, the cervix, and the vagina. All endometrial tissue, whether inside the uterus or not, responds to the sex hormones. It grows and thickens under the influence of estrogen and progesterone and then breaks down and bleeds at menstruation. There is no exit for this ectopic (out-of-place) discharge, however, and it remains within the body. This growing and bleeding tissue may cause pain (depending on location) and scar-tissue formation and may result in infertility.

There are several approaches to the treatment of endometriosis (Dawood, 1987b), the most effective of which involves the use of Danazol, a synthetic androgen that inhibits FSH, LH, and estrogen. Anovulation and amenorrhea occur, and the ectopic tissue regresses and dissolves. Another approach is to use a combined OC pill (containing both an estrogen and a progestin) or a progestin to cause a condition of pseudopregnancy. Again, the aim is to cause the ectopic endometrial tissue to regress. A third approach involves the surgical removal of ectopic endometrial material and may include complete hysterectomy and bilateral oophorectomy (removal of the uterus and both ovaries).

Premenstrual Syndrome

Premenstrual syndrome (PMS) includes many symptoms that occur only during the few days immediately preceding the onset of menstrual flow and are relieved when menses begins. These include (but are not limited to) anxiety, depression, irritability, headache, breast tenderness, water retention, abdominal bloating, peripheral edema, and increased appetite. Some of these symptoms (which are highly subjective) are experienced by nearly all women of reproductive age at some time. The severity and regularity of these symptoms marks the woman with PMS. Estimates of how many American women experience

PMS vary considerably, but most studies suggest that fewer than 10% experience severe symptoms (Johnson, 1987).

The most prevalent theory to explain PMS—that of a relative excess of estrogen and a deficiency of progesterone in the late luteal phase—has not enjoyed much clinical support (Marut, 1987). Although treatment of PMS with progesterone has been quite prevalent, the only controlled studies have demonstrated no difference in the relief of symptoms when compared to a placebo. Some researchers have claimed that estrogen stimulates the renin-angiotensin-aldosterone system, causing fluid retention. Salt restriction and the use of diuretics are usually prescribed by these advocates. Elevated levels of prolactin have also been implicated, particularly in regard to breast symptoms. However, women with hyperprolactinemia do not experience PMS.

Another prevalent theory is that the neurotransmitter dopamine, which functions as a prolactin inhibitor and suppresses aldosterone, is depleted. The recognition that vitamin B_6 acts as a coenzyme in the biosynthesis of dopamine (as well as serotonin) led to an enthusiasm for vitamin B_6 therapy. Controlled studies involving B_6 therapy have not been in agreement (early studies that showed a positive effect of B_6 on PMS have not been substantiated). Further discussion of the pathophysiology of PMS can be found in Reid (1985) and Marut (1987).

Probably the most successful therapy has been the suppression of cyclic steroid changes by the use of OCs. However, this is an unacceptable alternative for those women who wish to remain fertile or who are not willing to risk side effects.

Thus, although much has been written about PMS, the syndrome remains largely unexplained. Likewise, the effects of exercise on PMS are unclear (Shangold, 1984). Generally, women who exercise regularly experience fewer symptoms, but some women continue to report PMS in spite of exercising regularly. It could be that the rise in blood endorphins that occurs with exercise relieves some PMS symptoms. Recently, two reports on the same group of women (Prior, Vigna, & Alojado,

1986; Prior, Vigna, Sciarretta, Alojado, & Schulzer, 1987) documented that 3 months and 6 months of a program of gradually increasing running decreased premenstrual symptoms, but these women were not PMS sufferers. Nevertheless, these previously sedentary women reported decreases in breast tenderness, bloating, and personal stress with exercise training, whereas no changes occurred in the nontraining control group.

Menstrual Manipulation

One would expect athletic performance to be adversely affected by dysmenorrhea or PMS, but there are no objective reports of this. Most likely, an athlete who regularly experiences either malady will avoid competition during those days of the menstrual cycle or request hormonal manipulation of her cycle so she can compete at her best free of symptoms.

Shangold (1984) stated that inducing early menstruation by progestin withdrawal is preferable to delaying menstruation with estrogen and progestin because high concentrations of these hormones would then prevail during the event and possibly cause fluid retention. She also suggested restricting such manipulation to events of special importance to avoid promoting menstrual irregularity. Direct medical treatment of dysmenorrhea or PMS is preferable to menstrual manipulation.

Heavy Bleeding and Anemia

Some women experience exceptionally heavy menstrual bleeding (menorrhagia) with training. Menorrhagia may lead to iron deficiency, which is likely to impair oxygen delivery and lactate clearance and thus adversely affect performance (Shangold, 1984). Such women require hematological assessment and endometrial biopsy to rule out endometrial hyperplasia, endometrial polyps, and adenocarcinoma. Shangold (1984, p. 151) stated that "it is reasonable for all menstruating athletes to ingest supplementary iron (100 mg 2-3 times each week)" to prevent iron deficiency, anemia, or both (for an extensive discussion of so-called sports anemia, see chapter 12).

Short Luteal Phase

Many athletes with apparently normal menstrual cycles experience a *short luteal phase* (i.e., luteal insufficiency). This is characterized by a luteal phase of less than 10 days (some reported as short as 4 or 5 days), and inadequate progesterone levels during the latter half of the cycle. The total length of the menstrual cycle may be normal or slightly shorter than normal. Bonen (1986) cited several reports (including his own work) that short luteal phase (sometimes called *luteal phase defect*) is very common in athletes, although the overt appearance of menses leads one to believe that the menstrual cycle is normal.

Very likely, this phenomenon is attributable to deficient follicular phase gonadotropin levels that are possibly caused by a slowing of GnRH pulse frequencies. Both Prior, Yuen, Clement, Bowie, and Thomas (1982) and Shangold, Freeman, Thysen, and Gatz (1979) have presented data suggesting that the degree of luteal phase shortening is proportional to weekly training mileage. Prior (1988) described the sequence as follows:

1. Progressive hormonal changes with increasing exercise in women with ovulatory cycles
2. Decreased production of LH and FSH
3. Early follicular maturation with lower estradiol levels
4. Lessened progesterone output in a normal-length luteal phase
5. Less progesterone produced in a shortened luteal phase
6. Disruption of the midcycle estradiol feedback and LH surges so that no ovulation occurs

A shortened luteal phase is probably a benign condition that need not be treated unless fertility is desired. Although the minimum plasma progesterone threshold that is necessary to initiate or maintain a pregnancy is not known, luteal phase defect is associated with an inadequate secretory transformation of the endometrium so that infertility results. A menstrual cycle characterized by a shortened luteal phase may very likely progress to full-blown secondary amenorrhea.

Exercise and Prolapse

Most misconceptions that uterine damage can occur from strenuous activity involving jumping, falling, or body contact have been thoroughly discredited. The section on anatomical support of the pelvic viscera (chapter 4) documented that the pelvic contents are well protected. The analogy of an egg surrounded by water in a jar has been used to describe the protection afforded the uterus. If the egg is not resting against the side of the container and if the container does not break, it is impossible to break the egg by hitting the jar.

The supportive muscular and ligamentous components retain the pelvic contents as long as they are strong and firm. If they have been repeatedly traumatized in childbirth or if they are lacerated, atrophied, or in some way impaired or weakened, the uterus, bladder, or rectum may become displaced downward and even protrude. This is called *prolapse*. When the urinary bladder prolapses into the anterior wall of the vagina, it is called *cystocele*. When the rectum prolapses into the posterior wall of the vagina, it is called *rectocele*. Even though the uterus has more supporting structures than the other organs, it is the most likely to prolapse.

The pelvic organs and their associated connective tissue supports are sensitive to hormonal changes. During pregnancy, hormone levels are high, and the connective tissues will greatly increase in size (hypertrophy). The resulting support is more than sufficient for a full-term placenta and fetus.

For most women, childbearing and delivery are completely normal physiological processes that do not damage the reproductive organs or supportive tissues. Even though ligaments are stretched and soft tissue may lacerate during delivery, uterine supports remain firm and intact. Not all women are alike, however, and a few develop subsequent difficulties, especially after bearing several children. After menopause, supportive muscles and connective tissues are likely to atrophy. There is an increasing tendency to prolapse at this time, particularly if there is a previous history of childbirth damage to the supportive structures.

Prolapse will *not* result from strenuous exercise. Unless there is some previous weakening or rupture of the supporting structures, damage will not result from vigorous exercise. Prolapse can occur only when there are weakened or damaged tissues from previous traumatic events or a congenital soft-tissue deficiency.

Women with a prolapsed organ may be advised by their physicians to discontinue strenuous weight-bearing (i.e., upright and on the feet) exercise until after the prolapse has been surgically corrected. Strenuous bouncing-type exercise certainly could aggravate or contribute to further damage of prolapsed structures.

Summary

Many of the prevailing attitudes toward menstruation are extremely negative and based on misconceptions regarding the nature of menstrual function. A thorough understanding of this function will do much to improve such attitudes, which could deleteriously influence athletic performance.

There is little reason to avoid physical activity during menstruation. There appears to be no evidence to suggest that activity need be adjusted or curtailed (including swimming) during menses for any normally functioning woman. It has been shown that water does not enter the vagina and that bacteria shed by a swimmer is totally unrelated to her menstrual function. Consequently, there is no harm to either the participant or other swimmers.

The use of oral contraceptives to alter the menstrual cycle to fit the performance schedule of the athlete is not recommended because of the multiple side effects of "the pill." Quite possibly, the well-documented side effects will more seriously affect athletic performance than would the normal menstrual cycle.

Significant progress has been made in the treatment of dysmenorrhea, so one no longer needs to suffer from painful cramping, nausea, or backaches. Women with dysmenorrhea should consult a gynecologist. When a thorough pelvic examination fails to reveal organic pathology, a prostaglandin inhibitor should be prescribed.

There is still no clearly defined explanation for PMS. Many physicians and PMS clinics prescribe a regimen of aerobic exercise to reduce symptoms, but no controlled studies of the effect of exercise on PMS have been conducted.

Many athletes with apparently normal menstrual cycles are, in fact, experiencing short luteal phase cycles. Although such cycles are generally considered benign, these women are infertile, and the condition may progress to secondary amenorrhea.

Prolapse cannot be caused by exercise. No amount of jarring or jumping will result in an organ prolapse if pelvic support is normal. However, if pelvic supporting tissues are damaged by childbirth or weakened for some other reason, then the uterus, bladder, or rectum may become displaced downward. When this happens, strenuous weight-bearing exercise is not recommended until after the prolapse is corrected surgically.

Chapter 8

Athletic Amenorrhea

Twenty years ago, a vigorously active lifestyle might have been characterized by an hour of tennis two or three times a week. Now, more women are realizing the benefits of strenuous exercise and that being athletic is fun and rewarding. Today, many women are training all year-round. Running has gained tremendous popularity, and millions of girls and women are running harder and longer than ever before. They are also lifting weights, swimming, cycling, skiing, and playing tennis more intently than in earlier years. With this increase in exercise intensity, duration, and frequency has come an interesting and confusing problem for some: menstrual irregularity.

The fact that many highly active women and girls have experienced oligomenorrhea or amenorrhea has received a great deal of attention. The "problem" is extremely complex;

a review of chapter 4, which discussed the anatomy and physiology of the menstrual cycle, attests to the complexity of the normal menstrual cycle. Opening a discussion of disruptions in the normal menstrual cycle is like opening Pandora's box.

The following discussion of *athletic amenorrhea* begins with a section on the responses of the reproductive hormones to exercise and includes both basal and acute responses. This leads to an examination of a number of proposed mechanisms of athletic amenorrhea. The chapter concludes with a discussion of the health risks associated with athletic amenorrhea and current concepts of evaluation and treatment.

Hormonal Responses to Exercise

The topic of hormonal responses to exercise is one of great complexity and confusion. A discussion of athletic amenorrhea would be incomplete, however, without an attempt to clarify this issue for it is obviously at the core of the problem. The reader is urged to consult the latest literature.

The material that follows was taken from a number of reviews (see especially Loucks, 1986a; Loucks & Horvath, 1985; and Shangold, 1985) and research papers. Many papers have dealt with athletic amenorrhea. Those selected for inclusion here have the better experimental designs and controls and are most commonly cited in the literature. Space limitations prevent detailed descriptions of each study cited (for a critical review of such topics as research designs and methodological issues, see Loucks, 1986b).

Two types of hormonal responses are discussed: (a) the chronic, or *basal*, concentrations of hormones found at rest in trained women, and (b) changes in hormone concentrations, or the *acute* responses as a result of exercise (i.e., before, during, and after exercise). Emphasis is on comparing the hormonal status of eumenorrheic and amenorrheic athletes. The hormones that are discussed include the sex steroids (estrogens,

progesterone, and androgens), the gonadotropins (LH and FSH), the stress steroids (cortisol and DHEA), and the antireproductive hormones (β-endorphin, melatonin, and prolactin). These hormones are sometimes classified in other categories, and in some instances classification is purely arbitrary.

Basal Hormone Concentrations

Sex Steroids. Cyclic variations in plasma androgens occur in women. Testosterone (T) increases from a low value in the early-to-late follicular phase, peaks during the ovulatory period, and then decreases during the luteal phase (Abraham, 1974; Genazzanni et al., 1977). Elevated T concentrations, especially if prolonged, could cause early atresia (involution) of immature follicles (Speroff & Van de Wiele, 1971). These follicles would never mature and produce estradiol (E_2) to stimulate the LH surge, so no ovulation would occur. Under such a condition, gonadotropic feedback would be abnormal, and amenorrhea could occur.

Higher basal levels of T were reported in runners than in untrained control subjects by Dale, Gerlach, and Wilhite (1979). Testosterone concentrations could be elevated by increased ovarian or adrenal release due to stress, increased peripheral conversion of androstenedione (A) to T, or decreased conversion of T to E_2 (Loucks & Horvath, 1985) in adipose tissue. Fat cells are capable of aromatizing androgens to estrogens (E) (Longcope, Pratt, Schneider, & Fineberg, 1978; Nimrod & Ryan, 1975), and thus adipose tissue is a significant extragonadal source of E in women.

Because trained women have lesser amounts of body fat than untrained women, possibly less T is being converted to E. This mechanism has been proposed in support of the body fat hypothesis (Frisch, 1988) as the cause of athletic amenorrhea. However, no physiologically significant differences have been found in A, DHEA, DHEAS, or T between amenorrheic runners and cyclic runners or nonrunners (Baker et al., 1981; Boyden,

Pamenter, Stanforth, Rotkis, & Wilmore, 1983; Cumming & Belcastro, 1982; Schwartz et al., 1981). In fact, basal T levels have been reported to be higher in untrained than trained women (Keizer, Kuipers, de Haan, Beckers, & Habets, 1987). Therefore, there are no convincing data that elevated androgens are the cause of athletic amenorrhea.

Decreased basal levels of E and progesterone (P) have been reported in athletes repeatedly. Dale, Gerlach, and Wilhite (1979) concluded that their runners (not joggers) had depressed E and P levels that indicated chronically reduced ovarian function. Baker et al. (1981) reported that E and sex hormone–binding globulin (SHBG) were lower among amenorrheic runners than eumenorrheic runners or nonrunners. Schwartz et al. (1981) found similar levels of estrone (E_1) and E_2 among amenorrheic runners and eumenorrheic runners and nonrunners, although the ratio of E_1 to E_2 was significantly higher in the runners, an indication of an increased extraglandular conversion of A to E_1 or a decreased ovarian secretion of E_2. These changes could be due to variations in the rate of adrenal or ovarian synthesis and release of A.

Bonen, Belcastro, Ling, and Simpson (1981) reported lower values of luteal phase P and E_2 in teenage swimmers than in an untrained control group. These swimmers also showed a shortened luteal phase length than the controls. Depressed E_2 and elevated catecholestrogen values were found in young swimmers and middle-aged runners when compared to control subjects (Russell, Mitchell, Musey, & Collins, 1984). The investigators suggested that the elevated catecholestrogens and β-endorphin interacted to suppress the gonadotropins.

Boyden et al. (1983) reported that basal hormone levels changed after normally menstruating recreational runners increased their mileage to 30 and 50 mi per week. Values of E_1 fell progressively as mileage increased and were correlated with decreases in body fat. Values of E_2 were significantly decreased after the runners increased their mileage to 50 mi per week. Although the subjects did not become amenorrheic, menstrual irregularities occurred with increasing mileage.

Bullen et al. (1984) reported no changes in plasma E_2 but did report decreased excretion of E_1 and P with 8 weeks of moderate training. They interpreted their results to indicate disturbed ovarian function. Several recent studies have reported decreased basal E_2 values in amenorrheic runners (Ding, Sheckter, Drinkwater, Soules, & Bremner, 1988; Glass et al., 1987; Yahiro, Glass, Fears, Ferguson, & Vigersky, 1987).

In summary, the reviewed studies generally showed that basal concentrations of androgens were within normal ranges and that E_2 and E_1 were either low or within the low-to-normal range in amenorrheic athletes.

Gonadotropins.   Basal concentrations of the gonadotropins LH and FSH have been studied extensively. Decreased levels have been reported in runners (Dale, Gerlach, & Wilhite, 1979) and in swimmers (Russell et al., 1984). Bonen et al. (1981) found elevated LH and depressed FSH in the follicular phase and depressed FSH in the luteal phase in teenage swimmers with shortened luteal phases. Rogol (1988) found decreased LH pulse frequency in long-distance runners with amenorrhea or severe oligomenorrhea and attributed this to an alteration in hypothalamic regulatory centers that control the episodic release of endogenous GnRH. A similar result has been reported in regularly menstruating runners (Cumming, Vickovic, Wall, & Fluker, 1985).

Bullen et al. (1985) documented hormonal responses to 8 weeks of strenuous training in previously untrained college women. They reported a loss of LH surge as training progressed, especially in the weight-loss group. Lesser changes occurred in a weight-maintenance group. In an earlier study, these investigators found no changes in basal LH or FSH concentrations with moderate training (Bullen et al., 1984), a finding comparable to that of Schwartz et al. (1981). Loucks and Horvath (1984) reported that basal levels of FSH and LH were lower in amenorrheic runners than eumenorrheic runners. However, Glass et al. (1987) failed to find differences among amenorrheic and eumenorrheic Olympic tryout marathoners, and Yahiro et al. (1987) confirmed those results in less talented runners.

In summary, it appears that basal FSH levels are normal in trained women but that LH concentrations may be lower and LH pulsatility reduced in normally menstruating women following strenuous training. Amenorrheic athletes appear to have lower FSH and LH levels with no ovulatory peaks and reduced LH pulsatility, but not all studies agree.

Stress Hormones.   The classic indicators of stress are cortisol (F), epinephrine, and norepinephrine. Both DHEA and prolactin (PRL) may also be considered stress hormones but PRL is considered here as an antireproductive hormone and is discussed in a later section. Loucks and Horvath (1984) reported no significant differences in basal levels in any of these hormones between eumenorrheic and amenorrheic runners. Yahiro et al. (1987) also reported no differences between eumenorrheic and amenorrheic runners in basal levels of F or PRL. However, two other recent studies have reported that basal F concentrations were higher in amenorrheic runners than eumenorrheic runners (Ding et al., 1988; Glass et al., 1987). Ding et al. (1988) concluded that increased glucocorticoid levels may be an etiologic factor in athletic amenorrhea, but Glass et al. (1987) stated that there was no convincing evidence for such an effect.

Antireproductive Hormones.   Hyperprolactinemia has been suspected as a cause of athletic amenorrhea for some time. The nursing mother is the classic example of the amenorrheic woman, but high levels of serum PRL have also been reported in nonlactating women with secondary amenorrhea or oligomenorrhea (Pepperell, Bright, & Smith, 1977). Is hyperprolactinemic amenorrhea distinct from athletic amenorrhea?

Wakat and Sweeney (1979) reported that both eumenorrheic and oligomenorrheic (51% of the total group) cross-country runners exhibited higher than normal levels of PRL and human growth hormone. But Boyden et al. (1982, 1983) reported decreased basal PRL in trained runners. Ding et al. (1988) reported lower PRL in amenorrheic athletes than nonathletes, and Baker et al. (1981) reported lower PRL in amenorrheic than eumenorrheic runners. Bullen et al. (1984) saw no changes in basal PRL with 8 weeks of moderate endurance training, and Loucks and Horvath (1984), Glass et al. (1987), and Yahiro et al. (1987) reported no differences in basal PRL between eumenorrheic and amenorrheic runners.

Brisson, Volle, DeCarufel, Desharnais, and Tanaka (1980) suggested that elevated PRL levels in trained girls could explain the delayed onset of menarche observed in some young athletes. However, the work of Bonen et al. (1981) does not seem to support this concept as the young swimmers they studied who had anovulatory menstrual cycles had lower PRL concentrations than various control groups. Thus, the results regarding PRL are quite inconsistent.

Other antireproductive hormones include β-endorphin and melatonin, the basal levels of which did not change with training (Bullen et al., 1984). These substances are discussed further in the following section. A summary of basal hormone concentrations in trained women is given in Table 8.1.

Acute Hormonal Responses to Exercise

Sex Steroids.   Acute hormonal responses are difficult to interpret because it is not known from studying plasma hormone concentrations whether the results reflect glandular secretion, secretion from other sources (e.g., ovarian or adrenal sex steroids), peripheral conversion (metabolic degradation) of one substance to another, or metabolic clearance (renal and hepatic clearance). However, a considerable number of studies have been conducted on the acute exercise responses of all the hormones whose basal levels were previously discussed. The idea in regard to the cause of athletic

Table 8.1 Summary of Basal Hormone Concentrations in Eumenorrheic and Amenorrheic Athletes

Hormone	Subject groups	Results observed	References
		Sex steroids	
Testosterone (T)	Runners; untrained controls	Higher in runners	Dale, Gerlach, & Wilhite (1979)
Androgens, dehydroepiandrosterone, T, dehydroepiandrosterone sulfate	Amenorrheic & cyclic runners	No differences	Baker et al. (1981); Cumming & Balcastro (1982); Schwartz et al. (1981); Boyden et al. (1983)
T	Trained; untrained	Higher in untrained	Keizer et al. (1987)
Estrogens (E), progesterone (P)	Runners; joggers; untrained controls	Lower in runners	Dale, Gerlach, & Wilhite (1979)
E, sex hormone–binding globulin	Amenorrheic & eumenorrheic runners; untrained controls	Lower in amenorrhea	Baker et al. (1981)
Estrone (E_1), estradiol (E_2)	Amenorrheic & eumenorrheic runners; eumenorrheic controls	Similar	Schwartz et al. (1981)
$E_1:E_2$	Same as above	Higher in runners	Schwartz et al. (1981)
E_2, P	Teenage swimmers; untrained controls	Lower in luteal phase	Bonen et al. (1981)
E_2, catecholestrogens	Young swimmers; middle-age runners; untrained controls	Lower in athletes	Russell et al. (1984)
E_1, E_2	Eumenorrheic runners	Decreased as mileage increased	Boyden et al. (1983)
E_2	Subjects in training	No changes in E_2; decreased E_1 & P with training	Bullen et al. (1984)
E_2	Amenorrheic & eumenorrheic runners	Low basal levels	Glass et al. (1987); Yahiro et al. (1987); Ding et al. (1988); Drinkwater et al. (1984); Marcus et al. (1985)

(Cont.)

111

Table 8.1 (Continued)

Hormone	Subject groups	Results observed	References
Luteinizing hormone (LH), follicle-stimulating hormone (FSH)		Gonadotropins	
	Runners	Depressed	Dale, Gerlach, & Wilhite (1979)
	Swimmers	Depressed	Russell et al. (1984)
	Teenage swimmers	Elevated LH; depressed FSH in follicular phase	Bonen et al. (1981)
LH	Oligo-amenorrheic runners	Decreased pulse frequency	Rogol (1988)
LH	Subjects in training with weight loss	Loss of LH surge	Bullen et al. (1985)
LH, FSH	Moderate training	No change	Bullen et al. (1984); Schwartz et al. (1981)
LH, FSH	Amenorrheic & eumenorrheic runners	Lower with amenorrhea	Loucks & Horvath (1984)
LH, FSH	Amenorrheic & eumenorrheic marathon runners	No differences	Glass et al. (1987)
LH, FSH	Amenorrheic & eumenorrheic runners	No differences	Yahiro et al. (1987)

Hormone	Subjects	Response	Reference
Stress hormones			
Cortisol (F), epinephrine, norepinephrine	Amenorrheic & eumenorrheic runners	No differences	Loucks & Horvath (1984)
F	Amenorrheic & eumenorrheic runners	No differences	Yahiro et al. (1987)
F	Amenorrheic & eumenorrheic runners	Elevated with amenorrhea	Glass et al. (1987); Ding et al. (1988)
Antireproductive hormones			
Prolactin (PRL)	Cross-country runners	High levels	Wakat & Sweeney (1979)
PRL	Trained runners	Decreased	Boyden et al. (1982; 1983)
PRL	Amenorrheic athletes & nonathletes	Lower in athletes	Ding et al. (1988)
PRL	Amenorrheic & eumenorrheic runners	Lower with amenorrhea	Baker et al. (1981)
PRL, β-endorphin, melatonin	Moderate endurance training	No changes	Bullen et al. (1984)
PRL	Amenorrheic & eumenorrheic runners	No differences	Loucks & Horvath (1984); Glass et al. (1987); Yahiro et al. (1987)
PRL	Trained girls; control subjects	Elevated in trained girls	Brisson et al. (1980)
PRL	Teenage swimmers; control subjects	Lower in swimmers	Bonen et al. (1981)

amenorrhea is that seriously training athletes experience acute changes in reproductive hormones for several hours each day or even several times each day. Perhaps these temporary exercise-related changes interrupt delicate feedback mechanisms and thus cause athletic amenorrhea.

In men, the acute androgenic responses to exercise have been studied extensively. Serum androgen levels have been shown to increase with exercise if the work intensity is sufficiently strenuous. In women, although androgen levels have also been reported to increase with exercise, they always remain within normal limits. In highly trained girl swimmers aged 14.7 years, serum androgen rose significantly following maximal but not submaximal exercise (Sutton, Coleman, Casey, & Lazarus, 1973). The increase in androgen was independent of serum LH, the hormone generally accepted as the gonadotropin that controls T secretion. Shangold, Gatz, and Thysen (1981) reported an increase in T following 30 min of running in recreational runners. The rise was greater during the follicular than the luteal phase.

Jurkowski, Jones, Walker, Younglai, and Sutton (1978) studied responses to three levels of bicycle ergometer exercise in active but untrained women. Estradiol increased during all levels of exercise during both the follicular phase and the luteal phase. Progesterone increased at all levels of exercise during the luteal phase but only during exhausting work in the follicular phase. Bonen et al. (1979) reported that 30 min of exercise at 74% $\dot{V}O_2$max in untrained women resulted in a 40% rise in P during the luteal phase and menses and a 20% rise in E during the follicular phase. Hall, Younglai, Walker, Jones, and Sutton (1975) reported an elevation in E_2 and P following bicycle ergometer exercise at three levels of intensity.

In all these studies, the largest absolute changes in E_2 and P were found during the luteal phase, when these hormones are at their highest levels. Bonen's group also studied trained women. Apparently, the acute effects of exercise on the plasma levels of E_2 and P were extinguished by

training because no significant differences in these hormones were found after exercise in the trained women.

Cumming and Belcastro (1982) found elevated E_2 in cyclic trained and untrained women and in amenorrheic runners (but lower levels) following incremental ergometry exercise. Estrone increased in both groups of runners but not in the cyclic, untrained women. Androgens and DHEA also increased after exercise in all the groups. Loucks and Horvath (1984) found no changes in E_2, E_1, or T in either eumenorrheic or amenorrheic runners who ran for 40 min at 80% $\dot{V}O_2$max. Values of E_2 and A were lower in the amenorrheic runners. Significant increases occurred in A values that lasted for 30 min following exercise in the eumenorrheic runners only. After exercise, the amenorrheic group had higher ratios of E_1 to E_2 and T to E_2 and a lower ratio of A to E_1 than the eumenorrheic runners (as they had had at rest). Loucks and Horvath interpreted the stability of the E concentrations and steroid ratios to imply that submaximal exercise does not stimulate an ovarian response and that the increases in androgens were due to adrenal rather than ovarian activation.

Keizer (1986) reported that trained eumenorrheic runners showed no increment in E_2 during a treadmill run. In another group, he reported a pronounced increase in T, free T, A, and DHEAS in trained but not untrained women during 45 min at 80% $\dot{V}O_2$max. In another investigation, Keizer et al. (1987) showed a significant increase in E_2, P, T, and A in both trained and untrained women in incremental treadmill running irrespective of menstrual phase. The trained women had more pronounced increases in T and A than the untrained. It appears that some studies showed more extreme responses in untrained subjects than in both highly trained cyclic and amenorrheic subjects.

Gonadotropins.   The responses of the gonadotropins to the acute stress of exercise have not been studied extensively. In untrained subjects, Bonen et al. (1979) found no changes following exercise in

FSH or LH during menses or the luteal phase. In the trained subjects, however, a decrease was seen in FSH. Jurkowski et al. (1978) reported no change in LH during either the follicular or the luteal phase but did report an increase in FSH in the follicular phase with exhausting exercise. Cumming and Belcastro (1982) found that LH increased during 12 to 18 min of incremental ergometer exercise in eumenorrheic untrained and trained women; FSH increased in all groups, including amenorrheic runners.

Bullen et al. (1984) found essentially no changes in FSH and LH in response to 60 min of exercise after 8 weeks of strenuous training. After stimulating subjects with LH-releasing hormone (LH-RH), Yahiro et al. (1987) reported that amenorrheic runners had larger gonadotropin responses to LH-RH than the eumenorrheic runners. They suggested that the exaggerated gonadotropin responses to LH-RH may be a consequence of deficient LH-RH output per se or of increased estrogen sensitivity.

Stress Hormones.

It is well known that the classic stress hormones—epinephrine, norepinephrine, and growth hormone—are elevated with prolonged exercise. Bullen et al. (1984) showed that all three of these hormones increased following 60 min of exercise in cyclic women participating in a training program. In addition, F exhibited an increment peak response to exercise as training progressed; values were higher 30 min following than immediately after exercise (these investigators considered F an antireproductive hormone rather than a stress hormone).

Loucks and Horvath (1984) studied exercise-induced stress responses in eumenorrheic and amenorrheic runners. They found an elevation in F following a 40-min run at 80% $\dot{V}O_2$max that peaked at 30 min of recovery in the eumenorrheic but not the amenorrheic runners. Norepinephrine, epinephrine, and DHEA increased significantly following the run in both groups. The ratio of DHEA to F increased following the run in both

groups, but the ratio of DHEA to A increased in the amenorrheic group only.

Glass et al. (1987) found that F values following the 1984 Olympic marathon trials did not differ between eumenorrheic and amenorrheic runners, although baseline values were slightly higher in the amenorrheic group. Yahiro et al. (1987) reported essentially the same in a study of short-term treadmill exercise to exhaustion.

Antireproductive Hormones.

As with the other hormone groups, the data are conflicting as to the responses of the antireproductive hormones to acute exercise. Most of the available information is on PRL. Brisson et al. (1980) reported elevated PRL following 30 min of bicycle ergometry at 75% $\dot{V}O_2$max in women who had a past or present sport history. After 15 min, PRL had increased more than 40% and after 30 min had increased 100%. During recovery, PRL returned rapidly to near baseline levels. Women who had no prior sport experience showed a tendency toward decreased PRL levels with exercise. Shangold et al. (1981) reported increases in PRL that varied from 19% to 398% in recreational women runners after 30 min of running.

Cumming and Belcastro (1982) found that PRL increased and peaked after exercise in cyclic women (trained and untrained) but not in the amenorrheic runners. Loucks and Horvath (1984) found much the same thing, reporting markedly increased PRL (790%) following running at 80% $\dot{V}O_2$max in eumenorrheic but not amenorrheic runners. Bullen et al. (1984) found increases in PRL with exercise in women only after 4 weeks of endurance training. In the initial exercise tests, before the women had sport experience, the PRL results were like those of Brisson et al. (1980). Bullen's subjects experienced menstrual irregularity but not amenorrhea. Keizer et al. (1987) reported that PRL increased linearly with exercise intensity in cyclic marathon runners irrespective of menstrual phase but nonlinearly in untrained women. It seems that women must have prior sport experience and a menstrual cycle before they display this much-discussed response to exercise.

The results of Boyden et al. (1982) may partially explain this. They found that although basal PRL decreased significantly as cyclic women increased their training mileage by 30 and then 50 mi, PRL responsiveness to thyrotropin-releasing hormone (TRH) stimulation increased significantly. Yahiro et al. (1987), however, reported no differences in PRL responses to TRH stimulation between eumenorrheic and amenorrheic runners and concluded that, although increased PRL output may be a consequence of training, it was not the cause of athletic amenorrhea.

The secretion of GnRH may be suppressed by β-endorphin either directly or by stimulating dopamine. The endogenous opiates (endorphins and enkephalins) may be related to the so-called runner's high. β-endorphin has been shown to increase during or following endurance running (Carr et al., 1981). Several studies have shown that the endogenous opiates increase serum levels of PRL (Bruni, Van Vugt, Marshall, & Meites, 1977; Lien, Fenichel, Garsky, Sarantakis, & Grant, 1976; Rivier, Vale, Ling, Brown, & Guillemin, 1977; Shaar, Frederickson, Dininger, & Jackson, 1977) and growth hormone (Bruni et al., 1977; Shaar et al., 1977) and decrease serum LH (Bruni et al., 1977; Cicero, Schainker, & Meyer, 1979) and TRH (Bruni et al., 1977). These investigations suggest that the endogenous opiates produced during exercise may stimulate PRL by acting as a releasing factor and inhibit LH by competitively binding with the receptors that mediate proper LH response.

Bullen et al. (1984) found that β-endorphin (plus β-lipotropin) exhibited a progressive increment in peak responses to exercise as training progressed. This was similar to the response of PRL explained previously. In addition, another antireproductive hormone, melatonin, increased two- to threefold with exercise. Whether there is a link between the endogenous opiates, PRL, and amenorrhea remains unclear.

Table 8.2 provides a summary of acute hormonal responses to exercise.

Why So Much Variability in Results?

It is obvious from the previous discussion that considerable confusion remains regarding the effects of exercise on reproductive hormones and the substances suspected of controlling them. Although one study may indicate that a certain substance rises with exercise, another reports that it does not or even that it declines. In some cases, a substance will be reported to rise (or fall) in trained subjects only and in another in untrained subjects only. It does not appear that eumenorrheic and amenorrheic women respond differently. Why is there so much variability from study to study?

Loucks (1986a) discussed this problem at length and pointed out that inherent problems in research design and statistical analysis affect the interpretation of results. She discussed some of the pros and cons of each major type of research design (randomized prospective cohort, nonrandomized prospective cohort, cross sectional, case control, etc.) and some of the measurement errors that can occur.

From a less theoretical point of view, the investigator faces many problems. In addition to conflicts in the definitions (discussed in chapter 6) and criteria used to classify subjects into groups (trained-untrained, eumenorrheic-amenorrheic), it is difficult to recruit subjects and, once subjects are located, to get them to do everything the investigator wants (e.g., permit rectal probes or multiple blood samples, train or not train, exercise to exhaustion, show up early in the morning, keep detailed dietary records, or have a pelvic exam). Often, the absence of statistically significant differences occurs because the number of subjects studied was simply insufficient to attain a meaningful numeric difference with an acceptable error rate. It is unfortunate that no satisfactory animal models of the human menstrual cycle are available.

Table 8.2 Summary of Acute Hormonal Responses to Exercise

Hormone	Subject groups	Results observed	References
		Sex steroids	
Testosterone (T)	Highly trained girl swimmers	Significant increase with maximal exercise; no increase with sub-maximal exercise	Sutton et al. (1973)
T	Recreational runners	Increase after 30 min of running	Shangold et al. (1981)
Estradiol (E$_2$), progesterone (P)	Untrained women	Increased E$_2$ during all levels of exercise in both follicular & luteal phases; increased P during exhausting work in follicular phase	Jurkowski et al. (1978)
E$_2$, P	Untrained & trained women	Increase in E$_2$ (follicular phase), untrained; increase in P (luteal phase), untrained; no changes in trained	Bonen et al. (1979)
E$_2$, P	Untrained women	Increased at all levels of exercise; highest during luteal phase	Hall et al. (1975)
Estrone (E$_1$), E$_2$, androstenedione (A), dehydroepiandrosterone (DHEA)	Eumenorrheic & amenorrheic runners; untrained women	E$_2$ elevated in all groups with exercise; E$_1$ elevated in runners; A & DHEA increased in all subjects	Cumming & Belcastro (1982)
E$_1$, E$_2$, T, A	Amenorrheic & eumenorrheic runners	No changes in E$_1$, E$_2$, or T; increased A in eumenorrheic runners	Loucks & Horvath (1984)
E$_2$, T, free T, A, DHEA sulfate	Eumenorrheic runners; untrained controls	No change in E$_2$; increase in T, free T, A, & DHEAS in trained	Keizer (1986)
E$_2$, P, T, A	Trained & untrained women	Increased with running in both groups (more pronounced in trained)	Keizer et al. (1987)
		Gonadotropins	
Follicle-stimulating hormone (FSH), luteinizing hormone (LH)	Untrained women Trained women	No changes Decrease in FSH	Bonen et al. (1979)
FSH, LH	Untrained women	No change in LH; increase in FSH in follicular phase	Jurkowski et al. (1978)

(Cont.)

Table 8.2 (Continued)

Hormone	Subject groups	Results observed	References
FSH, LH	Eumenorrheic & amenorrheic runners; untrained women	LH increased in eumenorrheic women; FSH increased all groups	Cumming & Belcastro (1982)
FSH, LH	Subjects in training	No changes	Bullen et al. (1984)
FSH, LH	Amenorrheic & eumenorrheic runners	Larger FSH & LH responses following LH-RH in amenorrhea	Yahiro et al. (1987)
Stress Steroids			
Epinephrine (Epi), norepinephrine (NE), cortisol (F)	Subjects in training	Increased	Bullen et al. (1984)
F, NE, Epi, DHEA	Amenorrheic & eumenorrheic runners	F increased in eumenorrheic subjects; NE, Epi, DHEA increased in both groups	Loucks & Horvath (1984)
F	Eumenorrheic & amenorrheic marathoners	No difference	Glass et al. (1987)
F	Amenorrheic & eumenorrheic runners	No difference	Yahiro et al. (1987)
Antireproductive Hormones			
Prolactin (PRL)	Trained girls; untrained controls	Increased in girls with "sports history"	Brisson et al. (1980)
PRL	Recreational runners	Increased	Shangold et al. (1981)
PRL	Eumenorrheic & amenorrheic runners; untrained women	Increased in cyclic women	Cumming & Belcastro (1982)
PRL	Amenorrheic & eumenorrheic runners	Increased in cyclic women	Loucks & Horvath (1984)
PRL	Subjects in training	Increased	Bullen et al. (1984)
PRL	Trained & untrained women	Increased linearly in trained	Keizer et al. (1987)
PRL	Eumenorrheic runners	Increased responsiveness to TRH	Boyden et al. (1982)
PRL	Eumenorrheic & amenorrheic runners	No differences in responsiveness to TRH	Yahiro et al. (1987)
β-endorphin, melatonin	Subjects in training	Progressive increase as training progressed	Bullen et al. (1984)

Loucks (1986a) also discussed criteria for establishing causation in biological research and applied them to the question of athletic amenorrhea. Considerable liberty has been taken in paraphrasing her material in the following section. I also include some of my own ideas.

1. *Is there evidence from true experiments in humans that participation in athletics causes amenorrhea?* No. However, it is impossible to choose subjects randomly from the general population to study the etiology of athletic amenorrhea. The problem exists only in certain subsets of the population that may be particularly susceptible to athletic amenorrhea.

2. *Is the association in subexperiments strong?* The more reliable and valid cross-sectional studies have provided evidence of gonadotropin and sex steroid suppression in trained women with decreased LH pulsatility. The better longitudinal training studies also have shown a reduction or absence of a midcycle LH surge and a reduction in E levels. Thus, there is a limited but strong association of results across some studies.

3. *Is the association consistent from study to study?* The results have not been consistent across all studies, but the more stringently controlled studies have reported that the gonadotropins and ovarian steroids are suppressed in amenorrheic athletes.

4. *Is the temporal relationship correct?* The longitudinal training studies have documented that hormonal changes do occur *after* the onset of training.

5. *Is there a dose-response gradient?* There definitely appears to be more extreme hormonal changes with very strenuous training programs. This is obscured in some studies because training mileage, intensity, or both were not high enough.

6. *Does the association make epidemiological sense?* Yes. Menstrual irregularities develop most frequently among younger, more intensely trained, successful competitors rather than recreational athletes.

7. *Does the association make biological sense?* Of the hypothetical mechanisms proposed, not one has been satisfactorily demonstrated. Therefore, Loucks said "not yet." However, the association between extreme athletic training (physical stress coupled with other variables) and loss of normal menstrual function makes considerable intuitive sense (more on this later).

8. *Is the association specific?* Probably not. There appear to be many variables (physical, psychological, and dietary stress) that may be additive in their effect on the reproductive system.

9. *Is the association analogous to a previously proven causal association?* Not in humans. Physical, psychological, and dietary stress have never been established as the cause of reproductive failure in humans.

Proposed Mechanisms in Athletic Amenorrhea

With these criteria in mind, let us examine some proposed mechanisms in the etiology of athletic amenorrhea.

Body Fat Hypothesis

Currently, the popular notion is that loss of body weight, particularly loss of body fat, is *the* cause of athletic amenorrhea. Advocates of the concept (Frisch, 1977a, 1988; Frisch & McArthur, 1974; Frisch et al., 1980) have proposed that 17% body fat is needed for the onset of menarche and 22% to restore or maintain the menstrual cycle. This has been called the *critical fat hypothesis*. The logical extension of this hypothesis to athletic amenorrhea would be that strenuous and regular exercise results in excessive leanness (a low percent body fat). The low levels of body fat yield less aromatization of T to E, thus preventing the LH surge required for ovulation. The result could be elevated T levels, low gonadotropin stimulation, and secondary amenorrhea.

This hypothesis is intuitively attractive and has face validity. It seems that most (if not all) amenorrheic athletes are thin. Frisch's hypothesis, however, has been severely criticized because her data were retrospective and her method of body composition assessment indirect. Trussell (1978) argued that Frisch's index of fatness is not an accurate measure of fatness. In addition, many studies (some are cited in chapter 6) have reported that amenorrhea has occurred with the onset of weight loss, preceding weight loss, or without weight loss. For example, amenorrheic ballerinas who stopped training because of illness or injury experienced the return of menstruation without any discernible change in body weight or composition (Warren, 1980), and some anorexic patients do not resume menstruation until long after normal weight is restored.

More recently, several review papers have attacked Frisch's hypothesis (Loucks & Horvath, 1985; Sanborn & Wagner, 1988; Sinning & Little, 1987). The major problem with the body fat hypothesis is that some athletes with low body fat are eumenorrheic, some athletes with more body fat are amenorrheic, and some athletes regain menses with no change in weight (or fat). Menstrual function resumes with the cessation or reduction of training rather than weight gain. If the hypothesis were correct, it would be impossible to be below the critical fat level and experience menstrual flow.

It appears that athletic amenorrhea is not *caused* by weight loss or low body fat but is definitely *associated* (i.e., correlated) with it. It is incorrect to infer causation from correlational analysis.

Psychic Stress Theory

It has long been recognized that severe psychological stress and emotional disturbances are associated with a form of secondary amenorrhea that is usually called *psychogenic amenorrhea*. Almost all women who experience prolonged exposure to extreme dangers (or, e.g., to the harsh conditions encountered in concentration camps during war) also experience amenorrhea. Occasionally, relatively minor lifestyle changes (such as going away

to college or changing jobs) or emotional upheavals due to fear of pregnancy, marital conflicts, or financial worries (Wentz, 1977) have led to episodes of amenorrhea. Individuals, of course, vary widely in their perception and handling of these stresses, and in their vulnerability to becoming amenorrheic as a result.

In psychogenic amenorrhea, normal hormonal patterns are disrupted. The problem is thought to be basically one of hypothalamic dysfunction from higher brain involvement. The brain, after all, is really an endocrine gland that secretes hormones, releasing factors, and neurotransmitters in response to signals from the outside world. A large gap exists in our understanding of the effect of psychological trauma on biochemical alterations in the central nervous system and on reproductive function. Rapid progress is being made in this field, however, with the relatively new emphasis on research that deals with the neurotransmitters and behavior. Significant advances have been made in the study of drug addiction, depression, and schizophrenia, and such research may have ramifications for the study of athletic amenorrhea.

So far, no studies have successfully shown that amenorrheic athletes were under undue stress or more stress than eumenorrheic athletes. Most studies have shown that athletes in general display the "iceberg" psychological profile; that is, they score above the norm on the variable "vigor" and below the norm for negative attributes. Amenorrheic athletes appear to be typical of these other athletes. Either psychological stress plays no role in athletic amenorrhea, or our standardized psychological tests are not sensitive enough to detect small but critical differences in eumenorrheic and amenorrheic athletes.

Endocrine Conditioning (Adaptation) Theory

Prior (1982) has presented the concept that hormonal alterations associated with endurance training are analogous to cardiovascular and musculoskeletal training effects. She believes that "hypothalamic conditioning" is an adaptive, gradual, physiological process that is manifested by the development of menstrual cycle irregularity, amenorrhea, or infertility that serves some physiological purpose for the individual. Prior (1988) pointed out that the traditional "disease model" assumes that some aspect of sport participation is the cause of athletic amenorrhea and that the condition is stable or progressive unless it is treated.

However, the endocrine conditioning, or adaptation, model views reproductive changes associated with exercise as a complex interaction between physical training, nutrition, relative weight and weight change, past reproductive or hormonal history, and the athlete's sense of self in her social and cultural environment (Prior, 1988). It assumes that the changes are under continual adjustment and are fully reversible. Short-term, protective benefit is believed to result from the adaptation; thus, treatment is viewed as appropriate only if long-term harm is clear, the benefits outweigh any risks, or both. Therefore, therapy for chronic amenorrhea aims at preventing osteoporosis, vaginal atrophy, and unwanted pregnancy but not necessarily at correcting the amenorrhea.

In other words, this model takes the view that athletic amenorrhea is a natural phenomenon that occurs "in relationship to the effort of the body to conserve reproductive function for a time when the individual is in nutritional balance, psychological harmony, and under no excessive demands of exercise or physical illness" (Prior, 1988, p. 148).

The endocrine conditioning model also proposes that reproductive changes that occur with intense training are similar to those that occur with major weight loss, significant illness, or major psychological stress. Prior believes that a whole spectrum of reproductive hormonal changes are on a continuum and vary from cycle to cycle in the same woman and thus that factors of energetics and fecundity are highly interrelated (Prior, 1988).

Energy Drain Theory

Similarly, the energy drain theory is a multiple-factor hypothesis that has been developed to explain both primary and secondary amenorrhea associated with exercise. It was first proposed by Warren (1980), who stated that "energy drain may have an important modulatory effect on the hypothalamic pituitary set point at puberty and, in combination with low body weight, may prolong the prepubertal state and induce amenorrhea" (p. 1150). Whatever the mechanism, the energy drain hypothesis assumes that the common denominator of athletic amenorrhea is high energy expenditure from physical work.

The fact that high-mileage in runners is closely associated with the incidence of amenorrhea gives the hypothesis initial face validity, but the hypothesis is really more comprehensive than the simple relationship between exercise energy expenditure and menstrual function implies. Rather, it is a more inclusive view that very high energy expenditure—coupled with psychological stress (as with competition or performance demands) and inadequate rest and diet—results in an imbalance between energy output and energy availability. According to this theory, the hypothalamus acts to conserve as much energy as possible to maintain all required body functions by inducing a dormant state of reproductive function.

Hyperprolactinemia Theory

Amenorrhea in the nursing mother—*lactogenic amenorrhea*—is attributed to high levels of PRL, which is traditionally considered the lactogenic hormone. Prolactin is secreted from the anterior lobe of the pituitary gland by the nursing mother in response to episodes of suckling. Prolactin is known to be inhibited by dopamine (an intermediate biochemical by-product in the synthesis of norepinephrine). Thyrotrophic releasing hormone serves to stimulate its release. Prolactin exerts a luteotrophic effect on the ovary; that is, it prolongs the life of the corpus luteum and so inhibits ovulation. High levels of PRL suppress the gonadotropins and thus prevent ovulation.

Theoretically, intermittent surges of PRL might exert an influence similar to that of periodic suckling and thereby cause athletic amenorrhea. The data are not convincing, however (see the previous discussion of the acute responses to the antireproductive hormones). Whereas some studies found marked increases, particularly in trained runners, others did not. More important, comparisons of amenorrheic and eumenorrheic runners have shown that the PRL response to acute exercise was not greater in the amenorrheic subjects.

Is Athletic Amenorrhea Harmful?

Most of the published information about athletic amenorrhea has been directed toward identifying associated factors. However, the athlete, her coach, and her loved ones are far more interested in the consequences of athletically induced amenorrhea. Are there long-term effects from the loss of menstrual function due to strenuous physical training? Is there a lasting effect on menstrual function or fertility? As Stager (1984) pointed out, two lines of evidence suggest that athletic amenorrhea does not incur a lasting effect on future menstrual function or fertility. The first is a complete lack of evidence that amenorrhea in athletes results in permanent infertility. If this were so, there is every reason to believe that it would be widely documented.

The second line of evidence is purely anecdotal. Amenorrheic (or oligomenorrheic) athletes have been widely reported to resume regular menstrual cycles during periods of reduced training or at the end of a competitive season in such diverse activities as ballet, rowing, swimming, and distance running.

It appears that the reversibility of athletic amenorrhea is rapid. Most studies have reported that menstruation resumes in less than 2 months once training is either reduced or discontinued. Many athletes have borne children of normal weight after athletic careers that were marked by periods of oligomenorrhea and amenorrhea. Many athletes temporarily interrupt their athletic careers to begin families.

Are there health risks associated with athletic amenorrhea? Numerous studies have shown that hypoestrogenic amenorrheic women are at increased risk of osteopenia (bone mineral loss) as well as

atrophic vaginitis and urethritis (vaginal dryness and endothelial atrophy are discussed in chapter 10 in the section on menopausal symptoms). The most serious problem is the potential loss of bone mineral (discussed here extensively; see also chapter 10).

Osteopenia in Amenorrheic Athletes

Until recently, athletes (including those who were amenorrheic) were considered to be at minimal risk of early bone mineral loss. Numerous studies had shown that athletes had denser bones than nonathletes, indicating the beneficial effects of exercise on bone mineral. Weight-bearing exercise has long been prescribed for peri- or postmenopausal women on the assumption that it retarded or prevented the bone mineral loss associated with reduced estrogen levels at menopause. Consequently, it was a surprise when amenorrheic athletes were shown to have decreased bone density.

The first report of decreased bone mineral in amenorrheic athletes was the result of a study of 38 women who had several different types of amenorrhea (Cann, Martin, Genant, & Jaffe, 1984). The amenorrheic athletes (along with the other amenorrheic subjects) had 22% to 29% less spinal bone mass than the control subjects. The investigators concluded that a lack of estrogen was not mitigated by exercise.

A number of studies have now verified the results of this preliminary report. Drinkwater et al. (1984) compared the bone mass of 14 amenorrheic athletes to 14 regularly menstruating athletes to determine the effect of a hypoestrogenic status. The two groups of athletes were matched for age, height, weight, sport, and frequency and duration of daily training. Estradiol levels were significantly lower in the amenorrheic group, as were P and PRL levels. Dietary (including calcium) intake was similar between the groups. Regional bone mass at the distal radius (primarily hard, cortical bone) and the lumbar vertebrae (primarily softer, trabecular bone) was assessed. Bone mineral density at the radius did not differ between groups, but bone density at the lumbar vertebrae was significantly lower in the amenorrheic group of athletes. The bone mineral density of the lumbar spine in the menstruating athletes approximated that for their age-group, whereas the values for the amenorrheic athletes with low E levels were equivalent to those of women 51.2 years of age!

At least two other well-controlled studies have reported similar results. Lindberg et al. (1984) studied subjects grouped according to their menstrual and training status. Significant reductions in both radial and lumbar bone density were found in amenorrheic runners when compared to regularly menstruating runners and age-matched controls. The amenorrheic groups were similar in bone mineral to the postmenopausal control subjects.

Marcus et al. (1985) studied 17 distance runners from university track teams and running clubs who had the ability to complete a marathon within 3 h. The subjects ran distances of 65 km per week (40 mi). Eleven of these women had been amenorrheic for 1 to 7 years; six had regular menses. The amenorrheic runners were hypoestrogenic but had normal levels of PRL, LH, and FSH. The amenorrheic runners had lower bone mass (both radial and lumbar bone) than the normally menstruating runners and normal age-matched control subjects. They also had more running-related fractures.

One group of investigators reported no differences in bone mineral content between amenorrheic runners, regularly menstruating runners, and nonathletic women (Linnell, Stager, Blue, Oyster, & Robertshaw, 1984); however, only cortical bone (radius) was studied. Most researchers in this area of study believe that differences between such groups are less likely to appear in cortical bone than in the softer, more responsive (higher bone mineral turnover) trabecular bone. With extremely prolonged periods of amenorrhea, however, amenorrheic athletes are likely to have lower densities of both types of bone.

Another study (Jones, Ravnikar, Tulchinsky, & Schiff, 1985) compared cortical bone density in amenorrheic athletes, women with amenorrhea associated with weight loss, and women with premature menopause. No differences between groups were found; however, the authors concluded that radial bone density regressed linearly with increasing duration of amenorrhea regardless of etiology.

In summary, hypoestrogenic amenorrheic athletes lose bone mineral at a rate similar to that of postmenopausal women, perhaps greatly increasing their risk of developing osteoporotic fractures. In fact, some young female athletes have actually been diagnosed as osteoporotic (Carson, 1987). At least one investigation has shown that women athletes with menstrual irregularities have considerably more musculoskeletal injuries than athletes with regular menses (Lloyd et al., 1986). Fractures (documented by X ray) occurred in 9% of women athletes with regular menses and in 24% with irregular or absent menses. In ballerinas, Warren et al. (1986), reported a higher prevalence of scoliosis and more fractures with increasing menarcheal age. The dancers with stress fractures had a higher incidence and longer duration of amenorrhea. These results suggest that a delay in menarche and prolonged periods of hypoestrogenic amenorrhea may predispose ballerinas to the development of scoliosis and stress fractures.

A vast literature supports the concept that osteoporosis should be prevented before significant bone loss occurs. Therefore, it is imperative that hypoestrogenic amenorrhea in athletes not be ignored. Two studies have reported improvement in bone mineral density over 15 months with the reduction of running distance, gain in body weight, and resumption of menstrual flow. In a follow-up study of their original subjects, Drinkwater, Nilson, Ott, and Chesnut (1986) found a significant increase (6.3%) in lumbar bone mineral density for the formerly amenorrheic group. Two athletes who remained amenorrheic continued to lose bone (−3.4%). However, bone mineral in the cyclic women remained significantly higher than in the formerly amenorrheic athletes. This means that even after 15.5 months of normal menstrual function, the formerly amenorrheic athletes, although improving significantly, had not yet achieved the bone mineral density levels of the eumenorrheic women.

Lindberg, Powell, Hunt, Ducey, and Wade (1987) also conducted a follow-up study of their original runners who were identified as having secondary amenorrhea with osteopenia. Four of these runners took supplemental calcium, reduced their weekly running distances (by 43%), had increases in body weight (by 5%) and plasma E_2 levels, and became eumenorrheic. Their average vertebral bone mineral content increased by 6.5%. Three runners maintained their running distances and body weight, took supplemental calcium, continued to have abnormally low E_2 levels, and remained amenorrheic. There was no significant change in their bone mineral content. These two studies indicate that the primary factor for the increase in vertebral bone mineral density in formerly amenorrheic athletes was the resumption of menses.

Treatment of Menstrual Dysfunction

Menstrual dysfunction associated with heavy physical training should never be ignored. Rather, medical evaluation should be sought. Menstrual irregularity or amenorrhea can have many causes, among which are pituitary tumors, thyroid dysfunction, and premature menopause. Although these problems are relatively uncommon among amenorrheic athletes, the athlete is not immune to them. To assume that amenorrhea is simply associated with heavy exercise and therefore is nothing to be concerned about could result in dangerous consequences.

The diagnosis of exercise-associated menstrual dysfunction is one of exclusion and is based on ruling out significant causative pathologies (Shangold, 1985). Therefore, medical evaluation includes a careful menstrual history and a pelvic examination. Because pregnancy is the most common cause of amenorrhea in women of reproductive age (even among women who have been amenorrheic), this possibility must be thoroughly evaluated. Once pregnancy is ruled out, pituitary and thyroid

hormone levels are assessed. These measurements may be accompanied by a progestin challenge test to determine whether the endometrium has been stimulated by estrogen (Shangold, 1988).

Anovulatory amenorrheic women produce E but not P. As a result, the endometrium is continually stimulated by estrogen. Such stimulation without menstrual regression can result in endometrial hyperplasia, which has been associated with precancerous cellular growth. Withdrawal bleeding following a 5-day progestin trial indicates that the endometrium is being stimulated by E and that progestin therapy is required for protection. These women are classified as *euestrogenic*. No withdrawal bleeding after the progestin trial indicates that there has been no endometrial stimulation and probably that other target tissues are also in need of E (Shangold, 1988). These women are classified as *hypoestrogenic* and should receive E in some form to protect against vaginal and urethral atrophy and bone mineral loss.

Many amenorrheic athletes are concerned about their abnormal menstrual patterns. Still others claim that they prefer to be amenorrheic, and so they avoid medical evaluation. Two primary points can be made in such a case. First, it must not be assumed that amenorrhea protects against pregnancy. Spontaneous ovulation can occur at any time. The sexually active amenorrheic athlete is not likely to know for several months that her amenorrhea has changed from exercise-related causes to pregnancy. Second, as discussed previously, of the several potentially harmful outcomes of amenorrhea, the most serious is the loss of bone mineral (osteopenia) and thus an increased incidence of musculoskeletal injuries. Other outcomes include vaginal dryness, irritation, infection, and atrophy. It seems that for an athlete to remain amenorrheic for more than 3 months without treatment is potentially harmful.

Not all authorities agree on the exact treatment protocols for the amenorrheic athlete. However, the athlete does need protection from the risk of osteopenia, and some form of cyclic E and P should be given, possibly with an increased oral consumption of calcium in the form of either calcium supplementation or an improved diet that includes four to eight daily servings of dairy products. Oral contraceptives are used by some individuals, but many authorities believe they are not desirable (unless necessary for contraception) because they suppress cyclic hypothalamic-pituitary function. For a more thorough discussion of the treatment of the amenorrheic athlete, see Prior (1988), Prior and Vigna (1986), and Shangold (1988).

Summary

The actual cause (or causes) of exercise amenorrhea is not yet known. Although there are many prevailing opinions and theories, no conclusive evidence exists to support any of these hypotheses. The dominant thought is that exercise-associated amenorrhea is caused by a disruption of hypothalamic-pituitary function.

There may be harmful consequences of athletic amenorrhea, and no athlete should be allowed to remain in that state for a long period of time. Athletes with exercise-associated amenorrhea need to examine their daily routines to strike a better balance between their dietary, training, and psychophysiological needs. Assistance may be necessary to accomplish this.

PART III

Exercise and the Nonmenstruating Woman

A woman spends a great deal of her life in the nonmenstruating state. For each child born, a woman does not menstruate for a period of about 1 year or more (the 9-month gestation period plus a corresponding lactation period). This interval most often occurs during a period of one's life that would normally be characterized by vibrant health and youthful activity—time in one's life that would usually, without pregnancy, be filled with at least moderate levels of physical activity. The nonmenstruating state occurs again with the menopause at about 50 years of age—a period of time usually characterized by a more sedentary, less hectic lifestyle. And, of course, once menopause has occurred, a woman remains in the nonmenstruating state for the remainder of her life—a period that very likely will continue another 40 years or more.

Although much has been written about exercise and menstrual function (see Part II), relatively little information is available on exercise in the nonmenstruating women. Although there has always been concern that the pregnant woman or her unborn child might be harmed by strenuous exercise, there were few studies that dealt directly with the matter, and there was literally no research-based information available to the inquiring woman. This situation has changed considerably. With renewed interest in physical activity, sport, and physical fitness, more attention is being focused on the pregnant woman, the middle-aged woman, and the elderly woman. This part presents information, both basic and applied, on exercise during the nonmenstruating years.

Chapter 9 discusses the normal cardiovascular, respiratory, musculoskeletal, and general body changes that occur with pregnancy and emphasizes how these changes are affected by exercise. The acute effects of physical fitness and strenuous training are presented, as are the long-term effects on pregnancy and childbearing. Of considerable interest have been the effects of exercise on not only the pregnant woman but also her unborn child. Although the literature is still somewhat limited in this regard, information is presented on fetal responses to maternal exercise. Finally, a section of the chapter is devoted to consolidating this information into some practical suggestions and advice to pregnant women.

Chapter 10 outlines the effects of the female climacteric with particular attention to those changes that affect or are affected by exercise. Changes in aerobic power with age and changing levels of physical activity are discussed, as are the effects of physical training during the menopausal years. The effects of exercise on such menopausal symptoms as hot flashes, anxiety attacks, osteoporosis, stress incontinence, and prolapse are also discussed.

Chapter 11, unfortunately, remains relatively short. It presents a summary of the structural and physiological changes that accompany the years following the menopause and the responses to exercise during this period of life. It describes the effects of physical training in elderly women and profiles the older female athlete. Exercise adds life to years; hopefully, more research will soon be completed on the effects of exercise on the postmenopausal woman.

Chapter 9

Exercise During Pregnancy

Every pregnant woman experiences profound and multiple physiological changes that affect every system of her body. These changes begin at the moment of conception and continue throughout pregnancy. Some of these physiological adjustments are not reversed until approximately 6 weeks following delivery of the baby.

Everyone is, of course, different and unique. How a woman reacts and copes with these changes is influenced to a large extent by her personality, her lifestyle, her relationship with her partner and family, her feelings about herself and having a baby, and her level of physical fitness. This chapter presents some of the normal physiological changes that occur during pregnancy and emphasizes the alterations that are most likely to affect the performance of exercise. Maternal responses to exercise, fetal responses to exercise, training during pregnancy, and the effect of exercise on pregnancy outcome are covered at length. Some of the major concerns of both the medical and the lay communities, such as the possibility of fetal hypoxia, hyperthermia, or lengthened labor, are covered. A number of excellent reviews include Gorski (1985), Morton, Paul, and Metcalfe (1985), Lotgering (1988), Lotgering, Gilbert, and Longo (1984), and the edited volume of Artal and Wiswell (1986).

The last section of this chapter is informal and is titled "Advice on Exercise for Pregnant Women." It is directed to the pregnant athlete, her coach, and interested others.

Maternal Responses to Pregnancy and Exercise

With pregnancy come changes in cardiovascular dynamics, respiration, oxygen uptake, metabolism, and the functions of several organ systems. These changes and their impact on exercise in pregnancy are discussed in the sections that follow.

Cardiovascular Alterations

Changes in the cardiovascular system occur early in pregnancy to meet the demands of the enlarging uterus and placenta for more blood and oxygen. In pregnancy, the woman is oxygenating the blood of the fetus as well as her own, so the heart works harder. Cardiac output ($\dot{Q}$), the quantity of blood pumped by the heart per minute, begins to increase early in the first trimester, reaching levels approximately 40% above the nonpregnant state in the second trimester. The increase is due to an increase in both heart rate (HR) and stroke volume (SV). Heart rate during pregnancy increases approximately 15 beats per minute above the nonpregnant state, thus increasing myocardial oxygen needs. Stroke volume also increases as pregnancy progresses. Echocardiographic data indicate that left-ventricular size increases. Some have reported an increase in SV as high as 30%.

In the last trimester, the heart is pushed upward and to the left by the elevation of the diaphragm. During the last weeks, maternal $\dot{Q}$ becomes quite variable (and may be low in the supine position).

The position of the body may markedly affect circulatory dynamics. For example, if the pregnant uterus compresses the inferior vena cava, causing a reduced venous return of blood to the heart, SV and $\dot{Q}$ will decrease, as will arterial blood pressure.

Changes in blood pressure with pregnancy are small. Generally, there is a slight decrease in both systolic and diastolic pressures until about the 22nd week of gestation. Thereafter, these alterations are reversed, and blood pressure values rise toward prepregnancy levels.

Systemic vascular resistance is markedly reduced during pregnancy, leading to a generalized vascular dilation and an increase in venous distensibility as pregnancy progresses. This results in a sixfold increase in peripheral blood flow by the third trimester. The distribution of the elevated $\dot{Q}$ is also altered. Hepatic and cerebral blood flow remain unchanged, but renal and uterine blood flow is increased. Venous pooling tends to occur in the lower extremities as term approaches. The increased venous distensibility is responsible for the high incidence of varicosities in the lower extremities, vulva, and anus during pregnancy. These alterations may be caused in large part by the pressure of the enlarging uterus on the veins returning blood from the legs. Slowing of the circulation, coupled with the engorgement of the pelvic veins, sometimes causes blood to back up in the veins of the legs and to exert increasing pressure on their walls. Occasionally, pregnant women must avoid standing for long periods, elevate their legs whenever possible, or wear support hose to prevent discomfort from varicose veins.

Blood volume changes markedly with pregnancy (see Table 9.1). In the first half of pregnancy, the increase in blood volume exceeds that of the red cell mass, and hemoglobin concentration and hematocrit values decline. Later in pregnancy, the red cell mass increases more rapidly than the

Table 9.1   Blood Changes in Pregnancy

Parameter	Late pregnancy	Nonpregnant state	Percent increase
Blood volume (ml)	4,820	3,250	48
RBC volume (cells/mm³)	1,790	1,355	32
Hematocrit (%)	37.0	41.7	—

Note. From ''Maternal Physiology'' by E.J. Quilligan and I.H. Kaiser. In *Obstetrics and Gynecology* (4th ed., p. 332) by D.N. Danforth (Ed.), 1982, New York: Harper & Row. Reprinted by permission of Lippincott/Harper & Row. Data from Pritchard (1965).

plasma volume. Generally, the increase in plasma volume slightly exceeds the increase in red cell mass, and consequently the hematocrit value falls during pregnancy. If a woman's iron stores are adequate, there should be no problem with the slight fall in hematocrit and hemoglobin concentration.

Cardiovascular Responses to Exercise

Cardiac reserve is defined as (SV) × (maximum HR minus resting HR). Both pregnancy and increased physical fitness increase SV. However, pregnancy increases resting HR, whereas improved physical fitness decreases resting HR. Thus, cardiac reserve in a pregnant woman who is physically fit is influenced by competing factors (see Figure 9.1). Any change in the cardiac reserve with pregnancy would be a summation of these factors. The pregnant woman may be at some disadvantage regarding cardiac reserve, but this disadvantage is not large.

The $\dot{Q}$ of pregnant women has been measured during low-level work on the bicycle ergometer. As shown in Figure 9.2, exercise $\dot{Q}$ followed approximately the same progressive pattern of change with advancing gestation as resting values (Rose, Bader, Bader, & Braunwald, 1956). Resting $\dot{Q}$ increased during the 25th to 27th weeks to a maximum value 40% greater than values for nonpregnant women. Thereafter, $\dot{Q}$ fell progres-

sively until, at term, the values were only slightly higher than in nonpregnant women; $\dot{Q}$ decreased just before term. A similar pattern was observed in resting and exercise SV (Figure 9.2). Left-ventricular work was elevated between the 14th and 30th weeks of gestation but returned to normal levels before parturition. The investigators suggested that a redistribution of blood flow late in pregnancy—a decrease in the intrathoracic blood volume and pooling of blood in the lower extremities—may explain the reduction in $\dot{Q}$ in the presence of a markedly increased plasma volume. They also suggested that the placenta may behave as an arteriovenous shunt and that, as gestation progresses, obliteration of portions of the placenta maternal vascular bed subsequently reduces the shuntlike effect, accounting for the fall in $\dot{Q}$ before term. The $\dot{Q}$ response to exercise was normal in all respects in these subjects, and the investigators concluded that there was no impairment in cardiac reserve as a result of pregnancy.

In a similar study (Ueland, Novy, Peterson, & Metcalfe, 1969), $\dot{Q}$ increased to peak values between the 20th and 24th weeks of gestation and remained elevated until the 38th to 40th weeks. Heart rate increased throughout pregnancy, but SV showed a progressive decline from the 20th to 24th weeks until term. The increment in $\dot{Q}$ with light work (100 kpm • min⁻¹) appeared to be of the same magnitude throughout pregnancy as that in nonpregnant women. However, with moderate work (200 kpm • min⁻¹), the rise in SV and $\dot{Q}$

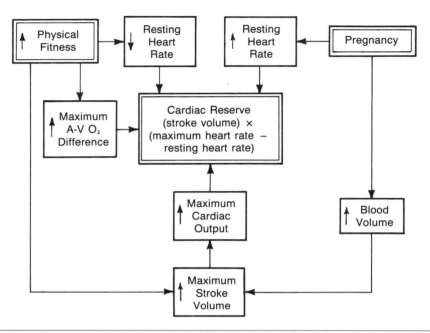

Figure 9.1 The influence of physical fitness and pregnancy on the parameters of cardiac output. *Note.* From "Physical Fitness in Pregnancy: Its Effects on Pregnancy Outcome" by J.J. Pomerance, L. Gluck, and V.A. Lynch, 1974, *American Journal of Obstetrics and Gynecology,* **119,** p. 874. Copyright 1974 by The C.V. Mosby Co. Reprinted by permission.

became progressively smaller with advancing pregnancy. These investigators concluded that there was a progressive decrease in cardiac reserve as pregnancy advanced that was attributable to peripheral pooling of blood and obstruction of venous return by the large gravid uterus.

In a very well designed study of maternal responses to exercise, 8 pregnant women performed monthly bicycle tests from the first trimester until delivery and again 3 months postpartum (Guzman & Caplan, 1970). At every work load throughout pregnancy, HR, SV, and Q̇ were significantly higher than in the postpartum test. The increments were somewhat less during the last 5 weeks of pregnancy, and the relative contribution of HR to Q̇ was greater in the later stages than was the contribution of SV. Because the increase in exercise Q̇ per unit increase in V̇O₂ was the same in all stages of pregnancy as the postpartum

measurements, the investigators concluded that their subjects demonstrated good cardiac reserve throughout pregnancy at the levels of work tested. However, because the heart was working harder during pregnancy, they noted that the pregnant woman would reach her maximum Q̇ at a lower level of work than when not pregnant.

Heart rate, SV, and Q̇ were measured during 6 min of low-intensity (50 W) bicycle exercise in late gestation and again postpartum (Morton, Paul, Compos, Hart, & Metcalfe, 1985). Resting and exercise Q̇ during pregnancy were not different from postpartum values, but HR was higher and SV lower. A precipitous drop in SV occurred at the end of exercise in late gestation but not during the postpartum test. The investigators concluded that the muscle pump of the legs was crucial for maintaining venous return during upright exercise in late gestation.

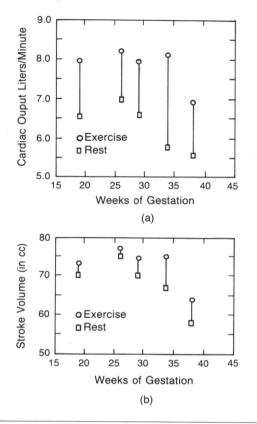

Figure 9.2 Cardiac output during low-level bicycle work during pregnancy. *Note.* From ''Catheterization Studies of Cardiac Hemodynamics in Normal Pregnant Women with Reference to Left Ventricular Work'' by D.J. Rose, M.E. Bader, R.A. Bader, and E. Braunwald, 1956, *American Journal of Obstetrics and Gynecology, 72,* pp. 237-238. Copyright 1956 by C.V. Mosby Co. Reprinted by permission.

Respiratory Alterations

As pregnancy progresses, the uterus rises in the abdominal cavity, elevating the diaphragm. The entire thoracic cavity compensates by increasing its dimensions so that more air can be inspired. The respiratory rate remains unchanged throughout pregnancy, but the tidal volume gradually increases. Figure 9.3 illustrates the functional changes in respiratory volumes in late pregnancy compared to the nonpregnant state. It can be seen that the expansion of tidal volume affects other lung volumes. For example, there is a decrease in expiratory and inspiratory reserve volumes even though the vital capacity remains unchanged. There is a decrease in residual volume (the volume of gas remaining in the lungs at the end of a maximal expiration) and in the functional residual capacity in pregnancy. Alaily and Carrol (1978) present a very complete analysis of changes in respiration with advancing pregnancy.

The increase in tidal volume with pregnancy, in association with a constant respiratory rate, yields an increase in respiratory minute volume ($\dot{V}_E$ = tidal volume × respiratory rate). The magnitude of the increase is approximately 40%. Because respiratory $\dot{V}_E$ increases to a greater extent than $\dot{V}O_2$, there is a relative hyperventilation that is even more pronounced with exercise. This *hyperventilation of pregnancy* is responsible for the decreased concentration of carbon dioxide in the alveoli and, subsequently, in the blood. This leads to a *compensated respiratory alkalosis* and an elevation of the blood pH (from 7.35 to approximately 7.42 at term). These changes (which occur to a lesser extent during the luteal phase of the normal menstrual cycle) probably result from the elevated blood progesterone seen with pregnancy.

Respiratory Responses to Exercise

Both $\dot{V}_E$ and alveolar ventilation are higher during pregnancy for both cycle and treadmill exercise (Pernoll, Metcalfe, Kovach, Wachtel, & Dunham, 1975). This increase is due to an increase in tidal volume rather than respiratory frequency and probably accounts for much of the respiratory distress and increased perceived exertion experienced by most pregnant women late in gestation.

Oxygen Uptake

Oxygen uptake ($\dot{V}O_2$) at rest increases 15% to 20% with pregnancy. The components of this increase are illustrated in Figure 9.4. Most of this is accounted for by the increasing $\dot{V}O_2$ of the

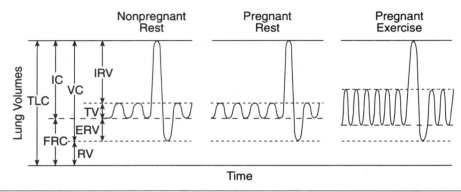

Figure 9.3 Effects of pregnancy and exercise on respiratory volumes. TLC = total lung capacity, IC = inspiratory capacity, FRC = functional residual capacity, VC = vital capacity, RV = residual volume, IRV = inspiratory reserve volume, TV = tidal volume, and ERV = expiratory reserve volume. *Note.* From "Pregnancy" by F.K. Lotgering. In *Women and Exercise: Physiology and Sports Medicine* (p. 149) by M.M. Shangold and G. Mirkin (Eds.), 1988, Philadelphia: F.A. Davis. Copyright 1988 by F.A. Davis. Reprinted by permission.

growing uterus, fetus, and placenta. About 4% of the increase is due to enhanced maternal costs of renal, cardiac, and respiratory work (Lotgering, 1988).

Four studies dealing with $\dot{V}O_2$ responses to exercise during pregnancy were located. Guzman and Caplan (1970) reported that $\dot{V}O_2$ at three bicycle ergometer work loads was unchanged throughout pregnancy. However, at every work load, $\dot{V}_E$ was significantly higher and arteriovenous oxygen difference notably lower during all stages of pregnancy. Although respiratory frequency was higher during the early stages of pregnancy at all work levels, the increment decreased with advancing gestation. Apparently, alterations in tidal volume made up the difference so that the result was a disproportionate increase in $\dot{V}_E$ per unit increase in $\dot{V}O_2$. Figure 9.5 illustrates the results.

Knuttgen and Emerson (1974) studied 13 women during pregnancy and again 6 weeks postpartum. The work tasks they selected were steady-state treadmill walking (4.5 km • h^{-1}, 4% grade) and ergometer cycling (60 W). In this way, they were able to examine exercise responses to both weight-bearing work (walking) and non-weight-bearing work (cycling). Oxygen uptake increased with pregnancy during treadmill walking but not during ergometer cycling. The increase in $\dot{V}O_2$ (13%) compared closely to the 15% increase in body weight. The investigators stated that activities that are not performed in a weight-bearing position or that do not involve lifting the body should not be expected to involve significant increases in energy cost during pregnancy. Nevertheless, both forms of exercise resulted in significantly elevated $\dot{V}_E$. These increases were out of proportion to the increases that occurred in $\dot{V}O_2$ during either walking or cycling. In other words, a definite hyperventilation occurred. This response occurred early in pregnancy and was accomplished primarily by increasing the tidal volume rather than the breathing frequency. A higher respiratory exchange ratio (R) during walking indicated that the subjects were utilizing carbohydrate substrates to a greater extent during pregnancy than during the postpartum period. Because R was also elevated at rest, the authors assumed that the role of carbohydrate as an energy source was enhanced during pregnancy, but this was not observed during cycling.

Another study of light bicycle work (50 W) at monthly intervals throughout pregnancy (Pernoll, Metcalfe, Schlenkar, Welch, & Matsumoto, 1975)

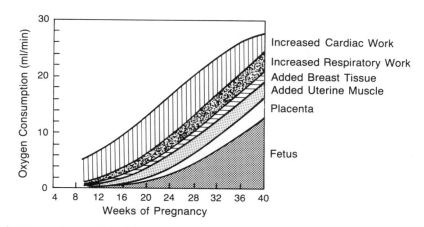

Figure 9.4 Components of increased oxygen uptake in pregnancy. *Note*. From *The Physiology of Human Pregnancy* (p. 100) by F.E. Hytten and I. Leitch, 1964, Oxford: Blackwell. Copyright 1964 by Blackwell Scientific Publications. Reprinted by permission.

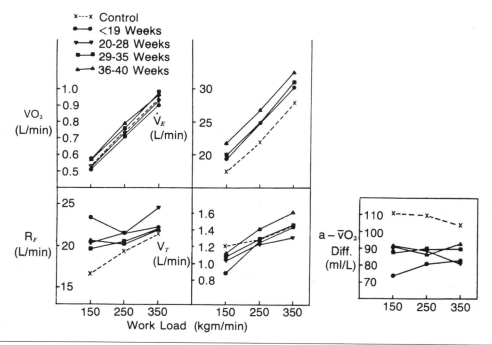

Figure 9.5 The effect of pregnancy on exercise oxygen uptake ($\dot{V}O_2$), minute ventilation ($\dot{V}_E$), respiratory frequency (R_f), tidal volume ($\dot{V}_T$), and arterial minus venous oxygen difference (a–$\bar{v}O_2$) at three work levels. *Note*. From "Cardiorespiratory Response to Exercise During Pregnancy" by C.A. Guzman and R. Caplan, 1970, *American Journal of Obstetrics and Gynecology*, **108**, pp. 602-603. Copyright 1970 by The C.V. Mosby Co. Reprinted by permission.

produced slightly different results. A significant increase in both $\dot{V}O_2$ (15%) and oxygen debt (14%) was observed in late pregnancy, and calculated work efficiency (work performed/$\dot{V}O_2$ in steady state) declined. The increase in $\dot{V}O_2$ was attributed to the increased cost of hyperventilation and $\dot{Q}$ with pregnancy. This group of investigators also reported a progressive increase with pregnancy in $\dot{V}_E$ (38%), carbon dioxide production (14%), and tidal volume (23%) during exercise. No alteration occurred in respiratory frequency during exercise. Alveolar ventilation was greater during pregnancy than at the postpartum period. The investigators suggested that the sensitivity of the respiratory center to carbon dioxide increased progressively during pregnancy.

Metabolic and respiratory responses were studied in pregnant and nonpregnant subjects at rest and at three levels of treadmill exercise: mild, moderate, and maximal (Artal, Wiswell, Romem, & Dorey, 1986). Significant differences were found between the groups during maximal exercise in tidal volume, $\dot{V}O_2$, $\dot{V}CO_2$, and R. There was no significant difference in $\dot{V}O_2$ with the mild or moderate exercise load. The authors concluded that there was a decrease in cardiorespiratory reserve during pregnancy.

In summary, it is important to take into account the increase in body weight and the type of exercise when considering the energy costs of exercise during pregnancy. The added energy expenditure of weight-bearing exercise is closely related to the gain in body weight, as would be expected. Non-weight-bearing exercise does not lead to an increased oxygen requirement. Thus, the apparent energy cost of exercise, independent of the increase in body weight, is not significantly altered during pregnancy.

It is interesting to speculate that because weight-bearing activities during pregnancy require a higher energy output, a training effect may occur. Two case studies reported that $\dot{V}O_2$max increased in pregnant women who maintained fairly strenuous activity during pregnancy (Dressendorfer, 1978; Ruhling, Cameron, Sibley, Christensen, & Bolen, 1981).

Metabolic Alterations

Fat accumulation in the expectant mother is one of the most obvious adaptations seen in pregnancy. Approximately 3.5 kg of fat accumulate, and the circulating free fatty acid concentration increases two- to fourfold (Gorski, 1985). Peak concentrations of glucose and insulin during a glucose tolerance test become increasingly higher as pregnancy progresses. It has been estimated that during late pregnancy sensitivity to insulin is reduced as much as 80% (Gorski, 1985).

Unfortunately, little is known about substrate utilization during exercise and pregnancy. Maternal blood glucose falls even with short-term exercise in pregnancy, perhaps because of the increased demand by the developing fetus as well as the mother. No significant differences have been reported in plasma lactate concentration during exercise between pregnant and nonpregnant subjects.

Musculoskeletal Changes

Under the influence of the hormone relaxin, the ligaments that hold the sacroiliac joints and the pubic symphysis soften and stretch, and the articulations between the joints widen and become more movable during pregnancy. There is a progressive relaxation of the joints that becomes maximal by the beginning of the third trimester. This increases the size of the pelvic cavity to make delivery easier.

The typical postural adaptations of pregnancy—increased swayback (lordosis) and upper spine extension to compensate for the enlarged abdomen—and the loosening of the sacroiliac joints often result in lower back pain. Exercises that strengthen the back and abdominal muscles often relieve these backaches. Figure 9.6 shows the development of postural changes during pregnancy. The increased curvature of the lumbar spine that occurs as the uterus gradually enlarges causes a change in the woman's center of gravity. She must gradually lean backward to compensate for the increasing weight of the uterus and its contents. This will, of course, have major ramifi-

Weeks

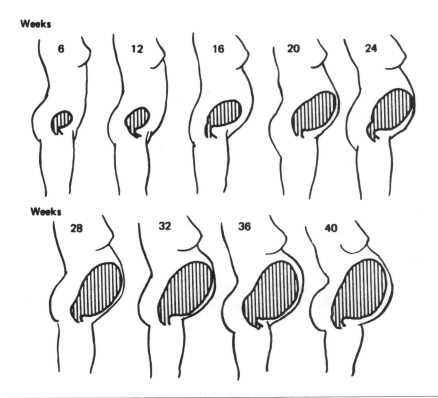

Figure 9.6 Development of postural changes during pregnancy. *Note*. From "Maternal Physiology" by E.J. Quilligan and I.H. Kaiser. In *Obstetrics and Gynecology* (4th ed., p. 338) by D.N. Danforth (Ed.), 1982, New York: Harper & Row. Reprinted by permission of Lippincott/Harper & Row.

cations for sport and exercise performance because a woman's center of gravity will change with the growth of the fetus. Modifications in movement patterns will occur. Some women develop a sort of waddling gait with advanced pregnancy.

Bruser (1968) stated that although the pubic symphysis is normally a solid, fixed structure, during pregnancy this junction softens and may separate "to the extent that on standing on one or the other leg, these bones can move upward and downward to the extent of a few millimeters, and in severe cases, up to 2 cm" (p. 723). This movement can be painful when walking, standing, or even rolling over in bed. Such a disability automatically excludes a woman from participating in sports activities.

Changes in the Central Nervous System

During the first trimester, the pregnant woman often experiences a desire to spend a large portion of time sleeping. The cause of this tendency to fatigue so easily is unknown but may be related to increased levels of progesterone, which in high doses can cause somnolence. Occasional vomiting (morning sickness) may also occur in the first trimester and is thought to be central in origin. The second trimester is often associated with feelings of euphoria and well-being and the third trimester with depression and chronic fatigue. These feelings are certainly not universal, however. Women frequently go through pregnancy with few or none of these reactions.

Women who normally exercise in the early morning may find that morning sickness interferes with exercise. When this occurs, the best solution is simply to exercise later in the day.

General Body Changes

There is probably no ideal value for weight gain in pregnancy, but the American College of Obstetricians and Gynecologists recommends that all women, regardless of prepregnant weight, gain between 22 and 26 lb. One's age, nutritional status, and physical activity level during pregnancy are modifying factors, but this range of weight gain is needed to support the changes that occur in the maternal as well as the fetal body. Such weight gain is commensurate with the fewest obstetric complications and the most favorable outcome. Because there is a positive relationship between maternal weight gain and infant birth weight (Pomerance, Gluck, & Lynch, 1974), insufficient maternal weight gain increases the likelihood of delivering an infant of low birth weight (Sloane, 1980, p. 280). Weight gains of 40 to 50 lb, however, result in excessive fat deposition that is difficult to lose after delivery and should be avoided.

The total accumulation of body weight is considered less significant than the *rate* of gain. By the end of the first trimester, when the fetus still weighs only 1 oz, the maternal weight gain should be about 2 to 4 lb. After that, the gain should average about 3/4 lb per week. During the last month, weight should be fairly stable. Figure 9.7 illustrates the usual distribution of weight gain in pregnancy. The fetus accounts for approximately 7 to 8 lb of the increase, the amniotic fluid for about 1.5 to 2 lb, the placenta for about 1 lb, the uterus for about 2.5 lb, and breast enlargement for about 2.5 to 3 lb. The remainder of the weight gain supports the increase seen in blood volume (about 3 lb), total body water, and other maternal adjustments. Table 9.2 provides an estimate of the extracellular and intracellular water added during pregnancy.

In 700 clinical patients (Abitbol, 1969), the increase in weight during pregnancy averaged 22 lb ($\pm$ 10 lb). The average loss during delivery was 13 lb ($\pm$ 3 lb). Weight loss at the 6-week postpartum checkup was an additional 5 lb ($\pm$ 2 lb). These 700 patients, then, had a 4-lb ($\pm$ 5 lb) weight gain following pregnancy. This "permanent" weight gain was thought to be due to tissue gain from a relatively long-term positive caloric balance influenced by endocrine and psychological factors.

Table 9.2   Estimate of Extracellular and Intracellular Water Added During Pregnancy

	Total water (ml)	Extracellular (ml)	Intracellular (ml)
Fetus	2,343	1,360	983
Placenta	540	260	280
Liquor amnii	792	792	0
Uterus	743	490	253
Mammary gland	304	148	156
Plasma	920	920	0
Red cells	163	0	163
Extracellular extravascular water	1,195	1,195	0
Total	7,000	5,165	1,835

Note. From *The Physiology of Human Pregnancy* (p. 287) by F.E. Hytten and I. Leitch, 1964, Oxford: Blackwell. Copyright 1964 by Blackwell Scientific Publications. Reprinted by permission.

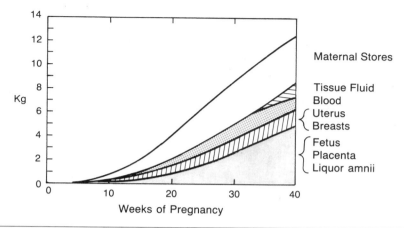

Figure 9.7 Distribution of maternal weight gain in a normal pregnancy. *Note.* From *The Physiology of Human Pregnancy* (p. 294) by F.E. Hytten and I. Leitch, 1964, Oxford: Blackwell. Copyright 1964 by Blackwell Scientific Publications. Reprinted by permission.

Changes in the Digestive System and Gastrointestinal Tract

Normally, physiological processes function at an increased level in pregnancy. Exceptions to this are found in systems dominated by smooth muscle, such as the gastrointestinal and urinary tracts. There is a generalized tendency for all smooth muscle to lose tone during pregnancy. One result is associated with a relaxation of the cardiac sphincter of the stomach with the consequent tendency to regurgitate gastric acid into the lower portion of the esophagus. The consequence is heartburn, a common annoyance during the last 3 months of pregnancy. The general decrease in motility of the alimentary tract leads to other common complaints, such as constipation and flatulence (gas). Apparently, the slower passage of food through the large bowel permits an increased absorption of water, resulting in dry, hard, and difficult-to-expel feces. The gallbladder also empties its contents more slowly, making the digestion of fatty foods more difficult.

Appetite often increases markedly during pregnancy. This may result from stimulation of the appetite control center in the hypothalamus but may also have an emotional basis. Occasionally, this increase in appetite takes a bizarre form, such as the proverbial craving for ice cream and pickles.

Urinary Tract Changes

Marked changes occur in kidney function during pregnancy, including increases in renal plasma flow, glomerular filtration rate, and values for renal function tests (such as clearances of urea and uric acid). The ureters leading from the kidneys to the bladder become dilated in pregnancy, possibly because of their being mechanically obstructed by the enlarging uterus, which also increases the pressure on the bladder. This may contribute to the relative stasis of urine in the ureter, the bladder, and even the renal pelvis, possibly predisposing the pregnant woman to urinary tract infections.

One of the most frequent complaints during pregnancy is that of increased micturition (urination). The sensation of often needing to urinate is annoying, but little can be done about this symptom. In late pregnancy, it is probably the result of lack of room for the bladder to fill. Occasionally with exercise during pregnancy, a woman will experience urinary incontinence. The use of minipads or panty shields will help one feel more secure about this annoyance.

Changes in the Reproductive System

The most dramatic changes in pregnancy, of course, are those taking place in the reproductive organs. The uterus, which normally weights 2 oz and measures 3 in. by 2 in. in the nonpregnant state, increases to about 2 lb and expands 5 to 6 times in size. Although its initial capacity is approximately 2 ml, it increases by 2,000 times to accommodate the developing fetus. This enlargement occurs by the growth of individual smooth muscle cells that become wider and longer. There is an enormous increase in the blood vessels that support and nourish this growth of muscle tissue. Uterine contractility is enhanced; in fact, irregular and painless contractions begin in the first trimester (these are called Braxton-Hicks contractions).

The height of the uterine fundus varies considerably at comparable gestation dates. Figure 9.8 illustrates the progression with successive weeks of pregnancy. After the first trimester, the uterus pushes progressively into the abdominal cavity and presses on the urinary bladder. By the fifth month, the fundus is at the level of the umbilicus.

The vagina becomes edematous and very pliable with pregnancy. There is an increased growth of muscle tissue, a thickening of the vaginal lining, and an increase in blood supply. The fallopian tubes undergo virtually no gross changes in pregnancy, but the ovaries become enlarged and elongated and tend to hang down along the uterus. The ovary that contains the corpus luteum enlarges the most and reaches its maximum development during the third month of pregnancy. When the placenta takes over the major production of progesterone, the corpus luteum regresses. No follicles mature or ovulate during pregnancy because large amounts of circulating steroid hormones inhibit the activity of the anterior pituitary gland.

There are major breast changes during pregnancy. The marked enlargement associated with

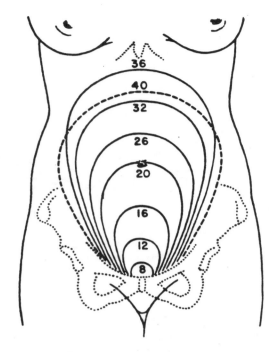

Spiegelberg's Table of Relation Between Linear Distance From Symphysis to Fundus and Length of Gestation

Linear Distance, Symphysis to Fundus (cm)	Estimated Fetal Age (Weeks)
26.7	28
30.0	32
32.0	36
37.7	40

Figure 9.8 Height of the uterine fundus with successive weeks of pregnancy. *Note*. From "Course and Conduct of Normal Pregnancy" by D.M. Haynes. In *Obstetrics and Gynecology* (4th ed., pp. 362, 363) by D.N. Danforth (Ed.), 1982, New York: Harper & Row. Reprinted by permission of Lippincott/Harper & Row.

pregnancy is due to a massive increase in the amount of ductal tissue and an increased deposition of fat. Each breast gains nearly 1 lb by the end of pregnancy. Tingling and soreness are common with these changes, and the breasts may become tender and nodular. The nipples become enlarged, more erectile, and deeply pigmented. The primary areolae widen, and Montgomery's glands (hypertrophied sebaceous glands) become more prominent. By the 10th week of pregnancy, a clear substance, *colostrum*, may ooze from the nipples, but actual milk synthesis does not occur until about the second or third day after delivery. During pregnancy, most women require good bra support, particularly during exercise. Some women even find it comfortable to wear a bra to bed.

Hormonal Alterations With Pregnancy

During pregnancy, steroid hormones are produced by the maternal-fetal-placental complex. The placenta, with precursors from the maternal and fetal compartments, synthesizes several forms of estrogen. There is also evidence that the placenta can convert circulating androgens to estrogen. Serum progesterone values steadily increase with advancing gestation. At term, progesterone values are elevated some 50-fold above the nonpregnant luteal phase values. Pregnanediol, a major metabolite of progesterone found in the urine, is commonly monitored throughout pregnancy.

The pituitary release of the gonadotropins and growth hormone is suppressed during gestation, but prolactin levels rise. In addition, elevated levels of adrenocorticotropic hormone (ACTH) and cortisol are seen in pregnancy, as are increased levels of circulating insulin and a rise in free fatty acids. Normal pregnancy is associated with a pronounced resistance to insulin, and thus pregnancy is often considered *diabetagenic*. Latent diabetes is frequently unmasked during pregnancy.

Hormonal Responses to Exercise

Hormonal responses to very light exercise were assessed in 23 women in their third trimester. A 15-min period of slow treadmill walking resulted in $\dot{V}O_2$ of less than 0.5 L • min^{-1} and yet induced a significant increase in glucagon, norepinephrine,

and epinephrine concentrations. These responses were reversed with 30 min of recovery. No changes occurred in glucose or cortisol concentrations. Because the increase in norepinephrine markedly exceeded the increase in epinephrine, the authors of this report (Artal, Platt, Sperling, Kammula, Jilek, & Nakamura, 1980) suggested that exercise stimulates the sympathetic nerves to a greater extent than the adrenal medulla. This sympathetic response is important because of its potential stimulating effect on uterine contractility. This response was seen in the nonpregnant subjects as well. None of the responses observed were considered inappropriate to pregnancy.

Swimming is often recommended during pregnancy because of the buoyant effect of water. When pregnant women were studied during ergometer exercise in water at 30 °C, cortisol levels declined from the elevated resting levels obtained on land (McMurray, Katz, Berry, & Cefalo, 1988). This was probably a response to immersion in water that was below body temperature. Plasma glucose levels also declined slightly, whereas triglycerides were elevated. Because plasma lactate levels rose, it was concluded that carbohydrates remained the primary energy source and that triglycerides were sequestered by the liver to replenish glucose levels.

Temperature Responses to Exercise

Severe maternal hyperthermia, especially during the first trimester, can affect fetal development. It is thought that maternal fever may be a teratogen (see section on fetal development, p. 148-150). This has been one of the main concerns voiced about exercise during pregnancy. Two investigations of maternal temperature response to exercise-induced heat stress were located. In one, thermoregulatory responses were studied in pregnant runners who ran at speeds estimated to require 80% to 90% $\dot{V}O_2$max at 12, 24, and 32 weeks of gestation (Jones, Botti, Anderson, & Bennett, 1985). Rectal temperature increased 0.6 to 1.0 °C above basal levels and never exceeded 39 °C. There were no differences in response throughout gestation.

Vaginal temperatures did not change either at rest or after exercise and were 0.1 to 0.3 °C less than rectal temperatures. Skin temperatures were quite variable. Sweat production did not change throughout pregnancy, and plasma volume decreased less than 4%. Fetal HRs after exercise increased 15 beats per minute (bpm) above resting values. It was concluded that thermal balance was well maintained by conditioned runners during pregnancy.

Clapp, Wesley, and Sleamaker (1987) studied 10 recreational runners 2 months before conception and at 19 to 22 weeks and 30 to 33 weeks of gestation. Each woman completed a 20-min steady-state run at her current training pace and intensity. Exercise intensity declined significantly as pregnancy progressed. Before conception, the subjects ran at 74% $\dot{V}O_2$max but at Weeks 20 and 32 at only 57% of the initial $\dot{V}O_2$max. Before pregnancy, rectal temperatures increased 1.5 °C (to about 39 °C) during the run. At both 20 and 32 weeks of gestation, the change in rectal temperature decreased in magnitude (an increase of 0.7 °C at 20 weeks and 0.4 °C at 32 weeks) and was accounted for by the decrease in exercise intensity; however, the rise in mean rectal temperature was, respectively, 22% and 38% less than expected. This suggests that the efficiency of heat dissipation may be increased during pregnancy. The investigators pointed out that similar mechanisms

are present in the physiological changes of pregnancy and in those of training and heat acclimatization. Further study of maternal temperature response to exercise seems warranted, particularly in untrained subjects.

No investigations were located on responses to exercise in the heat during pregnancy. However, because prolonged exercise in the heat is known to alter $\dot{Q}$ and blood flow distribution, it is probably best that pregnant women be very cautious about exercising in an environment that does not allow body temperatures to level off in proportion to exercise intensity. This could occur in hot-dry or warm-humid environments typical of the summer months.

Exercise Capacity During Pregnancy

No direct assessments of maximal physical working capacity have been made during human pregnancy. Submaximal exercise HRs show that exercise capacity is well maintained. However, the extra weight carried with pregnancy adds to the exercise effort; thus, in a practical sense, the apparent work capacity is reduced in many activities. At any rate, most exercise tasks would now require a greater percentage of maximal aerobic power. Exercise capacity is affected not only by $\dot{V}O_2$max, however, but also by somatic and psychic factors, including perception of effort;

Table 9.3   Summary of Maternal Changes With Pregnancy

Parameter	Percent increase	Percent decrease	Unchanged
Respiratory system			
Tidal volume	30-40		
Respiratory rate			x
Resistance of tracheobronchial tree		36	
Expiratory reserve		40	
Residual volume		40	
Functional residual capacity		25	
Vital capacity			x
Respiratory minute volume	40		

Parameter	Percent increase	Percent decrease	Unchanged
Cardiovascular system			
Heart			
Rate	0-20		
Stroke volume	20-30		
Cardiac output	40		
Blood pressure			x
Peripheral blood flow	600		
Blood volume	48		
Blood constituents			
Leukocytes	70-100		
Fibrinogen	50		
Platelets	33		
Carbon dioxide		25	
Standard bicarbonate		10	
Proteins		15	
Lipids	33		
Phospholipids	30-40		
Cholesterol	100		
Clotting factors I, VII, VIII, IX, X	x		
XIII		x	
Gastrointestinal system			
Cardiac sphincter tone		x	
Acid secretion		x	
Motility		x	
Gallbladder emptying		x	
Urinary tract			
Renal plasma flow	25-50		
Glomerular filtration rate	50		
Ureter tone		x	
Ureteral motility			x
Metabolism			
Nitrogen stores	x		
General stores of			
Sodium	x		
Potassium	x		
Calcium	x		
Oxygen consumption	14		

Note. From "Maternal Physiology" by E.J. Quilligan and I.H. Kaiser. In *Obstetrics and Gynecology* (4th ed., p. 339) by D.N. Danforth (Ed.), 1982, New York: Harper & Row. Reprinted by permission of Lippincott/Harper & Row.

143

subjectively, most women feel that they cannot maintain the same tasks as they did before pregnancy. Table 9.3 summarizes the maternal changes seen with pregnancy.

Physical Fitness and Pregnancy

How does one's physical fitness affect pregnancy? Do highly active women experience pregnancy differently than nonphysically fit women? Do physically fit women have fewer complications of pregnancy? Does maternal physical fitness benefit the fetus?

It seems logical to expect that a high level of physical fitness would enable a woman to better withstand the physical stresses of pregnancy. Unfortunately, these questions have not been systematically examined, and only one study was located that dealt specifically with physical fitness and pregnancy. In that investigation, women who were pregnant 35 to 37 weeks were given physical fitness scores (PFS) that were based on their $\dot{V}O_2max$ predicted from submaximal bicycle ergometer exercise (Pomerance et al., 1974). After delivery, correlation coefficients were calculated between PFS and numerous parameters. Physical fitness had a significant association with length of labor in multiparas (women having more than one pregnancy) but not in primiparas. Physically fit multiparas, however, tended to have shorter labors.

Physical fitness was not related to infant birth weight, length, head circumference, or Apgar score (a system used to evaluate the well-being of a newborn) or to length of gestation or complications of pregnancy. Birth weight was lower in infants born of women who smoked.

It is unfortunate that more information is not available regarding the benefits of an active lifestyle to pregnancy. The following two sections, however—one on training during pregnancy and the other on the long-term effects of exercise on pregnancy and childbearing—support my belief that in most cases strenuous exercise before and during pregnancy is not harmful to either the mother or the fetus and is generally beneficial to both.

Training During Pregnancy

Concern about the stresses of physical training during pregnancy is often voiced. Four studies (with control groups) of supervised exercise programs in women unaccustomed to regular exercise before pregnancy were located. They are presented here chronologically, and emphasis is placed on the physiological responses of the mothers.

Erkkola (1976) studied the influence of physical training during pregnancy on physical working capacity (PWC) on a bicycle ergometer. Two groups of pregnant women were studied. The training group performed strenuous exercise 1 h per day, three times per week, throughout pregnancy. They were instructed to raise HR to 140 bpm several times during the training hour. All subjects exceeded the 60-h exercise requirement, and some performed more than 80 h of training activities. Some of the exercises chosen were walking, running, climbing stairs, bicycling, swimming, and gymnastics (calisthenics?).

Increases in PWC were significant between the 10th and 38th weeks of pregnancy in both groups. In the control group, 94% of the improvement occurred between the 10th and 26th weeks and the remaining 6% between the 26th and 38th weeks. The increase in PWC in the training groups was 17.6% more than in the control group. With training, 73% of the total improvement occurred between the 10th and 26th weeks and 27% between the 26th and 38th weeks. The difference in PWC between the two groups was not significant until the 26th week of pregnancy. No negative effects from the training activities were observed.

Beginning in the second trimester, experimental subjects participated in a swimming conditioning program for 10 weeks, three times per week, with exercise HRs between 135 and 140 bpm (Sibley, Ruhling, Cameron-Foster, Christensen, & Bolen, 1981). A control group performed only their normal activities. Conditioning responses were assessed by estimating $\dot{V}O_2$max with the Balke treadmill test at 3.0 mph; exercise was terminated at the maternal HR of 142. The swimmers experienced a decline in aerobic capacity of 0.7% but increased their work rates by 6.2%. The control group decreased in both variables by 10.4% and 20.8%, respectively. The investigators stated that the findings demonstrate the effectiveness of swimming conditioning in countering a potential decrease in fitness with advancing pregnancy. In addition, they noted increased maternal well-being, appropriate weight gains in both groups, and high Apgar scores in the exercise group's babies.

Collings, Curet, and Mullin (1983) studied pregnant women who trained by cycling at 65% to 70% of their $\dot{V}O_2$max predicted from a submaximal exercise test. Each subject exercised 30 min, three times per week, for 14 weeks. A control group did not exercise regularly but was tested at the same periods (22 and 34 weeks) of gestation. The trained group's predicted $\dot{V}O_2$max (L · min^{-1}) increased 18% between the second and third trimesters. The control group declined by 4%. When these values were expressed per unit of body weight, the trained group increased by 8%, and the control group decreased by 10% at the third-trimester test. The investigators concluded that pregnant women are as trainable as their nonpregnant counterparts.

More recently, less dramatic results have been reported following 10 weeks of training on a cycle ergometer at 60% and progressing to 80% of the HR attained on a progressive exercise test to a minimum of 80% of maximal predicted HR (South-Paul, Rajagopal, & Tenholder, 1988). The exercise group increased its $\dot{V}O_2$ at maximal exercise by 225 ml, whereas the control group increased by 99 ml. The investigators concluded that pregnancy does not reduce aerobic power between the second and third trimesters of pregnancy and that improved efficiency in pulmonary function follows training.

In another study, training during pregnancy was shown to increase self-esteem and to decrease physical discomfort scores during pregnancy (Wallace, Boyer, Dan, & Holm, 1986). The exercise group reported significantly lower scores for symptoms of backache, headache, fatigue, shortness of breath, and hot flashes. There was a significant inverse relationship between amount of exercise and discomforts reported in the third trimester.

None of these studies dealt with women who were habitually active. How do women accustomed to an active lifestyle respond to strenuous exercise or training during pregnancy? Two studies were located that dealt with women who were physically active both before and during pregnancy. These reports are essentially case studies, and consequently the applicability of the results to the general population of pregnant women is somewhat limited. Nevertheless, the results are interesting and imply that strenuous exercise during pregnancy is not harmful.

Dressendorfer (1978) obtained an estimation of $\dot{V}O_2$max 1 day before delivery, 3 weeks postpartum, and at 2-1/2-month intervals throughout a second pregnancy. Distance-running performance was assessed by a 15-min-run test. At 3 weeks postpartum (first lactation period), the subject began a jogging program in which the weekly mileage progressively increased from about 10 to 35 mi when lactation ended and then to 50 mi at 14 months postpartum. The speed of running 1 mi also increased from about 12 to 8 min after 9 months. The subject became pregnant again 16 months after having her first child. Training mileage averaged 5 to 10 mi per week in the first trimester because of nausea, but thereafter she averaged 15 mi per week up to delivery. Training was resumed within 2 weeks of the second childbirth. Mileage was 20 mi per week at 4 months postpartum.

Figure 9.9 shows the effects of such training during pregnancy and lactation on $\dot{V}O_2$max and body weight. Childbirth had little effect on $\dot{V}O_2$max in this woman, although the weight-adjusted uptake increased 8% to 10% because of the loss of weight after each delivery. During the first lactation period, $\dot{V}O_2$max increased and body

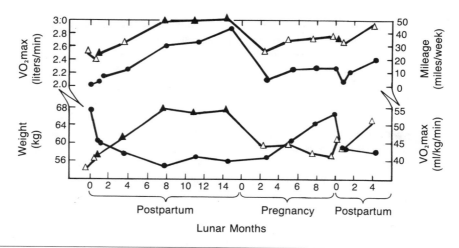

Figure 9.9 Effects of training during pregnancy and lactation on maximal oxygen uptake and body weight in a healthy women. Solid triangles show maximal oxygen uptake measured during graded treadmill exercise to exhaustion. Open triangles show maximal oxygen uptake obtained by extrapolation of the heart rate—oxygen uptake curve from values estimated to be about 90% of maximal. *Note.* From "Physical Training During Pregnancy and Lactation" by R.H. Dressendorfer, 1978, *The Physician and Sportsmedicine, 6*(2), p. 78. Reprinted by permission of *The Physician and Sportsmedicine.* Copyright McGraw-Hill, Inc.

weight decreased as the weekly mileage increased. Both variables plateaued after 8 months despite a continued increase in training mileage. The overall increase in $\dot{V}O_2$max during lactation was almost 25%. During the second pregnancy, $\dot{V}O_2$max was lower at the end of the first trimester, probably reflecting the reduced training mileage due to nausea. Part of this decrease was recovered later in pregnancy when the subject was able to increase her training mileage. The subject remained healthy throughout the investigation, and both pregnancies were normal and uncomplicated. Milk production was not affected by the high caloric cost and fluid loss of the running program. Obstetric and pediatric examinations indicated that all aspects of pregnancy, delivery, and lactation were normal. These findings indicate that endurance performance can be improved by strenuous physical training during pregnancy and lactation without having harmful effects on the mother or the child.

A similar study (Hutchinson, Cureton, & Sparling, 1981) involved a pregnant subject who had regularly engaged in running for 8 years before pregnancy. The investigators studied the metabolic and circulatory responses of this woman during monthly 10-min submaximal treadmill runs at 6 mph beginning at the third month of pregnancy. Ventilation, $\dot{V}O_2$, HR, and R at steady state increased substantially as the pregnancy progressed. The increase in $\dot{V}O_2$ was directly proportional to the weight gained, but HR, ventilation, and R were not. The investigators concluded that running became more stressful as the pregnancy advanced and recommended that pregnant women reduce their running speeds to maintain a constant level of physiological strain.

Long-Term Effects of Exercise on Pregnancy and Childbearing in Athletes

Concern about the long-term effects of strenuous exercise or training on pregnancy and childbearing has no basis. Myths abound about ruptured and sagging organs from jumping or falling. In reality, most studies indicate that women athletes are more likely to have normal pregnancies than sedentary women.

In the literature until the mid-1960s were two opinions about delivery in female athletes. One opinion held that extensive sport activity made the muscles of the pelvic floor and perineum rigid and led to difficulties during labor. The other opinion denied this supposition and emphasized the favorable effect of strengthened abdominal musculature during the second stage of labor. Erdelyi (1962) cited many European reports that supported the second opinion. His own clinical experience also confirmed that athletic women generally have shorter, easier labors than nonathletic women and completely normal deliveries. He studied 184 cases of pregnancy and delivery in 174 athletes. Complications of pregnancy were encountered in only 2.19%—less than in the nonathletic population. Threatened abortions did not reach the usual average, and those that did occur were not associated with sport participation. About two thirds of this sample continued their sport activities during the first 3 or 4 months of pregnancy. The duration of labor was shorter: 87% of the athletes delivered their babies faster than the established average age. The second stage of labor was completed in half the time considered average for nonathletes. Frequency of cesarean section was almost 50% less than in nonathletes, and forceps delivery also occurred with less frequency.

A pregnancy and maternity survey of Olympians at the Tokyo Games (Zaharieva, 1965) covered 13 women between the ages of 25 and 33 with sport careers ranging from 7 to 20 years. Most of the women had one pregnancy and one child. None of the athletes had spontaneous abortions. Pregnancy was normal in 91% of these women. In one case, delivery was prolonged over 48 h. Six had delivered without tissue ruptures, 6 had had ruptures, and 1 did not report data on this question. Ruptures were less common in the sportswomen than in working women and housewives. Most of these mothers reported resuming training 3 to 6 months following childbirth. The better athletes reported resuming training the earliest. The author concluded that childbearing was not a "barrier to top level performance" because 46% improved their performances by the end of their first year after childbirth. All the mothers in this study claimed they "became stronger, had greater stamina and were more balanced in every way after having a child" (p. 218).

More recently, Zaharieva (1972) reported data on the effects of participation in the Olympic Games on pregnancy and childbirth gathered over a period of 20 years (1952 to 1972). Pregnancy was totally normal in 70.4% of these athletes. Some felt more fit after childbirth than before (22.2%). Normal complaints of nausea, lack of appetite, or vomiting during the first stage of pregnancy were apparent in only 14.8%. The duration of the first phase of childbirth for the first child was identical to that for the nonathlete. The second, or expulsive, stage of childbirth was found to be 1.5 times shorter for the sportswomen. When protracted labor occurred among sportswomen, it was more frequent in the top performers than the more average performers. Zaharieva concluded that Olympic training and performance had no influence on the functional integrity of the sex organs and that the physical and functional condition of the athletes was actually improved after childbirth.

Jokl (1956) reviewed two European studies that dealt with childbirth in former participants in high-level athletic events. One study examined the obstetrical records of 94 Finnish women who had competed in national level baseball and swimming. The results included the following:

1. Major disorders during pregnancy were no more frequent among the athletes than among nonathletes.
2. The pelvic measurements of former champions did not depart from normal dimensions.
3. The athletes had shorter periods of labor (mean = 17 h, 27 min) than women who

had not competed in sports (mean = 21 h, 26 min).

4. The athletes had no disorders in uterine contractions or any indication that the elasticity of the cervix was lessened.
5. The incidence of tearing and of episiotomies was very low in the athletes.
6. The incidence of cesarean section, forceps use, manual removal of the placenta, or blood transfusion did not even approach the upper limit of what is considered normal.

Essentially, the same findings were reported for 107 outstanding German women athletes. In this group, the third phase of birth actually lasted half as long (1 h, 41 min) as in the control group. Fertility ratios of the ex-athletes were not different from those of the control data gathered from the Heidelberg Gynecological Clinic.

These reports should put to rest misconceptions about the "dangers" of long-term and strenuous sport performance to childbearing. Additionally, fears that sport participation during early adolescence may have an unfavorable effect on the development of the mature female bony pelvis are unfounded. Skeletal measurements by Erdelyi (1962) and Jokl (1958) indicated that pelvic dimensions of athletes, including former champion athletes, do not depart from normal in any way.

Another piece of information about the long-term effects of strenuous exercise on childbearing comes from Asia. To support their families, Japanese and Korean women divers, called *ama*, dive for pearls and for food year-round. In winter, the water temperature may be as low as 50 °F. They begin this profession as young girls and often continue until the age of 65. Childbearing does not interrupt their work (Hong & Rahn, 1967). A pregnant diver may work up to her day of delivery and thereafter nurse her baby between dives. There is no evidence that the diving women have different gynecologic or obstetric histories than the non-diving women of their communities. This is also true of former swimming competitors in the West. None of the subjects in the reports of Anderson (1965), Åstrand et al. (1963), or Eriksson et al.

(1978) had experienced obstetric, gynecologic, or fertility problems.

None of these studies are very current. As mentioned previously, present-day training practices and competitive schedules are much more strenuous and stressful than they were even 10 years ago. Although I do not believe that current athletic practices will prove harmful to women or their future obstetric concerns, I do believe that longitudinal data need to be collected on numerous variables before the question can be totally put to rest. In short, the old data may not apply to the athlete of today, and more current and complete data need to be collected on the long-term effects of strenuous physical training on menstrual function, fertility, and childbearing.

Exercise and Fetal Well-Being

This chapter would be incomplete without consideration of the fetus. Of major concern in the question of exercise during pregnancy is the safety and well-being of the baby. This discussion begins with a brief description of fetal development and then examines what research has indicated about fetal responses to maternal exercise.

Fetal Development

Fetal development may be divided into two distinct periods that follow the implantation of the zygote in the uterine endometrium. The *embryonic period* ranges from the third week to the eighth week and is the period during which the organs form. The *fetal period* extends from the ninth week until delivery and is the period of physiological development of the systems. Figure 9.10 illustrates the periods of human development. It indicates when an embryo or fetus is most susceptible to teratogens, or agents that may cause the development of malformations or functional abnormalities.

Gestation is more commonly divided into three parts (trimesters), each being 3 months in length.

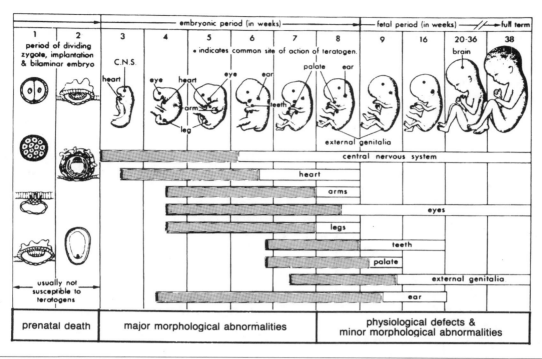

central nervous system

heart

arms

eyes

legs

teeth

palate

external genitalia

ear

Figure 9.10 The sensitive periods of human development in the uterus. The dark part of each horizontal bar indicates the most critical period in terms of the effects of a teratogen. The light part of the bar indicates a less sensitive stage. *Note.* From *Biology of Women* (p. 287) by E. Sloane, 1980, New York: John Wiley & Sons, Inc. Copyright © 1980 by John Wiley & Sons, Inc. Reprinted by permission of John Wiley & Sons, Inc.

The first trimester is a very critical period. By the end of this period, all the major organ systems are developed. The other two trimesters are primarily concerned with further growth and differentiation of the organs. At the end of the first trimester, the fetus weighs about 1 oz and is about the length of one's middle finger. By the end of the second trimester, the fetus weighs about 1-1/2 lb and is about the size of a closed fist. At term, the infant is about 20 to 21 in. long and weighs about 7-1/2 lb. In 9 months, the fetus increases in weight about 6 billion times! At that rate, a 10 year-old child would be 20 ft tall and outweigh the earth several trillion times (Sloane, 1980). Few studies dealing directly with fetal well-being have been completed because of the difficult nature of the research. Data

must be collected by noninvasive means so that the baby is not endangered. At this time, technology limits us to observing only a few variables.

Fetal heart rate (FHR) monitoring was developed as a clinical test to detect fetal distress and uteroplacental insufficiency. Severe bradycardia (less than 100 bpm), tachycardia (greater than 180 bpm), and loss of variability (slow responses) are clinically associated with poor fetal outcome (Lotgering, 1988). Accelerations and good variability are associated with well-being and good fetal outcome. Many studies have attempted to monitor FHR responses to maternal exercise and have had varying success. Maternal body movements can cause large artifacts, and FHR tracing may be difficult to interpret. The FHR responses varied, and only the investigations that were successful in monitoring FHR before, during, and after maternal exercise are reviewed here.

Dressendorfer and Goodlin (1980) studied FHR in third-trimester women who pedaled on a bicycle ergometer. Baseline FHRs averaged 142 bpm (range 135 to 152). The women exercised at 150, 300, 450, and 600 kpm • min^{-1} without fatigue (they all regularly participated in lap swimming). Maternal HRs rose to 146 bpm and $\dot{V}O_2$ to 1.85 L • min^{-1}. Fetal HR at peak exercise averaged 149 bpm ($SD = \pm 5$). Thus, although maternal HRs increased by 70 bpm, FHRs rose only 7 bpm. This means that FHR increased approximately 1 bpm for every 10 bpm increase in the mother. Collings et al. (1983) reported similar results during a 25-min cycling bout at 70% of maternal $\dot{V}O_2$max.

Transient fetal bradycardia was reported, however, during treadmill walking at 4 mph at an incline that elicited 80% predicted $\dot{V}O_2$max in the mother (Dale, Mullinax, & Bryan, 1982). This was described as an initial decline that continued for 2 to 3 min and was followed by recovery to normal ranges after 3 to 3.5 min. Fetal bradycardia was also reported when 6 subjects, who exercised at least twice per week during their pregnancies, cycled at 50% $\dot{V}O_2$max (Jovanovic, Kessler, & Peterson, 1985). Fetal HR before exercise was 142 bpm, decreased to 84 bpm during exercise, and rose to 143 bpm 1 min after exercise. Three of the fetuses had an average HR of 50 bpm during the 13 min of exercise. Although this is considered a lifethreatening event, recovery to a normal pattern occurred rapidly following exercise. Artal, Rutherford, Romem, Kammula, Dorey, and Wiswell (1986) obtained FHR at three levels of maternal exercise in 15 subjects. Mild exercise consisted of a 15-min walk at 2 mph (2.3 to 3.0 MET). For moderate exercise, the treadmill was elevated to a 10% grade (5 to 6 MET). Strenuous exercise consisted of a symptom-limited $\dot{V}O_2$max test at 2.5 mph with the treadmill grade elevated by 2% each minute. Bradycardia for at least 2 min was observed in 5 fetuses. In each instance, the bradycardia persisted beyond the exercise period.

Mean decreases in FHR were 9.7, 13.1, and 6.6 bpm for the mild, moderate, and strenuous exercise bouts, respectively. Paolone, Shangold, Paul, Minnitti, and Weiner (1987), however, concluded that apparent fetal bradycardia during maternal exercise is merely motion artifact from ergometer cycling and foot strides during walking. These investigators recommended M-mode echocardiography as the criterion method for monitoring FHR during maternal exercise.

Factors that might be related to FHR during and after maternal exercise include fetal arousal, placental transfer of elevated maternal catecholamines, maternal and fetal hyperthermia, and reduction in uterine blood flow. Fetal tachycardia *following* maternal exercise might be a compensatory response to undetected bradycardia *during* exercise.

Fetal Breathing Movements During Maternal Exercise

A transient and marked increase in fetal breathing movements during maternal exercise that did not elicit changes in FHR was observed by Marsäl, Löfgren, and Gennser (1979). The investigators suggested that breathing movement changes may be induced by acid-base variations that result from alterations in placental perfusion, increased catecholamines, or mechanical stimuli from maternal muscular tone. The breathing movements were not related to changes in maternal pH, PCO_2, or PO_2. Another group demonstrated a direct relationship between the level of sympathetic activity in the mother and the incidence of fetal breathing movements (Artal & Wiswell, 1988, p. 202). Because respiratory-like movements vary considerably with the activity of the fetus, it is not clear if the changes observed during exercise reflect the stress of exercise.

Fetal Injury During Maternal Exercise

The possibility of direct fetal injury caused by trauma during maternal exercise has been of major concern. No reports were located that dealt with this topic. None of the investigations or reports with which I am familiar have implied that there was any harm to the fetus. Most all the results from studies of maternal exercise or physical fitness were positive in terms of both maternal and newborn well-being.

Although some people believe that the jarring and jolting of maternal running may be detrimental to the fetus, most obstetricians point out that the amniotic fluid sac surrounding the fetus serves as a cushioning pillow. This issue remains unsettled, but so far fetal injury due to running or any other sport has not been reported despite the recent upsurge in athletic participation by pregnant women.

Uterine Blood Flow During Exercise

An adequate supply of well-oxygenated blood is essential for the fetus. Sudden and severe decreases in its supply is likely to cause hypoxic damage, whereas more chronic reduction may result in delayed development. Most of the information about fetal oxygenation and uterine blood flow comes from the study of animal models (pregnant sheep or pygmy goats). The data set is complicated and confused, so only the results that have been verified by replication are summarized here (for individual references, see the reviews cited in the introduction to this chapter).

The human fetus produces hemoglobin with an affinity for oxygen that differs from that of the mother. The fetal oxyhemoglobin dissociation curve is shifted to the left of that of maternal blood and consequently has an increased affinity for oxygen. Normal fetal umbilical venous blood actually has a higher oxygen content than the maternal blood. Apparently, the increased extraction of oxygen by fetal tissues compensates for the slight reduction (about 10%) in umbilical blood flow that occurs during exhaustive maternal exercise.

Although the dilated uterine vascular bed is less sensitive to vasoconstrictive agents than in the nonpregnant state, it responds to sympathetic stimulation and to circulating catecholamines and prostaglandins. Not all studies agree, but the consensus is that uterine blood flow decreases during exercise (possibly in direct relation to exercise intensity), perhaps as much as 59%. To compensate for reduced total blood flow to the uterus, blood flow within the uterus is redistributed. The decrease in blood flow to the uterine wall (myometrium) is greater than that to the placenta. Therefore, although a decrease in uterine blood flow during exercise seems likely to be detrimental to the fetus, several mechanisms may protect the fetus:

1. More oxygen is extracted by fetal tissues.
2. Uterine blood flow is redistributed to favor the placenta.
3. Hemoconcentration of maternal blood during exercise increases the oxygen content of the blood. The consequent delivery of oxygen to the uterus is only slightly lower during exercise than at rest.
4. The pregnant uterus compensates for reductions in oxygen delivery by increasing the extraction of oxygen from the blood.

The net result of these mechanisms is that the reduction in oxygen delivery is much smaller than the decrease in uterine blood flow would suggest. It appears that uterine and umbilical $\dot{V}O_2$ are constant.

Effects of Maternal Exercise on Offspring

Several studies were located that dealt with the effects of maternal exercise on offspring. Usually in such studies the stress on the pregnant animals was more extreme than most pregnant women would subject themselves to or researchers would impose. Perhaps, too, fear of electric shock or of drowning contributed to some of the responses seen. It is not possible to differentiate between responses due solely to exercise and responses due to the "flight-or-fight" mechanism.

In one study (Buffington, Newman, Bonner, Acosta, & Farrar, 1977), cultures were grown from the heart cells of 5-day-old neonatal offspring of exercised and control rats. In the cultures grown from the exercised rats, beating rates were reduced 19% to 26%, cell size was 27% greater, and the percent of single-cell contractility was elevated 18% to 26%. These cultures also colonized more rapidly and appeared more densely granulated than the cultures from the control rats. These results suggest that exercise during pregnancy may improve cell viability and produce hypertrophy in the cardiac cells of neonatal offspring.

No advantage, however, was transferred to offspring in terms of oxidative, glycolytic, or contractile properties of skeletal muscle (Corbett, Brassard, & Taylor, 1979). Endurance training during pregnancy had no effect on myosin adenosine triphosphatase (ATPase), succinate dehydrogenase (SDH), or phosphofructokinase (PFK) of the soleus, plantaris, or gastrocnemius muscles of 18-day-old rats.

The most thorough study of offspring was reported by Wilson and Gisolfi (1980). Four groups of rats were studied: T-T rats were trained before and during pregnancy, NT-T rats were trained only during pregnancy, T-NT rats were trained before but not during pregnancy, and C rats were not trained at all. Training was done by running the rats on a treadmill at 80% to 88% $\dot{V}O_2$max. The T-T rats had higher aerobic capacities than the NT-T rats (who were trained at a lower intensity during pregnancy) and the C rats. The exercised mothers (NT-T, T-T) had increased skeletal muscle cytochrome oxidase activity and ratios of left-ventricular weight to total heart weight.

Offspring mortality during the first 28 days was greater in the T-T group than the C group. This may have resulted from either increased susceptibility to death in the offspring or maternal factors. Both maternal neglect and maternal cannibalism were observed. The effect of electrical shock (to which the T-T mothers were exposed during pregnancy) on the offspring is unknown. Body dimensions and organ weights of offspring

were not different between the groups at 45 to 65 days. These data suggest that postuterine growth was not compromised by maternal exercise during pregnancy. Unfortunately, body weights and dimensions were not determined at birth.

Maternal exercise had no influence on $\dot{V}O_2$max in the offspring or on myocardial blood flow. Capillary density and fiber-to-capillary ratios were not different. Apparently, the mothers who exercised either before or during pregnancy did not "endow" their offspring with greater aerobic capacity.

Exercise and Pregnancy Outcome

Recently, meta-analysis was used to objectively and statistically integrate findings from 16 studies published between 1976 and 1988 on the effects of exercise training on pregnancy outcome (Lokey, 1988). Meta-analysis allows one to compile results from numerous investigations to form a complex data set. Statistical procedures are then used to organize and summarize data that would otherwise be impossible to review in an objective manner. This section reviews the results of Lokey's study. Only a few of the references she used are cited here (Berkowitz et al., 1983; Clapp & Dickstein, 1984; Collings et al., 1983; Dressendorfer, 1978; Erkkola, 1976; Hall & Kaufmann, 1987; Jarrett & Spellacy, 1983b; Kulpa, White, & Visscher, 1987; Ruhling et al., 1981; Sibley et al., 1981; Slavin, Lutter, Cushman, & Lee, 1988).

Exercise was characterized as occurring an average of 3.3 times per week at an HR of 144 bpm (which represented 81% of HRmax and 68% $\dot{V}O_2$max) for 43 min. Exercise modes included jogging, cycling, swimming, calisthenics, and weight training.

Table 9.4 is a compilation of Lokey's (1988) data, which represent 2,284 pregnant women (1,337 who were exercising, and 947 nonexercising control subjects). Only three significant differences were found between these two groups of subjects: The nonexercising subjects were higher

Table 9.4   Effect of Exercise on Pregnancy Outcome

Variable	Exercise group	Control group	Significance
Age (y)	28.2 (3.0)	26.8 (2.6)	N.S.
Height (m)	1.66 (.02)	1.66 (.01)	N.S.
Weight (kg)	56.5 (3.4)	62.1 (2.6)	$p < .01$
Weight gain (kg)	12.7 (1.8)	14.4 (0.6)	$p < .006$
Length of gestation (wk)	39.7 (1.1)	40.0 (0.2)	N.S.
Length of labor (h)	9.7 (4.7)	8.0 (0.0)	N.S.
Birth weight (gm)	3,397.6 (181.8)	3,545.2 (180.9)	$p < .07$
APGAR (1 min)	8.2 (1.0)	7.8 (1.1)	N.S.
APGAR (5 min)	9.2 (0.3)	8.7 (0.7)	N.S.
Cesarean delivery (%)	9.0	15.5	N.S.
Vaginal delivery (%)	91.0	84.5	N.S.
Pregnancy complications (#)			
Anemia	3	—	—
Prolonged labor	5	5	—
Meconium-stained amniotic fluid	16	31	—
Unexplained bleeding	15	—	—
Premature membrane rupture	9	11	—
Hypertension	2	—	—
Pitocin augmentation	6	4	—
Spontaneous abortion	5	—	—
Orthopedic	13	0	—

Note. Values are expressed as means. Standard deviations are in parentheses. N.S. = not significant. Data from Lokey (1988).

in prepregnancy body weight and weight gained with pregnancy, and they had heavier babies. Weight gain was 1.6 kg less for the exercising mothers; however, both groups were within the optimal range for weight gain (10 to 14.5 kg). No differences were found between groups in length of gestation, length of labor, condition of the child at birth (Apgar score), or rate of cesarean deliveries. Infants from both groups were very close to the 50th-percentile classification of newborn infants by birth weight and gestation (Jensen & Bobak, 1985, p. 1087).

Table 9.4 also shows the number of complications that occurred within each group. Twenty-four percent of the exercising subjects experienced complications during pregnancy or delivery com-

pared to 39% of the nonexercising subjects. This was not statistically significant. Prolonged labor occurred more frequently in the exercising subjects (6.6% compared to 3.3%). One infant mortality was reported in an exercising subject.

In conclusion, no detrimental effects of the intensity and duration described by these studies could be attributed to maternal exercise. Lokey concluded that a pregnant woman should be encouraged to remain physically fit by exercising during her pregnancy.

What does all this mean to the pregnant woman? The following summary is an informal treatment of the practical aspects of exercise during pregnancy and is written for the athlete, her coach or exercise leader, and interested others.

Advice on Exercise
for the Pregnant Woman

None of the evidence indicates any contraindications to exercise during normal pregnancy. Apparently, the mother and fetus are well equipped to tolerate the relatively minor reductions in cardiac reserve or uterine blood flow experienced with exercise. This statement is especially true for women who are physically fit before pregnancy. However, because most of the located studies on human subjects dealt with relatively short-term exercise, the effects of strenuous and prolonged exercise are still unknown.

In 1985, the American College of Obstetricians and Gynecologists (ACOG) introduced its *Guidelines for Exercise During Pregnancy and Postpartum*. Basically, the guidelines for exercise during pregnancy state that maternal HR should not exceed 140 bpm, strenuous activities should not exceed 15 min in duration, exercise should not be performed in the supine position after the fourth month, the Valsalva maneuver should be avoided, and maternal core temperature should not exceed 38 °C.

The ACOG guidelines have been debated within the medical and scientific communities. Many believe that these guidelines are too stringent for previously active women and that they are based on opinion and not data. Others say that the guidelines are too basic to be of use to anyone. Still others fear that the guidelines will become "a legal standard" in malpractice and litigation cases (Gauthier, 1986). Defenders of the guidelines say that they were written for the "average" woman, not for the sedentary and definitely not for the woman with a history of exercise. They also state that it is far better to err on the conservative side and that pregnant women were formerly without standards for exercise.

It is my opinion that, although they are somewhat helpful, the ACOG guidelines are too arbitrary. Ideally, exercise programs for pregnant women should be individualized, and habitually active women should continue their normal patterns of exercise and modify them as pregnancy progresses. As discomfort occurs, most women will follow the dictates of their perceived exertion levels and gradually slow down or shorten exercise periods in the latter months of pregnancy. Goal setting and a competitive attitude should be avoided, and care should be taken to avoid overheating and dehydration. This is essentially the position of the Melpomene Institute in Minneapolis. More specific recommendations for runners and swimmers can be found in Slavin et al. (1988), "Pregnancy and Exercise" (in *Sport Science Perspectives for Women*, edited by J. Puhl, C.H. Brown, & R. Voy. Champaign, IL: Human Kinetics).

Basically, a woman (whether pregnant or not) should listen to her body. Everyone is different, and what happens to one might not happen to another. If one experiences considerable discomfort, then either the intensity or the duration of exercise should be reduced. Problem signs include any evidence of vaginal bleeding or high blood pressure. Pain, membrane ruptures, or absence of fetal movements are warning signs that a physician should evaluate immediately.

Many changes will occur as pregnancy progresses. Weight gain is a natural occurrence and should not be avoided. A gain of around 20 to 24 lb will, of course, make exercise more difficult, especially weight-bearing exercise. House-cleaning activities, climbing stairs, jogging, and even walking responses will be altered. Heart rate will be higher, and there will be periods of breathlessness. Postural changes will occur to compensate for the added weight on the lower front of the trunk. The pregnant woman will find herself off balance more often than usual until she learns to adjust to this extra load. Sometimes backaches occur from increased lumbar lordosis (swayback). Although I found occasional mention in the literature of ligamentous relaxation and increased sacroiliac and pubic joint mobility with pregnancy, I was not able to find any mention of these variables in relation to exercise performance. Apparently, few women exercise strenuously enough during pregnancy to injure themselves. Whether this is because of needless avoidance of exercise during pregnancy or to wise management of exercise activity is unknown.

Part of a woman's weight gain during pregnancy and lactation results from changes in the breast. Usually, bra size increases one or two sizes. Most women will find bra support essential at these times, especially if exercise activities involve bouncing or jarring.

Sometimes, because cardiac reserve is reduced during pregnancy, blood will pool in the legs. Rhythmic exercise should aid venous return to the heart, whereas static forms of exercise may accentuate the problem. Periodic elevation of the legs will relieve this symptom, as will wearing stretch hose. One study mentioned that wrapping the legs with elastic bandages (Ace bandages) to prevent venous pooling in the upright posture caused immediate improvement in exercise tolerance (Bruce & Johnson, 1961).

During lactation, most women notice an increase in thirst. It is well known that the thirst mechanism is not sensitive enough to prevent dehydration in the heat or during exercise, so care should be taken to drink plenty of fluids both during and following exercise.

Obstetricians generally favor appropriate exercise during and following pregnancy. In fact, Gendel (1967) has reported that chronic lower backache and fatigue following pregnancy can be relieved (in patients without organic cause) by gradually improving physical fitness. Gendel is convinced that lack of physical activity and sport participation leads to underdeveloped, poorly toned abdominal musculature and weak fascial tissue—a major factor in chronic and severe lower backache following pregnancy.

How Much Exercise During Pregnancy?

Basically, the amount and type of exercise engaged in during pregnancy should be decided on in consultation with a physician. Pregnancy is not the time to begin a strenuous training program or to decide to lose weight, but sedentary women can gradually increase their physical activity during pregnancy without harm. Highly trained athletes might find it desirable to decrease their training schedules. Generally, there is no need to restrict exercise during the first 3 to 4 months. During the fifth and sixth months, it may be desirable to reduce exercise somewhat. If one regularly jogs, perhaps walking at a fast pace would be better. During the seventh to ninth months, most active women reduce their activity to light recreational activity.

Does Pregnancy Influence Athletic Performance?

Reportedly, three gold medal winners in the 1956 Olympics (Melbourne) were pregnant ("Pregnancy and Sports," 1974), and in 1952 a pregnant diver won third place (Bruser, 1968). Two pregnant athletes participated in the 1956 Olympics, one in discus and the other in weight lifting. Bruser (1968) cited many other athletic feats accomplished by pregnant athletes. Some women have completed marathons during their eighth month of pregnancy. Usually pregnancy has no effect on athletic performance up to the first 2 to 3 months. After the first trimester, an athlete may not do so well and may stop competing. After about the fourth month, most athletes stop competing ("Pregnancy and Sports," 1974). Erdelyi (1976) has pointed out that many athletes have competed and won medals without knowing they were pregnant. He does not object to competition for the pregnant athlete until about the third month. After that, he believes that each situation should be judged individually. Coaches should not pressure athletes into competing during pregnancy. A conservative approach is best, and pregnant athletes definitely should not try to prove anything by competing in strenuous sports during advanced gestation.

Twenty-four women who ran during pregnancy reported that they felt well, believed that running had bolstered their physical and mental condition, and thought that it had decreased the pain of their labor. The women ran an average of 26 mi per week, but only two raced while pregnant ("Women Say," 1981). Some of these women reported physical discomfort during running (backaches, breast soreness, fatigue, and increased urinary frequency) but said that these problems were associated with pregnancy and not running. Two miscarriages that may or may not have been due to running occurred in this group of women.

Performance After Pregnancy

Many well-known athletes have returned to competition after bearing children. Their performances indicate that childbearing is not a deterrent to athletic performance. Fanny Blankers-Koen, a Dutch track star, won three gold medals in the London Olympics after bearing two children, and Andrea Mead Lawrence won a gold medal after having her children ("Pregnancy and Sports," 1974). More recent examples are Margaret Smith Court, who won three legs of the Grand Slam of Tennis in 1973, 1 year after she had her first child; Evonne Goolagong Cawley, who won the Australian Open and Wimbledon after giving birth; Valerie Brisco, who won three gold medals in track at the 1984 Olympics when her son was 2 years old; Evelyn Ashford, who ran the best 100-m time in 1986, less than 10 months after giving birth; and Ingrid Kristiansen, who set new records in the 5,000-m, 10,000-m, and marathon runs after giving birth (Brownlee, 1988). Although these women's success could have been due to physiological factors such as stronger legs, a higher cardiac output, a larger blood volume, and improved heat dissipation, perhaps a psychological effect made the real difference. Many athletes feel that the pain of labor helps them discover mental and emotional resources that they never knew they had before they gave birth. Whether these phenomena are "real" awaits scientific validation.

According to Erdelyi ("Pregnancy and Sports," 1974), most athletes can return to competition in 5 to 6 weeks if the pregnancy was uncomplicated. Thomas points out that athletes should probably avoid cesarean section if possible ("Pregnancy and Sports," 1974) as the abdominal musculature is important in almost any athletic endeavor. The healing time required for an abdominal incision and severed abdominal muscles would mean that an athlete could not resume training as quickly as after a normal delivery.

Caveats Regarding Pregnancy and Exercise

Sometimes exercise and athletic competition cause skeletal or muscular injuries, aches, and pains. Physicians often prescribe anti-inflammatory agents to relieve these symptoms, but it is probably not a good idea to take anti-inflammatory drugs (even aspirin) during pregnancy as they may harm the fetus. Any physician who attends to a pregnant sport competitor should be made aware that she is pregnant.

Taking X rays during pregnancy is another problem. Many exercise injuries would be impossible to treat appropriately without a diagnostic X ray. Again, the attending physician and the X ray technician should know that the patient is pregnant. X rays of the abdominal region of a woman in early pregnancy may be hazardous to the fetus.

Physicians disagree whether swimming during the late stages of pregnancy is wise. Some believe that the cervix may be open during the last stages of gestation (especially in women who have had previous pregnancies) and may allow water to enter. Others doubt this and cite a study by Siegel (1960) (see chapter 7) that indicates that water does not enter the vagina either before or after delivery. Probably no danger is associated with swimming during pregnancy, but the best course of action is to consult the attending obstetrician. However, it is not wise to jump into water feet first or to water-ski during pregnancy because water could forcibly enter the vagina with these activities.

Summary

There appears to be no contraindication to exercise during pregnancy. It is best to take a conservative approach in matters so serious, however, and recommend physical activity in moderation relative to the mother's physical fitness and usual activity pattern. A few gynecologists, however, are braver than most and recommend that the pregnant athlete "be encouraged to continue her training so long as it is possible and reasonable for her to do so, and she ought to be encouraged to resume her training as soon as possible after parturition" (Bruser, 1968, pp. 724-725).

Chapter 10

Exercise and the Menopause

Menopause, that feared period of life that for some women represents a profound life crisis, refers rather simply to the cessation of menstrual function. The word comes from the Greek words for *month* and *cessation* and is sometimes used interchangeably with the broader term *climacteric* (from the Greek words meaning *rung of the ladder* and *critical time*). Actually, menopause refers specifically to the final menstrual period and is the biological marker of a gradual but persistent decrease in reproductive function that precedes the cessation of menstruation by about 15 years.

The climacteric (which occurs in men as well as women) is the gradual change from the reproductive to the nonreproductive stage of life (Sloane, 1980; Utian, 1980), a process that takes about 3 decades to fully accomplish. The climacteric really refers to all the time-related events associated with ''the change in life.'' In women, the early climacteric years occur between the ages of 35 and 45 (Notelovitz, 1988). The *perimenopause* represents the middle period of the climacteric and is the term used when characteristic symptoms and signs of ovarian failure are present (Gosden, 1985), usually around ages 46 to 55. In the United States, menopause typically occurs at about ages 50 to 51 and the late climacteric period from ages 56 to 65. Most people incorrectly use the word *menopause* to describe a vague period that is near the close of menstrual life. The more precise usage of these terms is used throughout this book.

The climacteric is often a difficult time of life. As some women emerge from childbearing age, they experience a change in social status, and their infertility becomes a great matter of concern to them. For these women, menopause is associated with being old and unwanted, with a loss of usefulness, with wrinkles and gray hair, with the end of the best time in one's life, and finally with the end of womanhood. These women tend to view fertility as femininity. They are the unfortunate victims of many cultural and societal attitudes and myths. They have succumbed to the Madison Avenue concept of ''youth culture.'' Much has been written on the adverse attitudes and conceptions of menopause (see, e.g., Delaney, Lupton, & Toth, 1976; Parker, 1960; Weideger, 1976).

Other women look forward to this period of life as being a release from the burdens of childbearing age and look forward to becoming freer, more fully active members of society. Some societies (unlike our own) reward women for having reached the end of the fertile period and welcome them into full cultural equality (Utian, 1980).

Whatever the woman's attitude toward or concept of menopause, some things in her life may change at about this period of life. For example, she may lose one or both of her parents; her children may leave home (college or marriage); she may become a mother-in-law, a grandmother, or both; or her husband may become ill. The single woman may suddenly find that her career is not as fulfilling as she once thought. Life's events (see

Sheehy, 1976) take on different meanings at different ages, and sometimes the menopausal years trigger severe psychological or emotional crises. This book, however, is not about the mental and emotional meanings of life but about the physiological events and responses that occur in a woman's life. Nevertheless, some of the profound physiological changes that occur with the climacteric and menopause have significant interactions with the mental and emotional meanings of life.

The remainder of this chapter outlines most of the responses or changes in body function that occur during the climacteric in women, emphasizes those changes that affect one's health and responses to exercise during and following this period, and discusses the role of exercise in the prevention or amelioration of climacteric symptoms.

Physiology of the Climacteric

The actual mechanism of menopause is not fully understood. Menstruation stops when ovarian hormonal secretion diminishes to the extent that it is insufficient to inhibit the pituitary gonadotropins FSH and LH. At that time, FSH and LH levels rise significantly, and the hypothalamic-pituitary-ovarian feedback system is altered so that the normal menstrual cycle stops (Sloane, 1980). The process of ovarian failure begins gradually (over a period of 5 to 10 years), and anovulatory cycles progressively increase during the perimenopause. This is usually attributed to irregular recruitment from a dwindling pool of follicles due to ovarian aging (Gosden, 1985). The concept of aging as a biological clock has been proposed to explain such peripheral organ failure (exhausted ovary theory), but the mechanism could lie in the hypothalamus. Research has yet to determine whether the loss of hypothalamic sensitivity to feedback information could be due to a loss of estrogen receptors.

Regardless of the etiology of menopause, certain facts have been well established, the most significant of which is that the loss of reproductive function is manifested by an absence of cyclic estrogen secretion. In addition, there is an elevation of FSH and LH for about 1 decade after menopause. These hormones are approximately 13 and 3 times higher, respectively, than in the early follicular phase of cyclic women (Gosden, 1985, p. 86). It is unclear if the elevated gonadotropins result from increased hormone production or decreased metabolic clearance.

Estrogen Levels Following Menopause

During the first few months following menopause, significant quantities of estrogen are produced intermittently from residual follicles that grow sporadically but fail to reach maturity. Plasma estrogen eventually falls, leveling off at approximately 20 mg · ml^{-1} for the remainder of life (Gosden, 1985, p. 28). The different forms of estrogen do not fall proportionately. Estrone becomes the most abundant estrogen of the postmenopausal period, and the ratio of plasma estradiol to estrone declines to levels characteristic of castrated women (0.42) and men (0.35) rather than of menstruating women (>1.0). Clearly, the circulating estrogens are no longer controlled by the gonadotropins following menopause.

The ovarian contribution to the circulating estrogens is insignificant in most postmenopausal women. The adrenal glands produce a large quantity of androgens (mainly androstenedione, DHEA and DHEAS, and some testosterone) plus a little estrone. Most of the circulating estrone is formed by the extraglandular conversion of adrenal androstenedione. The primary site for the conversion (aromatization) of androgen to estrogen is adipose tissue (for a discussion of aromatization of androgen to estrogen by adipose tissue and skeletal muscle, see chapter 8, pp. 108-110).

Circulating levels of both estrone and estradiol are significantly related to body weight and excess fat in postmenopausal women (Gannon, 1985, p. 156), presumably because of the increased rate of conversion made possible by larger amounts of fat.

In addition, body weight is negatively correlated with sex hormone–binding globulin (SHBG), a protein that binds estradiol, rendering it biologically inactive. Therefore, body fat has a dual effect on estrogen levels in that excess fat results in increased conversion of the androgens to estrogens, and lower levels of SHBG result in more biologically active estrogen. Presumably, this accounts for fewer menopausal symptoms such as hot flashes and osteoporosis (see following discussion) in obese postmenopausal women than thin women (Gannon, 1985, p. 157). It is possible to have too much estrogen, however. Excess estrogen in the postmenopause is associated with obesity as well as hepatic disease and hyperthyroidism. This is considered a risk factor for carcinoma of the endometrium and possibly of the breast (Gosden, 1985, p. 33).

With advancing age, androgen levels eventually drop because the adrenal glands become less sensitive to ACTH (Gosden, 1985, p. 30). Some refer to this as the *adrenopause* to contrast with the period of rising androgen levels of prepuberty called the *adrenarche* (see chapter 4). As body wasting advances because of aging, the aromatization of androgens to estrogens decreases, and estrogen levels decline further.

Effects of the Climacteric

The effects of chronological aging are difficult to distinguish from the biological effects of hormonal changes associated with the menopause. Nevertheless, the declining endocrine function of the ovaries is thought to affect many tissues and systems.

Changes in the Reproductive System

The two cardinal findings in postmenopausal women are the presence of low tonic estrogen output in conjunction with an elevation of the serum gonadotropins FSH and LH. Although estrogen levels in menopause are low, circulating estrogen is present, and peripheral estrogenic effects continue to be manifested (Jones & Wentz, 1977). The marked menstrual irregularity of the perimenopause represents the irregular maturation of ovarian follicles, which may or may not result in ovulation (Chang & Judd, 1981). For a time, vaginal bleeding may occur without a measurable increase in progesterone. This is characteristic of the perimenopause.

The effects of estrogenic deficiency are both immediate and delayed. The more or less immediate effect is the loss of menstrual cycling; other effects develop gradually. For example, epithelial tissues are affected. This includes atrophic thinning of the vaginal lining from 8 to 10 to 3 or 4 cell layers, and the vagina shrinks in both length and width. An impaired transudate response results in vaginal dryness, which leads to a change in microbial flora, a rise in pH above 5.0 (vaginal secretions are normally acidic with a pH in the range of 3.5 to 4.5), a higher risk for bacterial infection (vaginitis) manifested by itching and burning, and possibly pain during intercourse.

The uterus is reduced to less than one quarter of the dimensions it had as a fully functioning organ. The menopausal endometrium is atrophic, and the epithelial cells and glands are thin, flattened, and nonproliferating. Endogenous (or exogenous) estrogen can stimulate atrophic endometrial glands to proliferate and cells to hypertrophy even when progesterone is absent. This can lead to adenomas and adenocarcinomas in later life. Also, the oviducts shorten, cell linings thin, and the cilia gradually disappear.

The lower urinary tract undergoes essentially the same changes as the vagina. Estrogen deficiency may result in *stress incontinence* (loss of small amounts of urine on coughing, laughing, straining, jumping, or running), which is a result of the thinning and shrinking of the urethral epithelium and walls. Atrophic cystitis and urethritis may result. Because the vulvar skin is sensitive to the absence of estrogen, the labia majora and minora and the mons pubis shrink, and pubic hair becomes scant. The strength and elasticity of the muscles and ligaments of the pelvis are also affected. Pelvic muscle tone lessens, and prolapse of the uterus, bladder, or vagina can occur (see chapter 7, p. 105). Most of these atrophic changes can be reversed with estrogen replacement therapy (by means of a pill or skin patch) or vaginal application of creams or suppositories that contain estrogen.

Most women experience gradual changes in breast tissue during the climacteric. Glandular tissue gradually shrinks as estrogen and prolactin are lost. Fatter women will not experience as much change in breast size as leaner, smaller breasted women, but their breasts will become more pendulous.

Changes in the Circulatory System

One of the classic symptoms of the climacteric is the presence of *hot flashes* (flushes). When hot flashes occur at night, they are called *night sweats*. A hot flash, or *vasomotor flush*, is a sensation of warmth that usually starts in the face and progresses to the neck and chest. The skin surfaces over these regions of the body become reddened (flush). The sensation of heat is followed by a drenching sweat, an increase in heart rate, increased skin conductance indicating vasodilation, a rise in skin temperature, a decease in core temperature (Gannon, 1985; Gosden, 1985), and sometimes chills and shivering. At night, hot flashes are associated with waking episodes that contribute to the insomnia experienced by some perimenopausal women. The whole episode is over in 1 to 5 min.

The precise relationship between blood estrogen and hot flashes is still unclear. Generally, however, plasma estrogen levels are similar in women with and without these symptoms (Gannon, 1985, p. 175). Hot flashes occur at about the same time as the pulsatile release of LH, but it is not thought that LH pulses are the causal variable (Gosden, 1985). The current theory is that the hot flash is triggered by a hypothalamic mechanism that is the result of inappropriate activity of the central thermoregulatory mechanisms (Gosden, 1985, p. 130). The hot flash may be initiated by a transient fall in the set point of the hypothalamic thermostat, indicating that heat must be dissipated and peripheral changes effected that will lead to a lower core temperature (thus the sweating and vasodilation). The prevailing thought is that a decrease in catecholestrogen (a product of metabolizing estrone and estradiol in the hypothalamus) affects the stability of thermoregulatory synapses.

Hot flashes occur to some extent in nearly 85% of all perimenopausal and early postmenopausal women (Bates, 1981) but lessen with age. This annoying and embarrassing symptom, more than any other associated with menopause, drives women to seek the therapeutic relief of estrogen replacement therapy (ERT). The dramatic relief experienced with exogenous estrogen has made ERT the usual treatment of choice.

Cardiovascular Disease Risk

Cardiovascular disease is the leading cause of death among women in the United States, accounting for about 250,000 deaths annually. The two- to fourfold sex differential in mortality rates (Wingard, Suarez, & Barrett-Connor, 1983) has led to the popular notion that estrogen in some way "protects" the woman from cardiovascular disease. World Health Organization data from 1980 provide the following male-to-female ratios for annual mortality rates from coronary heart disease (CHD) in the United States:

Age (yr)				
35-44	45-54	55-64	65-74	> 75
4.3:1	4.1:1	3.0:1	2.2:1	1.3:1

Data from Johansson, Vedin, and Wilhelmsson (1983).

The decrease in the sex differential in mortality rates from CHD with advancing age has led to the notion that CHD increases markedly following menopause. However, careful study of mortality rates from CHD shows that the risk for females increases steadily with age and that there is no abrupt upward trend at the time of menopause but rather a gradual and steady increase (Jones &

Wentz, 1977). A recent prospective cohort study of a large sample of U.S. women who were followed for 6 years concluded that after age and cigarette smoking were controlled statistically, women who had had a natural menopause and who had never taken replacement estrogen had no more risk for CHD than premenopausal women (Colditz et al., 1987).

Nevertheless, whether the occurrence of menopause alters the risk of CHD remains controversial. Ryan (1976) observed that the decline with age of the sex advantage of women is due to a slower increment in the men's death rate than the women's and found no evidence that the natural menopause places women at greater risk. The death rate of men at an advanced age is thought to be incrementally less because of a prior "weeding out" of a coronary-prone group.

Oophorectomy (removal of the ovaries, also called *ovariectomy*) has been postulated as a predisposing factor for CHD. Ritterband, Jaffe, Densen, Magagna, and Reed (1963) studied oophorectomized women and a similar group of women who were undergoing hysterectomy without removal of the ovaries. They reported no difference in arteriosclerotic cardiovascular disease and myocardial infarction. More recent studies, however, support the hypothesis that women who have undergone bilateral oophorectomy and never taken estrogen have an increased risk for CHD (Colditz et al., 1987). The use of estrogens in these women appeared to eliminate the risk. These investigators concluded that, in contrast to a natural menopause, bilateral oophorectomy increased the risk for CHD, which could be prevented by ERT.

Menopause has been implicated in an increase in some of the identified risk factors associated with CHD. Both cross-sectional and longitudinal studies have shown that postmenopausal women have higher serum lipids (specifically increased serum cholesterol and triglycerides) and that more postmenopausal women smoke than other women (Johannsson et al., 1983). Notelovitz (1988, p. 164) reported age- and menopause-related increases in serum cholesterol as follows:

Age (yr)	Serum cholesterol (mg $\cdot$ dl^{-1})
35-34	170.5 $\pm$ 4.3
46-55 (menstruating)	203.2 $\pm$ 7.6
46-55 (nonmenstruating)	233.8 $\pm$ 5.9
56-65	230.1 $\pm$ 6.9
66-75	238.8 $\pm$ 6.7

A differential effect of menopause on serum cholesterol levels was found between black and white women in Georgia (Johnson, Heineman, Heiss, James, & Tyroler, 1986). Premenopausal total cholesterol levels were similar; however, after menopause, white women had a 20 mg $\cdot$ 100 ml^{-1} larger increase than black women. In this investigation, mortality from cardiovascular disease was significantly associated with systolic blood pressure in all women and with serum cholesterol in white women.

The causes of CHD are far from clear. The gradual upward trend of CHD with middle age in both men and women is thought to be related to risk factors including genetic endowment, hyperlipidemia, diabetes mellitus, obesity, hypertension, smoking, physical inactivity, and psychological stress. These multiple variables make it difficult to study the influence of menopause on CHD. Regular exercise before, during, and after the menopausal years is thought to counter several of these risk factors. Consequently, a lifestyle that includes a regular program of exercise is probably preventive for the development of heart and vascular disease in the menopausal years as well as in other stages of life (further discussion follows).

Changes in the Skeletal System

Hot flashes, genital atrophy, and osteoporosis are the three principal consequences of ovarian failure. Of these, osteoporosis represents the greatest health hazard to postmenopausal women (Worley, 1981). According to the National Institute of Arthritis, Diabetes, and Digestive and Kidney Disease, at least 15 million Americans have some degree of osteoporosis. At high risk for this epidemic disease are white, postmenopausal women, of whom it is estimated one out of four will experience fractures related to osteoporosis by age 65. About 150,000 hip fractures occur each year in the United States as a consequence of osteoporosis. Of this number, approximately 12% to 20% will die as a result of factors directly attributable to hip fracture (immobilization following a fracture may result in complications such as lung collapse or pneumonia). Only one third of the survivors will regain normal activity.

The economic consequences of osteoporosis are staggering. Short-term, direct costs for patient care are predicted to exceed 1 billion dollars annually. The total cost of osteoporosis has been estimated to be 7 to 10 billion dollars. As the world's population continues to live longer, it is anticipated that osteoporosis will become an even greater public health problem than it is today.

Osteoporosis means literally *holes in the bone*. The increased porosity of bone results from an excess of bone loss over bone formation and leads to increased fragility of bone. Osteoporosis is a chronic skeletal disorder associated with aging. Although peak bone mass is reached in both sexes at approximately age 35, the rate of bone loss after that is greater in women and is especially associated with menopause. Women over the age of 50 who are still menstruating lose bone mass at a lesser rate than postmenopausal women of comparable age.

Risk for Osteoporosis in Women.   Osteoporosis is eight times more common in women than in men. The primary reasons for this follow (National Dairy Council, 1984):

1. Women consume less calcium throughout their lives than do men (see chapter 12).
2. Women have less bone mass than do men because of their smaller body size and weight (i.e., less stress on bones).
3. Bone loss accelerates at menopause.
4. Pregnancy and breast feeding may lower a woman's skeletal reserve of calcium.

5. Women are more likely than men to go on weight-loss diets, which are typically low in calcium.

6. Women live longer than men, so they have an increased chance of developing osteoporosis.

Osteoporosis is less common in black women than in white women. This might be due to the black woman's larger body frame and muscle mass.

A number of risk factors for osteoporosis have been identified (USDHHS, 1986):

1. Being a woman, particularly a white woman of northern European descent
2. Early menopause (before age 45)
3. Chronic low calcium intake
4. Lack of physical activity
5. Being underweight
6. Family history of osteoporosis
7. Smoking cigarettes
8. Excessive use of alcohol (it is not known how much alcohol is too much)
9. High intake of caffeine-containing foods such as coffee
10. Extremely high protein intake
11. Consuming a high-fiber diet (reduces the benefits of calcium intake)

The Physiology of Bone.   Living bone is a dynamic tissue that is constantly being rebuilt, or *remodeled*. Old bone is *resorbed* (broken down) and replaced with new bone to keep the skeleton strong enough to withstand mechanical stress and to maintain the body's balance of essential minerals such as calcium. *Osteoblasts* and *osteoclasts* are the cells responsible, respectively, for the storage (deposition) and release (resorption) of the mineral within bone tissue. Hormonal and mechanical factors influence the activity of osteoblasts and osteoclasts.

Bone is not completely solid; rather, spaces in bone tissue accommodate blood vessels and nerves. The two types of bone structure found in the skeleton are trabecular and cortical bone. *Trabecular* (cancellous) *bone* consists of an irregular lattice network that is spongelike in appear-

ance. It predominates in the axial skeleton (i.e., the vertebral bodies) and the ends of long bones (e.g., the neck of the femur and the distal radius). *Cortical* (compact) *bone* consists of a more intricate network of tissue that is formed in a regular and consistent pattern. It is more solid than trabecular bone, and it constitutes the outer walls of the long bones (i.e., in the appendicular skeleton). Cortical bone is more abundant than trabecular bone as it composes 80% of the total skeletal mass (see Figure 10.1).

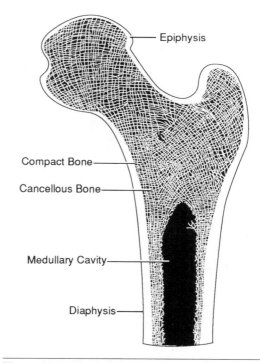

Figure 10.1   Cortical (compact) and trabecular (cancellous) bone. From *Functional Human Anatomy* (2nd ed., p. 82) by J.E. Crouch, 1972, Philadelphia: Lea & Febiger. Reprinted by permission of Lea & Febiger.

Differences in the structure and the distribution of these two forms of bone are of particular importance in the etiology of osteoporosis. Type I, or postmenopausal, osteoporosis is related to accelerated bone mineral loss in trabecular bone and often to the onset of menopause. Type II, or senile, osteoporosis has been attributed to the loss of both trabecular and cortical bone and is associated with advanced age.

In its most serious form, osteoporosis results in a predisposition to fractures. The principal sites are shown in Figure 10.2. When fractures occur in the thinned and weakened vertebrae that support the body weight, a progressive decrease in height and bending of the spine results. Approximately 25% of all white women over age 60 have spinal compression fractures that are due to osteoporosis (Vaughn & Hammond, 1981). A gradual loss of height and the formation of a so-called dowager's hump (humpback) with advanced age are common (Figure 10.3). One of the most severe consequences of osteoporosis is hip fracture due to complications of immobilization at advanced age. By age 90, a woman's risk of hip fracture has increased to 90% (Sloane, 1980).

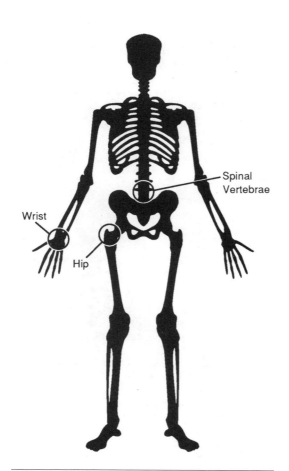

Figure 10.2 Three principal sites of osteoporotic fractures. *Note.* Adapted from National Dairy Council (1984).

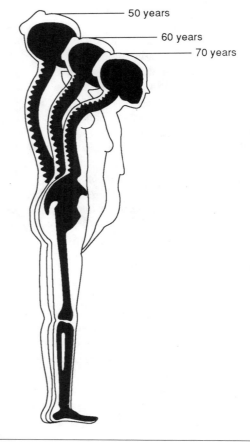

Figure 10.3 Loss of height with development of the dowager's hump with osteoporosis. *Note.* From *Calcium: A Summary of Current Research for the Health Professional*, courtesy of National Dairy Council® (1984, p. 16). Rosemont, IL: National Dairy Council.

Clearly, two practical issues need to be addressed:

1. Women need to acquire as much bone as possible before menopause (through exercise, a good diet, and other health-promoting habits).
2. The rate at which bone is lost after menopause needs to be reduced (again through exercise, good diet, health-promoting habits, and ERT).

Although age is clearly related to the loss of bone mineral, the hormonal factor seems to be the most important. Richelson, Wahner, Melton, and Riggs (1984) compared women (age 54) who had undergone oophorectomies during young adulthood, normal perimenopausal women (age 52), and normal postmenopausal women (age 73). Compared with the perimenopausal group, the other two groups had significantly lower bone mineral density at the midradius, femoral neck, femoral intertrochanteric area, and lumbar spine. It was concluded that estrogen deficiency rather than aging was the dominant causal factor.

The rate of bone formation is associated with several hormones. Parathyroid hormone and calcitonin are reciprocally involved in bone resorption and formation. Estrogen antagonizes the action of parathyroid hormone by decreasing glycolysis and interfering with citric acid formation (Jones & Wentz, 1977). Estrogen thus decreases the responsiveness of bone to endogenous parathyroid hormone and so decreases bone decalcification and resorption. Consequently, the loss of estrogen due to menopause accelerates bone loss. When administered before the onset of active osteoporosis, estrogen may delay the active phase of bone loss, cause a positive calcium balance, and reduce bone resorption. Because bone formation is not increased, the result of 3 to 9 months of estrogen therapy is a stabilized turnover rate of bone at a new level without a significant increase in net bone mass. There is no evidence that estrogen administration can totally prevent osteoporosis; it merely slows it down. Because of the controversy surrounding the risks of hormone replacement therapy (see the section on ERT), alternative treatments are being tested, including the administration of calcium, fluoride, vitamin D supplements, high-protein diets, and exercise programs (Sloane, 1980).

Changes in the Skin and Hair

Aging brings noticeable changes in the skin and hair. The presence of estrogen receptors in certain elements of the skin (in mice, anyway) suggests that estrogens have a direct effect on skin. With aging, there is a generalized thinning of the skin and a loss of water and elasticity that results in wrinkling. Skin also becomes more pigmented, an effect that is accelerated by regular exposure to the sun's ultraviolet rays. Head hair usually thins and grays with advanced age. However, as with other characteristics and responses to aging, there is a great deal of interindividual variability.

Menopausal Symptoms

In summary, multiple and extensive changes occur with the climacteric and menopause. The associated low estrogen level leads to atrophy of the breasts, labia, uterus, and urethral and vaginal epithelia. There is an increased susceptibility to vaginitis, bladder infections, and uterine prolapse. The fall in estrogen may be responsible for a rise in plasma low-density lipoprotein cholesterol, which in turn may be related to cardiovascular disease. Osteoporosis is an organic change in the bone associated with low estrogen levels and is seen in nearly all elderly women.

Besides the cardinal symptoms of the menopause (vasomotor flush and dryness and thinning of the vaginal walls) are a group of additional problems referred to as the *menopausal syndrome*. This includes fatigue, nervousness, sweating, headaches, insomnia, depression, irritability, joint and muscle pain, dizziness, palpitations, and formication (a feeling that is often said to be like ants crawling on the skin). Table 10.1 provides a partial listing and frequency of menopausal symptoms,

Table 10.1   Frequency of Symptoms During the Climacteric

Symptom	Incidence (%)
Flushing	67.0
Depression	38.5
Sweating	31.0
Insomnia	26.0
Atrophic vaginitis	20.0
Fatigue	18.5
Headache	11.0
All other	<10.0

Note. From "Limited Relationship of Maturation Index to Estrogen Therapy for Menopausal Symptoms" by S.A. Kaufmann. Reprinted with permission from the American College of Obstetricians and Gynecologists. (*Obstetrics and Gynecology*, **30**, 1967, p. 399.)

the severity and frequency of which are thought to be either the direct result of estrogen withdrawal or the result of biological changes that are induced by estrogen withdrawal.

Just as the physical and psychological reactions to the aging process are variable, so is the physical and psychological impact of the change in life. As a result, the clinical implications of menopause are usually considered from a symptomatic point of view.

Estrogen Replacement Therapy

Physicians often prescribe estrogen replacement therapy (ERT) for relief of troublesome symptoms. Both benefits and risks are associated with ERT.

Benefits of ERT

There is no question that ERT can control hot flashes and reduce vaginal and urethral symptoms (Gannon, 1985; Kase, 1987; Ragni, DeLauretis, Bestetti, Wyssling, & Crosignani, 1987; Stoppelli, Zanconato, & Guacci, 1987). Regardless of the method of administration, ERT has been shown to increase circulating estrogen levels and reduce the gonadotropins. In general, estrone increases to a greater extent than estradiol because the intestines and liver convert estradiol to the less active estrone. Vaginal (as opposed to oral) administration changes blood estrogen less but provides greater relief of vaginal symptoms. Empirical observations suggest that ERT can alleviate psychological disturbances as well. Although there is no evidence that the use of ERT is justified in the treatment of primary psychological problems, decreases in sleep latency and waking episodes and increases in sleep length and rapid-eye-movement (REM) sleep do occur. These effects are apparent in women with severe flashes, suggesting that these benefits may be secondary to the relief of hot flashes.

The estrogen compounds are "antibone resorbers in postmenopausal osteoporosis" (Chesnut, 1984, p. 44). The estrogen effect on bone health is two-fold: It has an overall effect on calcium balance because of improved intestinal calcium absorption and it retards bone mineral loss. Although ERT does not result in the restoration of lost bone mass, it significantly slows bone resorption. Therefore, for ERT to be effective in preventing osteoporosis, it must be instituted before serious loss of bone mineral has occurred. Women receiving ERT at menopause have significantly fewer osteoporotic fractures than women who never receive exogenous estrogen.

Exogenous estrogen use has been associated with a lower risk of mortality from all causes and most strongly in women reporting oophorectomy (Bush et al., 1983). Some of this benefit was accounted for by increased levels of high-density lipoprotein cholesterol (HDL-C). Numerous studies have shown that exogenous noncontraceptive estrogens increase HDL-C (which is associated with reduced risk of CHD) and reduce low-density lipoprotein cholesterol (LDL-C) and total triglycerides (Bush & Barrett-Connor, 1985). Therefore, many consider that ERT provides protection from ischemic heart disease.

Recent prospective studies have supported the hypothesis that postmenopausal ERT reduces the risk of severe CHD among postmenopausal women (Stampfer et al., 1985) and among women who have undergone bilateral oophorectomy (Colditz et al., 1987). Not all studies agree, however. In the well-known Framingham Heart Study (Wilson, Garrison, & Castelli, 1985), mortality from all causes and from cardiovascular disease did not differ between postmenopausal estrogen users and nonusers (this topic is more extensively reviewed by Bush & Barrett-Connor, 1985).

In summary, the benefits of ERT are the following:

- Control of hot flashes
- Reduction of vaginal and urethral symptoms
- Improved bone health (antiresorption)
- Increased HDL-C

Other agents have been shown to be effective in treating some climacteric symptoms. These include progestagens for hot flashes and calcitonin for the prevention of osteoporosis. Exercise has also been shown to prevent or retard osteoporosis.

Risks Associated With ERT

In the 1960s and 1970s when postmenopausal ERT was first introduced, the most commonly pre-scribed regimen was conjugated equine estrogen (Premarin) and was given without a progestin. At that time, the major benefits were thought to be decreased risks of osteoporosis and cardiovascular disease. However, considerable evidence began to show that exogenous estrogen treatment was associated with an increased risk of developing endometrial or breast cancer. Today there is general agreement that unopposed postmenopausal estrogen (i.e., estrogen given without a progestin) promotes endometrial growth (a known risk factor for endometrial carcinoma) and that the risk is dose related. Predisposing factors include obesity, hypertension, diabetes, and nulliparity (Barrett-Connor, 1987; Gannon, 1985). It is also known that the use of an orally active progestational agent (usually medroxyprogesterone) almost entirely prevents estrogen-induced endometrial growth.

The consensus is that sequential low-dose estrogen-progestin users are not at increased risk of developing either endometrial or breast cancer (Barrett-Connor, 1987; Cameron, 1982; Gambrell, Maier, & Sanders, 1983). However, there has been concern that the use of a progestin, which alone induces unfavorable serum lipid and lipoprotein changes, would negate any beneficial effects of ERT on CHD. A recent study compared different methods of administering estrogen and progestin in menopausal women and found that the sequential procedure (conjugated equine estrogen from Days 1 to 25 and medroxyprogesterone acetate from Days 16 to 25 of each 28-day cycle) did not induce adverse changes in the serum lipids (Luciano, Turksoy, Carleo, & Hendrix, 1988). It was concluded that *the sequential use of estrogen and progestin replacement therapy may be of therapeutic value against atherogenic disease as well as protect against endometrial growth.*

Figure 10.4 shows the death rates of U.S. women from myocardial infarction and breast and endometrial cancers. Heart disease is by far the most common cause of death in postmenopausal women. Although comparable data are not available for the death rate due to osteoporotic fracture, it most certainly exceeds that for endometrial

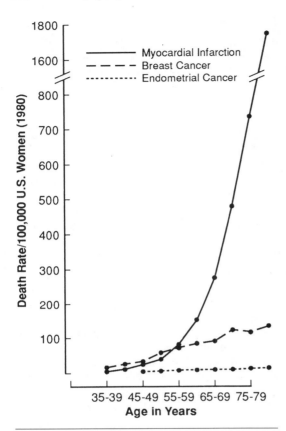

Figure 10.4 Death rates of U.S. women from myocardial infarction, breast and endometrial cancers. Appearing on p. 181 of Barrett-Connors, E., "Postmenopausal Estrogen, Cancer and Other Considerations." *Women and Cancer*, Vol. 11(3-4) of *Women and Health*, New York: The Haworth Press, 1987, pp. 179-195. Copyright 1987 by The Haworth Press. Reprinted by permission.

cancer (Barrett-Connor, 1987). In the final analysis, when one balances the benefits of ERT in preventing menopausal symptoms and osteoporosis against the possible risks, it is my opinion that the benefits far outweigh the risks.

Response to Exercise During the Climacteric

Studies of the relationship between aging and response to exercise in men are numerous, and a long list of declining responses can be compiled. With advancing age, there is a gradual degeneration in the man's physical working capacity and maximal heart rate, oxygen uptake, and cardiac output. A few studies have documented these functional decrements for women as well. The purpose of this section, however, is to compare exercise responses in pre- and postmenopausal women. This is a difficult task for the following reasons:

- There are very few investigations of exercise response in women aged 45 to 55.
- Most of the studies located studied either younger women (below 40) or older women (above 60).
- A few studies grouped subjects into decade age-groups but did not provide a statistical analysis decade by decade.
- The studies located were of cross-sectional design (rather than longitudinal) with all the inherent difficulties in the interpretation of the results.
- Few studies of middle-aged women differentiated between menstruating and postmenopausal women.
- Studies of aging always have multiple hidden variables that may or may not be related to aging itself (e.g., body weight, physical activity level, fatness, dietary differences, and genetic endowment).

With these limitations in mind, we turn to the following section, which focuses on reports of women in their 40s and 50s—the perimenopausal and early postmenopausal years, respectively.

Wessel, Small, Van Huss, Anderson, and Cederquist (1968) reported a consistent trend for higher oxygen uptake ($\dot{V}O_2$), oxygen pulse, and ventilation with increasing age for treadmill walking at 3.0 mph. They concluded that this trend reflected a decline in the ability to adjust to exercise stress with increasing age. They presented their data by age decades but provided no statistical analysis. There did not appear to be much difference, however, between the 40- to 49- and the 50- to 59-year age-groups in any of the variables they studied.

A more recent study reported essentially the same results (Zauner et al., 1984). Perimenopausal women (mean age 48.7) were studied to determine cardiorespiratory efficiency at work intensity equivalent to that required for daily activities. Their responses were compared to those of a younger group (mean age 24.7). The middle-aged women had higher $\dot{V}O_2$, higher heart rate (HR), and a higher ventilation. These results were interpreted to indicate a relative inefficiency in the middle-aged women.

The concept of a critical age of decline in physiological function has been studied for some time. Self-paced walking speed has been used as an index of "slowing down" in numerous studies of men. A recent study (Himann, Cunningham, Rechnitzer, & Paterson, 1988) showed that the age of 62 coincided with an accelerated decline in speed of walking in both men and women, an age well beyond the menopausal years. Age-group regression lines revealed little change between the ages of 40 and 59 in the female subjects.

Muscular strength and endurance was evaluated in a group of masters swimmers aged 24 to 71 (Dummer et al., 1985). Grip strength declined 16% from ages 30 to 39 through age 60, but differences among the age-groups were not statistically significant. Peak torque that was developed during knee and shoulder flexion and extension movements did not differ between the 40- to 49- and the 50- to 59-year age-groups. Although these swimmers experienced a decline in muscular strength as a function of advancing age, there was no indication that this gradual process was altered by menopause.

Kenny and Anderson (1988) compared the responses of postmenopausal women (mean age 56 years) with those of younger women (20- to 30-year-olds) to exercise in hot-dry and warm-humid heat without fluid replacement. In each environment, the postmenopausal women stored more heat as evidenced by their higher rectal temperatures. Four of these women were unable to complete some of the heat-stress exposures despite prior acclimation. In the hot-dry (but not the warm-humid) condition, the postmenopausal women's whole body and local sweat rates were

significantly lower than those of the younger subjects. Sweating did not appear to be limited at the sweat gland level as high local sweat rates could be artificially elicited. It was concluded that the ability of the sweat glands to maintain a high sweat rate was not diminished by sweat gland atrophy with aging skin; rather, this ability was due to the relative intolerance of the postmenopausal women to dehydration. This deserves further study, particularly because so many women beyond the age of 50 engage in endurance competition.

Aerobic Power During the Menopause

A large group of mostly sedentary women (only the data of the women in their fifth and sixth decades are discussed here) were tested for maximal aerobic capacity using the Bruce treadmill protocol (Profant et al., 1972). Maximal oxygen uptake ($\dot{V}O_2$max) decreased significantly from the fifth to the sixth decades ($p < .05$), as did maximal heart rate (HRmax). The overall decline in $\dot{V}O_2$ (from ages 20 to > 60) averaged 0.2 ml $\cdot$ kg^{-1} of body weight annually, confirming the inexorable decline in functional aerobic capacity with advancing years.

Although the $\dot{V}O_2$max values in this study sample indicated generally low cardiovascular fitness levels, the active women in each age-group (40 to 49 and 50 to 59) outperformed the sedentary women in $\dot{V}O_2$max and performance duration. Maximal HRs were virtually identical for active and sedentary women, but the active women had higher oxygen pulse values (milliliters of oxygen consumed per heartbeat). The average exercise duration and $\dot{V}O_2$max values of active 40- to 49-year-olds were higher than for the sedentary 30- to 39-year-olds; active 50- to 59-year-old women had values similar to the sedentary 40- to 49-year-olds. This demonstrated the "protective effect of approximately one decade of age in active women as noted before men" (Profant et al., 1972).

Three years following this study, Drinkwater, Horvath, and Wells (1975) determined how age and physical activity patterns affected women's

Table 10.2 Physiological Responses to Maximal Exercise in Women Above ($> M$) and Below ($< M$) Mean $\dot{V}O_2$max Values in the Fifth and Sixth Decades

Age	M	$\dot{V}O_2$max(L $\cdot$ min^{-1})	$\dot{V}O_2$max(ml $\cdot$ kg^{-1} $\cdot$ min^{-1})	$\dot{V}_E$BTPS (L $\cdot$ min^{-1})	HR	O$_2$pulse (ml/beat)
40-49	$> M$	2.36 ± 0.11	39.22 ± 0.74	82.6 ± 4.22	179 ± 7	13.2 ± 0.5
	$< M$	1.80 ± 0.05	29.52 ± 0.74	65.18 ± 1.76	177 ± 2	10.2 ± 0.3
50-59	$> M$	2.01 ± 0.18	34.64 ± 2.61	60.67 ± 2.61	176 ± 4	11.3 ± 1.2
	$< M$	1.55 ± 0.12	23.66 ± 1.41	56.58 ± 4.08	180 ± 6	8.6 ± 0.6

Note. From " Aerobic Power of Females, Ages 10-68'' by B.L. Drinkwater, S.M. Horvath, and C.L. Wells, p. 387. Copyright 1975 by the Gerontological Society of America. Adapted by permission of *The Journal of Gerontology*, Vol. 30, No. 4, 1975. Values are means ± standard deviations.

responses to maximal exercise (see Table 10.2). Within each age-group, the women were divided into two activity classifications: those above and those below the combined age-group means reported for Canadian and Scandinavian women. Generally, the $\dot{V}O_2$max values of this sample exceeded those found by Profant et al. (1972), indicating a higher level of cardiovascular fitness. In particular, the active subjects had $\dot{V}O_2$max values approximately 10 ml $\cdot$ kg^{-1} of body weight higher than the "moderately active" subjects of Profant et al. (1972).

Women who were above the mean aerobic power for their age-group also had a significantly lower body weight and body surface area than those below the average $\dot{V}O_2$max. Among other cardio-respiratory variables measured, only maximal ventilation volume ($\dot{V}_E$), oxygen debt, and post-exercise lactate discriminated significantly between the two activity groups. There were no differences in HRmax, excess carbon dioxide, or ventilation equivalent for oxygen. Pre- and postexercise hemoglobin, hematocrit, or plasma protein values did not differ between the high- and low-fitness groups.

Some aging effects were evident regardless of fitness category. The 40- to 49-year-old women had lower $\dot{V}O_2$max than the women in the three younger groups, and the 50- to 59-year-old women were lower than all the other groups whether $\dot{V}O_2$max was expressed in absolute or relative terms. Maximal ventilation volume dropped in the fifth decade. There were no significant changes in HRmax beyond the age of 30.

The authors of this study did not find a steady decrement across time but rather a plateau for many variables during the years from 20 to 49 and a sharp decrement from age 50 on. In other words, the effect of age was minimal up to age 50. The authors further noted that the 50- to 59-year-old group ($n = 12$) included 9 women who were past the menopause. Four of those were above average and five below average in fitness level.

Plowman, Drinkwater, and Horvath (1979) essentially repeated the previous study with 36 of Drinkwater's original sample some 6 years later.

This study added a longitudinal dimension to the study of the effects of age on aerobic power. Again, all age-groups showed a decrease in aerobic power expressed in liters per minute and relative to body weight but not when expressed relative to lean body mass. Because body weight remained constant but percent body fat increased, the decrease in aerobic power was "related to a decrease in utilization of oxygen due to loss of muscle tissue" (p. 519). The active women in their 40s "still maintained a cardiovascular endurance level comparable to that of sedentary 20 year olds" (p. 519). Despite their decline in aerobic power, the active women increased their walk time to exhaustion, whereas the sedentary women decreased their endurance time.

Blair, Lavey, Goodyear, Gibbons, and Cooper (1984) studied physiological responses to graded exercise in a large group of healthy women between the ages of 18 and 75. Essentially the same treadmill test protocol was used as in the studies of Drinkwater et al. (1975) and Plowman et al. (1979) discussed previously. Unfortunately, only estimated $\dot{V}O_2$max values were reported. Treadmill times used to estimate $\dot{V}O_2$max declined approximately 10% per decade, whereas HRs averaged 5 bpm lower per decade. The estimated $\dot{V}O_2$max values were somewhat lower than those reported by Drinkwater et al. (1975)—31 ml $\cdot$ kg^{-1} $\cdot$ min^{-1} for the 40- to 49-year-olds and 29 ml $\cdot$ kg^{-1} $\cdot$ min^{-1} for the 50- to 59-year-olds—and it appeared that these subjects were neither very physically active nor particularly fit.

Notelovitz, Fields, Caramelli, Dougherty, and Schwartz (1986) directly measured $\dot{V}O_2$max in healthy sedentary women using the same treadmill protocol. A decrement of 5.5% occurred with each succeeding decade between the ages of 35 and 75. However, the loss of aerobic power was not related to the menopause. A subgroup of subjects aged 45 to 55 were divided into premenopausal and postmenopausal groups and performed a bicycle ergometer test. No significant difference was found in their estimated $\dot{V}O_2$max values: 27.4 ± 6.3 versus 26.3 ± 4.7 ml $\cdot$ kg^{-1} $\cdot$ min^{-1}, respectively.

Body composition and $\dot{V}O_2$max were studied in two subsets of masters female swimmers ranging in age from 20 to 70 (Vaccaro et al., 1984). Only the data for the 40- to 49- and the 50- to 59-year-old groups are discussed in this chapter. The subjects classified as not highly trained (NHT) weighed more, were somewhat fatter, had higher HRs and systolic blood pressures at each stage of the treadmill test, and had higher HRmax and lower $\dot{V}O_2$max values than the trained (T) subjects. The 50- to 59-year-olds did not differ significantly from the 40- to 49-year-olds.

In summary, most of the studies discussed here reported a gradual decline in aerobic power with increasing age. Drinkwater, et al. (1975) showed a plateau up to about age 50 and then a decline. Blair et al. (1984) noted a plateau between 20 and 40, after which significant differences across age-groups appeared. The data of Vaccaro et al. (1984) and Notelovitz et al. (1986) indicated no plateau in values. Close examination of all these data revealed very little difference between the 40- to 49- (mostly premenopausal women) and the 50- to 59- (mostly postmenopausal women) year-old age-groups. It appears that the menopause does *not* significantly affect maximal aerobic power, but natural biological aging does. Still, more definitive studies should be conducted on this question.

Physical Training During the Menopausal Years

Few studies have dealt with the effects of menopause on responses to physical training. Most of the training studies reviewed here included a few middle-aged women but never stated which women were pre- or postmenopausal. Those studies are discussed in chapter 14 (Adaptation to Training). This section focuses only on those investigations that identified women as pre- or postmenopausal.

The effects of 6 months of either aerobic dancing or walking were examined in 51 postmenopausal women with a mean age of 56 (White et al., 1984). All training was performed four times per week for approximately 33 min at a mean HR of 116 bpm (about 70% of their predicted HRmax). Both groups showed significant increases in performance time to an HR of 145 bpm on a modified Balke treadmill test. Resting and recovery HRs decreased, as did rate-pressure products. There were no premenopausal women or a control group in this study.

Following a 9-week progressive walking program, premenopausal (mean age 41.3) and postmenopausal (mean age 55.7) women improved their submaximal $\dot{V}O_2$ at 80% age-adjusted HRmax by 12.1% and 19%, respectively (Cowan & Gregory, 1985). Both groups also experienced favorable changes in body composition. The two control groups did not improve in aerobic fitness or body composition. The investigators concluded that there was no difference in the relative trainability of these women due to menopausal status. It is unfortunate that this well-designed study did not directly measure $\dot{V}O_2$max.

Notelovitz (1988) reported that postmenopausal women (mean age about 55) who trained by treadmill walking or bicycle ergometry at the Center for Climacteric Studies (Gainesville, FL) increased their $\dot{V}O_2$max by 8.9% and 12.4%, respectively.

Interval bicycle ergometer training at 85% of age-predicted HRmax three times per week was used to assess plasma lipid fractions in a group of sedentary postmenopausal women whose mean age was 50.25 (Perry, Tapp, & Weeks, 1986). Their responses were compared to comparably aged sedentary men. Training caused a significant increase in estimated $\dot{V}O_2$max, but the women's plasma lipid responses were minimal—no change in very low density lipoprotein cholesterol (VLDL-C) or HDL-C and a 2% decrease in LDL-C—when compared to those of the men. However, the women's initial lipid profiles were surprisingly good (HDL-C = 66%), and it has been well established that individuals with the least favorable lipid profiles make the most beneficial changes following physical training.

Although these data are rather sparse, it appears that middle-aged women respond well to exercise training whether they are pre- or postmenopausal. It is hoped that a more definitive investigation of this topic will be completed soon.

Effects of Exercise on Menopausal Symptoms

With the exception of osteoporosis, little was located in the literature regarding exercise and its effects on menopausal symptoms. Pros (1962) reported in a rather vague abstract that almost none of the 85 climacteric sportswomen (aged 46 to 57) he clinically observed suffered "serious climacteric complaints." He also stated that exercises "leading to great exhaustion" were "unsuitable." Still, many of his subjects were "on top of their class," and I wonder how they could maintain that performance if they did not perform exhausting exercise at least occasionally.

Hot Flashes, Anxiety, and Exercise

Although documented evidence is not yet available, some researchers think that women who exercise regularly do not experience as many or as severe hot flashes as do women who are sedentary. If this is so, the basis for this effect is not clear. However, there could be several mechanisms. If the hot flash is stimulated by a sudden release of catecholamines, an exercise effect could be due to a lowering of catecholamine release. Regular exercise is known to reduce plasma catecholamine levels, which is one reason exercise is effective in reducing some forms of anxiety and depression.

If the hot flash is due to estrogen deficiency, then a possible explanation for a reduction in this symptom is that blood levels of both estrogen and progesterone are increased following exercise (Bonen et al., 1979; Hall et al., 1975; Jurkowski et al., 1978; see also Chapter 8, pp. 110-114). Possibly, regular exercise lessens the degree of perimenopausal estrogen deficiency.

If the basis of the hot flash is a pulsatile elevation in LH, then regular exercise might alleviate the hot flash by reducing LH concentrations. Dale, Gerlach, and Wilhite (1979) reported lower resting LH levels in runners than in occasional joggers or sedentary controls.

One study (Wallace, Lovell, Talano, Webb, & Hodgson, 1982) indicated that exercise can change the climacteric symptomatology in postmenopausal women and may delay the onset of menopause in premenopausal women. Two groups of women were classified as pre- or postmenopausal with 55% of the postmenopausal women experiencing symptoms of mild flushing. The women engaged in a 6-week conditioning program four times per week with exercise intensity set at 70% of maximal capacity using target HR determinations. Both groups significantly increased $\dot{V}O_2$max and decreased percent body fat. Estradiol increased significantly in both groups, and the postconditioning estrone-to-estradiol ratio for the postmenopausal women was characteristic of premenopause. Severity of flushing increased in 36% of the postmenopausal women and remained unchanged in 18%. The investigators suggested that physical conditioning may delay the onset of menopause through mechanisms that increase serum concentrations of estradiol.

Coronary Heart Disease and Exercise

Men who are more physically fit have previously been shown to have lower risk for CHD. This relationship appears to hold true for women as well, but far fewer studies of this relationship in women have been conducted.

At the Cooper Clinic, a large group of white, healthy, middle-class women were given a maximal treadmill test using the modified Balke procedure (3.3 mph) (Gibbons, Blair, Cooper, & Smith, 1983). Treadmill exercise time was used to determine physical fitness level. Multiple linear regression was used to control for the effects of age, weight, and year of exam on CHD risk factors. After adjustment, physical fitness was independently associated with triglycerides, HDL-C, total cholesterol/HDL-C, blood pressure, and cigarette smoking. The investigators concluded that their data support what was previously found in men, that is, that physical fitness is related to HDL-C levels in women. The strongest association with fitness was the relationship between fitness and total cholesterol/HDL-C, the factor most believe may be the best predictor of CHD risk among all the blood lipid indexes.

In white postmenopausal women (mean age 57.6 ± 4.3 years), physical activity, as measured by sport kilocalorie expenditure per week and an activity monitor that recorded body movements, was related to HDL-2 cholesterol, the protein subfraction most associated with reduction in CHD risk (Cauley et al., 1986). None of the women were on ERT. There was little difference in total HDL or HDL-2 over the four lower quintiles of physical activity, suggesting that a threshold may exist whereby women need to exceed a certain level of activity to positively affect their HDL-C. However, the data showed a "near linear relationship" between frequency of sport activity and HDL-2. Participation in aerobic sports at least three times per week at 70% to 80% HRmax is well established as the minimum necessary to improve cardiovascular fitness. In this group of women, most of the activity was not necessarily of this intensity. Apparently, such high activity is not needed to affect HDL levels in postmenopausal women.

Postmenopausal long-distance runners and joggers had significantly higher levels of HDL-C than a control group of relatively inactive women (Hartung, Moore, Mitchell, & Kappus, 1984). The lipid profiles of a simultaneously studied group of premenopausal women with normal lipid profiles were minimally affected by exercise. That exercise training does not affect already "normal" blood lipid values has been noted in earlier literature.

Notelovitz (1988) monitored serum lipids in a group of 50 healthy women between the ages of 40 and 65 who were invited to participate in a 12-week program of exercise, discussion sessions, or both. The exercise group walk-jogged for 30 min at a pace that maintained their HRs at 70% to 80% of their predicted HRmax. The exercise group had significant increases in $\dot{V}O_2$max and times to exhaustion on a treadmill but did not show significant changes in lipid or lipoprotein fractions at 6 or 12 weeks. This seems to verify the previous conclusion that exercise does not improve already normal blood lipid values. Obviously, more research is needed on the effects of moderate and strenuous conditioning exercise on the blood lipid profiles of menopausal women who have poor lipid profiles.

Osteoporosis and Exercise

There is considerable evidence that extreme muscular inactivity (e.g., bed rest, body casts, denervation, or prolonged space flight) results in bone demineralization. Conversely, there is growing evidence that muscular activity promotes bone mineralization and hypertrophy.

Bone is not merely an inert tissue; it responds to stress just as other tissues of the body do. In 1892, Wolff suggested that mechanical forces acting on bone could cause architectural bone changes (this became known as Wolff's law). Animal studies have shown that intermittent compression and deformation, such as that characterized by human locomotion, can produce a marked adaptive response in bone (Chamay & Tschantz, 1972; Goodship, Lanyon, & McFie, 1979). Some believe that a piezoelectric effect may be required. In bone, mechanical pressure is converted to electrical potential when the anions and cations of crystals in bone tissue separate. It is theorized that anions that are displaced to the convex side of the compressed bone stimulate osteoblastic activity, causing new bone growth.

Age is also a significant factor. Bone mass increases more readily in growing bone than mature bone. Furthermore, there is an optimal level beyond which increasing bone strain will no longer enhance bone mass but rather will have a negative effect. An osteogenic response from exercise is achieved by ensuring an adequate supply of the minerals (mainly calcium) that are needed to mineralize the newly formed bone.

Cross-sectional Studies of the Effect of Exercise on Bone.   Several studies have been completed on the bone characteristics of the playing and nonplaying arms of tennis players. Young adult male and female professional tennis players showed pronounced hypertrophy of the humerus on their playing side. In this study, every player had bone hypertrophy in the playing arm

(Jones, Priest, Hayes, Tichenor, & Nagel, 1977). Senior male tennis players (over 55 years old) had significantly greater volume and circumference measurements of the hand and forearm in the playing arm. Bone width and mineral content of the ulna, radius, and humerus were also greater in the playing arm. The length, total area, and cortical cross-sectional area of the second and third metacarpal bones were also greater in the playing arm, whereas skinfold thicknesses were not significantly different on the two sides (Montoye, Smith, Fardon, & Howley, 1980). In male lifelong tennis players (aged 70 to 84 years and with playing experience ranging from 25 to 72 years), the bone mass of the radius of the playing arm was greater than that of the nonplaying arm (Huddleston, Rockwell, Kulund, & Harrison, 1980). Because the quantity of bone mineral in the playing arms of this athletic population was greater than that in the dominant arms of nonathletes, the authors suggested that playing tennis throughout a lifetime produces a localized increase in bone mineralization that is greater than that found in nonathletes. Another study reported that male cross-country runners (mean age 55) who had practiced the sport at least 25 years had greater mineral content (10% to 20%) per centimeter of bone at seven sites on the arm, spine, and leg than did control subjects of the same age (Dalen & Olsson, 1974).

More recently, radial bone density was compared in women who had exercise-induced amenorrhea (mean age 26.5 years), amenorrhea associated with weight loss (mean age 24.3), or premature menopause (mean age 32.5) and a control group of nonathletic, normally menstruating women (mean age 28.9) (Jones, Ravnikar, Tulchinsky, & Schiff, 1985). Bone density in the amenorrheic athletes did not differ from that of the controls, but in the other two groups it was significantly lower. The vigorous exercise may have been a factor in preventing bone loss. The investigators concluded that inactive women with weight loss–associated amenorrhea or premature menopause were at risk for significant bone loss. (Note that exercise-induced amenorrhea is more closely associated with trabecular than cortical bone loss; see chapter 8.)

According to the studies cited in the beginning paragraph of this section, women who were college athletes might be expected to have higher bone density from their athletic activity and therefore be at lower risk of fractures in later life than nonathletes. A study of more than 5,000 women recently showed that former college athletes in each age decade from 20 to over 70 years reported a *higher* lifetime occurrence of bone fractures of all types than did nonathletes; however, when athletic activity was accounted for, there was *no* difference between the athletes and nonathletes in risk of bone fractures (Wyshak, Frisch, Albright, Albright, & Schiff, 1987).

Longitudinal Studies of the Effect of Exercise on Bone.

More directly related to the topic of exercise effects on osteoporosis are studies of middle-aged and elderly subjects. In 1973, Smith reported the effects of 8 months of exercise in elderly men and women (mean age 80 years). He divided his subjects into three subgroups: control, physical activity of 2 to 3 MET intensity, and physical therapy. Radial width and bone mineral mass were measured following the first, fifth, and eighth months. Bone mineral mass increased 2.6% in the physical activity group and 7.8% in the physical therapy group. The control group did not show a change in bone mineralization. Smith attributed the greater change in bone mineralization exhibited by the therapy group (individuals being rehabilitated from bed rest) to their lower bone mass at the beginning of the study. Smith cited four factors as possibly contributing to the increase in mineralization with exercise:

- Increased stress on the bone as a result of increased weight bearing
- Increased stress applied to bone by increased muscular contraction
- Increased bone growth as a result of physical activity
- Increased blood flow to the bone as a result of cardiovascular stimulation

Whereas bone mineral has been reported to decrease at a rate of about 0.7% per year in women between the ages of 30 and 70 (Mazess & Cameron, 1973), bone mineral loss is probably not a linear function of age. Measurement of radial bone mineral content in women aged 50 to 96 has revealed that the mean rate of mineral loss is not constant with aging (Smith, Khairi, Norton, & Johnston, 1976). Loss was significantly slower in the elderly subjects than among younger post-menopausal women. Because the more elderly women were less active, these findings suggest that factors in addition to decreased physical activity may be important in the rate of bone mineral loss. There are many possible explanations for these results, seemingly contrary to other studies indicating that physical activity reduces bone mineral loss. Perhaps the degree of activity or in-activity needed to affect mineral loss is greater than that which was measured in this study. Another possibility is that the change in activity status may be more important than absolute activity level. For example, the activity status of the younger women (50 to 65 years) may have been decreasing at a greater rate than in the older women (over 65), who may have been at relatively the same level for years and thus had reached a new equilibrium. Another possible explanation could be that the subjects with the highest rates of bone mineral loss died before the older survivors with the slower rate of bone mineral loss.

To ascertain whether exercise could prevent involutional bone loss, Aloia, Cohn, Ostuni, Cane, and Ellis (1978) compared 9 postmenopausal women (mean age 53 ± 5.6 years) who exercised 1 h three times a week for 1 year with a similar group who remained sedentary. In contrast to other studies, neither bone mineral content nor total body potassium (a measure of lean body mass) changed in their group. However, daily calcium balance was significantly different in the two groups. Because total body calcium increased in the exercise group but decreased in every seden-tary subject, the authors supported the concept that exercise can modify involutional bone loss.

Smith, Reddan, and Smith (1981) compared the effects of physical activity with dietary calcium and vitamin D supplementation on bone mineral content in elderly women (mean age 81) over 3 years. Four groups were formed: a physical activity group (1.5 to 3 METS), a dietary supple-mentation group, a physical activity plus supple-mentation group, and a control group that neither exercised nor received dietary supplementation. Bone mineral content (BMC) increased 2.29% in the activity group and 1.58% in the supplementa-tion group; the control group showed a decline of 3.29%. Contrary to expectation, the physical activity plus supplementation group did not change significantly. This group had a higher rate of over-all decline in physical and mental function, which may have been due to their older age. The investi-gators stated that the results clearly indicate "that bone loss in the aged female may be reversed" and BMC may be "maintained at a higher level . . . through physical activity or calcium and vita-min D supplementation" (p. 64).

After an 8-month program of weight-bearing and non-weight-bearing exercise performed for 1 h twice weekly, women aged 50 to 73 who had pre-vious Colles' fracture of the forearm had a 3.5% increase in bone mineral content in the lumbar spine (Krolner, Toft, Nielsen, & Tondevold, 1983). A nonexercising control group experienced a 2.7% decline in spinal bone mineral. No changes in bone mineral content were observed in the pre-viously fractured forearms of either group, but there was a decrease of 3.5% in the nonfractured forearms.

Various treatment programs were evaluated in women with postmenopausal spinal osteoporosis and back pain (Sinaki & Mikkelsen, 1984). Patients performed either extension exercises, flexion exer-cise, flexion and extension exercise, or no thera-peutic exercises. Heat and massage were included in all treatment programs. After 1 to 6 years, addi-tional wedging and compression fractures were observed in 16% of the extension exercise group, in 89% of the flexion group, in 53% of the flexion and extension group, and in 67% of the non-exercise group. The authors concluded that exten-sion but not flexion exercises were appropriate for the treatment of postmenopausal spinal osteo-porosis. This same laboratory (at the Mayo Clinic) later demonstrated a significant positive correlation between lumbar bone mineral density and back extensor strength (Sinaki, McPhee, Hodgson, Merritt, & Offord, 1986). This suggests that the strength of the back muscles may contribute to the bone mineral density of vertebral bodies.

Preliminary results from an ongoing study at the Center for Climacteric Studies indicated that an estrogen-replete state was necessary to induce an osteogenic effect from exercise in postmenopausal women (Notelovitz, 1988, p. 162). But the results of Snow-Harter (1987) do not confirm this. She studied the biochemical responses of two groups of postmenopausal women. The exercise group (mean age 54.1 years) met three times per week for 50 min and performed progressive calisthenic movements highlighted by extension, flexion, and rotation of the vertebral column. The control group (mean age 52.5) remained sedentary. The exercise group had higher serum alkaline phospha-tase (an indicator of bone deposition) and lower serum calcium than the controls. Urinary hydroxy-proline (an index of bone resorption) did not differ between the groups. These results may indicate increased bone deposition in response to the gravitational and mechanical demands of the exercises.

Can Exercise Prevent Osteoporosis?

In a short but excellent review, Block, Smith, Black, and Genant (1987) urged caution in interpreting these and other studies. They pointed out numer-ous methodological errors—lack of randomization, little control of extraneous events such as drug and medication use or dietary changes, inappropriate sample sizes to detect differences, and possible selection biases on the part of the investigators—in both cross-sectional and longitudinal prospective studies. They concluded that although " the assump-tion that exercise *prevents* [italics added] osteo-porosis has . . . been a widely held belief by many of the leading workers in the osteoporosis field" (p. 3115), "it is unwise to make confident recom-

mendations for the prophylactic use of exercise" (p. 3117) on the basis of the published studies.

Should Perimenopausal or Postmenopausal Women Be Screened for Osteoporosis?

It is the position of the American College of Physi-cians ("Bone Mineral Densitometry," 1987) that although the mortality and morbidity caused by hip fractures warrant routine screening, measure-ment of bone mineral density has uncertain value in assessing that risk. Measurements of spinal bone density are somewhat better able to reflect a woman's risk for vertebral fractures. The value of screening depends on whether findings would affect a woman's decision about using estrogen therapy. Serial measurements of bone mass to esti-mate rate of bone loss are relatively imprecise (see also Cummings & Black, 1986). "If prospective studies establish that densitometry is valuable in predicting hip and vertebral fractures, then screen-ing may be valuable for the post-menopausal women whose decision about taking estrogen therapy depends on an assessment of her risk for fracture" (p. 935).

Stress Incontinence, Prolapse, and Exercise

Although no data are available on uterine, rectal, or bladder prolapse due to or during exercise (see pp. 105 and 162), Christine Haycock, M.D. ("A Need to Know," 1981) and Ralph Hale, M.D. (1979) believe that exercise, including running, will not cause prolapse. Prolapse of a pelvic or-gan is caused by the stretching of supporting tissue during pregnancy and not by the stress of exercise. Neither physician believes that running is contra-indicated for women over 50. Occasionally, stress incontinence may develop if already weak liga-ments are subjected to the pounding of running. With surgical repair, a woman can continue regu-lar running.

Breast Support

Another concern of the aging woman is sagging breasts. Because breast tissues may become more lax during menopausal years, good bra support during running and other bouncing activities is even more essential than earlier in life.

Summary

To many, the menopausal years are hardly noticeable, but some women experience real problems. Menopausal symptoms may be less severe for those women who have always maintained a regular program of exercise, but only empirical observation, not specific data, is available on the matter. Whether regular exercise actually alleviates menopausal symptoms is not truly known. Perhaps the woman who exercises regularly is simply more tolerant of mild physical discomforts and therefore complains less often or is less likely to consult her physician about menopausal symptoms. The years from ages 45 to 55 are often characterized by a gradually decreasing level of physical activity and an accompanying gain in body weight (fat, of course). If for no other reason, this itself is a good motive to continue exercise or to begin a regular exercise program. An increasing amount of subcutaneous fat is not only psychologically distressing to many women but also potentially detrimental to health. Adult-onset diabetes, hyperlipidemia, and hypertension are related to increasing fat deposition as well as to cardiovascular disease.

Whether one utilizes estrogen replacement therapy to allay menopausal symptoms is an individual matter that should be discussed fully with a physician. It is probably best to consult a specialist who has current information and will discuss all the pros and cons freely. I believe that the benefits of the currently available low-dosage ERT in terms of possible prevention of osteoporosis and heart disease outweigh any associated risks. How long a program of ERT should be continued is a matter that needs attention by investigators.

For currently inactive women, the perimenopausal or postmenopausal years are a good time to start exercising regularly. Certainly this period of one's life does not contraindicate regular strenuous exercise. As always, it is desirable to have a thorough physical examination and a discussion of the planned exercise program with a physician before beginning. This is, of course, especially indicated if there are any basic physical health problems. After a physician's approval is secured, exercise should be started slowly and carefully to minimize aches, pains, and injuries. Starting a regular exercise program during the climacteric after years of inactivity is never easy, but it is rewarding, and it will probably never be any easier. Flexibility and stretching exercises should be included to prevent muscle soreness. It may be wise to begin exercising under adequate supervision, especially for those who have osteoporosis. Local classes are often available at a YWCA, YMCA, or YMHA or through preventive medicine programs in hospitals, health clinics, and university settings.

The increasing prevalence of competitive masters or senior events (running, swimming, tennis, and badminton are the most common) is encouraging. The competitive results, as well as the physiological data obtained, certainly indicate that the climacteric years, and the menopause, are not a hindrance to excellent physical performance or to the physical and social enjoyment associated with sport.

Chapter 11

Exercise and
the Elderly Woman

The previous chapter described changes occurring during the climacteric years (ages 45 to 55). This chapter concentrates on adaptations in the elderly woman, that is, in the woman over 60 years of age. There are two excellent reviews of exercise and aging (Shephard, 1978; Shephard & Sidney, 1978), and the reader is urged to consult these for a more elaborate treatment of that subject. Unfortunately, these reviews deal mostly with the aging man.

Structural and Physiological Changes in the Advanced Years

There is little evidence that women differ significantly from men in the manner in which their bodies change with age. In general, there is a shortening in stature because of compression of the intervertebral disks, weakening of the back muscles, and osteoporosis. Body weight usually declines with a general lessening of lean body mass and a loss in body density due to a concomitant lightening of the bones and atrophy of the skeletal musculature. Relative body fat, particularly internal body fat, increases. Reported percentages of body fat average about 38% in elderly women. However, body fat assessed by hydrodensitometry may be overestimated because of age-related alterations (e.g., loss of bone mineral, increased fat in bone marrow, and loss of water from connective tissues) in the constancy of the lean body mass. Changes in limb conformation generally reflect muscle wasting and the accumulation of subcutaneous fat. Although there is little net change, the body contours of the elderly have a less firm and muscular appearance than in middle age. Abdominal girth commonly increases 25% to 35% in women (Shephard, 1978).

Pulmonary dynamics markedly change because elastic tissue is lost. Resting $\dot{V}O_2$ decreases slightly relative to the loss of lean body mass. The decline in $\dot{V}O_2$, however, is less than the decline in resting cardiac output ($\dot{Q}$). Thus, the arteriovenous oxygen difference ($a-\bar{v}O_2$) increases with age. Resting HR does not change significantly, but stroke volume (SV) declines despite an increase in heart volume. It is well known that not all systems decline at the same rate as one ages.

Responses to Submaximal Exercise in the Elderly Woman

The regulation of homeostasis becomes less efficient with advancing age; therefore, the time required to attain steady state is prolonged, as is recovery time following exertion. The $\dot{V}O_2$ of a submaximal exercise task has been reported to increase (Wessel et al., 1968; Zauner et al., 1984), and anaerobic mechanisms may begin at a lower exercise intensity. Systemic and pulmonary blood pressures and arterial lactate concentrations are higher in the aged. All this indicates that more frequent and more prolonged rest periods are necessary to complete a submaximal work task with advancing age.

Responses to Maximal Exercise in the Elderly Woman

In the sedentary older person, effort is more often limited by dyspnea, fear of overexertion, muscular weakness, or poor motivation than by any limitation of oxygen transport. Some of the decline in performance may reflect a reluctance of the investigator to push women beyond the age of 60 to the point of exhaustion. However, HRmax, SV, and $\dot{Q}$ diminish, and there is a decline in the maximal $a-\bar{v}O_2$ difference, probably because more blood is directed to the skin because of peripheral changes (e.g., a reduced ratio of capillary to fiber in the muscles). The decrease in the maximal $a-\bar{v}O_2$ difference is an important reason why the loss of aerobic power is greater than the decrease in $\dot{Q}_{max}$ (Shephard & Sidney, 1978). Blair et al. (1984) reported a decrease of about 10% per decade (from 18 to 75 years) in treadmill walking time and a total decline in physical working capacity of about 41% by the seventh decade. Notelovitz et al. (1986) found a decline of 5.5% per decade in directly measured $\dot{V}O_2$max (from ages 35 to 75), a decline of approximately ± 1% per year. The correlation between age and $\dot{V}O_2$max (ml • kg^{-1} • min^{-1}) was −0.42 ($p < .0001$). Weight increased about 1 lb per decade in Blair et al.'s (1984) sample, and HRmax averaged 5 bpm lower in successive decades. Maximal HR was lower, and blood pressure responses were higher, in the less fit.

A mean functional capacity of 8.0 METS has been reported for 70-year-old social dancers, whereas a somewhat less active group of cardplayers achieved 6.8 METS (Goertzen, Serfass, Sopko, & Leon, 1984). (Note: The MET, or metabolic equivalent, is equal to 3.5 ml • kg^{-1} • min^{-1}.) The fittest woman in this study (a cardplayer) walked for 26 min on a treadmill and achieved a work capacity of 12 METS and a peak HR of 158 bpm. Table 11.1 summarizes some of the data reported in the literature for women aged 50 to 75.

The loss of aerobic power is significantly greater in sedentary than in active men, and this is certainly true of women as well. Maximal values for respiratory volume, alveolar ventilation, pulmonary

Table 11.1 Responses to Maximal Exercise in Women Aged 50 to 75

Reference	Age (yr)	Height (cm)	Weight (kg)	TMT (min)	Estimated $\dot{V}O_2$ (ml · kg^{-1} · min^{-1})	Measured $\dot{V}O_2$ (ml · kg^{-1} · min^{-1})	HRmax	SBP	DBP
Blair et al. (1984)	50-59	163 ± 5	61.3 ± 8.6	9:23[a]	28.0	—	171	168	76
	60-75	163 ± 8	60.8 ± 9.5	8:19	27.0	—	162	178	74
Notelovitz et al. (1986)	56-65	161 ± 6	61.2 ± 8	—	25.3 ± 5.3	25.9 ± 3.8[b]	—	—	—
	66-75	158 ± 6	59.1 ± 8	—	23.3 ± 3.1	24.2 ± 4.0	—	—	—
Goertzen et al. (1984)	70.4 ± 6.5 (dancers)	161.3 ± 6	62.3 ± 9	17:54[c]	—	—	155	175	—
	72.4 ± 7.3 (card players)	160.8 ± 6	64.5 ± 7	14:30	—	—	147	180	—
	60-69	—	—	—	—	29.4 ± 9.8	—	—	—
	70-79	—	—	—	—	24.5 ± 2.8	—	—	—
	80-86	—	—	—	—	20.6 ± 14.3	—	—	—
Adams & deVries (1973)	60-69	141.5	—	—	19.5[d]	—	—	131	76
	70-79	135.2	—	—	16.9[d]	—	—	132	73
Drinkwater et al. (1975)	60-69	162.5 ± 2	61.2 ± 3	—	—	25.6 ± 1.5	154	—	—
Vaccaro, Dummer, & Clarke (1981)	70-79	164.2	61.6	—	—	37.6	163	—	—

Note. TMT = treadmill time, SBP = systolic blood pressure, and DBP = diastolic blood pressure.

[a]Balke treadmill test at 3.3 mph.

[b]Balke-Ware treadmill test at 3.0 mph.

[c]Modified Balke-Naughton treadmill test.

[d]$\dot{V}O_2$ at 85% HRmax.

diffusing capacity, and the concentration of lactic acid following maximal exertion are reduced. These changes, of course, imply a diminished reserve capacity, and the quantity of work that can be performed in a given period is greatly reduced.

The American Heart Association provided the following guidelines for $\dot{V}O_2max$ (ml $\cdot$ kg^{-1} $\cdot$ min^{-1}) for healthy women in their menopausal or postmenopausal years:

Age	Poor	Fair	Average	Good	Excellent
50-59	< 15	15-20	21-27	28-37	38+
60-69	< 13	13-17	18-23	24-34	35+

Note. Adapted from AHA (1972, p. 15). Data from Preventive Medicine Center, Palo Alto, CA, and from a survey of published sources.

The Cooper Clinic provided the following fitness classifications, which are based on walking times on the modified Balke treadmill protocol (3.3 mph: 0% grade for first minute, 2% for second minute, with the grade increased 1% each minute thereafter):

Fitness category	50-59	60+
Very poor	< 5:38	< 4:00
Poor	5:38-6:59	4:00-5:32
Fair	7:00-9:29	5:33-7:59
Good	9:30-11:59	8:00-10:59
Excellent	12:00-14:59	11:00-11:59
Superior	> 15:00	> 12:00

Adapted from Gibbons et al. (1983).

Activity Patterns and Attitudes Toward Exercise

The well-known decline in physical activity with advanced age may be due to many factors other than true biological aging. Such factors as retirement, social and cultural expectations, lack of opportunity for exercise, institutionalization, accidents, or illnesses may also play a role. Gardening and walking appear to be the most common forms of physical activity in the elderly.

Many senior citizens believe that the need for exercise declines with age, that exercise is dangerous, and that their physical abilities are very limited (Conrad, 1976; cited in Shephard & Sidney, 1978). Frequently, the older individual has been conditioned to the attitude that at retirement a person should "slow down" and "enjoy a well-earned rest." Most elderly persons believe they are "active enough."

Sidney and Shephard (1976) have examined changes in attitudes toward physical activity in elderly men and women following a program of endurance training. The greatest changes were observed in the subjects who trained the hardest, showed the greatest gains in $\dot{V}O_2max$, or both.

Physical Training and the Elderly Woman

In an outstanding review of the topic, Shephard and Sidney (1978) commented that although some investigators believe that the training response is reduced in elderly subjects (particularly if they had been previously sedentary), others find at least as large a response in younger subjects. Problems such as initial fitness level, training methods employed, and methods of expressing the training response are some of the factors that have led to divergent conclusions.

The responses of the older woman to training seem comparable to those of the older man (Adams & deVries, 1973; Sidney & Shephard, 1976, 1977). Table 11.2 was originally adapted from Shephard and Sidney's (1978) review but has been expanded to include more recent data that indicate that the older woman is quite capable of undertaking a physical fitness program and benefiting from it.

Many studies have found significant decreases in resting systolic blood pressure but no changes in

Table 11.2 Effects of Physical Training on Aerobic Power of Healthy Men and Women Aged 60 and Older

| Investigator | Sex | Age (yr) | N | Training program | | | | $\dot{V}O_2$max (ml · kg⁻¹ · min⁻¹) | | | |
				Frequency (per wk)	Duration (min/session)	Intensity	Activity	Pre	Post	Δ	Δ%
Kilbom (1971)	F	51-64	12	2-3	7 wk (18 min)	77% $\dot{V}O_2$max	B (IT)	26.9	29.4	2.5	9
Sidney & Shephard (1978)	M/F	67	8	< 2	14 wk (45 min)	$f_H = 120 \cdot min^{-1}$	W, J, Cal	19.5[a]	19.2	-0.3	-2 (N.S.)
		63	5	< 2	14 wk (45 min)	$f_H = 140\text{-}150 \cdot min^{-1}$	W, J, Cal	24.1[a]	28.1	4.0	17
		64	13	2-4	14 wk (45 min)	$f_H = 120 \cdot min^{-1}$	W, J, Cal	21.7[a]	24.8	3.1	14
		61	8	2-4	14 wk (45 min)	$f_H = 140\text{-}150 \cdot min^{-1}$	W, J, Cal	23.4[a]	32.4	9.0	39
	M	65	10	1-4	52 wk (45 min)	$f_H = 120\text{-}145 \cdot min^{-1}$	W, J, Cal	23.7[a]	26.9	3.2	13.5
	F	65	11	1-4	52 wk (45 min)	$f_H = 120\text{-}145 \cdot min^{-1}$	W, J, Cal	24.2[a]	27.3	3.1	12.8
Suominen et al. (1977)	M	69	14	3-5	8 wk (60 min)	Submaximal	W, J, S, G, Cal	28.9[a]	32.0	3.1	10.7
	F	69	12	3-5	8 wk (60 min)	Submaximal	W, J, S, G, Cal	27.9[a]	31.3	3.4	12.2
Barry et al. (1966)	M/F	70	8	3	12 wk (16-25 min)	Submaximal and maximal	B (IT), Cal	16.1	22.3	6.2	38
Seals et al. (1984b)	M/F	63	14	LI-4.6	6 mo (27 min)	$f_H = 107$ min⁻¹	W	25.4	28.2	2.8	12%
				HI-3	6 mo (30-45 min)	75%-85% HR reserve	W, J, B	28.2	32.9	4.7	18%

Note. First four entries from "Exercise and Aging" by R.J. Shephard & K.H. Sidney, 1978, *Exercise and Sport Sciences Reviews*, **6**, pp. 20-21. Copyright 1979 by The Franklin Institute Press. Reprinted by permission.

[a]$\dot{V}O_2$max predicted from Åstrand-Ryhming nomogram.

W = walking, B = bicycling, S = swimming, IT = interval training, J = jogging, G = games/sports, Cal = calisthenics, f_H = heart rate, LI = low intensity, and HI = high intensity.

static or dynamic lung volumes. Usually, changes that indicate an increased economy of effort with submaximal work (variables such as lowered HR and blood lactate and higher oxygen pulse) occur in the elderly woman with training, but not all studies agree. Little change seems to occur in such variables as respiratory minute volume, diastolic blood pressure, or ventilatory equivalent for oxygen (Adams & deVries, 1973; Shephard & Sidney, 1978).

Adams and deVries (1973) reported significant improvements in women aged 52 to 79 (mean = 66) in physical working capacity (37%), $\dot{V}O_2$max (21%), and oxygen pulse (19%) after a program of walking and jogging. They concluded not only that the older woman is "trainable" but that "the magnitude of the capacity for training is not greatly different from that of the younger individual if compared on a percentage basis" (p. 53).

More recently, Seals, Hagberg, Hurley, Ehsani, and Holloszy (1984b) reported on an elaborate endurance training study of men and women aged 60 to 69. Unfortunately for our purposes, the responses of the subjects were not separated by sex (probably because they did not differ). Initially, training consisted of 20 to 30 min of walking at least three times per week for 6 months. This was termed low intensity (LI) training (subjects actually walked 4.6 times per week at an average HR of 107 bpm). This was followed by another 6 months of high intensity (HI) training characterized by either jogging, bicycle ergometry, or graded treadmill walking (depending on the orthopedic status of the subjects). Intensity was increased progressively from 75% HR reserve for 30 min to 85% HR reserve for 45 min. Some of the results are shown in Table 11.2. The LI training elicited a 12% increase in $\dot{V}O_2$max, and the additional HI training produced a further increase (18%). The increase in aerobic power was mediated primarily by an increase in the maximal $a-\bar{v}O_2$ difference with little augmentation of maximal $\dot{Q}$. Ventilation ($\dot{V}_E$) was increased by 11% and 29% in the LI and HI programs, respectively. These training

responses were greater than had been previously reported for individuals over 60 years of age. The investigators suggested that the training stimuli in earlier studies was neither great enough nor sufficiently prolonged to elicit the adaptations that were necessary to produce such marked increases in aerobic power.

These investigators also studied responses to submaximal exercise. After LI training, blood lactate, HR, $\dot{V}_E$, R, and mean blood pressures were significantly lower at the same absolute work rates; further reductions were seen in most of these variables with HI training (Seals, Hurley, Schultz, & Hagberg, 1984). Many of these reductions occurred also for relative (percent $\dot{V}O_2$max) work rates. The attenuated lactate responses were at least partially attributed to a shift in substrate utilization toward an increased oxidation of fat (and sparing of muscle glycogen); this had not been reported previously in older subjects. The results suggest that the capacity of the skeletal muscles for oxidative metabolism increased.

Body fat, glucose tolerance, and plasma lipid levels were also studied in the same men and women (Seals, Hagberg, Hurley, Ehsani, & Holloszy, 1984a). Body weight, percent body fat, and sum of skinfolds were unchanged after LI but significantly reduced after HI training. Glucose tolerance was unchanged after both LI and HI training. However, a significantly reduced plasma insulin concentration was interpreted to indicate that sensitivity to insulin improved substantially. The evidence suggested that this improvement was due to a reduction in the amount of insulin secreted by the pancreas. Total cholesterol and LDL-C were not significantly changed with either phase of training. However, after HI training, HDL-C was significantly increased (14%), resulting in a significantly lower ratio of total cholesterol to HDL-C after HI training. Plasma triglyceride concentration was also significantly lower (21%) after HI training. It appears that exercise training must be intense to elicit these blood lipid adaptations.

All these results have been reported previously in younger and middle-aged subjects. They are important because they demonstrate that older persons respond to prolonged, high-intensity endurance training similarly to younger individuals.

Increases in bone mineral content have been reported in several studies (see chapter 10, pp. 176-179) but not in all. Most physicians currently recommend exercise for elderly women to retard bone mineral loss and as a preventive measure for osteoporosis, which in this age-group takes a serious toll.

The Elderly Female Athlete

With the exception of three studies reported in the text that follows (Dummer et al., 1985; Vaccaro, Dummer & Clarke, 1981; Vaccaro et al., 1984), no scientific information is available on sports-women over 60 years of age. Shephard and Sidney (1978), however, reviewed data on elderly male athletes. This information is briefly reviewed here because there seems to be no reason to believe that female athletes over the age of 60 differ significantly in relative terms from male athletes over 60. We have already seen that older people respond to both acute and chronic exercise in the same manner as younger people and that elderly women respond much like elderly men.

Body build and body composition of elderly athletes are generally similar to those of younger competitors. There is little evidence of obesity and less lean body mass is lost than in elderly non-competitors.

Although some investigators have reported that $\dot{V}O_2$max deteriorates more slowly in the elderly athlete than in the sedentary subject, others have cited annual losses that are similar to those seen in the general population. Of course, the initial values are much higher in the athletic population, so the apparent loss is considerably less than in the average person. Basically, it appears that the functional adaptive capacity of aging athletes remains well above that of the less active population.

Vaccaro, Dummer, and Clarke (1981) have reported on two masters swimmers aged 70 and 71 who were members of the 1980 All-American Masters Swim Team. The physiological characteristics of these two women were compared with sedentary females of the same age and with younger female athletes. The swimmers had considerably lower percent body fat (23.5% vs. 44.6%) than normal sedentary women in their 70s and were well within the range for normal women aged 19 to 24. The $\dot{V}O_2$max values for the swimmers (37.56 ml $\cdot$ kg^{-1} $\cdot$ min^{-1}) were approximately twice those of sedentary women in their 70s and higher than those of sedentary 19- and 20-year-old women. The description of these two outstanding women is interesting and is quoted here:

[The 71-year-old subject] was generally active throughout her life, participating in a variety of sports including golf, tennis, dancing, and swimming. She began regular training for masters competitive swimming at age 65 and now swims five days a week, 1 hour a day, 1,500 yards per session. At the 1980 Short Course National Masters Swimming Championship, she placed second in the 50-yard butterfly (1:07.54), second in the 200-yard backstroke (4:41.10), third in the 200-yard freestyle (3:56.45), third in the 100-yard backstroke (2:13.14), and third in the 100-yard individual medley (2:20.72). She is ranked in the top ten nationally in nine events in her age-group (70 to 74).

[The 70-year-old subject] also has been generally active throughout her life. She worked as a physical education teacher and participated in a variety of sports including recreational swimming. She began masters competitive swimming at age 67 and holds national records for the 70 to 74 age-group in the 50-yard backstroke (54.15), 50-yard breaststroke (55.06), 100-yard breaststroke (2:02.0), 200-yard breaststroke (4:30.26), 100-yard individual medley (1:59.41), 400-yard individual medley (9:09.59),

50-meter breaststroke (1:03.38), 100-meter breaststroke (2:21.77), 200-meter breaststroke (5:03.45), and 400-meter individual medley (10:45.78). Her swimming training consists of four workouts a week covering distances ranging from 1,000 to 1,100 yards per session. (Vaccaro, Dummer, & Clark, 1981, p. 76)

Table 11.3 provides an interesting profile of 13 masters swimmers over 60 years of age (Vaccaro et al., 1984). The highly trained (T) women swam a minimum of three times per week, 1 h per session, and a minimum of 1,638 m. The not-highly-trained (NHT) swimmers swam a minimum of twice per week, at least 1/2 h per session, and a minimum of 455 m.

Aging is often associated with a gain in weight and body fat and a loss of lean tissue and aerobic power. These adverse changes are also associated with a loss of physical conditioning. The data in Table 11.3 indicate that although some decline in

function is inevitable, much can be reversed or delayed through vigorous physical training. The women studied here exhibited lower values for relative fat than untrained women of comparable age. In fact, the values of percent body fat for these highly trained 60-year-olds were within the range for healthy women aged 19.0 to 24.4 (21.5% to 29.1%) (Katch & McArdle, 1973). The values for the NHT subjects were only slightly above this level. As mentioned previously, the values of percent body fat are likely to be overestimated because of age-related changes in bone and fat-free tissues.

Many of the variables listed in Table 11.3 appear to be associated with the intensity, frequency, and duration of exercise undertaken because the NHT subjects differed significantly from the T subjects. The entire data set (not presented here) indicated that the $\dot{V}O_2$max of the T swimmers declined at a mean rate of about 7% per decade and that a significant decline first appeared at age 40. The NHT subjects declined at a rate of approximately

Table 11.3 Profile of Masters Female Swimmers Over Age 60

Variable	T	NHT
Height (cm)	163.4 ± 6.6	163.1 ± 5.6
Weight (kg)	60.6 ± 9.1	66.6 ± 6.0*
Body density	1.034 ± .01	1.015 ± .01*
Percent body fat	27.8 ± 3.5	36.0 ± 5.0*
Lean body mass	43.0 ± 5.0	41.6 ± 1.2*
Resting HR	68 ± 5	77 ± 8*
Resting BP	122 ± 17/77 ± 11	151 ± 27/90 ± 12
HR max	157 ± 7	157 ± 9
$V_E$max	66 ± 8	48 ± 8*
$\dot{V}O_2$max		
L · min⁻¹	1.93 ± .22	1.46 ± .22*
ml · kg⁻¹ · min⁻¹	32.1 ± 3.0	21.9 ± 3.5*
ml · kg⁻¹ LBM · min⁻¹	44.6 ± 4.2	34.3 ± 5.6*
Oxygen pulse		
ml · kg⁻¹ · beat⁻¹	.20 ± .01	.03 ± .02*

Note. T = trained, NHT = not highly trained. Data from Vaccaro et al. (1984).

* Significantly different from trained ($p < .05$).

8% per decade. Maximal aerobic power was 10 ml • kg⁻¹ • min⁻¹ higher in the T than the NHT swimmers. These highly trained swimmers had $\dot{V}O_2$max values comparable to those of sedentary women 20 to 30 years younger (Drinkwater, 1973). It is obvious that a fit elderly woman can have a body composition and aerobic capacity equivalent to that of a sedentary woman many years younger and to that of a physically fit woman 10 years younger.

Dummer et al. (1985) examined the muscular strength and endurance of these swimmers and reported that they exhibited higher grip strength and knee and shoulder flexion and extension strength than less active women of the same age. Nevertheless, there was an age-related decline in muscular strength that was not prevented by participating in swimming activities (none of the women trained with weights). Muscular endurance data did not reveal a pattern of age-related changes. It is obvious that training in competitive swimming helps older women maintain high functional levels.

Advice on Exercise for Elderly Women

There is a desirable exercise program for everyone, even for those confined to bed. For the healthy, nonathletic but reasonably active 60-year-old, the solution is easy. Simply initiate a progressive walking program. Start with a short distance (perhaps a block or half a block), do it every day for a week, and see how it goes. If aches and pains develop, advice may be needed about footwear, walking mechanics, posture, or general health. If there are no aches and pains, increase the work load *very gradually* by either (not both) walking faster or preferably walking farther (longer). The walking style can be made more strenuous by adding a vigorous arm swing. Some people are taking up race-walking, which is a style and not necessarily competitive despite its name (see Jacobson, 1980).

Other alternatives are tennis (but that could be hard on the elbows if tennis has not been played regularly), folk and square dancing, swimming, bicycling, or golf (carry the clubs or pull a golf cart—no electric carts!). Calisthenics (like slimnastics) or low-impact aerobic dance classes designed especially for women of this age-group are also excellent alternatives. Competitive situations where one is forced to keep up with others who may be younger or in better condition should be avoided.

Older women, particularly those who have not previously taken part in sport activities, should seek out activity classes for women of similar age. I suggest senior centers, YMCAs, YWCAs, or preventive medicine clinics. These classes usually begin with flexibility exercises and progress to daily walking, swimming, or bicycling programs. Professional leaders may be interested in reading about appropriate exercises for seniors such as those provided by Sager (1984), Piscopo (1985), and Aisenbrey (1987).

Women in their 80s and 90s should perform flexibility exercises from a solid base of support to prevent falling. Exercises that are done while sitting on a chair have been designed for this purpose. These exercises help maintain complete range of motion in the extremities and trunk. Consult senior centers, geriatrics clinics, or physical therapy clinics. Often a nearby medical school will have information about exercise classes.

Women who are quite elderly or infirm should also perform regular exercise. Flexibility exercises and some form of ambulation are very desirable. No one should be embarrassed to use a cane, crutch, or walker. Supervision or exercise guidance is highly desirable in such a case.

Regular exercise is a desirable part of life no matter what age. Nevertheless, one often encounters the attitude that it is useless to exercise in the advanced years because it is too late to reap the benefits. The information outlined here should adequately counter that attitude; still, a brief review of the specific benefits of regular exercise in the senior years follows.

Regular participation in exercise beyond the age of 60 aids in the maintenance of body weight. Although some sedentary older women literally waste away, others gain considerable body fat. Exercise contributes to the maintenance of lean body mass and prevents the deposition of body fat. In addition, the loss of bone mineral content is retarded or prevented and so osteoporosis is less severe. Joint flexibility and muscular strength are maintained or increased. These factors contribute to improved ambulation and the ability to perform life's tasks more adequately.

Performance of regular exercise in the advanced years helps to maintain or retard the loss of cardiovascular reserve. Even with mild forms of endurance exercise, the ability to transport and utilize oxygen is maintained or improved. The cardiovascular and pulmonary dynamics of elderly people who regularly exercise are generally superior to those who do not. There are many excellent examples of this. One is 80-year-old Ruth Rothfarb (Peitzmeier, 1981), who began running at the age of 72 after an active life that included bowling and dancing. Another is Mavis Lindgren (*Women's Sports & Fitness,* **10**(1) 1988, p. 95), whose goal is to become the first 80-year-old woman to run a marathon in under 5 h (the current record is 5 h, 10 s, held by Ida Mintz of Illinois). Then there is Rose Steward, 70, of Phoenix, Arizona. She is a masters swimmer as well as a triathlete and recently completed the USTS Phoenix Triathlon (the most difficult race on that circuit because of the heat and the hills) in 5 h 18 min. But competition is not the only arena in which elderly women shine. Hulda Crooks, now 92, has climbed more than 97 peaks since her 65th birthday, including 22 trips up Mt. Whitney (the highest peak in the lower 48 states) (Mills, 1987).

There are also psychological benefits from regular exercise in the advanced years. With regular participation in exercise programs, there are usually fewer medical complaints, an elevation in mood, a reduction in manifest anxiety, a relief of tension, favorable changes in body image, and the feeling that one is more in control of one's life. Whether these benefits accrue from gains in physical fitness or from such factors as increased interaction with others hardly matters. Nevertheless, improvements in social relationships usually occur as well.

It is never too late to begin an exercise program. The enrichment in the quality of one's life is well worth the effort at any age.

Summary

The decline in physical working capacity and the increase in body fat usually attributed to advancing age is probably more highly related to a decrease in daily physical activity level than to increasing age per se. There is, however, a gradual loss of lean body tissue (including cardiac tissue) after about age 50. This will eventually lead to a decrease in maximal cardiac output, maximal oxygen consumption, muscular strength, and subsequently performance. Nevertheless, older female athletes are capable of accomplishing much, particularly in endurance events.

There is no longer any doubt that one can reap the benefits of increased physical activity at any age and that a lifetime of regular physical activity enhances one's health and fitness during the senior years.

PART IV

Nutrition, Exercise, and Nutritional Disorders

Although there is a considerable amount of information available on diet and nutrition for people of all ages, relatively little of it is aimed specifically toward the active woman. I do not believe that athletes need any special diet, but there are many who do propagate such a belief. There is probably more misinformation on nutrition that is now considered "general knowledge" than on any other topic. Women who are seeking to lose weight are extremely susceptible to the unsubstantiated claims of those who advocate special diets for the loss of weight and body fat.

Chapter 12 presents the nutritional requirements of girls and women and advocates good dietary behaviors (e.g., reducing fat intake and increasing dietary fiber) for reducing risk factors associated with common health problems such as heart disease, hypertension, and cancer. Much of the chapter is devoted to the special nutritional needs of women and girls and includes discussions of such topics as iron deficiency, diet and bone health, nutrition and oral contraceptives, and body weight and body fat. The summary is directed to the active woman and includes eight guidelines for good nutrition.

Chapter 13 highlights a problem for many girls and women: obesity. The concept of caloric balance is described with an emphasis on the caloric cost of exercise. The effects of exercise on appetite and food intake are presented, as is a discussion of the effects of exercise on weight loss and body composition. The role of exercise in fatty acid mobilization and in adipose cellularity is described, and current information on the effects of exercise and weight loss on the serum lipids in women is presented. The chapter includes a description of two common eating disorders currently receiving considerable attention: anorexia nervosa and bulimia. The incidence of pathogenic weight control behaviors in women athletes is also discussed.

Chapter 12

Nutrition and the Active Woman

In the past 10 years, several U.S. governmental agencies and professional associations have led a major effort to establish a public health agenda for the United States. This is largely the result of the recognition that many of the prevalent causes of death and disability could have been prevented or reduced through improvements in diet, exercise, and other lifestyle practices. Thus, the Public Health Service authorized the Department of Health and Human Services to establish national goals of promoting health and preventing disease (hereafter referred to as the 1990 Objectives).

This chapter focuses on the nutritional needs of women, initially with particular attention to these national objectives and other guidelines for the promotion of health and prevention of disease and then to the special needs of the physically active woman.

Nutrition Basics

Nutrients are chemical substances obtained from food. They are assimilated by being digested (broken down to simple molecules) and then absorbed (passed through the walls of the digestive tract into the blood). *Essential nutrients* are substances the body either cannot synthesize or is unable to make in sufficient amounts. They must be obtained from the diet. About 50 nutrients are known to be needed by the human body and can be grouped into six classifications: proteins, carbohydrates, fats, vitamins, minerals, and water. We eat to obtain these nutrients for three general purposes:

1. To obtain energy for cellular metabolism
2. For the growth, repair, and maintenance of the body's cells
3. To regulate cellular processes

Energy can be obtained from the nutrients classified as proteins, carbohydrates, or fats. Protein and carbohydrates each supply about 4 kcal per gram, whereas fats, a more concentrated source of energy, supply about 9 kcal per gram. Some cells, such as the red blood cells and the cells of the nervous system, can utilize only carbohydrates for energy. Most cells can obtain energy from proteins, carbohydrates, or fats. However, energy from protein sources usually becomes available only when carbohydrate and fat are not sufficiently available, for example, during fasting, extreme dieting, and starvation. Protein is used mainly to synthesize hormones, enzymes, and body tissues. Whereas a few amino acids (the basic structural unit of protein), such as alanine, may play an important role in energy metabolism, protein is needed essentially and primarily for the growth, repair, and maintenance of body tissues. Proteins are not considered an important source of energy for the human body.

It is currently recommended that total caloric intake be 55% to 60% from carbohydrate sources, 30% from fat sources, and 15% from protein sources. It is usually assumed that nutritional adequacy cannot be achieved with a total caloric intake of less than 1,200 kcal per day.

Nutrient Requirements

How much of each nutrient is necessary or desirable? Recommended dietary allowances (RDAs) are the amounts of nutrients essential to meet the known nutritional needs of practically all healthy persons. They are based on age, weight, sex, and physical condition (such as pregnancy or lactation). Table 12.1 contains the 1989 revision of the recommended daily dietary allowances. Table 12.2 shows the estimated safe and adequate daily intakes of vitamins and minerals for which less information is available. Table 12.3 provides information to determine the recommended total caloric intake based on age, sex, and physical condition (pregnancy or lactation). The energy allowances for young adults are for men and women doing light work. The allowances for the two older groups represent mean energy needs and allow for a 2% decrease in basal (resting) metabolic rate per decade and a reduction in activity of 200 kcal per day for men and women between ages 51 and 75, 500 kcal for men over 75, and 400 kcal for women over 75.

Nutrition Guidelines for the Promotion of Health and the Prevention of Disease

Major health problems for women in the United States (and many other industrialized nations) include obesity, hypertension, diabetes mellitus, cardiovascular diseases (including coronary artery disease and stroke), cancer, and osteoporosis. Epidemiological studies have consistently revealed the role of various nutritional practices in the development of these health problems. Therefore, many of the 1990 Objectives (United States Department of Health, Education and Welfare [USDHEW], 1979) directly address the role of sound nutritional habits to promote health and prevent disease in women. It is especially noteworthy that the 1990 Objectives and the recent *Surgeon General's Report on Nutrition and Health* (United States Department of Health and Human

Services [USDHHS], 1988) reflect a shift in nutritional priorities in the United States from problems of nutrient deficiencies to those of dietary overconsumption.

Prior advice on nutrition focused on the consumption of foods containing fat and sugar and assigned foods to groups (the four food groups) to promote a more varied diet and to prevent nutrient deficiencies. Current advice now strongly emphasizes that the leading causes of death in the United States are associated with diets too high in fat, calories, salt, and alcohol and too low in fiber. Today, the primary dietary priority is to reduce one's consumption of fat, especially saturated fats and cholesterol.

Reduction of Fat and Cholesterol

Several of the 1990 Objectives relate to the reduction of fat and cholesterol in American diets. The objectives state that mean serum cholesterol for adults should be at or below 200 mg • dl^{-1} and for children at or below 150 mg • dl^{-1}. The Surgeon General's Report states that most people should reduce their consumption of fat (especially saturated fat) and cholesterol. The American Heart Association (AHA, 1986) is more specific in its *Dietary Guidelines for Healthy American Adults*. The AHA position statement claims the following:

- Total fat intake should be less than 30% of calories,
- Saturated fat intake should be less than 10% of calories,
- Cholesterol intake should be less than 100 mg per 1,000 calories and not exceed 300 mg per day.

The National Heart, Lung, and Blood Institute and the National Institutes of Health (NIH, 1985) consensus conference added the following:

- Polyunsaturated fat intake should be increased but to no more than 10% of total calories.
- Daily cholesterol intake should be 250 to 300 mg or less.

Saturated fats are oils from animal products and some plants (e.g., coconut and palm) that are solid at room temperature. Intake of saturated fat has been correlated with serum cholesterol values and coronary heart disease in many epidemiological studies. Americans currently consume 15% to 20% of their total calories from saturated fats. The AHA states that a 30% to 50% reduction in the current intake of these fats is necessary to meet the recommendation that less than 10% of calories be from saturated fat. Many favorite American foods are high in saturated fats, including fried foods, sour cream, butter, tender red meats, fast-food hamburgers, commercial baked goods, non-dairy creamers, whole milk, lunch meats, and potato chips.

Total fat intake in many Western industrialized nations is 40% of calories. The recommended reduction in total fat intake to 30% should be achieved mainly by reducing the intake of saturated fat, a calorically dense source of energy (9 kcal per gram). Monounsaturated and polyunsaturated fats are equally caloric but have no known undesirable effects on serum cholesterol. These fats are oils derived from vegetable products that are liquid at room temperature. Currently, monounsaturated fats contribute 15% to 20% of total calories in the American diet and polyunsaturated fats 5% to 7% of total calories (AHA, 1987). A few grams of polyunsaturated fats daily provide an adequate supply of the essential fatty acids.

There is evidence that substituting these fats for saturated fats reduces one's risk for heart disease. The NIH (1985) consensus conference report recommends that dietary intake of polyunsaturated fat intake be increased to no more than 10% of total calories. Vegetable oils from safflower and sunflower seeds, corn, soybeans, and cottonseeds are relatively high in polyunsaturated fats. Plant oils, such as olive and peanut oils, are high in monounsaturated fats (see Table 12.4).

Dietary cholesterol (as well as saturated fat) intake has been related to blood cholesterol levels in many studies. The NIH (1985) consensus conference report states that "a causal relationship between blood cholesterol levels and coronary heart disease comes from a wealth of congruent

Table 12.1 Recommended Daily Allowances,[a] Revised 1989, from the Food and Nutrition Board, National Academy of Sciences—National Research Council

Designed for the maintenance of good nutrition of practically all healthy people in the U.S.A.

Category	Age (y) or condition	Weight (kg)	Weight (lb)	Height (cm)	Height (in.)	Protein (g)	Vit. A (μg R.E.)[b]	Fat-soluble vitamins		
								Vit. D (μg)[c]	Vit. E (mg α-T.E.)[d]	Vit. K (μg)
Infants	0.0-0.5	6	13	60	24	13	375	7.5	3	5
	0.5-1.0	9	20	71	28	14	375	10	4	10
Children	1-3	13	29	90	35	16	400	10	6	15
	4-6	20	44	112	44	24	500	10	7	20
	7-10	28	62	132	52	28	700	10	7	30
Males	11-14	45	99	157	62	45	1,000	10	10	45
	15-18	66	145	176	69	59	1,000	10	10	65
	19-24	72	160	177	70	58	1,000	10	10	70
	25-50	79	174	176	70	63	1,000	5	10	80
	51+	77	170	173	68	63	1,000	5	10	80
Females	11-14	46	101	157	62	46	800	10	8	45
	15-18	55	120	163	64	44	800	10	8	55
	19-24	58	128	164	65	46	800	10	8	60
	25-50	63	138	163	64	50	800	5	8	65
	51+	65	143	160	63	50	800	5	8	65
Pregnant						60	800	10	10	65
Lactating	1st 6 months					65	1,300	10	12	65
	2nd 6 months					62	1,200	10	11	65

(Cont.)

Table 12.1 (Continued)

Category	Water-soluble vitamins							Minerals						
	Vit. C (mg)	Thiamin (mg)	Riboflavin (mg)	Niacin (mg N.E.)[e]	Vit. B6 (mg)	Folate (μg)	Vit. B12 (μg)	Ca (mg)	P (mg)	Mg (mg)	Fe (mg)	Zn (mg)	I (μg)	Se (μg)
Infants	30	0.3	0.4	5	0.3	25	0.3	400	300	40	6	5	40	10
	35	0.4	0.5	6	0.6	35	0.5	600	500	60	10	5	50	15
Children	40	0.7	0.8	9	1.0	50	0.7	800	800	80	10	10	70	20
	45	0.9	1.1	12	1.1	75	1.0	800	800	120	10	10	90	20
	45	1.0	1.2	13	1.4	100	1.4	800	800	170	10	10	120	30
Males	50	1.3	1.5	17	1.7	150	2.0	1,200	1,200	270	12	15	150	40
	60	1.5	1.8	20	2.0	200	2.0	1,200	1,200	400	12	15	150	50
	60	1.5	1.7	19	2.0	200	2.0	1,200	1,200	350	10	15	150	70
	60	1.5	1.7	19	2.0	200	2.0	800	800	350	10	15	150	70
	60	1.2	1.4	15	2.0	200	2.0	800	800	350	10	15	150	70
Females	50	1.1	1.3	15	1.4	150	2.0	1,200	1,200	280	15	12	150	45
	60	1.1	1.3	15	1.5	180	2.0	1,200	1,200	300	15	12	150	50
	60	1.1	1.3	15	1.6	180	2.0	1,200	1,200	280	15	12	150	55
	60	1.1	1.3	15	1.6	180	2.0	800	800	280	15	12	150	55
	60	1.0	1.2	13	1.6	180	2.0	800	800	280	10	12	150	55
Pregnant	70	1.5	1.6	17	2.2	400	2.2	1,200	1,200	320	30	15	175	65
Lactating	95	1.6	1.8	20	2.1	280	2.6	1,200	1,200	355	15	19	200	75
	90	1.6	1.7	20	2.1	260	2.6	1,200	1,200	340	15	16	200	75

Note. From *Recommended Dietary Allowances*, © 1989 by the National Academy of Sciences, National Academy Press, Washington, DC.

[a] The allowances, expressed as average daily intakes over time, are intended to provide for individual variations among most normal persons as they live in the United States under usual environmental stresses. Diets should be based on a variety of common foods in order to provide other nutrients for which human requirements have been less well defined. See text for detailed discussion of allowances and of nutrients not tabulated.

[b] Retinol equivalents. 1 retinol equivalent = 1 μg retinol or 6 μg β-carotene. See text for calculation of vitamin A activity of diets as retinol equivalents.

[c] As cholecalciferol. 10 μg cholecalciferol = 400 I.U. of vitamin D.

[d] α-Tocopherol equivalents. 100 mg d-α tocopherol = 1 α-T.E. See text for variation in allowances and calculation of vitamin E activity of the diet as α-tocopherol equivalents.

[e] 1 N.E. (niacin equivalent) is equal to 1 mg of niacin or 60 mg of dietary tryptophan.

199

Table 12.2 Estimated Safe and Adequate Daily Dietary Intakes of Selected Vitamins and Minerals

	Age (y)	Vitamins		Trace elements[a]				
		Biotin (µg)	Pantothenic acid (mg)	Copper (mg)	Manganese (mg)	Fluoride (mg)	Chromium (µg)	Molybdenum (mg)
Infants	0-0.5	10	2	0.4-0.6	0.3-0.6	0.1-0.5	10-40	15-30
	0.5-1	15	3	0.6-0.7	0.6-1.0	0.2-1.0	20-60	20-40
Children and adolescents	1-3	20	3	0.7-1.0	1.0-1.5	0.5-1.5	20-80	25-50
	4-6	25	3-4	1.0-1.5	1.5-2.0	1.0-2.5	30-120	30-75
	7-10	30	4-5	1.0-2.0	2.0-3.0	1.5-2.5	50-200	50-150
	11+	30-100	4-7	1.5-2.5	2.0-5.0	1.5-2.5	50-200	75-250
Adults		30-100	4-7	1.5-3.0	2.0-5.0	1.5-4.0	50-200	75-250

Note. From *Recommended Dietary Allowances*, © 1989 by the National Academy of Sciences, National Academy Press, Washington, DC.

Because there is less information on which to base allowances, these figures are not given in the main table of the RDA and are provided here in the form of ranges of recommended intakes.

[a]Because the toxic levels for many trace elements may be only several times the usual intakes, the upper levels for the trace elements given in this table should not be habitually exceeded.

Table 12.3 Medium Heights and Weights and Recommended Energy Intake

Category	Age (y) or condition	Weight (kg)	Weight (lb)	Height (cm)	Height (in.)	REE[a] (kcal/day)	Multiples of REE	Per kg	Per day[c]
								Average energy allowance (kcal)[b]	
Infants	0.0-0.5	6	13	60	24	320		108	650
	0.5-1.0	9	20	71	28	500		98	850
Children	1-3	13	29	90	35	740		102	1,300
	4-6	20	44	112	44	950		90	1,800
	7-10	28	62	132	52	1,130		70	2,000
Males	11-14	45	99	157	62	1,440	1.70	55	2,500
	15-18	66	145	176	69	1,760	1.67	45	3,000
	19-24	72	160	177	70	1,780	1.67	40	2,900
	25-50	79	174	176	70	1,800	1.60	37	2,900
	51+	77	170	173	68	1,530	1.50	30	2,300
Females	11-14	46	101	157	62	1,310	1.67	47	2,200
	15-18	55	120	163	64	1,370	1.60	40	2,200
	19-24	58	128	164	65	1,350	1.60	38	2,200
	25-50	63	138	163	64	1,380	1.55	36	2,200
	51+	65	143	160	63	1,280	1.50	30	1,900
Pregnant	1st trimester								+0
	2nd trimester								+300
	3rd trimester								+300
Lactating	1st 6 months								+500
	2nd 6 months								+500

Note. From *Recommended Dietary Allowances*, © 1989 by the National Academy of Sciences, National Academy Press, Washington, DC.

[a]Calculation of REE (Resting Energy Expenditure) based on FAO equations, then rounded.

[b]In the range of light to moderate activity, the coefficient of variation is ±20%.

[c]Figure is rounded.

results of genetic, experimental pathologic, epidemiologic, and intervention studies. These data establish beyond any reasonable doubt the close relationship between elevated blood cholesterol levels and coronary heart disease'' (p. 2081). The report states that the first step in the treatment of persons with high- to moderate-risk blood cholesterol levels is diet therapy and caloric restriction for weight normalization in those who are also overweight. The dietary approach should be to lower consumption of total fat, saturated fat, and cholesterol. Foods that are high in cholesterol (even if low in total proportion of fats) should be avoided. These include egg yolks, organ meats (livers, hearts, etc.), shrimp, lobster, and sardines. Plant foods such as fruits, vegetables, grains, cereals, nuts, and seeds contain no cholesterol and are highly recommended. Obese women frequently have elevated blood cholesterol levels and should be encouraged to follow this advice.

Table 12.4 Proportion (%) of Saturated, Monounsaturated, and Polyunsaturated Fats in Common Foods and Oils

Food	Saturated	Monounsaturated	Polyunsaturated
Butter, cream, milk	65	30	5
Bacon, pork	38	50	12
Lard	42	45	13
Chicken	33	39	28
Fish, shellfish	29	31	40
Coconut oil	92	6	2
Palm oil	86	12	2
Cocoa butter	63	34	3
Olive oil	15	76	9
Peanut oil	20	48	32
Soybean oil	16	24	60
Corn oil	13	26	61
Sunflower oil	11	22	57
Safflower oil	10	13	77

Recently, the *omega-3 fatty acids* have been extolled as providing positive health effects, including the reduction of risk factors for atherosclerosis and protection from immunologic reactions. These oils constitute an unusual class of polyunsaturated fatty acid (the first double bond is located three carbons from the terminal end of the molecule) and are a component of fish and fish oils. The omega-3 fatty acids appear to reduce the platelet aggregation that is associated with atherosclerosis, or plaque buildup on the inner surfaces of blood vessels (AHA, 1987). When large quantities of these oils are consumed, blood cholesterol and triglyceride levels decline. Studies have shown that diets high in fish oils help to reduce blood viscosity and tissue damage when blood flow is interrupted (ischemia) and to lower blood pressure (Harris, 1985). Fish from cold water (e.g., salmon, mackerel, and tuna) provide high amounts of omega-3 fatty acids and are commonly suggested

substitutes for red meats (which are high in saturated fats), but no specific dietary guidelines have yet been published.

Many people attempting to reduce their fat intake (much of it obtained from red meats) are concerned that their protein needs may not be met. The AHA (1987) guidelines address this issue by stating that protein intake should be approximately 15% of total calories. Protein can be obtained from grains, fish, poultry, and dairy products, but low saturated fat sources should be emphasized.

The remaining calories (30% or less from fat and 15% from protein sources) should be obtained from carbohydrates, particularly the complex carbohydrates of vegetables and grains. The current American diet consists of approximately 40% to 45% of calories from carbohydrates, and one third to one half of these calories come from the simple (refined) sugars. The AHA (1987) recommends that carbohydrate intake be increased to at least 50% to 55% of calories and emphasizes the increased consumption of vegetables, fruits, and grains. The Surgeon General's Report (USDHHS, 1988) states that most people should increase their consumption of whole-grain foods and cereal products, vegetables, and fruit to increase their intake of complex carbohydrate and fiber.

Although high blood cholesterol and atherosclerosis are more common in men than women, cardiovascular diseases are still the most common causes of death in women, who show very high rates of obesity, hypertension, and stroke.

Reduction of Obesity

Chapter 13 provides a more in-depth analysis of the problem of obesity in women. The extent of the problem is revealed by the emphasis given to obesity by the 1990 Objectives. One objective is that the prevalence of significant overweight (120% of desired weight) among the U.S. adult population be decreased to 17% in women (to 10% in men). Another objective states that 50% of the overweight population should adopt weight-loss regimens that attempt to achieve an appropriate balance of diet and physical activity. A third objective states that 90% of adults should come to understand that, to lose weight, one must consume foods that contain fewer calories, increase physical activity, or both (USDHEW, 1979).

The AHA (1987) statement recommends that the intake of total calories be reduced to correct obesity and then adjusted to maintain ideal body weight as defined by the 1959 Metropolitan Life Insurance Company tables (see Table 13.3). The AHA guidelines state that ''excess body fat is clearly related to an increase in the prevalence of high blood pressure, elevated serum cholesterol, and diabetes mellitus. . . . Even a moderate increase in adipose tissue, producing an excess body weight of 10 to 30% in young adults and middle-aged persons, is linked to heart disease'' (p. 1467A). The Surgeon General's Report (USDHHS, 1988) concludes that excesses in dietary intake can increase the risk of chronic

diseases. The report recommends achieving and maintaining a desirable body weight; choosing a dietary pattern in which caloric intake is consistent with energy expenditure; limiting the consumption of foods relatively high in calories, fats, and sugars; and increasing energy expenditure through regular and sustained physical activity.

Prevention of Hypertension

High salt (sodium) intake is associated with hypertension. The 1990 Objectives state that daily sodium ingestion for adults should be reduced at least to the 3- to 6-g range (USDHEW, 1979) The Surgeon General's Report recommends choosing foods low in sodium and limiting the amount of salt added both in food preparation and at the table. The AHA (1987) statement is more specific about this issue and states that there is compelling epidemiological evidence that a reduction in sodium intake to 1 g per 1,000 calories, not to exceed 3 g per day, is safe, feasible, and likely to prevent high blood pressure. Current consumption of salt is estimated at 4 to 5 g per day and is derived equally from naturally occurring food sources, sodium added during processing, and additions by the individual at the table. The AHA guidelines state that the body can function adequately with a sodium intake of less than 0.2 g per day.

A number of epidemiological studies have revealed an inverse relationship between dietary calcium and blood pressure, and a limited number of clinical trials have indicated that increasing calcium intake may lower high blood pressure. However, individuals vary in their blood pressure responses to increased calcium intake, and it has been deemed premature to make dietary recommendations regarding intake of this nutrient for the prevention of hypertension. Of particular interest to women is the association of low daily calcium intake and hypertension in pregnancy.

Because stroke is a common consequence of hypertension, lowering one's intake of dietary sodium and thus maintaining normal blood pressure is thought to decrease one's risk for stroke (cerebral vascular accident). Another issue of current nutritional concern is the prevention of cancer, the second leading cause of death in the United States.

Prevention of Cancer

Although the role of diet in the prevention of cancer remains a controversial issue, four national reports have made dietary recommendations to the American public in an effort to decrease the incidence of cancer. First, the National Research Council (1982) stated that evidence was sufficient to recommend a reduction in fat intake to prevent the risk of developing cancer. This statement recommended that fat intake not exceed 30% of caloric intake, that high-dosage vitamin-mineral supplements be avoided, and that the intake of salt-cured, pickled, and smoked foods be minimized.

Second, the American Cancer Society (1984) issued a report recommending that obesity be avoided, total fat intake be reduced, high-fiber foods be increased, high-dosage vitamin-mineral supplements be avoided, and intake of salt-cured, pickled, and smoked foods be minimal.

Third, the U.S. Department of Agriculture (USDA, 1985) provided a second edition of its dietary guidelines that added a statement about eating foods that contain adequate fiber.

Most recently, the National Cancer Institute has provided the most specific guideline yet, stating that fiber intake should increase to 20 to 30 g per day with an upper limit of 35 g. These guidelines also stated that one's diet should include a variety of fruits and vegetables; minimize consumption of salt-cured, pickled, or smoked foods; and contain no more than 30% of calories from fat. It also stated that obesity should be avoided (Butrum, Clifford, & Lanza, 1988).

Although all the evidence is not consistent, a high-fat diet has been implicated in breast and colon cancer (as well as prostate cancer). Total caloric intake may also be an important factor. Overweight women have a higher mortality rate for cancers of the ovary, breast, endometrium, gallbladder, and cervix than normal-weight women,

and obesity is associated with an increased risk of breast cancer in postmenopausal women (National Research Council, 1982).

Epidemiological studies have shown a correlation between the risk for colon cancer and a high-fat, low-fiber diet—a diet that is typical of Western society. The proposed hypothesis is that a high-fat diet increases the level of fecal bile acids, which act as promoters of colon cancer. Dietary fiber may play a protective role by (a) increasing the amount of fecal matter and thus reducing the concentration of potentially carcinogenic substances in the bowel, (b) reducing transit time through the colon and thus reducing contact between carcinogens and intestinal mucosa, or (c) altering bacterial metabolism (Greenwald & Lanza, 1986). Adult intakes of dietary fiber are typically about 20 g per day in industrialized nations. Common sources of fiber include vegetables (45%), cereals and legumes (35%), and fruits (20%) (Trowell & Burkitt, 1986).

Dietary fiber includes plant substances that are not digested or absorbed but that have important influences on the digestion and metabolism of carbohydrates and fats. Water-insoluble fiber includes cellulose and lignins. Wheat products are the most widely recognized sources of insoluble fiber, but vegetables and fruits also contain it. Soluble fiber includes pectins, gums, and storage polysaccharides. Primary sources include oat products, legumes, and fruits. Water-soluble fiber has been associated with the lowering of plasma lipid levels in hyperlipidemia and in the treatment of diabetes by lowering insulin requirements.

Another major health problem in the United States that is linked with dietary factors particularly affects women in their later years: osteoporosis.

Dietary Implications for the Prevention of Osteoporosis

Primary osteoporosis is an age-related disorder in which bone mass decreases and the risk of fractures—especially those of the vertebrae, hip, and wrist—increases (see chapter 10). Among the many factors associated with a decrease in bone mineral mass is a low intake of dietary calcium. Women consistently consume less calcium than their recommended daily allowance (RDA) (see Figure 12.1).

To address this issue, the government's second edition of its dietary guidelines (USDA, 1985) endorsed dairy products because calcium *may* play a role in preventing osteoporosis. The American Dietetic Association (1986) urged that one consume at least three to four daily servings of calcium-rich foods, and in 1988 the Surgeon General recommended that adolescent girls and adult women increase their consumption of low-fat dairy products that are high in calcium (USDHHS, 1988). Other dietary factors have been associated with the risk of osteoporosis, including high protein or fiber intake, vitamin D deficiency, alcohol abuse, and high caffeine intake (USDHHS, 1986).

Because most treatments for osteoporosis are ineffective in restoring lost bone and even in preventing further fractures, emphasis has been placed on preventing age-related bone loss *before* fractures occur. In 1984, the NIH Consensus Conference on Osteoporosis identified decreased estrogen production at menopause and a chronically

low intake of calcium as the most probable causes of osteoporosis. Thus, ERT has been advocated for the peri- and postmenopausal woman, and adequate calcium nutriture has been advocated throughout one's life.

Epidemiological evidence supports the concept that calcium intake during one's growing years may be especially important for the attainment of peak adult bone mass. In the later years, impaired calcium absorption related to aging (Type II, or senile, osteoporosis) may be responsive to increased calcium intake. However, increased calcium intake may have little effect on bone loss in women in the early stages of menopause without ERT.

The current RDA of 800 mg of calcium per day may be too low to maintain calcium balance in postmenopausal women. Many medical researchers are advocating a calcium intake of 1,000 mg per day for premenopausal and estrogen-treated women and 1,500 mg per day for postmenopausal women not receiving estrogen. Weight-bearing exercise (such as walking) is also advocated.

Table 12.5 includes a listing of calcium-rich foods as well as their caloric content. Because low-fat dairy foods are recommended, the third column

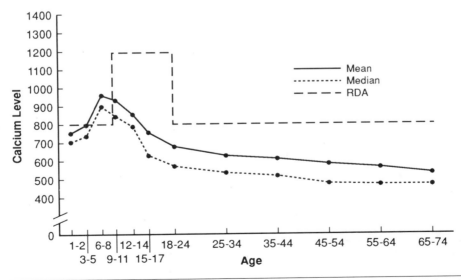

Figure 12.1 Daily calcium intake (mg) of U.S. women, 1976–1980. From "The Role of Calcium in Health" by the National Dairy Council, 1984, *Dairy Council Digest*, **55**(1), p. 2. Copyright 1984 by National Dairy Council. Courtesy of National Dairy Council.

Table 12.5 Sources of Dietary Calcium

Food	Calcium (mg)	Kcal	Calcium (mg)/Kcal	Cholesterol (gm)
Buttermilk (1 c)	285	100	2.8	9
Cheese				
American (1 oz)	174	106	1.6	27
Cheddar (1 oz)	204	114	1.7	30
Cottage, creamed (1/2 c)	68	108	.6	15
Cottage, low fat 2% (1/2 c)	77	101	.7	9
Mozzarella (1 oz)	147	80	1.8	22
Muenster (1 oz)	203	104	1.9	27
Swiss (1 oz)	272	105	2.5	26
Ice cream				
Hard, 11% fat (1/2 c)	88	135	.6	30
Hard 16% fat (1/2 c)	75	174	.4	44
Ice milk				
Hard, 4% fat (1 c)	176	185	.9	18
Soft, 3% fat (1 c)	274	225	1.2	13
Milk				
Whole (1 c)	291	150	1.9	33
Low fat, 2% (1 c)	297	121	2.4	18
Low fat, 1% (1 c)	300	100	3.0	10
Skim (1 c)	302	85	3.5	4
Yogurt				
Flavored, low fat (1 c)	389	194	2.0	10
Plain, low fat (1 c)	415	145	2.8	14
Fish and shellfish				
Oysters, raw (1 c)	226	160	1.4	120
Sardines, canned, with bones (3 oz)	371	175	2.1	85
Salmon, canned, with bones (3 oz)	167	120	1.4	34

Note. Data from United States Department of Agriculture Handbook No. 8 and United States Department of Agriculture/Department of Health and Human Services (1981).

in Table 12.5 indicates the milligrams of calcium obtained per calorie.

Nutritional Concerns Specific to Women

The extent to which the dietary requirements of women differ from those of men has only recently been recognized. The RDAs are the same for boys and girls until age 11. During adolescence, distinct changes in body composition result in different nutritional requirements. After adolescence, the woman requires slightly less vitamin A, vitamin E, vitamin B$_6$, thiamin, riboflavin, niacin, magnesium, protein, and energy intake because of her smaller body size and lean body mass. The larger body weight of the postpubertal male results in his expending more energy in performing the same task. It simply takes more energy to move a 70-kg body than a 55-kg body (refer to Table 12.3) and therefore more nutrients.

After approximately age 19, the fully mature menstruating woman requires more dietary iron than a man (see following discussion). Magnesium is the only major mineral with a higher RDA for the male than the female. There is no evidence that the requirements for the trace elements or the major electrolytes—sodium (Na^+), chloride (Cl^-) and potassium (K^+)—differ between the sexes.

There is no indication that girls or women utilize carbohydrates, fats, or proteins any differently than males. Although it has been suggested that women are especially adapted for endurance performance because they possess a larger quantity of storage fat (adipose tissue) than men, no study has yet shown that women are able to mobilize or utilize this storage fat better than men.

Nutritional Needs of Adolescence

The nutritional status of adolescents as a group is generally good, but low dietary intakes and marginal or subliminal deficiencies of iron, calcium, riboflavin, and vitamin A have been observed. Iron-deficient anemia, obesity, anorexia nervosa, and bulimia have been identified as special problems in young girls. Among the conditions that influence nutritional status are some special adolescent food habits such as skipping meals, snacking, eating at fast-food restaurants, and drug use. Teenage girls should have nutritional instruction directed at their specific dietary needs. The importance of adequate intake of calcium and iron should be emphasized, as should the need to develop good eating habits. Teenagers are the special ''prey'' of the health food and megavitamin

advocates, and many young girls will eat just about anything in an effort to achieve popularity and to ''fit in with the crowd.'' The obese teenager is especially vulnerable for she finds special prejudice everywhere she turns. It is no wonder that many of these girls try so many weight-loss gimmicks.

Nutritional Needs of Pregnancy and Lactation

Of course, there are special dietary needs for pregnancy and lactation. It is best that these topics be treated extensively elsewhere. It is sufficient to state here that these conditions require the additional intake of calories, protein, iron, calcium, vitamin D, and other nutrients. Current guidelines for weight gain, nutrient intake, and supplementation are available from the American College of Obstetricians and Gynecologists and the National Research Council.* Pregnant and lactating women who are also physically active must be very careful about fluid and caloric intake in particular and should consult either their physician or a nutritional counselor who is familiar with such matters to ensure that their nutritional status is adequately maintained with the extra stress of exercise.

Nutrition and Oral Contraceptives

Oral contraceptive (OC) agents are used by approximately 8.4 million women in the United States. Although few serious side effects have been reported, these agents may affect a number of metabolic and nutritional processes. However, much of the data is conflicting or inconsistent. For example, women using OCs have been found to have higher values for hematocrit, hemoglobin,

---

*Note. The address of the American College of Obstetricians and Gynecologists is 600 Maryland Avenue S.W., Suite 300 E., Washington, DC 20024. The address of the National Research Council is 2101 Constitution Avenue N.W., Washington, DC 20418.

serum vitamins (A, E, and K), total lipids, triglycerides, and iron and copper and lower values for thiamin, riboflavin, folacin, vitamin B_6, vitamin B_{12}, vitamin C, and zinc. However, an almost equal number of studies have found no significant differences between OC users and nonusers, especially when blood sampling was controlled for variations in the menstrual cycle (for brief reviews of this topic, see Grandjean, 1984, and "Nutrition and Women's Health Concerns," 1986).

Menstrual blood loss is less and iron-binding capacity higher in women taking OCs (Aftergood & Alfin-Slater, 1980). Therefore, the requirement for iron *may* be lower, but most probably still have inadequate iron intakes. Impairment of vitamin B_6 metabolism has been observed in some OC users as reflected by changes in tryptophan metabolism that in turn affect the availability of the neurotransmitter serotonin. This may cause menstrual depression. In such instances, daily supplements of 5 to 10 mg of vitamin B_6 have been suggested (Aftergood & Alfin-Slater, 1980).

Some physicians suggest that OC users ingest a low-level vitamin supplement (a maintenance rather than a therapeutic dose), but for women who consume a nutritionally adequate diet, vitamin and mineral supplements appear unnecessary.

Fad Dieting

One of the most commonly faced nutritional problems of girls and women is that of obesity or perceived obesity. It is so frequently a problem that almost every inactive American woman at some time in her life either "watches her weight" or very systematically "diets" to "reduce" (see chapter 13). Many women follow diets that are published in popular books and magazines or that are advocated by famous persons. Several studies have examined such weight-loss diets for nutrient quality, and most of these were found to be low in iron, calcium, magnesium, vitamins B_6 and B_{12}, thiamin, zinc, and copper. Whenever energy intake falls below about 1,200 kcal per day,

nutrient deficits are likely to occur. Many of these diets rely on some magical quality of a single food to somehow "melt" the excess fat away (e.g., the so-called grapefruit diet).

Iron Deficiency

Approximately 40% of women aged 20 to 50 have been estimated to show signs of iron inadequacy (Aftergood & Alfin-Slater, 1980). Males and non-menstruating, nonpregnant women lose about 1 mg of iron per day through the urine, feces, and sweat. Additional iron is lost in menstrual blood. Although the amount of iron lost per menstrual period is quite variable, the average loss is 0.5 mg per day (Haymes, 1980). This raises the adult woman's iron loss to 1.5 mg per day. The estimated iron requirement for the menstruating woman is 18 mg per day (only 10 mg per day for men) (see Table 12.1). It is difficult for women and teenage girls to obtain this much iron because the average American diet provides only about 6 mg of iron per 1,000 kcal (Aftergood & Alfin-Slater, 1980). If the average adult woman consumes 2,000 kcal (see Table 12.3), then she is consuming about 12 mg of iron per day. In addition, the absorbability of iron from different food sources is quite variable.

Basically, there are two major fractions of dietary iron. *Heme iron*, which is derived from animal sources, is well assimilated, and about 35% is absorbed. Although heme iron constitutes only about 5% to 10% of dietary iron in Western nations, it accounts for nearly one third of the absorbed iron (Cook, 1983). The bioavailability of nonheme iron (that from grains and vegetables) is much lower. Dietary nonheme iron forms a common pool in the intestinal tract, and its absorption is markedly influenced by the composition of the meal (Cook, 1983). The consumption of meat (as opposed to plant) proteins or vitamin C (ascorbic acid) has been shown to promote iron absorption (Lynch, 1980). Vitamin C is so efficient that a glass of orange juice containing 50 to 70 mg of vitamin C produces approximately a threefold increase in the nonheme iron absorption from a breakfast meal. Vitamin C has also been shown to reverse the inhibitory effects of substances such as coffee, tea, bran, egg, calcium, and phosphate. On the average, only about 10% of all consumed iron is actually absorbed. Therefore, the average woman consuming 12 mg of iron absorbs only about 1.2 mg of iron per day.

About 80% of the body iron resides in a *functional compartment* consisting of the proteins of oxygen storage and transport (hemoglobin and myoglobin). *Storage iron* makes up the rest of the body iron and is located in the liver, spleen, and bone marrow. Storage iron is metabolically inert and serves only to replenish losses from the functional compartment. Iron storage reflects the balance between dietary iron intake and iron losses from the body. In the United States, iron stores average about 300 mg in adult women (10% to 20% have zero iron stores) and about 1,000 mg in men (Cook, 1983). For comparison, a pint of blood contains 250 mg of iron, and the iron "cost" of a normal pregnancy is about 500 mg (Cook, 1983).

Because there is no mechanism for iron excretion, the level of body iron is regulated by the intestinal mucosa. Iron deficiency results from diminished dietary iron intake, excessive iron losses, or both. Women who do not menstruate and men have an iron loss of approximately 1 mg daily. Women who menstruate have an average daily loss of 1.5 to 2.0 mg. Because most of these women are replacing only about 1.2 mg of iron per day, the result is an iron deficit of 0.3 to 0.8 mg per day. This deficit must be obtained from the iron storage compartment. Iron deficiency occurs when these stores have been depleted. If we assume that a premenarcheal 12-year-old girl who weighs 45 kg has an iron storage of 20 mg • kg⁻¹ of body weight, then her total iron storage is 900 mg. With a daily iron deficit of about 0.3 mg, her iron storage will be depleted in about 8 years—by age 20 (Haymes, 1980). Presumably, this depletion could occur at an even faster rate with heavy menstrual flows. In one group of healthy (nonanemic) college women, two thirds had little or no iron stored in their bone

marrow (Scott & Pritchard, 1967). Iron depletion can occur without symptoms of iron deficiency anemia.

Anemia, iron deficiency anemia, or *nutritional anemia* is defined as a diminished concentration of circulating hemoglobin that can be corrected by increasing the intake of hematopoietic nutrients: iron, folate, and vitamin B_{12}. Some have added protein to this list (Cook, 1983). A woman is classified as anemic if her hemoglobin concentration falls below 12 mg per 100 ml of blood. About 22% of a group of women aged 17 to 44 with more than 10 mg of hemoglobin per 100 ml of blood had low plasma iron levels (USDHEW, 1972). This suggests that a large segment of the female population is iron deficient with or without anemia (Haymes, 1980).

There is considerable evidence that anemia has a detrimental effect on performance (Cook, 1983; Haymes, 1980). Even mild anemia is associated with decreased work output, although not all studies agree. Anemia in pregnancy is associated with increased risk of premature delivery, low birthweight, and placental hypertrophy (Cook, 1983). In children, iron deficiency is associated with impairment of intellectual performance. Iron deficiency may also lead to defects in cellular immunity and reduced activity of white blood cells, leading to increased numbers of bacterial infections.

To improve (or assure) iron status, women should consciously include iron-containing foods in their daily diet (particularly foods high in heme iron). To enhance absorption, citrus fruits or other vitamin C–containing foods should also be consumed. Foods cooked in cast-iron skillets (especially acidic foods) will contain additional iron. Table 12.6 lists the iron content of commonly eaten foods.

Diet and Bone Heath

The chapter on menopause included an extensive discussion of the role of exercise in the prevention of osteoporosis in menopausal and postmenopausal

Table 12.6 Iron Content of Commonly Eaten Foods

	Quantity	Iron (mg)
Heme Iron–Containing Foods		
Calf's liver[a]	100 g	9
Steak[a]	100 g	4.5
Pork chop[a]	100 g	4.5
Turkey, dark	100 g	2.5
Chicken, dark	100 g	2
Tuna	100 g	2
Chicken, light	100 g	1
Turkey, light	100 g	1
Non-Heme-Iron–Containing Foods		
Dried apricots	12	6
Prune juice	1/2 c	5
Baked beans	1/2 c	3
Raisins	1/2 c	2
Spinach	1/2 c	2
Tofu (well absorbed)	1/2 c	2
Enriched bread	1 slice	1
Enriched pasta	1/2 c	1
Wheat germ	1 tbsp	1

[a]Also high in cholesterol.

women. Because osteoporosis occurs in about 30% of all women, maintaining an active lifestyle that includes regular exercise in a weight-bearing position and making a conscious effort to eat foods known to be high in calcium were strongly recommended. This section treats the topic of diet and bone health more extensively. The question of whether osteoporosis is a nutritional disorder remains unclear, but several dietary constituents have been implicated as risk factors.

Increasing scientific evidence implicates calcium deficiency as a contributing factor in the development of osteoporosis. Dietary calcium deficiency (similar to that of iron deficiency) is largely a matter of decreased intake and bioavailability. When calcium intake is inadequate to offset the calcium needs of the body and the obligatory fecal and urinary losses, calcium must be withdrawn from the bones.

Data from national food consumption surveys indicate that a sizable number of adults ingest less calcium than the RDA of 800 mg. The calcium intake of women between ages 15 and 50 ranges from 400 to 1,050 mg per day, and the intake falls even lower after age 35. The mean intake is 540 mg per day. Evidence is accumulating to suggest that calcium intake in excess of the current RDA is necessary to achieve optimal bone health, particularly for the postmenopausal Caucasian woman and the elderly.

Various nutrient-nutrient, drug-nutrient, and disease-nutrient interactions affect absorption efficiency and calcium utilization. In addition, the efficiency of the intestinal absorption of calcium varies inversely with dietary calcium. This adaptability is present in variable degrees among individuals; however, the adaptation is rarely sufficient to compensate totally for a low calcium intake. Furthermore, the efficiency of calcium absorption decreases with age, beginning at about 45 years in females (60 in males), just at the time that calcium is most needed (i.e., the approaching menopausal years). The decline in calcium absorption efficiency with age is thought to be due to declining vitamin D metabolism ("Diet and Bone Health," 1982, p. 26).

High protein intake, particularly at levels exceeding the RDA for that nutrient, causes elevated urinary calcium excretion (hypercalciuria). It has been hypothesized that hypercalciuria induces negative calcium balance in adulthood, thereby increasing the risk of age-related osteoporosis ("Diet and Bone Health," 1982, p. 27). Apparently, high dietary protein consumption in adults increases the glomerular filtration rate and reduces the renal tubular reabsorption of calcium. Both factors contribute to an increased loss of calcium in urine and increase the amount of calcium required for calcium balance.

Nutritional Needs of Female Athletes

Physical training increases the requirement for total calories. A nutritionally balanced diet based on the four food groups (milk products; meat, fish, and poultry; fruits and vegetables; and grains) with sufficient calories to meet energy demands generally provides all the nutrients required by an athlete. The recommended proportion of carbohydrates, proteins, and fats remains about the same, but somewhat more emphasis is placed on complex carbohydrates. The position statement of the American Dietetic Association (1987) states that complex carbohydrates should account for "at least 50% to 55% of total calories for the athlete" (p. 933).

Protein needs *may* be a little higher as well because regular physical activity may cause a net catabolism of body protein. Athletes need protein for the maintenance of normal growth, for the restoration of tissues damaged by trauma, pro-

teinurea (loss of protein in urine), hemoglobinurea and myoglobinurea (loss of hemoglobin and myoglobin in urine), and losses of nitrogen during heavy sweating. Athletes also need protein for the development of increased muscle mass due to training. Obviously (in terms of this last category of protein need), the athlete who does not perform a great deal of heavy resistance weight training for the purpose of muscle building will not need as much protein as the one who does. The ADA recommends $1\ g \cdot kg^{-1}$ of body weight per day (rather than the RDA of $0.8\ g \cdot kg^{-1}$ per day) but states that this is more than adequately met by the typical American diet and so there is no need to supplement the usual athlete's diet. A diet providing 12% to 15% of calories from protein will provide sufficient protein unless the athlete is consuming less than 1,200 kcal daily (and some athletic women may be; see the following discussion).

The athlete may have an increased need for some vitamins and minerals that is easily met by a sound diet that also meets the extra caloric needs. Therefore, if an athlete is maintaining her body weight and the diet is well balanced, including foods from the four food groups in the recommended relative proportions, there should be no need to add vitamin or mineral supplements. A conscious effort to eat lots of fresh fruits and vegetables should provide any additional vitamins and minerals. This is the most desirable form of vitamin and mineral supplementation. It is important to realize that no single food or category of foods contains all the desired nutrients, so the best advice is to eat a wide variety of foods. Several studies have indicated that exercising women need more riboflavin, from 0.6 to 1.1 mg per 1,000 kcal (see Belko et al., 1983, 1985). However, riboflavin supplementation did not alter $\dot{V}O_2$max, and none of the subjects in these studies were athletes. Therefore, there is no conclusive evidence that performance is enhanced by any vitamin or mineral consumed in excess of the RDA. Supplementation carries the risk of toxicity from excessive blood vitamin levels.

Huse and Nelson (1977) have provided information on desirable diets for athletes. Table 12.7 gives caloric requirements of high school girls participating in various sporting events. Table 12.8 provides a daily diet of 2,300 kcal. Adjustments would need to be made to raise or lower the caloric intake to another level. Appropriate adjustments can be made simply by adjusting the size of a serving or adding or subtracting servings of the more caloric foods.

Consuming adequate iron and calcium is difficult if foods are not carefully selected or if one avoids some of the many high-fat foods (mainly meats and dairy products) that are excellent sources of these minerals. Female athletes are often susceptible to iron deficiency and may be at risk for bone mineral loss if they are amenorrheic.

Iron Deficiency Among Female Athletes

The topic of iron status among athletes is extremely complicated and confusing. For extensive reviews on this subject, the reader is referred to Clement and Sawchuk (1984); Eichner (1986); Newhouse and Clement (1988); Pate (1983), and Puhl, Van Handel, Williams, Bradley, and Harms (1985). For individual studies dealing with this topic in female athletes, refer to Blum, Sherman, and Boileau (1986); Diehl, Lohman, Smith, and Kertzer (1986); Lampe, Slavin, and Apple (1986); Manore, Besenfelder, Wells, Carroll, and Hooker (1989); Parr, Bachman, and Moss (1984); Risser et al. (1988); and Steenkamp, Fuller, Graves, Noakes, and Jacobs (1986). This section, rather than describing confusing and sometimes conflicting results, summarizes what appear to be the most important factors on which most investigators agree.

Athletes are at particular risk of developing iron deficiency because of inadequate dietary intake, poor absorption of iron (due to nonheme sources and rapid transport time through the intestine), increased iron losses in urine and sweat, gastrointestinal blood loss (particularly common in distance runners), and increased destruction of the red blood cells (foot-strike hemolysis). Female athletes are at particular risk for iron deficiency (low iron status) and iron deficiency anemia (low red cell iron) because of their low dietary intake of iron and menstrual losses.

Short-term sports anemia, or dilutional anemia, is not a true clinical anemia because it is caused by an expansion of the plasma volume while the red cell mass remains normal (i.e., the red blood cells are normal in size and hemoglobin content). In some cases there may also be a period of increased red blood cell destruction. The increased plasma volume enhances performance by improving the efficiency of cardiac output (increasing stroke volume) and maintaining blood pressure during peripheral dilation for temperature regulation. Most often, sports anemia is a transient response to training and is considered a normal, early adaptation to endurance training. Sports anemia is probably not detrimental to performance and does not progress to iron deficiency anemia.

Because bone marrow biopsies are highly invasive, iron storage (in the liver, spleen, and bone marrow) is usually determined by measuring serum ferritin or free erythrocyte porphyrin. Most studies have indicated that endurance athletes often have lower than normal iron stores. This is referred to as *iron depletion* and is considered the first stage of iron deficiency. Most investigators agree that there are no detrimental effects on performance due to iron depletion.

Iron deficiency erythropoiesis is determined by measuring serum iron, total iron-binding capacity, and transferrin saturation. Abnormal values indicate that the level of iron carried in the plasma, termed *transport iron*, is low. Many athletes experience this second stage of iron deficiency. There are no symptoms, and the condition is not considered detrimental to performance. Iron supplementation for these athletes remains controversial, and most investigations have shown that supplements do not benefit performance unless the subjects had a true anemia.

When full-blown iron deficiency anemia occurs (iron depletion, low transport iron, *and* low red

Table 12.7 Caloric Requirements of High School Girls Participating in Various Sports

Sport	Reference athlete		Daily caloric requirement for maintenance + light work (kcal)	Calories expended per minute of activity	Minutes of activity per event*	Calories expended per event	Approximate daily caloric requirement for maintenance + light work + event participation (kcal)
	Height	Weight (lb)					
Swimming	5' 4"	137	1,800	11.0	25	275	2,100
Tennis	5' 5"	115	1,600	7.1	60	420	2,000
Gymnastics (apparatus)	5' 7"	120	1,600	5.0	4.5	23	1,625
Basketball	5' 10"	160	2,200	8.6	32	275	2,500
Running (1 mi)	5' 7"	120	1,600	10.6	5.5	58	1,700

Note. From "Basic Balanced Diet Meets Requirements of Athletes," Huse and Nelson, **5**(1), 1977, *The Physician and Sportsmedicine*. Reprinted with permission of *The Physician and Sportsmedicine*. Copyright McGraw-Hill, Inc.

*The Athletic Department of Mayo High School, Rochester, MN, helped determine these values.

Table 12.8   A Daily 2,300-Kilocalorie Diet Suitable for an Athlete

Meat or substitute—8 oz daily
   1 oz of meat or its equivalent contains 7 g protein, 5 g fat, and 73 calories. Meat or substitutes include beef, veal, lamb, pork, fish, fowl, cold cuts,[a] cheese,[a] cottage cheese, egg,[a] shellfish,[a] and peanut butter[a].

Milk—3 c daily
   One cup of skim milk contains 8 g protein, 12 g carbohydrate, and 80 calories. Milk substitutes include whole,[a] 2%,[a] skim, evaporated milk[a], or ice cream[a].

Bread or substitute—8 servings daily
   One serving of bread or its equivalent contains 2 g protein, 15 g carbohydrate, and 68 calories. Bread or substitutes include bread, dinner rolls, biscuits, cereal, pancake,[a] waffle,[a] crackers, potato, rice, macaroni, noodles, popcorn, or pretzels.

Fat—8 servings daily
   One serving of fat contains 5 g fat and 45 calories. Fats or oils include butter,[a] margarine, oils, salad dressing, gravy,[a] bacon,[a] and cream.[a]

Vegetables—3 servings daily
   One serving of vegetable contains 2 g protein, 7 g carbohydrate, and 36 calories.

Fruit or fruit juice—6 servings daily
   One serving of fruit contains 10 g carbohydrate and 40 calories. Fruits may be fresh, frozen, cooked, or canned.

Dessert—1 serving daily
   One serving contains 3 g protein, 5 g fat, 30 g carbohydrate, and 200 calories. Desserts include pie, sweet roll, cookies, cake, or chocolate.

Sugars and sweets—1 serving daily
   One serving contains 15 g carbohydrate and 60 calories. Sugars and sweets include sugar, jelly, honey, syrup, hard candy, and carbonated beverage.

Note. From "Basic Balanced Diet Meets Requirements of Athletes," Huse and Nelson, **5**(1), 1977, *The Physician and Sportsmedicine.* Reprinted by permission of *The Physician and Sportsmedicine.* Copyright McGraw-Hill, Inc.
[a]Omit from diet to reduce cholesterol and/or saturated fat.

cell iron), performance capacity is decreased by the combined effects of reduced maximal oxygen uptake and muscle metabolism (tissue hypoxia). According to Eichner (1986), anemia is present if the hemoglobin concentration is less than 11.5 g • dl^{-1} for moderate exercisers or less than 11.0 g • dl^{-1} for elite aerobic athletes (this is because of the expanded plasma volume that results from exercise). This condition is medically treated with therapeutic doses of iron supplementation that, when successful in restoring normal hemoglobin levels, usually improve performance.

The American Dietetic Association (1987) recognizes that athletes may be at increased risk of developing iron deficiency but does not recom-mend iron supplementation without prior serum ferritin testing. Rather, the ADA recommends that all athletes make gradual changes in their training programs, maintain their body weight during the competitive season, and monitor their diets carefully to ensure adequate iron intake.

A recent study (Snyder, Dvorak, & Roepke, 1989) has confirmed what many believed previously: that women athletes who consume a primarily vegetarian diet may be at particular risk for developing low iron status. In that study, two groups of distance runners consumed comparable amounts of dietary iron, the bioavailability of which differed significantly. The vegetarian group (consuming primarily nonheme iron) had significantly lower iron status than the athletes who ate red meat.

In summary, women appear to be at greater risk of iron deficiency and anemia than men. This risk increases with strenuous training and particularly with endurance training. The lower serum iron seen in many women probably results from the interaction of a low dietary intake, increased red blood cell destruction, high menstrual iron loss, and high iron loss from sweating. Although there is little evidence that iron supplementation will aid performance when hemoglobin levels are normal, the routine use of low-dosage iron supplements may be beneficial. Another approach, of course, is to consciously consume more foods high in heme iron (see Table 12.6) with foods that are high in vitamin C to enhance absorption.

Dietary Studies of Female Athletes

Various reports have documented not only that female athletes eat poorly balanced diets but also that they lack basic knowledge of nutrition. Low intakes of energy and dietary iron, zinc, magnesium, calcium, folacin, and vitamin B_6 have been reported in gymnasts and ballerinas (Benson, Gillien, Bourdet, & Loosli, 1985; Cohen, Potosnak, Frank, & Baker, 1985; Loosli, Benson, Gillien, & Bourdet, 1986). Most of these athletes took vitamin and mineral supplements, usually in dosages several times the RDA for the vitamin B complex and vitamins A, C, and E. In addition, the proportion of total calories from carbohydrate sources was lower and the proportion from fat sources higher than the recommended quantities.

Elite Nordic skiers and college swimmers appear to consume better diets than the previously mentioned groups, which are normally extremely weight conscious. The Nordic skiers, however, had high fat and cholesterol intakes, a lower than recommended carbohydrate intake, and a low iron intake (Ellsworth, Hewitt, & Haskell, 1985). The swimmers had an elevated energy intake and low iron and vitamin D intakes (Adams, Porcello, & Vivian, 1982).

Two recent surveys of runners' attitudes and knowledge about nutrition have revealed a high incidence of self-reported eating disorders. In a recent survey of elite female runners, 13% reported a history of anorexia, 25% reported binge eating, 9% said they binged and purged, and 34% reported atypical eating behaviors (Clark, Nelson, & Evans, 1988). Responses to the recent National Runner's Survey on Dieting and Eating were interpreted by Brownell, Rodin, and Wilmore (1988) to indicate considerable "fear of fat," frequent dieting, preoccupation with being thinner, guilt feelings after eating, and frequent bingeing by female runners. These reports indicate that athletes have a considerable need for basic nutrition education. The following chapter discusses three common nutritional disorders in women.

Advice on Nutrition for Coaches and Athletes

What should a woman athlete eat? This commonly asked question has been partly answered in the preceding discussion, but this section briefly summarizes that discussion to directly and simply answer this question.

Eat a wide variety of foods. Follow the guidelines of the four food groups. Be sure to eat at least four servings a day of fruits and vegetables, and, for the most food value, eat them fresh and raw (as opposed to cooked or canned). Women especially need calcium, so eat a minimum of two servings of foods from the milk group. Skim or low-fat (2%) milk or yogurt is best. Different kinds of cheeses have different caloric values as well as calcium levels. You might want to consult food value tables such as *Nutritive Value of Foods* from the U.S. Department of Agriculture (Home and Garden Bulletin No. 72). This is available from the U.S. Government Printing Office (Washington, D.C. 20402) for $2.75 (Stock No. 001-000-03667-0). Ice cream (unfortunately) is not a particularly good way to get calcium (1 cup contains 194 mg of calcium) because of its high caloric value (about 255 kcal per cup).

Women have a special need for iron. Meats, particularly red meats, have much iron (the more easily absorbed heme iron) but are also high in fats. Other sources of iron are shrimp, almonds, spinach, raisins, cream of wheat, and dark-green leafy vegetables. To obtain as much iron as possible, eat these foods with some source of vitamin C, for example, an orange, orange juice, tomato, grapefruit, or broccoli (1 cup has 140 mg of vitamin C and 136 mg of calcium).

Women need vitamin B_6 and folic acid (folacin). Some foods that are recommended for these nutrients include dark-green leafy vegetables, bananas, lentils, dried beans, most fish and shellfish, muscle meats, and chicken.

By eating a wide variety of foods from the four food groups, you can be assured you are getting the proteins, essential fats, carbohydrates, vitamins, and minerals you need.

Maintain your ideal weight. If you are too fat, you need to do more aerobic exercise and eat somewhat less, particulary cutting down on foods that contain empty calories (see the following chapter). If you are too thin and lack the muscle mass needed for performance, engage in serious weight training.

Avoid too much fat (saturated fat in particular) and cholesterol. This advice is for good future health and for weight control. Choose *lean* meat, fish, poultry, dried beans and peas as protein sources. Limit your intake of butter, cream, hydrogenated margarines, shortenings, and foods made from such products. Broil, bake, or boil foods rather than fry them, and especially avoid deep-fat-fried foods.

Be sure to eat energy foods (carbohydrates) that do not contain too much sugar. In other words, avoid empty calories. Remember that about 58% of the total caloric intake should come from carbohydrate sources. "Carbos" are not bad! A diet high in sugar content is! Complex carbohydrates, such as beans, peas, nuts, seeds, fruits and vegetables, whole grain breads, cereals, and pasta, contain many essential nutrients not found in the refined sugars. Use as little of the sugars as you can. Avoid white sugar, brown sugar, raw sugar, honey, syrups (they are all basically the same thing despite merchandisers' claims), and as many of the foods that contain these substances as possible: candy, soft drinks, cake, cookies, pies. Do not avoid everything that is sweet, but eat as little of these as possible. When reading food labels, know that sucrose, glucose, maltose, dextrose, lactose, and fructose all mean *sugar*. The consumption of many complex carbohydrates also assures you of a good fiber content, which aids bowel regularity.

If you tend to gain weight (water retention) before your menstrual period, cut down on sodium intake about 5 days before your due date. The American diet tends to be too high in sodium anyway, so this is also good general advice. Some foods to avoid are table salt, potato chips, pretzels, salted nuts and popcorn, soy sauce, garlic salt, pickled foods, salted crackers, and cured meats.

Vitamin supplements are not necessary. This is particularly true for megadoses and megavitamins; you don't need them, and you will simply lose the vitamins your body does not need through your urine. Consequently, you will be wasting money, and some might even be harmful to you. If more vitamins and minerals are wanted, simply eat more fresh fruits and vegetables.

Drink plenty of water. Drink at least eight glasses of water a day, and if a great deal of sweat is lost during workouts, drink even more.

Finally, be critical of advertisements and the promotion of all miracle foods, supplements, and ergogenic (work-promoting) substances. Seek the expert advice of a qualified nutritionist (call your nearest university) with an advance degree from a reputable school before buying and consuming the "wonder" products that come along.

Summary

Many health problems can be traced to poor nutrition. Current nutritional guidelines are directed toward reducing dietary fat and cholesterol to prevent cardiovascular diseases, including hypertension and stroke. It was previously thought that these problems were limited to the male population, but today it is well recognized that women are also at risk.

Obesity is a major health problem among women today. Among the goals of the nation for 1990: limiting the consumption of foods high in calories, fats, and sugars and increasing energy expenditure through regular and sustained exercise. Additional dietary problems include the high consumption of salt (a risk factor related to hypertension) and, among women, the low consumption of calcium and iron.

The incidences of osteoporosis among post-menopausal women and of iron deficiency among women at any age are of special concern. These health problems need to be addressed more vigorously in the future.

Women have special nutritional needs because of pregnancy, lactation, and perhaps their use of oral contraceptives. Dietary studies of female athletes reveal not only that they tend to eat poorly balanced diets but also that they lack important nutritional information. Many athletes report atypical eating behaviors in their attempts to maintain a very low level of body fat. Often these athletes will consume large quantities of vitamins and minerals in an attempt to maintain energy levels while consuming very low calorie diets. Many of their efforts are counterproductive and in fact may lead to serious health problems such as iron deficiency and psychogenic eating disorders.

Chapter 13

Nutritional Disorders

Nutritional disorders are becoming more common in women, or at least women's awareness of these disorders has increased. This chapter discusses the prevalence, etiology, and role of exercise in obesity, anorexia nervosa, and bulimia.

Obesity

A major problem for many girls and women is overfatness, or *obesity*. A woman is considered obese if more than 30% of her body weight is fat (the corresponding standard for men is more than 20% body fat). Obesity is one of the most significant health problems in the United States today. Many illnesses are associated with obesity. Hypertension, coronary heart disease, thrombophlebitis, diabetes mellitus, respiratory problems, liver and gallbladder disorders, difficulties with pregnancy, osteoarthritis, increased surgical risk, and even increased incidence of accidents are all known to be related to excessive fatness (Sloane, 1980). In addition, being overweight is related to premature death. Statistics indicate that life expectancy is reduced when weight is increased as little as 5% over the theoretical limit for height. Obesity is also associated with increased emotional distress. In our society, overfat people are often stigmatized as "foodaholics" or "gluttons" and often experience job as well as social discrimination.

Prevalence of the Problem

Estimates of the prevalence of obesity range from 10% to 50% of the adult population, depending on the criterion used. Table 13.1 compares the prevalence of overweight women in 1960-62 with 1971-74 using the criterion of 20% or more from the desirable weight estimated from the regression of weight over height. National data reveal that more women than men are obese at all ages, that the frequency of overweightness increases in older age-groups, and that there is a decline in the percentage of the population that is overweight after age 55 (perhaps because of a higher mortality rate) (Bray, 1987). There are also some racial differences. Black women are more frequently overweight than white women by a ratio approaching or exceeding 2 to 1 (Kumanyika, 1987).

Body Fat Assessment

There are many ways to assess body fatness. The best methods involve laboratory techniques that require expensive equipment and considerable expertise (e.g., underwater weighing and skinfold assessment). These methods should always be used when assessing individuals for exercise or diet therapy prescriptions. However, they are too

Table 13.1 Prevalance of Overweight in U.S. Women

Age	1960-1962 (%)	1971-1974 (%)
20-74	25.1	23.8
20-24	9.1	9.6
25-34	14.8	17.1
35-44	23.2	24.3
45-54	28.9	27.8
55-64	38.6	34.7
65-74	38.8	31.5

Note. From "Overweight is Risking Fate" by G.A. Bray, 1987, *Annals of the New York Academy of Sciences, 499*, p. 19. (This volume is *Human Obesity*, edited by R.J. Wurtman and J.J. Wurtman.) Copyright 1987 by New York Academy of Sciences. Reprinted by permission. Data from the National Center for Health Statistics.

cumbersome for large-population epidemiological studies. Therefore, simple methods have evolved that use height and weight measures. The body mass index (BMI) is considered the most desirable of these methods because it has a better correlation with body fat (r between 0.7 and 0.8) measured from body density than do data derived from simple height and weight tables (Bray, 1987). The BMI is body weight (in kilograms divided by the square of the height (in meters), or BMI = kg/m^2.

Using life insurance data, Andres, Elahi, Tobin, Muller, and Brant (1985) calculated the BMI at which minimum mortality occurred at each decade of life. There was no sex difference. Table 13.2 presents the recommended age-adjusted ranges for BMI (sometimes called the *Quetelet index*). These values can be used to assess the magnitude of potential health risks associated with being overweight. Because major life insurance companies recognized the relationship between obesity and mortality long ago, tables were published for the

Table 13.2 Recommended Age-Adjusted Values for the Body Mass Index

Age-group	BMI (kg · m⁻²)
19-24	19-24
25-34	20-25
35-44	21-26
45-54	22-27
55-64	23-28
+65	24-29

Note. From "Overweight is Risking Fate" by G.A. Bray, 1987, *Annals of the New York Academy of Sciences, 499*, p. 17. (This volume is *Human Obesity*, edited by R.J. Wurtman and J.J. Wurtman.) Copyright 1987 by New York Academy of Sciences. Reprinted by permission.

most desirable weight ranges (least number of insurance claims). Probably the most commonly used table for women ages 18 and 25 was developed by the Metropolitan Life Insurance Company and is presented here as Table 13.3. This table may not be appropriate for weight-trained women, but it does provide an excellent guideline for most women. Table 13.4 presents similar information for younger girls.

A BMI exceeding 28 (the 85th percentile of the BMI for ages 20 to 29) is defined as *overweight* and one exceeding 32 as *severe overweight*. By this standard, 32.6 million adult Americans are overweight, and 11.5 million are severely overweight, according to National Center for Health Statistics data (Simopoulos, 1987). Table 13.5 documents the mean BMI values for women aged 30 to 39, 40 to 49, and 50 to 62 from three national studies.

Table 13.3 Desirable Weights for Women of Ages 25 and Over

Height (with 2-in. high shoes) Feet	Inches	Frame Small	Medium	Large
4	10	92-98	96-107	104-119
4	11	94-101	98-110	106-122
5	0	96-104	101-113	109-125
5	1	99-107	104-116	112-128
5	2	102-110	107-119	115-131
5	3	105-113	110-122	118-134
5	4	108-116	113-126	121-138
5	5	111-119	116-130	125-142
5	6	114-123	120-135	129-146
5	7	118-127	124-139	133-150
5	8	122-131	128-143	137-154
5	9	126-135	132-147	141-158
5	10	130-140	136-151	145-163
5	11	134-144	140-155	149-168
6	0	138-148	144-159	153-173

Note. For girls between 18 and 25, subtract 1 lb for each year under 25. Metropolitan Life Insurance Company, 1960.

Table 13.4 Height and Weight Table for Young Girls

Height (in.)	Age (yr)						
	6	8	10	12	14	16	18
38	33	—	—	—	—	—	—
40	36	—	—	—	—	—	—
42	39	—	—	—	—	—	—
44	42	42	—	—	—	—	—
46	47	48	—	—	—	—	—
48	52	52	53	—	—	—	—
50	56	57	59	62	—	—	—
52	—	64	64	67	—	—	—
54	—	69	70	71	—	—	—
56	—	—	78	79	83	—	—
58	—	—	84	86	93	101	—
60	—	—	91	95	101	108	111
62	—	—	—	105	109	115	118
64	—	—	—	114	117	120	123
66	—	—	—	—	124	128	130
68	—	—	—	—	133	136	138
70	—	—	—	—	136	140	144

Note. The following percentages of net weight have been added for clothing (shoes and sweaters not included): 35 to 65 lb: 3.0%; 66 to 82 lb: 2.5%; 83 lb and over: 2%.

From *Food, Nutrition and Diet Therapy* (5th ed., p. 700) by M. Krause and M. Hunscher, 1972, Philadelphia: W.B. Saunders. Copyright 1972 by W.B. Saunders Co. Reprinted by permission.

Excess Food Intake

Not only are Americans becoming heavier in relation to their height, but they are eating more as well. The most recent survey on food intake was completed on 1,503 women and 548 of their children (ages 1 to 5) in 1985. This study revealed a decrease in the mean intake of meat, poultry, and fish in comparison to data from 1977 (regardless of income level) but an increase in calories. Thus, excess intake has increased. Unfortunately, no data are available on energy expenditure. It is obvious, however, that activity levels have declined.

Overfat/"Overweight"

Strong, active people sometimes exceed the normal weight range for their sex, height, and frame size, but are rarely overfat. An obvious example is the football lineman who at 21 years of age is 6 ft 2 in. tall and weighs 200 lb. According to most height-and-weight tables, he is 26 lb overweight. He is probably quite lean and muscular, however, and not overfat.

Female athletes who train and compete regularly occasionally fall into the overweight but not overfat category, as the man in the previous example does. However, because most girls and women do not experience the large increase in lean body tissue (mostly muscle mass) that boys and men experience as they train, they need to pay much more attention to the type of weight they gain. Too many women athletes *are* overfat. There are numerous instances in which "also-ran" women athletes have lost considerable amounts of body weight (fat, of course) and become "winners."

Table 13.5 Mean Body Mass Index Values From Three National Studies

Study	Age		
	30-38	40-49	50-62
NHES	24.1 (5.12)	25.2 (5.49)	26.7 (5.24)
NHANES I	24.7 (5.71)	25.7 (5.61)	26.4 (5.69)
NHANES II	24.9 (5.79)	25.7 (6.07)	26.5 (5.56)

Note. Values are means; standard deviations are in parentheses. NHES = National Health Examination Survey, 1960-62; NHANES I = National Health and Nutrition Examination Survey I, 1971-74; NHANES II = National Health and Nutrition Examination Survey II, 1976-80.

From "Characteristics of Obesity: An Overview" by A.P. Simopoulos, 1987, *Annals of the New York Academy of Sciences,* **499**, pp. 7, 8. (This volume is *Human Obesity,* edited by R.J. Wurtman and J.J. Wurtman.) Copyright 1987 by New York Academy of Sciences. Used with permission.

For the inactive girl or woman, overfatness or obesity is a common problem. In fact, some extremely inactive women are overfat even though their weight is within the normal range for their age and height. This can occur in a woman with a very small lean body mass and indicates that one's level of fatness is more important than one's body weight alone.

Exercise and Weight Control

Physical inactivity is probably the single most important factor explaining the frequency of "creeping" overweight in modern societies. Despite much evidence to support this statement, people still widely believe two myths regarding exercise and weight loss:

- Myth 1. The amount of exercise needed to change caloric balance is too large to be practical.

- Myth 2. An increase in caloric expenditure through exercise will be accompanied by a corresponding increase in appetite and food intake. Exercise, according to this misconception, is self-defeating as a weight control measure because it only leads to eating more.

These incorrect notions can be refuted if we understand the concept of *caloric balance.*

Caloric Balance

Body weight is largely a function of *caloric energy balance.* When the caloric value of the foods eaten exactly balances the caloric value of the energy expended, body weight is maintained at a constant level (Figure 13.1a). *Positive energy balance* occurs when caloric intake exceeds caloric output (Figure 13.1b). A gain in body weight will result if a period of positive energy balance is not soon countered by a period of negative energy balance. *Negative energy balance* occurs when caloric expenditure exceeds caloric intake (Figure 13.1c). When negative energy balance persists for a period of time, a loss of body weight will occur.

A pound of body fat is equivalent to 3,500 kcal. A positive energy balance of 3,500 kcal will result in the gain of 1 lb of body fat. The opposite, of course, is also true. A negative energy balance of 3,500 kcal is necessary to lose 1 lb of body fat.

As Figure 13.1b shows, positive energy balance exists in the presence of a relatively increased food intake (overeating) or a relatively decreased exercise level. In either instance, the net effect is a gain in body fat, which is likely to result if caloric balance is not restored within a relatively short period of time. As Figure 13.1c illustrates, negative energy balance may occur as a result of diet restriction, a vigorous exercise program without a corresponding increase in food intake, or a combination of diet restriction and vigorous exercise.

Caloric Cost of Exercise

The metabolic cost of moving the body from one place to another is largely dependent on body weight. Table 13.6 indicates that weight-bearing

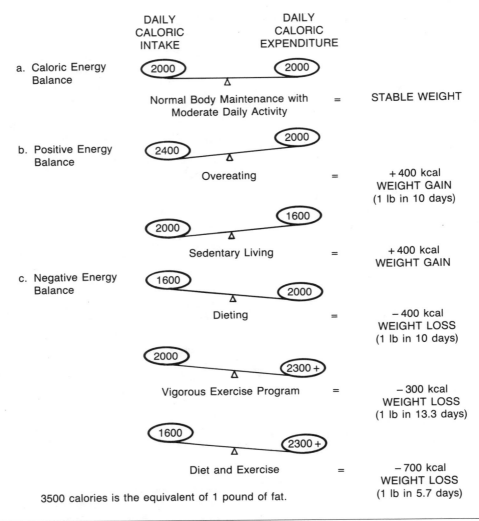

Figure 13.1 Caloric balance (a) Caloric energy balance leads to stable body weight. (b) Positive energy balance leads to a body weight gain whether due to overeating or inactivity. (c) Negative energy balance leads to weight loss whether due to dietary restriction, to vigorous exercise, or to a combination of dietary restriction and exercise.

activities that transport the body from one location to another require more energy expenditure in heavier people. For example, normal walking costs approximately 0.8 kcal $\cdot$ kg^{-1} $\cdot$ min^{-1}. For the petite girl of 110 lb, 1 min of walking costs 4 kcal. For the 190-pounder, however, that minute of walking costs 6.9 kcal. Note that the energy cost of running if one weighs 190 lb is nearly twice the cost than if one weighs 100 lb.

The MET is a useful index of caloric expenditure because it is adjusted for body weight. The MET, or metabolic equivalent, is a multiple of the resting metabolic rate and equals 3.5 milliliters of oxygen per kilogram of body weight per minute (3.5 ml $\cdot$ kg^{-1} $\cdot$ min^{-1}).

Exercise intensity can be classified using the MET

Table 13.6   The Effect of Body Weight on Energy Expenditure

Activity	Kcal • min^{-1} • kg^{-1}	50 kg (110 lb)	59 kg (130 lb)	68 kg (150 lb)	77 kg (170 lb)	86 kg (190 lb)
Walking (normal pace)	0.080	4.0[a]	4.7	5.4	6.2	6.9
Swimming (slow/crawl)	0.128	6.4	7.6	8.7	9.9	11.0
Running (9 min/mi)	0.193	9.7	11.4	13.1	14.9	16.6
Cycling (9.4 mph)	0.100	5.0	5.9	6.8	7.7	8.6

Note. From *Exercise Physiology: Energy, Nutrition and Human Performance* (Appendix D, pp. 486-493) by W.D. McArdle, F.I. Katch, and V.L. Katch, 1981, Philadelphia: Lea & Febiger. Copyright 1981 by Lea & Febiger. Adapted by permission. Data from Bannister and Brown (1968); Howley and Glover (1974); and Passmore and Durnin (1955).

[a]Caloric cost of the activity for 1 min (kcal).

Table 13.7   Classification of Exercise Intensity

Classification	HR	$\dot{V}O_2$ (L • min^{-1})	$\dot{V}O_2$ (ml • kg^{-1} • min^{-1})	Kcal • min^{-1}	METS
Light	100	.76	14.0	3.8	4.0
Moderate	135	1.55	28.4	7.8	8.1
Heavy	170	2.30	42.7	11.5	12.2

Note. Data are based on a 54-kg woman. $\dot{V}O_2$ is oxen uptake. One liter of oxygen uptake is equivalent to 5 kcal. MET (metabolic equivalent) is a multiple of resting metabolic rate, which is 0.250 L • min^{-1} or 3.5 ml • kg^{-1} • min^{-1}. Based on Sharkey (1979, p. 37).

concept. For example, consider Table 13.7. Light work is the equivalent of up to four times one's resting metabolism (or 4 METS) and requires approximately .76 L of oxygen uptake per minute ($\dot{V}O_2$ = .76 L • min^{-1}), or 14.0 ml of oxygen per kilogram of body weight (14 ml • kg^{-1} • min^{-1}). During light work, one is burning approximately 3.8 kcal. Moderate-intensity work requires between 1.09 to 2.0 L of oxygen per minute and, consequently, up to about 8.1 METS. Approximately 7.8 kcal are consumed per minute during moderate-intensity exercise.

Table 13.8 presents the energy cost of walking and running. Walking at 4 mph on flat terrain has a MET classification of 4.6 METS and requires approximately 4.4 kcal • min^{-1}. If one walked at this rate (a rather fast walk) for 1 h, 260 kcal would be expended. Jogging at a 10-minute-per-mile pace (6 mph) is equivalent to 10 METS. A 30-min jog at this pace would require the expenditure of about 285 kcal (95 kcal • min^{-1} × 30 min). Note that walking at 4 mph for 1 h is almost the equivalent of jogging at 6 mph for 30 min. The values in Table 13.8 are based on a body weight of 120 lb (54 kg), the "reference woman." At weights more or less than this, use the values in Table 13.6.

Table 13.9 presents the MET classifications for a number of useful and fun activities for weight loss and the development of physical fitness.

Table 13.8 Energy Cost of Walking, Jogging, and Running

Activity	Mph	Min • mi^{-1}	METS	Kcal • min^{-1}	Kcal • 30 min^{-1}
Walking	2.0	30:00	2.0	2.0	60
	2.5	24:00	2.5	2.4	70
	3.0	20:00	3.0	2.8	86
	3.5	17:08	3.5	3.3	100
	4.0	15:08	4.6	4.4	130
Jogging	4.5	13:20	5.7	5.4	162
	5.0	12:00	6.9	6.5	195
	5.5	10:55	8.3	7.9	237
	6.0	10:00	10.0	9.5	285
	7.0	8:35	11.5	10.9	330
Running	8.0	7:30	12.8	12.1	363
	9.0	6:40	14.2	13.4	402
	10.0	6:00	16.0	15.1	453
	12.0	5:00	20.0	18.9	570

Note. Data are based on a body weight of 120 lb (54 kg). One MET represents the oxygen requirement of the body sitting quietly. One MET equals 3.5 ml • kg^{-1} • min^{-1}.

From *Health and Fitness Through Physical Activity* (p. 134-135) by M.L. Pollock, J.H. Wilmore, and S.M. Fox III, 1978, New York: John Wiley & Sons, Inc. Copyright © 1978 by John Wiley & Sons, Inc. Adapted by permission of John Wiley & Sons, Inc.

Notice that the MET classification for rope skipping varies. This is dependent on the rate and style of skipping. Some women like to use bicycling as a means of increasing caloric expenditure. Cycling at slow speeds, however, is not very costly in terms of caloric expenditure. Cycling at 10 mph is equivalent to 6 METS, which points out that you must either cycle for long periods of time or cycle at fast rates to raise caloric expenditure significantly.

By increasing caloric expenditure 300 to 500 kcal per day through exercise, it is possible to lose a pound of fat (negative caloric balance equivalent to 3,500 kcal) in 7 to 12 exercise periods. For most people, this would mean a moderate jog for 30 min per day or a brisk walk for 45 to 60 min. If a modest diet were also followed, negative caloric balance would be greater and fat lost at a greater rate. For example, reducing daily food intake by one buttered slice of bread or one glass of dry white wine (approximately equivalent to 100 kcal),

combined with a jogging program of 30 min per day, 3 days per week, could result in a total weight loss of 20 to 30 lb per year, or about 1/2 lb per week. Furthermore, this gradual form of weight loss has been found to be more permanent than rapid losses of weight due to fasting or semi-starvation diets.

This information should convince anyone that the first myth regarding exercise and weight loss—that the amount of exercise needed to change caloric balance is too great to be practical—is totally false. Even a relatively small amount of regular exercise over and above what an individual usually does will contribute significantly to the total picture of caloric balance.

Effects of Exercise on Appetite and Food Intake

The second myth regarding exercise and weight loss is that exercise serves only to increase food

Table 13.9 Metabolic Equivalents (METS) Required by Various Activities

Activity	3	4	5	6	7	8	9	10	11	12
			METS							
Table tennis	x	x	Increasing demands with increasing skill and duration of rallies							
Golf		Pull cart	Carry clubs							
Badminton, volleyball, tennis		x	x	As with table tennis-----						
		x	x	x	x	x	As above----------			
		Social Doubles	Social Doubles				Singles			
						Competitive------------------				
Squash and handball				x	x	x	Competitive------------------			
Walking (mph)	3	3½	4							
Walking/jogging		x	x	x						
Jogging/running (mph)				5	5½	6	7	8	9	
Skating			x	x	x	x	x	x		
Rope skipping				x	x	x	x	x	x	x
Skiing (cross-country)			x	x[a]	x[a]	x[a]	x[a]	x[a]	x[b]	x[b]
Mountain hiking			x	x	x	x	x	x		
Horseback riding		x	Trot	x	Gallop----------					
Calisthenics, games, etc.		x	x	x	x	x				
Dynamic weight lifting			Disproportionate blood pressure rise may add to hazards.							
Dancing	x	x	x	x	x	x	x	x		
Cycling (mph)	4	6	8	10	12	13	14	15		
Rowing		x	x	x	x	x	x	x	x	
Swimming	x	x	x	x	x	x	Competitive--------------			

Note. From *Health and Fitness Through Physical Activity* (p. 342) by M.L. Pollock, J.H. Wilmore, and S.M. Fox III, 1978, New York: John Wiley & Sons, Inc. Copyright © 1978 by John Wiley & Sons, Inc. Reprinted by permission of John Wiley & Sons, Inc.

Adapted by S.M. Fox, M.D., from the table of Dr. Bruno Balke, and Aspen Health Center, Aspen, CO.

All intensities increase with commitment or competitiveness of approach.

[a]Intermittent. [b]Continuous.

intake and therefore is self-defeating in a weight-loss program.

Many animal studies have shown that vigorous exercise fails to stimulate the appetite. Mayer (1968) reported that food consumption in animals closely follows energy expenditure only within the range of so-called normal activity. Rats exercised 1 or 2 h daily did not eat more than sedentary animals; in fact, they ate somewhat less.

In another study, young, growing rats who ran on a treadmill 5 days per week, twice per day for 12 weeks, ate significantly less than sedentary controls and gained considerably less weight (Crews, Fuge, Oscai, Holloszy, & Shank, 1969). Oscai and Holloszy (1969) studied the effects of a strenuous swimming program 5 days per week over an 18-week period. Swimming periods were progressively increased from 10 min to 2 h each day. Exercise resulted in a chronically negative caloric balance that was reflected in a significant weight loss. The voluntary food intake of the exercised rats was significantly lower than that of the sedentary, free-eating animals, which gained weight throughout the study period.

Careful analysis of these and other studies suggests that the suppressive effect of exercise on appetite is related more to the severity than to the duration of exercise. Light-to-moderate exercise of extended duration does not affect the appetite; more severe exercise of shorter duration may actually suppress appetite. This observation tends to support the hypothesis that exercise-induced appetite suppression is mediated by the catecholamines epinephrine and norepinephrine, which are known to be close to resting levels during light-to-moderate exercise but to increase markedly in response to strenuous exercise.

There is also evidence of appetite suppression due to exercise in humans. Dempsey (1964) exercised obese and nonobese young men 1 h per day for 8 weeks at a sufficient intensity to cause a marked weight loss in both groups. Daily food intake records showed no effect on food intake. In another study, 45 min of jogging and calisthenics three times per week did not affect the food intake of middle-aged men (Holloszy, Skinner, Toro, & Cureton, 1964).

Katch, Michael, and Jones (1969) studied the effects of training on the dietary intake of college women. They studied tennis players and swimmers at the University of California at Santa Barbara. The tennis players practiced 1 h per day at an energy expenditure classified as moderate. The swimmers swam 2,000 to 4,000 m daily in a 2-h period. Their training was classified as strenuous.

During the 5-month period there were no changes in body weight, percent body fat, or lean body weight for either group of athletes. The use of a 7-day dietary inventory before and after the training period revealed no differences in caloric intake or in protein, fat, or carbohydrate consumption. More recently, sedentary obese women were studied during short periods (19 days) and longer periods (57 days) in which energy expenditure was increased to 110% or 125% of their sedentary level by treadmill exercise (Woo, Garrow, & Pi-Sunyer, 1982a, 1982b). The women did not increase their energy intake in proportion to the increase in energy expenditure, and they lost weight during the longer study period. Therefore, exercise does not necessarily lead to increased food intake and may even serve to suppress appetite.

Effects of Exercise on Weight Loss and Body Composition

When weight is lost solely by dieting, a substantial amount of that weight loss consists of lean body tissue and fluids. It is estimated that as much as 35% to 45% of the weight lost with severe dietary restriction is from the lean body component.

The advantage of exercise over diet restriction to accomplish negative energy balance (caloric deficit) is that exercise affords protection against the loss of body protein and lean body weight usually associated with dieting. There is considerable evidence to support this. In one study, two groups of rats lost the same amount of body weight. The exercising rats, however, lost significantly more fat and less than half as much body protein as the sedentary food-restricted rats. The exercised rats also lost significantly less body water (Oscai & Holloszy, 1969).

Table 13.10 presents data obtained on the effects of diet and exercise on the body composition of adult women (ages 20 to 45) during weight reduction (Zuti, 1972). Weight-reduction programs for the three groups were designed to achieve a caloric deficit of 500 kcal per day. The diet group achieved this through diet restriction alone. The exercise group performed exercise requiring 500 kcal and maintained its regular diet. The combination diet-exercise group achieved a 250-kcal reduction in diet and a 250-kcal expenditure through exercise.

Table 13.10 Effects of Diet and Exercise on the Body Composition of Adult Women

Group	Body weight	Body fat	Lean body tissue
Diet	−11.7	− 9.3	−2.4
Exercise	−10.6	−12.6	+2.0
Exercise-diet	−12.0	−13.0	+1.0

Note. Values are pounds.

From *Effects of Diet and Exercise on Body Composition of Adult Women During Weight Reduction* (doctoral dissertation) by W.B. Zuti, 1972, Kent State University. Reprinted by permission of W.B. Zuti.

The exercise regimen consisted of walking, walking and jogging, bench stepping, and calisthenics. All three groups lost weight. However, both exercise groups showed greater reductions in body fat than the diet group. The exercise groups not only maintained lean body weight but also increased it slightly as the result of training.

The loss of lean body tissue in the diet group is undesirable, of course, because it means a loss of muscle tissue. The exercise groups also showed evidence of increased cardiorespiratory endurance, but the diet group did not.

Body composition changes were assessed in normal and obese high school girls following 15 to 29 weeks of walking, jogging, and running (Moody, Wilmore, Girandola, & Royce, 1972). There were no dietary restrictions. The obese group demonstrated significant reductions in body weight and percent body fat and increases in body density and lean body mass. The normal-weight group showed no significant changes in body composition. Similar results have been reported in more recent studies. Hagan, Upton, Wong, and Whittam (1986) reported that a diet of 1,200 kcal per day, coupled with walking and running 5 days per week for 30 min, resulted in a 500-kcal deficit in significantly overweight women. The subjects who dieted *and* exercised lost significantly more body weight *and* fat weight than the groups that dieted without exercise or that exercised without dieting.

Two conclusions can be drawn from these studies:

1. Exercise affects body composition by lowering or preventing an increase in body fat and by increasing lean body tissue.
2. Exercise has a favorable effect on body composition with or without a change in body weight.

In explanation, exercise stimulates amino acid conservation and protein synthesis with a direct effect on muscle tissue. The anabolic effects of increased levels of growth hormone secondary to exercise not only conserves lean body mass during weight loss but also may contribute to an increase in muscle mass.

The water losses associated with diet restriction and low carbohydrate intake may eventually lead to depletion of the body's glycogen stores. With a loss of 1 g of glycogen, there is a corresponding loss of approximately 3 g of water. During severe dietary restriction, 3 to 5 lb of weight loss per week can result from water losses. This often occurs with the high-protein, low-carbohydrate diets. Water losses, of course, are not fat losses—another reason to include exercise in a weight-reduction program.

Fat-Mobilizing Effects of Exercise

Many of the differences occurring between the diet and the exercise groups described previously are due to the lipid- (or fat-) mobilizing effects of exercise. During prolonged exercise (which is usually considered longer than 20 min), fatty acid mobilization from body fat stores, a process called *lipolysis*, increases markedly. Furthermore, the fat-mobilizing effect of exercise may persist for a considerable period of time after exercise.

Lipolysis is probably mediated by increased activity of the sympathetic nervous system and the resultant surge in norepinephrine (also thought to be related to appetite suppression). Not only is lipolysis responsible for the greater loss of fat in exercising than in nonexercising, diet-restricted subjects, but it also aids the conservation of lean body tissue by making energy from fat stores available to muscle and organ cells. Consequently, with certain forms of exercise (and almost always with individuals who were previously very inactive), there is a slight increase in muscle mass at the same time that there is a loss of body fat. Thus, body weight may change very little during the first few weeks of an exercise program. This is sometimes discouraging to the exercise participant who expects to see massive weight losses almost immediately. Nevertheless, body composition is changing significantly, and that must not be overlooked. Rather than looking solely for weight losses on the bathroom scale, one should consider other indices of change in body composition.

Exercise, Weight Loss, and the Serum Lipids

Despite evidence of increased fatty acid mobilization during prolonged exercise, reports regarding changes in the serum lipids due to physical conditioning are contradictory. Substantial declines in serum cholesterol and *triglycerides* have been found in obese (Dudleston & Bennion, 1970) and overweight women (Zuti, 1972). The decrease in serum lipids paralleled body weight changes, and the subjects with the highest initial levels had the largest reductions. Some investigations, however, have failed to find changes in serum lipids with regular exercise. Björntorp et al. (1973), for example, did not find a posttraining reduction in serum triglycerides or cholesterol in women with juvenile-onset of obesity. (These women may have special problems: see next section.) Lewis et al. (1976) also failed to find a significant decline in serum lipids with training in obese women. They did report, however, a favorable change in the ratio of HDL-C to LDL-C, which indicates a desirable alteration in cholesterol metabolism and a decreased risk of cardiovascular disease.

These reports suggest that when serum cholesterol and triglycerides are within normal ranges,

they are not altered by weight reduction from increased physical activity. However, when higher than normal levels of these substances exist (*hyperlipidemia*), exercise may be effective in lowering initial values.

Facts About Body Fat

The study of *adipose tissue* (fat) in recent years has revealed at least two kinds of body fatness. *Fat cell hypertrophy* occurs when there is a normal number of *adipocytes* (fat cells) but the cells are greatly enlarged (or hypertrophied). Adult-onset obesity is characterized by enlarged adipocytes. *Fat cell hyperplasia* occurs when adipocytes are of normal size but excessive in number. An early onset of *hypercellularity* (increased number of fat cells) leads to the more severe form of obesity because fat cells, once formed, remain for life. There is no nonsurgical way a fat cell can be destroyed once it is formed; it can only be reduced in size.

People with hypercellular obesity usually have a difficult time throughout their lives trying to control their body weight. In fact, some weight-control specialists have referred to the "yo-yo" cycle of fat loss and fat gain among the long-term obese as the "plight of the starving fat cells" (Katch & McArdle, 1977, p. 141).

Most obese people have both more and larger (fatter) fat cells than nonobese people. Depending on the extent of adiposity, fat cells may be two or three times normal size. Some obese people have five to six times as many fat cells as do nonobese people (Puhl, 1977).

Apparently, fat cell number is subject to change at certain sensitive periods during maturation. Although much more needs to be learned in regard to this question, it appears that the last trimester of pregnancy, the first year of life, and the adolescent growth spurt are particularly vulnerable periods for an increase in the number of fat cells. This information points out the importance of weight control during pregnancy and the fact that a chubby baby and the preadolescent may be particularly vulnerable to the effects of prolonged positive energy balance (whether because of over-nutrition or underactivity) later in life. The facts clearly show that obese people who were obese as children have a higher number of fat cells and more difficulty controlling their level of body fat than people with ''middle-aged spread.'' However, adult hyperplasia may occur with certain types of obesity.

Fat loss is accomplished by a decrease in the size of fat cells; there is no change in fat cell number. Animal research indicates that exercise programs during growth periods result in a significant reduction in both cell size and number in later life (Booth, Booth, & Taylor, 1974; Oscai, Babirak, McGarr, & Spirakis, 1974). Apparently, exercise performed early in life (during growth) depresses the growth of new fat cells. This, of course, emphasizes the importance of a physically active life in the childhood years. Obviously, the early prevention of obesity through exercise and diet restriction is the most effective way to curb the problem of obesity in adult life.

Advice on Fat Loss

The minimum amount of body fat consistent with good health is approximately 7% to 10% for women. Somewhere between the lower extreme of 7% and the upper limit for obesity, 30%, is the level most desirable. Women over the age of 25 will tend to lose some lean body tissue, and body density will decrease and fat will be gained. Most women in their 30s and beyond need to either become more active physically or practice at least occasional dietary restriction. The ''battle of the bulge'' begins even earlier for physically inactive women.

Women who wish to lose body fat may be tempted to try some of the popular gimmicks advocated widely. Every day there are ''new and revolutionary'' diet plans. Beware! There is no sure or safe ''rapid method'' of fat reduction. Don't believe the hype of the popular press. Especially beware of the high-protein, low-carbohydrate diets so prevalent today.

Also, beware of the gimmicks of the health spa and figure salon. Unfortunately, there is no evidence that spot reduction works. Burn off the calories and the fat will come too. Sit-ups or other such exercises will tone or firm up the underlying musculature but will not selectively burn off the ''tummy roll'' or any other roll. Vibrating belts do not burn off excess fat and pounding or massage work does not reduce fatty layers. These techniques do not ''break up'' fat cells, and neither does body wrapping, which is dangerous for many people. Sitting in a sauna bath or using a sauna belt will cause one to lose body water, and that means body weight that is not fat.

Also beware of the ''special techniques and diets'' to remove *cellulite*, which is the name given by advertising promoters for large accumulations of fat that appear to be dimpled. Cellulite is not a special sort of fat. It is simply a large aggregation of fat cells supported by connective tissue.

The dimpling and patterning sometimes seen is caused by the connective tissue. There is no special way to remove this accumulation of fat other than the methods of dietary restriction and increased exercise previously described. Fat is fat and can be reduced only by prolonged negative caloric balance.

Using drugs for weight loss is often dangerous, especially without medical supervision. Amphetamines or their derivatives have been used for appetite suppression. These drugs can be addicting and dangerous. Laxatives and diuretics encourage the loss of body water and may cause severe dehydration. This is contraindicated for good health and physical performance.

In summary, exercise affects body composition by lowering or preventing an increase in body fat and by maintaining lean body tissue. It is possible to increase caloric expenditure sufficiently by means of regularly performed exercise without diet restriction to produce a marked decrease in body weight. As much as 78% of the long-term weight loss occurring in exercising subjects (both animals and humans) is due to loss of body fat. Exercise combined with food restriction appears to be the safest and fastest approach to weight reduction in obese individuals who desire to lose weight at a fairly rapid rate but who cannot tolerate severe caloric restriction for long periods of time.

The scientific literature on obesity is extensive. The interested reader is referred to the following reviews for further information: Hartung, 1984; Oscai, 1984; McNamara, 1987; "Symposium on Exercise," 1986; Wurtman and Wurtman, 1987; Fisler, 1987; Hagan, 1988.

Eating Disorders

Although obesity is considered by many to be an eating disorder, the term has generally been confined to anorexia nervosa and bulimia. These eating disorders are attracting considerable attention in the popular and medical press. The American College of Physicians (ACOP) (1986) estimated that anorexia nervosa and bulimia affect 10% to 15% of adolescent girls and young women. Persons with eating disorders "engage in various compulsive acts and rituals to lose or control weight, including abstaining from food, vomiting, ingesting cathartic or diuretic substances, and exercising vigorously to the point of exhaustion" (ACOP, 1986, p. 790). Athletic girls and women, especially those who participate in sports in which body weight is important for performance, may be at particular risk of developing an eating disorder.

Anorexia Nervosa

Anorexia nervosa is an endocrinologic and psychological syndrome characterized by extreme weight loss, body-image disturbance, intense preoccupation with food, and intense fear of becoming fat. Approximately 90% of those with anorexia are women. According to the American College Health Association (ACHA, 1984), an anorexic person displays some or all of the following characteristics:

- An intense and obsessive preoccupation with thinness
- Weight loss of at least 25% of the original body weight
- Distortion of body image ("sees" body as fat even when emaciated)
- No known physical illness that would account for weight loss

- Extreme self-imposed dieting, hyperactive exercise practices, or both
- Amenorrhea
- Depression, mood disturbance, chronic feelings of low self-esteem, and insomnia or other sleeping disorders
- Frequent weighings (e.g., several times a day)
- Hypothermia (because of the body's inability to maintain heat)
- Constipation (because the intestinal tract is disturbed by the failure to take in and retain normal amounts of foods and fluids)
- Inability to think clearly; lethargy

The incidence of anorexia nervosa has been estimated at 0.24 to 1.6 per 100,000 people but differs greatly in different populations. According to Warren (1985), at-risk populations include middle-class adolescent girls (1 of every 100) and professional ballet dancers (1 in 20 to 1 in 5, depending on the competitive level of the company). The syndrome is rare in men (female-to-male ratio is 9 to 1) but does occur in men who are training for competitive activity in which weight restriction is important.

Sociocultural factors may be important in the development of anorexia. Such factors may include the change from plumpness to slimness as an ideal for women and the pressure on women to achieve and be successful, independent, and competitive while maintaining more traditional roles (ACOP, 1986).

Bulimia

Bulimia (bulimarexia) is a syndrome separate from anorexia nervosa that is characterized by a behavior pattern of alternating extreme bingeing with self-induced vomiting, fasting, abuse of laxatives and diuretics, or all these. Bulimics are not extremely thin (like anorexics), and they are usually secretive about their addiction to food and to purging and therefore are not readily identifiable. According to the ACHA (1984), bulimia is characterized by the following:

- Hypokalemia due to low potassium intake or high loss of potassium from vomiting (the most serious medical consequence because it can lead to heart or kidney failure)
- Dehydration
- Internal bleeding, including gastric ulcers due to trauma from forceful vomiting
- Salivary gland enlargement
- Tooth and gum decay caused by stomach acids
- Cognitive disturbance secondary to starvation

The bulimic person generally appears healthy, but anxiety and depression have developed by the time medical help is sought, and about 5% have attempted suicide. Typically, bulimics are high achievers, socially ambitious, and have marked parental dependence. They often display impulsive behaviors, including drug abuse, kleptomania, and sexual promiscuity (ACOP, 1986).

Compared to anorexia nervosa, bulimia usually occurs in a slightly older age-group and more frequently in males. Its prevalence is higher than that of anorexia nervosa and is estimated between 7.8% and 19.6% of college women. It has been identified in jockeys, wrestlers, gymnasts, models, ballet dancers, and actors and actresses (ACOP, 1986).

Athletes and Eating Disorders

As early as 1980, excessive weight loss and food aversion was documented in young athletes (Smith, 1980). Yates, Leehey, and Shisslak (1983) proposed that running is an analogue of anorexia nervosa and therefore attracts persons with anorexic personalities. Blumenthal, O'Toole, and Chang (1984) contrasted the psychological traits of obligatory runners with those of patients with anorexia nervosa. The patients obtained more pathological scores than the runners on 8 of 10 subscales of the Minnesota Multiphasic Personality Inventory (MMPI). Another study (Weight & Noakes, 1987) reported the incidence of abnormal eating attitudes that are symptomatic of anorexia nervosa in 125 female distance runners. Of the 14% displaying abnormal eating attitudes, only 5 had a low body mass and a past history of amenorrhea, and 1 had been treated for anorexia nervosa. Neither of these studies (Blumenthal et al., 1984; Weight & Noakes, 1987) supported Yates's hypothesis that running was an analogue of anorexia nervosa.

Nevertheless, numerous studies have documented the incidence of pathogenic weight-control behaviors in female athletes. Of 182 athletes in 10 sports, 32% practiced at least one weight-control behavior defined as pathogenic: self-induced vomiting; bingeing more than twice weekly; use of laxatives, diet pills, or diuretics (Rosen, McKeag, Hough, & Curley, 1986). The gymnasts, field hockey players, and distance runners reported the highest incidence of pathogenic behaviors.

In a large group of accomplished young swimmers (ages 9 to 18), 15.4% of the girls and 24.8% of those who were postmenarcheal used pathogenic weight-loss techniques. Only 3.6% of the boys used such techniques (Dummer, Rosen, Heusner, Roberts, & Counsilman, 1987). The swimmers' attitudes about weight seemed more related to societal influences (to be attractive) than to the demands of swimming (to improve performance). In contrast to this latter finding, Rosen and Hough (1988) reported that all the women college gymnasts they studied were dieting to improve their performance as well as to lose weight. Sixty-two percent were using at least one form of pathogenic weight-control behavior, and 75% of the gymnasts who had been told by their coaches that they were too heavy used such behaviors. Borgen and Corbin (1987) reported the responses to the Eating Disorders Inventory of 168 college women, 101 nonathletes, 35 athletes whose sports emphasized leanness (ballet, bodybuilding, cheerleading, and gymnastics), and 32 athletes whose sports did not emphasize leanness (swimming, track and field, and volleyball). Six percent of the nonathletes, 20% of the athletes in sports emphasizing leanness, and 10% of all the athletes were either exceptionally preoccupied with weight or had tendencies toward eating disorders.

A recent survey of 695 athletes from 22 midwestern colleges concluded that 30.7% of female athletes and 16.9% of male athletes used self-induced vomiting, fasting, diuretics, or laxatives as a means of weight control. These numbers contrast markedly with those reported for 1,200 college freshman and seniors (nonathletes). Zuckerman et al. (1986) found that 23% of college women and 9% of college men reported the use of these behaviors. It is obvious that coaches and other individuals closely associated with athletes must be very careful not to set unrealistic standards of body weight or body fat for this very susceptible population.

In conclusion, a significant number of athletic subjects (both men and women) use a wide variety of pathogenic weight-control techniques and appear obsessed with body weight. Although performance seems an important incentive for most of these athletes, sociocultural factors prevail for some women in sports that do not emphasize leanness.

Diet and Athletic Amenorrhea

Amenorrhea is not generally considered an eating disorder. However, a number of studies have observed significant differences in the diets of amenorrheic and eumenorrheic subjects. Abnormal eating behaviors may well be a significant factor in the etiology of athletic amenorrhea.

Kemmann, Pasquale, and Skaf (1983) found that amenorrhea might be associated with *carotenemia*, which is an excessive intake of carotene (which is closely related to vitamin A). All their subjects were vegetarians. Carotenemia is frequently accompanied by skin discoloration (a yellow cast) on the palms and soles. This is also frequently seen in anorexia nervosa (Warren, 1985), in which amenorrhea is an associated symptom.

In a brief report, Brooks et al. (1984) compared the diets of amenorrheic and eumenorrheic runners. Of the amenorrheic group, 82% were vegetarians (only two of the eumenorrheic runners were vegetarians). The only other dietary difference was in fat consumption. Amenorrheic runners ate 68 g per day and eumenorrheic runners 98 g per day.

Three more extensive studies of the diets of amenorrheic and eumenorrheic athletes revealed significant differences between the two groups. Deuster et al. (1986) reported that highly trained amenorrheic runners consumed less fat, more vitamin A, and higher quantities of crude fiber. Zinc intake was considerably below the RDA in the amenorrheic runners, as was plasma zinc. Jaffee, Webster, and Lutter (1988) compared the diets of amenorrheic and eumenorrheic "active women." The amenorrheic women consumed fewer calories, less protein and fat, and more vitamin A. Only 15.4% of the amenorrheic women ate meat, and most of those ate only white meat. With vitamin and mineral supplementation, the intake of vitamin A by the amenorrheic subjects was more than three times that of the eumenorrheic athletes. Iron supplementation resulted in significantly higher iron intake levels for the eumenorrheic women.

Nelson and Fisher et al. (1986) reported significantly less energy intake (by 25%) and fat intake in amenorrheic than eumenorrheic subjects who were matched for amount of weekly training. Drinkwater et al. (1984) did not find differences in energy intake between their amenorrheic and eumenorrheic athletes, but training was significantly more vigorous in the amenorrheic group. Therefore, both these studies indicate significant differences in energy balance between their groups.

It was previously emphasized that athletic amenorrhea is a multifaceted entity. The data presented here imply a strong association between athletic amenorrhea and dietary behaviors. More precise answers await experimental verification.

Summary

Obesity among women is very prevalent in the United States, and it causes, both directly and indirectly, considerable morbidity and mortality. Obesity is mainly a problem of overconsumption relative in physical inactivity. Evidence has been presented that increased levels of exercise, coupled with caloric restriction, can lead to long-term reduction in body fat and body weight. However, much misinformation has been promulgated, and many dieting fads and gimmicks remain popular among the public.

The prevalence of eating disorders such as anorexia nervosa and bulimia seems to be increasing, especially among young athletes and physical fitness advocates. Excessive self-obsession with thinness can lead to severe medical and psychiatric problems. Athletes and coaches should be carefully advised on dietary matters and body weight goals so that athletes' performances can be enhanced without detrimental effects on their health. Nutritional supervision from well-qualified professionals is imperative.

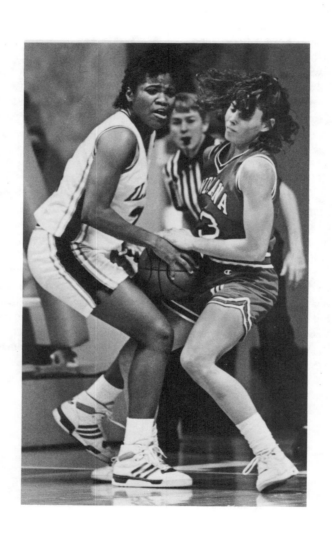

PART V

The Athletic Woman

Although most of this book has been directed toward girls and women in general, this section focuses specifically on the female athlete. Despite the fact that a considerable amount of information is available on the male athlete, there has always been (and continues to be) a dearth of information on the female athlete. And what information is available comes mainly from the intercollegiate sector, a population that has only relatively recently become "competitive" enough to truly be taken seriously. Before Title IX of the 1972 National Education Act, few women's intercollegiate teams "trained" or engaged in physical conditioning activities. They merely met to practice a few hours per week and played a rather meager competitive schedule. Much of the data seen in the scientific literature today is based on these athletes.

With Title IX and other sociopolitical influences, however, has come more money, which translates into scholarships; better equipment; more qualified coaches; more space and time for training, conditioning, and practice; and more interest. Intercollegiate athletic programs have, of course, improved tremendously. In addition, it can be argued that non-scholastic and noncollegiate athletic efforts have also benefited from Title IX. As awareness and interest on the part of many people increase, athletic programs of all sorts are bound to improve and become more competitive.

In an effort to be as selective as possible about the material presented in this section, I have chosen to include only those studies that dealt with outstanding athletes or highly successful teams. As girls' and women's athletic programs continue to improve and as female competitors of all ages progress in skill, technique, and physical conditioning, the information in this section will need to be updated.

Chapter 14 begins by outlining general training principles that serve to point out that adaptations to training are specific to the stresses applied. It continues with a discussion of women's adaptations to training and covers muscular, metabolic, and cardiovascular adaptations. Special attention is given to the training adaptations of the preadolescent and adolescent and to training in middle-aged and menopausal women.

Chapter 15 was written primarily to counter the misconception that girls and women incur more injuries with physical activity than do boys and men. The first part of the chapter deals with the incidence of athletic injuries in both sexes. The second part discusses athletic injuries that appear to be specific to girls and women, including such topics as pelvic and breast injuries and those that occur with running, contact sports, field hockey, figure skating, and ballet.

Chapter 16 presents a comprehensive profile of the female athlete in a wide variety of sports. Specifically, the chapter covers the body composition and physique characteristics of highly successful female athletes including adolescent and masters athletes. Data are also presented on metabolic characteristics such as cardiorespiratory endurance, anaerobic capacity and power, strength, and muscle fiber characteristics.

Chapter 14

Adaptation to Training

This book has dealt with the physiological responses of women to exercise. This chapter continues with that objective and thus is not about *how* women train or should train. There are already a number of excellent references on that topic (Daniels, Fitts, & Sheehan, 1978; Getchell, 1976; Katch & McArdle, 1977; Lamb, 1978; Ribisl, 1980; and Wilmore, 1982). Nevertheless, some basic training principles are outlined so that all readers will have a common starting ground. In the following sections, women's adaptations to training are reviewed using only those studies that adhered to the basic principles presented. Muscular, metabolic, and cardiovascular adaptations are emphasized because these are the areas of greatest general interest and because there are more than sufficient data available. Training adaptations in adolescents and preadolescents are also covered because of the controversy surrounding the topic of vigorous athletic training in children. Material is also included that deals with training adaptations during the menopausal years.

General Training Principles

Exercise provides considerable physiological stimulation, sometimes referred to as *stress*. There are numerous responses to this stimulation, but when the stress is removed, the organism gradually recovers and is essentially the same as before the stress was applied. This can be diagrammed very simply as follows:

ACUTE
PHYSICAL
STRESS

↓

SPECIFIC
RESPONSES

↓

RECOVERY (organism is
essentially unchanged)

Training implies repeated and systematic application of specific stresses. With training, responses gradually change, which means that *adaptations* occur.

CHRONIC
AND SYSTEMATIC
PHYSICAL STRESS

↓

SPECIFIC
RESPONSES

↓

ADAPTATIONS (the
organism is changed in
the sense that responses
are altered)

When one has adapted to chronic exercise, we say that one is trained. To study the effects of training means to study the adaptations of the organism to systematic and chronic exercise.

Adaptations to training are *specific* to the stresses applied. Only those systems that are sufficiently stressed will make adaptations. For example, if the muscles are chronically stressed, the responses of the muscles to that stress will gradually change. Unstressed systems will not be altered. If the muscle is chronically stressed by being required to lift heavier weights, the muscle will adapt by becoming stronger. Other adaptations will not occur; in other words, the muscle will not *necessarily* improve in speed of contraction or endurance. This is the concept of *specificity*, sometimes referred to as the *SAID principle* (an acronym for *specific adaptations to imposed demands*).

The process of applying stress is called *overloading*. A physiological system will adapt only if it is stimulated to adapt, that is, if stress to which it is not accustomed is gradually applied. The proper amount of overload is a very disputed and much discussed subject but is extremely important for at least two reasons. Too much overload could result in injury, and adaptations are specific to the nature of the overload.

Overload is a function of the frequency, duration, and intensity of exercise. *Frequency* usually refers to the number of times one engages in training activities per week. *Duration* is the period of time one performs the task, for example, 30 min per day or 30 s per 220-yd dash. The term *repetition* is used to describe the number of times a task is repeated, for example, the number of times a weight is lifted or the number of repeat intervals performed. *Intensity* refers to the difficulty of the task and is usually the most difficult of these variables to control or measure. Various methods are used to regulate exercise intensity. One involves prescribing a target heart rate. Another, applied in weight training, uses target weights on the basis of percentages of one's maximum strength. An exercise or training prescription must include specific instructions on frequency, duration, and intensity. As adaptations occur, the prescription must be adjusted so that overload is progressively applied.

To devise a training program, an athlete or coach must determine first what adaptations are necessary or desirable and then the exercise tasks that will specifically stress the systems necessary to accomplish the goal. This involves a basic knowledge of the physiology of exercise. Too often, coaches and athletes simply copy the training programs they know others use and do not take into account the specific needs, goals, strengths, or weaknesses of the individual. Training programs must be explicitly developed to achieve improvements in each component of physical performance: muscular strength and endurance, flexibility, cardiorespiratory endurance, and the various metabolic changes needed to improve aerobic or anaerobic capabilities.

Women's Adaptations to Training

It is difficult to compare studies dealing with physical adaptations because of the wide variation in training methods used. Different results will occur as the mode of exercise (e.g., running, stationary cycling, aerobic dance, or weight training), training frequency, duration, and intensity vary. Further complicating the task are the wide variations among studies in the initial fitness levels, ages, body types, and body composition of the subjects. These problems notwithstanding, the remainder of this chapter reviews the specific adaptations of a variety of training programs in women of all ages.

Most of the knowledge concerning adaptations to training comes from investigations involving animals (sometimes female) or men. Relatively few well-controlled training studies have been completed on either girls or women. Basically, however, girls and women adapt to the stresses of training in much the same manner as boys and men.

Strength Training

Until recently, strength training for women was not considered socially acceptable by many because of its suspected masculinizing effect. All but the most dedicated female athletes avoided strength training for fear of developing the enlarged, bulky muscles associated with the male athlete. This was, of course, quite unfortunate because many women have lacked sufficient strength to learn important skills and to progress in athletic achievement. Muscular strength is an important component of many physical skills and as such should be an important part of most training programs. In the United States, female athletes have largely neglected strength development, thus permitting other athletes (most notably the women of the eastern European countries) to excel in events requiring high levels of strength and power, such as the discus, javelin, and shot put. These women are noted for their aggressive approach to resistance training that uses near maximum loads, few repetitions, and multiple sets (Baechle, 1984). It appears that high-level athletes have much to gain from serious resistance training. Readers interested in learning about the design of strength-training programs and the special considerations for female athletes should refer to the excellent review article by Baechle (1984).

Women's fear of muscular hypertrophy has largely subsided. It is not uncommon today for the commercial health clubs to have as many women customers "pumping iron" as men. Much of this change in attitude has resulted from research studies that indicate that women who participate in weight training are capable of making strength improvements similar to men's without developing a massive body build. The factor most commonly cited for the differences in muscular hypertrophy between well-trained men and women is that of androgen secretion levels, particularly that of testosterone. The androgenic hormones are also anabolic and are thought to control muscle hypertrophy. There is a biological basis for women having significantly less muscle mass than do men because of their lower androgen levels.

Because strength gains have been conceptually linked with muscle mass, many have questioned the woman's potential for developing strength. However, comparisons of men and women who follow similar weight-training programs typically reveal not only that women respond with significant gains in strength but also that their rates of strength improvement *exceed* those of men. Of course, this may be because women begin training at a relatively lower level than men in terms of their strength potential. Certainly the quality of muscle tissue is identical between the sexes. Differences in strength can be simply attributed to the quantitative differences in muscle mass between men and women. Numerous studies have shown that women respond to weight training with significant gains in both absolute and relative strength.

Another question often posed is whether women can tolerate the stresses imposed by intensive resistance training programs. O'Shea and Wegner (1981) reported that women have the same ability as men to tolerate and adapt to the demanding physical stresses of power lifting. The belief that a woman cannot stand up to the rigors of a heavy weight-training program is totally unfounded.

The primary question regarding strength training and women, however, continues to be the one referred to previously: the relationship between strength development and muscular hypertrophy. It is quite clear that the acquisition of a massive body build is not a natural outcome of intensive strength training for most women. The typical woman responds to heavy weight training with slight increases in muscle girth, usually with a corresponding reduction in intramuscular and subcutaneous adipose tissue and little change in limb girth. Total body weight is likely to remain unchanged, but fat-free body weight (often referred to as lean body mass) is likely to increase because more muscle tissue is added. The increased muscle definition and protruding veins often observed in men who train strenuously with weights is not usually apparent in women, most likely because of the woman's larger amount of subcutaneous fat (thought to be related to her higher estrogen

levels). Competing bodybuilders go to considerable effort (by means of diet) not only to reduce subcutaneous fat but also to dehydrate themselves to achieve extreme muscle definition. Only women who compete at very high levels in power lifting or weight lifting show the muscle definition achieved by male bodybuilders.

In the most commonly cited study of sex differences in strength training (Wilmore, 1974), changes in the size and strength of untrained college-aged women and men were evaluated during a 10-week weight-training program. Before training, the men's strength exceeded the women's by 28% and 26% for muscle groups of the upper and lower body, respectively. After the training program, the men and women showed almost equal improvement in muscular strength with gains of approximately 30% in some areas of the body. Although the absolute differences in strength between the sexes still existed, the posttraining strength levels of the women were greater than the initial levels of the men. Most interesting, however, was the fact that these strength gains were accompanied by significant enlargements in the muscles of the men but *not* of the women.

Several studies have reported similar results: significant improvements in muscular strength without concomitant gains in muscular hypertrophy (Brown & Wilmore, 1974; Capen, Bright, & Line, 1961; Oyster, 1979; Wells, Jokl, & Bohanen, 1961). However, at least two studies have reported approximately equal gains between men and women in both strength and muscular hypertrophy (Cureton, Collins, Hill, & McElhannon, 1988; Hunter, 1985). Cureton et al.'s study is described in detail in the remainder of this section.

Most investigators have been limited to the use of gross indirect indicators of change in muscle size, such as limb circumference, skinfold measurements, and total body composition (estimates of the fat-free body and percent body fat by underwater weighing). These measures provide rather inexact estimations of changes in muscle mass. Cureton et al. (1988) applied a more direct measure of muscle size by measuring the cross-sectional areas of the muscles of the nondominant upper arm and thigh using computed axial tomography (CAT). The purpose of their investigation was "to compare skeletal muscle hypertrophy resulting from heavy-resistance training in men and women, using both traditional indirect indicators (anthropometric and body composition measures) as well as a direct measure (computed tomography scan) of muscle size" (p. 339). The results of their very well controlled 16-week individualized progressive heavy-resistance weight-training study differed from those of most previous investigations.

Cureton et al.'s strength-training program was designed to produce hypertrophy of the flexor and extensor muscles of the upper arms and thighs. There were no apparent differences between the men and women in terms of their past experience with heavy-resistance exercise. Results indicated that strength increased significantly for elbow flexion and extension as well as for knee flexion and extension. The percentage changes for men and women were not significantly different. Considerable muscular hypertrophy occurred in the upper arm, with cross-sectional area (CSA) increasing 16% for the men and 23% for the women. Neither absolute nor percentages changes in upper arm CSA differed between the sexes. Changes in bone and fat CSA were not statistically significant. However, no muscular hypertrophy occurred in the thigh in either group. The anthropometric indicators of muscle size were almost identical to those obtained with the CAT scan method. There were no significant changes from pre- to posttraining among the groups in any of the body composition measures.

The investigators concluded that although absolute changes tended to be larger in the men, percentage changes in both strength and muscular hypertrophy consequent to heavy-resistance training were similar in men and women. Examination of strength-to-CSA ratios before and after training indicated that the relative importance of neural and hypertrophic changes to increases in strength were quite similar between the men and women. This study, of course, needs replication but surely will open the door to more exact procedures for measuring changes in muscular growth with training.

Metabolic Adaptations in Previously Sedentary Women

Numerous studies have dealt with metabolic adaptations to training in nonathletic or sedentary subjects. It is often difficult to compare training studies because of the wide variation in training intensities used. Nevertheless, these studies are presented and interpreted in the sections that follow.

Early Studies. Kilbom (1971) conducted a comprehensive but brief (7 weeks) investigation of training in nonathletic women aged 19 to 64 years. Her most significant findings included the following:

- Maximal oxygen uptake ($\dot{V}O_2$max) improved in direct proportion to training intensity. Women who trained at less than 65% of their initial $\dot{V}O_2$max did not improve as much as those who trained at higher intensities.
- The training effect in subjects with higher initial fitness levels was less pronounced.
- The training effect in subjects older than 50 was less pronounced. No definite differences in training adaptations occurred between the 19- to 31-year-old subjects and those aged 34 to 48.
- Serum cholesterol values in the younger subjects were reduced. Values for the middle-aged and more elderly subjects were not affected.
- Serum iron in all age-groups was reduced, but hemoglobin, hematocrit, blood volume, and heart volume remained unchanged. Kilbom noted "that increased iron administration may be necessary during physical training" (p. 13).
- Heart rate (HR) and blood lactate levels decreased at comparable submaximal $\dot{V}O_2$ levels. Subjective work ratings also decreased at comparable $\dot{V}O_2$ levels but not at comparable HR levels. Maximal HR (HRmax) was not affected by training.

- Blood lactate concentration at maximal exertion was elevated, indicating an improvement in anaerobic capacity.

Significant increases in $\dot{V}O_2max$ have been reported following 9 weeks of treadmill walking at 50% and 64% of the HR reserve (Kearney, Stull, Ewing, & Strein, 1976) and after 6 weeks of training at 75% to 80% of HRmax (Flint, Drinkwater, & Horvath, 1974).

The effects of two levels of training intensity and two levels of training frequency were studied in sedentary college students in Japan (Atomi, Ito, Iwasaki, & Miyashita, 1978). Group 1 exercised on a bicycle ergometer at 80% $\dot{V}O_2max$ four times per week. Group 2 exercised at 80% twice a week. Group 3 exercised at 60% four times per week and Group 4 at 60% twice per week. Exercise was limited to 10 min per session and continued for 8 weeks. All groups significantly increased their $\dot{V}O_2max$ and lowered their HRs at submaximal work levels. Analysis of variance indicated that training frequency was not an important factor in increasing $\dot{V}O_2max$ but that training intensity was. These results indicate that training for 10 min twice a week at 60% $\dot{V}O_2max$ was sufficient to increase $\dot{V}O_2max$ by 16% to 17% in these sedentary women.

Anaerobic Threshold. Aerobic capacity ($\dot{V}O_2max$) and total exercise time to exhaustion improved with training at 40% above anaerobic threshold (AT+), at anaerobic threshold (AT), and at 40% below anaerobic threshold (AT−) (Gibbons, Jessup, Wells, & Werthmann, 1981). Posttraining anaerobic threshold was increased only in the AT training group. Training at 40% below AT was apparently not of sufficient intensity to effect a change in anaerobic metabolism. It was suggested that if the objective is to increase the anaerobic threshold, it is more productive to train at an exercise intensity equivalent to AT than to train above or below that level. The results of this study are quite interesting and need to be corroborated.

Aerobic Dance. This section would be incomplete without mentioning the benefits of aerobic dance. This form of exercise may be the most popular form of organized physical activity for women in the United States today (and other industrialized nations). The original form consisted of a combination of various dance movements and calisthenic exercises performed to popular music. Recent innovations include water aerobics, nonimpact or low-impact aerobics (requiring one foot on the floor at all times), the incorporation of specific dance movements (jazz and ballet), and the use of weight-assisted exercises using hand weights or resistive bands (Garrick & Requa, 1988).

Early studies (Foster, 1975; Weber, 1973) documented the metabolic cost of aerobic dance and declared that it met or exceeded the generally accepted minimum for training intensity and duration (Metcalf, Watson, Mathews, & Guynn, 1981). Others have noted significant improvements in $\dot{V}O_2max$ (Cearly, Moffatt, & Knutzen, 1984; Rockefeller & Burke, 1979) and 12-min run performance (Watterson, 1984) following aerobic dance performed three times per week for 10 and 6 weeks, respectively. No significant changes in $\dot{V}O_2max$ were observed in the twice-per-week classes (Cearly et al., 1984). In young middle-aged women (mean age 31.5 years), 10 weeks of aerobic dance performed three times per week at 70% to 85% of HR reserve resulted in a 16% increase in walking time on a treadmill test, a 5% to 7% improvement in $\dot{V}O_2max$, but no changes in body composition (Dowdy, Cureton, DuVal, & Ouzts, 1985). Current attention seems to be focused on the metabolic costs and effects of low-impact aerobics with and without weights. Although energy consumption may be higher with high-impact aerobic dance (Otto et al., 1986), it appears that low-impact aerobic dance can provide appreciable fitness benefits (Koszuta, 1986).

High-Intensity Training. Two studies were located that dealt with very high intensity training regimens. Significant improvements in aerobic power (10.5%), anaerobic power output (13%), and anaerobic capacity (12%) occurred with two 10-min all-out bouts on a bicycle ergometer (Weltman, Moffatt, & Stamford, 1978). Detraining (6 weeks) extinguished improvements in aerobic metabolism, but anaerobic parameters remained elevated. It was concluded that high-intensity, short-duration (anaerobic) training resulted in significant gains in aerobic power and in performance estimates of anaerobic capabilities.

The other study on supramaximal training intensity employed four combinations of training intensities and frequencies (Lesmes, Fox, Stevens, & Otto, 1978). The 8-week training program consisted of high-intensity, short-distance intervals (50, 101, and 201 m) or high-intensity, longer distance intervals (604, 805, and 1,208 m) for either 2 or 4 days per week. Estimates of training intensities were 170% and 130% $\dot{V}O_2max$ for the short and longer distances, respectively. After training, $\dot{V}O_2max$ was significantly increased (13%), as was maximal ventilation ($\dot{V}_E max$) (12%). Maximal HR, maximal lactic acid, and submaximal $\dot{V}O_2$ were not altered. Heart rate during submaximal exercise decreased significantly (6%). Statistical analysis revealed that these changes were independent of training frequency, distance, and intensity. It appears that high-intensity interval training programs are quite effective.

Fuel Source. Another topic of interest in regard to metabolic adaptations to training is that of fuel source. Trained subjects have a lower concentration of blood lactate and pyruvate and a lower respiratory exchange ratio (R) during submaximal exercise (Flint et al., 1974; Kilbom, 1971). The lower R reflects an increased rate of free fatty acid (FFA) oxidation by working skeletal muscles. Bransford and Howley (1979) sought to further evaluate the effects of training on substrate utilization by women. Previously sedentary women undertook a 4-week training program, 3 days per week, for 1 h each day. Work started at 300 kgm • min⁻¹ and progressed to 525 kgm • min⁻¹. A control group did not train. The trained subjects improved their aerobic capacity by 14% and decreased their HRs by approximately 15 bpm during a submaximal exercise test. No changes occurred in the control group. Although $\dot{V}O_2$ for the submaximal task did not change in either

group, the Rs of the trained group were significantly lower after training.

During a prolonged work task, plasma FFA and glycerol levels gradually increased in both groups, whereas lactate values remained essentially unchanged. In the trained subjects, however, FFA and glycerol levels were significantly lower than in the pretraining test (see Figure 14.1). The lower FFA levels following training may be due to the enhanced uptake and oxidation of FFA by skeletal muscle or to the reduced mobilization of FFA from

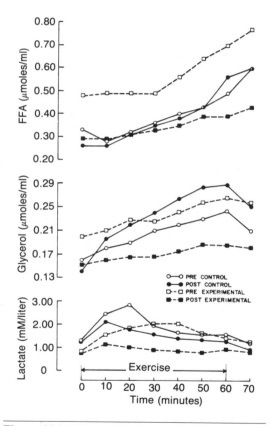

Figure 14.1 Changes in FFA, glycerol, and lactate during 60 minutes of exercise in the experimental (trained) group and control group. *Note.* From "Effects of Training on Plasma FFA During Exercise in Women" by D.R. Bransford and E.T. Howley, 1979, *European Journal of Applied Physiology,* **41,** p. 155. Copyright 1979 by Springer-Verlag. Reprinted by permission.

adipose tissue. The lowered R following training suggests that the cause was increased oxidation of fat. These results are similar to those previously observed in men after endurance training.

Blood Lipids.   Because lipoprotein abnormalities constitute a major risk for cardiovascular disease, considerable attention has been devoted to the chronic effects of training on lipid metabolism. Numerous investigations suggest that regular exercise produces favorable changes in serum lipid and lipoprotein cholesterol concentrations in men (Goldberg & Elliot, 1987). Considerably fewer investigations (sometimes with contradictory results) have been conducted on women. Lipid metabolism may differ in men and women because of the effect of estrogen on high-density lipoprotein cholesterol (HDL-C). It has been suggested that lipoprotein alterations after endurance exercise in women may differ from that in men (Brownell, Bachorik, & Ayerle, 1982).

Lokey and Tran (1989) used meta-analysis to statistically integrate the results of 27 studies on the relationship between exercise training and changes in serum lipid and lipoprotein cholesterol levels in women. This procedure utilized a total of 460 subjects, 379 of whom trained for an average of 12 weeks. The results indicated that cholesterol decreased by 4.1 mg $\cdot$ dl^{-1}, triglyceride decreased by 8.8 mg $\cdot$ dl^{-1}, and the ratio of cholesterol to HDL-C decreased by 0.12 (all significant results) in the subjects who trained. No significant changes were observed in HDL-C or LDL-C (low-density lipoprotein cholesterol). There was a significant correlation between changes in cholesterol and triglyceride and their initial levels; that is, decreases were larger in women who had initially higher levels. There was also a significant relationship between weight loss and cholesterol reduction. The investigators concluded that training, especially for those at high risk for heart disease, is beneficial to the lipid profile of women.

In summary, metabolic adaptations to training in previously sedentary women can be quite extensive and appear to be directly related to training intensity. Variations in frequency and duration

beyond the minimal requirements for a training effect seem to be less important. Aerobic capabilities are improved even with rather low intensity training activities in low-fit women. Some of the observed training responses are in direct proportion to body weight loss.

Metabolic Adaptations in Athletes

The metabolic adaptations to training in active women are similar to those in sedentary women although the extent or rate of improvement may be limited because of higher initial fitness levels. Members of the 1976-77 Illinois state women's championship cross-country team were tested just before and after the competitive season. The intervening 3-month training period consisted of weekly average distances of 38.8 mi, 8.3% of which was directed to interval training. Maximal oxygen consumption increased 9.1%, and 3-mi run time improved from 22.2 to 20.4 min. The percentage utilization of aerobic capacity during the 3-mi run remained unchanged at 89% (Knowlton, Miles, Sawka, Critz, & Blackman, 1978).

Preseason conditioning of seven international level lacrosse players resulted in significant gains in $\dot{V}O_2$max, anaerobic power, and lactic acid evoked by a short-duration maximal treadmill run. The players trained twice a day, 6 days a week, for a total of 10 h per week. About half the time was allotted to fitness and the other half to lacrosse skills. Circuit training was performed five times a week. Initially, training was continuous, but greater emphasis was gradually placed on interval training. Most of the improvements occurred within the first 2 months (Withers, 1978).

Cross-sectional studies have revealed a relationship between long-term exercise and lipid metabolism. Although most reports have dealt with male subjects, female joggers were reported to have higher HDL-C levels and female distance runners lower total cholesterol and triglyceride values than sedentary controls (Wood, Haskell, Stern, Lewis, & Perry, 1977). Serum HDL-C and percent HDL-C levels were significantly higher in female endurance runners than in female weight trainers or sedentary controls (Morgan et al., 1986). There were no significant differences between the weight-trained subjects and the controls, although an earlier study had reported that previously sedentary women had significantly reduced their total cholesterol, LDL-C, and the ratios of cholesterol to HDL-C and LDL-C to HDL-C after 16 weeks of weight training (Goldberg, Elliot, Schutz, & Kloster, 1984).

Cardiovascular Adaptations

Certain cardiovascular changes are expected with training, including increased $\dot{V}O_2max$, stroke volume, arterial-venous oxygen difference, and left-ventricular hypertrophy. The following sections discuss studies of these changes in women.

Previously Sedentary People.   As reported earlier, Kilbom (1971) studied the effect of low-intensity, relatively short duration training in women with low initial $\dot{V}O_2max$. She concluded that the improved $\dot{V}O_2max$ was due to the increase in stroke volume (SV) with no change in arterial-venous oxygen difference (a–$\bar{v}O_2$). These results contradict some observations in men. Saltin et al. (1968) and Rowell (1974) noted that increased aerobic capacity occurred with equal increments in SV and a–$\bar{v}O_2$ in men with initially low $\dot{V}O_2max$.

Cunningham and Hill (1975) examined this matter further. In their study, 17 women participated in a mild training program of jogging and walking two or three times per week for an initial 9-week period. Six subjects continued training for 1 year, and the remainder did not. Significant improvements in predicted $\dot{V}O_2max$ (34%) occurred during the initial period with an additional increase (+5%) during the final 52 weeks. Cardiac output ($\dot{Q}$) after 9 weeks of training increased considerably. At 50% predicted $\dot{V}O_2max$, training had resulted in about a 2-L increase; at 80% predicted $\dot{V}O_2max$, the increase was more than 3 L $\cdot$ min^{-1}. When SV was plotted against relative $\dot{V}O_2max$ values, large increases were observed. However, the values for a–$\bar{v}O_2$ indicated no change for work up to 80% predicted $\dot{V}O_2max$. Their results are shown in Figure 14.2.

Results for the subjects who completed a total of 61 weeks of training are shown in Figure 14.3. Cardiac output at 75% predicted $\dot{V}O_2max$ was increased 3 L $\cdot$ min^{-1} after 9 weeks but only 2.2 L $\cdot$ min^{-1} after 61 weeks. Thus, $\dot{Q}$ exhibited a large increase following the initial weeks of training but little change following the additional year of training. Stroke volume followed the same pattern as it increased considerably following 9 weeks of training with little change after that. However, the a–$\bar{v}O_2$ showed a continued increase with training. After 9 weeks a–$\bar{v}O_2$ difference showed a nonsignificant increase of 10 ml $\cdot$ L^{-1} at 75% predicted $\dot{V}O_2max$. Following a year of training, this value had significantly increased to 21 ml $\cdot$ L^{-1}.

An alteration in aerobic capacity should be reflected by either a central (SV) or a peripheral (a–$\bar{v}O_2$) adaptation. As noted previously, both Saltin et al. (1968) and Rowell (1974) reported approximately equal increases in SV and a–$\bar{v}O_2$ in men, whereas Kilbom (1971) had noted increases in SV but not in a–$\bar{v}O_2$ in women. The short-duration training results of Cunningham and Hill (1975) corroborate Kilbom's results. The subjects who trained for 9 weeks demonstrated a large and significant increase in SV with little or no change in a–$\bar{v}O_2$. With the additional year of training, however, the initial increase in SV was reduced, and a–$\bar{v}O_2$ increased significantly.

In conclusion, this study indicated that the initial adaptation to training in sedentary women was due to an increased central capacity (increased SV) and that the secondary adaptation to the longer period of training was due to peripheral mechanisms (a–$\bar{v}O_2$). This suggests that long-term training programs may be necessary to elicit both central and peripheral cardiovascular adaptations.

In a follow-up investigation, Cunningham, McCrimmon, and Vlach (1979) studied the time course of central and peripheral adaptations to short-term, high-intensity training programs in women. They also compared the effects of interval and continuous training methods. The total work done on a bicycle ergometer by each training group was held constant, as was the training period

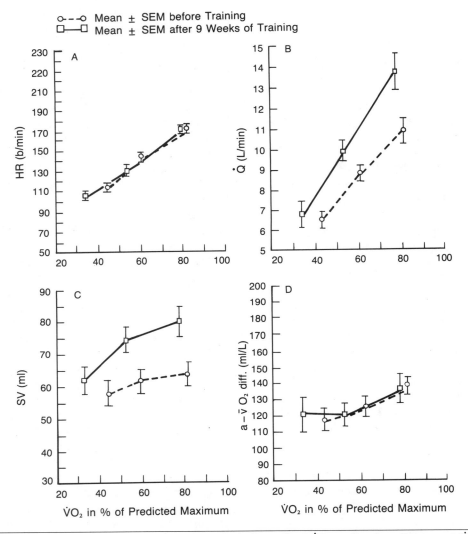

Figure 14.2 Relationship between oxygen uptake (as % of predicted $\dot{V}O_2$max) and cardiac output ($\dot{Q}$), stroke volume (SV), and arterial-venous oxygen difference (a–$\bar{v}O_2$ diff) from 17 subjects before and after 9 weeks of training. *Note.* From "Effect of Training on Cardiovascular Response to Exercise in Women" by D.A. Cunningham and J.S. Hill, 1975, *Journal of Applied Physiology, 39*, p. 893. Copyright 1975 by The American Physiological Society, Inc. Reprinted by permission.

of 12 weeks. The continuous training group (CTG) exercised at 70% $\dot{V}O_2$max for 20 min, four times per week. Intensity was increased 5% per week until 80% of each subject's $\dot{V}O_2$max was reached. The interval training group (ITG) exercised four times per week with 2-min work periods and 1 min

of rest at an initial work intensity of 90% $\dot{V}O_2$max. Work rate was increased 5% per week until 100% $\dot{V}O_2$max was reached.

Maximal oxygen uptake increased significantly in both groups over the 12 week period: 20.5% in the CTG and 23.2% in the ITG. Cardiac output

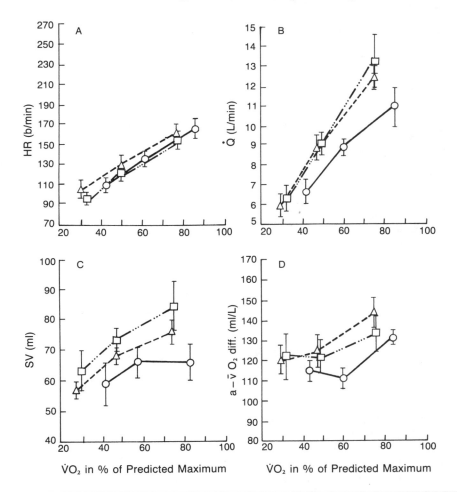

Figure 14.3 Relationship between oxygen uptake (as % of predicted $\dot{V}O_2$max) and cardiac output ($\dot{Q}$), stroke volume (SV), and arterial-venous oxygen difference (a–$\bar{v}O_2$) for 6 subjects who participated in 61 weeks of training. *Note.* From ''Effect of Training on Cardiovascular Response to Exercise in Women'' by D.A. Cunningham and J.S. Hill, 1975, *Journal of Applied Physiology,* **39,** p. 893. Copyright 1975 by The American Physiological Society, Inc. Reprinted by permission.

did not increase significantly. Stroke volume was increased at 4 weeks of training in the ITG, but the gain was extinguished at 12 weeks. Both exercise groups demonstrated significant increases in a–$\bar{v}O_2$ after 8 and 12 weeks, and the changes

were most marked at the higher submaximal work rates (65% to 85% $\dot{V}O_2$max).

These results differed from those of Kilbom (1971) and Cunningham and Hill (1975) on two counts. First, changes in cardiac function (SV and

$\dot{Q}$) did not occur in either group after 12 weeks of training. Second, both groups underwent a significant peripheral adaptation (a$-\overline{v}O_2$) after only 8 weeks. The training programs also differed in two ways from those of Kilbom and of Cunningham and Hill. First, both the IT and the CT programs were more intense than the training tasks of the other investigations. This suggests that a greater training intensity is required to achieve a peripheral adaptation. Second, the lack of change in cardiac function may have been related to the type of work performed. Training on a bicycle ergometer utilizes a smaller muscle mass than does jogging and may therefore place a lesser demand on the heart as a pump and emphasize extraction of oxygen by the working muscles. The authors suggested that when limited muscle mass is involved in an exercise task, the response is more peripheral than central. This study indicates that young women (like young men) can increase a$-\overline{v}O_2$ with short-term training *if* the work is of sufficient intensity.

Skeletal Muscle Capillarization.

Little is known about *skeletal muscle capillarization* in women. However, a Norwegian group (Ingjer & Brodal, 1978) completed a very interesting study utilizing muscle biopsies from the lateral part of the quadriceps muscle in untrained and endurance trained women (cross-country skiers). Mean fiber diameter did not differ significantly between the two groups; however, the number of capillaries per fiber, the average number of capillaries around each fiber, and the average number of capillaries per square millimeter was significantly higher in the trained group. The proportion of mitochondria-rich fibers was also higher in the trained women. The capillary densities of the women in this study were remarkably close to those found by the same investigators in untrained and endurance-trained men. The study concluded that the differences seen between the untrained and endurance trained women were due to training.

Ventricular Hypertrophy.

Males engaged in endurance training often show *cardiac ventricular hypertrophy*. Two studies were located that were concerned with this phenomenon in women. In one, 10 field hockey players were studied to determine if prolonged dynamic conditioning resulted in increased left-ventricular interval dimension at end diastole (LVIDD) and if any changes were correlated with $\dot{V}O_2$max (Zeldis, Morganroth, & Rubler, 1978). In both instances the answer was yes. The LVIDD index (LVIDD/body surface area) was significantly larger in the athletes than in a control group, and $\dot{V}O_2$max correlated significantly with LVIDD index ($r = 0.92$, $p < .001$). Ventricular septal and posterior wall thicknesses were compared (echocardiography) and were not different. The authors concluded that $\dot{V}O_2$max may be related to the ability of the heart to increase LVIDD because of high correlation between these two variables.

In swimmers (Lamont, 1980), various echocardiographic dimensions were studied before and after 13 weeks of interval training lasting 3 to 4 h per day, 5 days per week. The results documented a favorable adaptation in left-ventricular end-diastolic diameter, posterior wall thickness, and left-ventricular mass. Although statistically significant, the changes were small. A lengthened left-ventricular ejection time index and a lengthened electromechanical systole index resulted from an increased SV. Lamont concluded that short-term training appears to effect adaptive as well as functional changes within the hearts of collegiate swimmers.

A rather unique investigation of cardiovascular adaptations assessed the chronic effects of ballet training on the hearts of dancers in the American Ballet Theatre (Cohen, Gupta, Lichstein, & Chadda, 1980). The results of the dancers, who averaged 14 years of ballet training, were compared with a nondancing control group. The dancers had an increased incidence of sinus bradycardia and sinus arrhythmia. Their echocardiographic data showed significant increases in interventricular septal thickness, left-ventricular posterior wall thickness, left-ventricular end-diastolic interval dimension, and left-ventricular mass index. These results indicated combined left-ventricular hypertrophy and increased left-ventricular interval dimension consistent with the mixed isometric-isotonic nature of ballet exercises. It was concluded that, as in other athletes, physiological left-ventricular enlargements develop in ballet dancers in proportion to their training.

Echocardiograms were obtained from college women who were sedentary as well as athletes competing as sprinters, distance runners, swimmers, basketball players, and dancers (Rubal, Al-Muhailani, & Rosentswieg, 1987). The aerobic capacities of the athletes were 30% to 48% higher than the sedentary subjects. The athletes also exhibited higher left-ventricular end-diastolic dimensions, left-ventricular end-diastolic volumes, SVs, left-ventricular mass, and left-atrial dimensions when data were standardized for body surface area. The investigators concluded from these data that female athletes exhibit cardiac morphological features that resemble those reported for male endurance-conditioned athletes.

Further substantiating this conclusion, Rubal et al. (1987) added a longitudinal dimension to their study. They compared the aerobic capacity and echocardiographic responses of sedentary women and men to a 10-week running program equivalent to many recreational training programs. Both groups increased $\dot{V}O_2max$ approximately 20% and exhibited nonsignificant but similar changes in left-ventricular wall thickness, end-diastolic dimension, end-diastolic volume, and left-ventricular mass. These changes regressed within 10 weeks with discontinuation of running. This study verifies that the cardiac adaptations of men and women to modest levels of endurance training are similar.

Hematologic Changes

Reference was made to sports anemia in chapter 12, p. 212. As mentioned there, some believe that sports anemia is a transitory response to training. The work of Puhl, Runyan, and Kruse (1981) supports this contention. The hematologic status of 8 high school cross-country runners was assessed six times during an 8-week competition season and then compared with a nonrunning group. The runners had higher red blood cell (RBC) fragility at the initial assessment, although blood indices were within normal ranges throughout the study. During the competitive season, the runners had significant changes in all blood indices except reticulocyte count. After the first week of training, significant decreases were noted in hemoglobin (8%), hematocrit (7.7%), RBC count (6.8%), and osmotic fragility (21.5% and 42.0% in different salt solutions) and a significant increase in RBC volume (1.8%). By the eighth week of training, values were comparable to those at preseason except for RBC volume. Although blood volume expansion may have been responsible for some of these changes, the results suggest that increased RBC destruction was the cause of the altered hematologic status of these runners. The authors believe that the body iron reserves of the runners were stressed by increased erythropoiesis during recovery from these changes.

Heat Tolerance

The effects of 11 weeks of intensive interval training in a cool environment on heat tolerance was assessed in college women (Cohen & Gisolfi, 1982) because this method had been previously shown to be highly effective in men. Maximal oxygen consumption of the trained subjects increased 11%; heat-tolerance time increased from 1.44 to 3.25 h. The control group did not increase its heat-tolerance time. The improvement in heat tolerance of the trained subjects was attributed to the beneficial effects associated with the elevation in body core temperature during their training sessions.

Prescribing Exercise Intensity

There has been much discussion regarding the assignment of training intensity or level of effort to correspond to a desired metabolic load. Two commonly used methods in exercise prescription are (a) the Karvonen method, in which training heart rate (THR) = [(HRmax − HRrest)] × 60%-80% + HRrest, and (b) simple computation of THR as a chosen percentage of the measured HRmax (often the age-predicted HRmax). Numerous studies on men have shown remarkably similar regressions of percent $\dot{V}O_2$max on percent HRmax regardless of the muscle groups used and the fitness levels of the subjects. The major limitation to these methods appears to be the considerable individual variation in the relationships between HR and $\dot{V}O_2$ and between percent HRmax and percent $\dot{V}O_2$max.

Almost everyone prescribing exercise applies their preferred method of assigning work load to women as well as to men. Franklin, Hodgson, and Buskirk (1980) evaluated this procedure. First, they examined the pre- and posttraining relationship between percent HRmax and percent $\dot{V}O_2$max in women of different ages, body fatness, and $\dot{V}O_2$max and compared this relationship with those previously found in men. Second, they assessed the individual variation in the relationship between percent HRmax and percent $\dot{V}O_2$max.

The 12-week training program consisted of stretching and flexibility exercises and walk-jog bouts at the HR obtained at 75% $\dot{V}O_2$max. After training, $\dot{V}O_2$max increased 13% to 16%, but HRmax remained unchanged. These results are similar to those of several other studies cited in this chapter (Atomi et al., 1978; Kilbom, 1971; Lesmes et al., 1978). The pre- and posttraining regression equations are illustrated in Figure 14.4. At given percent HRmax values during the posttraining test, percent $\dot{V}O_2$max values were slightly lower ($p < .05$). This was particularly true at the lower work loads. Combined data from eight studies on men yielded a similar equation. Because relationships are quite similar, Franklin et al. (1980) concluded that the percent HRmax method of exercise prescription, when related to the individual capacity, could be used for both men and women. They also stated that the individual variability in the method suggests that the relative metabolic work load (percent $\dot{V}O_2$max) and conditioning response ($\Delta\dot{V}O_2$max) may differ consider-

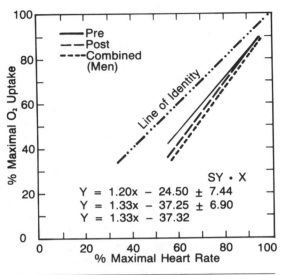

Figure 14.4 The relationship between % HR max and % $\dot{V}O_2$max in men and women. *Note.* From "Relationship Between Percent Maximal O_2 Uptake and Percent Maximal Heart Rate in Women" by B.A. Franklin, J. Hodgson, and E.R. Buskirk, 1980, *Research Quarterly for Exercise and Sport,* **51**, p. 622. Published by the American Alliance for Health, Physical Education, Recreation and Dance. Copyright 1980 by American Alliance for Health, Physical Education, Recreation and Dance. Reprinted by permission.

ably among individuals training at a given percent HRmax. Perhaps this partially explains the variability in training adaptations seen in some of the studies cited previously.

In a study that compared the cardiorespiratory responses of arm and leg ergometry in women, Vander, Franklin, Wrisley, and Rubenfire (1984) reported regression equations between percent $\dot{V}O_2$max and percent HRmax during arm exercise that were similar to those for leg exercise (see Figure 14.4). Thus, a given percent HRmax during arm exercise results in approximately the same percent $\dot{V}O_2$max as in leg exercise. This means that the same regression equations can be used for men and women in prescribing exercise regardless of the muscle groups involved.

Training in Preadolescence and Adolescence

The subject of training in young children has recently become quite an emotional issue. I believe this is largely because so many young children are entering (and completing) marathon races. Many pediatricians and child development experts are concerned about this. In 1979, *Runner's World* announced that it "would no longer carry age-group race times for children under 12 because publishing such records would irresistibly draw preadolescent runners, often urged by their parents, into high-intensity endurance training programs that can harm them psychologically if not physically" (Barnes, 1979, p. 114). The American Medical Joggers Association disagreed with this position. An article in its newsletter accused *Runner's World* of "dogmatically discouraging parents from introducing their children to marathoning" (Barnes, 1979, p. 114).

Such controversy has arisen mainly because of the concern that strenuous childhood training will lead to epiphyseal injury. Because this sort of injury could have a devastating impact on a child's life, it is not surprising that some believe that strenuous training is far too risky for children. A landmark study of this subject was Larson and McMahan's (1966) review of 1,338 athletic injuries seen by four orthopedists. They found that only 6% ($n = 23$) of the injuries in the 15-and-under age-group were epiphyseal. None of the injuries had a disastrous outcome. Although they acknowledged that some important injuries may have been missed in diagnosis, they concluded that the benefits of children's athletic programs outweighed the prospective risks to the epiphyses. This study, of course, was conducted at a time before children ran marathons and before many children (or their parents) took training very seriously.

Another aspect of the controversy stems from the realization that very little is known about the physical capabilities of children and pre-adolescents. Most of the physiological studies on children are dated. For example, Bengtsson (1956) studied the working capacity of children and found large variations (up to 400%) in the younger age-groups (7 to 9 years). He did not study the process of training in these children.

Anaerobic Performance

The ability of prepubertal girls (and boys) to perform anaerobic tasks is distinctly lower than that of adolescents and young adults (Bar-Or, 1983, 1988). The mechanism for low anaerobic performance in prepubescent girls is not known but may lie in the qualitative characteristics of the muscles and their neural control. Children of both sexes have lower maximal blood lactate levels than adolescents or adults. Presumably, low glycolytic capacity in prepubescents is the main cause of their low anaerobic performance. No studies regarding the trainability of anaerobic power or capacity have been completed on young children.

Physiological Indices

The classic study on training in young girls was that of Åstrand et al. (1963). The gynecologic aspects of this study and of the follow-up study (Eriksson & Thorén, 1978) were reported in other sections of this book. The physiological measures in the 1963 study showed that girl swimmers (aged 12 to 16 years) were advanced in functional development after 2.5 years of intensive swim training. Lung volume, total hemoglobin, blood volume, and heart volume were significantly higher than average in relation to body size. There was a high correlation between $\dot{V}O_2max$ and heart volume. Two girls had $\dot{V}O_2max$ values higher than the highest values previously reported for bicycle ergometer tests in women. In terms of training, the functional development of these girls was closely related to the amount and intensity of training, which varied considerably.

Many of the same physiological measurements were repeated 10 years after the original study, when the girls had given up swim training (Eriksson & Thorén, 1978). Heart volume had decreased but was still higher than normal. Total hemoglobin and blood volume had declined to normal values in relation to body size, and $\dot{V}O_2$max had dropped from 2.80 L • min^{-1} (51.4 ml • kg^{-1} • min^{-1}) to 2.18 L • min^{-1} (36.4 ml • kg^{-1} • min^{-1}). The authors concluded that the functional capacity of the cardiovascular system declined markedly in these girls when training ceased. It was interesting that most of the girls became sedentary after training ended. Six had medical problems. Three suffered mental depression, one developed petit mal epilepsy (perhaps training had masked this), another arthritis of the knee, and another arterial hypertension.

A more recent study of girl swimmers (Riddinger et al., 1978) examined cardiac function in girls aged 9 to 17 who engaged in high-intensity interval workouts 6 days per week. Total workout distance averaged 12,000 m per day. A control group did not engage in any type of endurance training. So that growth and maturation were controlled, the two groups were matched by skeletal wrist X ray, ponderal index, and body surface area. Unlike Åstrand et al.'s (1963) results, the heart volumes of these swimmers were not significantly larger than those of the control subjects. Although none of the subjects demonstrated left-ventricular hypertrophy, there was a significant difference between the groups. This would suggest that the swimmers had a greater ventricular mass resulting from physiological enlargement of the myocardial fibers. It was concluded that intense training of young female swimmers does not elicit greater heart volumes than would be expected from growth and that the functional adaptations are greater than structural changes.

Aerobic Performance

Bar-Or (1983, p. 45; 1988) cited a number of studies that showed that prepubescent children (girls and boys) fail to improve in $\dot{V}O_2$max following aerobic training programs despite improvements in athletic performance. However, in a group of 8- to 13-year-old girls, the effects of cross-country running increased $\dot{V}O_2$max by 18% at 6 weeks and 26% at 12 weeks (Brown, Harrower, & Deeter, 1972), and $\dot{V}_E$max was unchanged. However, HRs at submaximal and maximal work loads showed moderate but consistent declines. The results indicate that these preadolescent girls adapted to endurance training in the same manner as adult women. No detrimental effects were observed, although two runners experienced unexplained weight loss.

Krahenbuhl, Skinner, and Kohrt (1985) also addressed the controversy regarding the trainability of prepubescent children. They conducted an excellent critical analysis of the available data and then stated that "no definitive statement can be made about the optimal age of training. . . . It does appear, however, that the maximal aerobic power of children can be significantly increased in response to a vigorous, intensive training program and that this response is not different from that seen with adults" (pp. 528-529). Rowland (1985) also wrote a critical review of this issue and concluded that exercise programs for children that employed adult criteria of frequency, duration, and intensity to improve $\dot{V}O_2$max would result in training adaptations similar to those observed in older subjects.

Eisenman and Golding (1975) compared the effects of training on cardiorespiratory variables in 12- to 13-year-old girls and 18- to 21-year-old women. Training consisted of running and bench stepping for 30 min per session, 3 days per week, for 14 weeks. A treadmill test was used to elicit $\dot{V}O_2$max. The girls and women showed similar increases in both $\dot{V}O_2$max and in rate of change in $\dot{V}O_2$max during training. The most rapid improvement occurred during the first 2 weeks of training, but both groups improved throughout the 14-week period. The investigators concluded that within the ages of 12 to 21, the effect of training on $\dot{V}O_2$max is independent of age.

Drinkwater and Horvath (1972) studied the effects of *detraining* in 7 track athletes aged 15 to 17. These girls were tested for maximal aerobic capacity during their final month of formal track training and again 3 months after cessation of training. Maximum values for $\dot{V}O_2$, $\dot{V}_E$, oxygen pulse, rate of working, and 15-min oxygen debt decreased significantly in the detrained state. There were no differences in HRmax or blood lactate levels. The metabolic cost of submaximal walking was significantly higher in the detrained state. It appeared that 3 months without training had reduced the cardiovascular fitness of these young track athletes to levels found in nonathletic girls of the same age. Results like these certainly do much to demonstrate the transient nature of training adaptations.

Changes in $\dot{V}O_2$max and running economy were studied in teenage girls (mean age 15.6 years) following 20 weeks (5 days per week) of combined distance and interval training (Burkett, Fernhall, & Walters, 1985). The moderate-level training program produced a 9.3% increase in $\dot{V}O_2$max, a 4% reduction in submaximal $\dot{V}O_2$ at 9.66 km • h^{-1}, and a 12.2% reduction in the fractional utilization of $\dot{V}O_2$max at 9.66 km • h^{-1}. The most interesting aspect of this study was the change in running economy. The results indicate that there was both an absolute and a relative decrease in energy expenditure during submaximal running. The decrease in the respiratory exchange ratio (R), coupled with the lower $\dot{V}O_2$, indicated that the subjects were using fewer calories to run at the same speed than before training. Thus, it is likely that a lower anaerobic contribution was needed to sustain running at 9.66 km • h^{-1}. This could explain the usual improvement seen on posttraining performance times (even without $\dot{V}O_2$max changes).

Malina (1988) pointed out that the differences between trained and untrained girls in $\dot{V}O_2$max is largest during adolescence and that trained girls and boys differ by only 24% for absolute and 18% for relative values of aerobic power at age 16. This contrasts with the absolute difference of 56% and relative difference of 32% for $\dot{V}O_2$max in untrained 16-year-old girls and boys (Krahenbuhl et al., 1985).

The studies reviewed here indicate that preadolescent and adolescent girls adapt to training programs much like older girls and women and that these adaptations do not result in permanent changes in either structure or function. Training methods and intensities have changed considerably in recent years, however, as have the psychological stresses that young children and adolescents may face because of competitive pressures. The topic of strenuous and highly competitive physical training for children will no doubt generate much controversy for many years.

Training in Middle Age and Menopause

One often associates middle age (here defined as beginning at age 35) with being "over the hill." Can women on the "down slide" of life experience the same training adaptations that younger women do? The same problems mentioned at the beginning of this chapter about comparing research findings apply here (variations in training methods, etc.) but with one additional concern. Investigators are generally reluctant to push middle-aged persons on maximal performance tests for fear of medical repercussions. In my opinion, the exercise capacity of middle-aged and menopausal women is largely unexplored and considerably underestimated.

Training Benefits

The studies described in the following paragraphs are ordered in terms of the age of the subjects (for information about training in women beyond age 60, see chapter 11). It is unfortunate that no longitudinal data are available on the effects of training in active middle-aged and postmenopausal women.

Getchell and Moore (1975) studied sedentary middle-aged women (ages 28 to 50, mean = 35.5) and sedentary middle-aged men (ages 30 to 57, mean = 41.6) before and after a 10-week training program of 3 to 4 days per week with workout intensity approximating 75% to 85% HRmax. The exercise program resulted in improved cardiorespiratory fitness in both groups as evidenced by increased aerobic capacity and HR bradycardia during submaximal work. Although body weight did not change, body fat (skinfold method) decreased significantly. Table 14.1 presents some detailed data from the study. The results indicate that sedentary middle-aged women (some of whom were in the climacteric years) can benefit from a systematic exercise program of calisthenics and jogging. The women responded very much like the sedentary middle-aged men. The results confirm Kilbom's suggestion (1971) that there do not appear to be any sex differences in the ability to profit from physical training at any age.

Notelovitz (1988) documented several training studies completed at the Center for Climacteric Studies. In one, a group of women between the ages of 40 and 65 walk-jogged at an intensity sufficient to achieve 70% to 80% HRmax for 30 min, three times per week, for 12 weeks. They also took part (as did a control group) in a discus-

Table 14.1   Comparative Responses of Middle-Aged Adults to 10 Weeks of Training

Variable	Women ($n = 11$)		Men ($n = 12$)	
	Before	After	Before	After
Sitting heart rate	69.3	68.9	66.3	64.0
(bpm)	±2.8	±3.4	±1.5	±2.3
Systolic blood pressure	112.9	111.8	123.2	123.7
(mmHg)	±3.6	±3.2	±3.3	±2.7
Diastolic blood pressure	73.3	70.1	81.2	81.7
(mmHg)	±2.8	±3.1	±3.0	±1.7
Change in body weight	−0.7		−0.8	
(kg)				
Change in six skinfolds	−29.2		−38.2	
(mm)				
$\dot{V}_E$BTPS	69.6	95.4*	101.0	125.9*
(L · min^{-1})	±2.8	±4.4	±4.4	±5.2
$\dot{V}O_2$max	1.72	2.18*	2.78	3.42*
(L · min^{-1})	±0.04	±0.07	±0.13	±0.15
$\dot{V}O_2$max	29.2	37.4*	33.7	41.8*
(ml · kg^{-1} · min^{-1})				
HRmax	181.5	182.9	171.4	178.4
(bpm)	±3.2	±3.6	±3.0	±3.0
Lactic acid	63.4	81.9*	64.6	99.4*
(mg/100 ml)	±6.7	±7.5	±5.3	±6.5
HR at submax	131	124*	136	122*
walk (bpm)				
Mile-run time	—	9:13	—	8:14
(min:s)				

Note. From ''Physical Training: Comparative Responses of Middle-Aged Adults'' by L.H. Getchell and J.C. Moore, 1975, *Archives of Physical and Medical Rehabilitation,* **56**, pp. 251, 252. Copyright 1975 by American Congress of Rehabilitation Medicine. Adapted by permission.

*Significant increases.

sion group that focused on diet. The exercise group showed significant increases in $\dot{V}O_2$max and in the time required to reach 90% of $\dot{V}O_2$max but did not show changes in blood lipid profiles. In another study, several groups of postmenopausal women were evaluated over a 1-year period. Their training involved three weekly 20-min periods of treadmill or ergometer exercise at 70% to 85% HRmax. A third training group performed muscle-strengthening exercises. Two additional groups did not exercise at all. The treadmill and ergometer groups showed 8.9% and 12.4% increases, respectively, in $\dot{V}O_2$max and improvements in treadmill time. Neither the strength nor the nonexercise group had significant changes.

Cowan and Gregory (1985) compared groups of pre- and postmenopausal women in terms of their adaptations to aerobic conditioning. After a 9-week walking program 4 days per week at 80% of HRmax, the premenopausal women (mean age = 41) increased their submaximal $\dot{V}O_2$ by 12.1% and their treadmill walking time at 80% HRmax by 10.9%. The postmenopausal women (mean age = 57) increased their submaximal $\dot{V}O_2$ by 19% and their exercise time by 29.6%.

Finally, a group of women between the ages of 49 and 62 (mean age = 55) participated in a moderate-intensity aerobic training program 5 days per week that varied in exercise mode (3 days of walking, jogging, ergometry; 1 day of swimming; and 1 day of aerobic dancing) (Johannessen, Holly, Lui, & Amsterdam, 1986). First, these formerly sedentary women performed 3 to 5 min of interval exercise at 60% $\dot{V}O_2$max and then progressed to 30 min of continuous activity at 74% of $\dot{V}O_2$max. At the end of 10 weeks, the exercise group had increased its $\dot{V}O_2$max by 20%, but no body composition variables had changed. There were no orthopedic problems with this form of conditioning, an important factor to note when planning an exercise program for sedentary women.

The studies cited here (as well as those of older women cited in chapter 11) indicate that women can be aerobically conditioned at any age.

Obesity and Training

Two studies examined the results of physical training on middle-aged overweight and obese women. The obese women (mean age = 38.6, mean percent body fat = 45, mean weight = 96.6 kg) trained for 50 min per day, 3 days per week, for 12 weeks (Mandroukas et al., 1984). Light-intensity exercise (walking, jogging, and calisthenics) was alternated with heavy intervals performed on a bicycle ergometer. Although there were no significant changes in body weight or body composition, $\dot{V}O_2$max increased by 20%, and there were significant increases in isometric and isokinetic strength, capillary density of the vastus lateralis muscle, and several metabolic enzymes. This indicated that there were both central and peripheral adaptations to training in the obese subjects as well as the nonobese control subjects. Gillett and Eisenman (1987) studied the effects of 16 weeks of dance exercise on overweight women (mean age = 41.9). One group attended a well-regulated "intensity-controlled" class that emphasized a progressive, individualized approach. The other group attended a "typical" aerobic dance class that did not emphasize individualized exercise. No significant changes occurred in either group in body weight, body composition, blood chemistry, muscular endurance, or flexibility. However, $\dot{V}O_2$max increased 41% in the intensity-controlled class and 22% in the typical class. The investigators stated that fitness changes for overweight middle-aged women are greater when training intensity and progression are tailored to their age and fitness levels.

Detraining

There have been several studies of the effect of cessation of training, often called *detraining*, in females. One of these studies (Weltman et al., 1978) was reviewed in the section "Metabolic Adaptations in Previously Sedentary Women"; two others (Eriksson & Thorén, 1978; Drinkwater

& Horvath, 1972) were reviewed in the section "Training in Preadolescence and Adolescence." Two other studies dealt with this issue in young women (aged 17 to 28). One evaluated the effects of a 10-week intensive bicycle ergometer training program followed by a 5- or 10-week period of detraining (Fringer & Stull, 1974). Changes after training included higher maximal values of $\dot{V}O_2$, $\dot{V}_E$, oxygen pulse, HR, and total work output and a lower $\dot{V}_E$max. After the detraining periods, most of these variables regressed toward the pretraining values. Losses in maximal $\dot{V}O_2$, oxygen pulse, and $\dot{V}_E$ were greater following the longer period of detraining. Improvements in maximal HR, $\dot{V}_E$, and total work output were retained to some degree after 10 weeks of detraining.

Pedersen and Jorgensen (1978) investigated the effects of 7 weeks of bicycle ergometer training at an HR of 170 bpm, a 7-week detraining period, and another 7-week period of training. Increases in $\dot{V}O_2$max (10% to 14%) and work rate at target HR (24%) were observed in both training periods. Thus, the training response was similar in both periods. Gains were essentially extinguished following the detraining period, and there was no indication of beneficial effects during retraining from the previous activity. The 7-week period of inactivity between training periods was sufficient to neutralize the effects of the first training period.

These studies corroborate what has been found in men in regard to detraining: that most training adaptations are essentially lost at about the same rate they are gained. This indicates that athletes are well advised to engage in fitness maintenance programs during the off-season.

Testosterone and Trainability in Women

Greater androgen levels have often been associated with the development of larger muscle mass and lesser amounts of body fat. Androgen has also been believed to enhance *trainability*. Consequently, Krahenbuhl, Archer, and Pettit (1978) sought to establish the relationship between serum testos-terone (T) levels in untrained young women and strength, body fat, aerobic power, and improvement in these variables following training. Blood samples were obtained on the eighth day of the menstrual cycle before training. Static strength, percent body fat (hydrostatic weighing), and $\dot{V}O_2$max (treadmill) were determined before and after a 16-week training program. Training consisted of low-intensity running and weight training for 1 h, three times per week. Serum T was negatively related to percent body fat both before ($r = -.55$) and after ($r = -.77$) training but not to $\dot{V}O_2$max or static strength at either testing period. Improvement in $\dot{V}O_2$max with training, however, was significantly related to serum T ($r = .73$ for absolute improvement in ml • kg^{-1} • min^{-1}, and $r = .62$ for percent improvement in ml • kg^{-1} • min^{-1}). The investigators suggested that T may play a role in the trainability of women. (Author's note: Adipose tissue is known to convert T to estrogen. The fatter subjects in this investigation may have been converting more T to E and therefore would have lower T values. A relationship [correlation] does not imply causality, only association. The fact that lean body mass and strength were *not* related to serum T is of far greater significance than the relationship between body fat and T. I doubt if serum T has much to do with trainability, but the study is interesting and warrants a more elaborate follow-up investigation.)

Summary

This chapter has presented data from longitudinal training studies on girls and women. Little of the material has focused on the highly active or athletic woman because longitudinal studies have not been completed on those women. The information available on these groups is primarily cross-sectional and is presented elsewhere in this book (mainly chapter 16 but elsewhere when appropriate).

It is clear that the training adaptations of girls and women are not dissimilar from those of boys and men at any age. It is also clear that many girls and women have undertaken sport activities with little prior physical conditioning. However, this situation is rapidly changing. Athletic opportunities are expanding for women of all ages. With more participants, many of whom are serious competitors, have come improved performances. Those who strive to excel are finding they can no longer do so with only occasional practice. Serious physical conditioning and intense training programs are becoming prerequisites for success. With this metamorphosis has come the realization that many previous concepts about the coaching of female athletes are obsolete. Although some training methods may need to be specifically developed or altered for different age-groups (preadolescent, adolescent, and climacteric) of both sexes, it is clear that basic training techniques are suitable for all people. Good training methods for boys and men will yield basically the same qualitative results for girls and women. What is needed is a thorough understanding of the basic principles of specificity and overload, of how the body works, and of the techniques of sport. Therefore, today's coach must be an expert exercise physiologist and biomechanist (not to mention a psychologist). It is hoped that this book will provide some of the physiological knowledge and understanding necessary for successful coaching and performance.

Chapter 15

Athletic Injuries

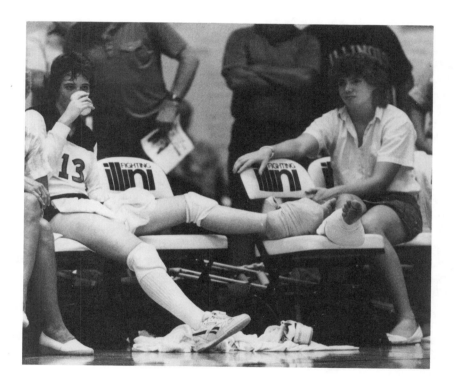

Are girls and women particularly vulnerable to athletic injuries? Many have thought so for a variety of reasons. Structurally (see chapter 1), women have narrower shoulders and wider hips, lesser bone density, and lesser muscle mass than men. Consequently, many have thought women too frail to participate in sports, especially sports that involve physical contact with other players or the ground. Also, fears that women would injure their reproductive organs in some way were very prevalent in earlier decades. Many have believed that women were just not built for sport and that frequent or strenuous play would ultimately lead to serious injury.

What are the facts? Are these concepts facts, or are they fallacies? The evidence discussed here is separated into four sections. The first deals with those studies that primarily compared athletic injuries in males and females. The second examines females' injuries in high school and college athletic programs. The third section discusses injuries and problems that are specific to the active female, and the fourth looks at sport-specific injuries to women.

Comparison of Athletic Injuries Between the Sexes

In the 1960s and 1970s, as more women began participating in sport, physicians noted that many women were being injured. This appeared to be a new phenomenon, probably because they were simply not accustomed to seeing women with sport-related injuries. Many physicians were quoted as saying that women experienced more sport injuries than men. In fact, this notion is simply not borne out by any statistical analysis of data. For example, a report by the Department of Health, Education and Welfare estimated that more than 1 million athletes were injured in high school and college programs during 1975-76 (Calvert, 1979). Football (male participants only) accounted for 326,000 of the 1.06 million injuries with an injury rate of 929 per 1,000 college-level participants! Injury rates in other contact sports were 74 per 1,000 for men and 54 per 1,000 for women. In noncontact sports, injury rates were 38 per 1,000 participants for men and 32 per 1,000 for women. Women made up nearly 29% of the varsity athletic squads but accounted for only 16% of the injuries.

Whiteside (1980) analyzed data from 29 states using the National Athletic Injury/Illness Reporting System (NAIRS) for the 1975-76 and 1976-77 seasons. Basketball players (both sexes) had the highest number and relative frequency of injuries, followed by gymnastics and baseball and softball (Table 15.1). The number of injuries was generally higher in practice than in game situations and was proportional to the time the athlete played. Sprains were the most common type of injury for both men and women.

Table 15.1   Number and Relative Frequency (R) of Men's and Women's Reportable Injuries, 1975-1977

Sport	No.	R
Women		
Basketball	383	19.5
Gymnastics	95	9.4
Softball	76	3.1
Men		
Basketball	566	15.9
Gymnastics	95	7.7
Baseball	133	2.9

Note. R = number of cases per 1,000 athletic exposures. From "Men's and Women's Injuries in Comparable Sports" by P.A. Whiteside, 1980, The Physician and Sportsmedicine, 8(3), p. 132. Reprinted by permission of Physician and Sportsmedicine. Copyright McGraw-Hill, Inc.

Whiteside also studied differences in the incidence of injury to various body parts for men and women. The ankle and foot, hip and leg, knee, and forearm and hand had the most frequently reported injuries in women's sports. The pattern of men's injuries was similar, but women had a higher relative frequency of ankle injuries. She concluded that there were more similarities than differences in injuries among men and women in comparable sports.

Clarke and Buckley (1980) ranked the average annual relative frequency of significant injuries in selected collegiate sports using NAIRS data from 1975 to 1978 (Table 15.2). The high ranking of women's gymnastics and basketball (and men's contact sports) is perhaps the most striking finding. However, they noted that matched sports demonstrated similar injury patterns and that the major differences were *among* sports. They concluded that sport injuries were sport related and not sex related.

More recently, the National Collegiate Athletic Association Injury Surveillance System (ISS) issued a report ("NCAA Survey Shows," 1987) showing not only higher values for the relative frequency of injury in collegiate sport, but also a slightly different ranking among sports. These values, shown in Table 15.2, indicate that women who participate in collegiate gymnastics have a high risk of injury.

A similar study was conducted to compare the incidence of injury between boys and girls in eight similar sports in the Oklahoma secondary schools (Shively, Grana, & Ellis, 1981). Results showed no difference in overall or individual sport injury rates: 25.4 and 27.4 injuries per 1,000 male and female participants, respectively (Table 15.3). The girls had a significantly larger number of ankle injuries and lost more playing time because of

them. Injuries were most common in the lower extremities, sprains and strains being the most common type. There was no difference in the occurrence of any specific type of injury between the sexes.

These studies reported the incidence of injury in terms of the number of participants. Data from sports medicine clinics, although interesting, cannot be analyzed in the same manner because there is no way to determine the total number of sport participants. Thus, considerable scientific control is lost. Nevertheless, two such reports are summarized here because of the general lack of published data in this area of inquiry.

The medical reports of orthopedic residents from the sports medicine clinic of Lenox Hill Hospital

Table 15.2   Relative Frequency of Significant Injury in Selected Collegiate Sports

	1975-1978[a]	1985-1986[b]
Spring football	6.3	—
Wrestling	4.2	10.84
Fall football	3.0	6.81
Women's gymnastics	2.7	9.38
Men's ice hockey	2.5	—
Women's basketball	2.5	—
Men's lacrosse	2.5	5.82
Men's soccer	2.3	—
Women's track and field	2.2	—
Men's basketball	2.1	—
Women's volleyball	2.1	5.44
Men's track and field	1.9	—
Women's softball	1.8	—
Men's gymnastics	1.5	—
Men's baseball	1.3	3.37
Women's field hockey	1.0	—
Women's tennis	0.6	—
Men's swimming and diving	0.6	—
Women's swimming and diving	0.2	—

Note. Frequencies are per 1,000 athletic exposures.

[a]Data from Clarke and Buckley (1980).

[b]Data from "NCAA Survey Shows Injury Trends" (1987).

Table 15.3 Injuries in Boys' and Girls' Sports

	Boys			Girls		
Sport	Participants	No. injuries	Rate/ 1,000	Participants	No. injuries	Rate/ 1,000
Track	1,682	28	16.6	1,141	8	7.0
Cross-country	389	9	23.1	187	0	0
Swimming	233	1	4.2	165	5	30.3
Tennis	430	0	0	457	3	6.6
Volleyball	19	0	0	429	2	4.6
Soccer	118	1	8.5	50	1	20.0
Basketball	1,638	98	59.8	1,605	105	65.4
Baseball/softball	1,969	28	14.2	773	9	11.6
Total	6,478	165	25.4	4,807	133	27.7

Note. From "High School Sports Injuries" by R.A. Shively, W.A. Grana, and D. Ellis, 1981, *The Physician and Sportsmedicine,* **9**(8), p. 48. Reprinted by permission of *The Physician and Sportsmedicine.* Copyright McGraw-Hill, Inc.

(New York City) were studied over a period of 4.5 years (Witman, Melvin, & Nicholas, 1981). Of 1,280 patients seen, 69% were male and 31% female, for a male-to-female ratio greater than 2 to 1. The age range of patients was 10 to 72 years (mean age 30.2). The most frequently injured areas of the body were the knee (45.5%), ankle (9.8%), and shoulder (7.7%). Unfortunately, the distribution of injuries was not analyzed according to sex. Most injuries were from running and jogging (35.2%), followed by racket sports (12.4%) and basketball (10.5%). Almost 76% of the injuries occurred during recreational activities.

More recently, injuries treated over a 7-year period at the University of Rochester Section of Sports Medicine were surveyed (DeHaven & Lintner, 1986). Males accounted for 80.3% of all injuries. For both sexes, the most commonly injured areas were the knee and ankle, sprains and strains being the most frequent injuries. Those of the patellofemoral articulation were significantly more frequent among women.

In summary, the literature indicates that injuries

are more sport specific than sex specific and that sprains and strains are the most common type of injury for both men and women. It is probable that better conditioning programs for both men and women would significantly lower the incidence of injury in sport, and this may be particularly true for women. Many girls and women are thrust into athletic participation without being adequately prepared in terms of prior conditioning, skill development, or knowledge about the sport.

Injuries in Girls' High School Athletic Programs

Four girls' high school athletic programs in the Seattle (Washington) area were studied for 2 years (Garrick & Requa, 1978). Specially trained athletic trainers examined each injured athlete and collected epidemiological data. There were 192 injuries, a rate of 220 injuries per 1,000 participants. Most of the victims were returned to full activity within 1 week. Three times more injuries occurred in practice than in competition, strains and sprains accounting for nearly two thirds of the injuries. Most of the injuries occurred in the lower extremities. Figure 15.1 gives more detail about each sport and indicates whether a physician or an X ray was needed. Some of the sports were being offered for the first time (badminton and softball), so these injury rates may be due largely to participant inexperience.

A more recent study ("Study Identifies," 1987) reported solely on high school girls' basketball injuries in the 1986-87 season using data from the National High School Injury Registry. Sixty-three percent of the injuries occurred during practice. Sixty percent of the game-related injuries occurred during the second half. One injury was reported for each of 429 players, which means that about 23% of the girls who played basketball that season were injured. Sprains and strains accounted for 57% of all injuries, and the ankle and foot was the most commonly injured (29.7%) part.

Injuries in Women's Collegiate Athletic Programs

Data from several surveys were incorporated into a report on injuries in women's intercollegiate athletic programs by Haycock and Gillette (1976).

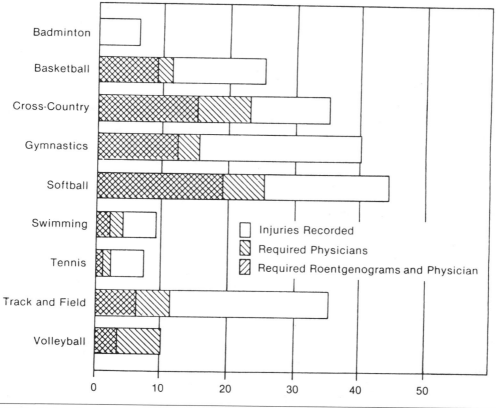

Figure 15.1 Rates of occurrence for injuries in four high school athletic programs for girls. *Note.* From "Girls' Sports Injuries in High School Athletics" by J.G. Garrick and R.K. Requa, 1978, *Journal of the American Medical Association,* **239**(1), p. 2246. Copyright 1978, American Medical Association. Reprinted by permission.

The largest number of injuries occurred in basketball, volleyball, gymnastics, and softball. The most serious injuries (fractures, head injuries, and dislocations) were in basketball, field hockey, softball, and gymnastics. Most of the injuries were not serious, the most common being sprained ankles, minor knee injuries, and contusions.

Eisenberg and Allen (1978) followed 110 female varsity athletes aged 17 to 23 years for one academic season. These women participated in eight sports and experienced a total of 114 injuries. Softball produced the largest number of (but not the most severe) injuries, followed by gymnastics, volleyball, track, basketball, swimming, golf, and tennis. As in the other studies reported previously, sprains and strains accounted for most of the injuries (60.5%), followed by contusions (15.8%), abrasions and lacerations (10.5%), and fractures and dislocations (7.9%). Chondromalacia was a chronic problem in both the track and the swim teams. Ankle and knee injuries made up most of the injuries (55.1%). Head, neck, and facial injuries were generally minor, the most serious being two nose fractures in basketball. No injuries were reported to the breast or pelvis.

Clarke and Buckley (1980) reported that college female athletes suffer more injuries than their high school counterparts because competition is more intense in college. They pointed out that this is also true in men's sports. They further stated that future investigations of injuries should be delimited to specific sports over a period of time so that attention can be given to the pattern of injury and to practical preventive measures.

Athletic Injuries Specific to Women

The remainder of this chapter is devoted to two questions: Are a girl's or woman's reproductive organs especially vulnerable to athletic injury? and, Are there any sport-specific injuries to which a woman is particularly vulnerable? In regard to the first question, attention is given to evidence of pelvic and breast injuries. The focus for the second question is on common orthopedic injuries associated with specific sports.

Pelvic Injuries

Pelvic injuries are rare even though it was once feared that girls and women would injure their reproductive organs in some way as a result of strenuous play or competitive sports. Occasionally, pelvic contusions occur from contact with the ground, a ball, or another player, but these bruises are strictly surface injuries and do not lead to internal injuries of the uterus, vagina, or ovaries. As was pointed out by at least one proponent of women's athletics (Ullyot, 1981), men are the ones in danger of athletic injuries to reproductive organs because their organs are exposed and relatively unsupported. As explained earlier in this text, the internal reproductive organs of women are extremely well protected by bony, ligamentous, and muscular structures (see chapter 4).

There are several reports in the literature (cited by Haycock & Gillette, 1976, p. 165) of "forceful vaginal douches in waterskiing leading to severe lacerations of the vulva." Large-bowel trauma, rectal lacerations, and injury to the bladder may also result (Kizer, 1980). This suggests that wearing nylon-reinforced neoprene rubber pants or a panty girdle while waterskiing may be wise.

Haycock and Gillette (1976) cited two severe pelvic injuries. In one case, the uterus was perforated by an IUD (intrauterine device) following a blow to the pelvis in a field hockey game. In the other, a liver was lacerated by a karate chop.

Breast Injuries and Problems During Sport

The American Medical Association's Committee on the Medical Aspects of Sports issued a special communication to the American Alliance for Health, Physical Education and Recreation (AAHPER) in 1975 that included the following statement: "Since breast tissue is susceptible to injury in contact and noncontact sports, appropriate and adequate protection should be provided and its use encouraged'' (Corbitt et al., 1975, p. 46). However, this statement failed to cite evidence that breast tissue is more susceptible to injury than is other tissue and what constituted ''appropriate and adequate protection.'' Indeed, Haycock stated that breast injuries are almost nonexistent and that contusions are very rare (Haycock, 1981; Haycock & Gillette, 1976).

Nevertheless, breast-related problems do occur in sport, including breast soreness from excessive movement; ''jogger's nipple'' (raw or bleeding nipples due to prolonged rubbing against a bra or shirt—men experience this too); abrasions from bra parts such as straps, metal hooks, clips, and underwires; and underarm chafing from material in shirts and athletic equipment (chest protectors in softball, backpacks, etc.). Haycock (1978) stated that of 115 survey respondents, 31% reported some type of breast discomfort during sport activity. Of these positive responses, 52% were due to specific injury and 48% simply to discomfort. A total of 72% reported breast tenderness following sport activity. A recent study (Lorentzen & Lawson, 1987) confirmed these statements. Fifty-six percent of a sample of women who varied widely in athletic participation reported breast-related pain or discomfort during sport that was mostly associated with excessive motion. Twenty-nine percent said they experienced no breast pain or discomfort during sport.

Occasionally, a laceration, contusion, or hematoma occurs in an athlete participating in a contact or racket sport. Few of these are dangerous. A laceration must be kept clean to prevent secondary infection, as abscesses are very painful. Applying a cold pack to a contusion or hematoma should control swelling and relieve discomfort. Haycock (1980) stated that occasionally a contusion results in fatty necrosis and the formation of a module of fibrous tissue that is of no consequence but that may remain for many years. Jogger's nipple can be prevented with a plastic bandage or application of petroleum jelly before running. Once an abrasion has occurred, it should be kept clean to prevent infection and covered to prevent recurrence.

Although absolutely no evidence suggests a relationship between an injury to the breast and cancer, the myth is prevalent. Women should be reassured that breast trauma does *not* lead to malignancy (Haycock, 1980, 1987).

Breast protection such as that offered by firm, impenetrable cup material (contact Fem-Gard Inc., Littleton, CO) is necessary only for such sports as fencing, ice hockey, and perhaps tackle football. This sort of protection is certainly not necessary for other sports, but good breast support is!

Breast Soreness. What causes breast soreness during or after sport activity? The answer appears to be that excessive movement of breast tissue causes strain to the fascial attachments of the breast to the underlying pectoralis major. A brief review of the structure of the breast reminds one that the breasts are glandular structures on the anterior chest wall and for support are entirely dependent on the skin, subcutaneous tissue, and rather flimsy fascial planes referred to as Cooper's ligaments. These ligaments are not ligaments in the usual sense in that they do not connect muscle to bone (as do tendons) or support joints (as do ligaments). Rather, these fascial planes divide the glandular elements in the breast into lobules from which ducts drain to the nipple during lactation (Haycock, 1978) (see chapter 4).

Breast motion during running and jumping has been studied by several groups (Gehlsen & Albohm, 1980; Haycock, 1978; Lorentzen & Lawson, 1987), and they discovered that the breasts move not only up and down but also in a spiral or circular motion. Vertical displacement during running is directly related to breast size. This indicates that women with cup sizes C and D should use a good supportive sport bra when running. Excessive motion apparently results in the fascial strain that leads to discomfort during physical activity and often delayed soreness following activity.

Athletic Bra Support. Opinions differ about going braless or using athletic bra support. Some believe that supporting the weight of the breasts diminishes the stress on the connective tissue network that supports fat and glandular tissue. Others believe that going braless (especially during the pubertal years) allows the tissues to adapt and become stronger and thus provides more support than would occur if a breast were continuously supported. There is no evidence that free-swinging breasts are more likely to sag than supported breasts except for the observation that women in primitive cultures who never wear bras do develop long, pendulous breasts (Haycock, 1988). The degree of each individual's need for breast support during physical activity is mostly contingent on breast size. Because most regular bras are designed primarily for reasons of aesthetics rather than athletic use, they provide minimal limitation of motion and usually only vertical support during static posture (Adrian, 1980). A key factor to providing the degree of support necessary during bouncing motions prevalent in sport is fit, both in the size and shape of the cup and the width of the circumference band. A complete rather than a partial cup is necessary to control upward motion as well as lateral and downward motions. The breasts should be limited in attaining high velocities and large displacements as they lift up and slap down on the chest wall. The ideal is probably a bra that keeps the breast motionless in reference to the body, allowing the breast to move only in unison with the trunk rather than bouncing separately. Haycock (1978, 1981) provided the following six criteria for a good sport bra:

1. The bra should provide good upward support.
2. It should limit the motion of the breast relative to the body.
3. It should be made of a material that is absorptive, nonallergenic, and nonabrasive with a minimal amount of elasticity.
4. All fasteners should be covered on both sides to prevent abrasions to the skin of the wearer as well as other players.
5. The straps should be wide, nonelastic, and designed so that they do not slip off the shoulders during movement.

6. There should be some provision at the base of the bra to prevent the bra "riding up" over the breasts. Usually a wide cloth band below the breast or a nonmetal underwire is sufficient.

There is probably no one ideal bra for all women. Gehlsen and Albohm (1980) studied horizontal and vertical breast displacement during jogging and found a difference in the support offered by eight different sport bras but not in size groups. Apparently, the mass of the breast is the most significant factor in breast discomfort during athletic activities. Occasionally women's sport magazines provide an analysis of the current sport bras on the market.

Injuries in Contact Sports

The AMA's Committee on the Medical Aspects of Sports (Corbitt et al., 1975) maintains that it is very unlikely that girls competing in contact sports will sustain more injuries than boys engaged in similar activities. It is even conceivable that girls may suffer fewer injuries because of their lesser muscle mass relative to body size, which means that they cannot generate the same momentum and potentially traumatic forces on body contact. This issue parallels one in the recent past regarding the advisability of boys playing tackle football. Medical authorities originally thought that boys would sustain a considerable number of fractures, but a study of more than 5,000 boys showed that fractures were rare and epiphyseal fractures even more infrequent in football. Apparently, young boys lack the strength and aggressiveness necessary to deliver a blow sufficient to cause a fracture. The same is thought to pertain to girls in contact sports. The committee is against girls' participating on boys' contact-sport teams, however. It believes that even if competitors were matched for weight, girls would still be exposed to potentially greater risk because the ratio of adipose tissue to lean body weight is to the disadvantage of girls after puberty (Corbitt et al., 1975).

The argument whether contact sports are appropriate for girls (and women) persists today. In the few cases in which girls have been allowed to participate in traditionally male-oriented sports (e.g., football and wrestling), there has not been an unusual instance of injury. Most physical educators, coaches, and physicians believe that girls and women desiring participation in traditional contact sports should have separate teams and coaches.

Orthopedic Injuries

Women are often said to have greater ligamentous laxity and hence to be more prone to ligamentous injuries than men. Whether this statement is true is debatable. Possibly, this concept stems from the woman's relatively lesser muscular strength. However, it should also be pointed out that the woman's shorter bone length results in less torque at a given joint. It is obvious that well-controlled studies of joint laxity need to be completed in both men and women.

Knee. A woman's wider hips increase the angle between the femur and the tibia, allowing the patella to move laterally when the leg is flexed (see chapter 1). This, combined with a relatively weak medial quadriceps muscle, tends to cause lateral tracking of the patella in the patellofemoral groove. This predisposes the woman to increased retropatellar pain (formerly referred to as *chondromalacia patella)* (Hunter, 1984, 1988; Hunter-Griffin, 1988). The problem may also be aggravated by foot pronation, which can usually be corrected with orthotics (shoe inserts), hamstring stretching, and exercises to strengthen the medial quadriceps rather than surgery. Readers interested in knee injuries in women should consult Hunter (1984, 1988) and Hunter-Griffin (1988).

Ankle. Ankle impingement (soft-tissue traumatization between bone prominences) and ankle sprains are common in sport and dance, particularly among gymnasts, ballerinas, ice skaters, and volleyball and basketball players. Ankle taping is common among volleyball and basketball players and may be a good preventive measure. Conditioning programs should include ankle evertor and invertor strengthening as well as dorsiflexor and plantar flexor strengthening. Achilles tendon stretching should also be included.

Foot. Bunions, an inflammation of the bursa overlying the medial prominence (or flare) of the great toe's head, appear to be more common in women than men. Shoes should be selected that have a wider toe box and forefoot area, and one should avoid shoes with heels that cause this area to be stressed. Conservative (nonoperative) therapy should be thoroughly explored before surgery is considered because foot mechanics are often altered by surgery, which can cause additional problems for the athlete (Hunter, 1988).

Shoulder. Shoulder impingement syndromes are often seen in swimmers and athletes participating in throwing or racket sports. Increased ligamentous laxity is often blamed for this weakening of the rotator cuff, which allows upward migration of the humeral head in the glenoid fossa (articulating surface). As this space becomes smaller, the tissues in that space become inflamed. Treatment usually includes anti-inflammatory medications, strengthening of the external rotator muscles of the shoulder, and careful analysis of training techniques. Steroid injection remains a controversial treatment for this problem (Hunter, 1984).

Back. Young female gymnasts have a high incidence of spondylolysis (a defect in the pars interarticularis) and vertebral apophysitis (irritation of the growth centers of the vertebral end plates). These problems appear related to repetitive hyperextension and flexion activities associated with movements typical of gymnastics, ice skating, and diving. Stress fractures of the lumbar vertebrae may also occur in these young girls and can be a source of persistent back pain. Rest, abdominal and back strengthening exercises, and anti-inflammatory medications are usually prescribed for these problems.

Stress Fractures. Stress fractures probably occur more frequently in women than men (Hunter, 1988; Hunter-Griffin, 1988). The problem is most commonly seen in runners, ballerinas, and gymnasts and may be related to decreased bone mineral density secondary to oligo-amenorrhea (Lloyd, Myers, Buchanan, & Demers, 1988; Lloyd et al., 1986; Warren et al., 1986; see also chapter 8). The tibia, pelvis, and metatarsals are the most frequent sites of stress fractures in female athletes and dancers (see the following discussion of running injuries). Many women experience recurrence of these injuries because, in my opinion, many physicians do not consider what probably is the ultimate cause: low circulating estrogen. Treatment should include rest (with gradual return to activity as pain allows), the dietary intake of minerals (particularly calcium), and a full evaluation of menstrual status.

Sport-Specific Injuries in Women

In this section, the focus shifts from injuries specific to women in sport to those specific to a particular sport. The sports examined are running, gymnastics, aerobic dance, field hockey, figure skating, and ballet.

Running

Most running injuries (60%) among long-distance runners are caused by training errors: excessive mileage, overly intensive workouts, rapid changes in training routines, or running on hills or hard surfaces. These extrinsic factors are not related

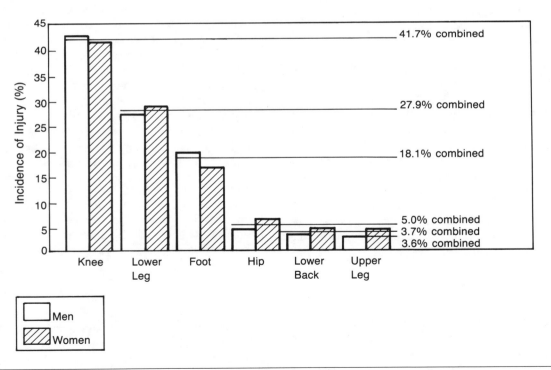

Figure 15.2 Incidence of overuse injuries in running, men and women. *Note.* From "A Survey of Overuse Running Injuries" by D.B. Clement, J.E. Taunton, G.W. Smart, and K.L. McNicol, 1981, *The Physician and Sportsmedicine, 9*(5), p. 49. Reprinted by permission of *The Physician and Sportsmedicine.* Copyright McGraw-Hill, Inc.

to gender. Some anatomic, or intrinsic, factors (e.g., excessive pronation, leg-length discrepancy, weakness of the vastus medialis, lack of sufficient flexibility, and increased joint laxity) are associated with overuse injuries common in running and may relate to sex differences (Nilson, 1986). Overuse injuries occur gradually and are not the result of trauma.

A Canadian group has reported an extensive retrospective survey of the clinical records of 1,650 running patients who had 1,819 overuse injuries during a 2-year period (Clement, Taunton, Smart, & McNicol, 1981). Forty percent of the patients were women who averaged 26 years in age and ran an average of 19 mi per week. Of the 709 patients who were 30 years or older, 28.3% were women. This led the authors to state that the younger female runners had the greater risk of developing overuse running injuries.

Figure 15.2 indicates the numbers and percent-ages of the overuse injuries by major anatomic region and by sex. The knee was the most common site of injury (41.7%), followed by the lower leg (27.9%). The areas least frequently injured were the lower back and upper leg. There were no apparent sex differences in susceptibility to injury by anatomic site. Table 15.4 lists the 10 most common overuse injuries found in the runners surveyed. These injuries accounted for 68.7% of all the injuries diagnosed. Patellofemoral pain syndrome was the most common disorder (25.8% of all injuries). The investigators (Clement et al., 1981) also provided a complete listing of the injuries by major anatomic region and by sex. Although both sexes were equally susceptible to injury in the major anatomic locations, certain conditions were observed more frequently in one sex than the other. For example, Achilles peritendinitis was seen more frequently in men and tibial stress syndrome in women. The authors

Table 15.4 Incidence of the 10 Most Common Overuse Injuries in Runners

Injury	Men		Women		Total	
	%	No.	%	No.	%	No.
Patellofemoral pain syndrome	24.3	262	27.9	206	25.8	468
Tibial stress syndrome	10.7	115	16.8	124	13.2	239
Achilles peritendinitis	7.9	85	3.2	24	6.0	109
Plantar fasciitis	5.3	57	3.9	28	4.7	85
Patellar tendinitis	5.6	60	2.8	21	4.5	81
Iliotibial band friction syndrome	4.6	50	3.8	28	4.3	78
Metatarsal stress syndrome	3.3	36	3.0	22	3.2	58
Tibial stress fracture	2.4	26	2.8	21	2.6	47
Tibialis posterior tendinitis	1.9	21	3.2	24	2.5	45
Peroneal tendinitis	2.0	22	1.6	12	1.9	34
Total	68.0	734	69.0	510	68.7	1,244

Note. From ''A Survey of Overuse Running Injuries'' by D.B. Clement, J.E. Taunton, G.W. Smart, and K.L. McNicol, 1981, *The Physician and Sportsmedicine,* **9**(5), p. 50. Reprinted by permission of *The Physician and Sportsmedicine.* Copyright McGraw-Hill, Inc.

believe that future studies should differentiate injuries by sex.

Truly definitive data on sex differences in anatomic factors and injuries due to running are nonexistent. Despite the belief that the wider female pelvis and resulting Q angle (see chapter 1) predisposes women to more patellofemoral problems, little data suggest that this is the case (Nilson, 1986). Although knee pain in runners is a common complaint, it appears to occur equally among men and women. Tibial stress syndrome (shinsplints) and stress fractures, however, may be more common in women. Stress fractures of the tibia, fibula, metatarsals, and pubic ramus seem to be occurring with increasing frequency as women run faster. This is possibly related to stride length and the tendency for many female runners to overstride (Atwater, 1986; Nilson, 1986).

Gymnastics

McAuley et al. (1987) published an extensive review of the literature on injuries in women's gymnastics. They concluded that the sport has a higher injury rate than any other, that the risk of injury increases with advancing levels of skill, and that floor exercise and tumbling involve the largest number of injuries, followed by the balance beam and uneven parallel bars. Two types of overuse injuries common in young female gymnasts are discussed at length by Walsh, Huurman, and Shelton (1984). Extensor mechanism dysfunction at the knee may manifest as patellar pain, patellar subluxation (dislocation), patellar tendinitis, or Osgood-Schlatter's disease (pain associated with the lowermost attachment of the knee extensors). Treatment involves strengthening the vastus medialis, controlling inflammation, rest, and sometimes functional bracing of the knee.

The other primary overuse injury in young gymnasts is to the bony structures of the spine, most often the lumbar spine. Such injury is usually related to a high incidence of vertical impact spinal loading, often in a hyperextended position. Hyper-

lordotic movements, typical of gymnastics, place extreme loads on the portion of the vertebral complex that is least resistant to compression, shear, and impact forces: the pars interarticularis. The result may be progressively debilitating pain in the mid-to-low back that results from repetitive microfracture with altered growth patterns. Treatments include rest, spinal immobilization with a body cast, and, in advanced cases, the discontinuation of a gymnastic career.

Aerobic Dance

The growth of aerobic dance has been phenomenal in the last decade and has become the most popular organized fitness activity for women in the United States. For many (about 40%), aerobic dance is their only form of exercise (Garrick & Requa, 1988), a factor that may predispose them to increased risk of injury.

Several studies have examined the incidence of injuries among aerobic dance students and instructors. Although the definition of *injury* and the method of reporting participation sometimes differed among studies, Garrick and Requa (1988) reported both agreement and disagreement among these investigations. For example, instructors were found to incur .22 (Francis, Francis, & Welshons-Smith, 1985), .29 (Richie, Kelso, & Bellucci, 1985), and .93 (Garrick, Gillien, & Whiteside, 1986) injuries per 100 h of activity. Students were found to incur 1.01 (Richie et al., 1985) and 1.16 (Garrick et al., 1986) injuries per 100 h of activity. Even more striking were the similarities among the percentages of participants reporting injuries. Among students, 43.3% (Richie et al., 1985) and 44.1% (Garrick et al., 1986) reported injuries. Among instructors, 76.3% (Francis et al., 1985), 75.9% (Richie et al., 1985), and 75% (Garrick et al., 1986) reported injuries. The injury rate among participants whose only fitness activity was aerobic dance was 1.90 per 100 h of activity compared to .64 per 100 h of activity among students involved in multiple fitness activities (Garrick et al., 1986).

Even closer agreement was found in the anatomic location of aerobic dance injuries. Among instructors, the leg, calf, and Achilles tendon accounted for 34.5% (Francis et al., 1985), 35.3% (Richie et al., 1985), and 24.1% (Garrick et al., 1986) of all injuries. For students, the leg, calf, and Achilles tendon accounted for 38.6% (Richie et al., 1985) and 28.7% (Garrick et al., 1986) of the injuries. Generally, foot, ankle, knee, and spine injuries occurred in descending order of incidence.

The role of shoes and floors are two extrinsic factors that have received attention in the study of aerobic dance injuries. Although not all studies agree, it appears that although it is important to wear shoes, no one shoe or type of floor is better than another (Garrick & Requa, 1988).

Field Hockey

Injuries in field hockey players were documented at California State University at Long Beach from 1976 to 1980 (Rose, 1981). Of the 81 injuries reported, 55 were seen by a physician, and only 16% were classified as major injuries. Ankle sprains were the most common injury. Of the serious injuries, there were four knee injuries, a shoulder subluxation, a cerebral concussion, a cheek contusion leading to nerve damage, and a foot fracture. Injuries decreased with increased team performance. This sport was equal to volleyball in leading the women's athletic program in total number of injuries.

Figure Skating

Smith and Micheli (1982) reported the nature and incidence of skating injuries in 15 female high-level competitors ranging in age from 11 to 16. These skaters trained 4 to 6 h a day, 6 days a week, and 48 to 51 weeks a year. Five skaters spent at least 30 min a day practicing triple jumps, and none did more than 5 min of warm-up activities, including on- or off-the-ice stretching. Only 4 skaters reported no skating injuries. The other 11

skaters reported 33 injuries, of which only 8 kept the skaters off the ice for more than 3 days and were classified as serious.

The authors, who are orthopedic surgeons, found an unusually high incidence of scoliosis in this group. Five of the 15 girls had clinically obvious curves, but the presence of a curve did not correlate with lower back pain. Seven girls had genu valgum (knock-knees), and in one it was severe. Acute injuries included torn knee ligaments, concussion, fifth metatarsal fracture, hamstring strain, rib bruise, groin strain, and chin laceration. Of the overuse injuries reported, lower back strain was most common, followed by malleolar swelling, medial shin pain, patellofemoral knee pain, ankle spurs, and lateral shin pain.

Ballet

Ballet is perhaps one of the most demanding of all physical activities as it requires very high levels of strength, flexibility, speed, coordination, agility, and balance. The professional ballerina attends dance classes and practices technique 6 to 7 h a day most weeks of the year. In fact, a professional dancer will seldom miss a single day of workout. The single most common complaint in ballet is plantar fascial strain. This is followed by Achilles tendinitis, first-metatarsal head pain, knee problems, and stress fractures ("Ballet Dancers' Injuries," 1976). The quality of the dance floor is thought to be an important factor. Most American dancing surfaces are wood that overlies concrete. This makes for a rigid, unyielding floor. Most Russian dance floors are wood that overlies a layer of air. This makes for loftier, less fatiguing jumps and leaps.

Ballet is multidirectional, requiring an extremely adaptable anatomic structure. Many ballet movements go beyond the normal ranges of joint motion. This is particularly true for the hip, knee, and foot joints. Weiker (1988) provided an excellent and thorough review of dance injuries of the knee, ankle, and foot and focused especially on the biomechanics of the *en pointe* position. In the same book, Micheli (1988) provided a similar review of injuries of the back, hip, and pelvis. Interested readers are referred to these extensive reviews.

Numerous foot and ankle problems arise from the *en pointe* position. These include talar dome fractures; problems of the os trigonum; stress fractures of the metatarsals, talus, or fibula; bone spurs; and tendinitis of the flexor hallucis longus. The dancer often has an amazing degree of foot deformity that includes calluses and corns, thickened bursae, interphalangeal joint enlargement of the toes, claw toes, and bunions (Hunter, 1984; Weiker, 1988).

Back pain is common among dancers and is usually associated with hyperlordotic posturing, which is often observable during *barre*, or floor work (Micheli, 1988). This may lead to disk herniation, spondylolysis (as with gymnastics), or stress fractures of the pelvis, hip, or vertebrae. The so-called snapping hip syndrome is also relatively common among dancers and is caused by repeated circumduction movements of the lower limb. Warren et al. (1986) reported that a delay in menarche and prolonged intervals of amenorrhea may predispose young dancers to a high incidence of scoliosis and stress fractures.

Plantar fascial strain occurs chiefly as the result of landing on the balls of the feet during frequent jumps and leaps. Force-platform tests reveal a landing force from such a maneuver as triple or quadruple that of body weight. Consequently, there is a tremendous risk of soft-tissue injury.

Ballet requires extreme external rotation of the leg at the hip. Women have less difficulty with this motion than men, and girls who start training early in life have less trouble with it than those who begin training later. It is often said that those who start ballet after age 14 are more prone to injury, and this is probably true.

Stress fractures in ballet dancers usually occur above the level of the foot, most often in the anterior part of the shin (tibia), where no muscles attach. They are caused by accumulated impact and rhythmic impact shock. Dancers seem to exhibit overuse injuries that are common among runners: posterior tibial myositis and tendinitis, medial arch strain, and medial collateral strain. Most ballet injuries occur during practice and late in the season, probably because the dancers are both physically and mentally overfatigued.

Summary

Women and girls do not appear to have a higher incidence of sport-related injuries than do boys or men. As in males, most injuries are relatively minor (sprains, strains, and contusions) and occur in the lower extremities. The ankle and knee are the most frequently injured areas. In high school and collegiate women's sports, more injuries occur in basketball, gymnastics, softball, and field hockey than in other sports. Apparently, the female's body structure does not offer a particular disadvantage in terms of the occurrence of athletic injury. Nevertheless, girls and women should probably not be encouraged to compete in contact sports either against boys or men or on boys' or men's teams.

Probably the best advice that can be given a girl or woman who wishes to engage in athletic activity is to carefully condition herself before beginning a stressful training program. Coaches should be well aware of this advice and provide some means for preseason physical conditioning. Because a busy competitive schedule sometimes allows for deconditioning (irregular practice and cumulative fatigue), a maintenance program for strength, flexibility, and cardiovascular efficiency should be encouraged.

A few injuries or potential injuries are unique to the female sport participant because of her physical structure and physiological function. These injuries have been described and discussed.

For further information on injuries in sport, contact the following organizations:

Big Ten Injury Surveillance Survey
1189 Carver Pavilion
University of Iowa Hospitals
Iowa City, IA 52242

Interscholastic Athletic Injury Surveillance
  System
International Institute of Sports Science and
  Medicine
1199 Hadley Road
Mooresville, IN 46158

National High School Athletic Injury Registry
c/o National Athletic Trainers' Association,
  Inc.
Box 3548
Oak Park, IL 60303

Chapter 16

The Female Athlete: A Profile

For what appear to be primarily psychological reasons, the physiological limits of the human body have not yet been approached by even the best athletes. Although the rate of improvement in athletic performance has slowed down somewhat in men, female athletes are still advancing rapidly. There are many reasons for this continuing advancement in athletic performance. One is that girls and women are now realizing the necessity for superior physical conditioning. In the early days of sport competition for women, recreational participants with high levels of "natural" skill simply entered an event without much thought to prior physical preparation. It was only as competition became more keen that serious thought and time went into preparing for a competitive event. It was then that athletic records for women began to suddenly and dramatically improve. In the United

States this did not begin until after World War II and in Europe some time before that. In many instances, women who desired to train and to excel in sport were restricted from doing so. These restrictions were both actual and implied. Until recently, women who wanted to train, practice, or receive coaching simply had no place to go. Membership in athletic clubs was strictly limited to men. School programs in girls' and women's athletics were either nonexistent or very meager (play days, etc.). No one knew anything about "women's sports," and it was just not "acceptable" to sweat and strain. In short, the athletic arena was traditionally the domain of the male.

Recent Cultural and Political Changes

The 1960s and 1970s, however, have changed all that. The women's rights movement has resulted in strides forward in political, academic, and economic affairs, and these gains have led to an athletic revolution as well. In fact, the advances in athletic participation far outstrip most other advances. Demands were made for equality in school and college athletic budgets, equipment, coaching, and competitive opportunities. Domains that were formerly all male—posh athletic clubs, gymnasiums, training rooms, and athletic fields—have either voluntarily (sometimes reluctantly) opened their doors to women or been taken to court and forced to do so. Women have today gained considerable status in the world of athletics, a status that is comparable to that enjoyed previously only by the male.

Today, it is commonplace to see a girl or woman jogging on a city street dressed in high-quality running shoes and up-to-date running attire. No longer does she feel the necessity to hide her athletic prowess in the confines of back alleys and "the girls' gym." She is right out there with the other millions of bicyclists, backpackers, runners, swimmers, scuba divers, tennis and racquetball players, golfers, and skiers. The sport industry has taken notice, creating for women of all sizes and ages well-made and stylish sport clothes that are practical as well as aesthetic. Young girls are playing soccer, T-ball (a form of baseball with no pitching), and Little League baseball and are swimming and running in highly competitive age-group teams. High school and college women are playing fiercely competitive games of field hockey, lacrosse, volleyball, basketball, and softball. Swimming and track records are being broken regularly in high school, collegiate, regional, national, and world categories. Women are now entering college, and some are leaving the ghettoes on athletic scholarships to some of the finest academic institutions in the world. Well-known female athletes give out autographs nearly as often as National Football League Players. Among many others, the names of women like Martina Navratilova, Chris Evert, Steffi Graf, Mary Lou Retton, Florence Griffith-Joyner, Grete Waitz, Joan Benoit-Samuelson, and Jackie Joyner-Kersee (to name a few) are household words in America and indeed throughout the world.

Olympic Games

One of the most recent political breakthroughs in the world of sport was the addition of the 3,000-m and marathon races for women in the 1984 Olympic Games. Before that, the longest women's running event was 1,500 m. Publication of the American College of Sports Medicine's (1979) opinion statement, "The Participation of the Female Athlete in Long-Distance Running," (see Appendix A) proved to be important in dispelling cultural myths as well as quasi-medical objections about female sport participation on the part of the International Olympic Committee (Hage, 1982). Women's rowing, a popular event on the international scene and long overdue as an Olympic event, was added at the 1976 Games along with basketball and team handball. In 1984, women's cycling (a road race only) and synchronized swimming were added, as were rhythmic gymnastics. In 1988, more women's events were added: the 1,000-m cycling sprint, the 10,000-m track race (illogically omitted from the 1984 Games), the heptathlon (in place of the pentathlon), team archery, air pistol, 50-m freestyle swimming, singles and doubles table tennis, and a separate yachting event (the 470 class). The Olympic movement has come a long way from the 1900 Paris Games, in which 6 women took part, to the 1988 Seoul Games, in which more than 2,476 women participated in medal and exhibition competition. Nevertheless, it should be pointed out that still many more events are open to men than to women.

Coaching

One area in which women have not advanced as rapidly as seems fitting is that of coaching. In fact, according to an 11-year longitudinal study by Acosta and Carpenter (1988), women are losing out on coaching positions at the collegiate level. They cited the following data:

- In 1988, only 48.3% of the coaches of women's teams were women. In 1972, more than 90% of women's teams were coached by women.
- In 1988, there were 5,757 head coaching positions of women's teams. Although this was an increase of 52 positions from the previous year, women did not share in the increase and actually held 7 fewer of those positions than in 1987.
- In 1972, more than 90% of women's programs were headed by a female administrator. In 1988, only 16% of women's programs were headed by a woman.
- In 1988, women held 29% of all administrative positions in women's intercollegiate programs. No women at all were involved in the administration of 32% of women's programs.

I am not sure of the reasons for these figures, but I suspect three main ones. One is that women seem more interested in the psychology and sociology of sport than in biomechanics and physiology. Although a coach must be well versed in personal relations, she must also have a thorough understanding of the scientific principles of sport.

A second possible reason has to do with social and cultural standards of acceptance. To many, including many top-flight female athletes, the expert is viewed as male. A third reason, which is very debatable, is the notion that women are not as competitive as men. A coach must constantly work and motivate athletes to perfection. Is it possible that men, with their longer history of competitive striving, are better at this than women? I think not, but women are generally seen as more caring and sympathetic persons than men and consequently are not considered "hard enough" to coach successfully at a highly competitive level. Unfortunately, misconceptions continue to stereotype both female and male coaches.

Athletic Profiles

Considerable variation exists within and among athletes relative to performance potential. Recent advances in sport physiology have led to the development of structural and physiological *profiles* to describe the characteristics and qualities of athletes, particularly elite athletes, in various sports. Detailed profiles have been established for male athletes in track-and-field events, rowing, gymnastics, swimming, orienteering, speed skating, wrestling, weight lifting, bodybuilding, horse racing, skiing, basketball, baseball, football, ice hockey, tennis, racquetball, and volleyball (Wilmore, 1982; Wilmore & Costill, 1988). These profiles have considerable application in developing a better understanding of a sport, its physical demands, and the characteristics of people who excel in it. Data from aspiring athletes can be compared to those from elite performers and thus can provide insight into those areas of training that should be emphasized. The physical potential of an athlete for a particular sport can be assessed, as can the need for specific physical conditioning.

Genetic endowment largely determines one's structural and physiological characteristics. If there are particular traits necessary to excel in a sport, it is likely that these attributes will be evident in a sport profile. There has been some interest among coaches and sport scientists in the past about identifying the necessary characteristics and abilities required for championship performance and then "choosing" likely candidates for such excellence. Largely, this has not come to fruition, but Wilmore (1982, p. 98) cited one successful example of such an effort. Soviet sport scientists, following an exhaustive analysis, established a comprehensive anthropometric, biomechanical, physiological, and performance profile of the characteristics needed by a world-class sprinter. A careful search and screening of Soviet athletes led to the selection of a group of men that included Valeri Borzov, who was a long jumper at the time. Following months of highly specialized training at the Physical Education Institute at Kiev, Borzov became one of the top sprinters in the world, winning gold medals in the 1972 Olympic Games.

With few possible exceptions, world-class women's sports have not developed to the extent that such an example is applicable yet, and possibly such an application is not desirable. There is something very cold and dehumanizing about the thought of selecting children for specialized training at an early stage of their development so they can win medals in international competition. Still, athletic profiling can be of considerable use in a more limited sense: in helping us to better understand sport and training practices and in more wisely advising girls and women about their sport performance. For example, in a study of 9 of the top 11 pentathletes in the United States, Krahenbuhl et al. (1979) came to the conclusion that the most successful performers were exceptionally strong and possessed a high lean body mass. Aerobic capacity was not exceptional in these athletes and did not prove to be an important factor in predicting success.

The largest volume of data on female athletes exists for the areas of body composition, physique, and cardiorespiratory endurance capacity. The remainder of this chapter presents data gleaned from the literature on highly skilled female athletes of various ages and discusses each area of data collection.

Body Composition and Physique of Female Athletes

Currently, many methods are available for estimating body composition. The usually accepted criterion method is body densitometry using the underwater-weighing method (with measurement of residual lung volume using a gas dilution, or washout, method). Unfortunately, this method is based on a number of basic assumptions derived from a few male cadavers. Numerous other methods have also been devised, some using skinfolds, some using circumference measurements, and others combining skinfolds and circumferences. Ultrasound and bioelectric impedance methods have also been developed recently. The data presented here were culled from studies that used underwater-weighing and skinfold techniques.

Sinning and Wilson (1984) conducted a study on the validity of generalized equations for analysis of body composition in women athletes. They compared the results of nine different skinfold formulas with underwater-weighing data on 79 intercollegiate athletes. It is recommended on the basis of their results that future investigators utilize the four-site generalized skinfold formula of Jackson, Pollock, and Ward (1980) as follows:

$$BD = 1.096095 - 0.0006952(X_1) + 0.0000011(X_1)^2 - 0.0000714(X_2)$$

where X_1 = sum of triceps, oblique suprailiac, abdominal, and midanterior thigh skinfolds and X_2 = age in years (to the nearest tenth of a year).

Wide variability in results may exist, however, even when experts use skinfold prediction formulas. One group of highly experienced investigators of body composition methods reported a mean percent body fat range of 7% in a group of women athletes that was due merely to the use of different calipers by different investigators (Lohman, Pollock, Slaughter, Brandon, & Boileau, 1984).

With these caveats in mind, refer to the body composition data from a wide variety of female athletes (beyond high school age) in Table 16.1. It is apparent that most of the athletes are leaner than untrained women (who have approximately 22% to 26% body fat). The exceptions appear to be women in those events or activities that require considerable strength and body mass, such as the weight events (discus, shot put, javelin, and hammer throw). These women are the heaviest women listed in the table. Remember that most of these women are successful in weight events *because* of their large body mass or size. Unfortunately, much of this large body mass is due to an accumulation of considerable body fat, which does not contribute to strength or power. One wonders how much performance could improve if lean body mass were substituted for much of this body fat. Wilmore (1982) stated that one of the shot-putters with whom he worked lost a considerable amount of body fat and gained lean body mass through a combination of weight training and dieting. As she did so, her performance continued to improve. Today, field athletes appear to be much leaner than the athletes documented here.

Lean-to-Fat Ratio

The lean-to-fat ratio (shown in Table 16.1) is a derived index that expresses lean mass relative to fat mass. Not surprisingly, highly competitive bodybuilders have a very high lean-to-fat ratio. Top performance in bodybuilding is determined by high muscularity, extreme muscle definition, and low body fat. Although elite distance runners appear much less muscular, they too have a high lean-to-fat ratio, as do cyclists and gymnasts. Swimmers have relatively lower lean-to-fat ratios than other athletes. In comparison, reference woman has a lean-to-fat ratio of 2.8.

Also evident from Table 16.1 is that athletes with lower performance levels than athletes designated as Olympians, national athletes, or elite performers tend to be fatter. As noted formerly for men, female athletes in sports that require that the body mass be moved through space (either verti-

cally as in jumping or horizontally as in running) are the leanest and lightest in body weight. The better jumpers, pentathletes, gymnasts, divers, rowers, cyclists, ballerinas, and runners were really quite low in relative body fat. Elite distance runners had similar skeletal diameters to those reported for gymnasts and bodybuilders but smaller skinfolds and circumferences and lower total body weight (Graves, Pollock, & Sparling, 1987). This suggests that elite runners carry less fat and lean body mass on a frame similar in size to bodybuilders and gymnasts.

Body Fat and Health

The question of how much body fat is "essential" in the female body is of interest here. The mature woman has large amounts of fat tissue in the breast and in (or surrounding) other sex-specific organs. The following important questions remain to be answered:

- How much fat is essential for life, for reproduction, and for good health?
- How much additional fat should a woman athlete possess?
- At what points do high or low levels of body fat hinder performance in each sport?
- What is the ideal range of relative body fat for each sport?
- At what point is being too lean unhealthful?

(See chapter 10 for material on osteopenia, chapter 6 for material on delayed menarche, and chapter 13 for material on eating disorders.)

Variability in Body Composition

Figure 16.1 points out the important observation that highly successful performers can vary considerably from one another. Note that elite distance runners between the ages of 20 and 30 varied from about 6% to about 20% body fat. Graves et al. (1987) also noted this in a more recent sample. The leanest elite runner (successful national and international competitor) had 9.7% body fat and the fattest 20.8% body fat. Thus, although the best

Table 16.1 Body Composition Values of Female Athletes

Athletic group or sport	Level[a]	Age (yr)	Height (cm)	Weight (kg)	Relative fat (%)	Lean/fat ratio[b]	Reference
Basketball	C	19.1	169.1	62.6	20.8	3.8	Sinning (1973)
	C	19.4	167.0	63.9	26.9	2.7	Conger & MacNab (1967)
Bodybuilders	NT, N	27.0	160.8	53.8	13.2	6.9	Freedson et al. (1983)
	SF	28.0	164.0	55.0	14.4	5.9	Elliot et al. (1987)
Cycling	E	—	167.7	61.3	15.4	5.5	Burke (1980)
Dancers							
Ballet	E	23.7	165.6	49.5	—	—	Cohen, Kim, et al. (1982)
	E	23.7	167.4	54.2	14.1	6.1	Chmelar et al. (1988)
	C	19.3	166.1	53.5	14.2	6.0	Chmelar et al. (1988)
Modern	C	—	—	—	13.4	—	Chambers (1981)
	E	30.4	161.8	53.3	12.2	7.2	Chmelar et al. (1988)
	C	26.4	163.0	54.4	14.7	5.8	Chmelar et al. (1988)
Diving	O	18.5	160.9	54.1	13.9	6.2	McArdle et al. (1981)
	O	21.1	160.4	52.3	11.5	7.7	McArdle et al. (1981)
Field events							
Discus	C	21.1	168.1	71.0	25.0	3.0	Malina et al. (1971)
Shot put	C	21.5	167.6	78.1	28.0	2.6	Malina et al. (1971)
Shot, discus	O	26.2	170.4	79.0	33.8	1.9	McArdle et al. (1981)
	O	19.9	170.9	73.5	28.5	2.5	McArdle et al. (1981)
Shot, discus, javelin	E	18.8	173.9	80.8	27.0	2.7	Wilmore et al. (1977)
Jumpers, hurdlers	C	20.3	165.9	59.0	20.7	3.8	Malina et al. (1971)
Jumpers	O	23.6	169.5	60.2	14.1	6.1	McArdle et al. (1981)
	O	21.5	169.4	56.4	8.4	10.9	McArdle et al. (1981)
Gymnastics	C	19.4	163.0	57.9	23.8	3.2	Conger & MacNab (1967)
	C	20.0	158.5	51.5	15.5	5.4	Sinning & Lindberg (1972)
	O	19.0	163.5	52.5	13.3	6.5	Novak et al. (1977)
		23.0	—	—	11.0	—	Pařízková (1973)
		23.0	—	—	9.6	—	Pařízková & Poupa (1963)
	O	22.7	157.0	52.0	14.7	5.8	McArdle et al. (1981)
	O	17.8	156.9	49.8	11.0	8.1	McArdle et al. (1981)
Orienteering	E	29.0	—	58.1	18.7	4.3	Knowlton et al. (1980)
Pentathalon	N, E	21.5	175.4	65.4	11.0	8.1	Krahenbuhl et al. (1979)
Rowing	N	23.0	173.0	68.0	14.0	6.1	Hagerman et al. (1979)
	O	—	174.3	67.4	—	—	Hebbelinck et al. (1981)
Running							
Distance	C	19.9	161.3	52.9	19.2	4.2	Malina et al. (1971)
	E	25.0	166.8	54.3	16.9	4.9	Wilmore et al. (1977)
	E	32.4	169.4	57.2	15.2	5.6	Wilmore & Brown (1974)
	HT	23.5	166.2	52.1	—	—	Daniels et al. (1977)
	T	24.1	159.7	49.3	15.5	5.4	Conley et al. (1981)

Athletic group or sport	Level[a]	Age (yr)	Height (cm)	Weight (kg)	Relative fat (%)	Lean/fat ratio[b]	Reference
	E	27.6	161.0	47.2	14.3	6.0	Graves et al. (1987)
	HT	28.6	162.0	49.4	16.8	4.6	Graves et al. (1987)
Marathon	T	28.5	166.6	52.0	11.4	7.8	Wells et al. (1981)
Sprint	C	20.1	164.9	56.7	19.3	4.2	Malina et al. (1971)
	O	22.7	166.0	56.6	12.4	7.1	McArdle et al. (1981)
	O	20.7	165.0	56.8	13.7	6.3	McArdle et al. (1981)
Sprint, middle distance	E	18.3	171.5	57.8	11.1	8.0	Wilmore et al. (1977)
Cross-country	C	19.3	163.0	54.7	12.7	6.9	Kollias et al. (1987)
Rugby							
Forwards	C	20.4	166.4	69.2	22.6	3.4	Sedlock et al. (1988)
Backs	C	21.0	162.2	54.1	17.5	4.7	Sedlock et al. (1988)
Skiing, Alpine	E	19.5	165.1	58.8	20.6	3.8	Haymes & Dickenson (1980)
Skiing, cross-country	E	20.2	163.4	55.9	15.7	5.2	Haymes & Dickenson (1980)
	HT, N	24.3	163.0	59.1	21.8	3.6	Rusko et al. (1978)
Swimming	N, O	20.4	175.4	66.7	19.09	4.2	Haan (1979)
	C	19.4	168.0	63.8	26.3	2.8	Conger & MacNab (1967)
Sprint	C	—	165.1	57.1	14.6	5.8	Wilmore et al. (1977)
Middle distance	C	—	166.6	66.8	24.1	3.2	Wilmore et al. (1977)
Distance	C	—	166.3	60.9	17.1	4.8	Wilmore et al. (1977)
Unspecified	O	18.6	166.3	59.7	16.6	5.0	McArdle et al. (1981)
	O	17.7	167.0	60.1	18.9	4.3	Novak et al. (1977)
Synchronized	N	20.1	166.2	55.8	24.0	3.2	Roby et al. (1983)
Tennis	Class B, C	39.0	163.3	55.7	20.3	3.9	Vodak et al. (1980)
Volleyball	C	19.4	166.0	59.8	25.3	3.0	Conger & MacNab (1967)
	C	19.9	172.2	64.1	21.3	3.7	Kovaleski et al. (1980)
	E	21.6	183.7	73.4	—	—	Spence et al. (1980)
	N	24.4	173.8	63.0	—	—	Spence et al. (1980)
	E	21.6	178.3	70.5	17.9	4.6	Puhl et al. (1982)

[a]Levels of performance indicated as follows: E = elite, HT = highly trained, N = national, O = Olympic, C = collegiate, T = trained, R = regionally ranked, and SF = steroid free.

[b]Lean/fat ratio calculated from data.

runners usually have low relative body fat values, some successful runners are considerably fatter than others. This should remind us that athletes are individuals and that if there is one axiom that must be understood, it is that there are always exceptions to commonly accepted principles.

Relationship of Body Build to Athletic Performance

One's body build, or physique, is determined largely by genetics. Basic physical characteristics

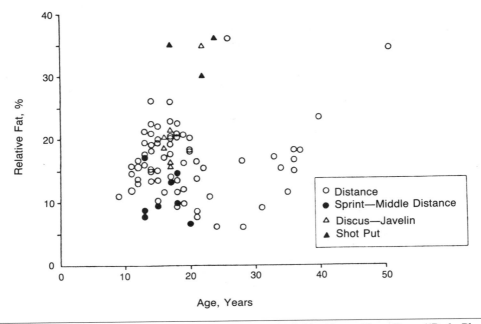

Figure 16.1 Relative body fat values for elite female track and field athletes. *Note.* From ''Body Physique and Composition of the Female Distance Runner'' by J.H. Wilmore, C.H. Brown, and J.A. Davis, 1977, *Annals of the New York Academy of Sciences,* **301,** p. 770. Copyright 1977 by New York Academy of Sciences. Reprinted by permission.

are inherited from parents and vary only within rather narrow limits. Body size (height) and general physique is one characteristic so established. With this understanding, it is often evident that some sports require a particular body type for successful performance. One example is basketball, a sport in which tall people excel. Therefore, to succeed, an athlete should select a sport in which her physical characteristics will prove an asset.

As mentioned in an earlier chapter, body build is often assessed by somatotyping. Figure 16.2 illustrates a somatochart, which can be used for plotting the somatotypes of athletes in various sports. This has been done fairly extensively with Olympic athletes (see deGaray, Levine, & Carter, 1974; Tanner, 1964 [males only]). The results typically indicate that there is more than moderate similarity in the somatotypes of successful athletes within each sport, that is, that somatotypes

tend to cluster in specific areas of a somatochart for different sports. This suggests that body size and type are important factors in determining success in many sports.

Table 16.2 presents some somatotype values for women athletes culled from several sources. The athletes were generally low in endomorphy (roundness), had moderate values for mesomorphy (muscularity), and ranged from low to moderate in ectomorphy (linearity).

Figure 16.3 illustrates a number of mean somatoplots for athletes in various sports. It is obvious that the basketball and tennis players were more similar in physique than were the middle- and long-distance runners. The basketball players were more endomorphic-mesomorphic than the gymnasts, who were more similar to the skaters and skiers. Most of the athletes were fairly tightly grouped within their sports, but note the wide

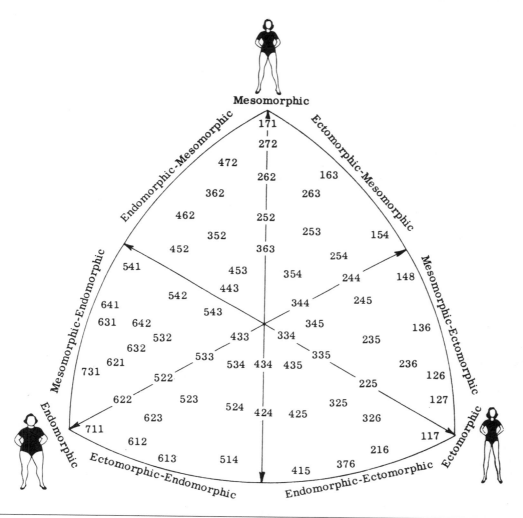

Figure 16.2 A somatochart. *Note.* From *Movement Fundamentals: Figure, Form, Fun* (3rd ed., p. 223) by J.A. Wessel, 1972, Englewood Cliffs, NJ: Prentice-Hall, Inc. Reprinted by permission of J.A. Wessel.

variety of somatotypes among the field-event competitors.

The following generalizations can be made regarding the available somatotype data on female athletes (Carter, 1981). Generally, throwers are more endomorphic, more mesomorphic, and less ectomorphic than other sport groups. Gymnasts, divers, swimmers, and sprinters are close to the 3-4-3 somatotype. Gymnasts and track-and-field athletes are lower in endomorphy than rowers or swimmers. The highest values of endomorphy are found in shot and discus throwers and in some golfers, tennis players, swimmers, and rowers. The lowest endomorphy values are found in distance runners, gymnasts, and high jumpers. The highest values for mesomorphy are found in rowers and shot and discus throwers, whereas the lowest values are found in high jumpers, distance

Table 16.2   Somatotypes of Women Athletes

Athletic group or sport	Level[a]	Age (yr)	Height (cm)	Weight (kg)	Somatotype Endo	Meso	Ecto	Reference
Basketball								
USSR	E	—	173.0	71.4	4.3	4.5	3.0	Carter (1981)
Canada	N	20.0	170.6	63.9	4.0	3.5	2.7	Carter (1981)
Diving	O	21.1	160.4	52.3	2.9	4.0	2.9	deGaray et al. (1974)
Golf	E	27.8	167.6	62.4	4.1	4.0	2.7	Carter (1981)
Gymnastics								
Mexico City (1968)	O	17.8	156.9	49.8	2.7	4.2	2.8	Carter (1981)
Munich (1972)	O	19.0	163.5	52.5	2.6	3.8	3.4	Carter (1981)
Montreal (1976)	O	17.0	161.5	50.9	2.1	4.0	3.4	Carter (1981)
AIAW placers	C, N	19.4	161.5	55.1	2.6	4.4	2.6	Carter (1981)
USSR	—	—	157.0	53.9	3.8	5.2	1.6	Carter (1981)
Nordic skiers: USA	N	23.5	164.5	56.9	3.5	4.2	2.3	Carter (1981)
1968 Olympic athletes (canoeing, diving, gymnastics, swimming, track and field)	O	19.5	163.8	57.1	2.8	4.0	3.0	Carter (1981)
1976 Olympic athletes (all sports)	O	20.9	169.6	60.8	2.8	3.8	3.1	Carter (1981)
Orienteers	E	29	—	58.1	3.9	3.7	2.5	Knowlton et al. (1980)
Pentathlon	O	22.5	169.5	60.0	2.4	3.6	3.1	deGaray et al. (1974)
Rowing	O	23.8	174.3	67.4	3.1	3.9	2.8	Carter (1981)
Runners								
Middle distance	O	20	166.9	54.3	2.0	3.3	3.7	deGaray et al. (1974)
Sprint	O	21	165.0	56.8	2.7	3.9	2.9	deGaray et al. (1974)
400 m	O	19.5	165.4	53.4	2.0	3.4	3.6	Carter (1981)
Swimming								
Munich (1972)	O	17.7	167.0	60.1	3.2	4.6	2.6	Carter (1981)
Tennis	C	20.4	166.4	57.9	4.6	3.9	3.0	Carter (1981)
Professionals	E	24.1	167.3	60.7	3.1	3.9	2.6	Carter (1981)
Throwers	O	22	169.4	56.4	2.2	3.3	3.7	deGaray et al. (1974)
Shot, discus	O	20	170.9	73.5	5.3	5.2	1.7	deGaray et al. (1974)
Volleyball	C	20	172.2	64.1	4.2	3.7	3.3	Kovaleski et al. (1980)

[a]Levels of performance indicated as follows: E = elite, N = national, O = Olympic, and C = collegiate.

runners, tennis players, and synchronized swimmers. The highest values for ectomorphy are found in high jumpers, some basketball and volleyball players, and distance runners. The lowest values for ectomorphy, not surprisingly, are found in shot and discus throwers.

In general, the following five conclusions have been drawn (Carter, 1981):

1. Top-class female athletes in most sports are more mesomorphic and less endomorphic than nonathletes.

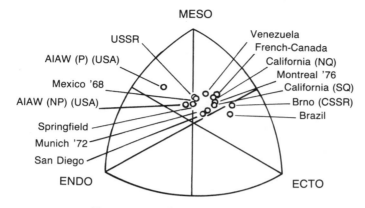

Mean somatoplots of female gymnasts.

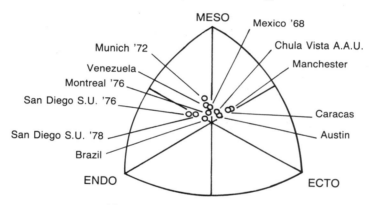

Mean somatoplots of female swimmers.

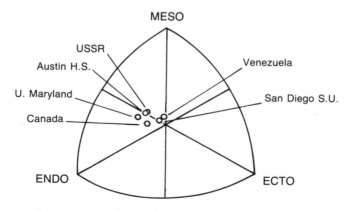

Mean somatoplots of female basketball players.

(Cont.)

Figure 16.3 Somatoplots for female athletes. *Note.* From "Somatotypes of Female Athletes" by J.E.L. Carter. In *The Female Athlete* (*Medicine and Sport*, Vol. 15, pp. 91, 93, 96, 98, 100, 104, 105, 108), 1981, Basel: S. Karger AG. Copyright 1981 by S. Karger AG. Reprinted by permission.

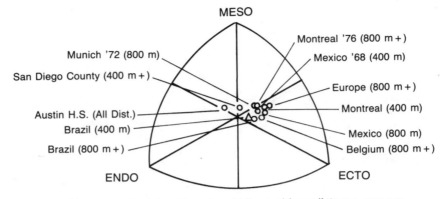

Mean somatoplots of female middle- and long-distance runners.

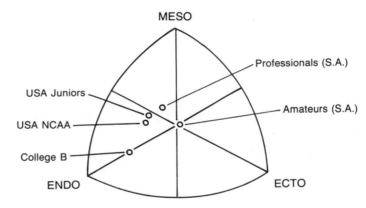

Mean somatoplots of female tennis players.

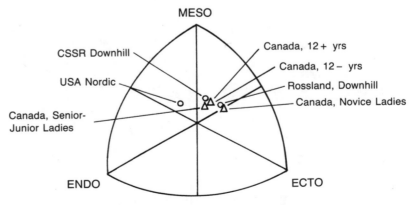

Mean somatoplots of female skaters and skiers.

Figure 16.3 (Continued)

288

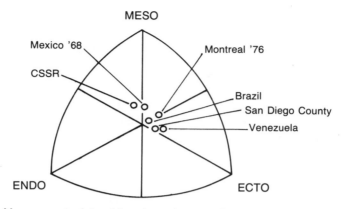

Mean somatoplots of female sprinters and hurdlers.

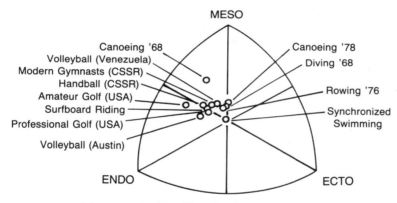

Mean somatoplots of female athletes from different sports.

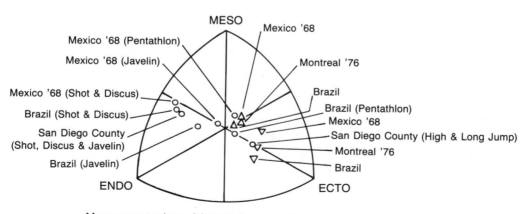

Mean somatoplots of female field event competitors.

Figure 16.3 (Continued)

2. Quite similar somatotypes appear necessary for success in some sports, but there are widely differing somatotypes represented in other sports.

3. Somatotype means for most sports have a wide range along or near the ectomorphic axis of the somatochart.

4. Means for a large number of sports and events are bounded by somatotypes 4-4-3, 3-4-3, 2-4-4, and 3-3-3.

5. Successful young female athletes have somatotypes similar to those of older athletes.

Metabolic Characteristics of Women Athletes

Muscular activity depends on the production of the energy substrate adenosine triphosphate (ATP), which can be synthesized for physical activity in several ways. The duration and relative intensity of the activity determines the primary metabolic process used by the athlete to produce ATP. Various systems have been devised to classify sports into categories according to the primary metabolic pathway (or pathways) used to produce energy to drive muscular contraction. The system used by Skinner and Morgan (1985) is used here (for a more complete explanation, see Haymes, 1988; Skinner & Morgan, 1985).

In brief, athletes who perform very high intensity but short-duration (less than 10 s) events (e.g., 100-m sprint; long, high, or triple jumps; discus, shot, or javelin; diving; or gymnastics) must have high *anaerobic power*, which is the ability to utilize stored high-energy phosphate compounds (ATP and creatine phosphate, or CP) for instant energy production. For activities that last longer than 10 s but less than 1 min, muscle glycogen is utilized anaerobically to produce ATP. Unfortunately, relying on this process results in the accumulation of high amounts of lactic acid, a metabolic by-product associated with fatigue. Athletes performing events of somewhat lesser

relative intensity (e.g., 200- and 400-m sprints, swim sprints, skating sprints, and downhill slalom skiing) must have high *anaerobic capacity*. Events lasting between about 1 min and 9 or 10 min (e.g., 800- to 3,000-m runs, 200- and 400-m swim events, rowing, floor exercise in gymnastics, fencing, figure skating, 1,000- and 3,000-m skating, and giant slalom and downhill ski races) require high *lactate tolerance* because so much energy is produced by the combined anaerobic and aerobic production of ATP from muscle glycogen and blood glucose.

Longer events depend more on the aerobic production of ATP from glycogen stores, blood glucose, and free fatty acids liberated from adipose stores. These events are performed at a lower relative intensity but often for a very prolonged period of time and thus are recognized as requiring high *aerobic power*, or cardiorespiratory endurance. Such events include distance-running events (5,000 m and longer), cross-country skiing, cycling, biathlon and triathlon events, race walking, and possibly team sports such as soccer, basketball, and field hockey. The information available on women athletes is classified according to the above system as much as is currently possible. Unfortunately, although cardiorespiratory endurance can be easily determined, few valid or reliable tests are available to adequately measure anaerobic power, anaerobic capacity, or lactate tolerance.

Anaerobic Power

Anaerobic power is required to generate maximal force through distance in a minimum of time. This quality is thought to be important in jumping and throwing events, sprinting, volleyball, and possibly basketball. The Margaria-Kalamen Stair Run (Fox & Mathews, 1981, pp. 621-623) represents an objective measure of lower body power (it is a very brief stair-running test). Other anaerobic power tests commonly used are the long jump, the vertical jump, short sprints lasting 3 to 10 s, and the Wingate Anaerobic Power Test (maximal rpm on a cycle ergometer during a 5-s interval). Unfortunately, these tests have no established standards and are not widely used. The small amount of available data on the anaerobic power of female athletes is shown in Table 16.3.

It is difficult to compare athletes from the various sports listed in Table 16.3 because of the different tests used. In fact, it is not altogether clear that each of these tests actually measures anaerobic power. Nevertheless, examination of the stair-run data reveals that the field-event participants (high jump, long jump, and shot put) have high anaerobic power, followed by basketball players and Alpine skiers. Using the vertical jump test as the criterion reveals that volleyball players, followed by Alpine and cross-country skiers, have the highest anaerobic power.

Probably one of the best tests of anaerobic power is the score of the first 5 s of the Wingate Anaerobic Power Test (a description of the complete test follows). The adolescent runners for whom data were available did not do well in relation to older athletes. Bar-Or (1983) has previously commented on the relatively poor anaerobic power of preadolescents. The college-age throwers, basketball players, and volleyball players had the highest scores on this test.

Anaerobic Capacity

The sole test currently advocated as a test of anaerobic capacity is the Wingate Anaerobic Power Test, an all-out 30-s performance on a bicycle ergometer with the resistance set according to one's body weight (.075 kg resistance per kilogram of body weight). Limited information is available on anaerobic capacity performance scores of female athletes. Williams (1985) tested six groups of intercollegiate athletes (anaerobic power results are shown in Table 16.3). The anaerobic capacity results revealed that the gymnasts (2,221 W) scored significantly below the other athletes. The basketball players (3,103 W), volleyball players (3,260 W), and throwers (3,552 W) did not differ significantly from one another

and had the highest scores. Intermediate scores were achieved by the swimmers (2,691 W) and runners (2,645 W).

Williams further analyzed these scores in terms of body weight and lean body mass. Expressing anaerobic capacity in relative terms reduced differences among the athletic groups considerably. In terms of watts per unit of body mass, the volleyball players (47 W • kg⁻¹) had the highest scores and the throwers (42 W • kg⁻¹) and swimmers (42.5 W • kg⁻¹) the lowest. In terms of watts per unit of lean body mass, the basketball players (56 W • kg⁻¹) and volleyball players (56.5 W • kg⁻¹) had the highest scores and the gymnasts (51 W • kg⁻¹) the lowest.

Chmelar et al. (1988) assessed professional and collegiate ballet and modern dancers on the Wingate test but, rather than reporting performance scores, reported blood lactate values 4 to 6 min following the test. The professional ballerinas had significantly lower blood lactate values (6.0 mM) than the professional modern dancers (9.7 mM), the collegiate ballerinas (9.5 mM), and the modern dancers (9.0 mM). It is interesting here that fat-free mass did not differ among these four groups but that maximal aerobic capacity was lower in the professional ballerinas. Roby, Buono, Constable, Lowdon, and Tsao (1983) measured the ability of national level synchronized swimmers to produce leg work (isokinetic knee flexion and extension at 180° per second over a 1-min period). When work output was expressed relative to body weight, the synchronized swimmers' scores were 12% lower than those of the intercollegiate swimmers and 7% less than those of the intercollegiate volleyball players.

Lactate Tolerance

Tests for lactate tolerance have not yet been standardized but usually include the measurement of blood lactate over the same distance at two velocities. This can be done using a cycle ergometer or treadmill or while swimming or rowing. The effectiveness of a training program can be monitored

Table 16.3 Anaerobic Power of Female Athletes

Athletic group or sport	Level[a]	Margaria stair-run ($kgm \cdot s^{-1}$)	Vertical jump (cm)	Standing long jump (m)	50-yd dash (s)	20-yd dash (s)	Wingate test (W)	Reference
Adolescents								
Runners								
10-11 yr	HT	—	—	—	—	—	282	Tharp et al. (1984)
12-13 yr	HT	—	—	—	—	—	447	Tharp et al. (1984)
14-15 yr	HT	—	—	—	—	—	531	Tharp et al. (1984)
Alpine skiers	E	115.2	47.0	—	—	—	—	Haymes & Dickinson (1980)
Basketball	C	116.6	42.1	—	—	—	—	Haymes (1988a)
	C	95.9	—	—	—	—	671.5	Williams (1985)
Cross-country skiers	E	100.8	47.2	—	—	—	—	Haymes & Dickinson (1980)
Figure skaters (adolescent)	HT	—	35.0	1.98	—	—	—	Niinimaa (1982)
Field events	C	129.1	—	—	—	—	—	Haymes (1988a)
Throwers	C	125.0	—	—	—	—	835.2	Williams (1985)
Field hockey	N	83.0	—	—	—	—	—	Withers & Roberts (1981)
	N	—	40.6	1.82	—	—	—	Bale & McNaught-Davis (1983)
Gymnasts	C	70.5	—	—	—	—	488.7	Williams (1985)
Orienteers	E	76.6	—	—	—	—	—	Knowlton et al. (1980)
Pentathletes	N	—	—	—	6.31	—	—	Krahenbuhl et al. (1979)
Rugby	C	91.9	—	—	—	—	—	Sedlock et al. (1988)
Runners	C	88.8	—	—	—	—	—	Haymes (1988a)
	C	85.1	—	—	—	—	586.2	Williams (1985)
	C	104.1	—	—	—	—	—	Haymes (1988a)
Sprinters	N	81.7	—	—	—	—	—	Withers & Roberts (1981)
Softball	C	84.7	—	—	—	—	571.7	Williams (1985)
Swimmers	C	98.7	—	—	—	—	738.0	Williams (1985)
Volleyball	E	—	45.9	—	—	3.14	—	Puhl et al. (1982)
	N	—	47.3	—	—	3.08	—	Spence et al. (1980)
	E	—	52.5	—	—	—	—	

Note. From ''Metabolism and Performance'' by E.M. Haymes. In *Sport Science Perspectives for Women* (p. 89) by J. Puhl, C.H. Brown, and R.O. Voy (Eds.), 1988, Champaign, IL: Human Kinetics Books. Copyright 1988 by Human Kinetics Publishers. Adapted and expanded by permission.
[a]Levels of performance indicated as follows: HT = highly trained, E = elite, N = nationally ranked, and C = collegiate.

by the changes in blood lactate level over time. No data have yet been published on women athletes and lactate tolerance.

Aerobic Power

The most widely used test of aerobic power is the maximal oxygen uptake ($\dot{V}O_2$max) test. Aerobic power, or cardiorespiratory endurance, is an important variable in many sports. Table 16.4 provides some insight into the aerobic power (measured as $\dot{V}O_2$max in ml $\cdot$ kg^{-1} $\cdot$ min^{-1}) required for success in various sports. The athletes with the highest $\dot{V}O_2$max values included distance runners, cross-country skiers, rowers, Alpine skiers, and cyclists. Moderately high $\dot{V}O_2$max values are reported for swimmers, modern dancers, speed skaters, orienteers, pentathletes, figure skaters, and mountaineers. Gymnasts and volleyball and basketball players have relatively low $\dot{V}O_2$max values.

It is generally thought that a woman must have a $\dot{V}O_2$max in excess of 60-65 ml $\cdot$ kg^{-1} $\cdot$ min^{-1} to achieve elite status in endurance events. An accurate understanding of the importance of aerobic power for successful performance in a sport is paramount. Although the relative contribution of genetic endowment to aerobic power is an argued point, most exercise physiologists agree that proper training methods can increase $\dot{V}O_2$max 10% to 25% (the exact amount depends to a large extent on pretraining condition). It is highly unlikely that a woman with only a low level of cardiorespiratory endurance will be very successful as a middle-distance runner, cross-country skier, or rower even with considerable aerobic training.

Although aerobic power is an extremely important predictor of performance in sports such as middle- and long-distance running and cross-country skiing, it is certainly not all that is required. Running economy (steady-state $\dot{V}O_2$ at standardized speeds) and the fractional utilization of $\dot{V}O_2$max at submaximal speeds (percent $\dot{V}O_2$max) may also be important factors (Conley, Krahenbuhl, Burkett, & Millar, 1981; Daniels et al., 1977). Another important variable in endurance performance may be the running (or cycling, swimming, etc.) velocity at the onset of the blood lactate or lactate threshold, which is usually established at the 4-mM level. These variables possibly reflect one's lactate clearance capacity. These factors most likely determine success when the $\dot{V}O_2$max of competitors is similar.

Pate, Sparling, Wilson, Cureton, and Miller (1987) recently conducted a study that compared elite with "good" distance runners (see Table 16.4). Mean $\dot{V}O_2$max expressed relative to body weight was 14% higher in the elite group, and metabolic and cardiorespiratory responses at two submaximal running velocities were lower, indicating that running economy was clearly superior in the elite group. In addition, blood lactate response to submaximal running was a sensitive discriminator between the groups. Lactate following the submaximal run protocol was clearly elevated in the good but not the elite runners. The results of this study demonstrate that the current population of elite women distance runners have markedly higher maximal aerobic power than nationally ranked women runners of the 1970s.

Strength of Women Athletes

Strength is another very important variable in athletic performance. Unfortunately, many different factors are involved in defining muscular strength and in measuring it. For example, there is isometric, or static, strength; isotonic, or dynamic, strength; eccentric strength (lengthening contraction); isokinetic strength (movement at a constant speed against an accommodating resistance); and possibly explosive strength (power?). Numerous methods to assess strength intend to clarify the measurement of muscular strength but instead have only confused the matter. Probably the most useful method is the repetition maximum test (1-RM), which determines the heaviest weight an individual can lift one time. Measuring strength

Table 16.4 Aerobic Power of Women Athletes

Athletic group or sport	Level[a]	Age (yr)	Height (cm)	Weight (kg)	$\dot{V}O_2$max ml · kg⁻¹ · min⁻¹	Reference
Basketball	C	19	169.1	62.6	42.95	Sinngin (1973)
	C	19	167.0	63.9	42.3	Conger & MacNab (1967)
	C	20	165.3	61.5	35.75	McArdle et al. (1971)
	C	19.4	173.0	68.3	49.63	Vaccaro et al. (1979)
	C	20.7	166.4	61.3	38.3	Sinning & Adrian (1968)
Bicycling	E	—	167.7	61.3	57.4	Burke (1980)
	E	20	165.0	55.0	50.2	Burke et al. (1977)
Bodybuilders	SF	28	164.0	55.0	39.5	Elliot et al. (1987)
Dance	C	21.2	162.7	51.2	41.5	Novak et al. (1978)
Modern	C	—	—	—	50.0	Chambers (1981)
	E	30.4	161.8	53.3	49.1	Chmelar et al. (1988)
	C	26.5	163.0	54.4	47.5	Chmelar et al. (1988)
Ballet	E	23.7	165.6	49.5	43.7	Cohen et al. (1982)
	E	23.7	167.4	54.2	42.2	Chmelar et al. (1988)
	C	19.3	166.1	53.5	47.0	Chmelar et al. (1988)
Gymnastics	HT	17.2	162.3	56.5	42.54	Sprynarova & Pařízková (1969)
	HT	18.6	157.0	46.6	61.77	Noble (1975)
	C	19	163.0	57.9	36.3	Conger & MacNab (1967)
Orienteering	E	29	—	58.1	46.1	Knowlton et al. (1980)
Pentathlon	N, E	21	175.4	65.4	45.9	Krahenbhl et al. (1979)
Rowing	N	23.0	173.0	68.0	60.3	Hagerman et al. (1979)
Rugby						
Forwards	C	20.4	166.4	69.2	41.4	Sedlock et al. (1988)
Backs	C	21.0	162.2	54.1	43.2	Sedlock et al. (1988)

Running						
400-800 m	N	23	—	—	56.0	Saltin & Åstrand (1967)
Cross-country	C	19.3	163.0	54.7	59.5	Kollias et al. (1978)
	N	23.7	166.2	52.1	59.1-59.6	Daniels et al. (1977)
	C	20.6	166.4	53.7	48.8	Bransford & Howley (1977)
	N, E	15-26	164.0	50.4	68.8	Brown & Wilmore (1971)
	E	32	169.4	57.2	59.1	Wilmore & Brown (1974)
10 km	HT	24.1	159.7	49.3	53.0	Conley et al. (1981)
Middle distance (1,500-5,000 m)	E	25.8	161.3	46.9	68.0	Sparling et al. (1987); Pate et al. (1987)
Long distance (10-42 km)	E	28.3	161.3	47.0	66.4	Sparling et al. (1987); Pate et al. (1987)
Long distance	HT	28.6	161.5	49.3	58.6	Sparling et al. (1987); Pate et al. (1987)
Marathon	T	29.2	165.2	52.2	53.5	Jordan (1977)
	HT	28.5	166.6	52.0	59.2	Wells et al. (1981)
	HT	33.0	172.3	65.3	72.5	Davies & Thompson (1979)
Skating						
Speed	N	21.5	164.5	60.8	46.1	Maksud et al. (1970)
Figure	—	19.3	—	57.6	47.93	Gordon et al. (1969)
Skiing, cross-country	N, E	22.9	164.3	58.5	63.8	Saltin & Åstrand (1967)
	E	20	163.4	55.9	61.5	Haymes & Dickenson (1980)
	HT, N	24.3	163.0	59.1	68.2	Rusko et al. (1978)
Alpine	E	19	165.1	58.8	52.7	Haymes & Dickenson (1980)
Swimmers	HT	19.5	166.2	63.8	45.95	Sprynarova & Pařízková (1969)
	N, O	20.4	175.4	66.7	49.52	Haan (1979)
	O	17.7	167.0	60.1	43.4	Novak et al. (1977)
Synchronized	N	20.1	166.2	55.8	43.2	Roby et al. (1983)
Tennis	Class B, C	39	163.3	55.7	44.2	Vodak et al. (1980)
Volleyball	N	24.4	173.8	63.0	44.2	Spence et al. (1980)
	E	21.6	183.7	73.4	41.7	Spence et al. (1980)
	C	19	166.0	59.8	43.5	Conger & MacNab (1967)
	C	20	172.2	64.1	56.0	Kovaleski et al. (1980)
	E	21.6	178.3	70.5	50.6	Puhl et al. (1982)

aLevels of performance indicated as follows: HT = highly trained, E = elite, C = collegiate, N = nationally ranked, O = Olympian, and SF = steroid free.

in this way requires only basic weight-training equipment but with inexperienced lifters can require considerable time. Usually, three or four exercises, such as the bench press, leg press, standing press, and curl, are chosen to represent the major muscle groups. Additional methods are available that use rather elaborate and sometimes extremely expensive equipment. Because there is no standardization in the measurement of strength from one laboratory to another, it is nearly impossible to compare what little strength data is available on female athletes. Some information on strength is provided in Table 16.5 and illustrates this point rather well.

Muscle Fiber Characteristics of Female Athletes

A few years ago, the technique of muscle biopsy became a useful tool. The purpose of the technique was to determine the number and relative distribution of fast-twitch and slow-twitch muscle fibers. This research has shown a direct relationship between the endurance component (aerobic) of performance and the percentage of slow-twitch muscle fibers one possesses. Far more studies have been completed on male subjects than female, but in the few studies in which men and women have been compared, it is evident that there are few sex differences. Although men may have larger muscle fibers, a larger muscle fiber area, and possibly a larger number of muscle fibers, there appears to be no difference in the relative distribution of fibers. Table 16.6 presents the data available on female athletes.

The highest percentages of slow-twitch muscle fibers appeared in the cross-country skiers and the middle- and long-distance runners—the same groups of athletes that have the highest cardiorespiratory endurance values (compare Tables 16.6 and 16.4). A recent study by Costill, Fink, Flynn, and Kirwan (1987) showed that when elite runners were subdivided on the basis of their best

events, the percentage of slow-twitch fibers in lower leg muscles was highest among the marathon runners (80%) and lowest among the 1,500- and 3,000-m runners (62%). The highest individual values for slow-twitch fibers in male distance runners have been reported to range from 92% to 98% (Costill et al., 1976). The highest individual values among the women runners in the study by Costill et al. (1987) ranged from 90% to 96%. A very low value for percentage of slow-twitch fibers was obtained from the gastrocnemius muscles of the sprinters. Thus, it appears that successful long-distance runners are characterized by slow-twitch fibers and middle-distance runners and sprinters by fast-twitch fibers.

These runners also had a very high number of capillaries per muscle fiber (elite = 2.50, good runners = 2.30). This has previously been associated with high $\dot{V}O_2$max. Enhanced capillarization occurs with endurance training and increases oxygenation to all parts of the muscle fiber. The activity of the oxidative enzyme did not differ between the elite and good runners but was significantly higher than in the untrained women.

Because most of the power in swimming comes from the arms, it would be interesting to know the relative distribution of muscle fibers in the upper body and arm muscles of elite female swimmers. In men, the percentage of slow-twitch fibers in the vastus lateralis was reported to be 57.7% but in the deltoid was 74.3% (Gollnick, Armstrong, Saubert, Piehl, & Saltin, 1972).

The Adolescent Female Athlete

Although children of both sexes compete in sport, prepubescent and adolescent girls are more successful at the national and international levels. This is particularly evident in such sports as gymnastics, figure skating, and swimming. Adolescence marks a period of rapid change in growth and maturation. In girls, relative body fat increases, secondary sex characteristics appear

Table 16.5 Strength of Female Athletes

Athletic group or sport	Level[a]	Variable[b]	Score	Reference
Alpine skiers	E	Isometric knee extension (8)	2,194 N	Haymes & Dickinson (1980)
		Isokinetic knee extension at 30°/s (1)	189.1 Nm	
		at 180°/s	104.9 Nm	
Basketball	C	Bench press at 20°/s (2)	43.2 kg	Morrow & Hosler (1981)
		Leg press at 20°/s	177.7 kg	
Cross-country skiers	E	Isometric knee extension (8)	1,176 N	Haymes & Dickinson (1980)
Field events (throwers)	N	Bench press (3)	52-85 kg	Brown & Wilmore (1974)
		Leg press	56-79 kg	
Figure skaters (adolescent)	HT	Grip strength	30.5 kg	Niinimaa (1982)
		Knee extension	257.8 kg	
Modern dancers	C	Leg extension at 60°/s (1)	116 ft lb	Chambers (1981)
		Leg flexion at 60°/s	71.8 ft lb	
		Hip flexion at 60°/s	66.6 ft lb	
		Hip extension at 60°/s	163 ft lb	
		Abdominal strength at 0°/s	45.4 ft lb	
		Back hyperextension at 0°/s	84.6 ft lb	
	E	Leg extension at 60°/s	75.7 ft lb/lb	Chmelar et al. (1988)
		Leg extension at 180°/s	47.9 ft lb/lb	
		Leg flexion at 60°/s	43.2 ft lb/lb	
		Leg flexion at 180°/s	36.4 ft lb/lb	
	C	Leg extension at 60°/s	78.8 ft lb/lb	Chmelar et al. (1988)
		Leg extension at 180°/s	50.9 ft lb/lb	
		Leg flexion at 60°/s	45.1 ft lb/lb	
		Leg flexion at 180°/s	37.4 ft lb/lb	
Ballet Dancers	E	Leg extension at 60°/s (1)	73.7 ft lb/lb	Chmelar et al. (1988)
		Leg extension at 180°/s	46.5 ft lb/lb	
		Leg flexion at 60°/s	50.5 ft lb/lb	
		Leg flexion at 180°/s	42.3 ft lb/lb	

(Cont.)

Table 16.5 (Continued)

athletic group or sport	Level[a]	Variable[b]	Score	Reference
	C	Leg extension at 60°/s	74.7 ft lb/lb	Chmelar et al. (1988)
		Leg extension at 180°/s	45.5 ft lb/lb	
		Leg flexion at 60°/s	46.2 ft lb/lb	
		Leg flexion at 180°/s	35.5 ft lb/lb	
Pentathletes	N	Squat (3)	89.7 kg	Krahenbuhl et al. (1979)
		Power clean	59.7 kg	
		Horizontal bench press	61.5 kg	
		Pull-down	60.0 kg	
		Inclined bench press	44.9 kg	
		Leg curl	36.3 kg	
Rugby				
Forwards	C	Isometric knee extension at 90° (4)	48.0 kg	Sedlock et al. (1988)
		Isometric elbow flexion at 90°	26.1 kg	
Backs	C	Isometric knee extension at 90°	43.0 kg	
		Isometric elbow extension at 90°	23.8 kg	
Rowers	E	Knee extension at 0°/s	220 Nm	Clarkson et al. (1984)
		Elbow flexion at 0°/s	60.1 Nm	
Tennis				
(Adolescent)	HT	Grip strength, dominant arm (5)	34.2 kg	Powers & Walker (1982)
		Nondominant arm	28.0 kg	
(Middle-aged)	Class B, C	Grip strength, dominant arm (6)	351 N	Vodak et al. (1980)
		Nondominant arm	294 N	

Volleyball				
	N	Isometric leg extension at 90° (7)	73.2 psi	Spence et al. (1980)
	E	Isometric leg extension at 90°	76.2 psi	Spence et al.. (1980)
	C	Bench press at 20°/s (2)	40.7 kg	Morrow & Hosler (1981)
		Leg press at 20°/s	143.8 kg	
	E	Knee extension at 30°/s (1)	140 Nm	Puhl et al. (1982)
		Knee extension at 180°/s	60 Nm	
		Knee flexion at 30°/s	105 Nm	
		Knee flexion at 180°/s	60 Nm	
		Elbow extension at 30°/s	32 Nm	
		Elbow extension at 180°/s	17.5 Nm	
		Elbow flexion at 30°/s	36 Nm	
		Elbow flexion at 180°/s	19 Nm	
		Shoulder extension at 30°/s	55 Nm	
		Shoulder extension at 180°/s	36 Nm	
		Plantar flexion at 30°/s	57 Nm	
		Plantar flexion at 180°/s	11 Nm	

[a]Levels of performance indicated as follows: HT = highly trained, E = elite, C = collegiate, and N = nationally ranked.

[b](1) = Cybex II dynamometer, (2) = Lumex bench and leg press, (3) = free weights, (4) = load cell force monitor, (5) = Lafayette grip dynamometer, (6) = JAMAR hand dynamometer, (7) = Elgin multiple angle strength testing table, and (8) = cable tensiometer.

Table 16.6 Muscle Fiber Characteristics of Women Athletes

Athletic group or sport	Age (yr)	Height (cm)	Weight (kg)	ST fibers (%)	ST area μM²	ST area (%)	Reference
Bicyclists	20	165	55.0	55.5[a]	5,487	47.6	Burke et al. (1977)
Field hockey	23	161	57.7	48.2[a]	4,305	27.5	Prince et al. (1977)
Javelin	21	169	65.3	41.6[b]	4,864	42.9	Costill et al. (1976)
Long/high jumpers	22	177	61.1	48.7[b]	4,163	44.0	Costill et al. (1976)
Rowers, elite	—	175	74.6	53.6[c]	—	51.9	Clarkson et al. (1984)
				62.5[a]	—	64.0	
Shot put, discus	24	171	77.0	51.2[b]	5,192	46.9	Costill et al. (1976)
Skiers, cross-country	24	163	59.1	60.0[a]	—	—	Rusko et al. (1978)
				61.0[b]			
Runners, sprint	19	168	55.6	27.4[b]	3,752	26.8	Costill et al. (1976)
Runners, middle distance	20	166	52.5	60.6[b]	6,069	60.4	Costill et al. (1976)
Runners, elite middle-long distance	27.6	161	47.0	68..8[b]	4,441	69.4	Costill et al. (1987)
Runners, good long-distance	28.6	162	49.3	60.8[b]	4,392	64.0	Costill et al. (1987)
Skiers, cross-country	17.6	166.9	57.9	59.9[a]	—	—	Rusko et al. (1980)

Note. Adapted from Wilmore (1982, pp. 157-158). [a]Biopsy from vastus lateralis. [b]Biopsy from gastrocnemius. [c]Biopsy from biceps brachii.

(breast development, pubic hair, etc.), menarche occurs, and physical activity generally declines.

Late maturation has often been associated with better motor performance in girls (the opposite is true in boys), and it is notable that prepubescence favors success in such sports as gymnastics, figure skating, ballet, and running. Early maturation favors performance in swimming (increased body fat?), basketball, volleyball, and tennis. It is unfortunate that no longitudinal studies of young female athletes as they progress through their athletic careers are available. However, data from some cross-sectional studies are presented in Tables 16.7, 16.8, and 16.9.

Lohman, Boileau, and Slaughter (1984) have proposed that the density of lean tissue is less in children than in adults. This means that current methods for assessing body composition in children overestimate their body fat. Perhaps the data in Table 16.7 inadequately reflect the leanness of these adolescent athletes. Thorland, Johnson, Tharp, Housh, and Cisar (1984) cross-validated a skinfold prediction equation for adolescent female athletes (mean age 16.5 years) as follows:

$$BD = 1.0987 - 0.00122 (X) + 0.00000263 (X)^2$$

where X = sum of triceps, subscapular, and suprailiac skinfolds. Future investigators may wish to use this formula when measuring adolescent female athletes.

Table 16.8 reveals that adolescent athletes are rather low in endomorphy (relative to adults). For the most part, their general somatotype appears to be in the ectomorphy-mesomorphy category.

Table 16.7 Body Composition of Adolescent Athletes

Athletic group or sport	Level[a]	Age (yr)	Height (cm)	Weight (kg)	Relative fat (%)	Lean/fat ratio	Reference
Ballet	HT	15.0	161.1	48.4	16.4	5.5	Clarkson et al. (1985)
Figure skating	HT	16.5	158.8	48.6	12.5	7.0	Niinimaa (1982)
Gymnastics	—	14.0	—	—	17.0	—	Pařízková (1973)
	S	15.2	161.1	50.4	13.1	6.6	Moffatt et al. (1984)
Running							
Cross-country	S	15.6	163.3	50.9	15.4	5.5	Butts (1982a)
Track	E	~16	—	55.1	15.5	5.5	Housh et al. (1984)
Skiing							
Cross-country	N	17.6	166.9	57.7	22.7	3.4	Rusko et al. (1980)
Swimming	N	14.6	163.4	52.0	15.9	5.2	Haan (1979)
	O	16.3	164.4	56.9	14.5	5.9	McArdle et al. (1981)
	JO	~16	—	58.5	19.8	4.0	Housh et al. (1984)
Tennis	R	15.8	168.7	58.0	23.3	3.3	Powers & Walker (1982)

[a]Levels of performance indicated as follows: E = elite, HT = highly trained, N = national, O = Olympic, R = ranked, S = scholastic, and JO = Junior Olympics.

Table 16.8 Somatotypes of Adolescent Athletes

Athletic group or sport	Level[a]	Age (yr)	Height (cm)	Weight (kg)	Somatotype			Reference
					Endo	Meso	Ecto	
Figure skaters	N	15.7	156.8	48.6	2.6	3.8	3.0	Carter (1981)
	N	14.0	154.1	45.5	2.5	4.1	3.2	Carter (1981)
Swimming	O	16.0	164.4	56.9	3.4	4.0	3.0	deGaray et al. (1974)
	O	16.3	164.0	56.9	3.1	4.0	3.0	Carter (1981)
	N	14.2	161.3	52.2	2.4	3.4	2.8	Carter (1981)
Runners								
Cross-country	S	15.6	164.2	51.1	2.8	3.2	4.0	Butts (1982b)

[a]Levels of performance indicated as follows: N = nationally ranked, O = Olympian, and S = Scholastic.

Maximal aerobic power of adolescent athletes (Table 16.9) is comparable to that of adult athletes in those sports that are not highly dependent on aerobic power. Notably, the adolescent runners and cross-country skiers, whose performance is highly dependent on maximal aerobic power, have much lower values than highly successful adult athletes in those sports. It appears that a long period of training is necessary to develop world-class $\dot{V}O_2$max for endurance sports.

Table 16.9   Aerobic Power of Adolescent Athletes

Athletic group or sport	Level[a]	Age (yr)	Height (cm)	Weight (kg)	VO₂max (ml · kg⁻¹ · min⁻¹)	Reference
Ballet	HT	15.0	161.1	48.4	48.9	Clarkson et al. (1985)
Gymnastics	S	15.0	—	50.4	45.2	Moffatt et al. (1984)
Runners						
Sprinters	S	15.0	—	—	43.9	Raven et al. (1972)
	S	16.0	—	—	58.5	Raven et al. (1972)
Unspecified	N	—	—	—	54.0	Novak et al. (1973)
	S	12-13	152.9	44.8	48.7	Drinkwater & Horvath (1971)
	S	14-15	162.2	52.2	48.5	Drinkwater & Horvath (1971)
	S	16-18	163.2	54.2	51.1	Drinkwater & Horvath (1971)
	HT	16.2	162.2	48.6	63.2	Burke & Brush (1979)
Cross-country	S	15.6	163.3	50.9	50.8	Butts (1982a)
	HT	12-14	157.5	42.6	52.6	Wells et al. (1973)
Track	E	9-15	—	—	59.9	Van Huss et al. (1988)
Figure skating	HT	16.5	158.8	48.6	48.9	Niinimaa (1982)
Skiing						
Cross-country	HT	16-18	158.8	52.8	50.2	Wells et al. (1973)
	N	17.6	166.9	57.7	47.3	Rusko et al. (1980)
Swimmers	—	12.0	154.8	43.3	46.2	Cunningham & Eynon (1973)
	—	13.0	160.0	52.1	43.4	Cunningham & Eynon (1973)
	N	14.6	163.4	52.0	56.4	Haan (1979)
	—	15.0	164.8	—	40.5	Cunningham & Eynon (1973)
Tennis	R	15.8	168.7	58.0	48.0	Powers & Walker (1982)

[a]Levels of performance indicated as follows: HT = highly trained, E = elite, N = nationally ranked, S = scholastic, and R = ranked.

The Woman Masters Athlete

The woman masters athlete has been studied even less than the adolescent athlete. The most likely reason for this scientific disinterest is that masters competition for women is so new. Although many women have pursued active lifestyles well into their 60s, only recently has organized sport been made available to them. Others have recently begun to exercise and have met with unqualified success.

Drinkwater (1988) stated that whether the woman masters athlete is a recent convert or has been active all her life, she is likely to be at least 1 or 2 decades physiologically younger than the sedentary woman of the same age. Active 50-year-olds may have VO₂max values equal to sedentary 20- or 30-year-olds! Vacarro, Dummer, and Clarke (1981) agreed, stating that the 70-year-old masters swimmers they studied could match sedentary 20-year-olds in VO₂max. Obviously, masters athletes are forcing the reevaluation of what is commonly believed to be normal physiological aging processes.

Table 16.10 presents characteristics of women masters athletes aged from the mid 30s to over 70. Upton, Hagan, Rosentswieg, and Gettman (1983) and Upton et al. (1984) showed that middle-aged (mean age 37.8 years) distance runners had lower body weight and body fat and higher aerobic power than both sedentary women of the same age and active but untrained women (Drinkwater et al., 1975). The middle-aged marathoners did not differ significantly in $\dot{V}O_2$max from the 25-year-old marathoners (Upton et al., 1984).

The data in Table 16.10 for the Vaccaro, Morris, and Clarke (1981) reference include only the distance runners who were older than 45. These runners were lighter in body weight and had less body fat than nonathletes. Of course, this is not too surprising when one considers the average distance these women ran (46 mi per week). These women also had lower values for relative body fat than those reported by Katch and McArdle (1973) for women athletes aged 19 to 24.4 (21.5% to 29.1% body fat). Mean $\dot{V}O_2$max values in the masters runners were superior to those reported by Drinkwater (1973) for normal sedentary women of the same age and by Profant et al. (1972), Drinkwater et al. (1975; see Table 10.2), Getchell and Moore (1975), and Plowman et al. (1979). Rather, the aerobic power values of these masters runners were comparable to values achieved by college basketball players (Vaccaro, Clarke, & Wrenn, 1979) and Olympic speed-skating candidates (Maksud, Hamilton, & Coutts, 1971).

Perhaps the most interesting question about the woman masters athlete is whether menopause has any effect on her physiological profile or competitive performance. A comprehensive investigation of premenopausal, perimenopausal, and postmenopausal masters athletes is needed.

Summary

The purpose of this chapter was to pull together concepts and data discussed earlier in the text—body composition, aerobic capacity, muscle fiber characteristics, and so on—that dealt exclusively

with highly successful female athletes. A considerable amount of data was perused and consolidated into tables to accomplish this. Although the "big picture" was sought, however, much has also been lost in this approach. The topic could have been presented in an entirely different manner, and in fact the initial attempt was to profile each sport or activity separately. Although that method had some merit, using concepts as highlighted material, rather than detailed descriptions of each sport, seemed more relevant and simply "hung together" better. With this approach, however, the coach or athlete, although getting the big picture, will have to dig for the details he or she may want. Perhaps this process, plus seeing how particular athletes compare with others, may yield much that might have been missed with the specific-sport approach.

Obviously, many problems remain in terms of standardizing methods of measurement and methods of reporting data. A running $\dot{V}O_2$max test on a treadmill, for example, is known to give a higher value than either a pedaling $\dot{V}O_2$max test on a bicycle ergometer or a tethered swimming test. Most of the $\dot{V}O_2$max values reported here were obtained using a treadmill test, a procedure that may not be particularly appropriate for swimmers, cyclists, rowers, or other athletes. Problems in data reporting are particularly evident in the descriptions of muscular strength and anaerobic power. Although the newton may be a meaningful unit to the scientist, it is probably not too useful to the athlete or coach, who is more familiar with feet, inches, seconds, and pounds. Obviously, there is a great necessity for uniformity in measurement techniques and data reporting.

In addition, the elite female athlete has not been studied as comprehensively as one would desire. An excellent model is provided by the monograph edited by P.B. Sparling (1987), titled "A Comprehensive Profile of Elite Women Distance Runners." Longitudinal data are also needed to study the development of elite performers. Because most outstanding athletes come through the ranks of age-group participation (tennis, track, and swimming), a great deal is missed by not studying these

Table 16.10 Characteristics of Women Masters Athletes

Athletic group or sport	Age (yr)	Height (cm)	Weight (kg)	Relative fat (%)	LBM (kg)	Lean/fat ratio	$\dot{V}O_2$max (ml · kg^{-1} · min^{-1})	$\dot{V}_E$ (L · min^{-1})	HRmax	Reference
Mountaineers	35.6	168.6	63.6	21.1	50.2	3.7	43.7	96.4	184	Kramár & Drinkwater (1980)
Runners										
10 km	33.1	165.2	57.4	—	—	—	48.5	102.1	182	Upton et al. (1984)
Marathon	37.8	165.1	54.1	15.5	45.6	5.4	55.5	103.0	180	Upton et al. (1983)
Distance	47.0	159.0	51.1	16.3	42.8	5.2	44.7	84.4	179	Vaccaro, Morris, & Clarke (1981)
Swimmers										
31-40		—	—	18.6	—	—	42.1	79.0	178	Drinkwater (1988)
51-60		—	—	23.8	—	—	35.9	75.0	163	Drinkwater (1988)
61-70		—	—	27.8	—	—	32.1	66.0	159	Drinkwater (1988)
71-80		164.2	61.6	23.5	—	—	37.6	78.9	162	Vaccaro, Dummer, & Clarke (1981)

Note. Adapted and expanded from Drinkwater (1988, p. 167).

young performers more extensively. Much of the blame for the lack of an integrated, well-organized, and uniform approach can be placed on the lack of adequate funding resources: money and politics (the roots of all things?). Without funding, the research exercise physiologist and biomechanist can do very little. Shoestring budgets usually mean poor equipment, limited procedures, and no graduate students to help with the work.

Most of sport's national governing bodies have recognized that research and development in their sports is important not only to improve the performance of a few but also to promote the future development of that sport for all people. With improved knowledge come breakthroughs of all sorts—in conditioning and training, in equipment, and in technique. The future application of scientific principles to sport performance has never looked more promising than it does today. The

work of the U.S. Olympic Training Center in Colorado Springs, as well as the establishment of regional training centers, is particularly promising. Fairly comprehensive attempts to study performance are being made by such groups as the U.S. Ski Team Nordic Sportsmedicine Council (an example are its ongoing studies of junior skiers). Corporate funding is being tapped, and public solicitation is also reasonably successful. With all these ongoing activities, we should have more information available on young and adult female athletes.

As a final encouraging note, it currently appears that girls' and women's sports have captured the imaginations of scientists, participants, and spectators. Participation, whether as a fun activity, a fitness activity, or a competitive venture, is rapidly improving. It is hoped that this book will encourage all women to achieve their full potential.

Chapter 17

Epilogue

The preceding chapters contain a considerable amount of information on women and exercise. My criteria for including or excluding a topic or piece of information was the test of peer review in a reputable journal, a process that is considered the ultimate test in science. I sought to include all the physiological information that is relevant to girls and women engaged in exercise and sport.

   The purpose of this concluding chapter is to synthesize some of the more important aspects of the preceding information and to point the way for further study of the exercising woman. Perhaps this chapter should be titled "Future Directions in Sport Science for Women" because it attempts to answer the question, Where do we go from here? The material I have chosen to include is more philosophical and personal than in the preceding chapters.

It is only natural to have some personal feelings and opinions about current issues after gathering and integrating so much information. For the most part, those feelings and opinions were subdued in earlier chapters. This, finally, is my "soapbox" chapter. I discuss some problems and issues that involve the physiological aspects of the exercising woman as I see them. My purpose is to stimulate future scientific study as well as to point out where current practice (policy) could well be altered for the betterment of women of all ages, that is, to effect change. Citations are not given because the material is largely based on my impressions of the massive amount of literature I have reviewed.

I believe that two primary issues have arisen as a result of the material presented in this book. Both are related to women's health. The first issue is related to the lack of exercise, or, more precisely, to health as it relates to inactivity. The second issue is health as it relates to high levels of physical training.

Health Issues Related to Inactivity

According to Christine Brooks (assistant professor, University of Michigan), approximately 35% of Americans are irregularly active, and 45% seem to never exert themselves at all. Only one in five adult Americans (20% of the U.S. population) engages in moderate-to-vigorous physical activity more than 60 days per year—that's once every 6 days.

The President's Council on Physical Fitness and Sports claims that less than 50% of the American adult population exercise regularly and that only 20% of those exercise at a level sufficient to produce cardiorespiratory benefits. The Council further states that 40% of children between the ages of 5 and 8 already show at least one risk factor for heart disease.

In general, women are less physically active than men. Therefore, it is evident that the so-called U.S. fitness boom is not affecting a significant number of individuals, whether male, female, child, or adult. Significant health problems are associated with a sedentary lifestyle, and most of these are probably well known to the readers of this book. This is a critical issue for the health and welfare of American women.

Obesity

The majority of women in America (as well as in other industrialized nations) are, in my opinion, too fat. Their overfatness or obesity is related to underactivity (low caloric expenditure) and overeating (high caloric intake coupled with high consumption of saturated fat), both of which predispose them to increased risk for heart disease, hypertension, adult-onset diabetes, gallbladder disease, and possibly cancer.

Many of these women have high levels of blood cholesterol and relatively high ratios of low-density lipoprotein cholesterol (so-called bad cholesterol) to high-density lipoprotein cholesterol (so-called good cholesterol). In their younger years, many of these women are protected from heart disease by normal levels of plasma estrogen, probably because the proportion of low-density to high-density lipoprotein cholesterol is kept in check. Before menopause, the greatest health risks for these women are adult-onset diabetes, gallbladder disease, and cellular changes that are associated with developing cancer in later life.

With advancing age, however, the relative risk factors for disease change. It is well documented that we are living longer today than ever before and it is not uncommon for a woman to live 40 to 50 years beyond menopause. Because her body has lower estrogen levels for a longer period of time, protection is lost, and the risk factors associated with high levels of body fat become more ominous. The relationship between obesity and high blood pressure has long been recognized. Hypertension, particularly in the elderly, is highly associated with stroke and other cerebrovascular diseases. After age 50, the prevalence of hypertension and various forms of cardiovascular disease increase considerably.

Body shape often changes too. In particular, abdominal fat increases. Studies are now showing that individuals with more body fat in the abdominal region (the so-called apple shape) are at greater risk of cardiovascular disease than persons with relatively more body fat in the hips and buttocks (the so-called pear shape). Most women display the characteristic pear shape, but with advancing age, the pattern of fat deposition changes to form a more applelike pattern. Fat lost from the extremities is redistributed to the abdomen.

With increasing age, being overweight also predisposes one to osteoarthritic changes in the hips, back, knees, and ankles. These painful symptoms obviously lead to further inactivity and ultimately to increased fatness and a loss of lean body mass.

The American Cancer Society's data on mortality in relation to body weight show that the death rate due to cancer increases considerably as body weight increases. In women, cancers of the gallbladder, breast, cervix, endometrium, uterus, and ovaries all show increased incidence with excessive body weight (which usually means overfatness).

Much of this is well known. Most would agree that being 100 to 200 pounds overweight is bad for your health and your physical fitness. But what about those who are only 30 to 50 pounds overweight? Many of these women are aware of the health issues associated with fatness but are far more conscious of the social stigma of being overfat. These women are more often driven by sociological forces to lose weight. In fact, it appears that we are rapidly becoming a nation of dieters. Nearly all these women have dieted to lose weight, and some have been moderately successful. Others, however, continue a cycle of "yo-yo" dieting (dieting to lose weight, regaining it, only to diet again), which is largely nonproductive. One simply loses lean body mass and becomes more fat. As lean body mass declines, the body seems to go into a protective mode to conserve its reserves of fat. The result is twofold. First, basal and resting metabolic rates decline, and future weight loss becomes increasingly difficult. Second, there is a gain in relative levels of body fat and the continued high risk for developing chronic health problems.

Osteoporosis

Another problem associated with a sedentary lifestyle is advanced bone mineral loss. In older age, this leads to osteoporosis, or porous bones, and its accompanying postural changes and risk of spontaneous fractures (described in chapter 10). Because osteoporosis is difficult to treat and current (nonexperimental) treatment is not very effective, it is important to take preventive measures to reduce the risks associated with osteoporosis. A sedentary lifestyle is one such risk factor.

However, we know relatively little about the relationship between exercise and bone mineral deposition or resorption. How much exercise is needed? Is weight-bearing exercise essential for the bones of the lower extremity and spine? What are appropriate types of exercise for increasing bone density of the upper body? Is there an ideal combination of dietary calcium and exercise for either the prevention or the treatment of osteopenia? What is the role of estrogen in bone mineral deposition and exercise? What are the mechanisms that effect earlier bone mineral losses in high-risk women (Caucasians, those of northern European background, smokers, caffeine and alcohol consumers) than in other women? Is exercise particularly effective for high-risk women? What is the exact affect of menopause on bone tissues? Is it important to maximize peak bone mass before menopause? If so, how can that best be accomplished?

What Can Be Done About These Problems?

I have presented two major problems facing women today that are related to the lack of regular physical exercise. How can we (as teachers, coaches, exercise physiologists, voters, and political activists) get women to exercise sufficiently to maintain desirable levels of body weight and fat and to prevent (or treat) osteoporosis in later life? In my opinion, the problem requires a massive, multi-faceted effort on a national level. The most obvious steps are as follows:

Promoting Physical Activity

1. Various professional associations and governmental agencies must launch a massive public education program depicting exercise as preventive medicine. Particular emphasis should be placed on women. To a certain extent, this is already taking place (e.g., the American Heart Association's so-called war on cholesterol and the federal government's objectives for the nation), but there is little emphasis on obesity specifically and on women in general.

2. There must be a well-organized training program (and possibly certification) at the federal level for persons providing exercise leadership. Otherwise, charlatans take advantage of the gullible, a phenomenon we have already seen in fitness spas, in fitness videos, and in the organic foods movement.

3. There must be sufficient incentives for those who do not normally like to exercise. We already have reduced automobile insurance for "safe drivers" and reduced health insurance premiums for nonsmokers. I suggest reduced health or life insurance premiums (or both) for persons who develop good fitness habits and reduce and maintain their body weight from overweight to normal for their age and sex classifications. Data from major insurance companies indicate that obese persons who successfully lose weight and maintain a lower weight can reduce their risk of mortality to within the normal limits for their age and sex. Women who exercise regularly throughout a lifetime may have fewer osteoporotic fractures. These facts mean dollars to insurance companies.

4. Grants should be given to colleges, universities, YWCAs, Girl Scouts, Campfire, church groups, ethnic associations, and so on to develop model programs for teaching lifetime fitness concepts and practices and encouraging exercise as preventive medicine (we brush our teeth daily, so why not exercise daily?).

5. Quality physical education must be available in every school in America on a daily basis. There must be federal imperatives and incentives for such programs as well as assistance from professional associations. There are many possible forms, including direct subsidies to schools that adopt such programs and tax credits for the taxpayers in those school districts.

6. Community-based exercise programs must be established and then assisted financially by state, federal, or professional foundations and associations such as the National Dairy Council, the American Medical Association, and the American Heart Association. This latter group has already worked extensively with the American Alliance for Health, Physical Education, Recreation and Dance on the child-based Jump Rope for Heart program. Now it is time for a nationally focused exercise promotion program for adult women. Child care facilities and early-morning or evening hours must be available for working women for such programs to be successful.

As you can see, I envision nothing less than a massive effort requiring a high degree of cooperation among governmental, educational, professional, and corporate business groups. This would take considerable dedication, money, man- and womanpower, and motivation.

Many of us who love to exercise and who do so regularly simply because we experience joy in physical effort often find it difficult to understand that most women in the United States do not share this same love. New ways must be found to help women learn to truly enjoy physical activity. Although I firmly believe that exercise *is* preventive medicine, it must not be viewed like simply taking a pill. Women will not exercise throughout their lives simply because exercise is good for them. They will continue exercise throughout a lifetime only if it is enjoyable and socially rewarding and if they perceive that they are successful at it. Unfortunately, many of our current exercise programs are not based on this premise.

The best way to accomplish our goals may be by providing good role models at every age level. Perhaps that is why some of our movie stars have been so successful in the aerobics and fitness business and "professionals" have enjoyed only a modicum of success in their appeal to the masses. Effective leadership and public relations are absolutely essential. As professionals, we need to pay more attention to basic principles of public relations and product promotion.

Health Issues Related to High Levels of Physical Training

If it is possible to exercise too little (and I sincerely believe it is), can it also be possible to exercise too much?

Women's athletics has changed considerably since Title IX. Formerly, physically active and highly talented women participated in many sports, usually without adequate conditioning or training, without coaching, and certainly without high levels of organization. Before Title IX, there was hardly any support for women's athletics, and women's performances reflected this. For the most part, women's performance levels were far below the quality of men's. Today, women train hard; work with coaches on conditioning, technique, and strategy; travel extensively to high-level competitions; go to college on scholarships; and even turn professional. Women's athletics has changed from a "play day" approach to a highly competitive business. As reported in chapter 3, women's performances have improved significantly. Today, women's records are very close to those of men because women's opportunities to train, to be coached, and to specialize in sports, often at a very early age, have improved.

Unfortunately, along with these "improvements" have come some less desirable changes.

The training that is necessary to become truly competitive is so intense today that being a champion performer often means being thoroughly dedicated at an early age. Of course, this is also true in other fields of endeavor, such as music, theater, and art, but these are far less physically demanding. The effort and dedication necessary to excel in sport requires a fine balance between training, diet, and rest. There is a delicate edge between being finely tuned for performance and being so physically stressed and fatigued that health problems result. In my opinion, we are seeing evidence of this today in many avenues of women's sport. It is not at all uncommon to hear of menstrual irregularities, eating disorders, and stress injuries. What is the reason for this?

Relative Energy Drain

The term *relative energy drain* (see chapter 8) is used here to indicate a multifactorial situation in which physical and psychological stressors are not adequately balanced by the quality and quantity of one's dietary intake, sleep, rest, and relaxation. In short, the physical and psychological needs of the body (and mind) are not in proper balance: there is a relative energy drain.

The concept of relative energy drain is not a new one. It has been used in various forms to explain the fluctuation in population dynamics in such diverse fields as wildlife biology and anthropology. For example, if deer face starvation because of a long-term drought, the females fail to conceive that season. They must search for food more extensively and, if they survive, will conceive in another season when the food supply is improved. The herd will thus survive. Similar explanations have been offered in terms of human survival in hunter-gatherer societies. It is well documented that women facing starvation temporarily become infertile by losing menstrual function. When food is more plentiful, they regain menstrual function, successfully conceive, and bear normal children. Thus, the tribe survives. I contend that the same thing is occurring today in many female athletes. I refer to this as relative energy drain. A possible scenario might be as follows.

A female athlete (a gymnast or runner perhaps) is successful during her high school years and subsequently receives a college scholarship. Her college coach has a history of being very successful (in fact, that is why the athlete chose this college over others) and is highly motivated to continue producing winning teams and outstanding performers. Ritual team weigh-ins (often including skinfold measurements) are held each week because an important factor, body weight, has been identified with excellent performance. Our hypothetical athlete dreads these weekly weigh-ins (as do her teammates). The coach is adamant that body weight and body fat be monitored very carefully and threatens that athletes will be removed from the team if they exceed certain arbitrary weight or body fat levels. There is little understanding by either the coach or the athletes regarding the limitations of the body weight or skinfold measurements in assessing body composition. The coach constantly admonishes the athletes to lose weight but gives little guidance regarding a suitable diet. Most of the athletes eat cafeteria-style dorm food, fast foods at the student union, or packaged foods from the grocery store that are quick and easy to prepare. Typical college social life encourages the frequent consumption of pizza, ice cream, soda, and beer. Typically, college students (even athletes) gain weight (the freshman 15!) and experience considerable stress associated with that weight gain.

Two sorts of behaviors often develop in this kind of situation. Excessive and compulsive training practices are used to expend calories and lose weight, or extreme dietary habits (psychogenic eating disorders) develop (see chapter 13). In either case, body weight is lost, sometimes with a corresponding loss of lean body mass (including muscle mass). With relative energy drain there is a loss of both body fat and lean body mass. At the same time, psychological stresses are quite high: the need to maintain good grades, the normal stresses of college life, and the excessive stress imposed by the coach to maintain a preconceived body weight or fat level as well as to improve performance—and the need to hide all this from the scrutiny of others.

The physiological ramifications are considerable. Usually the athlete becomes quite thin and sometimes even emaciated (but often a well-developed muscular appearance hides this). Menstrual function is lost (see chapter 8). Frequently (but not always), fatigue and overtraining occur, and performance is "disappointing." This usually brings on further excesses. In other instances, considerable success serves to reinforce the extraordinary behaviors of the athlete. Not unlikely, this scenario ends with a series of overuse injuries to the musculoskeletal system that is frequently characterized by a stress fracture (see chapter 15). The result is an injured athlete who cannot complete the season or whose performance is seriously compromised.

It is my belief that variations on this scenario occur throughout women's sports today at both professional and amateur levels. It is commonplace to read of the recurring injuries of famous female athletes, most of whom are extremely thin, well trained, and amenorrheic.

The high incidence of musculoskeletal injuries in amenorrheic athletes with eating disorders stems from their loss of bone mineral (see chapters 8 and 15). This occurs despite their high levels of exercise, primarily because they are hypoestrogenic. Dietary factors are secondary and include consuming insufficient calories, too little calcium and iron, too much fat in relation to total caloric intake (particularly saturated fat), and too few complex carbohydrates. Additional factors (which remain undocumented in the scientific literature) include inadequate rest and recovery from heavy training and high levels of psychological stress.

What can be done to halt this devastating cycle of events? The problem involves many factors and thus requires a multifactorial approach. I suggest the following:

- Professional associations (including coaches' associations) must take the position that extreme pressures to perform must not take the form of imposing body weight, body composition, or dietary restrictions on athletes (both men and women). Coaches must be educated about the dangers of imposing such restrictions on athletes in terms of injury and performance. A balance must be sought between the demands on the body and the ability to recuperate. Instead of restrictions being imposed, a means must be found by which dietary guidance and health-promoting foods can be made available to the athletes. I suggest that every team and coach have access to the services of a registered dietitian. Both coaches and athletes need considerable guidance in regard to the nutritional demands of training and proper food selection for health and performance. I contend that physical conditioning and the development of outstanding skill and technique go hand in hand with rest and optimal nutrition.

- In addition, coaches and athletes must be more accurately informed regarding the validity and reliability of the various techniques of assessing body composition that are available today. Many believe that these methods are infallible. In my opinion, many coaches impose strict body weight or body fat restrictions on their athletes while being ignorant of the possible effects of these restrictions on their athletes. Such lack of knowledge must be eliminated. When the dangers of such practices are fully realized, only those coaches who are solely interested in winning at all costs will continue to impose extreme restrictions on their athletes. This, in time, will be seen as unethical behavior.

- Many universities have "training tables" available for athletes in the high-revenue sports (i.e., men's football and basketball). Of course, this is a discriminatory practice. It should be not eliminated but expanded to include *all* athletes rather than a select few. Such a practice should be coupled not only with the availability of high-quality foods but also with dietary advice and information. This has been done quite successfully at the U.S.

Olympic Training Center in Colorado Springs. Certainly the monitoring of body weight or body fat levels of athletes should not be done without corresponding dietary advice and the means for providing a good diet.

- Female athletes (and their coaches) should be informed of the potential dangers of long-term amenorrhea (often viewed as a blessing) to their ultimate bone health and potential risk for injury. Many athletes remain completely unaware of the possible relationship between their high incidence of injury and their menstrual dysfunction and dietary habits. Furthermore, female athletes must be made aware of their personal rights in regard to issues that affect their future health and welfare.

- The American system of integrating the knowledge gained from exercise science and sports medicine with the practical aspects of coaching leaves much to be desired. It is ironic that the nation that contributes most to the development of the scientific and medical aspects of sport fails so miserably in delivering that knowledge to the athlete and coach. It is my opinion that intermediary positions between scientists and coaches need to be created to bridge the gap between available scientific knowledge and improved practical application. This task could be within the realm of the U.S. Olympic Committee and the various national governing bodies of national sport associations. The President's Council on Physical Fitness and Sports could also play a more active role, as could a wide variety of professional and medical associations.

Optimistic Signs in Women's Sports

Despite such discouraging information as the continuing decline in the number of women coaches,

the increasing fatness of American society in general (and of women in particular), and the fact that only about 20% of Americans are physically active, I remain optimistic about the future role of women in sport for the following five reasons:

1. Women's performance levels are improving rapidly.
2. Intercollegiate athletics for women appears to be quite healthy even though there has been a general cutback in minor sports (this is also true in men's sports).
3. Opportunities for older women to engage in masters competitions (e.g., tennis, swimming, walking, running, cycling, and triathlon) are increasing.
4. More events are added to each Olympiad that are specifically for women.
5. Women are becoming more interested in health and fitness, at least white women in the middle to upper socioeconomic levels. There are encouraging signs that we may be eating better (e.g., increasing awareness of the high levels of saturated fat in our diets) than in previous years. And it is fashionable today to wear athletic clothes and shoes, which implies that women are at least interested in looking like they are physically active (a good first step).

Nevertheless, much remains to be done to increase the physical activity levels of women, especially minority women, poor women, women in the inner cities, handicapped women, elderly women, women living in rural communities, and the millions of overweight women who are at high risk for chronic disease. This will require the continued effort of everyone interested in exercise, sport, and the health and welfare of women everywhere.

Appendix

American College of Sports Medicine Opinion Statement on

The Participation of the Female Athlete in Long-Distance Running

In the Olympic Games and other international contests, female athletes run distances ranging from 100 meters to 3,000 meters, whereas male athletes run distances ranging from 100 meters through 10,000 meters as well as the marathon (42.2 km). The limitation on distance for women's running events has been defended at times on the grounds that long-distance running may be harmful to the health of girls and women.

Opinion Statement

It is the opinion of the American College of Sports Medicine that females should not be denied the opportunity to compete in long-distance running. There exists no conclusive scientific or medical evidence that long-distance running is contraindicated for the healthy, trained female athlete. The American College of Sports Medicine recommends that females be allowed to compete at the national and international level in the same distances in which their male counterparts compete.

Supportive Information

Studies (10, 20, 32, 41, 54) have shown that females respond in much the same manner as males to systematic exercise training. Cardiorespiratory function is improved as indicated by significant increases in maximal oxygen uptake (4, 6, 13, 16, 30). At maximal exercise, stroke volume and cardiac output are increased after training (30). At standardized submaximal exercise intensities after training, cardiac output remains unchanged, heart rate decreases, and stroke volume increases (6, 30, 31). Also, resting heart rate decreases after training (30). As is the case for males, relative body fat content is reduced consequent to systematic endurance training (33, 35, 51).

Long-distance running imposes a significant thermal stress on the participant. Some differences do exist between males and females with regard to thermoregulation during prolonged exercise. However, the differences in thermal stress response are more quantitative than qualitative in nature (36, 38, 47). For example, women experience lower evaporative heat losses than do men exposed to the same thermal stress (29, 40, 53) and usually have higher skin temperatures and deep body temperatures upon onset of sweating (3, 18, 45). This may actually be an advantage in reducing body water loss so long as thermal equilibrium can be maintained. In view of current findings (10, 11, 15, 40, 48, 49, 50), it appears that earlier studies which indicated that women were less tolerant to exercise in the heat than men (36, 53) were misleading because they failed to consider the women's relatively low level of cardiorespiratory fitness and heat acclimatization. Apparently, cardiorespiratory fitness as measured by maximum oxygen uptake is a most important functional capacity as regards a person's ability to respond adequately to thermal stress (9, 11, 15. 47). In fact, there has been considerable interest in the seeming cross-adaptation of life style characterized by physical activity involving regular and prolonged periods of exercise hyperthermia and response to high environmental temperatures (1, 37, 39). Women trained in long-distance running have been reported to be more tolerant of heat stress than nonathletic women matched for age and body surface area (15). Thus, it appears that trained female long-distance runners have the capacity to deal with the thermal stress of prolonged exercise as well as the moderate-to-high environmental temperatures and relative humidities that often accompany these events.

The participation of males and females in road races of various distances has increased tremendously during the last decade. This type of competition attracts the entire spectrum of runners with respect to ability—from the elite to the novice. A common feature of virtually all of these races is that a small number of participants develop medical problems (primarily heat injuries) which frequently require hospitalization. One of the first documentations of the medical problems associated with mass participation in this form of athletic competition was by Sutton and co-workers (46). Twenty-nine of 2,005 entrants in the 1971 Sydney City-to-Surf race collapsed; seven required hospitalization. All of the entrants who collapsed

were males, although 4% of the race entrants were females. By 1978 the number of entrants increased approximately 10 fold with females accounting for approximately 30% of the entrants. In the 1978 race only nine entrants were treated for heat injury and again all were males (43). In a 1978 Canadian road race, in which 1,250 people participated, 15 entrants developed heat injuries—three females and 12 males, representing 1.3% and 1.2% of the total number of female and male entrants, respectively (27). Thus, females seem to tolerate the physiological stress of road race competition at least as well as males.

Because long-distance running competition sometimes occurs at moderate altitudes, the female's response to an environment where the partial pressure of oxygen is reduced (hypoxia) should be considered. Buskirk (5) noted that, although there is little information about the physiological responses of women to altitude, the proportional reduction in performance at Mexico City during the Pan American and Olympic Games was the same for males and females. Drinkwater et al. (13) found that women mountaineers exposed to hypoxia demonstrated a similar decrement in maximal oxygen uptake as that predicted for men. Hannon et al. (23, 24) have found that females tolerate the effects of altitude better than males because there appears to be both a lower frequency and shorter duration of mountain sickness in women. Furthermore, at altitude women experience less alteration in such variables as resting heart rate, body weight, blood volume, electrocardiograms, and blood chemistries than men (23, 24). Although one study has reported that women and men experience approximately the same respiratory changes with altitude exposure (44), another (22) reports that women hyperventilate more than men, thereby increasing the partial pressure of arterial oxygen and decreasing the partial pressure of arterial carbon dioxide. Thus, females tolerate the stress of altitude at least as well as men.

Long-distance running is occasionally associated with various overuse syndromes such as stress fracture, chondromalacia, shinsplints, and tendonitis. Pollock et al. (42) have shown that the incidence of these injuries for males engaged in a program of jogging was as high as 54% and was related to the frequency, duration, and intensity of the exercise training. Franklin et al. (19) recently reported the injury incidence of 42 sedentary females exposed to a 12-week jogging program. The injury rate for the females appeared to be comparable to that found for males in other studies although, as the investigators indicated, a decisive interpretation of presently available information may be premature because of the limited orthopedic injury data available for women. It has been suggested that the anatomical differences between men's and women's pelvic width and joint laxity may lead to a higher incidence of injuries for women who run (26). There are no data available, however, to support this suggestion. Whether or not the higher intensity training programs of competitive male and female long-distance runners result in a difference in injury rate between the sexes is not known at this time. It is believed, however, that the incidence of injury is due to running surfaces encountered, biomechanics of the back, leg and foot, and to foot apparel (28).

Of particular concern to female competitors and to the American College of Sports Medicine is evidence which indicates that approximately one-third of the competitive female long-distance runners between the ages of 12 and 45 experience amenorrhea or oligomenorrhea for at least brief periods (7, 8). This phenomenon appears more frequently in those women with late onset of menarche, who have not experienced pregnancy, or who have taken contraceptive hormones. This same phenomenon also occurs in some competing gymnasts, swimmers, and professional ballerinas as well as sedentary individuals who have experienced some instances of undue stress or severe psychological trauma (25). Apparently, amenorrhea and oligomenorrhea may be caused by many factors characterized by loss of body weight (7, 21, 25). Running long distances may lead to decreased serum levels of pituitary gonadotrophic hormones in some women and may directly or indirectly lead to amenorrhea or oligomenorrhea. The role of running and the pathogenesis of these menstrual irregularities remains unknown (7, 8).

The long-term effects of these types of menstrual irregularities for young girls that have undergone strenuous exercise training are unknown at this time. Eriksson and co-workers (17) have reported, however, that a group of 28 young girl swimmers, who underwent strenuous swim training for 2.5 years, were normal in all respects (e.g., childbearing) 10 years after discontinuing training.

In summary, a review of the literature demonstrates that males and females adapt to exercise training in a similar manner. Female distance runners are characterized by having large maximal oxygen uptakes and low relative body fat content (52). The challenges of the heat stress of long-distance running or the lower partial pressure of oxygen at altitude seem to be well tolerated by females. The limited data available suggest that females, compared to males, have about the same incidence of orthopedic injuries consequent to endurance training. Disruption of the menstrual cycle is a common problem for female athletes. While it is important to recognize this problem and discover its etiology, no evidence exists to indicate that this is harmful to the female reproductive system.

Abbreviations

AAHPER or AAHPERD—American Alliance for Health, Physical Education, Recreation and Dance

A—Androstenedione

ACOG—American College of Obstetricians and Gynecologists

ACS—American Cancer Society

ACSM—American College of Sports Medicine

ACTH—Adrenocorticotropic hormone

AHA—American Heart Association

AMA—American Medical Association

AT—Anaerobic threshold

ATP—Adenosine triphosphate (the major energy substrate)

$a-\bar{v}O_2$—Arterial minus mixed venous oxygen difference

BE—Bicycle ergometer

Db—Body density

BMC—bone mineral content

BMD—Bone mineral density

BMI—Body mass index (weight/height^2)

BMR—Basal metabolic rate

bpm—Beats per minute (heart rate)

BSA—Body surface area (in square meters)

b.w.—Body weight

Ca—Calcium

CAT—Computed axial tomography

CHD—Coronary heart disease

CHOL—Cholesterol

CP—Creatine phosphate

CSA—Cross-sectional area

DHEA, DHEAS—Dehydroepiandrosterone, DHEA sulfate

DHEW—Department of Health, Education, and Welfare

dl—Deciliter

E, E$_1$, E$_2$—Estrogen, estrone, 17 β-estradiol

Epi—Epinephrine

ERT—Estrogen replacement therapy

F—Cortisol

Fe—Iron

FFA—Free fatty acid

FFB—Fat-free body

FFM—Fat-free mass

FG—Fast-twitch glycolytic muscle fiber

FHR—Fetal heart rate

FOG—Fast-twitch oxidative-glycolytic muscle fiber

FSH—Follicle-stimulating hormone

g—Gram

GnRH—Gonadotropin-releasing hormone

Hb—Hemoglobin

Hct—Hemocrit

HDL-C—High-density lipoprotein cholesterol

HDL-2—Subfraction 2 of high-density lipoprotein

HGH—Human growth hormone

HR—Heart rate (beats per minute)

HRmax—Heart rate maximum

%HRmax—Percent heart rate maximum

IUD—Intrauterine device

kcal—Kilocalorie

kg—Kilogram

L—Liter

LBM—Lean body mass

LDL-C—Low-density lipoprotein cholesterol

LH—luteinizing hormone

LT—Lactate threshold

M—Mean (or average) value

m^2—Square meter

MBC—Maximum breathing capacity

MET—Metabolic equivalent, equal to 3.5 milliliters of oxygen per kilogram of body weight per minute ($ml \cdot kg^{-1} \cdot min^{-1}$)

mg—Milligram

ml—Milliliter

mm—Millimeter

NAIRS—National Athletic Injury/Illness Reporting System

NCAA—National Collegiate Athletic Association

NCYFS—National Children and Youth Fitness Study

NE—Norepinephrine

O_2 pulse—Oxygen pulse (oxygen uptake per heart beat)

OC—Oral contraceptive

$\dot{Q}$—Cardiac output

$\dot{Q}_{max}$—Maximal cardiac output

P—Progesterone

PMS—Premenstrual syndrome

PRL—Prolactin

PWC—Physical working capacity

R—Respiratory exchange ratio

r—Correlation coefficient

RBC—Red blood cell

RDA—Recommended daily allowance

RV—Residual lung volume

SD—Standard deviation

SDH—Succinate dehydrogenase, an oxidative mitochondrial enzyme

SHBG—Sex hormone–binding globulin

ST—Slow-twitch muscle fiber (oxidative)

SV—Stroke volume of the heart (quantity of blood pumped per beat)

SV_{max}—Stroke volume maximum

T—Testosterone

TM—Treadmill

THR—Training heart rate

TRH—Thyrotrophic releasing hormone

TLC—Total lung capacity

TV—Tidal volume of lung

μg—Microgram

VC—Vital lung capacity

$\dot{V}_E$—Minute volume of respiration ($L \cdot min^{-1}$)

VLDL-C—Very low density lipoprotein cholesterol

$\dot{V}O_2$—Oxygen consumption or uptake ($L \cdot min^{-1}$, $ml \cdot kg^{-1}$ body weight $\cdot min^{-1}$, or $ml \cdot kg^{-1}$ LBM $\cdot min^{-1}$)

$\dot{V}O_2max$—Maximal oxygen uptake

%$\dot{V}O_2max$—Percent of maximal oxygen uptake

Glossary

Adipocyte—Fat cell or adipose tissue cell

Adipose tissue—Fat tissue

Aerobic—Requires metabolic processes that utilize oxygen

Aerobic power—See Maximal oxygen uptake

Amenorrhea—Cessation of menstrual function without menopause

Anaerobic—Utilizes metabolic processes that do not utilize oxygen

Anaerobic power—Explosive power; the ability to perform anaerobic work

Anaerobic threshold—The initial appearance of elevated venous blood lactate

Body composition—The description of the components of the body, usually the lean body mass and the percent body fat (by weight)

Climacteric—The gradual transition from the reproductive stage to the nonreproductive stage

Cooper's droop—Sagging breasts (ptosis)

Cooper's ligaments—Fibrous bands within the breast that serve to support the glandular and fatty tissue and that divide the breast into lobules

Dysmenorrhea—Painful menstrual periods

Ectomorphy—The linear component of body build

Endometriosis—Occurrence of endometrial tissue outside the uterus

Endometrium—Inner lining of the uterus that undergoes cyclic changes during the menstrual cycle

Endomorphy—The fat (roundness) component of body build

Eumenorrhea—Normal menstrual function

Graffian follicle—The maturing primary oocyte from which an ova will come

Hyperlipidemia—Having excess serum lipids

Hypertrophy—Enlargement from normal size

Lean body—The "metabolically active part of the body, the muscles, bone, nervous tissue, organs

Lipolysis—The liberation of free fatty acids from adipose tissue

Lipoprotein—A form of lipid and protein in blood, as in high- and low-density-lipoprotein cholesterol

Maximal oxygen uptake—The maximal amount of oxygen that one can utilize through the oxidative process per minute ($l \cdot min^{-1}$, $ml \cdot kg^{-1}$ body weight $\cdot min^{-1}$, or $ml \cdot kg^{-1}$ LBM $\cdot min^{-1}$)

Menarche—First menstrual flow

Menopause—Last menstrual flow

Menses—Menstrual flow

Mesomorphy—The muscular component of body build

Morphology—The study of the structure of the body

Obesity—The state of being overly fat

Oligomenorrhea—Scanty and/or infrequent menstrual flow

Osteoporosis—The loss of bone density, usually occurring after menopause

Overweight—Having a body weight in excess of the standard for one's height, body frame, sex, and age

Oxygen pulse—Quantity of oxygen consumed per heartbeat

Pelvic diaphragm—The muscles and connective tissue of the pelvic outlet

Perimenopause—The period of time surrounding the menopause (approximately ages 45-55 years)

Physique—Body build (sometimes quantified by a somatotype)

Prolapse—A "fallen" organ (usually the uterus, bladder, or rectum)

Somatotype—A quantitative description of physique or body build

Triglycerides—A form for fatty acid transport in blood; a molecule of glycerol with three fatty acids attached by an ester bond

Bibliography

Abitbol, M.M. (1969). Weight gain in pregnancy. *American Journal of Obstetrics and Gynecology,* **104**, 140-157.

Abraham, G. (1974). Ovarian and adrenal contribution to peripheral androgens during the menstrual cycle. *Journal of Clinical Endocrinology and Metabolism,* **39**, 340-346.

Abraham, S.F., Beaumont, P.J.V., Fraser, I.S., & Llewellyn-Jones, D. (1982). Body weight, exercise, and menstrual status among ballet dancers in training. *British Journal of Obstetrics and Gynecology,* **89**, 507-510.

Acosta, R.V., & Carpenter, L.J. (1988). *Women in intercollegiate sport: A longitudinal study—Eleven year update.* Unpublished manuscript, Brooklyn College, Brooklyn.

Adams, G.M., & deVries, H.A. (1973). Physiological effects of an exercise training regimen upon women aged 52-70. *Journal of Gerontology,* **28**, 50-55.

Adams, M.M., Porcello, L.P., & Vivian, V.M. (1982). Effect of a supplement on dietary intakes of female swimmers. *The Physician and Sportsmedicine,* **10**(7), 122-124.

Adrian, M. (1980). Protection for the female athlete. *Athletic Purchasing and Facilities,* **4**, 74, 76.

Adrian, M. (1972). Sex differences in biomechanics. In D.V. Harris (Ed.), *Women and sport: A national research conference* (pp. 289-297) (HPER Series No. 2). University Park: Pennsylvania State University.

Aftergood, L., & Alfin-Slater, R.B. (1980). Women and nutrition. *Contemporary Nutrition,* **5**(3), n.p.

Aisenbrey, J.A. (1987). Exercise in the prevention and management of osteoporosis. *Physical Therapy,* **67**, 1100-1104.

Alaily, A.B., & Carrol, K.B. (1978). Pulmonary ventilation in pregnancy. *British Journal of Obstetrics and Gynecology,* **85**, 518-524.

Allsen, P.E., Parsons, P., & Bryce, G.R. (1977). Effect of the menstrual cycle on maximum oxygen uptake. *The Physician and Sportsmedicine,* **5**(7), 53-55.

Aloia, J.F., Cohn, S.H., Ostuni, J.A., Cane, R., & Ellis, K. (1978). Prevention of involutional bone loss by exercise. *Annals of Internal Medicine,* **89**, 356-358.

American Alliance for Health, Physical Education, Recreation and Dance. (1976). *AAHPERD Youth Fitness Test manual* (rev. ed.). Reston, VA: Author.

American Alliance for Health, Physical Education, Recreation and Dance. (1980). *Lifetime Health Related Physical Fitness Test manual.* Reston, VA: Author.

American Cancer Society. (1984). Nutrition and cancer: Cause and Prevention—a special report. *Cancer Journal of Clinicians,* **34**, 121.

American College Health Association. (1984). *Eating disorders.* Rockville, MD: Author.

American College of Obstetricians and Gynecologists. (1985). *Exercise during pregnancy and the postnatal period.* Washington, DC: Author.

American College of Physicians. (1986). Eating disorders: Anorexia nervosa and bulimia [Position paper]. *Annals of Internal Medicine,* **105**, 790-794.

American College of Sports Medicine. (1979).

The participation of the female athlete in long-distance running [Opinion statement]. *Medicine and Science in Sports,* **11**(4), ix-xi.

American Dietetic Association. (1986). The American Dietetic Association's nutrition recommendations for women. *Journal of the American Dietetic Association,* **86**, 1663-1664.

American Dietetic Association. (1987). Position of the American Dietetic Association: Nutrition for physical fitness and athletic performance for adults. *Journal of the American Dietetic Association,* **87**(7), 933-939.

American Heart Association. (1972). *Exercise testing and training in apparently healthy individuals: A handbook for physicians.* Dallas: Author.

American Heart Association. (1987). Dietary guidelines for healthy American adults: A statement for physicians and health professionals by the Nutrition Committee, American Heart Association. *Circulation,* **74**, 1465A-1468A.

Andersen, H.T., & Barkve, H. (1970). Iron deficiency and muscular work performance. *Scandinavian Journal of Clinical and Laboratory Investigation,* **25**(Suppl. 114), 1-62.

Anderson, T. (1965). Swimming and exercise during menstruation. *Journal of Health, Physical Education, and Recreation,* **36**(8), 66-68.

Anderson, M., Coté, R., Coyle, E., & Roby, F. (1979). Leg power, muscle strength, and peak EMG activity in physically active college men and women. *Medicine and Science in Sports,* **11**, 81-82.

Andres, R., Elahi, D., Tobin, J.D., Muller, D.C., & Brant, L. (1985). Impact of age on weight goals. *Annals of Internal Medicine,* **103**(6, Pt. 2), 1030-1033.

Artal, R., Platt, L.D., Sperling, M., Kammula, R.K., Jilek, J., & Nakamura, R. (1980, October). *Maternal exercise: I. Cardiovascular and metabolic responses in normal pregnancy.* Paper presented at the meeting of the Pacific Coast Obstetrical and Gynecological Society, Monterey, CA.

Artal, R., Rutherford, S., Romem, Y., Kammula, R.K., Dorey, F.J., & Wiswell, R.A. (1986). Fetal heart rate responses to maternal exercise. *American Journal of Obstetrics and Gynecology,* **155**, 729-733.

Artal, R., & Wiswell, R.A. (Eds.) (1986). *Exercise in pregnancy.* Baltimore: Williams & Wilkins.

Artal, R., Wiswell, R., Romem, Y., & Dorey, F. (1986). Pulmonary responses to exercise in pregnancy. *American Journal of Obstetrics and Gynecology,* **154**, 378-383.

Åstrand, I. (1960). Aerobic capacity in men and women with special reference to age. *Acta Physiologica Scandinavia,* **49**(Suppl. 169), 1-92.

Åstrand, P.-O., Cuddy, T.E., Saltin, B., & Stenberg, J. (1964). Cardiac output during submaximal and maximal work. *Journal of Applied Physiology,* **19**, 268-274.

Åstrand, P.-O., Engström, I., Eriksson, B.O., Karlberg, P., Nylander, I., Saltin, B., & Thorén, C. (1963). Girl swimmers, with special reference to respiratory and circulatory adaptation and gynaecological and psychiatric aspects. *Acta Paediatrica Scandinavia* (Suppl. 147), 1-75.

Åstrand, P.-O., & Rodahl, K. (1977). *Textbook of work physiology* (2nd ed.). New York: McGraw-Hill.

Atomi, Y., Ito, K., Iwasaki, H., & Miyashita, M. (1978). Effects of intensity and frequency of training on aerobic work capacity of young females. *Journal of Sports Medicine and Physical Fitness,* **18**, 3-9.

Atwater, A.E. (1988). Biomechanics and the female athlete. In J. Puhl, C.H. Brown, & R.O. Voy (Eds.), *Sport science perspectives for women* (pp. 1-12). Champaign, IL: Human Kinetics.

Auster, M. (1944). *The menstrual function of college women.* Unpublished master's thesis,

Pennsylvania State University, University Park.

Baechle, T.R. (1984). Women in resistance training. *Clinics in Sports Medicine, 3*(4), 791-808.

Baker, E.R., Mathur, R.S., Kirk, R.F., & Williamson, H.O. (1981). Female runners and secondary amenorrhea: Correlation with age, parity, mileage, and plasma hormonal and sex-hormone-binding globulin concentrations. *Fertility and Sterility, 36*, 183-187.

Bale, P., & McNaught-Davis, P. (1983). The physiques, fitness and strength of top class women hockey players. *Journal of Sports Medicine and Physical Fitness, 23*, 80-88.

Ballet dancers' injuries pose sportsmedicine challenge. (1976). *The Physician and Sportsmedicine, 4*(11), 44-57.

Bannister, E.W., & Brown, S.R. (1968). The relative energy requirements of physical activity. In H.B. Falls (Ed.), *Exercise Physiology.* New York: Academic Press.

Barnes, L. (1979). Preadolescent training—How young is too young? *The Physician and Sportsmedicine, 7*(10), 114-119.

Bar-Or, O. (1983). *Pediatric sports medicine for the practitioner.* New York: Springer.

Bar-Or, O. (1988). The prepubescent female. In M. Shangold & G. Mirkin (Eds.), *Women and exercise: Physiology and sports medicine* (pp. 109-119). Philadelphia: F.A. Davis.

Barrett-Connor, E. (1987). Postmenopausal estrogen, cancer and other considerations. In *Women and Cancer* (pp. 179-195, Vol. 11 [3-4] of *Women and Health* series). New York: The Haworth Press.

Barry, A.J., Daly, J.W., Pruett, E.D.R., Steinmetz, J.R., Page, H.F., Birkhead, N.C., & Rodahl, K. (1966). The effects of physical conditioning on older individuals. I. Work capacity, circulatory-respiratory function, and electrocardiogram. *Journal of Gerontology, 21*, 182-191.

Bates, G.W. (1981). On the nature of the hot flash.

Clinical Obstetrics and Gynecology, 24, 231-241.

Beals, R.K. (1976). The normal carrying angle of the elbow. *Clinical Orthopaedics, 119*, 194-196.

Becklake, M.R., Frank, H., Dagenais, G.R., Ostiguy, G.L., & Guzman, C.A. (1965). Influence of age and sex on exercise cardiac output. *Journal of Applied Physiology, 20*, 938-947.

Behnke, A.R. (1969). New concepts in height-weight relationships. In N. Wilson (Ed.), *Obesity.* Philadelphia: F.A. Davis.

Behnke, A.R., & Wilmore, J.H. (1974). *Evaluation and regulation of body build and composition.* Englewood Cliffs, NJ: Prentice-Hall.

Belko, A.Z., Meredith, M.P., Kalkwarf, H.J., Obarzanek, E., Weinberg, S., Roach, R., McKeon, G., & Roe, D.A. (1985). Effects of exercise on riboflavin requirements: Biological validation in weight reducing women. *American Journal of Clinical Nutrition, 41*, 270-277.

Belko, A.Z., Obarzanek, E., Kalkwarf, J.H., Rotter, M.A., Bogusz, S., Miller, D., Haas, J.D., & Roe, D.A. (1983). Effects of exercise on riboflavin requirements of young women. *American Journal of Clinical Nutrition, 37*, 509-517.

Bengtsson, E. (1956). The working capacity in normal children, evaluated by submaximal exercise on the bicycle ergometer and compared with adults. *Acta Medica Scandinavica, 154*, 91-109.

Benson, J., Gillien, D.M., Bourdet, K., & Loosli, A.R. (1985). Inadequate nutrition and chronic calorie restriction in adolescent ballerinas. *The Physician and Sportsmedicine, 13*(10), 79-90.

Berkowitz, G.S., Kelsey, J.L., Holford, T.R., & Berkowitz, R.L. (1983). Physical activity and the risk of spontaneous preterm delivery. *Journal of Reproductive Medicine, 28*, 581-588.

Billewicz, W.Z., Fellowes, H.M., & Hytten, C.A. (1976). Comments on the critical metabolic mass and the age of menarche. *Annals of Human Biology, 3*, 51-59.

Birch, W.G. (1980). *A doctor discusses pregnancy.* Chicago: Budlong Press.

Bishop, P., Cureton, K., & Collins, M. (1987). Sex difference in muscular strength in equally-trained men and women. *Ergonomics, 30*, 675-687.

Björntorp, P., deJounge, K., Krotkiewski, M., Sullivan, L., Sjöstrom, L., & Stenberg, J. (1973). Physical training in human obesity: III. Effects of long-term physical training on body composition. *Metabolism, 22*, 1467-1475.

Black, D.R., & Burckes-Miller, M.E. (1988). Male and female college athletes: Use of anorexia nervosa and bulimia nervosa weight loss methods. *Research Quarterly for Exercise and Sport, 59*, 252-256.

Blair, S.N., Lavey, R.S., Goodyear, N., Gibbons, L.W., & Cooper, K.H. (1984). Physiologic responses to maximal graded exercise testing in apparently healthy white women aged 18 to 75 years. *Journal of Cardiac Rehabilitation, 4*, 459-468.

Block, J.E., Smith, R., Black, D., & Genant, H.K. (1987). Does exercise prevent osteoporosis? *Journal of the American Medical Association, 257*, 3115-3117.

Blum, S.M., Sherman, A.R., & Boileau, R.A. (1986). The effects of fitness-type exercise on iron status in adult women. *American Journal of Clinical Nutrition, 43*, 456-463.

Blumenthal, J.A., O'Toole, L.C., & Chang, J.L. (1984). Is running an analogue of anorexia nervosa? An empirical study of obligatory running and anorexia nervosa. *Journal of the American Medical Association, 252*, 520-523.

Boileau, R.A., Lohman, T.G., Slaughter, M.H., Ball, T.E., Going, S.B., & Hendrix, M.K. (1984). Hydration of the fat-free body in children during maturation. *Human Biology, 56*, 651-666.

Bone mineral densitometry. (1987). [Position statement of the American College of Physicians]. *Annals of Internal Medicine, 107*, 932-936.

Bonen, A. (1986). Endocrine alterations with exercise and training. In J. Puhl & C.H. Brown (Eds.), *The menstrual cycle and physical activity* (pp. 81-100). Champaign, IL: Human Kinetics.

Bonen, A., Belcastro, A.N., Ling, W.Y., & Simpson, A.A. (1981). Profiles of selected hormones during menstrual cycles of teenaged athletes. *Journal of Applied Physiology: Respiratory, Environmental and Exercise Physiology, 50*(3), 545-551.

Bonen, A., Haynes, F.J., Watson-Wright, W., Sopper, M.M., Pierce, G.N., Low, M.P., & Graham, T.E. (1983). Effects of menstrual cycle on metabolic responses to exercise. *Journal of Applied Physiology: Respiratory, Environmental and Exercise Physiology, 55*, 1506-1513.

Bonen, A., & Keizer, H.A. (1984). Athletic menstrual cycle irregularity: Endocrine response to exercise and training. *The Physician and Sportsmedicine, 12*(8), 78-94.

Bonen, A., Ling, W.Y., MacIntyre, K.P., Neil, R., McGrail, J.C., & Belcastro, A.N. (1979). Effects of exercise on the serum concentrations of FSH, LH, progesterone, and estradiol. *European Journal of Applied Physiology, 42*, 15-23.

Booth, M.A., Booth, M.J., & Taylor, A.W. (1974). Rat fat cell size and number with exercise training, detraining and weight loss. *Federation Proceedings, 33*, 1959-1963.

Booyens, J., & Keatinge, W.R. (1957). The expenditure of energy by men and women walking. *Journal of Physiology (Lond.), 138*, 165-171.

Borgen, J.S., & Corbin, C.B. (1987). Eating disorders among female athletes. *The Physician and Sportsmedicine, 15*(2), 89-95.

Boyden, T.W., Pamenter, R.W., Grosso, D., Stanforth, P., Rotkis, T., & Wilmore, J.H. (1982). Prolactin responses, menstrual cycles, and body composition of women runners. *Journal of Clinical Endocrinology and Metabolism, 54*(4), 711-714.

Boyden, T.W., Pamenter, R.W., Stanforth, P., Rotkis, T., & Wilmore, J.H. (1983). Sex steroids and endurance running in women. *Fertility and Sterility, 39*, 629-632.

Bransford, D.R., & Howley, E.T. (1977). Oxygen cost of running in trained and untrained men and women. *Medicine and Science in Sports, 9*, 41-44.

Bransford, D.R., & Howley, E.T. (1979). Effects of training on plasma FFA during exercise in women. *European Journal of Applied Physiology, 41*, 151-158.

Bray, G.A. (1987). Overweight is risking fate: Definition, classification, prevalence, and risks. *Annals of the New York Academy of Sciences, 499*, 14-28.

Brisson, G.R., Dulac, S., Péronnet, F., & Ledoux, M. (1982). The onset of menarche: A late event in pubertal progression to be affected by physical training. *Canadian Journal of Applied Sport Sciences, 7*, 61-67.

Brisson, G.R., Volle, M.A., DeCarufel, D., Desharnais, M., & Tanaka, M. (1980). Exercise-induced dissociation of the blood prolactin response in young women according to their sports habits. *Hormones and Metabolic Research, 12*, 201-205.

Brook, C.G.D. (1985). *All about adolescence.* Chichester, England: Wiley.

Brooke, M., & Engel, W. (1969). The histographic analysis of human muscle biopsies with regard to fiber types. *Neurology, 19*, 221-233.

Brooks, S.M., Sanborn, C.F., Albrecht, B.H., & Wagner, W.W., Jr. (1984, March 10). Diet in athletic amenorrhoea. *Lancet, 1*(8376), 559-560.

Brooks-Gunn, J., Gargiulo, J.M., & Warren, M.P. (1986a). The effect of cycle phase on the performance of adolescent swimmers. *The Physician and Sportsmedicine, 14*(3), 182-192.

Brooks-Gunn, J., Gargiulo, J., & Warren, M.P.

(1986b). The menstrual cycle and athletic performance. In J.L. Puhl & C.H. Brown (Eds.), *The menstrual cycle and physical activity* (pp. 13-28). Champaign, IL: Human Kinetics.

Brown, C.H., Harrower, J.R., & Deeter, M.F. (1972). The effects of cross-country running on pre-adolescent girls. *Medicine and Science in Sports, 4*, 1-5.

Brown, C.H., & Wilmore, J.H. (1971). Physical and physiological profiles of champion women long distance runners [Abstract]. *Medicine and Science in Sports, 3*, h.

Brown, C.H., & Wilmore, J.H. (1974). The effects of maximal resistance training on the strength and body composition of women athletes. *Medicine and Science in Sports, 6*, 174-177.

Brownell, K.D., Bachorik, P.S., & Ayerle, R.S. (1982). Changes in plasma lipids and lipoprotein levels in men and women after a program of moderate exercise. *Circulation, 65*, 477-484.

Brownell, K.D., Rodin, J., & Wilmore, J.H. (1988). Eat, drink and be worried? *Runner's World, 23*(8), 28-34.

Brownlee, S. (1988, May 30). Moms in the fast lane. *Sports Illustrated*, pp. 57-60.

Bruce, R.A., & Johnson, W.P. (1961). Exercise tolerance in pregnant cardiac patients. *Clinical Obstetrics and Gynecology, 4*, 665-676.

Bruni, J.F., Van Vugt, D., Marshall, S., & Meites, J. (1977). Effects of nalozone, morphine and methionine enkephalin on serum prolactin, luteinizing hormone, follicle stimulating hormone, thyroid stimulating hormone and growth hormone. *Life Sciences, 21*, 461-466.

Bruser, M. (1968). Sporting activities during pregnancy. *Obstetrics and Gynecology, 32*, 721-725.

Buffington, C., Newman, J., Bonner, H., Acosta, D., & Farrar, R. (1977). Rat neonatal heart cell response to exercise during pregnancy [Abstract]. *Medicine and Science in Sports, 9*, 54.

Bullen, B.A., Skrinar, G.S., Beitins, I.Z., Carr, D.B., Reppert, S.M., Dotson, C.O., Fencl, M. de M., Gervino, E.V., & McArthur, J.W. (1984). Endurance training effects on plasma hormonal responsiveness and sex hormone excretion. *Journal of Applied Physiology: Respiratory, Environmental and Exercise Physiology,* **56**, 1453-1463.

Bullen, B.A., Skriner, G.S., Beitins, I.Z., von Mering, G., Turnbull, B.A., & McArthur, J.W. (1985). Induction of menstrual disorders by strenuous exercise in untrained women. *New England Journal of Medicine,* **312**, 1349-1353.

Burke, E.R. (1980). Physiological characteristics of competitive cyclists. *The Physician and Sportsmedicine,* **8**(7), 79-84.

Burke, E.R., & Brush, F.C. (1979). Physiological and anthropometric assessment of successful teenage female distance runners. *Research Quarterly,* **50**, 180-187.

Burke, E.R., Cerny, F., Costill, D.K., & Fink, W. (1977). Characteristics of skeletal muscle in competitive cyclists. *Medicine and Science in Sports,* **9**, 109-112.

Burkett, L.N.., Fernhall, B., & Walters, S.C. (1985). Physiologic effects of distance running training on teenage females. *Research Quarterly for Exercise and Sport,* **56**, 215-220.

Bush, T.L., & Barrett-Connor, E. (1985). Noncontraceptive estrogen use and cardiovascular disease. *Epidemiologic Reviews,* **7**, 80-104.

Bush, T.L., Cowan, L.D., Barrett-Connor, E., Criqui, M.H., Karon, J.M., Wallace, R.B., Tyroler, H.A., & Rifkind, B.M. (1983). Estrogen use and all-cause mortality. *Journal of the American Medical Association,* **249**, 903-906.

Butrum, R.R., Clifford, C.K., & Lanza, E. (1988). NCI dietary guidelines: Rationale. *American Journal of Clinical Nutrition,* **48**, 888-895.

Butts, N.K. (1982a). Physiological profiles of high school female cross-country runners. *Research Quarterly for Exercise and Sport,* **53**, 8-14.

Butts, N.K. (1982b). Physiological profile of high school female cross-country runners. *The Physician and Sportsmedicine,* **10**(11), 103-111.

Byrne-Quinn, E., Weil, I.V., Sodal, I.E., Filley, G.F., & Grover, R.F. (1971). Ventilatory control in the athlete. *Journal of Applied Physiology,* **30**, 91-98.

Byrnes, W.C. (1988). Female and male skeletal muscle fiber composition and performance. In J. Puhl, C.H. Brown, & R.O. Voy (Eds.), *Sport science perspectives for women* (pp. 23-35). Champaign, IL: Human Kinetics.

Calabrese, L.H., Kirkendall, D.T., Floyd, M., Rapoport, S., Williams, G.W., Weiker, G.G., & Bergfeld, J.A. (1983). Menstrual abnormalities, nutritional patterns and body composition in female classical ballet dancers. *The Physician and Sportsmedicine,* **11**(2), 86-98.

Calvert, R. (1979). *Athletic injuries and deaths in secondary schools and colleges, 1975-1976* (National Center for Education Statistics, Department of Health, Education, and Welfare). Washington, DC: U.S. Government Printing Office.

Cameron, N. (1976). Weight and skinfold variation at menarche and the critical body weight hypothesis. *Annals of Human Biology,* **3**, 279-282.

Cameron, W.J. (1982). Use of hormones for treatment of the menopausal female. *Advances in Clinical Obstetrics and Gynecology,* **1**, 219-224.

Campaigne, B.N. (1977). *Breast volume and body composition in females.* Unpublished master's thesis, University of Michigan, Ann Arbor.

Cann, C.E., Martin, M.C., Genant, H.K., & Jaffe, R.B. (1984). Decreased spinal mineral content in amenorrheic women. *Journal of the American Medical Association,* **251**, 626-629.

Capen, E.K., Bright, J.A., & Line, P.A. (1961). The effects of weight training on strength, power, muscular endurance, and anthropometric measurements on a selected group of college women. *Journal of the Association for Physical and Mental Rehabilitation,* **15**, 169-173, 180.

Carlberg, K.A., Buckman, M.T., Peake, G.T., & Riedesel, M.L. (1983). A survey of menstrual function in athletes. *European Journal of Applied Physiology,* **51**, 211-222.

Carr, D.B., Bullen, B.A., Skrinar, G.S., Arnold, M.A., Rosenblatt, M., Beitins, I.Z., Martin, J.B., & McArthur, J.W. (1981). Physical conditioning facilitates the exercise-induced secretion of beta-endorphin and beta-lipotrophin in women. *New England Journal of Medicine,* **305**, 560-563.

Carson, E. (1987). A young runner faces osteoporosis. *Women's Sports and Fitness,* **9**(1), 58-59.

Carter, J.E.L. (1981). Somatotypes of female athletes. *Medicine and Sport Science,* **15**, 85-116.

Cauley, J.A., LaPorte, R.E., Sandler, R.B., Orchard, T.J., Slemenda, C.W., & Petrini, A.M. (1986). The relationship of physical activity to high density lipoprotein cholesterol in postmenopausal women. *Journal of Chronic Diseases,* **39**, 687-697.

Cavanagh, J.R. (1963). *Fundamental marriage counseling: A catholic viewpoint.* Milwaukee: Bruce Publishing.

Cearly, M.L., Moffatt, R.J., & Knutzen, K.M. (1984). The effects of two- and three-day-per-week aerobic dance programs on maximal oxygen uptake. *Research Quarterly for Exercise and Sport,* **55**, 172-174.

Chamay, A., & Tschantz, P. (1972). Mechanical influence in bone remodelling. Experimental research on Wolff's Law. *Journal of Biomechanics,* **5**, 173-180.

Chambers, B. (1981). Fitness of dancers and varsity athletes. *Journal of Physical Education, Recreation and Dance,* **52**(5), 46-49.

Chang, R.J., & Judd, H.L. (1981). The ovary after menopause. *Clinical Obstetrics and Gynecology,* **24**, 181-191.

Chestnut, C.H. (1984). Treatment of postmenopausal osteoporosis. *Comprehensive Therapy,* **10**, 41-47.

Chmelar, R.D., Schultz, B.B., Ruhling, R.O., Shepherd, T.A., Zupan, M.F., & Fitt, S.S. (1988). A physiologic profile comparing levels and styles of female dancers. *The Physician and Sportsmedicine,* **16**(7), 87-96.

Cicero, T.J., Schainker, B.A., & Meyer, E.R. (1979). Endogenous opioids participate in the regulation of the hypothalamic-pituitary-luteinizing hormone axis and testosterone's negative feedback control of luteinizing hormone. *Endocrinology,* **104**, 1286-1291.

Cimons, M. (1981, July). How women got to run the distance, *Ms,* **10**(1), 47-50.

Clapp, J.F., III, & Dickstein, S. (1984). Endurance exercise and pregnancy outcome. *Medicine and Science in Sports and Exercise,* **16**, 556-562.

Clapp, J.F., III, Wesley, M., & Sleamaker, R.H. (1987). Thermoregulatory and metabolic responses to jogging prior to and during pregnancy. *Medicine and Science in Sports and Exercise,* **19**, 124-130.

Clark, N., Nelson, M., & Evans, W. (1988). Nutrition education for female runners. *The Physician and Sportsmedicine,* **16**(2), 124-136.

Clarke, H.H. (Ed.) (1975). Exercise and fat reduction. *Physical fitness research digest* (Series 5, No. 2). Washington, DC: President's Council on Physical Fitness and Sports.

Clarke, K.S., & Buckley, W.E. (1980). Women's injuries in collegiate sports: A preliminary comparative overview of three seasons. *American Journal of Sports Medicine,* **8**, 187-191.

Clarkson, P.M., Freedson, P.S., Keller, B., Carney, D., & Skrinar, M. (1985). Maximal oxygen uptake, nutritional patterns and body composition of adolescent female ballet dancers. *Research Quarterly for Exercise and Sport,* **56**, 180-184.

Clarkson, P.M., Graves, J., Melchionda, A.M., & Johnson, J. (1984). Isokinetic strength and endurance and muscle fiber type of elite oars-women. *Canadian Journal of Applied Sport Sciences, 9*, 127-132.

Clement, D.B., & Sawchuk, L.L. (1984). Iron status and sports performance. *Sports Medicine, 1*, 65-74.

Clement, D.B., Taunton, J.E., Smart, G.W., & McNicol, K.L. (1981). A survey of overuse running injuries. *The Physician and Sportsmedicine, 9*(5), 47-58.

Cohen, J.L., Gupta, P.K., Lichstein, E., & Chadda, K.D. (1980). The heart of a dancer: Noninvasive cardiac evaluation of professional ballet dancers. *American Journal of Cardiology, 45*, 959-965.

Cohen, J.L., Kim, C.S., May, P.B., & Ertel, N.H. (1982). Exercise, body weight, and professional ballet dancers. *The Physician and Sportsmedicine, 10*(4), 92-101.

Cohen, J.L., May, P.B., Kim, C.S., Ertel, N.J. (1980). Exercise and amenorrhea in professional ballet dancers. *Clinical Research, 28*(1), 23.

Cohen, J.L., Potosnak, L., Frank, O., & Baker, H. (1985). A nutritional and hematologic assessment of elite ballet dancers. *The Physician and Sportsmedicine, 13*(5), 43-54.

Cohen, J.L., Segal, K.R., Witriol, I., & McArdle, W.D. (1982). Cardiorespiratory response to ballet exercise and the $\dot{V}O_2$max of elite ballet dancers. *Medicine and Science in Sports and Exercise, 14*, 212-217.

Cohen, J.S., & Gisolfi, C.V. (1982). Effects of interval training on work-heat tolerance of young women. *Medicine and Science in Sports and Exercise, 14*, 46-52.

Colditz, G.A., Willett, W.C., Stampfer, M.J., Rosner, B., Speizer, F.E., & Hennekens, C.H. (1987). Menopause and the risk of coronary heart disease in women. *New England Journal of Medicine, 316*, 1105-1110.

Collings, C.A., Curet, L.B., & Mullin, J.P. (1983). Maternal and fetal responses to a maternal aerobic exercise program. *American Journal of Obstetrics and Gynecology, 145*, 702-707.

Comroe, J.H., Jr., Forster, R.E., II, DuBois, A.B., Briscoe, W.A., & Carlsen, E. (1962). *The lung: Clinical physiology and pulmonary function tests* (2nd ed.). Chicago: Year Book Medical Publishers.

Conger, P.R., & MacNab, R.B.J. (1967). Strength, body composition, and work capacity of participants and nonparticipants in women's intercollegiate sports. *Research Quarterly, 38*, 184-192.

Conley, D.L., Krahenbuhl, G.S., Burkett, L.N., & Millar, A.L. (1981). Physiological correlates of female road racing performance. *Research Quarterly for Exercise and Sport, 52*, 441-448.

Cook, J.D. (1983). Nutritional anemia. *Contemporary Nutrition, 8*(4), p. 600. (Published by General Mills)

Coping with Eve's curse. (1981, July 27). *Time*, p. 59.

Corbett, K., Brassard, L., & Taylor, A.W. (1979). Skeletal muscle metabolism in the offspring of trained rats [Abstract]. *Medicine and Science in Sports, 11*, 107.

Corbitt, R.W., Cooper, D.L., Erickson, D.J., Kriss, F.C., Thornton, M.L., & Craig, T.T. (1975). Female athletics. *Journal of Physical Education and Recreation, 46*(1), 45-46.

Costill, D., Daniels, D., Evans, W., Fink, W., Krahenbuhl, G., & Saltin, B. (1976). Skeletal muscle enzymes and fiber composition in male and female track athletes. *Journal of Applied Physiology, 40*, 149-154.

Costill, D.L., Fink, W.J., Flynn, M., & Kirwan, J. (1987). Muscle fiber composition and enzyme activities in elite female distance runners. *International Journal of Sports Medicine, 8*(Suppl. 2), 103-106.

Costill, D.L., Fink, W.J., Getchell, L.H., Ivy, J.L., & Witzmann, F.A. (1979). Lipid metabolism in skeletal muscle of endurance-trained males and females. *Journal of Applied Physiology, 47,* 787-791.

Costill, D.L., Fink, W.J., & Pollock, M.L. (1976). Muscle fiber composition and enzyme activities of elite distance runners. *Medicine and Science in Sports and Exercise, 8,* 96-100.

Cowan, M.M., & Gregory, L.W. (1985). Responses of pre- and post-menopausal females to aerobic conditioning. *Medicine and Science in Sports and Exercise, 17,* 138-143.

Crawford, J.D., & Osler, D.C. (1975). Body composition at menarche: The Frisch-Revelle hypothesis revisited. *Pediatrics, 56,* 449-458.

Crews, E.L., Fuge, K.W., Oscai, L.B., Holloszy, J.O., & Shank, R.E. (1969). Weight, food intake, and body composition: Effects of exercise and of protein deficiency. *American Journal of Physiology, 216,* 359-363.

Crouch, J.E. (1972). *Functional human anatomy* (2nd ed.). Philadelphia: Lea & Febiger.

Cumming, D.C., & Belcastro, A.N. (1982). The reproductive effects of exertion. *Current Problems in Obstetrics and Gynecology, 5*(8), 1-42.

Cumming, D.C., Vickovic, M.M., Wall, S.R., & Fluker, M.R. (1985). Defects in pulsatile LH release in normally menstruating runners. *Journal of Clinical Endocrinology and Metabolism, 60,* 810-818.

Cummings, S.R., & Black, D. (1986). Should perimenopausal women be screened for osteoporosis? *Annals of Internal Medicine, 104,* 817-823.

Cunningham, D.A. (1980). Physical working capacity of children and adolescents. In G.A. Stull (Ed.), *Encyclopedia of physical education, fitness, and sports* (Vol. 2, pp. 481-494). Salt Lake City: Brighton Publishing.

Cunningham, D.A., & Eynon, R.B. (1973). The working capacity of young competitive swimmers, 10-16 years of age. *Medicine and Science in Sports, 5,* 227-231.

Cunningham, D.A., & Hill, J.S. (1975). Effect of training on cardiovascular response to exercise in women. *Journal of Applied Physiology, 39,* 891-895.

Cunningham, D.A., McCrimmon, D., & Vlach, L.F. (1979). Cardiovascular response to interval and continuous training in women. *European Journal of Applied Physiology, 41,* 187-197.

Cunningham, D.J., & Cabanac, M. (1971). Evidence from behavioral thermoregulatory responses of a shift in setpoint temperature related to the menstrual cycle. *Journal of Physiology* (Paris), *63,* 236-238.

Cureton, K., Bishop, P., Hutchinson, P., Newland, H., Vickery, S., & Zwiren, L. (1986). Sex difference in maximal oxygen uptake: Effect of equating haemoglobin concentration. *European Journal of Applied Physiology, 54,* 656-660.

Cureton, K.J., Collins, M.A., Hill, D.W., & McElhannon, F.M. (1988). Muscle hypertrophy in men and women. *Medicine and Science in Sports and Exercise, 20,* 338-344.

Cureton, K., & Sparling, P.B. (1980). Distance running performance and metabolic responses to running in men and women with excess weight experimentally equated. *Medicine and Science in Sports and Exercise, 12,* 288-294.

Daggett, A., Davies, B., & Boobis, L. (1983). Physiological and biochemical responses to exercise following oral contraceptive use [Abstract]. *Medicine and Science in Sports and Exercise, 15*(2), 174.

Dale, E., Gerlach, D.H., Martin, D.E., & Alexander, C.R. (1979). Physical fitness profiles and reproductive physiology of the female distance runner. *The Physician and Sportsmedicine, 7*(1), 83-95.

Dale, E., Gerlach, D.H., & Wilhite, A.L. (1979). Menstrual dysfunction in distance runners. *Obstetrics and Gynecology, 54,* 47-53.

Dale, E., Mullinax, K.M., & Bryan, D.H. (1982). Exercise during pregnancy: Effects on the fetus. *Canadian Journal of Applied Sport Sciences, 7*, 98-103.

Dalen, N., & Olsson, K.E. (1974). Bone mineral content and physical activity. *Acta Orthopedica Scandinavica, 45*, 170-174.

Dalton, K. (1960). Effect of menstruation on schoolgirls' weekly work. *British Medical Journal, 5169*, 326-328.

Daniel, W.A., Jr. (1983). Pubertal changes in adolescence. In J. Brooks-Gunn & A.C. Petersen (Eds.), *Girls at puberty* (pp. 59-60). New York: Plenum Press.

Daniels, J., Fitts, R., & Sheehan, G. (1978). *Conditioning for distance running*. New York: Wiley.

Daniels, J., Krahenbuhl, G., Foster, C., Gilbert, J., & Daniels, S. (1977). Aerobic responses of female distance runners to submaximal and maximal exercise. *Annals of the New York Academy of Sciences, 301*, 726-733.

Davies, C.T.M., & Thompson, M.W. (1979). Aerobic performance of female marathon and male ultramarathon athletes. *European Journal of Applied Physiology, 41*, 233-245.

Davies, C.T.M., Barnes, C., & Godfrey, S. (1974). Body composition and maximal exercise performance in children. *Human Biology, 44*, 195-214.

Dawood, M.Y. (1987a). Dysmenorrhea and prostaglandins. J.J. Gold & J.B. Josimovich (Eds.), *Gynecologic endocrinology* (4th ed., pp. 405-421). New York: Plenum Medical.

Dawood, M.Y. (1987b). Endometriosis. In J.J. Gold & J.B. Josimovich (Eds.), *Gynecologic endocrinology* (4th ed., pp. 387-404). New York: Plenum Medical.

Degaray, A.L., Levine, L., & Carter, J.E.L. (1974). *Genetic and anthropological studies of Olympic athletes*. New York: Academic Press.

DeHaven, K.E., & Lintner, D.M. (1986). Athletic injuries: Comparison by age, sport, and gender. *American Journal of Sports Medicine, 14*, 218-224.

Delaney, J., Lupton, M.J., & Toth, E. (1976). *The curse: A cultural history of menstruation*. New York: E.P. Dutton.

Dempsey, J.A. (1964). Anthropometric observations on obese and nonobese young men undergoing a program of vigorous physical exercise. *Research Quarterly, 35*, 275-287.

Deuster, P.A., Kyle, S.B., Moser, P.B., Vigersky, R.A., Singh, A., & Schoomaker, E.B. (1986). Nutritional intakes and status of highly trained amenorrheic and eumenorrheic women runners. *Fertility and Sterility, 46*, 636-643.

DeVries, H. (1980). *Physiology of exercise for physical education and athletics* (3rd ed.). Dubuque, IA: Wm. C. Brown.

Diehl, D.M., Lohman, T.G., Smith, S.C., & Kertzer, R. (1986). Effects of physical training and competition on the iron status of female field hockey players. *International Journal of Sports Medicine, 7*, 264-270.

Diet and bone health. (1982). *Dairy Council Digest, 55*(5), 25-30.

Diet, exercise, and health. (1985). *Dairy Council Digest, 56*(3), 13-18.

Diet, nutrition, and cancer: New findings. (1986). *Dairy Council Digest, 57*(2), 7-12.

Ding, J.-H., Sheckter, C.B., Drinkwater, B.L., Soules, M.E., & Bremner, W.J. (1988). High serum cortisol levels in exercise-associated amenorrhea. *Annals of Internal Medicine, 108*, 530-534.

Doolittle, T.L., & Engebretsen, J. (1972). Performance variations during the menstrual cycle. *Journal of Sports Medicine and Physical Fitness, 12*, 54-58.

Dowdy, D.B., Cureton, K.J., DuVal, H.P., & Ouzts, H.G. (1985). Effects of aerobic dance on physical work capacity, cardiovascular function and body composition of middle-aged women. *Research Quarterly for Exercise and Sport, 56*, 227-233.

Dressendorfer, H. (1978). Physical training during pregnancy and lactation. *The Physician and Sportsmedicine, 6*(2), 74-80.

Dressendorfer, R.H., & Goodlin, R.C. (1980). Fetal heart rate response to maternal exercise testing. *The Physician and Sportsmedicine,* **8**(11), 91-95.

Drinkwater, B.L. (1973). Physiological responses of women to exercise. In J.H. Wilmore (Ed.), *Exercise and sport sciences reviews* (Vol. 1). New York: Academic Press.

Drinkwater, B.L. (1986). Gender and heat tolerance. In B.L. Drinkwater (Ed.), *Female endurance athletes* (pp. 113-124). Champaign, IL: Human Kinetics.

Drinkwater, B.L. (1988). Exercise and aging: The female masters athlete. In J. Puhl, C.H. Brown, & R.O. Voy (Eds.), *Sport science perspectives for women* (pp. 161-169). Champaign, IL: Human Kinetics.

Drinkwater, B.L., & Horvath, S.M. (1971). Responses of young female track athletes to exercise. *Medicine and Science in Sports, 3,* 56-62.

Drinkwater, B.L., & Horvath, S.M. (1972). Detraining effects in young women. *Medicine and Science in Sports, 4,* 91-95.

Drinkwater, B.L., Horvath, S.M., & Wells, C.L. (1975). Aerobic power of females, ages 10-68. *Journal of Gerontology, 30,* 385-394.

Drinkwater, B.L., Nilson, K., Chestnut, C.H., III, Bremner, W.J., Shainholtz, S., & Southworth, M.B. (1984). Bone mineral content of amenorrheic and eumenorrheic athletes. *New England Journal of Medicine,* **311,** 277-281.

Drinkwater, B.L., Nilson, K., Ott, S., & Chesnut, C.H., III. (1986). Bone mineral density after resumption of menses in amenorrheic athletes. *Journal of the American Medical Association,* **256**(3), 380-382.

Dudleston, A.K., & Bennion, M. (1970). Effect of diet and/or exercise on obese college women. *Journal of the American Dietetic Association,* **156,** 126-129.

Duentzer, E., & Hellendall, M. (1930). The influence of physical education activities upon constitution, child-bearing and menstruation of women. *Journal of Health and Physical Education,* **1**(9), 47.

Dummer, G.M., Clarke, D.H., Vaccaro, P., VanderVelden, L., Goldfarb, A.H., & Sockler, J.M. (1985). Age-related differences in muscular strength and muscular endurance among female masters swimmers. *Research Quarterly for Exercise and Sport,* **56,** 97-110.

Dummer, G.M., Rosen, L.W., Heusner, W.W., Roberts, P.J., & Counsilman, J.E. (1987). Pathogenic weight-control behaviors of young competitive swimmers. *The Physician and Sportsmedicine,* **15**(5), 75-84.

Dyer, K. (1977). Female athletes are catching up. *New Scientist,* **75,** 722-723.

Edgerton, V.R., Smith, J.L., & Simpson, D.R. (1975). Muscle fiber type populations of human leg muscles. *Histochemistry Journal,* **7,** 259-266.

Edstrom, L., & Nystrom, L. (1969). Histochemical types and sizes of fibers in normal human muscles. *Acta Neurologica Scandinavica,* **45,** 257-269.

Eichner, E.R. (1986). The anemias of athletes. *The Physician and Sportsmedicine,* **14**(9), 122-130.

Eisenberg, I., & Allen, W.C. (1978). Injuries in a women's varsity athletic program. *The Physician and Sportsmedicine,* **6**(3), 112-120.

Eisenman, P.A., & Golding, L.A. (1975). Comparison of effects of training on $\dot{V}O_2$max in girls and young women. *Medicine and Science in Sports, 7,* 136-138.

Elliot, D.L., Goldberg, L., Kuehl, K.S., & Catlin, D.H. (1987). Characteristics of anabolic-androgenic steroid-free competitive male and female bodybuilders. *The Physician and Sportsmedicine,* **15**(6), 169-179.

Ellison, P.T. (1981a). Physical growth and reproductive maturity in humans [Abstract]. *American Journal of Physical Anthropology,* **54,** 216.

Ellison, P.T. (1981b). Threshold hypotheses, developmental age, and menstrual function.

American Journal of Physical Anthropology, **54**, 337-340.

Ellsworth, N.M., Hewitt, B.F., & Haskell, W.L. (1985). Nutrient intake of elite male and female Nordic skiers. *The Physician and Sportsmedicine,* **13**(2), 78-92.

Enzi, G., Gasparo, M., Biondetti, P.R., Fiore, D., Semisa, M., & Zurlo, F. (1986). Subcutaneous and visceral fat distribution according to sex, age, and overweight, evaluated by computer tomography. *American Journal of Clinical Nutrition,* **44**, 739-746.

Erdelyi, G.J. (1962). Gynecological survey of female athletes. *Journal of Sports Medicine and Physical Fitness,* **2**, 174-179.

Erdelyi, G.J. (1976). Effects of exercise on the menstrual cycle. *The Physician and Sportsmedicine,* **4**(3), 79-81.

Eriksson, B.O., Engstrom, I., Karlberg, P., Lundin, A., Saltin, B., & Thorén, C. (1978). Long-term effect of previous swimtraining in girls: A 10-year follow-up of the "girl swimmers." *Acta Paediatrica Scandinavica,* **67**, 285-292.

Eriksson, B.O., & Thorén, C. (1978). Training girls for swimming from medical and physiological points of view, with special reference to growth. In B. Eriksson & B. Furberg (Eds.), *Swimming medicine IV* (International Series on Sports Sciences, Vol. 6, pp. 3-15). Baltimore: University Park Press.

Erkkola, R. (1976). The influence of physical training during pregnancy on physical work capacity and circulatory parameters. *Scandinavian Journal of Clinical and Laboratory Investigation,* **36**, 747-754.

Eston, R.G., & Burke, E.J. (1984). Effects of the menstrual cycle on selected responses to short constant-load exercise. *Journal of Sports Sciences,* **2**, 145-153.

Feicht, C.B., Johnson, T.S., Martin, B.J., Sparkes, K.E., & Wagner, W.W., Jr. (1978, November 25). Secondary amenorrhea in athletes [Letter]. *Lancet,* **2**(8100), 1145-1146.

Feicht, C.B., Martin, B.J., & Wagner, W.W., Jr. (1980). Is athletic amenorrhea specific to runners? [Abstract 536]. *Federation Proceedings,* **39**(3, Pt. 1), 371.

Ferguson, J. (1976). *Habits, not diets: The real way to weight control.* Palo Alto, CA: Bull Publishing.

Finally, drugs that work for menstrual pain. (1981). *Consumer Reports,* **46**(2), 92-93.

Fisler, J.S. (1987). Starvation and semistarvation diets in the management of obesity. *Annual Review of Nutrition,* **7**, 465-484.

Flint, M.M., Drinkwater, B.L., & Horvath, S.M. (1974). Effects of training on women's response to submaximal exercise. *Medicine and Science in Sports,* **6**, 89-94.

Foster, C. (1975). Physiological requirements of aerobic dancing. *Research Quarterly for Exercise and Sport,* **46**, 120-122.

Fox, E.L., & Mathews, D.K. (1981). *The physiological basis of physical education and athletics* (3rd ed.). Philadelphia: Saunders College Publishing.

Francis, L.L., Francis, P.R., & Welshons-Smith, K. (1985). Aerobic dance injuries: A survey of instructors. *The Physician and Sportsmedicine,* **13**(2), 105-111.

Franklin, B.A., Hodgson, J., & Buskirk, E.R. (1980). Relationship between percent maximal O_2 uptake and percent maximal heart rate in women. *Research Quarterly for Exercise and Sport,* **51**, 616-624.

Freedson, P.S. (1981). The influence of hemoglobin concentration on exercise cardiac output. *International Journal of Sports Medicine,* **2**, 81-86.

Freedson, P.S. (1988). Body composition and performance. In J. Puhl, C.H. Brown, & R.O. Voy (Eds.), *Sport science perspectives for women* (pp. 13-21). Champaign, IL: Human Kinetics.

Freedson, P., Katch, V.L., Sady, S., & Weltman, A. (1979). Cardiac output differences in males and females during mild cycle ergometer exercise. *Medicine and Science in Sports,* **11**, 16-19.

Freedson, P.S., Mihevic, P.M., Loucks, A.B., & Girandola, R.N. (1983). Physique, body composition, and psychological characteristics of competitive female body builders. *The Physician and Sportsmedicine, 11*(5), 85-93.

Fringer, M.N., & Stull, G.A. (1974). Changes in cardiorespiratory parameters during periods of training and detraining in young adult females. *Medicine and Science in Sports, 6*, 20-25.

Frisch, R.E. (1977a). Fatness and the onset and maintenance of menstrual cycles. *Research in Reproduction, 6*(1), 1.

Frisch, R.E. (1977b). Food intake, fatness, and reproductive ability. In R.A. Vigersky (Ed.), *Anorexia nervosa* (pp. 149-160). New York: Raven Press.

Frisch, R.E. (1988). Fatness and fertility. *Scientific American, 258*(3), 88-95.

Frisch, R.E., Gotz-Welbergen, A.V., McArthur, J.W., Albright, T., Witschi, J., Bullen, B., Birnholz, J., Reed, R.B., & Hermann, H. (1981). Delayed menarche and amenorrhea of college athletes in relation to age of onset of training. *Journal of the American Medical Association, 246*, 1559-1563.

Frisch, R.E., & McArthur, J.W. (1974, September 13). Menstrual cycles: Fatness as a determinant of minimum weight for height necessary for their maintenance or onset. *Science, 185*, 949-951.

Frisch, R.E., & Revelle, R. (1970). Height and weight at menarche and a hypothesis of critical body weights and adolescent events. *Science, 169*, 397-399.

Frisch, R.E., & Revelle, R. (1971). Height and weight at menarche and a hypothesis of menarche. *Archives of Diseases in Children, 46*, 695-701.

Frisch, R.E., Revelle, R., & Cook, S. (1973). Components of weight at menarche and the initiation of the adolescent growth spurt in girls: Estimated total water, lean body weight and fat. *Human Biology, 45*, 469-483.

Frisch, R.E., Wyshak, G., & Vincent, L. (1980). Delayed menarche and amenorrhea in ballet dancers. *New England Journal of Medicine, 303*, 17-19.

Frye, A.J., Kamon, E., & Webb, M. (1982). Responses of menstrual women, amenorrheal women, and men to exercise in a hot, dry environment. *European Journal of Applied Physiology, 48*, 279-288.

Gamberale, F., Strindberg, L., & Wahlberg, I. (1975). Female work capacity during the menstrual cycle: Physiological and psychological reactions. *Scandinavian Journal of Work, Environment and Health, 1*, 120-127.

Gambrell, R.D., Maier, R.C., & Sanders, B.I. (1983). Decreased incidence of breast cancer in postmenopausal estrogen-progestogen users. *Obstetrics and Gynecology, 62*, 435-443.

Gannon, L.R. (1985). *Menstrual disorders and menopause: Biological, psychological, and cultural research*. New York: Praeger.

Garlick, M.A., & Bernauer, E.M. (1968). Exercise during the menstrual cycle: Variations in physiological baselines. *Research Quarterly, 39*, 533-542.

Garrick, J.G., Gillien, D.M., & Whiteside, P. (1986). The epidemiology of aerobic dance injuries. *American Journal of Sports Medicine, 14*, 67-72.

Garrick, J.G., & Requa, R.K. (1978). Girls' sports injuries in high school athletics. *Journal of the American Medical Association, 239*, 2245-2248.

Garrick, J.G., & Requa, R.K. (1988). Aerobic dance: A review. *Sports Medicine (New Zealand), 6*, 169-179.

Gauthier, M.M. (1986). Guidelines for exercise during pregnancy: Too little or too much? *The Physician and Sportsmedicine, 14*(4), 162-169.

Gehlsen, G., & Albohm, M. (1980). Evaluation of sports bras. *The Physician and Sportsmedicine, 8*(10), 89-97.

Gehlsen, G., & Dill, D.B. (1977). Comparative performance of men and women in grade walking. *Human Biology, 49*, 381-388.

Gehlsen, G., & Stoner, L.J. (1987). The female breast in sports and exercise. *Medicine and Sport Science, 24*, 13-22.

Genazzanni, A.R., Magrini, G., Faccinetti, F.,

Romagnino, S., Pintor, C., Felber, J.P., & Fioretti, P. (1977). Behavior and origin of plasma androgens throughout the menstrual cycle. In L. Martini & M. Motta (Eds.), *Androgens and antiandrogens* (pp. 247-261). New York: Raven Press.

Gendel, E.S. (1967). Pregnancy, fitness, and sports. *Journal of the American Medical Association,* **201**(10), 125-128.

Gendel, E.S. (1976). Psychological factors and menstrual extraction. *The Physician and Sportsmedicine,* **4**(3), 72-75.

Getchell, B. (1976). *Physical fitness: A way of life.* New York: Wiley.

Getchell, L.H., & Moore, J.C. (1975). Physical training: Comparative responses of middle-aged adults. *Archives of Physical and Medical Rehabilitation,* **56**, 250-254.

Gibbons, L.W., Blair, S.N., Cooper, K.H., & Smith, M. (1983). Association between coronary heart disease risk factors and physical fitness in healthy adult women. *Circulation,* **67**, 977-983.

Gibbons, E.S., Jessup, G.T., Wells, T.D., & Werthmann, D.S. (1981). The effects of various training intensities on anaerobic threshold, aerobic power, and aerobic capacity in young females [Abstract 16]. *Medicine and Science in Sports and Exercise,* **13**(2), 100.

Gillett, P.A., & Eisenman, P.A. (1987). The effect of intensity controlled aerobic dance exercise on aerobic capacity of middle-aged, overweight women. *Research in Nursing and Health,* **10**, 383-390.

Glass, A.R., Deuster, P.A., Kyle, S.B., Yahiro, J.A., Vigersky, R.A., & Schoomaker, E.B. (1987). Amenorrhea in Olympic marathon runners. *Fertility and Sterility,* **48**, 740-745.

Goertzen, D., Serfass, R., Sopko, G., & Leon, A. (1984). The functional capacity and physical activity levels of women over 60 years of age. *Journal of Sports Medicine and Physical Fitness,* **24**, 30-36.

Goldberg, L., & Elliot, D.L. (1987). The effect of exercise on lipid metabolism in men and women. *Sports Medicine (New Zealand),* **4**, 307-321.

Goldberg, L., Elliot, D.L., Schutz, R.W., & Kloster, F.E. (1984). Changes in lipid and lipoprotein levels after weight training. *Journal of the American Medical Association,* **252**, 504-506.

Gollnick, P.D., Armstrong, R.B., Saubert, C.W., IV, Piehl, K., & Saltin, B. (1972). Enzyme activity and fiber composition in skeletal muscle of untrained and trained men. *Journal of Applied Physiology,* **33**, 312-319.

Goodship, A.E., Lanyon, L.E., & McFie, H. (1979). Functional adaptation of bone to increased stress. *Journal of Bone and Joint Surgery,* **61**(A), 539-546.

Gordon, T.I., Bannister, E.W., & Gordon, B.P. (1969). The caloric cost of competitive figure skating. *Journal of Sports Medicine and Physical Fitness,* **9**, 98-103.

Gorski, J. (1985). Exercise during pregnancy: Maternal and fetal responses. A brief review. *Medicine and Science in Sports and Exercise,* **17**, 407-416.

Gosden, R.G. (1985). *Biology of menopause: The causes and consequences of ovarian ageing.* London: Academic Press.

Grandjean, A.C. (1984). Nutritional concerns for the woman athlete. *Clinics in Sports Medicine,* **3**(4), 923-938.

Graves, J.E., Pollock, M.L., & Sparling, P.B. (1987). Body composition of elite female distance runners. *International Journal of Sports Medicine,* **8**(Suppl. 2), 96-102.

Gray, D.P., & Dale, E. (1983). Variables associated with secondary amenorrhea in women runners. *Journal of Sports Sciences,* **1**, 55-67.

Gray, D.P., Harding, E., & Dale, E. (1983). Effects of oral contraceptives on serum lipid profiles of women runners. *Fertility and Sterility,* **39**, 510-514.

Greenwald, P., & Lanza, E. (1986). Dietary fiber and colon cancer. *Contemporary Nutrition,* **11**(1), n.p.

Gregor, R.J., Edgerton, V.R., Perrine, J.J., Campion, D.S., & DeBus, C. (1979). Torque-velocity relationships and muscle fiber composition in elite female athletes. *Journal of Applied Physiology: Respiratory, Environmental, Exercise Physiology, 47*, 388-392.

Guzman, C.A., & Caplan, R. (1970). Cardiorespiratory response to exercise during pregnancy. *American Journal of Obstetrics and Gynecology, 108*, 600-605.

Haan, A.L. (1979). *An anthropometrical and physiological study of outstanding female swimmers.* Unpublished master's thesis, Arizona State University, Tempe.

Hagen, R.D. (1988). Benefits of aerobic conditioning and diet for overweight adults. *Sports Medicine, 5*, 144-155.

Hagan, R.D., Upton, S.J., Wong, L., & Whittam, J. (1986). The effects of aerobic conditioning and/or caloric restriction in overweight men and women. *Medicine and Science in Sports and Exercise, 18*, 87-94.

Hage, P. (1982). American College of Sports Medicine: New growth, new future? *The Physician and Sportsmedicine, 10*(5), 123-127.

Hagerman, F.C., Hagerman, G.R., & Nickelson, T.C. (1979). Physiological profiles of elite rowers. *The Physician and Sportsmedicine, 7*(7), 74-83.

Hale, R. (1979, May). *Effects of exercise and athletic competition on women.* Paper presented at the meeting of the American College of Obstetricians and Gynecologists, New Orleans.

Hall, D.C., & Kaufmann, D.A. (1987). Effects of aerobic and strength conditioning on pregnancy outcomes. *American Journal of Obstetrics and Gynecology, 157*, 1199-1203.

Hall, J.E., Younglai, E.V., Walker, C., Jones, J.L., & Sutton, J.R. (1975). Ovarian hormonal responses to exercise [Abstract]. *Medicine and Science in Sports, 7*, 65.

Hall-Jurkowski, J.E., Jones, N.L., Toews, C.J., & Sutton, J.R. (1981). Effects of the menstrual cycle on blood lactate, oxygen delivery and performance during exercise. *Journal of Applied Physiology: Respiratory, Environmental and Exercise Physiology, 51*, 1493-1499.

Harris, W.S. (1985). Health effects of omega-3 fatty acids. *Contemporary Nutrition, 10*(8), n.p.

Hartung, G.H. (1984). Diet and exercise in the regulation of plasma lipids and lipoproteins in patients at risk of coronary disease. *Sports Medicine, 1*, 413-418.

Hartung, G.H., Moore, C.E., Mitchell, R., & Kappus, C.M. (1984). Relationship of menopausal status and exercise level to HDL cholesterol in women. *Experimental Aging Research, 10*, 13-18.

Haycock, C.E. (1978). Breast support and protection in the female athlete. In C.B. Corbin (Ed.), *AAHPER Research Consortium Symposium papers: Sport, health, fitness and dance* (Vol. 1, Bk. 2, pp. 50-53). Washington, DC: *American Alliance for Health, Physical Education and Recreation.*

Haycock, C.E. (1980). Soft-tissue injuries. In C.E. Haycock (Ed.), *Sports medicine for the athletic female* (pp. 199-205). Oradell, NJ: Medical Economics Co.

Haycock, C.E. (1981). Breast problems—Jogging and other sports. *Nautilus Magazine, 3*(4), 50-52.

Haycock, C.E. (1987). How I manage breast problems in athletes. *The Physician and Sportsmedicine, 15*(3), 89-95.

Haycock, C.E. (1988). The breast. In M.M. Shangold & G. Mirkin (Eds.), *Women and exercise: Physiology and sports medicine* (pp. 181-185). Philadelphia: F.A. Davis.

Haycock, C.E., & Gillette, J.V. (1976). Susceptibility of women athletes to injury. *Journal of the American Medical Association, 236*, 163-165.

Haymes, E. (1973). Iron deficiency and the active woman. In D.V. Harris (Ed.), *D.G.W.S. research reports: Women in sports* (Vol. 2, pp. 91-97). Washington, DC: American

Association for Health, Physical Education and Recreation.

Haymes, E. (1980). Nutrition for the female athlete. In G.A. Stull (Ed.), *Encyclopedia of physical education, fitness, and sports* (Vol. 2, pp. 237-245). Salt Lake City: Brighton Publishing.

Haymes, E.M. (1984). Physiological responses of female athletes to heat stress: A review. *The Physician and Sportsmedicine, 12*(3), 45-59.

Haymes, E.M. (1988a). Metabolism and performance. In J.L. Puhl, C.H. Brown, R.O. Voy (Eds.), *Sport science perspectives for women* (pp. 85-95). Champaign, IL: Human Kinetics.

Haymes, E.M. (1988b) Temperature and exercise. In J. Puhl, C.H. Brown, & R.O. Voy (Eds.), *Sport science perspectives for women* (pp. 37-47). Champaign, IL: Human Kinetics.

Haymes, E.M., & Dickinson, A.L. (1980). Characteristics of elite male and female ski racers. *Medicine and Science in Sports and Exercise, 12*, 153-158.

Haymes, E.M., & Wells, C.L. (1986). *Environment and human performance*. Champaign, IL: Human Kinetics.

Haynes, D.M. (1977). Course and conduct of normal pregnancy. In D.N. Danforth (Ed.), *Obstetrics and gynecology* (3rd ed.). New York: Harper & Row.

Hebbelinck, M., Ross, W.D., Carter, J.E.L., & Borms, J. (1981). Body build of Olympic female rowers. *Medicine and Sports, 15*, 201-205.

Hellebrandt, F.A., & Meyer, M.H. (1939). Physiological data significant to participation by women in physical activities. *Research Quarterly, 10*, 10-23.

Hermansen, L. (1974). Individual differences. In L.A. Larson (Ed.), *Fitness, health and work capacity* (p. 408). New York: Macmillan.

Heyward, V.H., Johannes-Ellis, S.M., & Romer, J.F. (1986). Gender differences in strength. *Research Quarterly for Exercise and Sport, 57*, 154-159.

Higgs, S.L., & Robertson, L.A. (1981). Cyclic variations in perceived exertion and physical work capacity in females. *Canadian Journal of Applied Sport Sciences, 6*, 191-196.

Himann, J.E., Cunningham, D.A., Rechnitzer, P.A., & Paterson, D.H. (1988). Age-related changes in speed of walking. *Medicine and Science in Sports and Exercise, 20*, 161-166.

Hodgkins, J., & Skubic, V. (1968). Women's track and field records: Analysis and predictions. *Journal of Sports Medicine and Physical Fitness, 8*, 36-42.

Holloszy, J.O., Skinner, J.S., Toro, G., & Cureton, T.K. (1964). Effects of a six month program of endurance exercise on the serum lipids of middle-aged men. *American Journal of Cardiology, 14*, 753-760.

Hong, S.K., & Rahn, H. (1967). The diving women of Korea and Japan. *Scientific American, 216*(5), 34-43.

Horvath, S.M., & Drinkwater, B.L. (1982). Thermoregulation and the menstrual cycle. *Aviation, Space, and Environmental Medicine, 53*, 790-794.

Hosler, W.W., & Morrow, J.R. (1982). Arm and leg strength compared between young women and men after allowing for difference in body size and composition. *Ergonomics, 25*, 309-313.

Housh, T.J., Thorland, W.G., Johnson, G.O., Tharp, G.D., Cisar, C.J., Refsell, M.J., & Ansorge, C.J. (1984). Body composition variables as discriminators of sports participation of elite adolescent female athletes. *Research Quarterly for Exercise and Sport, 55*, 302-304.

Howley, E.T., & Glover, M.E. (1974). The caloric costs of running and walking one mile for men and women. *Medicine and Science in Sports, 6*, 235.

Huddleston, A.L., Rockwell, D., Kulund, D.N., & Harrison, R.B. (1980). Bone mass in lifetime tennis athletes. *Journal of the American Medical Association, 244*, 1107-1109.

Hunter, G.R. (1985). Changes in body composition, body build and performance associated with different weight training frequencies in males and females. *National Strength and Conditioning Association Journal, 7*(1), 26-28.

Hunter, L.Y. (1984). Women's athletics: The orthopedic surgeon's viewpoint. *Clinics in Sports Medicine, 3*(4), 809-827.

Hunter, L.Y. (1988). The frequency of injuries in women's sports. In J.L. Puhl, C.H. Brown, & R.O. Voy (Eds.), *Sport science perspectives for women* (pp. 49-58). Champaign, IL: Human Kinetics.

Hunter-Griffin, L.Y. (1988). Orthopedic concerns. In M.M. Shangold & G. Mirkin (Eds.), *Women and exercise: Physiology and sports medicine* (pp. 195-219). Philadelphia: F.A. Davis.

Huse, D.M., & Nelson, R.A. (1977). Basic, balanced diet meets requirements of athletes. *The Physician and Sportsmedicine, 5*(1), 52-56.

Hutchinson, P.L., Cureton, K.J., & Sparling, P.B. (1981). Metabolic and circulatory responses to running during pregnancy. *The Physician and Sportsmedicine, 9*(8), 55-61.

Ingjer, F., & Brodal, P. (1978). Capillary supply of skeletal muscle fibers in untrained and endurance trained women. *European Journal of Applied Physiology, 38*, 291-299.

Ingman, O. (1953). Menstruation in Finnish top-class sportswomen. In M.J. Karvonen (Ed.), *Sports medicine.* Helsinki: Finnish Association of Sports Medicine.

Jackson, C.W., & Jackson, C.W. (1977). Sex gap in swimming performance narrows. *American Corrective Therapy Journal, 31*, 172.

Jackson, A.S., Pollock, M.L., & Ward, A. (1980). Generalized equations for predicting body density of women. *Medicine and Science in Sports and Exercise, 12*, 175-182.

Jacobson, H. (1980). *Racewalk to Fitness.* New York: Simon & Schuster.

Jaffe, R.B., & Josimovich, J.B. (1977). Endocrine physiology of pregnancy. In D.N. Danforth (Ed.), *Obstetrics and Gynecology* (3rd ed., pp. 178-185). New York: Harper & Row.

Jaffee, L., Webster, M., & Lutter, J.M. (1988). Dietary differences of amenorrheic and eumenorrheic athletes. *The Melpomene Journal, 7*(3), 15-19.

James, S.L., Bates, B.J., & Osternig, L.R. (1978). Injuries to runners. *American Journal of Sports Medicine, 6*(2), 40-50.

Jarrett, J.C., II, & Spellacy, W.N. (1983a). Contraceptive practices of female runners. *Fertility and Sterility, 39*, 374-375.

Jarrett, J.C., II, & Spellacy, W.N. (1983b). Jogging during pregnancy: An improved outcome? *Obstetrics and Gynecology, 61*, 705-709.

Jensen, M.D., & Bobak, I.M. (1985). *Maternity and gynecologic care* (3rd ed.). St. Louis: C.V. Mosby.

Johannessen, S., Holly, R.G., Lui, H., & Amsterdam, E.A. (1986). High-frequency, moderate-intensity training in sedentary middle-aged women. *The Physician and Sportsmedicine, 14*(5), 99-102.

Johansson, S., Vedin, A., & Wilhelmsson, C. (1983). Myocardial infarction in women. *Epidemiological Reviews, 5*, 67-95.

Johnson, G. (1932). The effects of periodicity on learning to walk a tight-wire. *Journal of Comparative Psychology, 13*, 133-141.

Johnson, J.L., Heineman, E.F., Heiss, G., James, C.G., & Tyroler, H.A. (1986). Cardiovascular disease risk factors and mortality among black women and white women aged 40-64 years in Evans County, Georgia. *American Journal of Epidemiology, 123*(2), 209-220.

Johnson, R.B. (1977). Effects of frequency and duration of training on attrition and incidence of injury. *Medicine and Science in Sports, 9*, 31-36.

Johnson, S.R. (1987). The epidemiology and social impact of premenstrual symptoms.

Clinical Obstetrics and Gynecology, 30, 367-376.

Johnston, F.E. (1974). Control of age at menarche. *Human Biology, 46,* 159-171.

Johnston, F.E. (1982). Relationships between body composition and anthropometry. *Human Biology, 54,* 221-245.

Johnston, F.E., Malina, R.M., & Galbraith, M.A. (1971). Height, weight and age at menarche and the "critical weight" hypothesis. *Science, 174,* 1148-1149.

Johnston, F.E., Roche, A.F., Schell, L.M., & Wettenhall, H.N.B. (1975). Critical weight at menarche: Critique of a hypothesis. *American Journal of Disease in Childhood, 129,* 19-23.

Jokl, E. (1956). Some clinical data on women athletes. *Journal of the Association for Physical and Mental Rehabilitation, 10*(2), 48-49.

Jokl, E. (1958). *The clinical physiology of physical fitness and rehabilitation.* Springfield, IL: Charles C Thomas.

Jones, G.S., & Wentz, A.W. (1977). Adolescence, menstruation, and the climacteric. In D.N. Danforth (Ed.), *Obstetrics and gynecology* (3rd ed., pp. 178-185). New York: Harper & Row.

Jones, H.H., Priest, J.D., Hayes, W.C., Tichenor, C.C., & Nagel, D.A. (1977). Humeral hypertrophy in response to exercise. *Journal of Bone and Joint Surgery, 59,* 204-208.

Jones, K.P., Ravnikar, V.A., Tulchinsky, D., & Schiff, I. (1985). Comparison of bone density in amenorrheic women due to athletics, weight loss, and premature menopause. *Obstetrics and Gynecology, 66,* 5-7.

Jones, R.L., Botti, J.J., Anderson, W.M., & Bennett, N.L. (1985). Thermoregulation during aerobic exercise in pregnancy. *Obstetrics and Gynecology, 65,* 340-345.

Jordan, D.B. (1977). Analysis of exercise stress test responses of adult women marathon runners. *Journal of Sports Medicine and Physical Fitness, 17,* 59-64.

Jovanovic, L., Kessler, A., & Peterson, C.M. (1985). Human maternal and fetal response to graded exercise. *Journal of Applied Physiology, 58,* 1719-1722.

Jurkowski, J.E., Jones, N.L., Walker, W.C., Younglai, E.V., & Sutton, J.R. (1978). Ovarian hormonal responses to exercise. *Journal of Applied Physiology: Respiratory, Environmental and Exercise Physiology, 44,* 109-114.

Kalamen, J. (1968). *Measurement of maximum power in man.* Unpublished doctoral dissertation, The Ohio State University, Columbus.

Kase, N.G. (1987). The management of the postmenopausal woman. In P. Fioretti, C. Flamigni, V.M. Jasonni, & G.B. Melis (Eds.), *Postmenopausal hormonal therapy: Benefits and risks* (pp. 35-54). New York: Raven Press.

Katch, V.L., Campaigne, B., Freedson, P., & Sady, S. (1980). Contribution of breast volume and weight to body fat distribution in the female. *American Journal of Physical Anthropology, 53,* 93-100.

Katch, F.I., & Katch, V.L. (1980). Measurement and prediction errors in body composition assessment and the search for the perfect prediction equation. *Research Quarterly for Exercise and Sport, 51,* 249-260.

Katch, F.I., & McArdle, W.D. (1973). Prediction of body density from simple anthropometric measurements in college-age men and women. *Human Biology, 45,* 445-455.

Katch, F.I., & McArdle, W.D. (1977). *Nutrition, weight control, and exercise.* Boston: Houghton-Mifflin.

Katch, F.I., Michael, E.D., Jr., & Jones, E.M. (1969). Effects of physical training on the body composition and diet of females. *Research Quarterly, 40,* 99-104.

Kaufman, S.A. (1967). Limited relationship of maturation index to estrogen therapy for menopausal symptoms. *Obstetrics and Gynecology, 30,* 399.

Kearney, J.T., Stull, G.A., Ewing, J.L., & Strein, J.W. (1976). Cardiorespiratory responses of sedentary college women as a function of training intensity. *Journal of Applied Physiology, 41*, 822-825.

Keenan, B.A. (1958). *The effect of the menstrual cycle on selected measures of balance, kinesthesis, strength, and steadiness.* Unpublished master's thesis, State University of Iowa, Ames.

Keizer, H.A. (1986). Exercise- and training-induced menstrual cycle irregularities (AMI). *International Journal of Sports Medicine, 7,* 38-44.

Keizer, H.A., Kuipers, H., de Haan, J., Beckers, E., & Habets, L. (1987). Multiple hormonal responses to physical exercise in eumenorrheic trained and untrained women. *International Journal of Sports Medicine, 8*(Suppl. 3), 139-151.

Keizer, H.A., Poortmans, J., & Bunnik, G.S.J. (1980). Influence of physical exercises on sex-hormone metabolism. *Journal of Applied Physiology: Respiratory, Environmental and Exercise Physiology, 48*, 765-769.

Kemmann, E., Pasquale, S.A., & Skaf, R. (1983). Amenorrhea associated with carotenemia. *Journal of the American Medical Association, 249*, 926-929.

Kenny, W.L., & Anderson, R.K. (1988). Responses of older and younger women to exercise in dry and humid heat without fluid replacement. *Medicine and Science in Sports and Exercise, 20*, 155-160.

Kilbom, A. (1971). Physical training in women. *Scandinavian Journal of Clinical and Laboratory Investigation, 28*(Suppl. 119), 7-34.

Kindig, L.E., Soares, P.L., Wisenbaker, J.M., & Mrvos, S.R. (1984). Standard scores for women's weight training. *The Physician and Sportsmedicine, 12*(10), 67-74.

Kizer, K.W. (1980). Medical hazards of the water skiing douche. *Annals of Emergency Medicine, 9*, 268-269.

Knowlton, R.G., Ackerman, K.J., Fitzgerald, P.I., Wilde, S.W., & Tahamont, M.V. (1980). Physiological and performance characteristics of United States championship class orienteers. *Medicine and Science in Sports and Exercise, 12*, 164-169.

Knowlton, R.G., Miles, D.S., Sawka, M.N., Critz, J.B., & Blackman, C. (1978). Cardiorespiratory adaptations of females to cross-country training. *Journal of Sports Medicine and Physical Fitness, 18*, 391-398.

Knuttgen, H.G., & Emerson, K., Jr. (1974). Physiological response to pregnancy at rest and during exercise. *Journal of Applied Physiology, 36*, 549-553.

Kollias, J., Barlett, H.L., Mendez, J., & Franklin, B. (1978). Hemodynamic responses of well-trained women athletes to graded treadmill exercise. *Journal of Sports Medicine and Physical Fitness, 18*, 365-372.

Koszuta, L.E. (1986). Low-impact aerobics: Better than traditional aerobic dance? *The Physician and Sportsmedicine, 14*(7), 156-161.

Kovaleski, J.E., Parr, R.B., Hornak, J.E., & Roitman, J.L. (1980). Athletic profile of women college volleyball players. *The Physician and Sportsmedicine, 8*(2), 112-118.

Krahenbuhl, G.S., Archer, P.A., & Pettit, L.L. (1978). Serum testosterone and adult female trainability. *Journal of Sports Medicine and Physical Fitness, 18*, 359-364.

Krahenbuhl, G.S., Skinner, J.S., & Kohrt, W.M. (1985). Developmental aspects of maximal aerobic power in children. *Exercise and Sport Sciences Reviews, 13*, 503-538.

Krahenbuhl, G.S., Wells, C.L., Brown, C.H., & Ward, P.E. (1979). Characteristics of national and world class female pentathletes. *Medicine and Science in Sports, 11*, 20-23.

Kramár, P., & Drinkwater, B.L. (1980). Women on Annapurna. *The Physician and Sportsmedicine, 8*(3), 93-99.

Krause, M., & Hunscher, M. (1972). *Food,*

nutrition and diet therapy (5th ed.). Philadelphia: W.B. Saunders.

Krølner, B., Toft, B., Nielsen, S.T., & Tøndevold, E. (1983). Physical exercise as prophylaxis against involutional vertebrae bone loss: A controlled trial. *Clinical Science, 64*, 541-546.

Kulpa, P.J., White, B.M., & Visscher, R. (1987). Aerobic exercise in pregnancy. *American Journal of Obstetrics and Gynecology, 156*, 1395-1403.

Kumanyika, S. (1987). Obesity in black women. *Epidemiologic Reviews, 9*, 31-50.

Lamb, D.R. (1978). *Physiology of exercise: Responses and adaptations*. New York: Macmillan.

Lamb, D.R. (1984). *Physiology of exercise: Responses and adaptations* (2nd ed.). New York: Macmillan.

Lamont, L.S. (1980). Effects of training on echocardiographic dimensions and systolic time intervals in women swimmers. *Journal of Sports Medicine and Physical Fitness, 20*, 397-404.

Lamont, L.S. (1986). Lack of influence of the menstrual cycle on blood lactate. *The Physician and Sportsmedicine, 14*(11), 159-163.

Lampe, J.W., Slavin, J.L., & Apple, F.S. (1986). Poor iron status of women runners training for a marathon. *International Journal of Sports Medicine, 7*, 111-114.

Larson, R.L., & McMahan, R.O. (1966). The epiphyses and the childhood athlete. *Journal of the American Medical Association, 196*, 99-104.

Laubach, L. (1976). Comparative muscular strength of men and women: A review of the literature. *Aviation, Space, and Environmental Medicine, 47*, 534-542.

Leaf, D.A. (1981). *A review of current information and research exploring the controversy of exercise and pregnancy with particular reference to running*. Unpublished manuscript.

Lesmes, G.R., Fox, E.L., Stevens, C., & Otto, R. (1978). Metabolic responses of females to high intensity interval training of different intensities. *Medicine and Science in Sports, 10*, 229-232.

Lewis, S., Haskell, W.L., Wood, P.D., Manoogian, N., Bailey, J., & Pereira, M. (1976). Effects of physical activity on weight reduction in obese middle-aged women. *American Journal of Clinical Nutrition, 29*, 151-156.

Lien, E.L., Fenichel, R.L., Garsky, V., Sarantakis, D., & Grant, N.H. (1976). Enkephalin-stimulated prolactin release. *Life Sciences, 19*, 837-840.

Lindberg, J.S., Fears, W.B., Hunt, M.M., Powell, M.R., Boll, D., & Wade, C.E. (1984). Exercise-induced amenorrhea and bone denisty. *Annals of Internal Medicine, 101*, 647-648.

Lindberg, J.S., Powell, M.R., Hunt, M.M., Ducey, D.E., & Wade, C.E. (1987). Increased vertebral bone mineral in response to reduced exercise in amenorrheic runners. *Western Journal of Medicine, 146*, 39-42.

Linnell, S.L., Stager, J.M., Blue, P.W., Oyster, N., & Robertshaw, D. (1984). Bone mineral content and menstrual regularity in female runners. *Medicine and Science in Sports and Exercise, 16*, 343-348.

Linse, J., & Lutter, J.M. (1987). Physical activity and menstrual cycle discomfort: New evidence. *The Melpomene Report, 6*(3), 15-18.

Lloyd, T., Myers, C., Buchanan, J.R., & Demers, L.M. (1988). Collegiate women athletes with irregular menses during adolescence have decreased bone density. *Obstetrics and Gynecology, 72*, 639-641.

Lloyd, T., Triantafyllou, S.J., Baker, E.R., Houts, P.S., Whiteside, J.A., Kalenak, A., & Stumpf, P.G. (1986). Women athletes with menstrual irregularity have increased musculoskeletal injuries. *Medicine and Science in Sports and Exercise, 18*, 374-379.

Lohman, T.G., Boileau, R.A., & Slaughter, M.H. (1984). Body composition in children and youth. In R.A. Boileau (Ed.), *Advances in pediatric sport sciences: Vol. 1. Biological issues* (pp. 29-57). Champaign, IL: Human Kinetics.

Lohman, T.G., Pollock, M.L., Slaughter, M.H., Brandon, L.J., & Boileau, R.A. (1984). Methodological factors and the prediction of body fat in female athletes. *Medicine and Science in Sports and Exercise,* **16,** 92-96.

Lokey, E.A. (1988). *The effect of exercise training on pregnancy outcomes.* Unpublished master's thesis, Arizona State University, Tempe.

Lokey, E.A., & Tran, Z.V. (1989). Effects of exercise training on serum lipid and lipoprotein concentrations in women: A meta-analysis. *International Journal of Sports Medicine,* **10,** 424-429.

Longcope, C., Pratt, J.H., Schneider, S.H., & Fineberg, S.E. (1978). Aromatization of androgens by muscle and adipose tissue *in vivo. Journal of Clinical Endocrinology and Metabolism,* **46,** 146-152.

Loosli, A.R., Benson, J., Gillien, D.M., & Bourdet, K. (1986). Nutrition habits and knowledge in competitive adolescent female gymnasts. *The Physician and Sportsmedicine,* **14**(8), 118-130.

Lorentzen, D., & Lawson, L. (1987). Selected sports bras: A biomechanical analysis of breast motion while jogging. *The Physician and Sportsmedicine,* **15**(5), 128-139.

Lotgering, F.K. (1988). Pregnancy. In M.M. Shangold & G. Mirkin (Eds.), *Women and exercise: Physiology and sports medicine* (pp. 145-155). Philadelphia: F.A. Davis.

Lotgering, F.K., Gilbert, R.D., & Longo, L.D. (1984). The interactions of exercise and pregnancy: A review. *American Journal of Obstetrics and Gynecology,* **149,** 560-568.

Loucks, A.B. (1986a). Does exercise training affect reproductive hormones in women? *Clinics in Sports Medicine,* **5,** 535-557.

Loucks, A.B. (1986b). Problems in methodology. In J.L. Puhl & C.H. Brown (Eds.), *The*

menstrual cycle and physical activity (pp. 143-157). Champaign, IL: Human Kinetics.

Loucks, A.B., & Horvath, S.M. (1984). Exercise-induced stress responses of amenorrheic and eumenorrheic runners. *Journal of Clinical Endocrinology and Metabolism,* **59,** 1109-1120.

Loucks, A.B., & Horvath, S.M. (1985). Athletic amenorrhea: A review. *Medicine and Science in Sports and Exercise,* **17,** 56-72.

Loucks, A.B., Horvath, S.M., & Freedson, P.S. (1984). Menstrual status and validation of body fat prediction in athletes. *Human Biology,* **56,** 383-392.

Loucks, J., & Thompson, J. (1968). Effect of menstruation on reaction time. *Research Quarterly for Exercise and Sport,* **39,** 407-408.

Lucas, A.R. (1978). Anorexia nervosa. *Contemporary Nutrition,* **3**(8), n.p. (Published by General Mills)

Lucas, A.R. (1981). Bulimia and vomiting syndrome. *Contemporary Nutrition,* **6**(4), n.p. (Published by General Mills)

Luciano, A.A., Turksoy, R.N., Carleo, J., & Hendrix, J.W. (1988). Clinical and metabolic responses of menopausal women to sequential versus continuous estrogen and progestin replacement therapy. *Obstetrics and Gynecology,* **71,** 39-43.

Lutter, J.M. (1983). Contraceptive practices of female runners [Correspondence]. *Fertility and Sterility,* **40,** 551.

Lutter, J.M., & Cushman, S. (1982). Menstrual patterns in female runners. *The Physician and Sportsmedicine,* **10**(9), 60-72.

Lynch, S. (1980). Ascorbic acid and iron nutrition. *Contemporary Nutrition,* **5**(9), n.p.

MacDougall, J.D., Roche, P.D., Bar-Or, O., & Moroz, J.R. (1983). Maximal aerobic capacity of Canadian schoolchildren: Prediction based on age-related oxygen cost of running. *International Journal of Sports Medicine,* **4,** 194-198.

Malina, R.M. (1978). Adolescent growth and maturation: Selected aspects of current research. *Yearbook of Physical Anthropology*, **21**, 63-94.

Malina, R.M. (1980). Growth, strength, and physical performance. In G.A. Stull (Ed.), *Encyclopedia of physical education, fitness, and sports* (Vol. 2, pp. 443-470). Salt Lake City: Brighton Publishing.

Malina, R.M. (1983). Menarche in athletes: A synthesis and hypothesis. *Annals of Human Biology*, **10**, 1-24.

Malina, R.M. (1988). Growth, performance, activity, and training during adolescence. In M. Shangold & G. Mirkin (Eds.), *Women and exercise: Physiology and sports medicine* (pp. 120-128). Philadelphia: F.A. Davis.

Malina, R.M., Harper, A.B., Avent, H.H., & Campbell, D.E. (1971). Physique of female track and field athletes. *Medicine and Science in Sports*, **3**, 32-38.

Malina, R.M., Harper, A.B., Avent, H.H., & Campbell, D.E. (1973). Age at menarche in athletes and nonathletes. *Medicine and Science in Sports*, **5**, 11-13.

Malina, R.M., Spirduso, W.W., Tate, C., & Baylor, A.M. (1978). Age at menarche and selected menstrual characteristics in athletes at different competitive levels and in different sports. *Medicine and Science in Sports*, **10**, 218-222.

Maksud, M.G., Hamilton, L.H., & Coutts, K.D. (1971). Pulmonary function measurements of Olympic speed skaters for the U.S. *Medicine and Science in Sports*, **3**, 66-71.

Maksud, M.G., Wiley, R.L., Hamilton, L.H., & Lockhart, B. (1970). Maximal $\dot{V}O_2$, ventilation, and heart rate of Olympic speed skating candidates. *Journal of Applied Physiology*, **29**, 186-190.

Mandroukas, K., Krotkiewski, M., Hedberg, M., Wroblewski, Z., Björntorp, P., & Grimby, G. (1984). Physical training in obese women: Effects of muscle morphology, biochemistry and function. *European Journal of Applied Physiology*, **52**, 355-361.

Manore, M.M., Besenfelder, P.D., Wells, C.L., Carroll, S.S., & Hooker, S.P. (1989). Nutrient intakes and iron status in female long-distance runners during training. *Journal of the American Dietetic Association*, **89**, 257-259.

Marcus, R., Cann, C., Madvig, P., Minkoff, J., Goddard, M., Bayer, M., Martin, M., Gaudiani, L., Haskell, W., & Genant, H. (1985). Menstrual function and bone mass in elite women distance runners. *Annals of Internal Medicine*, **102**, 158-163.

Margaria, R., Aghemo, P., & Rovelli, E. (1966). Measurement of muscular power (anaerobic) in man. *Journal of Applied Physiology*, **21**, 1662-1664.

Märker, K. (1981). Influence of athletic training on the maturity process of girls. *Medicine and Sport Science*, **15**, 117-126.

Marples, M.J. (1969). Life on the human skin. *Scientific American*, **220**, 108-115.

Marsäl, K., Löfgren, O., & Gennser, G. (1979). Fetal breathing movements and maternal exercise. *Acta Obstetrics and Gynecology Scandinavica*, **58**, 197-201.

Martin, F.L. (1976). *Effects of the menstrual cycle on metabolic and cardiorespiratory responses*. Unpublished doctoral dissertation, Ohio State University, Columbus.

Marut, E.L. (1987). Premenstrual tension and idiopathic edema. In J.J. Gold & J.B. Josimovich (Eds.), *Gynecologic endocrinology* (4th ed., pp. 447-457). New York: Plenum Medical.

Mayer, J. (1968). *Overweight: Causes, cost, and control*. Englewood Cliffs, NJ: Prentice-Hall.

Mazess, R.B., & Cameron, J.R. (1973). Bone mineral content in normal U.S. whites. In R.B. Mazess (Ed.), *International Conference on Bone Mineral Measurement* (DHEW Publication No. NIH 75-683). Bethesda, MD: Public Health Service.

McArdle, W.D., Katch, F.I., & Katch, V.L. (1981). *Exercise physiology: Energy, nutrition, and human performance*. Philadelphia: Lea & Febiger.

McArdle, W.D., Magel, J.R., & Kyvallos, L.C.

(1971). Aerobic capacity, heart rate and estimated energy cost during women's competitive basketball. *Research Quarterly, 42*, 178-186.

McAuley, E., Hudash, G., Shields, K., Albright, J.P., Garrick, J., Requa, R., & Wallace, R.K. (1987). Injuries in women's gymnastics: The state of the art. *American Journal of Sports Medicine, 15*, 558-565.

McClintock, M.K. (1971). Menstrual synchrony and suppression. *Nature, 229*, 244-245.

McMurray, R.G., Katz, V.L., Berry, M.J., & Cefalo, R.C. (1988). The effect of pregnancy on metabolic responses during rest, immersion, and aerobic exercise in the water. *American Journal of Obstetrics and Gynecology, 158*, 481-486.

McNamara, D.J. (1987). Effects of fat-modified diets on cholesterol and lipoprotein metabolism. *Annual Review of Nutrition, 7*, 273-290.

Mellits, E.D., & Cheek, D.B. (1970). The assessment of body water and fatness from infancy to adulthood. *Monogram of Social Research in Child Development, 35*, 12-26.

Metcalf, J.A., Watson, H., Mathews, R., & Guynn, G. (1981). ECG effects of aerobic dance. *Post-Graduate Medicine, 70*, 219-223.

Micheli, L.J. (1988). Dance injuries: The back, hip, and pelvis. In P.M. Clarkson, & M. Skrinar (Eds.), *Science of dance training* (pp. 193-207). Champaign, IL: Human Kinetics.

Milligan, D., Drife, J.O., & Short, R.V. (1975). Changes in breast volume during normal menstrual cycle and after oral contraceptives. *British Medical Journal, 4*, 494-496.

Mills, J. (1987). Life in the nineties. *Women's Sports and Fitness, 9*(11), 61.

Moffatt, R.J., Surina, B., Golden, B., & Ayres, N. (1984). Body composition and physiological characteristics of female high school gymnasts. *Research Quarterly for Exercise and Sport, 55*, 80-84.

Montoye, H.J., & Lamphiear, D.E. (1977). Grip and arm strength in males and females, age 10 to 69. *Research Quarterly for Exercise and Sport, 48*, 109-120.

Montoye, H.J., Smith, E.L., Fardon, D.E., &

Howley, E.T. (1980). Bone mineral in senior tennis players. *Scandinavian Journal of Sports Science, 2*(1), 26-32.

Moody, D.L., Wilmore, J.H., Girandola, R.N., & Royce, J. (1972). The effects of a jogging program on the body composition of normal and obese high school girls. *Medicine and Science in Sports, 4*, 210-213.

Morgan, D.W., Cruise, R.J., Girardin, B.W., Lutz-Schneider, V., Morgan, D.H., & Qi, W.M. (1986). HDL-C concentrations in weight-trained, endurance-trained, and sedentary females. *The Physician and Sportsmedicine, 14*(3), 166-181.

Morrow, J.R., Jr., & Hosler, W.W. (1981). Strength comparisons in untrained men and trained women athletes. *Medicine and Science in Sports and Exercise, 13*, 194-198.

Morton, M.J., Paul, M.S., Campos, G.R., Hart, M.V., & Metcalfe, J. (1985). Exercise dynamics in late gestation: Effects of physical training. *American Journal of Obstetrics and Gynecology, 152*, 91-97.

Morton, M.J., Paul, M.S., & Metcalfe, J. (1985). Exercise during pregnancy. *Medical Clinics of North America, 61*, 97-108.

National Center for Health Statistics. (1977, November 30). Weight by height and age of adults 18-74 years: United States, 1971-1974. *Advancedata* (Vital and Health Statistics of the National Center for Health Statistics), No. 14. Washington, DC.

National Dairy Council. (1982). *Guide to wise food choices*. Rosemont, IL: Author.

National Dairy Council. (1984). *Calcium: A summary of current research for the health professional*. Rosemont, IL: Author.

National Institutes of Health. (1985). Lowering blood cholesterol to prevent heart disease [Consensus development conference report]. *Journal of the American Medical Association, 253*(14), 2080-2086.

National Research Council. Food and Nutrition Board. (1989). *Recommended dietary allowances* (10th ed.). Washington, DC: National Academy of Sciences.

National Research Council. National Academy of Sciences. (1982). *Diet, nutrition and cancer*. Washington, DC.

NCAA survey shows injury trends (1987). *The Physician and Sportsmedicine, 15*(2), 30.

A need to know. (1981). *The Physician and Sportsmedicine, 9*(12), 17.

Nelson, J.K., Thomas, J.R., Nelson, K.R., & Abraham, P.C. (1986). Gender differences in children's throwing performance: Biology and environment. *Research Quarterly for Exercise and Sport, 57*, 280-287.

Nelson, M.E., Fisher, E., Catsos, P.D., Meredith, C.N., Turksoy, R.N., & Evans, W.J. (1986). Diet and bone status in amenorrheic runners. *American Journal of Clinical Nutrition, 43*, 910-916.

Newhouse, I.J., & Clement, D.B. (1988). Iron status in athletes: An update. *Sports Medicine, 5*, 337-352.

Niinimaa, V. (1982). Figure skating: What do we know about it? *The Physician and Sportsmedicine, 10*(1), 51-56.

Nilson, K.L. (1986). Injuries in female distance runners. In B.L. Drinkwater (Ed.), *Female endurance athletes* (pp. 149-161). Champaign, IL: Human Kinetics.

Nimrod, A., & Ryan, K.J. (1975). Aromatization of androgens by human abdominal and breast fat tissue. *Journal of Clinical Endocrinology and Metabolism, 40*, 367-375.

Noble, L. (1975). Heart rate and predicted $\dot{V}O_2$ during women's competitive gymnastic routines. *Journal of Sports Medicine and Physical Fitness, 15*, 151-157.

Notelovitz, M. (1988). The menopause. In M.A. Shangold & G. Mirkin (Eds.), *Women and exercise: Physiology and sports medicine* (pp. 156-177). Philadelphia: F.A. Davis.

Notelovitz, M., Fields, C., Caramelli, K., Dougherty, M., & Schwartz, A.L. (1986). Cardiorespiratory fitness evaluation in climacteric women: Comparison of two methods. *American Journal of Obstetrics and Gynecology, 154*, 1009-1013.

Notelovitz, M., Zauner, C., McKenzie, L., Suggs, Y., Fields, C., & Kitchens, C. (1987). The effect of low-dose oral contraceptives on cardiorespiratory function, coagulation, and lipids in exercising young women: A preliminary report. *American Journal of Obstetrics and Gynecology, 156*, 591-598.

Novak, L.P. (1972). Aging, total body potassium, fat-free mass, and cell mass in males and females between ages 18 and 85 years. *Journal of Gerontology, 27*, 438-443.

Novak, L.P., Bierbaum, M., & Mellerowicz, H. (1973). Maximal oxygen consumption, pulmonary function, body composition, and anthropometry of adolescent female athletes. *Internationale Zeitschrift angewandte Physiologie, 31*, 103-119.

Novak, L.P., Magill, L.A., & Schutte, J.E. (1978). Maximal oxygen intake and body composition of female dancers. *European Journal of Applied Physiology, 39*, 277-282.

Novak, L.P., Woodward, W.A., Bestit, C., & Mellerowicz, H. (1977). Working capacity, body composition and anthropometry of Olympic female athletes. *Journal of Sports Medicine and Physical Fitness, 17*, 275-283.

Nunneley, S.A. (1978). Physiological responses of women to thermal stress: A review. *Medicine and Science in Sports, 10*, 250-255.

Nutrition and women's health concerns. (1986). *Dairy Council Digest, 57*(1), 1-6.

Oscai, L.B. (1973). The role of exercise in weight control. *Exercise and Sport Sciences Reviews, 1*, 103-123.

Oscai, L.B. (1984). Recent progress in understanding obesity. *American Academy of Physical Education Papers, 17*, 42-48.

Oscai, L.B., Babirak, S.P., McGarr, J.A., & Spirakis, C.N. (1974). Effect of exercise on adipose tissue cellularity. *Federation Proceedings, 33*, 1956-1958.

Oscai, L.B., & Holloszy, J.O. (1969). Effects of weight changes produced by exercise, food restriction, or overeating on body composition. *Journal of Clinical Investigation, 48*, 2124-2128.

O'Shea, J.P., & Wegner, J. (1981). Power weight training and the female athlete. *The Physician and Sportsmedicine, 9*(6), 109-120.

Osler, D.C., & Crawford, J.D. (1973). Examination of the hypothesis of a critical weight at menarche in ambulatory and bedridden mentally retarded girls. *Pediatrics, 51*, 674.

Otto, R.M., Parker, C.A., Smith, T.K., Wygand, J.W., & Perez, H.R. (1986). The energy cost of low impact and high impact aerobic dance exercise [Abstract 113]. *Medicine and Science in Sports and Exercise, 18*(Suppl.), S23-S24.

Oyster, N. (1979). Effects of a heavy-resistance weight training program on college women athletes. *Journal of Sports Medicine and Physical Fitness, 19*, 79-83.

Paolone, A.M., Shangold, M., Paul, D., Minnitti, J., & Weiner, S. (1987). Fetal heart rate measurement during maternal exercise—Avoidance of artifact. *Medicine and Science in Sports and Exercise, 19*, 605-609.

Pappenheimer, J.R., Comroe, J.H., Cournand, A., Ferguson, J.K., Filley, G.F., Fowler, W.S., Gray, J.S., Helmholtz, H.F., Otis, A.B., Rahn, H., & Riley, R.L. (1950). Standardization of definitions and symbols in respiratory physiology. *Federation Proceedings, 9*, 602-605.

Pařízková, J. (1973). Body composition and exercise during growth and development. In G.L. Rarick (Ed.), *Physical activity, human growth and development* (pp. 97-124). New York: Academic Press.

Pařízková, J., & Poupa, D. (1963). Some metabolic consequences of adaptation to muscular work. *British Journal of Nutrition, 17*, 341-343.

Parker, E. (1960). *The seven ages of woman.* Baltimore: Johns Hopkins Press.

Parr, R.B., Bachman, L.A., & Moss, R.A. (1984). Iron deficiency in female athletes. *The Physician and Sportsmedicine, 12*(4), 81-86.

Passmore, R., & Durnin, J.V.G.A. (1955). Human energy expenditure. *Physiological Reviews, 35*, 801.

Pate, R.R. (1983). Sports anemia: A review of the current research literature. *The Physician and Sportsmedicine, 11*(2), 115-131.

Pate, R.R., Barnes, C., & Miller, W. (1985). A physiological comparison of performance-matched female and male distance runners. *Research Quarterly for Exercise and Sport, 56*, 245-250.

Pate, R.R., & Kriska, A. (1984). Physiological basis of the sex difference in cardiorespiratory endurance. *Sports Medicine (New Zealand), 1*, 87-98.

Pate, R.R., Sparling, P.B., Wilson, G.E., Cureton, K.J., & Miller, B.J. (1987). Cardiorespiratory and metabolic responses to submaximal and maximal exercise in elite women distance runners. *International Journal of Sports Medicine, 8*(Suppl. 2), 91-95.

Paul, B. (1983). Running before menarche: Does it affect later menstrual function? *Melpomene Institute for Women's Health Research Newsletter, 2*(1), 5-6.

Pedersen, P.K., & Jorgensen, J. (1978). Maximal oxygen uptake in young women with training, inactivity, and retraining. *Medicine and Science in Sports, 10*, 233-237.

Peitzmeier, J. (1981, November 20). Jogger beats odds in race against years. *The Scottsdale Daily Progress,* p. 15.

Peltenburg, A.L., Erich, W.B.M., Bernink, M.J.E., Zonderland, M.L., & Huisveld, I.A. (1984). Biological maturation, body composition, and growth of female gymnasts and control groups of schoolgirls and girl swimmers, aged 8 to 14 years: A cross-sectional survey of 1064 girls. *International Journal of Sports Medicine, 5*, 36-42.

Pepperell, R.J., Bright, M., & Smith, M.A. (1977). Serum prolactin levels in normal women and in women with disorders of menstruation. *Medical Journal of Australia, 1*, 85-89.

Pernoll, M.L., Metcalfe, J., Kovach, P.A., Wachtel, R., & Dunham, M. (1975). Ventilation during rest and exercise in pregnancy and postpartum. *Respiratory Physiology, 25*, 295-310.

Pernoll, M.L., Metcalfe, J., Schlenkar, T.L., Welch, J.E., & Matsumoto, J.S.A. (1975). Oxygen consumption at rest and during exercise in pregnancy. *Respiratory Physiology,* **25,** 285-293.

Perry, A.C., Tapp, J., & Weeks, L. (1986). The effects of interval aerobic training on plasma lipid fractions of male and post-menopausal sedentary faculty. *Journal of Sports Medicine and Physical Fitness,* **26,** 186-193.

Petrofsky, J.S., LeDonne, D.M., Rinehart, J.S., & Lind, A.R. (1976). Isometric strength and endurance during the menstrual cycle. *European Journal of Applied Physiology,* **35,** 1-10.

Phillips, M. (1962, April 10). *The effect of the menstrual cycle on selected measures of steadiness, reaction and movement time, blood pressure and heart rate.* Paper presented at the meeting of the American Association for Health, Physical Education and Recreation, Research Section, Cincinnati.

Phillips, M. (1968). Effect of the menstrual cycle on pulse rate and blood pressure before and after exercise. *Research Quarterly,* **39,** 327-333.

Piscopo, J. (1985). Prescriptive exercise for older adults. *Journal of Physical Education, Recreation and Dance,* **56**(8), 65-69.

Plowman, S. (1974). Physiological characteristics of female athletes. *Research Quarterly,* **45,** 349-362.

Plowman, S.A., Drinkwater, B.L., & Horvath, S.M. (1979). Age and aerobic power in women: A longitudinal study. *Journal of Gerontology,* **34,** 512-520.

Pollock, M.L., Wilmore, J.H., & Fox, S.M., III. (1978). *Health and fitness through physical activity.* New York: Wiley.

Pomerance, J.J., Gluck, L., & Lynch, V.A. (1974). Physical fitness in pregnancy: Its effect on pregnancy outcome. *American Journal of Obstetrics and Gynecology,* **119,** 867-876.

Powers, S.K., & Walker, R. (1982). Physiological and anatomical characteristics of outstanding female junior tennis players. *Research Quarterly for Exercise and Sport,* **53,** 172-175.

Pregnancy and sports. (1974). *The Physician and Sportsmedicine,* **2**(5), 35-41.

Prince, F.P., Hikida, R.S., & Hagerman, F.C. (1977). Muscle fiber types in women athletes and non-athletes. *Pflügers Archives,* **371,** 161-165.

Prior, J.C. (1982). Endocrine "conditioning" with endurance training: A preliminary review. *Canadian Journal of Applied Sports Sciences,* **7,** 148-157.

Prior, J.C. (1988). Reproductive changes with exercise: When and how to evaluate, who and why to treat. In J.L. Puhl, C.H. Brown, & R.O. Voy (Eds.), *Sport science perspectives for women* (pp. 131-150). Champaign, IL: Human Kinetics.

Prior, J.C., & Vigna, Y. (1985). Gonadal steroids in athletic women: Contraception, complications and performance. *Sports Medicine (New Zealand),* **2,** 287-295.

Prior, J.C., & Vigna, Y. (1986). The therapy of reproductive system changes associated with exercise training. In J.L. Puhl & C.H. Brown (Eds.), *The menstrual cycle and physical activity* (pp. 105-114). Champaign, IL: Human Kinetics.

Prior, J.C., Vigna, Y., & Alojado, N. (1986). Conditioning exercise decreases premenstrual symptoms: A prospective controlled three month trial. *European Journal of Applied Physiology,* **55,** 349-355.

Prior, J.C., Vigna, Y., Sciarretta, D., Alojado, N., & Schulzer, M. (1987). Conditioning exercise decreases premenstrual symptoms: A prospective, controlled 6-month trial. *Fertility and Sterility,* **47,** 402-408.

Prior, J.C., Yuen, B.H., Clement, P., Bowie, L., & Thomas, J. (1982). Reversible luteal phase changes and infertility associated with marathon training. *Lancet,* **2,** 269-270.

Pritchard, J.A. (1965). Changes in the blood volume during pregnancy and delivery. *Anesthesiology,* **26,** 393-399.

Profant, G.R., Early, R.G., Nilson, K.L., Kusumi, F., Hofer, V., & Bruce, R.A. (1972). Responses to maximal exercise in healthy middle-aged women. *Journal of Applied Physiology, 33*, 595-599.

Pros, J.R. (1961). The prevention of climacteric complaints by means of sport. *Cs. Gynekologie,* **XXVI**, 1-2. (From *Journal of Sports Medicine and Physical Fitness*, 1962, **2**, 125-126) (Abstract)

Puhl, J. (1977). Nutrition and weight control. In L.I. Gedvilas & M.E. Kneer (Eds.), *Proceedings of the NCPEAM/NAPECW National Conference* (pp. 85-102). Chicago: University of Illinois at Chicago Circle, Office of Publications Services.

Puhl, J.L. (1986). Women and endurance: Some factors influencing performance. In B.L. Drinkwater (Ed.), *Female endurance athletes* (pp. 41-58). Champaign, IL: Human Kinetics.

Puhl, J., Case, S., Fleck, S., & Van Handel, P. (1982). Physical and physiological characteristics of elite volleyball players. *Research Quarterly for Exercise and Sport,* **53**, 257-262.

Puhl, J.L., Runyan, W.S., & Kruse, S.J. (1981). Erythocyte changes during training in high school women cross-country runners. *Research Quarterly for Exercise and Sport,* **52**, 484-494.

Puhl, J.L., Van Handel, P.J., Williams, L.L., Bradley, P.W., & Harms, S.J. (1985). Iron status and training. In N.K. Butts, T.T. Gushiken, & B. Zarins (Eds.), *The elite athlete* (pp. 209-236). New York: Medical and Scientific Books.

Quilligan, E.J., & Kaiser, I.H. (1982). Maternal physiology. In D.N. Danforth (Ed.), *Obstetrics and gynecology* (4th ed.). New York: Harper & Row.

Ragni, G., DeLauretis, L., Bestetti, O., Wyssling, H., & Crosignani, P.G. (1987). Effects of combined hormonal-antiinflammatory therapy in the postmenopausal vaginitus. In P. Fioretti, C. Flamigni, V.M. Jasonni, & C.B. Melis (Eds.), *Postmenopausal hormonal therapy: Benefits and risks* (pp. 103-109). New York: Raven Press.

Raine, C.A. (1978). An examination of men's and women's Olympic performance since 1960. *Athletic Coach,* **12**, 26-28.

Raven, P.B., Drinkwater, B.L., & Horvath, S.M. (1972). Cardiovascular responses of young female track athletes during exercise. *Medicine and Science in Sports,* **4**, 205-209.

Recommended dietary allowances revised. (1980). *Dairy Council Digest,* **51**(2), n.p.

Reid, R.L. (1985). The endocrinology of premenstrual syndrome. In M.Y. Dawood, J.L. McGuire, & L.M. Demers (Eds.), *Premenstrual syndrome and dysmenorrhea* (pp. 51-66). Baltimore: Urban & Schwarzenberg.

Ribisl, P.M. (1980). Guidelines and principles of cardiovascular conditioning and exercise prescription. In G.A. Stull (Ed.), *Encyclopedia of physical education, fitness, and sports: Vol. 2. Training, environment, nutrition, and fitness* (pp. 4-19). Salt Lake City: Brighton Publishing.

Richelson, L.S., Wahner, H.W., Melton, L.J., III, & Riggs, B.L. (1984). Relative contributions of aging and estrogen deficiency to postmenopausal bone loss. *New England Journal of Medicine,* **311**, 1273-1275.

Richie, D.H., Kelso, S.F., & Bellucci, P.A. (1985). Aerobic dance injuries: A retrospective study of instructors and participants. *The Physician and Sportsmedicine,* **13**(2), 130-140.

Riddinger, R.R., Steinmetz, C.W., Robinson, P.S., Caffrey, G.P., Bartels, R.L., Fox, E.L., & Shaffer, T.E. (1978). Chronic, intensive physical training and cardiac function in female swimmers. In C.B. Corbin (Ed.), *AAHPER Research Consortium Symposium papers: Sport, health, fitness and dance* (Vol. 1, Bk. 2, pp. 13-17). Reston, VA: American Alliance for Health, Physical Education and Recreation.

Risser, W.L., Lee, E.J., Poindexter, H.B., West, M.S., Pivarnik, J.M., Risser, J.M.H., & Hickson, J.F. (1988). Iron deficiency in female athletes: Its prevalence and impact on performance. *Medicine and Science in Sports and Exercise,* **20**, 116-121.

Ritterband, A.B., Jaffe, I.A., Densen, P.M., Magagna, J.F., & Reed, E. (1963). Gonadal function and the development of coronary heart disease. *Circulation, 27*, 237-251.

Rivier, C., Vale, W., Ling, N., Brown, M., & Guillemin, R. (1977). Stimulation *in vivo* of the secretion of prolactin and growth hormone by β-endorphin. *Endocrinology, 100*, 238-241.

Robinton, E.D., & Mood, E.W. (1966). A quantitative and qualitative appraisal of microbial pollution of water by swimmers: A preliminary report. *Journal of Hygiene* (Cambridge), **64**, 489-499.

Roby, F.B., Buono, M.J., Constable, S.H., Lowdon, B.J., & Tsao, W.Y. (1983). Physiological characteristics of champion synchronized swimmers. *The Physician and Sportsmedicine, 11*(4), 136-147.

Rockefeller, K.A., & Burke, E.J. (1979). Psychophysiological analysis of an aerobic dance programme for women. *British Sports Medicine, 13*, 77-80.

Rockwell, M.H. (1962). *The effect of the menstrual cycle on cardiovascular and muscular efficiency of college women.* Unpublished master's thesis, Pennsylvania State University, University Park.

Rogol, A.D. (1988). Pubertal development in endurance-trained female athletes. In E.W. Brown & C.F. Branta (Eds.), *Competitive sports for children and youth* (pp. 173-193). Champaign, IL: Human Kinetics.

Rose, C.P. (1981). Injuries in women's field hockey: A four-year study. *The Physician and Sportsmedicine, 9*(3), 97-100.

Rose, D.J., Bader, M.E., Bader, R.A., & Braunwald, E. (1956). Catheterization studies of cardiac hemodynamics in normal pregnant women with reference to left ventricular work. *American Journal of Obstetrics and Gynecology, 72*, 233-246.

Rosen, L.W., & Hough, D.O. (1988). Pathogenic weight-control behaviors of female college gymnasts. *The Physician and Sportsmedicine, 16*(9), 141-146.

Rosen, L.W., McKeag, D.B., Hough, D.O., & Curley, V. (1986). Pathogenic weight-control behavior in female athletes. *The Physician and Sportsmedicine, 14*(1), 79-86.

Rowell, L.B. (1974). Human cardiovascular adjustments to exercise and thermal stress. *Physiological Reviews, 54*, 75-159.

Rowland, T.W. (1985). Aerobic response to endurance training in prepubescent children: A critical analysis. *Medicine and Science in Sports and Exercise, 17*, 493-497.

Rubal, B.J., Al-Muhailani, A.-R., & Rosentswieg, J. (1987). Effects of physical conditioning on the heart size and wall thickness of college women. *Medicine and Science in Sports and Exercise, 19*, 423-429.

Ruhling, R.O., Cameron, J., Sibley, L., Christensen, C., & Bolen, T. (1981). Maintaining aerobic fitness while jogging through a pregnancy! A case study. *Medicine and Science in Sports and Exercise, 13*, 93.

Rusko, H., Hara, M., & Karvinen, E. (1978). Aerobic performance capacity in athletes. *European Journal of Applied Physiology, 38*, 151-159.

Rusko, H., Rahkila, P., & Karvinen, E. (1980). Anaerobic threshold, skeletal muscle enzymes and fiber composition in young female cross-country skiers. *Acta Physiologica Scandinavica, 108*, 263-268.

Russell, J.B., Mitchell, D., Musey, P.I., & Collins, D.C. (1984). The relationship of exercise to anovulatory cycles in female athletes: Hormonal and physical characteristics. *Obstetrics and Gynecology, 63*, 452-456.

Ryan, K.J. (1976). Estrogens and atherosclerosis. *Clinical Obstetrics and Gynecology, 19*, 805-815.

Sady, S.P., & Freedson, P.S. (1984). Body composition and structural comparisons of female and male athletes. *Clinics in Sports Medicine, 3*, 755-777.

Sager, K. (1984). Exercises to activate seniors. *The Physician and Sportsmedicine, 12*(5), 144-151.

Saltin, B., & Åstrand, P.-O. (1967). Maximal oxygen uptake in athletes. *Journal of Applied Physiology, 23*, 353-358.

Saltin, B., Blomquist, G., Mitchell, J.H., Johnson, R.L., Jr., Wildenthal, K., & Chapman, C.B. (1968). Response to exercise after bed rest and after training: A longitudinal study of adaptive changes in oxygen transport and body composition. *Circulation, 38*(Suppl. 7), 1-78.

Saltin, B., Henriksson, J., Nygaard, E., & Anderson, P. (1977). Fiber types and metabolic potentials of skeletal muscles in sedentary man and endurance runners. *Annals of the New York Academy of Science, 301,* 3-29.

Sanborn, C.F., Martin, B.J., & Wagner, W.W., Jr. (1982). Is athletic amenorrhea specific to runners? *American Journal of Obstetrics and Gynecology, 143,* 859-861.

Sanborn, C.F., & Wagner, W.W., Jr. (1988). The female athlete and menstrual irregularity. In J.L. Puhl, C.H. Brown, & R.O. Voy (Eds.), *Sport science perspectives for women* (pp. 111-130). Champaign, IL: Human Kinetics.

Saunders, N.A., Leeder, S.R., & Rebuck, A.S. (1976). Ventilatory response to carbon dioxide in young athletes: A family study. *American Review of Respiratory Diseases, 113,* 497-502.

Schantz, P., Randall-Fox, E., Hutchinson, W., Tyden, A., & Åstrand, P.O. (1983). Muscle fibre type distribution, muscle cross-sectional area and maximal voluntary strength in humans. *Acta Physiologica Scandinavica, 117,* 219-226.

Schoene, R.B., Robertson, H.T., Pierson, D.J., & Peterson, A.P. (1981). Respiratory drives and exercise in menstrual cycles of athletic and nonathletic women. *Journal of Applied Physiology: Respiratory, Environmental and Exercise Physiology, 50,* 1300-1305.

Schwartz, B., Cumming, D., Riordan, E., Selye, M., Yen, S., & Rebar, R. (1981). Exercise-associated amenorrhea: A distinct entity? *American Journal of Obstetrics and Gynecology, 141,* 662-670.

Scott, D.E., & Pritchard, J.A. (1967). Iron deficiency in healthy young college women. *Jour-nal of the American Medical Association, 199,* 897-900.

Scott, E.C. (1984). Estimation of total water and fatness from weight and height: Inaccurate for lean women. *American Journal of Physical Anthropology, 64,* 83-87.

Scott, E.C., & Johnston, F.E. (1982). Critical fat, menarche, and the maintenance of menstrual cycles: A critical review. *Journal of Adolescent Health Care, 2,* 249-260.

Scott, M.G., & Tuttle, W.W. (1932). The periodic fluctuation in physical efficiency during the menstrual cycle. *Research Quarterly, 3,* 137-144.

Secondary amenorrhea linked to stress. (1978). *The Physician and Sportsmedicine, 6*(10), 24.

Seals, D.R., Hagberg, J.M., Hurley, B.F., Ehsani, A.A., & Holloszy, J.O. (1984a). Effects of endurance training on glucose tolerance and plasma lipid levels in older men and women. *Journal of the American Medical Association, 252,* 645-649.

Seals, D.R., Hagberg, J.M., Hurley, B.F., Ehsani, A.A., & Holloszy, J.O. (1984b). Endurance training in older men and women: I. Cardiovascular responses to exercise. *Journal of Applied Physiology: Respiratory, Environmental and Exercise Physiology, 57,* 1024-1029.

Seals, D.R., Hurley, B.F., Schultz, J., & Hagberg, J.M. (1984). Endurance training in older men and women: II. Blood lactate response to submaximal exercise. *Journal of Applied Physiology: Respiratory, Environmental and Exercise Physiology, 57,* 1030-1033.

Sedlock, D.A., Fitzgerald, P.I., & Knowlton, R.G. (1988). Body composition and performance characteristics of collegiate women rugby players. *Research Quarterly for Exercise and Sport, 59,* 78-82.

Selden, G. (1981). Frailty, thy name's been changed. *Ms., 10*(1), 51-53, 96.

Shaar, G.J., Frederickson, R.C.A., Dininger, N.B., & Jackson, L. (1977). Enkephalin analogues and naloxone modulate the release of growth hormone and prolactin—Evidence for regulation by an endogenous opioid peptide in brain. *Life Sciences, 21*, 853-860.

Schaffer, T.E.. (1972). Physiological considerations of the female participant. In D.V. Harris (Ed.), *Women and sport: A national research conference* (pp. 321-331). (HPER Series No. 2). University Park: Pennsylvania State University.

Shangold, M.M. (1984). Effects of exercise on reproductive function. *Advances in Clinical Obstetrics and Gynecology, 2*, 146-157.

Shangold, M.M. (1985). Causes, evaluation, and management of athletic oligo-/amenorrhea. *Medical Clinics of North America, 69*, 83-95.

Shangold, M.M. (1988). Menstruation. In M.M. Shangold & G. Mirkin (Eds.), *Women and exercise: Physiology and sports medicine* (pp. 129-144). Philadelphia: F.A. Davis.

Shangold, M.M., Freeman, R., Thysen, B., & Gatz, M. (1979). The relationship between long-distance running, plasma progesterone, and luteal phase length. *Fertility and Sterility, 31*, 131-133.

Shangold, M.M., Gatz, M.L., & Thysen, B. (1981). Acute effects of exercise on plasma concentrations of prolactin and testosterone in recreational women runners. *Fertility and Sterility, 35*, 699-702.

Shangold, M.M., & Levine, H.S. (1982). The effect of marathon training upon menstrual function. *American Journal of Obstetrics and Gynecology, 143*, 862-869.

Sharkey, B.J. (1979). *Physiology of fitness*. Champaign, IL: Human Kinetics.

Sharkey, B., Wilson, D., Whiddon, T., & Miller, K. (1978). Fit to work? *Journal of Physical Education and Recreation, 49*, 18-21.

Sheehy, G. (1976). *Passages: Predictable crises of adult life*. New York: E.P. Dutton.

Shephard, R.J. (1977). *Endurance fitness*. Toronto: University of Toronto Press.

Shephard, R.J. (1978). *Physical activity and aging*. Chicago: Year Book Medical Publishers.

Shephard, R.J., & Sidney, K.H. (1978). Exercise and aging. In R.S. Hutton (Ed.), *Exercise and sport sciences reviews* (Vol. 6, pp. 1-57). Philadelphia: Franklin Institute Press.

Shively, R.A., Grana, W.A., & Ellis, D. (1981). High school sports injuries. *The Physician and Sportsmedicine, 9*(8), 46-50.

Sibley, L., Ruhling, R.O., Cameron-Foster, J., Christensen, C., & Bolen, T. (1981). Swimming and physical fitness during pregnancy. *Journal of Nurse-Midwifery, 26*(6), 3-12.

Sidney, K.H., & Shephard, R.J. (1976). Attitudes toward health and physical training in the elderly: Effects of a physical training program. *Medicine and Science in Sports, 8*, 246-252.

Sidney, K.H., & Shephard, R.J. (1977). Maximum and submaximum exercise tests in men and women in the seventh, eight, and ninth decades of life. *Journal of Applied Physiology, 43*, 280-287.

Siegel, P. (1960). Does bath water enter the vagina? *Obstetrics and gynecology, 15*, 660-661.

Simopoulos, A.P. (1987). Characteristics of obesity: An overview. *Annals of the New York Academy of Sciences, 499*, 4-13.

Sinaki, M., McPhee, M.C., Hodgson, S.F., Merritt, J.M., & Offord, K.P. (1986). Relationship between bone mineral density of spine and strength of back extensors in healthy postmenopausal women. *Mayo Clinical Proceedings, 61*, 116-122.

Sinaki, M., & Mikkelsen, B.A. (1984). Postmenopausal spinal osteoporosis: Flexion versus extension exercises. *Archives of Physical Medicine and Rehabilitation, 65*, 593-596.

Sinning, W.E. (1973). Body composition, cardiovascular function, and rule changes in women's basketball. *Research Quarterly, 44*, 313-321.

Sinning, W.E., & Adrian, M.J. (1968). Cardiorespiratory changes in college women due to a season of competitive basketball. *Journal of Applied Physiology, 25*, 720-724.

Sinning, W.E., & Lindberg, G.D. (1972). Physical characteristics of college age women gymnasts. *Research Quarterly, 43,* 226-234.

Sinning, W.E., & Little, K.D. (1987). Body composition and menstrual function in athletes. *Sports Medicine (New Zealand), 4,* 34-45.

Sinning, W.E., & Wilson, J.R. (1984). Validity of "generalized" equations for body composition analysis in women athletes. *Research Quarterly for Exercise and Sport, 55,* 153-160.

Skinner, J.S., & Morgan, D.W. (1985). Aspects of anaerobic performance. In D.H. Clarke & H.M. Eckert (Eds.), *Limits of human performance* (pp. 31-44). Champaign, IL: Human Kinetics.

Slavin, J.L., Lutter, J.M., Cushman, S., & Lee, V. (1988). Pregnancy and exercise. In J. Puhl, C.H. Brown, & R. Voy (Eds.), *Sport science persepctives for women* (pp. 151-160). Champaign, IL: Human Kinetics.

Sloane, E. (1980). *Biology of women.* New York: Wiley.

Smith, A.D., & Micheli, L.J. (1982). Injuries in competitive figure skaters. *The Physician and Sportsmedicine, 10,* 36-47.

Smith, D.M., Khairi, M.R.A., Norton, J., & Johnston, C.C., Jr. (1976). Age and activity effects on rate of bone mineral loss. *Journal of Clinical Investigation, 58,* 716-721.

Smith, E.L. (1974). The effects of physical activity in bone in the aged. In R.B. Mazess (Ed.), *International Conference on Bone Mineral Measurement* (DHEW Publication No. NIH 75-683, pp. 397-407). Bethesda, MD: Public Health Service.

Smith, E.L., Reddan, W., & Smith, P.E. (1981). Physical activity and calcium modalities for bone mineral increase in aged women. *Medicine and Science in Sport and Exercise, 13,* 60-64.

Smith, N.J. (1980). Excessive weight loss and food aversion in athletes simulating anorexia nervosa. *Pediatrics, 66,* 139-142.

Snow-Harter, C. (1987). Biochemical changes in postmenopausal women following a muscle fitness program. *The Physician and Sportsmedicine, 15*(8), 90-96.

Snyder, A.C., Dvorak, L.L., & Roepke, J.B. (1989). Influence of dietary iron source on measures of iron status among female runners. *Medicine and Science in Sports and Exercise, 21,* 7-10.

South-Paul, J.E., Rajagopal, K.R., & Tenholder, M.F. (1988). The effect of participation in a regular exercise program upon aerobic capacity during pregnancy. *Obstetrics and Gynecology, 71,* 175-179.

Southam, A.L., & Gonzaga, F.P. (1965). Systemic changes during the menstrual cycle. *American Journal of Obstetrics and Gynecology, 91,* 142-165.

Sparling, P.B. (1980). A meta-analysis of studies comparing maximal oxygen uptake in men and women. *Research Quarterly for Exercise and Sport, 51,* 542-552.

Sparling, P.B. (Ed.) (1987). A comprehensive profile of elite women distance runners [Monograph]. *International Journal of Sports Medicine, 8*(Suppl. 2).

Sparling, P.B., Wilson, G.E., & Pate, R.R. (1987). Project overview and description of performance, training, and physical characteristics in elite women distance runners. *International Journal of Sports Medicine, 8*(Suppl. 2), 73-76.

Spence, D.W., Disch, J.G., Fred, H.L., & Coleman, A.E. (1980). Descriptive profiles of highly skilled women volleyball players. *Medicine and Science in Sports and Exercise, 12,* 299-302.

Speroff, L., & Redwine, D.B. (1980). Exercise and menstrual function. *The Physician and Sportsmedicine, 8*(5), 42-52.

Speroff, L., & Van de Wiele, R.L. (1971). Regulation of the human menstrual cycle. *American Journal of Obstetrics and Gynecology, 109,* 234-247.

Sports during pregnancy, other questions answered. (1976). *The Physician and Sportsmedicine,* **4**(3), 82-85.

Sprynarova, S., & Pařízková, J. (1969). Comparison of the functional, circulatory and respiratory capacity in girl gymnasts and swimmers. *Journal of Sports Medicine and Physical Fitness,* **9**, 165-172.

Stager, J.M. (1984). Reversibility of amenorrhoea in athletes. *Sports Medicine (New Zealand),* **1**, 337-340.

Stager, J.M., Robertshaw, D., & Miescher, E. (1984). Delayed menarche in swimmers in relation to age of onset of training and athletic performance. *Medicine and Science in Sports and Exercise,* **16**, 550-555.

Stampfer, M.J., Willett, W.C., Colditz, G.A., Rosner, B., Speizer, F., & Hennekens, C.H. (1985). A prospective study of postmenopausal estrogen therapy and coronary heart disease. *New England Journal of Medicine,* **313**, 1044-1049.

Stauffer, R. (1976). *Comparison of United States Military Academy men and women on selected physical performance measures.* West Point, NY: Office of Physical Education, United States Military Academy.

Steenkamp, I., Fuller, C., Graves, J., Noakes, T.D., & Jacobs, P. (1986). Marathon running fails to influence RBC survival rates in iron-replete women. *The Physician and Sportsmedicine,* **14**(5), 89-95.

Stephenson, L.A., Kolka, M.A., Wilkerson, J.E. (1982a). Metabolic and thermoregulatory responses to exercise during the human menstrual cycle. *Medicine and Science in Sports and Exercise,* **14**, 270-275.

Stephenson, L.A., Kolka, M.A., & Wilkerson, J.E. (1982b). Perceived exertion and anaerobic threshold during the menstrual cycle. *Medicine and Science in Sports and Exercise,* **14**, 218-222.

Stoppelli, I., Zanconato, G., & Guacci, A.M. (1987). Hormonal treatment of the post-menopausal genito-urinary syndrome. In P.

Fioretti, C. Flamigni, V.M. Jasonni, & G.B. Melis (Eds.), *Postmenopausal hormonal therapy: Benefits and risks* (pp. 95-101). New York: Raven Press.

Study identifies girls' basketball injury trends. (1987). *The Physician and Sportsmedicine,* **15**(8), 62.

Summary of findings from National Children and Youth Fitness Study. (1985). *Journal of Physical Education, Recreation and Dance,* **56**(1), 43-90.

Summary of findings from National Children and Youth Fitness Study II. (1987). *Journal of Physical Education, Recreation and Dance,* **58**(9), 49-96.

Suominen, H., Heikkinen, E., & Parkatti, T. (1977). Effects of eight weeks' physical training on muscle and connective tissue of the M. Vastus Lateralis in 69 year old men and women. *Journal of Gerontology,* **32**, 33-37.

Sutton, J.R., Coleman, M.J., & Casey, J.H. (1974). The adrenal cortical contribution to serum androgens in physical exercise [Abstract]. *Medicine and Science in Sports,* **6**, 72.

Sutton, J.R., Coleman, M.J., Casey, J.H., & Lazarus, L. (1973). Androgen responses during physical exercise. *British Medical Journal,* **1**, 520-522.

Symposium on exercise in the treatment of obesity. (1986). *Medicine and Science in Sports and Exercise,* **18**, 1-30.

Tanner, J.M. (1962). *Growth at adolescence* (2nd ed.). Oxford: Blackwell Scientific Publications.

Tanner, J.M. (1964). *The physique of the Olympic athlete.* London: Allen & Unwin.

Tharp, G.D., Johnson, G.O., & Thorland, W.G. (1984). Measurement of anaerobic power and capacity in elite young track athletes using the Wingate test. *Journal of Sports Medicine and Physical Ftiness,* **24**, 100-105.

Thomas, C.L. (1974). Special problems of the female athlete. In A.J. Ryan & F.L. Allman, Jr. (Eds.), *Sports medicine* (pp. 347-373). New York: Academic Press.

Thomas, J.C., & Riding, D.E. (1978). Physical performance standards for women. In L.L. Gedvilas & M.E. Kneer (Eds.), *Proceedings of the NAPECW/NCPEAM National Conference* (pp. 232-239). Chicago: University of Illinois at Chicago Circle, Office of Publications Services.

Thomas, J.R., & French, K.E. (1985). Gender differences across age in motor performance: A meta-analysis. *Physiological Bulletin, 98,* 260-282.

Thorland, W.G., Johnson, G.O., Tharp, G.D., Housh, T.J., & Cisar, C.J. (1984). Estimation of body density in adolescent athletes. *Human Biology, 56,* 439-448.

Trowell, H., & Burkitt, D. (1986). Physiological role of dietary fiber: A ten-year review. *Contemporary Nutrition, 11*(7), n.p.

Trussell, J. (1978). Menarche and fatness: Re-examination of the critical body composition hypothesis. *Science, 200,* 1506-1509.

Trussell, J. (1980). Statistical flaws in evidence for the Frisch hypothesis that fatness triggers menarche. *Human Biology, 52,* 711-720.

Tuttle, W.W., & Frey, H. (1930). A study of the physical efficiency of college women as shown by the pulse-ratio test. *Research Quarterly, 1,* 17-25.

Ueland, K., Novy, M.J., Peterson, E.N., & Metcalfe, J. (1969). Maternal cardiovascular dynamics: IV. The influence of gestational age on the maternal cardiovascular response to posture and exercise. *American Journal of Obstetrics and Gynecology, 104,* 856-864.

Ullyot, J. (1976). *Women's running.* Mountain View, CA: World Publications.

United States Department of Agriculture. Department of Health and Human Services. (1981). *Nutritive value of foods* (Home and Garden Bulletin No. 72) (GPO Stock No. 001-000-030667-0). Washington, DC: U.S. Government Printing Office.

United States Department of Agriculture. Department of Health and Human Services. (1985). *Nutrition and your health: Dietary guidelines for Americans* (2nd ed.) (Home and Garden Bulletin No. 232). Washington, DC: U.S. Government Printing Office.

United States Department of Health, Education and Welfare. (1972). *Ten State Nutrition Survey 1968-1970: Biochemical: V. Dietary* (DHEW Publication No. HMS 72-8133). Washington, DC: U.S. Government Printing Office.

United States Department of Health, Education and Welfare. (1979, August). *Promoting health/preventing disease.* Washington, DC: U.S. Government Printing Office.

United States Department of Health and Human Services. Public Health Service. (1986). *Osteoporosis: Cause, treatment, prevention* (NIH Publication No. 86-2226). Washington, DC: U.S. Government Printing Office.

United States Department of Health and Human Services. (1988). *The surgeon general's report on nutrition and health: Summary and recommendations* (Publication No. PHS 88-50210). Washington, DC: U.S. Government Printing Office.

Upton, S.J., Hagan, R.D., Lease, B., Rosentswieg, J., Gettman, L.R., & Duncan, J.J. (1984). Comparative physiological profiles among young and middle-aged female distance runners. *Medicine and Science in Sports and Exercise, 16,* 67-71.

Upton, S.J., Hagan, R.D., Rosentswieg, J., & Gettman, L.R. (1983). Comparison of the physiological profiles of middle-aged women distance runners and sedentary women. *Research Quarterly for Exercise and Sport, 54,* 83-87.

Utian, W.H. (1980). *Your middle years: A doctor's guide for today's woman.* New York: Appleton-Century-Crofts.

Vaccaro, P., Clarke, D.H., Wrenn, J.P. (1979). Physiological profiles of elite women basketball players. *Journal of Sports Medicine and Physical Fitness, 19,* 45-54.

Vaccaro, P., Dummer, G., & Clarke, D.H. (1981). Physiological characteristics of female masters swimmers. *The Physician and Sports-medicine,* **9**(12), 75-78.

Vaccaro, P., Morris, A.F., & Clarke, D.H. (1981). Physiological characteristics of masters female distance runners. *The Physician and Sportsmedicine,* **9**(7), 105-108.

Vaccaro, P., Ostrove, S.M., Vandervelden, L., Goldfarb, A.H., Clarke, D.H., & Dummer, G.M. (1984). Body composition and physiological responses of masters female swimmers 20 to 70 years of age. *Research Quarterly for Exercise and Sport,* **55**, 278-284.

Van Huss, W., Evans, S.A., Kurowski, T., Anderson, D.J., Allen, R., & Stephens, K. (1988). Physiological characteristics of male and female age-group runners. In E.W. Brown & C.F. Branta (Eds.), *Competitive sports for children and youth* (pp. 143-158). Champaign, IL: Human Kinetics.

Vander, L.B., Franklin, B.A., Wrisley, D., & Rubenfire, M. (1984). Cardiorespiratory responses to arm and leg ergometry in women. *The Physician and Sportsmedicine,* **12**(5), 101-106.

Vander, A.J., Sherman, J.H., & Luciano, D.S. (1985). *Human physiology: The mechanisms of body function* (4th ed.). New York: McGraw-Hill.

Van't Hof, M., & Roede, H.J. (1977). A Monte Carlo test of weight as a critical factor in menarche, compared with bone age and measures of height, width, and sexual development. *Annals of Human Biology,* **4**, 581-585.

Vaughn, T.C., & Hammond, C.B. (1981). Estrogen replacement therapy. *Clinical Obstetrics and Gynecology,* **24**, 253-281.

Vodak, P.A., Savin, W.M., Haskell, W.L., & Wood, P.D. (1980). Physiological profile of middle-aged male and female tennis players. *Medicine and Science in Sports and Exercise,* **12**, 159-163.

Wagner, J.A., & Horvath, S.M. (1985a). Cardiovascular reactions to cold exposures differ with age and gender. *Journal of Applied Physiology,* **58**, 187-192.

Wagner, J.A., & Horvath, S.M. (1985b). Influences of age and gender on human thermoregulatory responses to cold exposures. *Journal of Applied Physiology,* **58**, 180-186.

Wakat, D.K., & Sweeney, K.A. (1979). Etiology of athletic amenorrhea in cross-country runners [Abstract]. *Medicine and Science in Sports,* **11**(1), 91.

Wakat, D.K., Sweeney, K.A., & Rogol, A.D. (1982). Reproductive system function in women cross-country runners. *Medicine and Science in Sports and Exercise,* **14**, 263-269.

Wallace, A.M., Boyer, D.B., Dan, A., & Holm, K. (1986). Aerobic exercise, maternal self-esteem, and physical discomforts during pregnancy. *Journal of Nurse-Midwifery,* **31**(6), 255-262.

Wallace, A.M., & Engstrom, J.L. (1987). The effects of aerobic exercise on the pregnant woman, fetus, and pregnancy outcome: A review. *Journal of Nurse-Midwifery,* **32**, 277-290.

Wallace, J., Lovell, S., Talano, C., Webb, M.L., & Hodgson, J.L. (1982). Changes in menstrual function, climacteric syndrome, and serum concentrations of sex hormones in pre- and post-menopausal women following a moderate intensity conditioning program [Abstract]. *Medicine and Science in Sports and Exercise,* **14**(2), 154.

Walsh, W.M., Huurman, W.W., & Shelton, G.L. (1984). Overuse injuries of the knee and spine in girls' gymnastics. *Clinics in Sports Medicine,* **3**, 829-850.

Warren, M.P. (1980). The effects of exercise on pubertal progression and reproductive function in girls. *Journal of Clinical Endocrinology and Metabolism,* **51**, 1150-1157.

Warren, M.P. (1985). Anorexia nervosa and related eating disorders. *Clinical Obstetrics and Gynecology,* **28**, 588-597.

Warren, M.P., Brooks-Gunn, J., Hamilton, L.H., Warren, L.F., & Hamilton, W.G. (1986). Scoliosis and fractures in young ballet dancers: Relation to delayed menarche and secondary amenorrhea. *New England Journal of Medicine,* **314**, 1348-1353.

Washburn, R.A., & Seals, D.R. (1984). Peak oxygen uptake during arm cranking for men and women. *Journal of Applied Physiology: Respiratory, Environmental and Exercise Physiology,* **56**, 954-957.

Watterson, V.V. (1984). The effects of aerobic dance on cardiovascular fitness. *The Physician and Sportsmedicine,* **12**(10), 138-145.

Weber, H. (1973). The energy cost of aerobic dancing. *Medicine and Science in Sports,* **5**, 65-66.

Weideger, P. (1976). *Menstruation and menopause: The physiology, and psychology, the myth and the reality.* New York: Knopf.

Weight, L.M., & Noakes, T.D. (1987). Is running an analog of anorexia? A survey of the incidence of eating disorders in female distance runners. *Medicine and Science in Sports and Exercise,* **19**, 213-217.

Weiker, G.G. (1988). Dance injuries: The knee, ankle, and foot. In P.M. Clarkson & M. Skrinar (Eds.), *Science of dance training* (pp. 147-192). Champaign, IL: Human Kinetics.

Wells, C.L. (1971). The menstrual cycle and physical activity. In D.V. Harris (Ed.), *DGWS research reports: Women in sports* (Vol. 1, pp. 71-80). Washington, DC: American Alliance for Health, Physical Education and Recreation.

Wells, C.L. (1977). Sexual differences in heat stress response. *The Physician and Sportsmedicine,* **5**(9), 78-90.

Wells, C.L., & Ballinger, D. (1988). Women's performances—the last decade. In J. Puhl, C.H. Brown, & R.O. Voy (Eds.), *Sport science perspectives for women* (pp. 221-233). Champaign, IL: Human Kinetics.

Wells, C.L., Hecht, L.H., & Krahenbuhl, G.S. (1981). Physical characteristics and oxygen utilization of male and female marathon runners. *Research Quarterly for Exercise and Sport,* **52**, 281-285.

Wells, C.L., & Horvath, S.M. (1973). Heat stress responses related to the menstrual cycle. *Journal of Applied Physiology,* **35**, 1-5.

Wells, C.L., & Horvath, S.M. (1974). Responses to exercise in a hot environment as related to the menstrual cycle. *Journal of Applied Physiology,* **36**, 299-302.

Wells, C.L., & Plowman, S.A. (1988). Relationship between training, menarche, and amenorrhea. In E.W. Brown & C.F. Branta (Eds.), *Competitive sports for children and youth* (pp. 195-211). Champaign, IL: Human Kinetics.

Wells, C.L., Scrutton, E.W., Archibald, L.D., Cooke, W.P., & DeLaMothe, J.W. (1973). Physical working capacity and maximal oxygen uptake of teenage athletes. *Medicine and Science in Sports,* **5**, 232-238.

Wells, J.B., Jokl, E., & Bohanen, J. (1961). The effect of intensive physical training upon body composition of adolescent girls. *Journal of the Association for Physical and Mental Rehabilitation,* **17**, 68-72.

Weltman, A., Moffatt, R.J., & Stamford, B.A. (1978). Supramaximal training in females: Effects of anaerobic power output, anaerobic capacity, and aerobic power. *Journal of Sports Medicine and Physical Fitness,* **18**, 237-244.

Wentz, A.C. (1977). Psychogenic amenorrhea and anorexia nervosa. In R. Givens (Ed.), *Endocrine causes of menstrual disorders* (pp. 87-113). Chicago: Year Book Medical Publishers.

Wessel, J.A. (1972). *Movement fundamentals: Figure, form, fun* (3rd ed.). Englewood Cliffs, NJ: Prentice-Hall.

Wessel, J.A., Small, A., Van Huss, W.D., Anderson, D.J., & Cederquist, D. (1968). Age and physiological responses to exercise in women 20-69 years of age. *Journal of Gerontology,* **23**, 269-278.

White, M.K., Yeater, R.A., Martin, R.B., Rosenberg, B.S., Sherwook, L., Weber, K.C., & Della-Gustina, D.E. (1984). Effects of aerobic dancing and walking on cardiovascular function and muscular strength in postmenopausal women. *Journal of Sports Medicine and Physical Fitness, 24*, 159-166.

Whiteside, P.A. (1980). Men's and women's injuries in comparable sports. *The Physician and Sportsmedicine, 8*(3), 130-140.

Widholm, O. (1985). Epidemiology of premenstrual tension syndrome and primary dysmenorrhea. In M.Y. Dawood, J.L. McGuire, & L.M. Demers (Eds.), *Premenstrual syndrome and dysmenorrhea* (pp. 3-12). Baltimore: Urban and Schwarzenberg.

Williams, L.M. (1985). *Anaerobic power/capacity of college women athletes in various sports.* Unpublished master's thesis, Arizona State University, Tempe.

Williams, M.H. (1976). *Nutritional aspects of human physical and athletic performance.* Springfield, IL: Charles C Thomas.

Wilmore, J.H. (1974). Alterations in strength, body composition and anthropometric measurements consequent to a 10-week weight training program. *Medicine and Science in Sports, 6*, 133-138.

Wilmore, J.H. (1977). *Athletic training and physical fitness: Physiological principles and practices of the conditioning process.* Boston: Allyn & Bacon.

Wilmore, J.H. (1979). The application of science to sport: Physiological profiles of male and female athletes. *Canadian Journal of Applied Sport Sciences, 4*, 103-115.

Wilmore, J.H. (1982). *Training for sport and activity: The physiological basis of the conditioning process* (2nd ed.). Boston: Allyn & Bacon.

Wilmore, J.H., & Brown, C.H. (1974). Physiological profiles of women distance runners. *Medicine and Science in Sports, 6*, 178-181.

Wilmore, J.H., Brown, C.H., & Davis, J.A. (1977). Body physique and composition of the female distance runner. *Annals of the New York Academy of Sciences, 301*, 764-776.

Wilmore, J.H., & Costill, D.L. (1988). *Training for sport and activity* (3rd ed.). Dubuque, IA: Wm. C. Brown.

Wilmore, J.H., Parr, R.B., Girandola, R.N., Ward, P., Vodak, P.A., Barstow, T.J., Pipes, T.V., Romero, G.T., & Leslie, P. (1978). Physiological alterations consequent to circuit weight training. *Medicine and Science in Sports, 10*, 79-84.

Wilson, N.C., & Gisolfi, C.V. (1980). Effects of exercising rats during pregnancy. *Journal of Applied Physiology: Respiratory, Environmental and Exercise Physiology, 48*, 34-40.

Wilson, P.W.F., Garrison, R.J., & Castelli, W.P. (1985). Postmenopausal estrogen use, cigarette smoking, and cardiovascular morbidity in women over 50. *New England Journal of Medicine, 313*, 1038-1043.

Wingard, D.L., Suarez, L., & Barrett-Connor, E. (1983). The sex differential in mortality from all causes and ischemic heart disease. *American Journal of Epidemiology, 117*(2), 165-172.

Wirth, J.C., & Lohman, T.G. (1982). The relationship of static muscle function to use of oral contraceptives. *Medicine and Science in Sports and Exercise, 14*, 16-20.

Withers, R.T. (1978). Physiological responses of international female lacrosse players to preseason conditioning. *Medicine and Science in Sports, 10*, 238-242.

Withers, R.T., & Roberts, R.G.D. (1981). Physiological profiles of representative women softball, hockey and netball players. *Ergonomics, 24*, 583-591.

Witman, P.A., Melvin, M., & Nicholas, J.A. (1981). Common problems seen in a metropolitan sports injury clinic. *The Physician and Sportsmedicine, 9*(3), 105-110.

Women say running helped pregnancy, labor. (1981). *The Physician and Sportsmedicine, 9*(3), 24-25.

Woo, R., Garrow, J.S., & Pi-Sunyer, F.X. (1982a). Effect of exercise on spontaneous calorie intake in obesity. *American Journal of Clinical Nutrition, 36*, 470-474.

Wood, R., Garrow, J.S., & Pi-Sunyer, F.X. (1982b). Voluntary food intake during prolonged exercise in obese women. *American Journal of Clinical Nutrition, 36,* 478-484.

Wood, P.D., Haskell, W.L., Stern, S., Lewis, M.P., & Perry, C. (1977). Plasma lipoprotein distributions in male and female runners. *Annals of the New York Academy of Sciences, 301,* 748-763.

Worley, R.J. (1981). Age, estrogen, and bone density. *Clinical Obstetrics and Gynecology, 24,* 203-218.

Wurtman, R.J., & Wurtman, J.J. (Eds.) (1987). Human obesity. *Annals of the New York Academy of Sciences, 499,* 1-348.

Wyrick, W. (1971). How sex differences affect research in physical education. In D.V. Harris (Ed.), *DGWS research reports: Women in sports* (Vol. 1, pp. 21-30). Washington, DC: American Alliance for Health, Physical Education and Recreation.

Wyshak, G., Frisch, R.E., Albright, T.E., Albright, N.L., & Schiff, I. (1987). Bone fractures among former college athletes compared with nonathletes in the menopausal and postmenopausal years. *Obstetrics and Gynecology, 69,* 121-126.

Yahiro, J., Glass, A.R., Fears, W.B., Ferguson, E.W., & Vigersky, R.A. (1987). Exaggerated gonadotropin response to luteinizing hormone-releasing hormone in amenorrheic runners. *American Journal of Obstetrics and Gynecology, 156,* 586-591.

Yates, A., Leehey, K., & Shisslak, C.M. (1983). Running—An analogue of anorexia? *New England Journal of Medicine, 308,* 251-255.

Zacharias, L., & Wurtman, R.J. (1964). Blindness: Its relation to age of menarche. *Science, 29,* 1154.

Zaharieva, E. (1965). Survey of sportswomen at the Tokyo Olympics. *Journal of Sports Medicine and Physical Fitness, 5,* 215-219.

Zaharieva, E. (1972). Olympic participation by women: Effects on pregnancy and childbirth. *Journal of the American Medical Association, 221,* 992-995.

Zauner, C.W., Notelovitz, M., Fields, C.D., Clair, K.M., Clair, W.J., & Vogel, R.B. (1984). Cardiorespiratory efficiency at submaximal work in young and middle-aged women. *American Journal of Obstetrics and Gynecology, 150,* 712-715.

Zeldis, S.M., Morganroth, J., & Rubler, S. (1978). Cardiac hypertrophy in response to dynamic conditioning in female runners. *Journal of Applied Physiology: Respiratory, Environmental and Exercise Physiology, 44,* 849-852.

Zuckerman, D.M., Colby, A., Ware, N.C., & Lazerson, J.S. (1986). The prevalance of bulimia among college students. *American Journal of Public Health, 76,* 1135-1137.

Zuti, W.B. (1972). *Effects of diet and exercise on body composition of adult women during weight reduction.* Unpublished doctoral dissertation, Kent State University, Kent, Ohio.

Zwiren, L.D., Cureton, K.J., & Hutchinson, P. (1983). Comparison of circulatory responses to submaximal exercise in equally trained men and women. *International Journal of Sports Medicine, 4,* 255-259.

Index

Physical Education &
Sports Studies
Resources